International Business
The Challenges of Globalization

Canadian Edition

John J. Wild
University of Wisconsin-Madison, US

Kenneth L. Wild
University of London, UK

Halia M. Valladares Montemayor
Mount Royal University, Canada

Toronto

Vice-President, Editorial Director: Gary Bennet
Managing Editor: Claudine O'Donnell
Acquisitions Editor: Deana Sigut
Senior Marketing Manager: Leigh-Anne Graham
Lead Project Manager: Avinash Chandra
Program Manager: Karen Townsend
Project Manager: Sarah Gallagher
Developmental Editor: Johanna Schlaepfer
Copy Editor: Carolyn Zapf
Proofreader: Tara Tovell
Full-Service Project Management: Niraj Bhatt/Aptara®, Inc.
Production Services: Aptara®, Inc.
Permissions Project Manager: Joanne Tang
Photo Permissions Research: Rebecca O'Malley, Q2A/Bill Smith
Text Permissions Research: Khalid Shakhshir, Electronic Publishing Services Inc., NYC
Cover Art Director: Jayne Conte
Cover Designer: Suzanne Behnke
Interior Designer: Electronic Publishing Services., NYC
Cover Image: Shutterstock

Credits and acknowledgments for material borrowed from other sources and reproduced, with permission, in this textbook appear on the appropriate page within the text.

Original edition published by Pearson Education, Inc., Upper Saddle River, New Jersey, USA. Copyright © 2013 Pearson Education, Inc. This edition is authorized for sale only in Canada.

If you purchased this book outside the United States or Canada, you should be aware that it has been imported without the approval of the publisher or the author.

10 9 8 7 6 5 4 3 2 [WC]

Library and Archives Canada Cataloguing in Publication

Wild, John J., author
    International business : the challenges of globalization / John J. Wild, Kenneth L. Wild,
    Halia M. Valladares Montemayor. — First [Canadian] edition.
    Includes index. ISBN 978-0-13-286688-0 (pbk.)

    1. International business enterprises—Management—Textbooks.   2. International trade—Textbooks.
    3. Canada—Commerce—Textbooks.   I. Wild, Kenneth L., author
    II. Valladeres Montemayor, Halia Mayela, author   III. Title.

HD62.4.W587 2013
658'.049   C2013-907220-9

ISBN 978-0-13-286688-0

*To my parents, Elena and Hugo, for educating and teaching me to pursue higher goals;
to Jan and Vanessa—I hope this book opens your eyes to the world. A special thank you
to Dr. Manuel Diaz Avila and Victoria Calvert for their words of encouragement and for being
with me on this journey.*

BRIEF CONTENTS

CONTENTS

Welcome to the first Canadian edition of *International Business: The Challenges of Globalization*. As with previous US editions, this book is the result of extensive research, chapter reviews, and correspondence with instructors and students. We are delighted that instructors agree with a fresh approach to international business, and the reception of this textbook has exceeded expectations.

This book presents international business in a comprehensive yet concise framework. Real-world examples and engaging features bring the concepts of international business to life and make international business accessible for all students. A main goal in this first Canadian edition is to continue to deliver the most readable, current, and concise international business textbook available with a Canadian perspective and examples in mind.

This book is our means of travel on an exciting tour through the study of international business. It motivates the reader by making international business challenging yet fun. It also embraces the central role of people and their cultures in international business. Each chapter is infused with real-world discussion, while underlying theory appears in the background where it belongs. Terminology is used consistently, and theories are explained in direct and concise terms. The book's visual style is innovative yet subtle and uses photos, illustrations, and features sparingly. The result is an easy-to-read and clutter-free design.

Features of the Canadian Edition

- This first Canadian edition of *International Business* captures and explains Canada's business environment and compares it to several countries around the world. For example, in Chapter 2, Canadian culture is explained using Hofstede's cultural dimensions. In the same chapter, the subcultures section has a Canadian emphasis, and both the company profile and the international management case feature successful Canadian companies.
- The latest available data and reference sources are put forward in each chapter. For example, the "Measuring Globalization" section in Chapter 1 presents the latest Index of Globalization (2012) developed by the KOF institute. In Chapter 3, political risk levels are presented with an updated map. Chapter 5 gives an analysis of a new index called the UN World Risk Index, and the Big Mac Index and the Human Development Index provide the most recent data focusing on Canadian numbers in comparison to other countries.
- Chapter 4 (International Ethics) is entirely new, and contains topics such as codes of ethics, corporate social responsibility, sustainability, fair trade, and the principles of responsible investment from the UN. This chapter also includes examples of ethical dilemmas that international managers may encounter.
- The crucial role that emerging markets play in the global economy and international business is an ongoing focus in this edition. For example, the Culture Matters feature box in Chapter 5, titled "Foundations of Development," discusses how ambition and fear in emerging markets has created $3000 autos, $300 computers, and $30 mobile phones that appeal to customers worldwide. Additionally, the chapter's company profile features Datawind, a Canadian-owned technology company that developed the world's cheapest tablet for the Indian market.
- This edition keeps pace with current events and integrates them into chapter-opening company profiles, feature boxes, and end-of-chapter mini cases. For example, the company profile in Chapter 7 describes a new trend in foreign direct investment where companies in developed countries, such as Calgary-based Nexen Inc., are being acquired by foreign investors from developing countries.
- Key changes were made based on suggestions from instructors. For example, coverage of international finance (Chapter 9) has been streamlined, removing extended calculations using cross rates and coverage of discounts and premiums.

● Each part in the Canadian edition concludes with the *Teaming Up* project, a course-long, critical- and creative-thinking exercise for students to develop a market research analysis—from the Canadian perspective—for a product or service comparing two selected countries.

Hallmark Features of International Business

Culture Early and Often

Culture is a fundamental element of all international business activity. This book's presentation of culture sensitizes students to the lives of people in other nations. Culture appears early (Chapter 2) and is integrated throughout the text, using culture-rich chapter openers and lively examples of how culture affects international business. Covering culture in this way gets students interested in chapter material because it illustrates how concepts relate to the real world.

Accessible Material

A successful book for the first course in international business must be accessible to students. We describe conceptual material and specialized business activities in concrete, straightforward terms and illustrate them appropriately. For example, we introduce the concepts of absolute and comparative advantage in Chapter 6 by discussing whether Kevin O'Leary should install his own hot tub or let a professional installer perform the job. This approach—presenting complex material in an accessible manner—helps students to better master the material.

Integrative Approach

International business is not simply a collection of separate business functions and environmental forces. The model shown here (and detailed in Chapter 1) is a unique organizing framework

FIGURE 1.6

The Global Business Environment

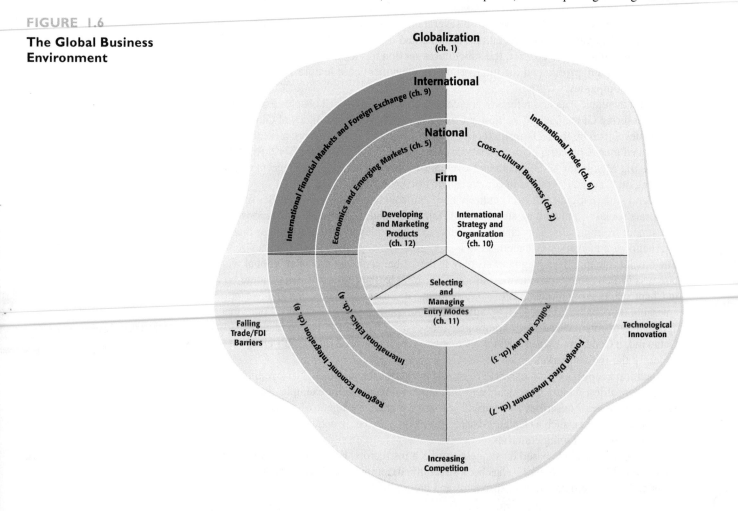

that helps students to understand how the elements of international business are related. It depicts a dynamic, integrated system that weaves together national business environments, the international business environment, and international business management. It also shows that characteristics of globalization (new technologies and falling barriers to trade and investment) are causing greater competition.

Innovative Pedagogy

This book's pedagogy stands apart from the competition:

- *Chapter-opening company profiles* are brief, easy-to-read introductions to each chapter's content. Companies profiled are on the leading edge of their industries and inherently interesting to students. They include YouTube, Cirque Du Soleil, PepsiCo, Air Canada, Datawind, Walmart, Nexen, Bombardier, Nintendo, Lululemon, Spin Master, and Red Bull.
- *Entrepreneur's Toolkit* boxes underscore the key roles that entrepreneurs and small businesses play in our global economy. This feature profiles successful international entrepreneurs and highlights issues especially relevant for entrepreneurs.
- *Global Manager's Briefcase* boxes address issues that pose special problems for managers of global companies. Topics include corruption issues, doing business in Mexico, surprises that can occur when investing aboard, and negotiating market entry strategies.
- *Culture Matters* boxes present the relation between culture and a key chapter topic. For example, Chapter 2 presents the importance of businesspeople developing a global mindset and avoiding cultural bias.
- *Global Challenges* boxes present special obstacles facing the world that concern businesses, such as global organized crime (illustrated by the Japanese *yakuza*) and improving the health of the world's poor.
- *Bottom Line for Business* sections conclude chapters and explain the impact on managers and their firms' policies, strategies, and activities abroad.
- *Quick Study* concept checks help students to verify that they have learned the section's key terms and important concepts before moving on.
- *Full-Colour World Atlas*, which appears as an appendix to Chapter 1, is a primer for students to test their knowledge of world geography and acts as a reference tool throughout the course.
- *Learning Objectives* focus on the main lessons students should take away from the material and are summarized in bullet-point format at the end of the chapter.
- *Beacons* provide students with a "roadmap" of how chapters relate to one another. These beacons appear at the start of each chapter and are appropriately titled "A Look Back," "A Look at This Chapter," and "A Look Ahead."

Culture Matters | Creating a Global Mindset

In this era of globalization, companies need employees who function without the blinders of ethnocentricity. Here are some ways managers can develop a *global mindset*:

- **Cultural Adaptability.** Managers need the ability to alter their behaviour when working with people from other cultures. The first step is to develop one's knowledge of unfamiliar cultures; one way to begin is to join an organization such as another culture's Chamber of Commerce and attend meetings where nationals of that culture will be present.[2] The second step is to act on that knowledge to alter behaviour to suit cultural expectations. The manager with a global mindset can evaluate others in a culturally unbiased way, and can motivate and lead multicultural teams.

- **Bridging the Gap.** A large gap can emerge between theory and practice when Western management ideas are applied in Eastern cultures. Whereas North American management principles are often accepted at face value in businesses throughout the world, North American business customs are not. In Asia, for example, Western managers may try implementing "collective leadership" practices more in line with Asian management styles.

- **Building Global Mentality.** Companies can apply personality-testing techniques to measure the global aptitude of managers. A global mindset test evaluates an individual's openness and flexibility, understanding of global principles, and strategic implementation abilities. It can also identify areas in which training is needed and generate a list of recommended programs. A global mindset requires managers to swallow personal pride, put aside ego, and ignore cultural preconceptions.

- **Flexibility Is Key.** The more behavioural are the issues, the greater is the influence of local cultures. Japanese and Korean managers are more likely than North American managers to wait for directions and consult peers on decisions. Western managers posted in the Middle East must learn to work within a rigid hierarchy to be successful. And although showing respect for others is universally valued, respect is defined differently from country to country.

- **Want to Know More?** Visit the Centre for Creative Leadership (www.ccl.org); The Globalist (www.theglobalist.com); and Transnational Management Associates (www.tmaworld.com).

Tools for Active Learning

Well-planned end-of-chapter assignment materials span the full range of complexity to test students' knowledge and ability to apply key principles. They are often experiential in nature to help students develop international business skills and make business decisions. Assignment material includes the following:

Practising International Management Case

Is Canada Open for Business?

As you may recall from Chapter 5, Canada is considered one of the freest economies in the world, ranking sixth on the Index of Economic Freedom (published annually by *The Wall Street Journal* and Washington's Heritage Foundation). Although many consider Canada to have a free market economy, no country in the world is a completely "free" market—all governments try to protect or restrict investment in sectors they consider strategic for the country's economy or its national security. In 2010, Canada had to deal with a tough decision that raised the question: Is Canada truly open for business?

The fight was over Potash Corporation of Saskatchewan (Potash Corp), the world's leading producer of potash and key to the economy of Saskatchewan. When Australian-based mining giant BHP Billiton (BHP) suddenly launched a $38.6 billion hostile takeover bid for the Saskatchewan company in August of 2010, both the federal and provincial levels of government got involved.

Why would the acquisition decision not rest solely in the hands of the executives and stakeholders of both companies? The proposed transaction exceeded the CAD $299 million–defined monetary threshold established by the Canadian government for foreign investment, and therefore had to be approved by the Investment Canada Act (ICA).

The Investment Canada Act is designed to ensure that foreign investments benefit Canada economically and contribute to opportunities for employment in Canada. ICA applies to all acquisitions of a Canadian business by non-Canadians, and it conducts a "net benefit test" on any foreign investments that exceed its defined monetary threshold.

Historically, ICA has approved acquisition requests if the investor makes binding commitments that satisfy ICA criteria for net benefit to Canada. To date about 99 percent of applications have been given the green light. As part of its application and review process for the takeover, BHP promised to establish the headquarters of the business in Saskatoon, Saskatchewan, where the president and management group would be located; maintain current levels of employment for at least five years; give up all tax benefits; and sponsor the creation of a Centre of Excellence at the University of Saskatchewan.

To many people's surprise, ICA ruled against BHP's application on the grounds that it did not pass the net benefit test. BHP was given 30 days to make further representations or to submit revised proposals in order to prove a net benefit for Canada. However, BHP refused to make further concessions and dropped the bid.

Many external factors may have influenced ICA's decision. First, potash is considered by many to be a strategic natural resource as countries around the world work to maximize crop yields. The media, therefore, were able to make a case against the acquisition through articles addressing "the loss of a strategic resource to a foreign investor."

Second, it was an election year for both the federal and provincial governments. Brad Wall, then premier of Saskatchewan, voiced his concerns to the federal Minister of Industry and to the public, stating that BHP's bid failed the net benefit test in three areas: jobs and investment, Canadian control of a strategic resource, and provincial revenues—the government stood to lose about $100 million annually in corporate tax.

Certainly the takeover bid had the potential to destabilize Saskatchewan's finances, since Potash Corp is a significant source of tax revenue for the provincial government. The expatriation of revenues was also a concern: If the takeover were to be approved, revenues would go to BHP stakeholders in Australia rather than to Saskatchewan, where profits were being re-invested to fund roads, schools, and hospitals. The revenue to the province also allowed the local government to keep tax levels at a lower rate, which made the local economy more competitive.

Two weeks before the decision date, Premier Wall told the media, "The people of Saskatchewan deserve a potash industry unequivocally managed, operated and marketed for the benefit of Canada and Saskatchewan." Clearly he had done his research: His statement echoed a 2001 statement made by the government of Australia. That year, Shell was denied acquisition of a controlling stake in an Australian natural gas company because it was "in Australia's best interest to have offshore reserves unequivocally managed, operated and marketed for Australia."

Thinking Globally

1. Why do you think BHP was not able to prove a "net benefit" for Canada?
2. Why did ICA approve the acquisition of Nexen but not that of Potash Corp?
3. Was it correct for the Canadian government to restrict FDI in this case? Explain your answer.
4. What are the global implications for Canadian business because of ICA's decision?
5. Do you think the decision might have been different if it had not been an election year?

Sources: Lawson A. W. Hunter, Ashley M. Weber, and Maris Berswick, "A Guide to Navigating Canada's Foreign Ownership Laws for New Investors," *Competition Law International,* January 2012, 8(1), pp. 37–42; Eric J. Dufour and Imran Ahmad, "The Investment Canada Act—Canada's Waking Giant?," *International Law Office* (www.internationallawoffice.com), November 24, 2010; Don Newman, "The Case Against Selling Saskatchewan's Potash Corp," CBC News (www.cbc.ca), October 1, 2010.

231

- *Talk It Over* questions can be used for in-class discussion or as homework assignments. These exercises raise important issues currently confronting entrepreneurs, international managers, policy makers, consumers, and others.
- *Take It to the Web* assignments ask students to conduct research using the Internet. *Web Site Report* exercises send students to specific Web sites to research a single company, or ask students to locate information using the Web.
- *Practising International Management* cases ask students to analyze the responses of real-world companies to the issues, problems, and opportunities discussed in each chapter.

Teaching and Learning Support

Instructor's Resource Centre

The instructor resources can be downloaded from Pearson Canada's online catalogue at www.pearsoncanada.ca/highered.

- **Instructor's Manual:** This manual is a complete instruction toolkit containing a wealth of teaching aids, including detailed lecture outlines and suggested answers to all the Quick Study, Talk It Over, Practising International Management case, and Teaming Up questions.
- **MyTest (www.pearsonmytest.com):** MyTest is a powerful assessment generation program that helps instructors easily create and print quizzes, tests, and exams, as well as homework or practice handouts. Questions and tests can all be authored online, allowing instructors ultimate flexibility and the ability to efficiently manage assessments at any time, from anywhere. MyTest for *International Business*, Canadian edition, includes questions in multiple-choice, true/false, short answer, and fill-in-the-blank format.
- **Test Item File:** This test bank includes all the questions from the MyTest version in Microsoft Word format.
- **PowerPoints:** Engaging PowerPoint slides draw students into the lecture with interesting information and rich visuals. Written teaching notes are provided, and question slides can be used as in-class comprehension checks

Pearson Custom Library

For enrolments of at least 25 students, you can create your own textbook by choosing the chapters that best suit your own course needs. To begin building your custom text, visit www.pearsoncustomlibrary.com. You may also work with a dedicated Pearson Custom editor to create your ideal text—publishing your own original content or mixing and matching Pearson content. Contact your local Pearson representative to get started.

CourseSmart for Instructors

CourseSmart goes beyond traditional expectations, providing instant, online access to the textbooks and course materials you need at a lower cost for students. And even as students save money, you can save time and hassle with a digital eTextbook that allows you to search for the most relevant content at the very moment you need it. Whether it's evaluating textbooks or creating lecture notes to help students with difficult concepts, CourseSmart can make life a little easier. See how when you visit www.coursesmart.com/instructors.

CourseSmart for Students

CourseSmart goes beyond traditional expectations, providing instant, online access to the textbooks and course materials you need at an average savings of 60 percent. With instant access from any computer and the ability to search your text, you'll find the content you need quickly, no matter where you are. And with online tools like highlighting and note-taking, you can save time and study efficiently. See all the benefits at www.coursesmart.com/students.

Learning Solutions Consultants

Pearson's Learning Solutions consultants work with faculty and campus course designers to ensure that Pearson products, assessment tools, and online course materials are tailored to meet your specific needs. This highly qualified team is dedicated to helping schools take full advantage of a wide range of educational resources by assisting in the integration of a variety of instructional materials and media formats. Your local Pearson Education sales representative can provide you with more details on this service program.

Acknowledgments

I would like to express thanks to the many people who offered thoughtful suggestions and recommendations for updating and improving this book. I especially thank the following instructors for providing formal reviews for the Canadian Edition:

Ron Chaikin	*Seneca College*
Choon Hian Chan	*Kwantlen Polytechnic University*
Hoshiar Gosal	*Langara College*
Renata Kobe	*University of Windsor*
Michael MacColl	*Vancouver Island University*
Gordon D. McFarlane	*University Canada West*
Charles Scott	*University of Northern British Columbia*
Ronald J. Thompson	*Okanagan College*
Frank Vuo	*Lethbridge College*
Michael Wade	*Seneca College*
Vasile Zamfirescu	*Kwantlen Polytechnic University*
David Di Zhang	*University of Saskatchewan*

It takes a dedicated group of individuals to take a textbook from first draft to final manuscript. Special recognition goes to Professor Victoria Calvert, Dr. Manuel Diaz Avila, and Laurie Jensen for reviewing the chapters in their first draft and providing valuable feedback. In addition, I want to thank Gerry Taft, the supplemental/developmental author, for the dedication to provide high quality power point slides, with amazing photos that capture the international business environment and for the superb instructor's manual. Thanks to my partners at Pearson Canada for their tireless efforts in bringing the first Canadian edition of this book to fruition. Special thanks on this project go to Deana Sigut, Acquisitions Editor; Johanna Schlaepfer, Development Editor; Sarah Gallagher, Project Manager; Leigh-Anne Graham, Marketing Manager; Niraj Bhatt, Project Manager; and Carolyn Zapf, Copy Editor.

John Wild, Kenneth Wild, and Halia M. Valladares Montemayor provide a blend of skills uniquely suited to writing an international business textbook. They combine award-winning teaching and research with a global view of business gained through years of living and working in cultures around the world. Their writing makes the topic of international business practical, accessible, and enjoyable.

John J. Wild

John J. Wild is a distinguished Professor of Business at the University of Wisconsin at Madison. He previously held appointments at the University of Manchester in England and Michigan State University. He received his B.B.A., M.S., and Ph.D. from the University of Wisconsin at Madison.

Teaching business courses at both the undergraduate and graduate levels, Professor Wild has received several teaching honours, including the Mabel W. Chipman Excellence-in-Teaching Award, the Teaching Excellence Award from the 2003 and 2005 business graduates from the University of Wisconsin, and a departmental Excellence-in-Teaching Award from Michigan State University. He is a prior recipient of national research fellowships from KPMG Peat Marwick and the Ernst and Young Foundation. Professor Wild is also a frequent speaker at universities and at national and international conferences.

The author of more than 60 publications, in addition to five best-selling textbooks, Professor Wild conducts research on a wide range of topics, including corporate governance, capital markets, and financial analysis and forecasting. He is an active member of several national and international organizations, including the Academy of International Business, and has served as associate editor and editorial board member for several prestigious journals.

Kenneth L. Wild

Kenneth L. Wild is affiliated with the University of London, England. He previously taught at the Pennsylvania State University. He received his Ph.D. from the University of Manchester (UMIST) in England and his B.S. and M.S. degrees from the University of Wisconsin. Dr. Wild also undertook postgraduate work at École des Affairs Internationale in Marseilles, France.

Having taught students of international business, marketing, and management at both the undergraduate and graduate levels, Dr. Wild is a dedicated contributor to international business education. An active member of several national and international organizations, including the Academy of International Business, he has spoken at major universities and at national and international conferences.

Dr. Wild's research covers a range of international business topics, including market entry modes, country risk in emerging markets, international growth strategies, and globalization of the world economy.

Halia Mayela Valladares Montemayor

Halia Valladares Montemayor is the Chair of Entrepreneurship, Nonprofit Studies, International Business and Aviation at the Bissett School of Business at Mount Royal University in Calgary, Alberta. She is also an Associate Professor of International Business. She earned her doctoral degree in economics and business administration from Burgos University, Spain. In addition, she holds a MBA in international trade and a Master of Science in international logistics from Texas A & M International University, and is a Certified International Trade Professional (CITP) by the Forum of International Trade Training (FITT).

Dr. Valladares Montemayor has been a university professor and scholar for over a decade. She also has international business experience in the private sector, and was the traffic, shipping, and receiving supervisor for a Fortune 100 corporation. She has participated in several international research conferences as a speaker, and has authored a number of research publications for journals in Mexico, Spain, Canada, Cuba, Venezuela, and Colombia.

Dr. Valladares Montemayor's research covers an array of international business topics, including management accounting systems and cost control in international logistics, the principles of responsible investment under Jonas theory, agency theory applied to international operations, foreign direct investment by emerging economies in developed countries, and globalization applying econophysics models. She is an active member of several organizations, such as the Forum of International Trade Training (FITT), the Production and Operations Management Society (POMS), Academia de Ciencias Administrativas (ACACIA), the Administrative Science Association of Canada (ASAC), and the Econometric Society.

International Business
The Challenges of Globalization

CHAPTER ONE

Globalization

Learning Objectives

After studying this chapter, you should be able to

1. Describe the process of globalization and how it affects markets and production.

2. Identify the two forces causing globalization to increase.

3. Summarize the evidence for each main argument in the globalization debate.

4. Identify the types of companies that participate in international business.

5. Describe the global business environment and identify its four main elements.

A LOOK AT THIS CHAPTER

This chapter defines the scope of international business and introduces us to some of its most important topics. We begin by presenting globalization—describing its influence on markets and production and the forces behind its growth. Each main argument in the debate over globalization is also analyzed in detail. We then identify the key players in international business today. This chapter closes with a model that depicts international business as occurring within an integrated global business environment.

A LOOK AHEAD

Part 2, encompassing Chapters 2, 3, 4, and 5, introduces us to different national business environments. Chapter 2 describes important cultural differences among nations. Chapter 3 examines different political and legal systems. Chapter 4 examines different approaches to business ethics, corporate social responsibility, and sustainability for international businesses. Chapter 5 presents the world's various economic systems and discusses issues surrounding economic development.

Source: ShutterStock.

YouTube's Global Impact

SAN MATEO, California—YouTube (www.youtube.com) is the world's most popular service for sharing video clips through Web sites, mobile devices, blogs, and e-mail. YouTube launched in December 2005, and was purchased by Google for $1.65 billion less than a year later. People view more than 6 billion videos daily on the site, making YouTube about 30 times more popular than its nearest rival. YouTube's spectacular success illustrates the opportunities that globalization creates for entrepreneurs.

YouTube founders Chad Hurley and Steve Chen (pictured here in Paris, France) created a truly global medium to capitalize on exploding demand for user-created video content. "This is just the beginning," says Chen. "If we had the resources, we would be launching in 140 countries."

Most people visit YouTube's Web site to catch up on current events and find videos about their hobbies and interests. Wannabe pop stars and filmmakers also share their creative efforts with the world by uploading them to YouTube. And YouTube's CitizenNews (www.youtube.com/citizennews) gives a voice to citizen journalists and vloggers (video bloggers) who report firsthand accounts of events where they live—whether their home is in Toronto or New Delhi.

Source: Christophe Morin/Newscom.

Freedom sparks the creativity of artists and journalists, but it also draws the attention of heavy-handed governments. Nations that have at times blocked access to YouTube include China, Iran, Pakistan, Tunisia, and Turkey. Pakistan banned YouTube for one week in an effort to contain what it considered "blasphemous" content. YouTube and local providers of similar services must then employ their entrepreneurial creativity to overcome this government censorship.

As you read this chapter, consider how globalization is reshaping our personal lives and altering the activities of international companies.[1]

Globalization is reshaping our lives and leading us into uncharted territory. As *new technologies* drive down the cost of global communication and travel, we are increasingly exposed to the traits and practices of other cultures. As countries *reduce barriers to trade and investment*, globalization forces their industries to grow more competitive if they are to survive. And as multinationals from advanced countries and emerging markets seek out customers, *competition intensifies* on a global scale. These new realities of international business are altering our cultures and transforming the way companies do business.

International Business Involves Us All

The dynamic nature of international business affects each of us personally. In our daily communications, we encounter terms such as outsourcing, emerging markets, competitive advantage, multiculturalism, sustainability, and social responsibility. And each of us experiences the result of dozens of international transactions every day.

The General Electric alarm clock/radio (www.ge.com) that woke you up this morning was likely made in *China*. The breaking news broadcast on your TV was produced by *CNN International* (www.cnn.com); your Birkenstock sandals (www.birkenstock.com) were made in *Germany*; your Gap T-shirt (www.gapcanada.ca) was made in *Jordan*; and your Roots jeans (www.canada.roots.com) were made in *India*. You may have pulled the charger off your Blackberry phone (www.ca.blackberry.com), which was designed in *Canada* and manufactured in *Mexico* with parts from *China and Japan* before you headed out the door. You might hop into your *Korean* Hyundai (www.hyundaicanada.com) that was manufactured in *Bromont, Quebec,* and pop in a CD performed by the *English* band Coldplay (www.coldplay.com). You could swing by the local Starbucks (www.starbucks.com) to charge your own batteries with coffee brewed from a blend of beans harvested in *Colombia* and *Ethiopia*. Your day is just one hour old, but in some sense, you have already taken a virtual trip around the world. A quick glance at the "Made in" tags on your jacket, backpack, watch, wallet, or other items with you right now will demonstrate the pervasiveness of international business transactions.

International business is any commercial transaction that crosses the borders of two or more nations. You don't have to set foot outside a small town to find evidence of international business. No matter where you live, you'll be surrounded by **imports**—goods and services purchased abroad and brought into a country. Your counterparts around the world will undoubtedly spend some part of their day using your nation's **exports**—goods and services sent out of a country and sold abroad. Every year, all the nations of the world export goods and services worth more than $18 trillion.[2] This figure is approximately 41 times the annual global revenue of all Walmart stores (www.walmart.com), which is the biggest company in the world based on revenue.

international business
Commercial transaction that crosses the borders of two or more nations.

imports
Goods and services purchased abroad and brought into a country.

exports
Goods and services sent out of a country and sold abroad.

Technology Makes It Possible

Technology is perhaps the most remarkable facilitator of societal and commercial changes today. Consumers use technology to reach out to the world on the Internet—gathering and sending information and purchasing all kinds of goods and services. Companies use technology to acquire materials and products from distant lands and to sell goods and services abroad.

When businesses or consumers use technology to conduct transactions, they engage in **e-business (e-commerce)**—the use of computer networks to purchase, sell, or exchange products; service customers; and collaborate with partners. E-business is making it easier for companies to make their products abroad, not simply import and export finished goods.

e-business (e-commerce)
Use of computer networks to purchase, sell, or exchange products; service customers, and collaborate with partners.

Consider how Hewlett-Packard (HP) (www.hp.com) designed and built a computer server for small businesses. Once HP identified the need for a new low-cost computer server, it seized the rewards of globalization. HP dispersed its design and production activities throughout a specialized manufacturing system across five Pacific Rim nations and India. This helped the company minimize labour costs, taxes, and shipping delays yet maximize productivity when designing, building, and distributing its new product. Companies use such innovative production and distribution techniques to squeeze inefficiencies out of their international operations and boost their competitiveness.

Global Talent Makes It Happen

Media companies today commonly engage in a practice best described as a global relay race. Fox and NBC Universal created Hulu, one competitor of YouTube, as a cool venue for fans to watch TV

Workers at a factory in Indonesia inspect electronic parts bound for global markets. Today, companies can go almost anywhere in the world to tap into local expertise and favourable business climates. For example, Canadian businesses exploit technology by subcontracting work to Indian companies that write computer software code, and then e-mail their end product to the Canadian clients. In this way, companies can lower costs, increase efficiency, and grow more competitive. In what other ways might technology and global talent facilitate international business activity?

Source: AFP Photo/Bob Low/Newscom.

shows online. Hulu employs two technical teams—one in the United States and one in China—to manage its Web site. Members of the team in Santa Monica, California, work late into the night detailing code specifications that it sends to the team in Beijing, China. The Chinese team then writes the code and sends it back to Santa Monica before the US team gets to work in the morning.[3]

Some innovative companies use online competitions to tap global talent. InnoCentive (www.innocentive.com) connects companies and institutions seeking solutions to difficult problems using a global network of more than 300 000 creative thinkers. These engineers, scientists, inventors, and businesspeople with expertise in life sciences, engineering, chemistry, mathematics, computer science, and entrepreneurship compete to solve some of the world's toughest problems in return for significant financial awards. InnoCentive is open to anyone, is available in seven languages, and pays cash awards that range from as little as $5000 to over $1 million.[4]

Korn/Ferry International (www.kornferry.com) is a company dedicated to assisting its clients recruit world-class leadership talent. The company has over 80 offices in 40 countries, including Canada, France, The Netherlands, Turkey, Indonesia, Ecuador, India, Brazil, Ukraine, and Norway. Korn/Ferry offices around the world assist organizations to attract, engage, develop, and retain global talent, which is a key competitive advantage in our increasingly integrated and competitive environment.

This chapter begins by presenting globalization—we describe its powerful influence on markets and production and explain the forces behind its expansion. Following coverage of each main point in the debate over globalization, we examine the key players in international business. We then explain why international business is special by presenting the dynamic, integrated global business environment. Finally, the appendix at the end of this chapter contains a world atlas to be used as a primer for this chapter's discussion and as a reference throughout the remainder of the book.

Quick Study

1. Define the term *international business,* and explain how it affects each of us.
2. What do we mean by the terms *imports* and *exports*?
3. Explain how *e-business* (*e-commerce*) is affecting international business.

Globalization

globalization

Trend toward greater economic, cultural, political, and technological interdependence among national institutions and economies.

Although nations historically retained absolute control over the products, people, and capital crossing their borders, economies are becoming increasingly intertwined. **Globalization** is the trend toward greater economic, cultural, political, and technological interdependence among national institutions and economies. Globalization is a trend characterized by *denationalization* (national boundaries becoming less relevant) and is different from *internationalization* (entities cooperating across national boundaries). The greater interdependence that globalization is causing means an increasingly freer flow of goods, services, money, people, and ideas across national borders.

As its definition implies, globalization involves much more than the expansion of trade and investment among nations. Globalization embraces concepts and theories from political science, sociology, anthropology, and philosophy as well as economics. As such, it is not a term exclusively reserved for multinational corporations and international financial institutions. Nor is globalization the exclusive domain of those with only altruistic or moral intentions. In fact, globalization has been described as going "well beyond the links that bind corporations, traders, financiers, and central bankers. It provides a conduit not only for ideas but also for processes of coordination and cooperation used by terrorists, politicians, religious leaders, anti-globalization activists, and bureaucrats alike."[5]

For our purposes, this discussion focuses on the business implications of globalization. Two areas of business in which globalization is having profound effects are the globalization of *markets* and *production*.

Globalization of Markets

Globalization of markets refers to convergence in buyer preferences in markets around the world. This trend is occurring in many product categories, including consumer goods, industrial products, and business services. Clothing retailer Lululemon (www.lululemon.com), shoe producer Aldo (www.aldoshoes.com), and cell phone maker Blackberry (www.ca.blackberry.com) are all examples of companies that sell *global products*—products marketed worldwide, essentially without any changes to them. For example, Apple's iPad qualifies as a global product because of its highly standardized features and the company's global marketing strategy and global brand.[6]

Global products and global competition characterize many industries and markets, including semiconductors (Intel, Philips), aircraft (Bombardier, Boeing), construction equipment (Caterpillar, Mitsubishi), oil and gas (Suncor, Pemex, Shell), autos (Volvo, Volkswagen), financial services (ING, HSBC), air travel (Lufthansa, Air Canada, Quantas, KLM), accounting services (Ernst & Young, KPMG), consumer goods (Procter & Gamble, Unilever), and fast food (Subway, New York Fries, McDonald's). The globalization of markets is important to international business because of the benefits it offers companies. Let's now look briefly at each of these benefits.

REDUCES MARKETING COSTS Companies that sell global products can reduce costs by *standardizing* certain marketing activities. A company selling a global consumer good, such as shampoo, can make an identical product for the global market and then simply design different packaging to account for the language spoken in each market and to comply with the labelling rules for each country. Companies can achieve further cost savings by keeping an ad's visual component the same for all markets but dubbing TV ads and translating print ads into local languages.

CREATES NEW MARKET OPPORTUNITIES A company that sells a global product can explore opportunities abroad if the home market is small or becomes saturated. For example, China holds enormous potential for e-business with more than 500 million Internet users, which is more than 10 times the population of Canada. But while more than 77 percent of people in Canada actively surf the Web, just 30 percent of people in China do. So, the battle for market share in the Middle Kingdom is raging between the top two online search engines—Google (www.google.cn) and Yahoo! (www.cn.yahoo.com).[7] Seeking sales growth abroad can be absolutely essential for an entrepreneur or small company that sells a global product but has a limited home market such as Canada.

Ecstatic customers display their new iPads in Mexico City. The iPad is Apple's (www.apple.com) first tablet computer and a global success that excites style-lovers the world over. The iPad lets users surf the Web, write e-mail, flip through photos, and watch movies—all on a device that is only 1.3 cm thick. Thousands of applications expand the iPad's capabilities even further and more are created daily. Apple standardized the iPad to reduce production and marketing costs and to support its powerful global brand.

Source: STR/AFP/Getty Images/Newscom.

LEVELS UNEVEN INCOME STREAMS A company that sells a product with universal, but seasonal, appeal can use international sales to level its income stream. By supplementing domestic sales with international sales, the company can reduce or eliminate wide variations in sales between seasons and steady its cash flow. For example, a firm that produces extreme winter weather outwear, such as Canada Goose (www.canada-goose.com), can match product distribution with the winter seasons in the northern and southern hemispheres in alternating fashion, thereby steadying its income from these global yet highly seasonal products. Put differently, Canada Goose could start marketing a new jacket in Canada, Germany, Switzerland, and Sweden in September to distribute and sell it for the winter months of November to February in those markets. Then in March the company could begin marketing the same jacket in Chile and Argentina to distribute and sell it for their winter months of June to August.

YET LOCAL NEEDS ARE IMPORTANT Despite the potential benefits of global markets, managers must constantly monitor the match between the firm's products and markets to not overlook the needs of buyers. The benefit of serving customers with an adapted product may outweigh the benefit of a standardized one. For instance, soft drinks, fast food, and other consumer goods are global products that continue to penetrate markets around the world. But sometimes these products require small modifications to better suit local tastes. In southern Japan, Coca-Cola (www.cocacola.com) sweetens its traditional formula to compete with sweeter-tasting Pepsi (www.pepsi.com). In India, where cows are sacred and the consumption of beef is taboo, McDonald's (www.mcdonalds.com) markets the "Maharaja Mac"—two all-mutton patties on a sesame-seed bun with all the usual toppings.

Globalization of Production

Many production activities are also becoming global. *Globalization of production* refers to the dispersal of production activities to locations that help a company achieve its cost-minimization or quality-maximization objectives for a good or service. This includes the sourcing of key production inputs (such as raw materials or products for assembly) as well as the international outsourcing of services. Let's now explore the benefits that companies obtain from the globalization of production.

ACCESS LOWER-COST WORKERS Global production activities allow companies to reduce overall production costs through access to low-cost labour. For decades, companies located their factories in low-wage nations to churn out all kinds of goods, including toys, small appliances, inexpensive electronics, and textiles. Yet whereas moving production to low-cost locales traditionally meant *production of goods* almost exclusively, it increasingly applies to the *production of services* such as accounting and research. Although most services must be produced where they are consumed, some services can be performed at remote locations where labour costs are lower. Many European and North American businesses have moved their customer service and other nonessential operations to places as far away as India to slash costs by as much as 60 percent.

ACCESS TECHNICAL EXPERTISE Companies also produce goods and services abroad to benefit from technical know-how. Film Roman (www.filmroman.com) produces the TV series *The Simpsons*, but it provides key poses and step-by-step frame directions to AKOM Production Company (www.akomkorea.com) in Seoul, South Korea. AKOM then fills in the remaining poses and links them into an animated whole. But there are bumps along the way, says animation director Mark Kirkland. In one middle-of-the-night phone call, Kirkland was explaining to the Koreans how to draw a shooting gun. "They don't allow guns in Korea; it's against the law," says Kirkland. "So they were calling me [asking]: How does a gun work?'" Kirkland and others put up with such cultural differences and phone calls at odd hours to tap a highly qualified pool of South Korean animators.[8]

ACCESS PRODUCTION INPUTS Globalization of production allows companies to access resources that are unavailable or more costly at home. The quest for natural resources draws many companies into international markets. Japan, for example, is a small, densely populated island

Global Challenges — Managing Security in the Age of Globalization

The globalization of markets and production creates new challenges for companies. As well as the need to secure lengthy supply chains and distribution channels, companies must secure their facilities, information systems, and reputations.

- **Facilities Risk.** Careful planning and facilities assessment (around $12 000 for a medium-sized company; $1 million for a large firm) can be well worth the cost. Large companies with top-notch property risk management programs are said to produce more stable earnings. And companies practising weak risk management experience 55 times greater risk of property loss due to fire and 29 times greater risk of property loss caused by natural hazards.

- **Information Risk.** Computer viruses, software worms, malicious code, and cyber criminals cost companies around the world many billions of dollars each year. The usual suspects include disgruntled employees and dishonest competitors, but often are hackers who steal customers' personal and financial data that is then sold worldwide to the highest bidder. Upon quitting their jobs, some employees simply walk away with digital devices containing confidential memos, competitive data, and private e-mails.

- **Reputational Risk.** News regarding the actions of today's largest corporations spreads worldwide quickly.

Reputational risk is anything that can harm a firm's image, including accounting irregularities, product recalls, workers' rights violations, and involvement in a lawsuit. The damaged reputation of Goldman Sachs following its $550 million settlement with the Securities and Exchange Commission (for its actions before and during the financial meltdown on Wall Street) is estimated to have cost the firm nearly 40 percent ($6 billion) of its brand value in one year.

- **The Challenge.** Like the risks themselves, the challenges are also varied. First, companies should identify all potential risks to their facilities and develop a best-practice property risk program. Second, employees should change passwords often, guard computers and mobile devices with software patches, and return company-owned digital devices when leaving the firm. Third, as they come under ever-increasing scrutiny, companies should act ethically and within the law to protect their reputations.

- **Want to Know More?** Visit leading risk consultancy Kroll (www.krollworldwide.com), leading Internet security firm Check Point Software Technologies (www.checkpoint.com), and Internet security agency CERT Coordination Center (www.cert.org).

Sources: Douglas McIntyre, "The 10 Biggest Brand Disasters of 2010," Daily Finance Web site (www.dailyfinance.com), July 21, 2010; Erik Schatzker and Christine Harper, "Goldman Could Have Managed Reputational Risks Better, Cohn Says," *Bloomberg Businessweek* (www.businessweek.com), July 1, 2010; *The Risk/Earnings Ratio: New Perspectives for Achieving Bottom-Line Stabililty* (Johnston, RI; FM Global, June 2010); *An Introduction to the Business Model for Information Security* (Rolling Meadows, IL: ISACA, 2009).

nation with very few natural resources of its own—especially forests. But Japan's largest paper company, Nippon Seishi, does more than simply import wood pulp. The company owns huge forests and corresponding processing facilities in Australia, Canada, and the United States. This gives the firm not only access to an essential resource but also control over earlier stages in the papermaking process. As a result, the company is guaranteed a steady flow of its key ingredient (wood pulp) that is less subject to swings in prices and supply associated with buying pulp on the open market. Likewise, to access cheaper energy resources used in manufacturing, a variety of Japanese firms are relocating production to China and Vietnam, where energy costs are lower.

Despite its benefits, globalization also creates new risks and accentuates old ones for companies. To read about several key risks that globalization heightens and how companies can better manage them, see this chapter's Global Challenges feature, titled "Managing Security in the Age of Globalization."

Quick Study

1. Define *globalization*. How does denationalization differ from internationalization?
2. List each benefit a company might obtain from the globalization of markets.
3. How might a company benefit from the globalization of production?

Forces Driving Globalization

Two main forces underlie the globalization of markets and production: *falling barriers to trade and investment* and *technological innovation*. These two features, more than anything else, are increasing competition among nations by levelling the global business playing field. Greater competition is simultaneously driving companies worldwide into more direct confrontation *and* cooperation. Local industries once isolated by time and distance are increasingly accessible to large international companies based many thousands of miles away. Some small and medium-sized local firms are compelled to cooperate with one another or with larger international firms to remain competitive. Other local businesses revitalize themselves in a bold attempt to survive the competitive onslaught. And on a global scale, consolidation is occurring in many industries as former competitors link up to challenge others on a worldwide basis. Let's now explore in greater detail the pivotal roles of the two forces driving globalization.

Falling Barriers to Trade and Investment

In 1947, political leaders of 23 nations (12 developed and 11 developing economies) made history when they created the **General Agreement on Tariffs and Trade (GATT)**—a treaty designed to promote free trade by reducing both tariffs and nontariff barriers to international trade. *Tariffs* are essentially taxes levied on traded goods, and *nontariff barriers* are limits on the quantity of an imported product or bureaucratic procedures required to import the goods. The treaty, which came into effect in 1948, was successful in its early years. After four decades, world merchandise trade had grown 20 times larger, and average tariffs had fallen from 40 percent to 5 percent.

Significant progress occurred again with a 1994 revision of the GATT treaty. Nations that had signed on to the treaty further reduced average tariffs on merchandise trade and lowered subsidies (government financial support) for agricultural products. The treaty's revision also clearly defined *intellectual property rights*—giving protection to copyrights (including computer programs, databases, sound recordings, and films), trademarks and service marks, and patents (including trade secrets and know-how). A major flaw of the original GATT was that it lacked the power to enforce world trade rules. Likely the greatest accomplishment of the 1994 revision was the creation of the *World Trade Organization*.

WORLD TRADE ORGANIZATION   The **World Trade Organization (WTO)**, established January 1, 1995, is the international organization that enforces the rules of international trade. It was created by the Uruguay Round of negotiations held between 1986 and 1994, and replaced

General Agreement on Tariffs and Trade (GATT)
Treaty designed to promote free trade by reducing both tariffs and nontariff barriers to international trade.

World Trade Organization (WTO)
International organization that enforces the rules of international trade.

the GATT treaty. The three main goals of the WTO (www.wto.org) are to help the free flow of trade, help negotiate the further opening of markets, and settle trade disputes among its members. WTO specifies that its "main function is to ensure trade flows as smoothly, predictably, and freely as possible."[9]

While the WTO replaced the *institution* of GATT, it absorbed the GATT *agreements* (such as those on services, intellectual property, and agriculture) into its own agreements. One key component that was carried over from the GATT treaty into the WTO is the principle of non-discrimination—formerly known as "most favoured nation status" and now referred to as **normal trade relations**—a requirement that WTO members extend the same favourable terms of trade to all members as they extend to any single member. For example, if Japan were to reduce its import tariff on German automobiles to 5 percent, it must reduce the tariff it levies against auto imports from all other WTO nations to 5 percent.

It is the power of the WTO to settle trade disputes that really sets it apart from its predecessor, the GATT. Under the GATT, a nation could file a complaint against another member, and a committee would investigate the matter. If appropriate, the GATT would identify the unfair trade practices, and member countries would pressure the offender to change its ways. But in reality, GATT rulings were usually given only after very long investigative phases that could last years, and they were likely to be ignored.

By contrast, the various WTO agreements are essentially contracts between member nations committed to maintain fair and open trade policies. When one WTO member files a complaint against another, the Dispute Settlement Body of the WTO takes swift action. Decisions must be rendered within 9 months if the case is urgent and within 15 months if the case is appealed. The WTO dispute settlement system is faster and more automatic, and its rulings cannot be ignored or blocked by members. Offenders must realign their trade policies according to WTO guidelines or suffer financial penalties, perhaps even trade sanctions. Because of its ability to penalize offending member nations, the WTO's dispute settlement system has become key to the global trading system.

The WTO also settles disputes involving "dumping" and the granting of subsidies. When a company exports a product at a price that is either lower than the price normally charged in the domestic market or lower than the cost of production, it is said to be **dumping**. Charges of dumping are made against companies from almost every nation and can occur in any type of industry. For example, Western European plastic producers considered retaliating against Asian competitors whose prices were substantially lower in European markets than at home. More recently, US steel producers and their powerful union charged that steelmakers in Brazil, Japan, and Russia were dumping steel on the US market at low prices. The problem arose as those nations tried to improve their economies through increased exporting of all products, including steel.

When a company is accused of dumping, the WTO cannot penalize the country in which the company is based. Dumping is an act carried out by a company, not a country. The WTO can respond only to the actions of a country that retaliates against a company for dumping. The WTO allows a nation to act against dumping if it can prove that dumping is actually occurring, can calculate the damage to its own companies, and can show that the damage is significant. The usual way a country retaliates is by charging an **antidumping duty**—an additional tariff placed on an imported product that a nation believes is being dumped on its market. Such measures must expire within five years of the time they are initiated, unless a country can demonstrate that circumstances warrant their continuation. A large number of antidumping cases have been brought before the WTO in recent years.

Governments often retaliate when subsidies another country pays to its own domestic producers threaten the competitiveness of their companies. As with antidumping measures, nations can take action against product(s) that receive an unfair subsidy by charging a **countervailing duty**—an additional tariff placed on an imported product that a nation believes is receiving an unfair subsidy. Unlike dumping, however, the payment of a subsidy is an action carried out by a country. In this instance, the WTO regulates the actions of both parties: the government that reacts to the subsidy as well as the government that originally paid the subsidy.

Today, the WTO recognizes 159 members and 29 "observer" members. The newest members are Russia, which joined the WTO on August 22, 2012, after 19 years of negotiations; Laos, which joined on February 2, 2013; and Tajikistan, which joined on March 2, 2013.[10]

---

normal trade relations (formerly "most favoured nation status")
Requirement that WTO members extend the same favourable terms of trade to all members as they extend to any single member.

dumping
Exporting a product at a price that is either lower than the price normally charged in the domestic market or lower than the cost of production.

antidumping duty
Additional tariff placed on an imported product that a nation believes is being dumped on its market.

countervailing duty
Additional tariff placed on an imported product that a nation believes is receiving an unfair subsidy.

The WTO launched a new round of negotiations in Doha, Qatar, in late 2001. The renewed negotiations were designed to lower trade barriers further and to help poor nations in particular. Agricultural subsidies that rich countries pay to their own farmers are worth $1 billion per day—more than six times the value of their combined aid budgets to poor nations. Because 70 percent of poor nations' exports are agricultural products and textiles, wealthy nations had intended to further open these and other labour-intensive industries. Poor nations were encouraged to reduce tariffs among themselves and were to receive help in integrating themselves into the global trading system. Although the Doha Round was to conclude by the end of 2004, negotiations are proceeding more slowly than was anticipated.[11] Some consider the Doha Round to be at a critical stage, as negotiations have been ongoing for more than a decade with disagreement centred on two main topics: eliminating subsidies and decreasing antidumping policies.

REGIONAL TRADE AGREEMENTS   In addition to the WTO, smaller groups of nations are integrating their economies as never before by fostering trade and boosting cross-border investment. For example, the *North American Free Trade Agreement (NAFTA)* gathers three nations (Canada, Mexico, and the United States) into a free-trade bloc. The more ambitious *European Union (EU)* combines 28 countries. The *Asia Pacific Economic Cooperation (APEC)* consists of 21 member economies committed to creating a free-trade zone around the Pacific. The aims of each of these smaller trade pacts are similar to those of the WTO but are regional in nature. Moreover, some nations are placing greater emphasis on regional pacts because of resistance to worldwide trade agreements.

TRADE AND NATIONAL OUTPUT   Together, the WTO agreements and regional pacts have boosted world trade and cross-border investment significantly. Trade theory tells us that openness to trade helps a nation to produce a greater amount of output. Figure 1.1 illustrates that growth in national output over a seven-year period is significantly positive, with the exception of the 2008–2009 years. As shown in Map 1.1, economic growth is greater in nations that have recently become more open to trade, such Brazil, China, India, and Russia (the BRIC countries), than it is in many other countries. Much of South America is also growing rapidly, while Africa's experience is mixed.

Let's take a moment in our discussion to define a few terms that we will encounter time and again throughout this book. **Gross domestic product (GDP)** is the value of all goods and services produced by a domestic economy over a one-year period. GDP excludes a nation's income generated from exports, imports, and the international operations of its companies. We can speak in terms of world GDP when we sum all individual nations' GDP figures. GDP is a somewhat narrower figure than **gross national product (GNP)**—the value of all goods and services produced by a country's domestic and international activities over a one-year period. A country's **GDP or GNP per capita** is simply its GDP or GNP divided by its population.

gross domestic product (GDP)
Value of all goods and services produced by a domestic economy over a one-year period.

gross national product (GNP)
Value of all goods and services produced by a country's domestic and international activities over a one-year period.

GDP or GNP per capita
Nation's GDP or GNP divided by its population.

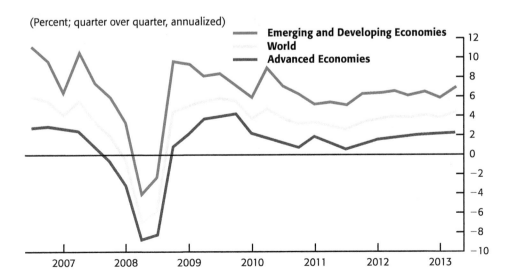

(Percent; quarter over quarter, annualized)

Emerging and Developing Economies
World
Advanced Economies

FIGURE 1.1

Global GDP Growth

Source: Based on data from IMF (http://www.imf.org/external/pubs/ft/weo/2012/update/01/)

MAP 1.1

Growth in National Output

http://data.worldbank.org/indicator/NY.GDP.MKTP.
KD.ZG/countries?display=map

GREENLAND

ARCTI

ALASKA

ICELAND

C A N A D A

UNITED KINGDOM
IRELAND
NETHERLA
G
BELGIUM
LUXEMBO
FRANCE
SWIT
MONACO
ANDORRA
SPAIN
PORTUGAL

PACIFIC
OCEAN

UNITED STATES
OF AMERICA

NORTH

ATLANTIC

OCEAN

MOROCCO

ALGERIA

WESTERN
SAHARA

HAWAII

MEXICO

CUBA
JAMAICA
BELIZE
HONDURAS
GUATEMALA
EL SALVADOR NICARAGUA
COSTA RICA
PANAMA

DOMINICAN
REPUBLIC
HAITI PUERTO
RICO

MAURITANIA MALI N

SENEGAL
GAMBIA
GUINEA-BISSAU GUINEA
BURKINA
FASO
NIG
SIERRA LEONE IVORY
COAST
GHANA
TOGO
BENIN
LIBERIA

EQUATORI
GUINEA
GA

GALAPAGOS
ISLANDS

TRINIDAD &
TOBAGO

VENEZUELA
GUYANA FRENCH
GUIANA
SURINAME

COLOMBIA

ECUADOR

B R A Z I L

SWEDEN LATVIA
DENMARK
LITHUANIA
RUSSIA
NETHERLANDS
BELGIUM GERMANY
LUXEMBOURG
FRANCE
LICHTENSTEIN AUSTRIA
SWITZERLAND
SLOVENIA
SAN
MARINO BOSNIA-
MONACO
ANDORRA HERZEGOVINA
ITALY
MONTENEGRO
MACEDONIA
ALBANIA
ALGERIA

TUNISIA MALTA

POLAND
BELARUS

CZECH
REP.
SLOVAKIA

UKRAINE

MOLDOVA
HUNGARY
CROATIA ROMANIA
SERBIA Black Sea
BULGARIA

GREECE T U R K E Y

CYPRUS

LIBYA

PERU

BOLIVIA

PARAGUAY

URUGUAY

ARGENTINA

CHILE

FALKLAND/MALVINAS
ISLANDS

SOUTH

ATLANTIC

OCEAN

Average annual GDP growth
rate, 1998–2007, (%)

negative
less than –2.5

–2.5 to 0

no data available

positive
0 to 1

1 to 2

2 to 3

3 to 4

4 to 5

over 5

Technological Innovation

Although falling barriers to trade and investment encourage globalization, technological innovation is accelerating its pace. Significant advancements in information technology and transportation methods are making it easier, faster, and less costly to move data, goods, and equipment around the world. Let's examine several innovations that have had a considerable impact on globalization.

E-MAIL AND VIDEOCONFERENCING Operating across borders and time zones complicates the job of coordinating and controlling business activities. But technology can speed the flow of information and ease the tasks of coordination and control. Electronic mail (e-mail) is an indispensable tool that managers use to stay in contact with international operations and to respond quickly to important matters. Videoconferencing allows managers in different locations to meet in virtual face-to-face meetings. Primary reasons for 25 to 30 percent annual growth in videoconferencing include lower-cost bandwidth (communication channels) used to transmit information, lower-cost equipment, and the rising cost of travel for businesses. Videoconferencing equipment can cost as little as $5000 and as much as $340 000. A company that does not require ongoing videoconferencing can pay even less by renting the facilities and equipment of a local conference centre.[12] Another option is to use Skype (www.skype.com), which allows registered users to conduct Internet phone calls and video conferences free of charge.

INTERNET AND WORLD WIDE WEB Companies use the Internet to quickly and cheaply contact managers in distant locations, for example, to inquire about production runs, revise sales strategies, and check on distribution bottlenecks. They also use the Internet to achieve longer-term goals, such as sharpen their forecasting, lower their inventories, and improve communication with suppliers. The lower cost of reaching an international customer base especially benefits small firms, which were among the first to use the Web as a global marketing tool. Further gains arise from the ability of the Internet to cut postproduction costs by decreasing the number of intermediaries a product passes through on its way to the customer. Eliminating intermediaries greatly benefits online sellers of books, music, and travel services, among others.

COMPANY INTRANETS AND EXTRANETS Internal company Web sites and information networks (*intranets*) give employees access to company data using personal computers. A particularly effective marketing tool on Volvo Car Corporation's (www.volvocars.com) intranet is a quarter-by-quarter database of marketing and sales information. The cycle begins when headquarters submits its corporate-wide marketing plan to Volvo's intranet. Marketing managers at each subsidiary worldwide then select those activities that apply to their own market, develop their marketing plan, and submit it to the database. This allows managers in every market to view every other subsidiary's marketing plan and to adapt relevant aspects to their own plan. In essence, the entire system acts as a tool for the sharing of best practices across all of Volvo's markets.

Extranets give distributors and suppliers access to a company's database to place orders or restock inventories electronically and automatically. These networks permit international companies (along with their suppliers and buyers) to respond to internal and external conditions more quickly and more appropriately.

ADVANCEMENTS IN TRANSPORTATION TECHNOLOGIES Retailers worldwide rely on imports to stock their storerooms with finished goods and to supply factories with raw materials and intermediate products. Innovation in the shipping industry is helping globalize markets and production by making shipping more efficient and dependable. In the past, a cargo ship would sit in port up to 10 days while it was unloaded one pallet at a time. But because cargo today is loaded onto a ship in 20- and 40-foot containers that are quickly unloaded onto railcars or truck chassis at the final destination, a 700-foot cargo ship is routinely unloaded in just 15 hours.

Operation of cargo ships is now simpler and safer due to computerized charts that pinpoint a ship's movements on the high seas using Global Positioning System (GPS) satellites. Combining GPS with radio frequency identification (RFID) technology allows continuous monitoring of individual containers from port of departure to destination. RFID can tell whether a container's doors are opened and closed on its journey and can monitor the temperature inside refrigerated containers.[13]

Measuring Globalization

Although we intuitively feel that our world is becoming smaller, researchers have created ways to measure the extent of globalization. One index of globalization was created by A.T. Kearney (www.atkearney.com), a management consultancy, and by *Foreign Policy* magazine (www.foreignpolicy.com).[14] This index ranked 72 nations, which altogether accounted for 97 percent of the world's GDP and 88 percent of its population in 2007. In 2007, Singapore ranked number 1, followed by Hong Kong, The Netherlands, and Switzerland. Canada was ranked number 8 overall in this globalization index, but ranked 34 out of 72 in terms of economic integration.

The KOF Index of Globalization, a current and more comprehensive index, was developed by Dr. Axel Dreher at the KOF Swiss Economic Institute.[15] This index measures 24 different variables within three dimensions: economic, social, and political globalization. Its records show changes in globalization by comparing 187 countries over a long-term period (1970–2012). The globalization of a country is measured on a scale from 1 to 100, with higher numbers indicating greater levels of globalization. Following are some of the factors considered for each of the three main dimensions:

1. **Economic globalization:** Trade and investment flows, and trade barriers.
2. **Social globalization:** Flow of ideas and information.
3. **Political globalization:** Degree of political cooperation between countries.

The KOF Index of Globalization 2012 still shows the impact of the 2009 financial and world economic crisis. Nonetheless, overall there has been a progressive upward trend in globalization since the 1970s (see Figure 1.2).

By incorporating a wide variety of variables, the KOF Index is apt to cut through cycles occurring in any one of the three dimensions listed above. And by encompassing social factors, in addition to economic influences, it tends to capture the broad nature of globalization.

Figure 1.3 shows the 15 highest-ranking nations in the latest KOF Index of Globalization. It shows each nation's overall rank and its rank for each of the three dimensions described earlier: (1) economic globalization; (2) social globalization; and (3) political globalization. Europe accounts for 9 of the top 10 spots, while Canada appears as number 15. Belgium, Ireland, The Netherlands, and Austria are the most globalized nations. In the KOF Index 2012, Singapore ranks number 5, but remains number 1 in terms of economic globalization.

Large nations often do not make it into the higher ranks in the economic globalization dimension, because they tend to depend less on external trade and investment. For example, Germany and the United States rank as numbers 44 and 79, respectively. Among the leaders of the economic globalization dimension are Luxemburg, Malta, Ireland, and Belgium, all of them relatively small countries with open economies.

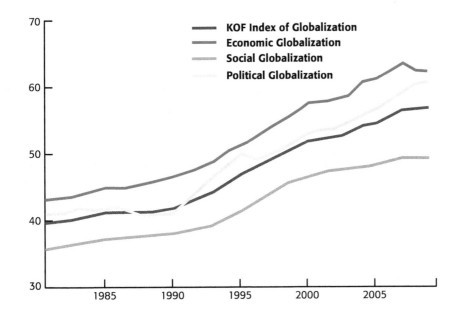

Legend:
- KOF Index of Globalization
- Economic Globalization
- Social Globalization
- Political Globalization

FIGURE 1.2

KOF Index of Globalization Worldwide 1970–2012

Source: KOF Press Release March 16, 2012 (http://globalization.kof.ethz.ch/), Dreher, Axel (2006): Does Globalization Affect Growth? Evidence from a new Index of Globalization, Applied Economics 38, 10: 1091–1110. Reprinted with permission

FIGURE 1.3

The World's 15 Most Globalized Countries

Source: KOF Press Release March 16, 2012 (http://globalization.kof.ethz.ch/), Dreher, Axel (2006): Does Globalization Affect Growth? Evidence from a new Index of Globalization, Applied Economics 38, 10: 1091–1110. Reprinted with permission

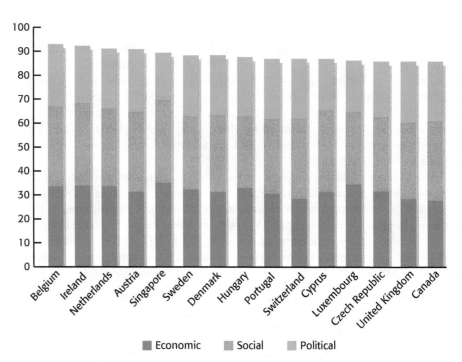

Canada ranks number 35 in the KOF Index of Globalization, with a score of 76.05 in the economic dimension. One could argue that the efforts the Canadian government has put into diversification of trade over the past five years by negotiating and signing several trade agreements have not yet paid off. On the other hand, Canada ranked number 7 in terms of social globalization, scoring 88.72, and number 10 in political globalization, scoring 94.16.

The world's least globalized nations include: Timor-Leste, Kiribati, Equatorial Guinea, Laos, Solomon Islands, Eritrea, Bhutan, Afghanistan, Comoros, the West Bank and Gaza, Liberia, Burma, Sao Tome and Principe, Burundi, and the Central African Republic. One remarkable commonality among these nations is their low levels of technological connectivity. These nations will likely continue to encounter economic challenges if they do not overcome their lack of global integration.

Some of the least-global nations are characterized by ongoing political unrest, corruption, and terrorism. Other nations with large agricultural sectors face trade barriers in developed countries and are subject to highly volatile prices on commodity markets. Others have recurring environmental catastrophes, terrorism, and burdensome visa regulations that hurt tourism. To deepen their global links, each of these nations will need to make great strides in their economic, social, technological, and political environments.

Quick Study

1. What two main forces underlie the expansion of globalization?
2. How have global and regional efforts to promote trade and investment advanced globalization?
3. How does technological innovation propel globalization?
4. What factors make some countries more global than others?
5. What measures does Canada need to take in order to rank higher in the KOF Index of Globalization?

Untangling the Globalization Debate

Globalization means different things to different people. A businessperson may see globalization as an opportunity to source goods and services from lower-cost locations and to pry open new markets. An economist may see it as an opportunity to examine the impact of globalization on jobs and standards of living. An environmentalist may be concerned with how globalization affects our environment. An anthropologist may want to examine the influence of globalization on the culture of a group of people. A political scientist may be concerned with the impact of globalization on the power of governments relative to that of multinational companies. And an employee may view globalization either as an opportunity for new work or as a threat to his or her current job.

It is because of the different lenses through which we view events around us that the globalization debate is so complex. Entrepreneurs, small business owners, and globetrotting managers need to understand globalization and the arguments of those who oppose it. In the pages that follow, we explain the main arguments of those opposed to globalization and the responses of those in favour of it. But before we address the intricacies of the debate, it is helpful to put today's globalization into its proper context.

Today's Globalization in Context

Many people forget that there was a first age of globalization that extended from the mid-1800s to the 1920s.[16] In those days, labour was highly mobile, with 300 000 people leaving Europe each year in the 1800s and 1 million people leaving each year after 1900.[17] Other than in wartime, nations did not even require passports for international travel before 1914. And like today, workers in wealthy nations back then feared competition for jobs from high- and low-wage countries.

Trade and capital flowed more freely than ever during that first age of globalization. Huge companies from wealthy nations built facilities in distant lands to extract raw materials and produce all sorts of goods. Large cargo ships plied the seas to deliver their manufactures to distant markets. The transatlantic cable (completed in 1866) allowed news between Europe and the United States to travel faster than ever before. The drivers of that first age of globalization included the steamship, telegraph, railroad, and, later, the telephone and airplane.

That first age of globalization was abruptly halted by the arrival of the First World War, the Russian Revolution, and the Great Depression. A backlash to fierce competition in trade and unfettered immigration in the early 1900s helped usher in high tariffs and barriers to immigration. The great flows of goods, capital, and people common before the First World War became a mere trickle. For 75 years, from the start of the First World War to the end of the Cold War, the world remained divided. There was a geographic divide between East and West and an ideological divide between communism and capitalism. After the Second World War, the West experienced steady economic gains, but international flows of goods, capital, and people were confined to their respective capitalist and communist systems and geographies.

Fast-forward to 1989 and the collapse of the wall separating East and West Berlin (end of the Cold War period). One by one, Central and Eastern European nations broke with the former Soviet bloc, becoming more liberalized and adopting free market economic systems. But it took until the 1990s for international capital flows, in absolute terms, to recover to levels seen prior to the First World War. Lowering the cost of telecommunications and binding our world more tightly together are the drivers of this second age of globalization—communication satellites, fibre optics, microchips, and the Internet.

Introduction to the Debate

In addition to the World Trade Organization presented earlier, several other supranational institutions play leading roles in fostering globalization. The **World Bank** is an agency created to provide financing for national economic development efforts. The initial purpose of the World Bank (www.worldbank.org) was to finance European reconstruction following the Second World War. It later shifted its focus to the general financial needs of developing countries, and today it finances many economic development projects in Africa, South America, and Southeast Asia. The **International Monetary Fund (IMF)** is an agency created to regulate fixed exchange rates and enforce the rules of the international monetary system. Today, the IMF (www.imf.org) has 188 member countries. Some of the purposes of the IMF include promoting international monetary cooperation; facilitating expansion and balanced growth of international trade; avoiding competitive exchange devaluation; and making financial resources temporarily available to members.

At this point we should note one caveat. Each side in the debate over globalization tends to hold up results of social and economic studies they say show "definitive" support for their arguments. Yet many organizations that publish studies on globalization have political agendas, such as decreasing

World Bank
Agency created to provide financing for national economic development efforts.

International Monetary Fund (IMF)
Agency created to regulate fixed exchange rates and enforce the rules of the international monetary system.

Employees of Brazilian company Volkswagen do Brasil cheerfully celebrate at Volkswagen's (www.vw.com) factory in Anchieta, close to Sao Paulo, Brazil. Factory employees are celebrating the production of more than 15 million vehicles in VW's 50-plus years in Brazil. The country is one of the strongest emerging markets in the world and one that benefited tremendously by embracing the opportunities offered by globalization. Can you identify other emerging markets in which globalization helped create good jobs and rising incomes for people?

Source: Z6334 Ralf Hirschberger Deutsch Presse Agentur/Newscom.

government regulation or expanding government programs. This can make objective consideration of a group's claims and findings difficult. A group's aims may influence the selection of the data to analyze, the time period to study, the nations to examine, and so forth. It is essential to take into account such factors any time we hear a group arguing the beneficial or harmful effects of globalization.

Let's now engage the debate over globalization by examining its effects on (1) jobs and wages; (2) labour and environmental regulation; (3) income inequality; (4) national sovereignty; and (5) cultures.

Quick Study

1. How does this current period of globalization compare with the first age of globalization?
2. Explain the original purpose of the *World Bank* and its mandate today.
3. What are the main purposes of the *International Monetary Fund*?

Globalization's Impact on Jobs and Wages

We open our coverage of the globalization debate with an important topic for both developed and developing countries—the effect of globalization on jobs and wages. We begin with the arguments of those against globalization and then turn our attention to how supporters of globalization respond.

AGAINST GLOBALIZATION Groups opposed to globalization blame it for eroding standards of living and ruining ways of life. Specifically, they say globalization *eliminates jobs* and *lowers wages* in developed nations and *exploits workers* in developing countries. Let's explore each of these arguments.

Eliminates Jobs in Developed Nations Some groups claim that *globalization eliminates manufacturing jobs in developed nations*. They criticize the practice of sending good-paying manufacturing jobs abroad to developing countries where wages are a fraction of the cost for international firms. It is argued that a label reading "Made in China" translates to "Not Made Here." Although critics admit that importing products from China (or another low-wage nation) lowers consumer prices for televisions, sporting goods, and so on, they say this is little consolation for workers who lose their jobs.

A G-20 2010 protest in Toronto, Ontario. This summit was the fourth meeting of the group of countries with the 20 largest economies in the world. One of the summit's objectives was to evaluate progress on promoting open markets. As you can see in the picture, people are protesting the economic conditions created by the current system.

Source: KOZAK NICK/SIPA/ ASSOCIATED PRESS

To illustrate their argument, globalization critics point to the activities of big-box retailers such as Costco (www.costco.com) and Walmart (www.walmart.com). It is difficult to overstate the power of these retail giants and symbols of globalization. It is said that by relentlessly pursuing low-cost goods, these retailers force their suppliers to move to China and other low-wage nations.[18]

Lowers Wages in Developed Nations   Opposition groups say *globalization causes worker dislocation that gradually lowers wages*. They allege that when a manufacturing job is lost in a wealthy nation, the new job (assuming new work is found) pays less than the previous one. Some evidence does suggest that a displaced manufacturing worker, especially an older one, receives lower pay in a subsequent job. Those opposed to globalization say this decreases employee loyalty, employee morale, and job security. They say this causes people to fear globalization and any additional lowering of trade barriers.

Big-box retailers come under fire in this discussion also. Globalization critics say powerful retailers continually force manufacturers in low-wage nations to accept lower profits so the retailers can slash prices to consumers. As a result of these business practices, critics charge, powerful retailers force down wages and working conditions worldwide.

Exploits Workers in Developing Nations   Critics charge that *globalization and international outsourcing exploit workers in low-wage nations*. One notable critic of globalization is Naomi Klein (www.naomiklein.org). She vehemently opposes the outsourced call centre jobs of Western companies, such as Victoria's Secret (www.victoriassecret.com) and Delta Airlines (www.delta.com). Klein says such jobs force young Asians to disguise their nationality, adopt fake Midwestern accents, and work nights when their North American customers are awake halfway around the world. Klein maintains that free trade policies are "a highly efficient engine of dispossession, pushing small farmers off their land and laying off public-sector workers."[19]

FOR GLOBALIZATION   Supporters of globalization credit it with improving standards of living and making possible new ways of life. They argue that globalization *increases wealth and efficiency in all nations, generates labour market flexibility in developed nations,* and *advances the economies of developing nations.* Let's now examine each of these arguments.

Increases Wealth and Efficiency in All Nations   Some economists believe *globalization increases wealth and efficiency in both developed and developing nations.* Globalization supporters argue that openness to international trade (the ratio of trade to national output) increases national production (by increasing efficiency) and raises per capita income (by passing savings on to consumers). For instance, by squeezing inefficiencies out of the retail supply chain, powerful global retailers help restrain inflation and boost productivity. Some economists predict that removing all remaining barriers to free trade would significantly boost worldwide income and greatly benefit developing nations.

Generates Labour Market Flexibility in Developed Nations   Globalization supporters believe *globalization creates positive benefits by generating labour market flexibility in developed nations.* It is claimed that benefits derive from worker dislocation, or "churning" as it is called when there is widespread job turnover throughout an economy. Flexible labour markets allow workers to be redeployed rapidly to sectors of the economy where they are highly valued and in demand. This also allows employees, particularly young workers, to change jobs easily with few negative effects. For instance, a young person can gain experience and skills with an initial employer and then move to a different job that provides a better match between employee and employer.

Advances Economies of Developing Nations   Those in favour of globalization argue that *globalization and international outsourcing help to advance developing nations' economies.* India initially became attractive as a location for software-writing operations because of its low-cost, well-trained, English-speaking technicians. More recently, telephone call centres that provide all sorts of customer services offer bright futures to young graduates who will not become doctors and lawyers. Millions of young Indians view such a job as a ticket to working for an international firm at a good salary.

Today, the relentless march of globalization is making India a base for business process outsourcing—including financial, accounting, payroll, and benefits services. A bourgeoning back-office industry worth billions of dollars in India is significantly elevating living standards. The reason is simple. The world's largest corporations and law firms now outsource legal work such as document review, due diligence, contract management, and other activities to Indian law firms for one-tenth to one-third what they pay Western firms.[20] Figure 1.4 illustrates why India is also popular as a location to outsource information technology (IT) jobs. The salary of an IT worker in Canada is nearly 11 times that of an IT worker in India. So long as such economic disparities exist, international outsourcing will continue to grow more popular.[21]

SUMMARY OF THE JOBS AND WAGES DEBATE   All parties appear to agree that dislocation in labour markets is a by-product of globalization. In other words, although globalization eliminates some jobs in a nation, it creates jobs in other sectors of the nation's economy. Yet, while some people lose their jobs and find new employment, it can be very difficult for others to find new work. The real point of difference between the two sides in the debate, it seems, is whether overall gains that (may or may not) accrue to *national economies* are worth the lost livelihoods that *individuals* (may or may not) suffer. Those in favour of globalization say individual pain is worth the collective gain, whereas those against globalization say it is not.

FIGURE 1.4

Comparing Salaries of IT Workers (in US Dollars)

Source: Based on data from www. payscale.com, June 26, 2012.

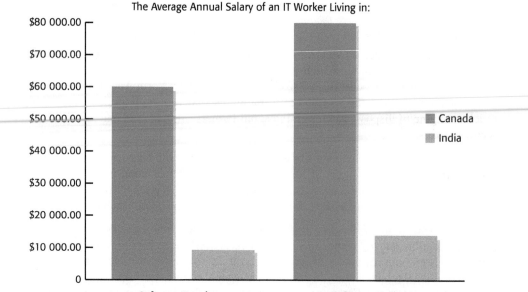

The Average Annual Salary of an IT Worker Living in:

Globalization's Impact on Labour, the Environment, and Markets

Critics of globalization say companies locate operations to where labour and environmental regulations are least restrictive and, therefore, least costly. They argue this puts downward pressure on labour and environmental protection laws in all countries as nations compete to attract international firms. Let's now examine these claims and the responses of globalization supporters.

LABOUR STANDARDS Trade unions claim globalization reduces labour's bargaining power and lowers global labour standards when international firms are permitted to continually move to nations with lower labour standards. One place to test this assertion is in developing nations' *export-processing zones (EPZs)*—special areas in which companies engage in tariff-free importing and exporting. EPZs have spread rapidly in the last two decades. The International Labour Organization EPZ database counted 176 such zones in 47 countries in 1986; by 2006, there were 3500 in 130 countries, employing 68 million people worldwide.[22] Yet, a study by the International Labour Organization (www.ilo.org), hardly a pro-business group, found no evidence to support the claim that nations with a strong union presence suffered any loss of investment in their EPZs. In fact, another study by the World Bank found that the higher occupational safety and health conditions an EPZ had in place, the greater foreign investment it attracted.[23] The evidence fails to support critics' allegations that economic openness and foreign investment contribute to lower labour standards.

ENVIRONMENTAL PROTECTION Some environmental groups say globalization causes a "race to the bottom" in environmental conditions and regulations. Many developing nations, including Mexico, Argentina, Brazil, Malaysia, and Thailand, liberalized their foreign investment environment while simultaneously enacting *stricter* environmental legislation. If large international companies were eager to relocate to nations having poor environmental protection laws, they would not have invested in these countries for decades. Additional evidence that closed, protectionist economies are worse than open ones at protecting the environment includes Mexico before NAFTA, Brazil under military rule, and the former Warsaw Pact of communist nations—all of which had extremely poor environmental records. Again, the evidence does not support claims of lower environmental standards as a result of economic openness and globalization.

FUTURE MARKETS Opponents to globalization claim international firms exploit local labour markets and the environment to produce goods that are then exported back to the home country. Such claims may not only perpetuate a false image of corporations but may also have no factual basis. International firms today support reasonable labour and environmental laws because (if for no other reason) they want to expand future local markets for their goods and services. When analyzing a country prior to investing, companies today often examine a location for its potential as a future market as well as a production base. For additional insights into how managers today succeed by respecting unfamiliar markets, see the Global Manager's Briefcase, titled "The Keys to Global Success."

Globalization and Income Inequality

Perhaps no controversy swirling around globalization is more complex than the debate over its effect on income inequality. Here, we focus on three main branches of the debate: inequality within nations, inequality between nations, and global inequality.

INEQUALITY WITHIN NATIONS The first inequality debate is whether globalization is increasing income inequality among people *within* nations. Opponents of globalization argue that freer trade and investment allows international companies to close factories in high-wage developed nations and to move them to low-wage developing nations. They argue this increases the wage gap between white-collar and blue-collar occupations within rich nations.

Two studies of *developed and developing nations* find contradictory evidence on this argument. The first study of 38 countries over nearly 30 years supports the increasing inequality argument. The study finds that, as a nation increases its openness to trade, income growth among the poorest 40 percent of a nation's population declines, while income growth among other groups increases.[24] The second study of 80 countries over 40 years fails to support the increasing inequality argument. It finds that incomes of the poor rise one-for-one with overall economic growth and concludes that the poor benefit from international trade along with the rest of a nation.[25] The mixed findings of these two studies are typical of a large set of research examining inequality between developed *and* developing nations.

Global Manager's Briefcase   The Keys to Global Success

Making everything from English muffins (Maple Leaf) to aircraft (Bombardier), managers of global companies must overcome obstacles when competing in unfamiliar markets. Global managers acknowledge certain common threads in their approaches to management and offer the following advice:

- **Communicate Effectively.** Cultural differences in business relationships and etiquette are central to global business and require cross-cultural competency. Effective global managers welcome uniqueness and ambiguity while demonstrating flexibility, respect, and empathy.

- **Know the Customer.** Successful managers understand how a company's different products serve the needs of international customers. Then, they ensure that the company remains flexible enough and able to customize products to meet those needs.

- **Emphasize Global Awareness.** Good global managers integrate foreign markets into business strategy from the outset. They ensure that products and services are designed and built with global markets in mind, and not used as dumping grounds for the home market's outdated products.

- **Market Effectively.** The world can beat a path to your door to buy your "better mousetrap" only if it knows about it. A poor marketing effort can cause great products to fade into obscurity, while an international marketing blunder can bring unwanted media attention. Top global managers match quality products with excellent marketing.

- **Monitor Global Markets.** Successful managers keep a watchful eye on business environments for shifting political, legal, and socioeconomic conditions. They make obtaining accurate information a top priority.

Quick Study

1. What are the claims of those who say globalization eliminates jobs, lowers wages, and exploits workers?
2. Identify the arguments of those who say globalization creates jobs and boosts wages.
3. Why do critics say globalization adversely affects labour standards, environmental regulations, and future markets?
4. How do supporters of globalization argue that it does not harm labour standards, environmental regulations, and future markets?

Two studies of *developing nations only* are more consistent in their findings. One study finds that an increase in the ratio of trade to national output of 1 percent raises average income levels by 0.5 to 2 percent. Another study shows that incomes of the poor keep pace with growth in average incomes in economies (and periods) of fast trade integration, but that the poor fall behind during periods of declining openness.[26] Results of these two studies suggest that by integrating their economies into the global economy, developing nations (by far the nations with the most to gain) can boost incomes of their poorest citizens.

A new approach being developed takes a multidimensional view of poverty and deprivation. Proponents of this approach say that the problem with focusing on income alone is that higher income does not necessarily translate into better health or nutrition. The new approach examines whether a household lacks any of 10 basic things, including whether the family home has a dirt floor, a decent toilet, electricity service; whether children are enrolled in school; and whether family members are malnourished or must walk more than 30 minutes to obtain clean drinking water. A household is considered poor if it is deprived on over 30 percent of the indicators. This new approach reveals important differences among poor regions. For example, while material measures contribute more to poverty in sub-Saharan Africa, malnutrition is a bigger factor in South Asia.[27]

INEQUALITY BETWEEN NATIONS   The second inequality debate is whether globalization is widening the gap in average incomes *between* rich and poor nations. If we compare average incomes in high-income countries with average incomes in middle- and low-income nations, we do find a widening gap. But *averages* conceal differences between nations.

On closer inspection, it appears the gap between rich and poor nations is not occurring everywhere: one group of poor nations is closing the gap with rich economies, while a second group of poor countries is falling further behind. For example, China is narrowing the income gap between itself and Canada as measured by GDP per capita, but the gap between Africa and Canada is widening. China's progress is no doubt a result of its integration with the world economy. Its annual economic growth rates for 2012 and estimates for 2013 are above 8 percent. Another emerging market, India, is also narrowing its income gap with Canada by embracing globalization.[28]

Developing countries that embrace globalization are increasing personal incomes, extending life expectancies, and improving education systems. In addition, post-communist countries that welcomed world trade and investment experienced high growth rates in GDP per capita. But nations that remain closed off from the world economy have performed far worse.

GLOBAL INEQUALITY   The third inequality debate is whether globalization is increasing *global inequality*—widening income inequality between all people of the world, no matter where they live. A recent study paints a promising picture of declining poverty. This study finds that the percentage of the world population living on less than a dollar a day (a common poverty gauge) fell from 17 percent to just 7 percent over a 30-year period, which reduced the number of people in poverty by roughly 200 million.[29] Yet a widely cited study by the World Bank finds that the percentage of the world population living on less than a dollar a day fell from 33 percent to 18 percent over a 20-year period, which reduced the number of people in poverty from 1.5 billion to 1.1 billion.[30]

For a variety of reasons, the real picture likely lies somewhere in between these two studies' estimates. For example, whereas the World Bank study used population figures for developing countries only, the first study used global population in its analyses, which lowered poverty estimates, all else being equal. What is important is that most experts agree that global inequality has fallen, although they disagree on the extent of the fall.

What it must be like to live on less than a dollar a day in abject poverty in sub-Saharan Africa, South Asia, or elsewhere is too difficult for most of us to comprehend. The continent of Africa presents the most pressing problem. Home to 13 percent of the world's population, Africa accounts for just 3 percent of world's GDP. Rich nations realize they cannot sit idly by while so many of the world's people live under such conditions.

What can be done to help the world's poor? First of all, rich nations could increase the amount of foreign aid they give to poor nations—foreign aid as a share of donor country GDP is at historically low levels. Second, rich nations can accelerate the process of forgiving some of the debt burdens of the most heavily indebted poor countries (HIPCs). The HIPC initiative is committed to reducing the debt burdens of the world's poorest countries. This initiative would

We see the result of embracing globalization in this photo of skyscrapers in the Lujiazui Financial and Trade Zone of the Pudong New Area in Shanghai, China. After years of stunning economic growth and expansion, Shanghai has emerged as a key city for companies entering China's marketplace. China developed Pudong to reinvigorate Shanghai as an international trade and financial centre. Pudong is now a modern, cosmopolitan district.

Source: © Zhang Ming/Xinhua Press/ CORBIS.

enable these countries to spend money on social services and greater integration with the global economy instead of on interest payments on debt.[31]

Summary of the Income Inequality Debate For the debate over inequality *within nations*, studies suggest that developing nations can boost incomes of their poorest citizens by embracing globalization and integrating themselves into the global economy. In the debate over inequality *between nations*, nations open to world trade and investment appear to grow faster than rich nations do. Meanwhile, economies that remain sheltered from the global economy tend to be worse off. Finally, for the debate over *global inequality*, although experts agree inequality has fallen in recent decades, they disagree on the extent of the drop.

Globalization and National Sovereignty

National sovereignty generally involves the idea that a nation-state (1) is autonomous; (2) can freely select its government; (3) cannot intervene in the affairs of other nations; (4) can control movements across its borders; and (5) can enter into binding international agreements. Opposition groups allege that globalization erodes national sovereignty and encroaches on the authority of local and state governments. Supporters disagree, saying that globalization spreads democracy worldwide and that national sovereignty must be viewed from a long-term perspective.

GLOBALIZATION: MENACE TO DEMOCRACY? A main argument levelled against globalization is that it empowers supranational institutions at the expense of national governments. It is not in dispute that the World Trade Organization, the International Monetary Fund, and the United Nations are led by appointed, not democratically elected, representatives. What is debatable, however, is whether these organizations unduly impose their will on the citizens of sovereign nations. Critics argue that by undercutting the political and legal authority of national, regional, and local governments, such organizations undercut democracy and individual liberty.

Opponents of globalization also take issue with the right of national political authorities to enter into binding international agreements on behalf of citizens. Critics charge that such agreements violate the rights of sub-federal (local and provincial) governments. For example, at the international level, Canada is subject to the same provisions as other countries regarding fulfillment of treaty guidelines. Article 27 of the 1969 *Vienna Convention on the Law of Treaties* prohibits countries from using domestic law (at any level) as justification for violating international treaty obligations. The WTO also incorporates a similar clause. Article 105 of NAFTA stipulates that "all necessary measures" be taken to ensure the compliance of federal, provincial, and local governments.[32]

GLOBALIZATION: GUARDIAN OF DEMOCRACY? Globalization supporters argue that an amazing consequence of globalization has been the spread of democracy worldwide. In recent decades, the people of many nations have thrown off the chains of authoritarianism and are now better educated, better informed, and more empowered. Supporters say globalization has not sent democracy spiralling into decline but instead has been instrumental in spreading democracy to the world.

Backers of globalization also contend that it is instructive to take a long-term view on the issue of national sovereignty. Witnessing a sovereign state's scope of authority altered is nothing new, as governments have long given up trying to control issues that they could not resolve. In the mid-1600s, governments in Europe surrendered their authority over religion because attempts to control it undermined overall political stability. Also, Greece in 1832, Albania in 1913, and the former Yugoslavian states in the 1990s had to protect minorities in exchange for international recognition. And over the past 50 years, the United Nations has made significant progress on worthy issues such as genocide, torture, slavery, refugees, women's rights, children's rights, forced labour, and racial discrimination. Pointing to the positive results achieved through the loss of sovereignty over these issues, globalization supporters say lost sovereignty over some economic issues may actually enhance the greater good.[33]

Globalization's Influence on Cultures

National culture is a strong shaper of a people's values, attitudes, customs, beliefs, and communication. Whether globalization eradicates cultural differences between groups of people or reinforces cultural uniqueness is a hotly debated topic.

Protesters complain that globalization is homogenizing our world and destroying its rich diversity of cultures. Critics say that in some drab, new world we all will wear the same clothes bought at the same brand-name shops, eat the same foods at the same brand-name restaurants, and watch the same movies made by the same production companies.

But supporters argue that globalization allows us all to profit from our differing circumstances and skills. Trade allows countries to specialize in producing the goods and services they can produce most efficiently. Nations can then trade with each other to obtain goods and services they desire but do not produce. In this way, France still produces many of the world's finest wines, South Africa yields much of the world's diamonds, Japan continues to design some of the world's finest-engineered autos, and Canada is one of the biggest suppliers in the world of wheat and lumber. Other nations then trade their goods and services with these countries to enjoy the wines, diamonds, wheat, lumber, and autos that they do not, or cannot, produce. To learn more about the interplay between culture and globalization, see this chapter's Culture Matters feature, titled "The Global Consumer."

Quick Study

1. What does the evidence suggest for each branch of the debate over globalization and income inequality?
2. What are each side's arguments in the debate over globalization's impact on national sovereignty?
3. Summarize the claims of each side in the debate over globalization's influence on cultures.

Culture Matters   The Global Consumer

The debate over globalization's influence on culture evokes strong opinions. Some say globalization promotes sameness among cultures while others say it fosters cultural individuality. Here are a few main arguments in this debate.

- **Material Desire.** Critics say globalization fosters the "Coca-Colanization" of nations through advertising campaigns that promote material desire. They also argue that global consumer-goods companies destroy cultural diversity (especially in developing nations) by putting local companies out of business.

- **Artistic Influence.** Evidence suggests that the cultures of developing nations are thriving and that the influence of their music, art, and literature has grown (not shrunk) throughout the past century. African cultures, for example, have influenced the works of artists including Picasso, the Beatles, and Sting.

- **Western Values.** Businesses reach far and wide through the Internet, global media, increased business travel, and local marketing by international companies. Critics say local values and traditions are being replaced by North American companies promoting "Western" values.

- **A Force for Good.** Globalization tends to foster two important values: tolerance and diversity. Globalization advocates say nations should be more tolerant of opposing viewpoints and welcome diversity among their peoples. This view interprets globalization as a potent force for good in the world.

- **Deeper Values.** Globalization can cause consumer purchases and economic ideologies to converge, but these are rather superficial aspects of culture. Deeper values that embody the true essence of cultures may be more resistant to a global consumer culture.

- **Want to Know More?** Visit the globalization page of the Global Policy Forum (www.globalpolicy.org), The Globalization Website (www.sociology.emory.edu/faculty/globalization), or The Globalist (www.theglobalist.com).

Sources: "Economic Globalization and Culture: A Discussion with Dr. Francis Fukuyama," Merrill Lynch Forum Web site (www.ml.com); "Globalization Issues," The Globalization Web site (www.sociology.emory.edu/faculty/globalization); "Cultural Diversity in the Era of Globalization," UNESCO Culture Sector Web site (http://portal.unesco.org/culture).

Key Players in International Business

Companies of all types and sizes and in all sorts of industries become involved in international business, yet they vary in the extent of their involvement. A small shop owner might only import supplies from abroad, while a large company may have dozens of factories located around the world. Large companies from the wealthiest nations still dominate international business, but firms from emerging markets (such as Brazil, China, and India) are increasingly important in international business activity. Small and medium-sized companies also account for a greater portion of international business largely because of advances in technology.

Multinational Corporations

multinational corporation (MNC)

Business that has direct investments abroad in multiple countries.

A **multinational corporation (MNC)** is a business that has direct investments (in the form of marketing or manufacturing subsidiaries) abroad in multiple countries. Multinationals generate significant jobs, investment, and tax revenue for the regions and nations they enter. Likewise, they can leave thousands of people out of work when they close or scale back operations. Mergers and acquisitions between multinationals are commonly worth billions of dollars and increasingly involve companies based in emerging markets.

Some companies have more employees than many of the smallest countries and island nations have citizens. Walmart has more than 2 million employees—the most of any company. We see the enormous economic clout of multinational corporations when we compare the revenues of the Global 500 ranking of companies to the value of goods and services that countries generate. Figure 1.5 shows the world's 10 largest companies (measured in revenue) inserted into a ranking of nations according to their national output (measured in GDP). If Walmart (www.walmart.ca) were a country, it would weigh in as a rich nation ranking just below Sweden. Even the retail food chain Kroger (www.kroger.com) exceeds the output of Iraq.[34]

FIGURE 1.5

Comparing the Global 500 with Selected Countries

Source: Data obtained from D. Steven White, "The Top 175 Global Economic Entities, 2010" (www.dstevenwhite.com).

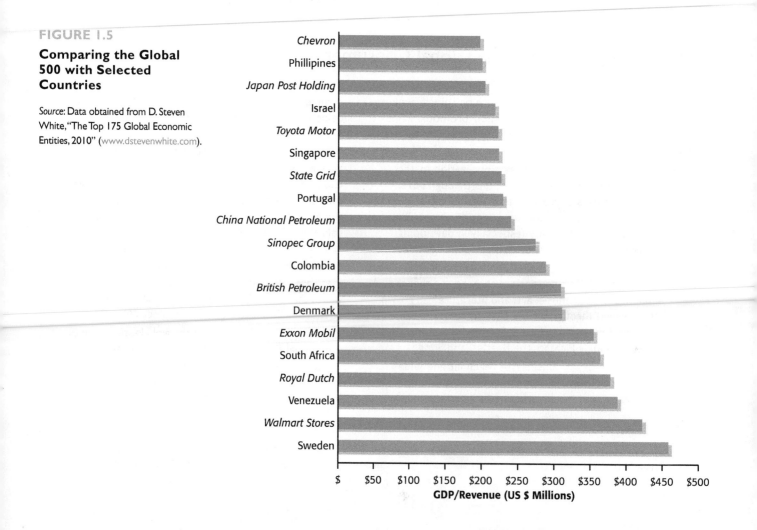

Entrepreneurs and Small Businesses

In this age of globalization, small companies are increasingly active in international trade and investment. Companies are exporting earlier and growing faster, often with help from technology. Whereas traditional distribution channels often gave only large companies access to distant markets, electronic distribution is a cheap and effective alternative for small businesses that sell digitized products. Small companies that sell traditional products also benefit from technology that lowers the cost and difficulties of global communication.

Globalization has given rise to a new international entity, the **born global firm**—a company that adopts a global perspective and engages in international business from or near its inception. Key characteristics of born global firms are an innovative culture and knowledge-based organizational capabilities. Although these firms first appeared in nations having small domestic markets, today they arise from all major trading nations. Remarkably, many of these companies rise to the status of international competitor in less than three years.

Perhaps the extreme example of a born global firm is one that reaches out to customers around the world solely through the Internet. Alessandro Naldi's Weekend a Firenze (Weekend in Florence) Web site (www.firenze.waf.it) offers global villagers more authentic Florentine products than they'll find in the scores of overpriced tourist shops in downtown Florence. A Florentine himself, Naldi established his site to sell high-quality, authentic Italian merchandise made only in the small factories of Tuscany. Weekend a Firenze averages 20 000 visitors each month, with 40 percent coming from Japan, 30 percent from the United States, and the remainder from Greece, Australia, Canada, Mexico, Saudi Arabia, and Italy.[35] An example of a successful small business Canadian exporter is McKenney Custom Sports, Inc. Founded in 1996, McKenney produces and sells goalie pads, blockers, and gloves, to name a few products. The equipment is made in Scarborough, Ontario, and is exported to the United States, Russia, the United Kingdom, and Japan.[36]

Unfortunately, many small businesses capable of exporting have not yet begun to do so. By some estimates, only 10 percent of US companies with fewer than 100 employees export—the number is twice as high for companies of all sizes. Although there are certain real obstacles to exporting for small businesses, such as a lack of investment capital, some common myths create

born global firm
Company that adopts a global perspective and engages in international business from or near its inception.

Entrepreneur's Toolkit   ## Myths of Small Business Exporting

- **Myth 1:** Only large companies can export successfully. **Fact:** According to data from the Exporter Register, roughly 34 percent of small and medium-sized enterprises (SMEs) in Canada export. In The Netherlands and Spain, the percentage of SMEs exporting is 55 percent and 66 percent, respectively. Exporting can reduce the dependency of small firms on domestic markets and can help them avoid seasonal sales fluctuations. A product popular domestically, or perhaps even unsuccessful at home, may be wanted elsewhere in the global market.

- **Myth 2:** Small businesses can find little export advice. **Fact:** Novice and experienced exporters alike can receive comprehensive export assistance from federal agencies such as Export Development Canada (www.edc.ca), the Canadian Trade Commissioner Service (infoexport.gc.ca), and the Business Development Bank of Canada (www.bdc.ca).

International trade specialists such as those certified by the Forum for International Trade Training (FITT) (www.fitt.ca) can help small businesses locate and use federal, provincial, local, and private-sector programs. They are also an excellent source of market research, trade leads, financing, and trade events.

- **Myth 3:** Licencing requirements needed to export are too complicated. **Fact:** Most products do not need export licences. Exporters need only to write "NLR" for "no licence required" on their Shipper's Export Declaration. A licence is generally needed only for high-tech or defence-related goods.

- **Myth 4:** Small businesses cannot obtain export financing. **Fact:** Export Development Canada (www.edc.ca), the Business Development Bank of Canada (www.bdc.ca), and HSBC Canada International Business Solutions (www.hsbc.ca) work in lending money to small businesses.

Sources: Fisher and Reuber, "The State of Entrepreneurship in Canada," Statistics Canada, International Trade Division, Exporter Register, 2010.

artificial obstacles. To explore some of these myths and the facts that dispute them, see this chapter's Entrepreneur's Toolkit, titled "Myths of Small Business Exporting."

Why International Business Is Special

As we've already seen in this chapter, international business differs greatly from business in a purely domestic context. The most obvious contrast is that nations can have entirely different societies and commercial environments. Let's now take a moment to examine what makes international business special by introducing a model unique to this book—a model we call the *global business environment*.

The Global Business Environment

International business is special because it occurs within a dynamic, integrated system that weaves together four distinct elements:

1. The forces of *globalization*
2. The *international* business environment
3. Many *national* business environments
4. International *firm* management

The model in Figure 1.6 identifies each of these main elements and their subparts that together comprise the *global business environment*. Thinking about international business as occurring within this global system helps us understand its complexities and the interrelations between its distinct elements. Let's now preview each of the four main components in the global business environment.

Globalization is a potent force transforming our societies and commercial activities in countless ways. Globalization, and the pressures it creates, forces its way into each element shown in Figure 1.6. In this way, the drivers of globalization (technological innovation, and falling trade and investment barriers) influence every aspect of the global business environment.

FIGURE 1.6

The Global Business Environment

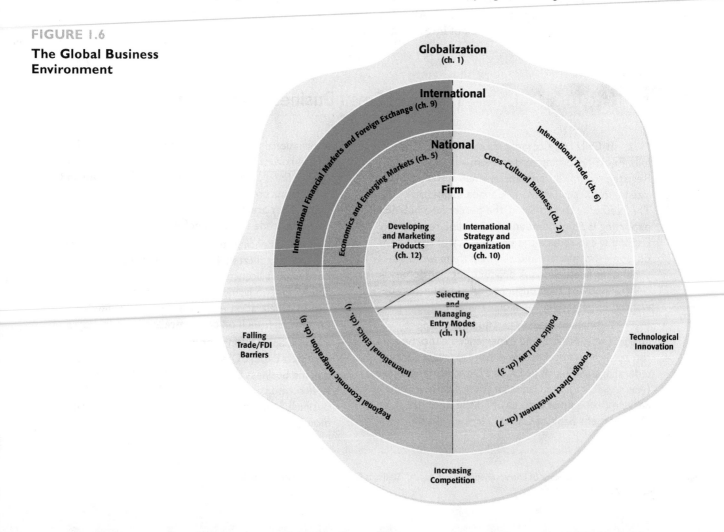

The dynamic nature of globalization also creates increasing competition for all firms everywhere, as managers begin to see the entire world as an opportunity. At home and abroad, firms must remain vigilant to the fundamental societal and commercial changes that globalization is causing.

The *international business environment* influences how firms conduct their operations in both subtle and not-so-subtle ways. No business is entirely immune to events in the international business environment, as evidenced by the long-term trend toward more porous national borders. The drivers of globalization are causing the flows of trade, investment, and capital to grow and become more entwined—often causing firms to search simultaneously for production bases *and* new markets. Companies today must keep their finger on the pulse of the international business environment to see how it may affect their business activities.

Each *national business environment* is composed of unique cultural, political, legal, and economic characteristics that define business activity within that nation's borders. This set of national characteristics can differ greatly from country to country. But, as nations open up and embrace globalization, their business environments are being transformed. Globalization can cause powerful synergies and enormous tensions to arise within and across various elements of a society. Company managers must be attentive to such nuances, adapting their products and practices as needed.

International firm management is vastly different from managing a purely domestic business. Companies must abide by the rules in every market in which they choose to operate. Therefore, the context of international business management is defined by the characteristics of national business environments. Because of widely dispersed production and marketing activities today, firms commonly interact with people in distant locations within the international business environment. Finally, managers and their firms are compelled to be knowledgeable about the nations in which they operate because of the integrating power of globalization. Businesses should try to anticipate events and forces that can affect their operations by closely monitoring globalization, national business environments, and the international business environment.

The Road Ahead for International Business

The coverage of international business in this book follows the model of the global business environment displayed in Figure 1.6. In this chapter, we learned how *globalization* is transforming our world and how elements of the global business environment are becoming increasingly intertwined. As globalization penetrates deeper into the national context, every aspect of international business management is being affected.

In Part 2 (Chapters 2 through 5), we explore how *national business environments* differ from one nation to another. We examine how people's attitudes, values, beliefs, and institutions differ from one culture to another and how this affects business. This section also covers how nations differ in their political, legal, and economic systems, as well as how they differ in their ethical philosophies. This material is placed early in the text because these differences between countries help frame subsequent topics and discussions, such as how companies modify business practices and strategies abroad.

We describe major components of the *international business environment* in Part 3 (Chapters 6 through 9). Our coverage begins with an examination of trade and investment theories, and why governments encourage or discourage these two forms of international business. We explore the process of regional economic integration sweeping the globe and outline its implications for international business. Finally, we discuss how events in global financial markets affect international business and examine the methods for payment of international transactions.

In Part 4 (Chapters 10 through 12), our coverage turns to ways in which *international business management* differs from management of a purely domestic firm. We explain how a company creates an international strategy, organizes itself for international business, and analyzes and selects the markets it will pursue. We also explore different potential entry modes. The book closes by discussing how a firm markets products to specific nations, regions, or the entire world.

Quick Study

1. Why do large *multinational corporations* dominate international business?
2. Explain why small companies and *born global firms* are increasingly involved in international business.
3. Describe the global business environment and how its main elements interact.

Bottom Line for Business

The main theme of this chapter is that the world's national economies are becoming increasingly intertwined through the process of globalization. Cultural, political, legal, and economic events in one nation increasingly affect the lives of people in other countries. Companies must pay attention to how changes in nations where they do business can affect operations. In this section, we briefly examine several important business implications of globalization.

Harnessing Globalization's Benefits

People opposed to globalization say it negatively affects wages and environmental protection, reduces political freedom, increases corruption, and inequitably rewards various groups. Yet there is evidence that the most globalized nations have the strongest records on equality, the most robust protection of natural resources, the most inclusive political systems, and the lowest levels of corruption. People in the most global nations also live the healthiest and longest lives, and women there have achieved the most social, educational, and economic progress.

As mentioned earlier in this chapter, Canada is among the most globalized countries in the world according to the KOF Index of Globalization, ranking fifteenth. In Canada, some of the benefits from globalization include increased demand for Canada's commodities, increased foreign direct investment, a growing service sector, access to new markets that were previously not accessible, increased diversity of products for the Canadian consumer, and so forth. Those opposing globalization could argue that jobs have been lost, as some labour-intensive industries have moved manufacturing production to developing countries.

One thing the debate over globalization has achieved is a dialogue on the merits and demerits of globalization. What has emerged is a more sober, less naive notion of globalization. Those on each side of the debate understand that it can have positive effects on people's lives, but globalization cannot, by itself, alleviate the misery of the world's poor. Both sides in the debate are now working together to harness the benefits of globalization while minimizing its costs.

Intensified Competition

The two driving forces of globalization (lower trade and investment barriers and increased technological innovation) are taking companies into previously isolated markets and increasing competitive pressures worldwide. And innovation is unlikely to slow any time soon.

As the cost of computing power continues to fall and new technologies are developed, companies will find it easier and less costly to manage widely dispersed marketing activities and production facilities. Technological developments may even strengthen the case for outsourcing more professional jobs to low-cost locations. As competition intensifies, international companies will increase their cooperation with suppliers and customers.

Wages and Jobs

Some labour groups in wealthy nations contend that globalization is forcing companies to join the "race to the bottom" in terms of wages and benefits. But to attract investment, a location must offer low-cost, adequately skilled workers in an environment with acceptable levels of social, political, and economic stability.

Rapid globalization of markets and production is making delivery a complex engineering task. And as companies cut costs by outsourcing activities, supply and distribution channels grow longer and more complex. Corporate logistics departments and logistics specialist firms are helping international players respond to such challenges. Logistics experts are helping companies untangle lengthy supply chains, monitor shipping lanes, and forecast weather patterns. High-wage logistics jobs represent the kind of high-value-added employment that results from the "churning" in labour markets caused by globalization.

The Policy Agenda

Countless actions could be taken by developed and developing nations to lessen the negative effects of globalization. The World Bank calls on rich countries to (1) open their markets to exports from developing countries; (2) slash their agricultural subsidies that hurt poor-country exports; and (3) increase development aid, particularly in education and health. It calls on poor countries to improve their investment climates and improve social protection for poor people in a changing economic environment.

The Peterson Institute for International Economics (www.iie.com) proposed a policy agenda for rich nations on two fronts. On the *domestic front*, it proposes (1) establishing on-the-job training to help workers cope with globalization; (2) offering "wage insurance" to workers forced by globalization to take a lower-paying job; (3) subsidizing health insurance costs in case of lost work; and (4) improving education and lifetime learning. On the *international front*, it proposes (1) enforcing labour standards more effectively; (2) clarifying the relation between international trade and environmental agreements; and (3) reviewing the environmental implications of trade agreements.

This chapter has only introduced you to the study of international business—we hope you enjoy the rest of your journey!

Chapter Summary

1. Describe the process of globalization and how it affects markets and production.
   - *Globalization* is the trend toward greater economic, cultural, political, and technological interdependence among national institutions and economies.
   - It is marked by "denationalization," in which national borders are becoming somewhat less relevant.
   - The globalization of *markets* helps a company to (1) reduce costs by standardizing marketing activities; (2) explore international markets if the home market is small or saturated; and (3) level income streams, especially for makers of seasonal products.
   - The globalization of *production* helps a company to (1) access low-cost labour and become more price-competitive and (2) access technical know-how or natural resources nonexistent or too expensive at home.

2. Identify the two forces causing globalization to increase.
   - *Falling barriers to trade and investment* is one major force behind globalization.
   - Trade barriers have been drastically reduced through institutions such as the *General Agreement on Tariffs and Trade* and the *World Trade Organization*.
   - Groups of several or more nations are reducing trade barriers by creating regional trade agreements.
   - *Technological innovation* is a second main force driving globalization.
   - Companies can manage global business activities with the use of e-mail, videoconferencing, intranets, and extranets.
   - Technology increases the speed and ease with which companies can manage far-flung operations.
   - Innovations in transportation technologies are making the shipment of goods between nations more efficient and dependable.
   - The KOF Index of Globalization records show changes in globalization by comparing 187 countries over a long-term period (1970–2012).

3. Summarize the evidence for each main argument in the globalization debate.
   - Regarding *jobs and wages*, both sides agree that globalization causes dislocation in labour markets: those supporting globalization believe overall gains of national economies are worth lost jobs for individuals, but globalization critics do not.
   - Labour unions argue globalization causes a "race to the bottom" in *labour and environmental regulation*, though they lack supporting evidence.
   - Regarding inequality *within nations*, developing nations can boost incomes of their poorest citizens by integrating themselves into the global economy.
   - In the debate over *inequality between nations*, nations that embrace world trade and investment grow faster than rich nations, whereas sheltered economies become worse off.
   - Groups agree that *global inequality* has fallen in recent decades but differ on the extent of the drop.
   - In terms of *national sovereignty*, globalization has helped spread democracy worldwide and aided progress on many global issues.
   - Evidence suggests that *cultures* of developing nations are thriving in an age of globalization and that deeper elements of culture are not easily abandoned.

4. Identify the types of companies that participate in international business.
   - Entrepreneurs and small firms are increasingly active in international business because the Internet and other technologies help them overcome high advertising and distribution costs.
   - Large *multinational corporations (MNCs)* still conduct most international business transactions.
   - MNCs have great economic and political muscle, and their deals are often worth billions of dollars.
   - Globalization has given rise to the *born global firm*—a company that adopts a global perspective and engages in international business from or near its inception.
   - Born global firms tend to have an innovative culture and knowledge-based organizational capabilities.
   - Many born global firms rise to the status of international competitor in less than three years.

5. Describe the global business environment and identify its four main elements.
   - International business occurs within an integrated, *global business environment* consisting of four elements.
   - *Globalization* is transforming business and society, and increasing competition for all firms.
   - The *international business environment* influences how firms conduct operations, while globalization further entwines the flows of trade, investment, and capital.
   - Separate *national business environments* comprise unique cultural, political, legal, and economic characteristics that define business activity within a nation.
   - *International business management* differs from management of a purely domestic firm in all respects.

Key Terms

antidumping duty 10	General Agreement on Tariffs and Trade	International Monetary Fund (IMF) 17
born global firm 27	(GATT) 9	normal trade relations 10
countervailing duty 10	globalization 6	multinational corporation (MNC) 26
dumping 10	gross domestic product (GDP) 11	World Bank 17
e-business (e-commerce) 4	gross national product (GNP) 11	World Trade Organization (WTO) 9
exports 4	imports 4	
GDP or GNP per capita 11	international business 4	

Talk It Over

1. Today, international businesspeople must think globally about production and sales opportunities. Many global managers will eventually find themselves living and working in cultures altogether different from their own. Many entrepreneurs will find themselves booking flights to places they had never heard of. What do you think companies can do now to prepare their managers for these new markets? What can entrepreneurs and small businesses with limited resources do?

2. In the past, national governments greatly affected the pace of globalization through agreements to lower barriers to international trade and investment. Is the pace of change now outpacing the capability of governments to manage the global economy? Will national governments become more or less important to international business in the future? Explain your answer.

3. Information technologies are developing at a faster rate than ever before. How have these technologies influenced globalization? Give specific examples. Do you think globalization will continue until we all live in one "global village"? Why or why not?

4. Consider the following statement: "Globalization and the resulting increase in competition harm people, as international companies play one government against another to get the best deal possible. Meanwhile, governments continually ask for greater concessions from their citizens, demanding that they work harder and longer for less pay." Do you agree? Why or why not?

Take It to the Web

1. **Video Report.** Visit YouTube (www.youtube.com) and type "globalization" into the search engine. Watch one of videos from the results of your search and then summarize it in a half-page report. Reflecting on the contents of this chapter, which aspects of globalization can you identify in the video? How might a company engaged in international business act on the information contained in the video?

2. **Web Site Report.** In this chapter, we've seen how globalization is fundamentally changing business and society. Managers can be more effective if they know what drives globalization and are familiar with its positive and negative aspects.

   Select a controversial globalization topic that interests you, and visit the Web sites of two organizations that have opposing views on this topic. (Hint: You might begin by visiting an organization noted in this chapter.) For the topic you've chosen, report on the (1) specific argument(s) of each side; (2) evidence each side uses to support its position(s); and (3) policy agenda, if any, each side promotes.

   Which argument(s) do you agree with most? Have your views on this topic changed as a result of your research? If yes, explain how. Which types of firms/industries do you think this topic affects most? Explain. Write a short summary of your findings and include key Web sites you found helpful.

Ludia Plays Global

Do you want to get together to play a board game? That's a question that you are unlikely to hear from teenagers and young adults nowadays.

One industry that has greatly benefited from globalization is the online gaming industry. Video games are now a global mass medium with global revenues of approximately US $68.4 billion. The global video gaming market is expected to grow annually at 5.1 percent during the 2009 to 2014 period. In the same period, the online gaming market is forecast to grow 13.9 percent per year, and social gaming will grow approximately 27.2 percent per year. The video game industry in Canada employs approximately 16 000 people and is comprised of 350 companies, making Canada's the third-largest video game industry in the world behind only the United States and Japan. According to Exportwise (www.exportwise.ca), video game development is forecast to grow 29 percent annually over the next few years. At least 90 percent of the revenues for the Canadian video game industry are generated through export sales.

One Canadian company that has hit the jackpot in this industry is Montreal-based Ludia. Established in 2007 with only five employees, Ludia has become the developer of many of the world's most successful games, including *The Price Is Right®*, *Family Feud®*, *Where's Waldo?®*, *Are You Smarter than a 5ᵗʰ Grader®*, *Hell's Kitchen*, *The Amazing Race*, and *Who Wants to Be a Millionaire?*

Ludia creates cross-platform downloadable interactive game show video games with mass consumer appeal (www.ludia.com). Ludia's mission "is to provide entertainment to adults that remind them of what it's like to have fun."

Ludia delivers one-of-a-kind games with components including performance, online community, and social networking. Ludia's games are available in applications for iPhone, iPad, iPod touch, Facebook, Wii, XBox360, Nintendo, and PS™. According to Ludia's Linkedin page, "Ludia's social game division creates casual Facebook games based on popular television game shows. The already established title *The Price Is Right®* has gained international recognition and has built a community of over 2 million users."

Ludia has clearly benefited from the globalization of markets, enjoying strong growth and selling its games globally, essentially without changes to them. Ludia signed its first multi-year exclusive partnership agreement with FremantleMedia (one of the world's largest entertainment producers) in July 2007. In 2010, FremantleMedia became the majority shareholder of Ludia, purchasing 80 percent of the company, with the deal stipulating that the existing management team be maintained, including its founder and CEO Alex Thabet. By 2012 Ludia planned to launch more than 20 new games and had approximately 200 employees.

Thinking Globally

1. Some say globalization is homogenizing the attitudes and spending habits of young consumers worldwide. As one journalist puts it, "It may still be conventional wisdom to 'think globally and act locally,' but in the youth market, it is increasingly a case of one size fits all." Do you agree or disagree? Why or why not?

2. Do you think Ludia fits the definition of a born global firm? Explain your answer based on the case.

3. Advances in technology, including the Internet, made it possible for Ludia to sell its product worldwide. Can you think of other technological innovations that have helped companies to think globally?

4. Advances in technology often spur evolution in the entertainment industry. How might new products and services, such as the iPhone, YouTube, and Ludia's games, affect entertainment in years to come?

Sources: "Business Insights 2011," Smart Brief Web site (www.smartbrief.com), August 22, 2011; Canada Newswire (CNW), "Canada Shines at This Year's E3 with Major Blockbuster Titles," CNW Telebec Web site (www.newswire.ca), June 7, 2011; Danny Kucharsky, "This Ain't Kid Stuff," *ExportWise.ca*, Export Development Canada's online magazine for Canadian Exporters (www.exportwise.ca), Summer 2010, pp. 10–13; Ludia's Web site (www.ludia.com); Ludia's LinkedIn page (www.linkedin.com/company/ludia); PR Newswire, "Ludia Signs Deal with FremantleMedia to Launch *The Price Is Right* Video Game Across All Major Platforms," July 16, 2007; The Canadian Press, "Interactive Company Ludia Hiring 100 Workers in Montreal over the Next Year," November 1, 2011.

As globalization marches across the globe, international business managers can make more informed decisions if they know the locations of countries and the distances between them. This atlas presents the world in a series of maps and is designed to assist you in understanding the global landscape of business. We encourage you to return to this atlas frequently to refresh your memory, especially when you encounter the name of an unfamiliar city or country.

Familiarize yourself with each of the maps in this appendix, and then try to answer the following 20 questions. For each question, select all answers that apply.

Map Exercises

1. Which of the following countries border the Atlantic Ocean?

   a. Bolivia
   b. Australia
   c. South Africa
   d. Japan
   e. United States

2. Which of the following countries are found in Africa?

   a. Guyana
   b. Morocco
   c. Egypt
   d. Pakistan
   e. Niger

3. Which one of the following countries does not border the Pacific Ocean?

   a. Australia
   b. Venezuela
   c. Japan
   d. Mexico
   e. Peru

4. Prague is the capital city of:

   a. Uruguay
   b. Czech Republic
   c. Portugal
   d. Tunisia
   e. Hungary

5. If transportation costs for getting your product from your market to Japan are high, which of the following countries might be good places to locate a manufacturing facility?

   a. Thailand
   b. Philippines
   c. South Africa
   d. Indonesia
   e. Portugal

6. Seoul is the capital city of (capital cities are designated with red dots):

   a. Vietnam
   b. Cambodia
   c. Malaysia
   d. China
   e. South Korea

7. Turkey, Romania, Ukraine, and Russia border the body of water called the _____ Sea.

8. Thailand shares borders with:

   a. Cambodia
   b. Pakistan
   c. Singapore
   d. Indonesia
   e. Malaysia

9. Which of the following countries border no major ocean or sea?

   a. Austria
   b. Paraguay
   c. Switzerland
   d. Niger
   e. all of the above

10. Oslo is the capital city of:

    a. Germany
    b. Canada
    c. Brazil
    d. Norway
    e. Australia

11. Chile is located in:

    a. Africa
    b. Asia
    c. the Northern Hemisphere
    d. South America
    e. Central Europe

12. Saudi Arabia shares borders with:

    a. Jordan
    b. Kuwait
    c. Iraq
    d. United Arab Emirates
    e. all of the above

13. The body of water located between Sweden and Estonia is the _____ Sea.

14. Which of the following countries are located on the Mediterranean Sea?

    a. Italy
    b. Croatia
    c. Turkey
    d. France
    e. Portugal

15. The distance between Sydney (Australia) and Tokyo (Japan) is shorter than that between:

    a. Tokyo and Cape Town (South Africa)
    b. Sydney and Hong Kong (China, SAR)
    c. Tokyo and London (England)
    d. Sydney and Jakarta (Indonesia)
    e. all of the above

16. Madrid is the capital city of:

    a. Madagascar
    b. Italy
    c. Mexico
    d. Spain
    e. United States

17. Which of the following countries is not located in central Asia?

    a. Afghanistan
    b. Uzbekistan
    c. Turkmenistan
    d. Kazakhstan
    e. Suriname

18. If you were shipping your products from your production facility in Pakistan to market in Australia, they would likely cross the _____ Ocean.

19. Papua New Guinea, Guinea-Bissau, and Guinea are alternative names for the same country.

    a. true
    b. false

20. Which of the following countries are island nations?

    a. New Zealand
    b. Madagascar
    c. Japan
    d. Australia
    e. all of the above

Answers

(1) c. South Africa, e. United States; (2) b. Morocco, c. Egypt, e. Niger; (3) b. Venezuela; (4) b. Czech Republic; (5) a. Thailand, b. Philippines, d. Indonesia; (6) e. South Korea; (7) Black; (8) a. Cambodia, e. Malaysia; (9) e. all of the above; (10) d. Norway; (11) d. South America; (12) e. all of the above; (13) Baltic; (14) a. Italy, c. Turkey, d. France; (15) a. Tokyo and Cape Town (South Africa), c. Tokyo and London (England); (16) d. Spain; (17) e. Suriname; (18) Indian; (19) b. false; (20) e. all of the above.

Self-Assessment

If you scored 15 correct answers or more, well done! You seem well prepared for your international business journey. If you scored fewer than 8 correct answers, you may wish to review this atlas before moving on to Chapter 2.

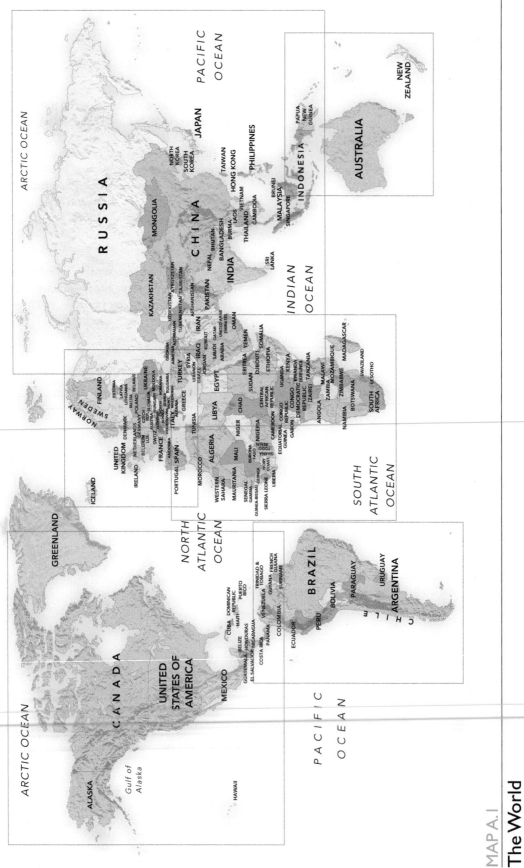

The World

This global view identifies each continent and acts as a reference for the six maps that follow.

MAP A.2

North America

MAP A.4

Europe

Asia

MAP A.6

Africa

MAP A.7

Oceania

Teaming Up   GLOBALIZATION

With a group of classmates, select two countries other than Canada that you are interested in comparing. Next, choose an industry and product or service, and assume you and your teammates own a Canadian company in this area. Your company has to choose between your two selected countries for making a $150 million investment. Both investments promise the same long-run return, so your choice is driven by challenges in international business. Assess the various challenges—economic, political, legal, ethical, and cultural—of doing business in each of these countries. By the end of the course, you should be able to determine which country you would select for your investment and why.

Start your research by answering the following questions: Can you obtain a benefit from the globalization of production in the countries you selected? Which one(s) and why? What is the KOF index for the two countries that you selected?

CHAPTER TWO

Cross-Cultural Business

Learning Objectives

After studying this chapter, you should be able to

1. Describe culture and explain the significance of both national culture and subcultures.

2. Identify the components of culture and describe their impact on international business.

3. Describe cultural change and explain how companies and culture affect each other.

4. Explain how the physical environment and technology influence culture.

5. Describe the two main frameworks used to classify cultures and explain their practical use.

6. Explain the three different types of staffing policies used by international companies.

7. Describe the recruitment, selection, and cultural training issues facing international companies.

8. Explain how companies compensate managers and workers in international markets.

A LOOK BACK

Chapter 1 introduced us to international business. We examined the impact of globalization on markets and production, the forces behind its expansion, and each main argument in the debate over globalization. We also profiled the kinds of companies engaged in international business.

A LOOK AT THIS CHAPTER

This chapter introduces the important role of culture in international business. We explore the main elements of culture and how they affect business policies and practices. We learn different methods of classifying cultures and how these methods can be applied to business. We study how a company acquires and manages its most important resource—its employees. We also learn about culture shock and how employees can deal with its effects.

A LOOK AHEAD

Chapter 3 describes the political and legal systems of nations. We will learn how different national systems affect international businesses and how managers can reduce political risk.

Source: ShutterStock.

Connecting Cultures

MONTREAL, Quebec—Cirque du Soleil (www.cirquedusoleil.com) is the world's leading circus and Canada's largest cultural export. Founded in 1984 by a group of 20 street performers, the company employs over 5000 people, including approximately 1300 performers from more than 50 countries, and generates $800 million in annual revenue.

Cirque du Soleil has staged productions in over 300 cities worldwide and has resident shows in the United States and China. To achieve success in foreign markets, Cirque du Soleil employed Canadian delegates abroad as intermediaries. They assisted the company to understand cultural differences, provided information about local market trends, and furnished business contacts. With its entrance into foreign markets, Cirque du Soleil extended its touring season to countries with warmer climates than Canada.

Many internal factors contribute to Cirque du Soleil's international success. Its shows have no spoken language, making them accessible to diverse audiences. The company's ability to adapt and change,

Source: NetPhotos/Alamy.

and to tolerate uncertainty (the opposite of Hofstede's uncertainty avoidance, discussed in this chapter) has helped it maintain a culture of innovation. Cirque du Soleil focuses on geocentric staffing, recruiting talent from around the world, including support staff such as physiotherapy and fitness specialists. It relies on a casting team supported by a global network of partners who act as eyes and ears in the field, discovering and recommending artists from around the world.

Recruiting artists is a challenge, because the shows have a 15-year lifespan: Cirque du Soleil must not only find the best performers in the world, but must also retain them for a long run. The talent team holds auditions worldwide throughout the year. The company has a Web site (available in seven languages) dedicated to recruiting and also recruits through social networking sites. More than half the artists Cirque du Soleil hires are athletes whose competitive careers are ending. The company also hires from circus schools and has training programs in China and Russia.

As you read this chapter, consider how culture influences international business. Think about the human resource issues that arise when international companies manage their employees around the world and about how company actions affect culture.[1]

This chapter is the first of four that describe the links between international business activity and a nation's business environment. We introduce these topics early because of their strong influence on how commerce is conducted in different countries. Success in international business can often be traced directly to a deep understanding of some aspect of a people's commercial environment. This chapter explores the influence of *culture* on international business activity and examines how companies acquire and manage their employees. Chapter 3 presents the roles of *political and legal systems*; Chapter 4 describes the different approaches to ethics and the ethical dilemmas that arise; and Chapter 5 looks at the impact of *economic systems and emerging markets* on international business.

An assessment of any nation's overall business climate is typically the first step in analyzing its potential as a host for international commercial activity. This means addressing some important questions, such as the following: What language(s) do the people speak? What is the climate like? Are the local people open to new ideas and new ways of doing business? Do government officials and the people want our business? Is the political situation stable enough so that our assets and employees are not placed at unacceptable levels of risk? Answers to these kinds of questions—plus statistical data on items such as income level and labour costs—allow companies to evaluate the attractiveness of a location as a place for doing business.

We address culture first in our discussion of national business environments because of its pivotal role in all international commercial activity. Whether we are discussing an entrepreneur running a small import/export business or a huge global firm directly involved in more than 100 countries, *people* are at the centre of all business activity. When people from around the world come together to conduct business, they bring with them different backgrounds, assumptions, expectations, and ways of communicating—in other words, *culture*.

We begin this chapter by exploring the influence of nation-states and subcultures on a people's overall cultural image. Next we learn the importance of values, attitudes, manners, and customs in any given culture. We then examine ways in which social institutions, religion, language, and other key elements of culture affect business practices and national competitiveness. We also look at two alternative methods for classifying cultures.

Finally, we focus on how a company acquires and manages *people*. People are a company's most important resource, and, as mentioned earlier, culture affects business practices. Therefore, we look at the different types of staffing policies international companies use; at the recruitment, selection, and cultural training issues these companies face; and at the ways in which they compensate managers and workers in international markets.

What Is Culture?

When travelling in other countries, we often perceive differences in the way people live and work. In Canada dinner is commonly eaten around 6:00 p.m.; in Spain and Mexico it's not served until 8:00 or 9:00 p.m. In Canada most people shop in large supermarkets once or twice a week; Italians and the Dutch tend to shop in smaller local grocery stores nearly every day. Essentially, we are experiencing differences in **culture**—the set of values, beliefs, rules, and institutions held by a specific group of people. Culture is a highly complex portrait of a people. It includes everything from high tea in England to the tropical climate of Barbados, to Mardi Gras in Brazil, to segregation of the sexes in Saudi Arabian schools.

Before we learn about the individual components of culture, let's look at one important concept that should be discouraged and one that should be fostered.

culture

Set of values, beliefs, rules, and institutions held by a specific group of people.

AVOIDING ETHNOCENTRICITY **Ethnocentricity** is the belief that one's own ethnic group or culture is superior to that of others. Ethnocentricity can seriously undermine international business projects. It causes people to view other cultures in terms of their own and, therefore, disregard the beneficial characteristics of other cultures. Ethnocentricity played a role in many stories, some retold in this chapter, of companies that failed when they tried to implement a new business practice in a subsidiary abroad. The failures occurred because managers ignored a fundamental aspect of the local culture, which provoked a backlash from the local population, their government, or nongovernmental groups. As suppliers and buyers increasingly treat the world as a single, interconnected marketplace, managers should eliminate the biases inherent in ethnocentric thinking. For more information on how companies can foster a non-ethnocentric

ethnocentricity

Belief that one's own ethnic group or culture is superior to that of others.

| Culture Matters | Creating a Global Mindset |

In this era of globalization, companies need employees who function without the blinders of ethnocentricity. Here are some ways managers can develop a *global mindset*:

- **Cultural Adaptability.** Managers need the ability to alter their behaviour when working with people from other cultures. The first step is to develop one's knowledge of unfamiliar cultures; one way to begin is to join an organization such as another culture's Chamber of Commerce and attend meetings where nationals of that culture will be present.[2] The second step is to act on that knowledge to alter behaviour to suit cultural expectations. The manager with a global mindset can evaluate others in a culturally unbiased way, and can motivate and lead multicultural teams.

- **Bridging the Gap.** A large gap can emerge between theory and practice when Western management ideas are applied in Eastern cultures. Whereas North American management principles are often accepted at face value in businesses throughout the world, North American business customs are not. In Asia, for example, Western managers may try implementing "collective leadership" practices more in line with Asian management styles.

- **Building Global Mentality.** Companies can apply personality-testing techniques to measure the global aptitude of managers. A global mindset test evaluates an individual's openness and flexibility, understanding of global principles, and strategic implementation abilities. It can also identify areas in which training is needed and generate a list of recommended programs. A global mindset requires managers to swallow personal pride, put aside ego, and ignore cultural preconceptions.

- **Flexibility Is Key.** The more behavioural are the issues, the greater is the influence of local cultures. Japanese and Korean managers are more likely than North American managers to wait for directions and consult peers on decisions. Western managers posted in the Middle East must learn to work within a rigid hierarchy to be successful. And although showing respect for others is universally valued, respect is defined differently from country to country.

- **Want to Know More?** Visit the Centre for Creative Leadership (www.ccl.org); The Globalist (www.theglobalist.com); and Transnational Management Associates (www.tmaworld.com).

perspective, see this chapter's Culture Matters feature, titled "Creating a Global Mindset," and read about geocentric staffing toward the end of the chapter.

DEVELOPING CULTURAL LITERACY   As globalization continues, people directly involved in international business increasingly benefit from a certain degree of **cultural literacy**—detailed knowledge about a culture that enables a person to function effectively within it. Cultural literacy improves people's ability to manage employees, market products, and conduct negotiations in other countries. Global brands such as Procter & Gamble (www.pg.com) and Apple (www.apple.com) provide a competitive advantage because consumers know and respect these highly recognizable names. Yet cultural differences often dictate alterations in some aspect of a business to suit local tastes and preferences. The culturally literate manager who compensates for local needs and desires brings his or her company closer to customers and improves the firm's competitiveness.

cultural literacy
Detailed knowledge about a culture that enables a person to function effectively within it.

As you read through the concepts and examples in this chapter, try to avoid reacting with *ethnocentricity* while developing your own *cultural literacy*. Because these two concepts are central to the discussion of many international business topics, you will encounter them throughout this chapter and this book.

National Culture and Subcultures

Rightly or wrongly, we tend to invoke the concept of the *nation-state* when speaking of culture. In other words, we usually refer to British and Indonesian cultures as if all Britons and all Indonesians were culturally identical. We do this because we are conditioned to think in terms of *national culture*. But this is at best a generalization. In Great Britain, campaigns for greater Scottish and Welsh independence continue to make progress. And people in remote parts of Indonesia build homes in treetops even as people in the nation's developed regions pursue ambitious economic development projects. Let's now take a closer look at the diversity that lies beneath the veneer of national culture.

Subculture members define themselves by their style (such as clothing, hair, tattoos) and rebel against mass consumerism. London, England's Camden district is famous for its historic markets and as a gathering place for alternative subcultures such as goth, punk, and emo. Businesses like YouTube help subcultures to spread quickly worldwide. Can you think of a company that targets an international subculture with its products?

Source: Nik Wheeler Danita Delimont Photography/Newscom.

NATIONAL CULTURE   Nation-states *support* and *promote* the concept of national culture by building museums and monuments to *preserve* the legacies of important events and people. Nation-states also intervene in business to preserve national culture. Most nations, for example, regulate culturally sensitive sectors of the economy, such as filmmaking and broadcasting. France continues to voice fears that its language is being tainted with English and its media with North American programming. To stem the English invasion, French laws limit the use of English in product packaging and storefront signs. At peak listening times, at least 40 percent of all radio station programming is reserved for French artists. Similar laws apply to television broadcasting. The French government even fined the local branch of a US university for failing to provide a French translation on its English-language Web site.

Cities, too, get involved in enhancing national cultural attractions, often for economic reasons. Lifestyle enhancements to a city can help it attract companies, which benefit by having an easier task retaining top employees. The Guggenheim Museum in Bilbao, Spain (www.guggenheim-bilbao.es), designed by Frank Gehry, revived that old Basque industrial city. And Hong Kong's government enhanced its cultural attractions by building a Hong Kong Disneyland to lure businesses that might otherwise locate elsewhere in Asia.

SUBCULTURES   A group of people who share a unique way of life within a larger, dominant culture is called a **subculture**. A subculture can differ from the dominant culture in language, race, lifestyle, values, attitudes, or other characteristics.

subculture
A group of people who share a unique way of life within a larger, dominant culture.

Although subcultures exist in all nations, they are often glossed over by our *impressions* of national cultures. For example, the customary portrait of Chinese culture often ignores the fact that China's population includes more than 50 distinct ethnic groups. Decisions regarding product design, packaging, and advertising should consider each group's distinct culture. Marketing campaigns also need to recognize that Chinese dialects in the Shanghai and Canton regions differ from those in the country's interior; not everyone is fluent in the official Mandarin dialect.

Canada also has many subcultures, the three largest of which are English, French, and Chinese Canadians. Both French Canadians and Chinese Canadians tend to be extremely family-oriented and respond to advertising that understands their heritage and reinforces traditional family values. French Canadians make up over 15 percent of the total Canadian population. The majority of them live in Quebec, and over 50 percent speak only French. In terms of culture, French Canadians tend to be more individualistic, liberal, and autonomy-seeking than Canadians from other cultural backgrounds, and place a higher value on work–life balance. French Canadians also drink more coffee but less tea, and try to eat more organic food.[3]

Chinese Canadians are the largest visible minority population in Canada and the second largest subculture. Chinese (if Mandarin and Cantonese are combined) is the third most spoken language in Canada. Chinese Canadians are concentrated in five major cities: Toronto, Vancouver, Montreal, Calgary, and Edmonton. Chinese Canadians value education and are interested in luxury goods and brand name products as a way of gaining status (see the Social Status section later in this chapter).[4]

Cultural boundaries do not always correspond to political boundaries. In other words, subcultures sometimes exist across national borders, especially if the boundaries have been arbitrarily drawn after a conflict. People who live in different nations but who share the same subculture can have more in common with one another than with their fellow nationals. Arab culture, for example, extends from northwest Africa to the Middle East, with pockets of Arabs in many European countries and North America. Because Arabs share a common language and tend to share purchasing behaviours related to Islamic religious beliefs, marketing to Arab subcultures can sometimes be accomplished with a single marketing campaign.

Quick Study

1. Define *culture*. How does ethnocentricity distort one's view of other cultures?
2. What is *cultural literacy*? Why should businesspeople understand other cultures?
3. How do nation-states and *subcultures* influence a nation's cultural image?

Components of Culture

The actions of nation-states and the presence of subcultures help define the culture of a group of people. But a people's culture also includes what they consider beautiful and tasteful, their underlying beliefs, their traditional habits, and the ways in which they relate to one another and their surroundings. Let's take a detailed look at each main component of culture (see Figure 2.1): *aesthetics*, *values* and *attitudes*, *manners* and *customs*, *social structure*, *religion*, *personal communication*, *education*, and *physical* and *material environments*.

Aesthetics

What a culture considers "good taste" in the arts (including music, painting, dance, drama, and architecture), the imagery evoked by certain expressions, and the symbolism of certain colours is called **aesthetics**.

Aesthetics are important when a company does business in another culture. The selection of appropriate colours for advertising, product packaging, and even work uniforms can improve the

aesthetics
What a culture considers "good taste" in the arts, the imagery evoked by certain expressions, and the symbolism of certain colours.

FIGURE 2.1

Components of Culture

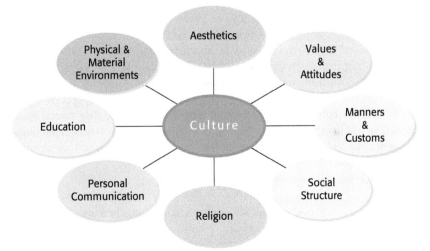

Entrepreneur's Toolkit | Giving Web Sites Local Appeal

When going global with an Internet presence, the more a company localizes the better. Online customers want an experience corresponding to their cultural context offline. Here are a few tips for entrepreneurs launching an online presence.

- **Choosing Colours.** A black-and-white Web site is fine for many countries, but in Asia visitors may think you are inviting them to a funeral. In Japan and across Europe, Web sites in pastel colour schemes often work best.
- **Selecting Numbers.** Many Chinese-speaking cultures consider the number four unlucky, although eight and nine symbolize prosperity. Be careful that your Web address and phone numbers do not send the wrong signal.
- **Watching the Clock.** If marketing to countries that use the 24-hour clock, adjust times stated on the site so it reads, "Call between 9:00 and 17:00" instead of "Call between 9 a.m. and 5 p.m."

- **Avoiding Slang.** English in Britain is different from that in the United States, Spanish in Spain is different from that in Mexico, and French in France is different from that in Quebec. Avoid slang to lessen the potential negative impact of such differences.
- **Waving the Flag.** Using national flags as symbols for buttons that access different language versions of your site should be done carefully. Mexican visitors to your site may be put off by a Spanish flag to signify the site's Spanish-language version, for example.
- **Doing the Math.** Provide conversions into local currencies for buyer convenience. For online ordering, be sure your site calculates any shipping costs, tax rates, tariffs, and so on. Also allow enough blanks on the order form to accommodate longer international addresses.
- **Getting Feedback.** Finally, talk with customers to know what they want to accomplish on your Web site. Then, thoroughly test the site to ensure it functions properly.

odds of success. For example, green is a favourable colour in Islam and adorns the national flags of most Islamic nations, including Jordan, Pakistan, and Saudi Arabia. Companies take advantage of the emotional attachment to the colour green in these countries by incorporating it into a product, its packaging, or its promotion. Across much of Asia, on the other hand, green is associated with sickness. In Europe, Mexico, and Canada, the colour of death and mourning is black; in Japan and most of Asia, it's white.

Shoe manufacturer Nike (www.nike.com) experienced first-hand the importance of imagery and symbolism in international marketing. The company emblazoned a new line of shoes with the word "Air" written to resemble flames or heat rising off blacktop. The shoes were given various names, including *Air Bakin'*, *Air Melt*, *Air Grill*, and *Air B-Que*. But what Nike did not realize was that the squiggly lines of the "Air" logo resembled Arabic script for "Allah," the Arabic name for God. Under threat of a worldwide boycott by Muslims, who considered it a sacrilege, Nike apologized and recalled the shoes.

Music is deeply embedded in culture and, when used correctly, can be a clever and creative addition to a promotion; if used incorrectly, it can offend the local population. The architecture of buildings and other structures should also be researched to avoid making cultural blunders attributable to the symbolism of certain shapes and forms.

The importance of aesthetics is just as great when going international using the Internet. Many companies exist that teach corporations how to globalize their Internet presence. These companies often provide professional guidance on how to adapt Web sites to account for cultural preferences such as colour scheme, imagery, and slogans. The advice of specialist firms can be particularly helpful for entrepreneurs and small businesses because they rarely have in-house employees well versed in other cultures. To read how small business owners can tailor a Web site to suit local aesthetics and other cultural variables, see the Entrepreneur's Toolkit, titled "Giving Web Sites Local Appeal."

Values and Attitudes

values
Ideas, beliefs, and customs to which people are emotionally attached.

Ideas, beliefs, and customs to which people are emotionally attached are called **values**. Values include concepts such as honesty, marital faithfulness, freedom, and responsibility. Values are important to business because they affect a people's work ethic and desire for material possessions.

For example, whereas people in Singapore value hard work and material success, people in Greece value leisure and a modest lifestyle. The United States and Canada value individual freedom; Japan and South Korea value group consensus.

The influx of values from other cultures can be fiercely resisted. Many Muslims believe drugs, alcohol, and certain kinds of music and literature will undermine important Islamic values. This is why nations under Islamic law (including Iran and Saudi Arabia) exact severe penalties against anyone possessing illegal items such as drugs and alcohol. Deeply held conservative values are why the Arab world's reality TV programs tend to be short-lived. In Bahrain, the local version of *Big Brother* was cancelled after people objected to the program's format, which involved young unmarried adults of both sexes living under the same roof. The Lebanon-based program *Hawa Sawa* (*On Air Together*) was shut down because its "elimidate" format (in which a young man would gradually eliminate young women to finally select a date) was perceived by many people as too Western.

Attitudes are positive or negative evaluations, feelings, and tendencies that individuals harbour toward objects or concepts. Attitudes reflect underlying values. For example, a Westerner would be expressing an attitude if he or she were to say, "I do not like the Japanese purification ritual because it involves being naked in a communal bath." The Westerner quoted here might hold conservative beliefs regarding exposure of the body.

attitudes
Positive or negative evaluations, feelings, and tendencies that individuals harbour toward objects or concepts.

Similar to values, attitudes are learned from role models, including parents, teachers, and religious leaders. Attitudes also differ from one country to another because they are formed within a cultural context. But unlike values (which generally concern only important matters), people hold attitudes toward both important and unimportant aspects of life. And whereas values remain quite rigid over time, attitudes are more flexible.

A "European" attitude has sunk into the psyche of young people there as companies from different countries merge, industries consolidate, and nations grow closer together in the European Union. Many young people in Europe today consider themselves to be "European" as much as they identify with their individual national identities. Still, the underlying values of young Europeans tend to remain similar to those of their parents. Such cultural knowledge can help managers decide whether to adapt promotions to local attitudes for maximum effectiveness.

Let's now look at how people's attitudes differ toward three important aspects of life that directly affect business activities: time, work and achievement, and cultural change.

ATTITUDES TOWARD TIME People in many Latin American and Mediterranean cultures are casual about their use of time. They maintain flexible schedules and would rather enjoy their time than sacrifice it to unbending efficiency. Businesspeople, for example, may arrive after the scheduled meeting time and prefer to build personal trust before discussing business. Not surprisingly, it usually takes longer to conduct business in these parts of the world than in the United States or northern Europe.

By contrast, people in Japan and Canada typically arrive promptly for meetings, keep tight schedules, and work long hours. The emphasis on using time efficiently reflects the underlying value of hard work in both these countries. Yet people in Japan and Canada sometimes differ in how they use their time at work. For example, Canadian employees strive toward workplace efficiency and may leave work early if the day's tasks are done, reflecting the value placed on producing individual results. But in Japan, although efficiency is prized, it is equally important to look busy in the eyes of others even when business is slow. A Japanese employee would not leave work early even if he finished the day's task ahead of schedule. Japanese workers want to demonstrate their dedication to superiors and co-workers—an attitude grounded in values such as the concern for group cohesion, loyalty, and harmony.

ATTITUDES TOWARD WORK Whereas some cultures display a strong work ethic, others stress a more balanced pace in juggling work and leisure. People in southern France like to say they work to live, while people in North America live to work. The French say work is a means to an end for them, whereas work is an end in itself in North America. Not surprisingly, the lifestyle in southern France is slower-paced. People tend to concentrate on earning enough money to enjoy a relaxed, quality lifestyle. Businesses practically close down during August, when many workers take month-long paid holidays, often outside the country.

People tend to launch their own businesses when capital is available for new business start-ups and when the cultural stigma of entrepreneurial failure is low. In European countries, start-ups are considered quite risky, and capital for entrepreneurial ventures can be scarce. Moreover, if an entrepreneur's venture goes bust, he or she can find it very hard to obtain financing for future projects because of the stigma of failure. This remains true despite some progress recently. The opposite attitude tends to prevail in North America. Reference to prior bankruptcy in a business plan is sometimes considered a valuable learning experience (assuming lessons were learned). As long as Canadian bankers or venture capitalists see or hear about promising business plans, they are generally willing to lend money. An example of this attitude is the popular TV show *Dragon's Den,* where aspiring entrepreneurs pitch their business ideas to a panel of Canadian business investors. Today, many European nations are working to foster an entrepreneurial spirit similar to that of North America.

cultural trait

Anything that represents a culture's way of life, including gestures, material objects, traditions, and concepts.

ATTITUDES TOWARD CULTURAL CHANGE   A **cultural trait** is anything that represents a culture's way of life, including gestures, material objects, traditions, and concepts. Such traits include bowing to show respect in Japan (gesture), a Buddhist temple in Thailand (material object), relaxing in a tearoom in Kuwait (tradition), and practising democracy in North America (concept). Let's look more closely at the role of cultural traits in causing cultural change over time and the relation between international companies and cultural change.

cultural diffusion

Process whereby cultural traits spread from one culture to another.

CULTURAL DIFFUSION   The process whereby cultural traits spread from one culture to another is called **cultural diffusion**. As new traits are accepted and absorbed into a culture, *cultural change* occurs naturally and, as a rule, gradually. Globalization and technological advances are increasing the pace of both cultural diffusion and cultural change. Satellite television, videoconferencing, and videos on the Internet increase the frequency of international contact and expose people of different nations to new ideas and practices.

When Companies Change Cultures   International companies are often agents of cultural change. As trade and investment barriers fall, for example, US consumer-goods and entertainment companies are moving into untapped markets. Critics in some of these places charge that in exporting the products of such firms, the United States is practising **cultural imperialism**—the replacement of one culture's traditions, folk heroes, and artifacts with substitutes from another.

cultural imperialism

Replacement of one culture's traditions, folk heroes, and artifacts with substitutes from another.

Fears of cultural imperialism still drive some French to oppose the products of the Walt Disney Company (www.disney.com) and its Disneyland Paris theme park. They fear "Mickey and Friends" could replace traditional characters rooted in French culture. McDonald's (www.mcdonalds.com) is also sometimes charged with cultural imperialism. It is reported that the average Japanese child thinks McDonald's was invented in Japan and exported to the United States. Chinese children consider "Uncle" McDonald "funny, gentle, kind, and understanding." Meanwhile, politicians in Russia decry the Snickerization of their culture—a snide term that refers to the popularity of the candy bar made by Snickers (www.snickers.com). And when the Miss World Pageant was held in India, conservative groups criticized Western corporate sponsors for spreading the message of consumerism and portraying women as sex objects.

Sensitivity to the cultures in which they operate can help companies avoid charges of cultural imperialism. Firms must focus not only on meeting people's product needs but also on how their activities and products affect people's traditional ways and habits. Rather than view their influence on culture as the inevitable consequence of doing business, companies can take several steps to soften those effects. For example, policies and practices that are at odds with deeply held beliefs can be introduced gradually. Managers could also seek the advice of highly respected local individuals such as elders, who fulfill key societal roles in many developing countries. And businesses should always make clear to local workers the benefits of any proposed changes that are closely linked to cultural traits.

When Cultures Change Companies   Culture often forces companies to adjust their business policies and practices. Managers from the United States, for example, often encounter cultural differences that force changes in how they motivate employees in other countries. Managers sometimes use *situational management*—a system in which a supervisor walks an employee through every step of an assignment or task and monitors the results at each stage. Although time-consuming, this technique helps employees fully understand the scope of their jobs and clarifies the boundaries of their responsibilities.

Other types of changes might also be needed to suit local culture. Vietnam's traditional, agriculture-based economy means people's concept of time revolves around the seasons. The local

A student in Krakow, Poland, pedals his way to an outlet of Sweden-based IKEA. Sweden historically dominated other Scandinavian nations, including Denmark. Now some in Denmark say IKEA is a "cultural imperialist" for portraying Denmark as Sweden's doormat because it assigns Danish names to doormats and rugs, but reserves Swedish names for expensive items such as beds and chairs. IKEA says the product names are simply a coincidence.

Source: Jean Pierre Amet/Corbis.

"timepiece" is the monsoon, not the clock. Western managers, therefore, modify their approach and take a more patient, long-term view of business by modifying employee evaluation and reward systems. For example, individual criticism should be delivered privately to save employees from "losing face" among co-workers. Individual praise for good performance can be delivered either in private or in public, if done carefully. The Vietnamese place great value on group harmony, so an individual can be embarrassed if singled out publicly as being superior to the rest of the work unit.

Is a Global Culture Emerging?   What does the rapid pace of cultural change worldwide mean for international business? Are we witnessing the emergence of a new, truly global culture in which all people share similar lifestyles, values, and attitudes? The rapid pace of cultural diffusion today is causing cultures to converge to some extent. The successful American TV show *So You Think You Can Dance* (www.fox.com/dance), where aspiring dancers compete for a chance to become a celebrity, is one example of global pop culture. The show has many clones around the world. It is available in Armenia, Australia, Benelux, Denmark, Finland, France, Germany, Israel, Malaysia, Scandinavia, South Africa, and Vietnam, although it was recently cancelled in Canada.

It might be true that people in different cultures are developing similar perspectives on certain issues. But it seems that just as often as we see signs of an emerging global culture, we discover some new habit unique to one culture. When that happens, we are reminded of the roles of history and tradition in defining culture. Though values and attitudes are under continually greater pressure from globalization, their transformation will be gradual rather than abrupt because they are deeply ingrained in culture. This is why the managers of tomorrow must work to develop their knowledge and understanding of other cultures.

Quick Study

1. What is meant by a culture's *aesthetics*? Give several examples.
2. How can businesses incorporate aesthetics into their Web sites?
3. Compare and contrast *values* and *attitudes*. How do cultures differ in their attitudes toward time, work, and cultural change?
4. Describe the process of *cultural diffusion*. Why should international businesses be sensitive to charges of *cultural imperialism*?

Manners and Customs

When doing business in another culture, it is important to understand a people's manners and customs. At a minimum, understanding manners and customs helps managers avoid making embarrassing mistakes or offending people. In-depth knowledge, meanwhile, improves the ability to negotiate in other cultures, market products effectively, and manage international operations. Let's explore some important differences in manners and customs around the world.

manners
Appropriate ways of behaving, speaking, and dressing in a culture.

MANNERS   Appropriate ways of behaving, speaking, and dressing in a culture are called **manners**. In Arab cultures, for example, one does not extend a hand to greet an older person unless the elder first offers the greeting. In going first, a younger person would be displaying bad manners. Moreover, because Arab culture considers the left hand the one used for personal hygiene, using it to pour tea or serve a meal is considered very bad manners.

Jack Ma founded Alibaba (www.alibaba.com) as a way for suppliers and buyers to increase efficiency by cutting through layers of intermediaries and trading companies. But he realized early that his Chinese clients needed training in business etiquette to cross the cultural divide and do business with people from Western cultures. So Alibaba offers seminars on business manners that instruct clients to spend more time chitchatting with clients and conversing more casually.[5]

Conducting business during meals is common practice in Canada. In Mexico, however, it is poor manners to bring up business at mealtime unless the host does so first. Business discussions in Mexico typically begin when coffee and tequila arrive. Likewise, toasts in Canada tend to be casual and sprinkled with light-hearted humour. In Mexico, where a toast should be philosophical and full of passion, a light-hearted toast would be offensive. See the Global Manager's Briefcase, titled "A Globetrotter's Guide to Manners," for additional pointers on appropriate manners when abroad on business.

customs
Habits or ways of behaving in specific circumstances that are passed down through generations in a culture.

CUSTOMS   When habits or ways of behaving in specific circumstances are passed down through generations, they become **customs**. Customs differ from manners in that they define appropriate habits or behaviours in *specific situations*. Sharing food gifts during the Islamic holy month of Ramadan is a custom, as is the Japanese tradition of throwing special parties for young women and men who turn age 20. Let's examine two types of customs and see how instances of each vary around the world.

folk custom
Behaviour, often dating back several generations, that is practised by a homogeneous group of people.

popular custom
Behaviour shared by a heterogeneous group or by several groups.

Folk and Popular Customs   A **folk custom** is behaviour, often dating back several generations, that is practised by a homogeneous group of people. The wearing of turbans by Muslims in southern Asia and the art of belly dancing in Turkey are both folk customs. A **popular custom** is behaviour shared by a heterogeneous group or by several groups. Popular customs can exist in just one culture or in two or more cultures at once. Wearing blue jeans and playing golf are both popular customs across the globe. Folk customs that spread by cultural diffusion to other regions develop into popular customs.

Despite their appeal, popular customs can be seen as a threat by some members of a culture. Authorities in a devoutly religious district of Indonesia's Aceh province banned Muslim women from wearing tight clothing, short skirts, and blue jeans. Islamic police set up raids to distribute long skirts to women found violating the ban and to confiscate their offending garments. Violators were released from custody after they provided their identities to police and received advice from Islamic preachers.[6]

We can also distinguish between folk and popular food. Popular Western-style fast food, for instance, is rapidly replacing folk food around the world. Widespread acceptance of "burgers 'n' fries" (born in the United States) and "fish 'n' chips" (born in Britain) is altering deep-seated dietary traditions in many Asian countries, especially among young people. In Japan and South Korea today, these popular foods are even becoming a part of home-cooked meals.

The Business of Gift Giving   Although giving token gifts to business and government associates is customary in many countries, the proper type of gift varies. A knife, for example, should not be offered to associates in Russia, France, or Germany, where it signals the severing of a relationship. In Japan, gifts must be wrapped in such a delicate way that it is wise to ask someone trained in the practice to do the honours. It is also Japanese custom for the giver to protest that the gift is small and unworthy of the recipient, and for the recipient not to open the gift in front of the giver. This tradition does not endorse trivial gifts but is simply a custom.

Global Manager's Briefcase	A Globetrotter's Guide to Manners

Large multinationals need top managers who are comfortable living, working, and travelling worldwide. Here are a few guidelines for a manager to follow when meeting colleagues from other cultures:

- **Familiarity.** Avoid the temptation to get too familiar too quickly. Use titles such as "doctor" and "mister." Switch to a first-name basis only when invited to do so, and do not shorten people's names from, say, Catherine to Cathy.
- **Personal Space.** Culture dictates what is considered the appropriate distance between two people. Middle Eastern and Latin American nations close the gap significantly. And in Latin America the man-to-man embrace can occur regularly in business.
- **Religious Values.** Be cautious so that your manners do not offend people. Former Secretary of State Madeline Albright acquired the nickname "The Kissing Ambassador" for kissing the Israeli and Palestinian leaders of these two religious peoples.
- **Business Cards.** In Asia, business cards are considered an extension of the individual. Business cards in Japan are typically exchanged after a bow, with two hands extended, and the wording facing the recipient. Leave the card on the table for the entire meeting—don't quickly stuff it in your wallet or toss it into your briefcase.
- **Comedy.** Use humour cautiously because it often does not translate well. Avoid jokes that rely on wordplay and puns or events in your country, of which local people might have little or no knowledge.
- **Body Language.** Do not "spread out" by hanging your arms over the backs of chairs, but don't be too stiff either. Look people in the eye lest they deem you untrustworthy, but don't stare too intently in a challenging manner.

Cultures differ in their legal and ethical rules against giving or accepting bribes. Large gifts to business associates are particularly suspicious. To reduce ethical or legal issues in this regard, the Canadian federal government developed guidelines with suggested gift values for presents offered to foreign dignitaries by or on behalf of ministers. The list puts a limit of $800 on gifts to foreign heads of state, $600 for foreign ministers, $400 for officials such as state governors or mayors, $300 for senior bureaucrats, and $50 for security staff, drivers, translators, and so forth. Appropriate gifts include contemporary arts and crafts or items representative of Canadian culture, such as silver-plated maple leaf business card cases, maple leaf cufflinks, and wool scarves with maple leaves.[7]

Yet in many cultures bribery is woven into a social fabric that has worn well for centuries. In Germany, bribe payments may even qualify for tax deductions. Though many governments worldwide are adopting stricter measures to control bribery, in some cultures large gifts are still an effective way to obtain contracts, enter markets, and secure protection from competitors.

Social Structure

Social structure embodies a culture's fundamental organization, including its groups and institutions, its system of social positions and their relationships, and the process by which its resources are distributed. Social structure plays a role in many business decisions, including production-site selection, advertising methods, and the costs of doing business in a country. Three important elements of social structure that differ across cultures are social group associations, social status, and social mobility.

social structure
A culture's fundamental organization, including its groups and institutions, its system of social positions and their relationships, and the process by which its resources are distributed.

SOCIAL GROUP ASSOCIATIONS   People in all cultures associate themselves with a variety of **social groups**—collections of two or more people who identify and interact with each other. Social groups contribute to each individual's identity and self-image. Two groups that play especially important roles in affecting business activity everywhere are family and gender.[*]

social group
Collection of two or more people who identify and interact with each other.

---

[*]We put these two "groups" together for the sake of convenience. Strictly speaking, a gender is not a group. Sociologists regard it as a category—people who share some sort of status. A key to group membership is mutual interaction. Individuals in categories know that they are not alone in holding a particular status, but the vast majority remain strangers to one another.

Family   There are two different types of family groups:

- The *nuclear family* consists of a person's immediate relatives, including parents, brothers, and sisters. This concept of family prevails in Australia, Canada, the United States, and much of Europe.
- The *extended family* broadens the nuclear family and adds grandparents, aunts and uncles, cousins, and relatives through marriage. It is an important social group in much of Asia, the Middle East, North Africa, and Latin America.

Extended families can present some interesting situations for businesspeople unfamiliar with the concept. In some cultures, owners and managers obtain supplies and materials from another company in which someone from the extended family works. Gaining entry into such family arrangements can be difficult because quality and price are not sufficient motives to ignore family ties.

In extended-family cultures, managers and other employees often try to find jobs for relatives inside their own companies. This practice (called "nepotism") can present a challenge to the human resource operations of a Western company, which typically must establish explicit policies on the practice.

Gender   *Gender* refers to socially learned traits associated with, and expected of, men or women. It includes behaviours and attitudes such as styles of dress and activity preferences. It is not the same thing as sex, which refers to the biological fact that a person is either male or female.

Though many countries have made great strides toward gender equality in the workplace, others have not. In countries where women are denied equal opportunity in the workplace, their unemployment rate can easily be double that for men and their pay half that for men in the same occupation. Women's salaries can be so low and the cost of childcare so high that it simply makes more sense for mothers to stay home with their children. Caring for children and performing household duties are also likely considered women's work and not the responsibility of the entire family.

Countries operating under Islamic law sometimes segregate women and men in public schools, universities, and social activities, and restrict women to certain professions. Yet women are sometimes allowed teaching careers in all-female classrooms only, or they can become physicians for female patients only.

SOCIAL STATUS   Another important aspect of social structure is the way a culture divides its population according to *status*—that is, according to positions within the structure. Although some cultures have only a few categories, others have many. The process of ranking people into social layers or classes is called **social stratification**.

Three factors that normally determine social status are family heritage, income, and occupation. In most industrialized countries, royalty, government officials, and top business leaders occupy the highest social layer. Scientists, medical doctors, and others with a university education occupy the middle layer. Below are those with vocational training or a secondary-school education, who dominate the manual and clerical occupations. Although rankings are fairly stable, they can and do change over time. For example, because Confucianism (a major Chinese religion) stresses a life of learning, not commerce, Chinese culture frowned on businesspeople for centuries. In modern China, however, people who have obtained wealth and power through business are now considered important role models for younger generations.

SOCIAL MOBILITY   Moving to a higher social class is easy in some cultures but difficult or impossible in others. **Social mobility** is the ease with which individuals can move up or down a culture's "social ladder." For much of the world's population today, one of two systems regulates social mobility: a *caste system* or a *class system*.

Caste System   A **caste system** is a system of social stratification in which people are born into a social ranking, or *caste*, with no opportunity for social mobility. India is the classic example of a caste culture. Although the Indian constitution officially bans discrimination by caste, its influence persists. Little social interaction occurs between castes, and marrying out of one's caste is taboo. Opportunities for work and advancement are defined within the system, and certain occupations are reserved for the members of each caste. For example, a member of a lower caste cannot supervise someone of a higher caste because personal clashes would be inevitable.

social stratification
Process of ranking people into social layers or classes.

social mobility
Ease with which individuals can move up or down a culture's "social ladder."

caste system
System of social stratification in which people are born into a social ranking, or caste, with no opportunity for social mobility.

The caste system forces Western companies to make some hard ethical decisions when entering the Indian marketplace. They must decide whether to adapt to local human resource policies in India or import their own from the home country. As globalization penetrates deeper into Indian culture, the nation's social system and international companies will face many challenges to overcome.

Class System   A **class system** is a system of social stratification in which personal ability and actions determine social status and mobility. It is the most common form of social stratification in the world today. But class systems vary in the amount of mobility they allow. Highly class-conscious cultures offer less mobility and, not surprisingly, experience greater class conflict. Across Western Europe, for example, wealthy families have retained power for generations by restricting social mobility. Countries there must sometimes deal with class conflict in the form of labour–management disputes that can increase the cost of doing business.

Conversely, lower levels of class consciousness encourage mobility and lessen conflict. A more cooperative atmosphere in the workplace tends to prevail when people feel that a higher social standing is within their reach. Most Canadians share the belief that hard work can improve their standard of living and social status. People attribute higher status to greater income or wealth but often with little regard for family background.

class system
System of social stratification in which personal ability and actions determine social status and mobility.

Quick Study

1. How do *manners* and *customs* differ? Give examples of each.
2. List several manners that managers should consider when doing business abroad.
3. Define *folk* and *popular* customs. How can a folk custom become a popular custom?
4. Define *social structure*. How do social rank and *social mobility* affect business?

Religion

Human values often originate from religious beliefs. Different religions take different views of work, savings, and material goods. Identifying why they do so may help us understand business practices in other cultures. Knowing how religion affects business is especially important in countries with religious governments.

Map 2.1 shows where the world's major religions are practised. Religion is not confined to national political boundaries but can exist in different regions of the world simultaneously. It is also common for several or more religions to be practised within a single nation. In the following sections, we explore Christianity, Islam, Hinduism, Buddhism, Confucianism, Judaism, and Shinto. We examine their potential effects, both positive and negative, on international business activity.

CHRISTIANITY   Christianity was born in Palestine around 2000 years ago among Jews who believed that God sent Jesus of Nazareth to be their saviour. Although Christianity boasts more than 300 denominations, most Christians belong to the Roman Catholic, Protestant, or Eastern Orthodox churches. With two billion followers, Christianity is the world's single largest religion. The Roman Catholic faith asks its followers to refrain from placing material possessions above God and others. Protestants believe that salvation comes from faith in God and that hard work gives glory to God—a tenet known widely as the "Protestant work ethic." Many historians believe this conviction to be a main factor in the development of capitalism and free enterprise in nineteenth-century Europe.

Christian organizations sometimes get involved in social causes that affect business policy. For example, some conservative Christian groups have boycotted the Walt Disney Company (www.disney.com), charging that in portraying young people as rejecting parental guidance, Disney films impede the moral development of young viewers worldwide.

The Church itself has been involved in some highly publicized controversies. Ireland-based Ryanair (www.ryanair.com), Europe's leading low-fare airline, ruffled the feathers of the Roman Catholic Church with an ad campaign. The ad depicted the pope (the head of the Church) claiming

MAP 2.1

World Religions

 C OCEAN

NORWAY
SWEDEN
FINLAND
ESTONIA
DENMARK
LATVIA
LITHUANIA
RUSSIA
BELARUS
GERMANY
POLAND
JRG
CZECH
REP.
SLOVAKIA
UKRAINE
AUSTRIA
HUNGARY
MOLDOVA
Z.
SLOVENIA
ROMANIA
IT.
CROATIA
SERBIA AND
BOSNIA
MONTENEGRO
HERZEGOVINA
BULGARIA
ITALY
MACEDONIA
ALBANIA
GREECE
TURKEY
GEORGIA
ARMENIA
AZERBAIJAN
TUNISIA
CYPRUS
SYRIA
LEBANON
ISRAEL
IRAQ
JORDAN
LIBYA
EGYPT
KUWAIT
QATAR
UNITED ARAB
EMIRATES
SAUDI
ARABIA
OMAN
GER
CHAD
ERITREA
YEMEN
SUDAN
DJIBOUTI
CENTRAL
AFRICAN
REPUBLIC
ETHIOPIA
SOMALIA
ROON
UGANDA
CONGO
REPUBLIC
KENYA
CONGO
DEMOCRATIC
RWANDA
REPUBLIC
BURUNDI
(ZAIRE)
TANZANIA
ANGOLA
MALAWI
ZAMBIA
MOZAMBIQUE
NAMIBIA
ZIMBABWE
MADAGASCAR
MAURITIUS
BOTSWANA
RÉUNION
SWAZILAND
SOUTH
LESOTHO
AFRICA

RUSSIA

KAZAKHSTAN
MONGOLIA
UZBEKISTAN
KYRGYZSTAN
TURKMENISTAN
TAJIKISTAN
AFGHANISTAN
CHINA
IRAN
PAKISTAN
NEPAL
BHUTAN
BANGLADESH
INDIA
MYANMAR
(BURMA)
LAOS
THAILAND
VIETNAM
CAMBODIA
SRI
LANKA
BRUNEI
MALAYSIA
SINGAPORE
INDONESIA

NORTH
KOREA
SOUTH
KOREA
JAPAN

TAIWAN

PHILIPPINES

PAPUA
NEW
GUINEA
SOLOMON
ISLANDS

VANUATU
FIJI

NEW
CALEDONIA

AUSTRALIA

NEW
ZEALAND

INDIAN
OCEAN

PACIFIC
OCEAN

Christianity   Buddhism

Judaism   Nature religion

Hinduism   Chinese religion

Islam   Other groups

that the fourth secret of Fatima was Ryanair's low fares. The Church sent out a worldwide press release accusing the airline of blaspheming the pope. But much to the Church's dismay, the press release generated an enormous amount of free publicity for Ryanair.

Hyundai (www.hyundai.com) offended the Catholic Church when it ran a television commercial during the 2010 World Cup. The spot showed a "church" in Argentina with a stained glass window of a soccer ball, a soccer ball topped with a crown of thorns, and parishioners receiving slices of pizza instead of communion hosts. The Catholic Church took offence at the images of people worshipping soccer and at the mocking of its practice of receiving Holy Communion. Hyundai put a stop to the ad two days after it began airing, saying that upon review the ad was found to be unintentionally insensitive.[8]

ISLAM   With 1.3 billion adherents, Islam is the world's second-largest religion. The prophet Muhammad founded Islam around 600 CE in Mecca, the holy city of Islam located in Saudi Arabia. Islam thrives in north-western Africa, the Middle East, Central Asia, Pakistan, and some Southeast Asian nations, including Indonesia. Muslim concentrations are also found in most European and US cities. *Islam* means "submission to Allah" and *Muslim* means "one who submits to Allah." Islam revolves around the "five pillars": (1) reciting the *Shahada* (profession of faith); (2) giving to the poor; (3) praying five times daily; (4) fasting during the holy month of *Ramadan*; and (5) making the *Hajj* (pilgrimage) to the Saudi Arabian city of Mecca at least once in one's lifetime.

Religion strongly affects the kinds of goods and services acceptable to Muslim consumers. Islam, for example, prohibits the consumption of alcohol and pork. Popular alcohol substitutes are soda pop, coffee, and tea. Substitutes for pork include lamb, beef, and poultry (all of which must be slaughtered in a prescribed way so as to meet *halal* requirements). Because hot coffee and tea often play ceremonial roles in Muslim nations, the markets for them are quite large. And because usury (charging interest for money lent) violates the laws of Islam, credit card companies collect management fees rather than interest, and each cardholder's credit line is limited to an amount held on deposit.

Nations governed by Islamic law (see Chapter 3) sometimes segregate the sexes at certain activities and in locations such as schools. In Saudi Arabia, women cannot drive cars on public streets. In orthodox Islamic nations, men cannot conduct market research surveys with women at home unless they are family members. Women visiting Islamic cultures need to be especially sensitive to Islamic beliefs and customs. In Iran, for example, the Ministry of Islamic Guidance and Culture posts a reminder to visiting female journalists: "The body is a tool for the spirit and the spirit is a divine song. The holy tool should not be used for sexual intentions." Although the issue of *hejab* (Islamic dress) is hotly debated, both Iranian and non-Iranian women are officially expected to wear body-concealing garments. They are also expected to wear scarves over their hair because hair is considered enticing.

HINDUISM   Hinduism formed around 4000 years ago in present-day India, where more than 90 percent of its 900 million adherents live. It is also the majority religion of Nepal and a secondary religion in Bangladesh, Bhutan, and Sri Lanka. Considered by some to be a way of life rather than a religion, Hinduism recalls no founder and recognizes no central authority or spiritual leader. Integral to the Hindu faith is the caste system described earlier.

Hindus believe in reincarnation—the rebirth of the human soul at the time of death. For many Hindus the highest goal of life is *moksha*—escaping from the cycle of reincarnation and entering a state of eternal happiness called *nirvana*. Hindus tend to disdain materialism. Strict Hindus do not eat or wilfully harm any living creature because it may be a reincarnated human soul. Because Hindus consider cows sacred animals, they do not eat beef; consuming milk is considered a means of religious purification. Firms such as McDonald's (www.mcdonalds.com) must work closely with government and religious officials in India to respect Hindu beliefs. In many regions, McDonald's has removed all beef products from its menu and prepares vegetable and fish products in separate kitchen areas. And for those Indians who do eat red meat (but not cows because of their sacred status), the company sells the Maharaja Mac, made of lamb, in place of the Big Mac.

In India, there have been attacks on Western consumer-goods companies in the name of preserving Indian culture and Hindu beliefs. Some companies, such as Pepsi-Cola (www.pepsi.com), have been vandalized, and local officials even shut down a KFC restaurant (www.kfc.com)

for a time. Although it currently operates in India, Coca-Cola (www.cocacola.com) once left the market completely rather than succumb to demands that it reveal its secret formula to authorities. India's investment environment has improved greatly in recent years. Yet labour–management relations sometimes deteriorate to such a degree that strikes cut deeply into productivity.

BUDDHISM   Buddhism was founded about 2600 years ago in India by a Hindu prince named Siddhartha Gautama. Today, Buddhism has around 380 million followers, mostly in China, Tibet, Korea, Japan, Vietnam, and Thailand, and there are pockets of Buddhists in Europe and the Americas. Although founded in India, Buddhism has relatively few adherents there. Unlike Hinduism, Buddhism rejects the caste system of Indian society. But like Hinduism, Buddhism promotes a life centred on spiritual rather than worldly matters. In a formal ceremony, Buddhists take refuge in the "three jewels": the Buddha, the *dharma* (his teachings), and the *sangha* (community of enlightened beings). They seek *nirvana* (escape from reincarnation) through charity, modesty, compassion for others, restraint from violence, and general self-control.

Although monks at many temples are devoted to lives of solitary meditation and discipline, many other Buddhist priests are dedicated to lessening the burden of human suffering. They finance schools and hospitals across Asia and are active in worldwide peace movements. In Tibet, where most people still acknowledge the exiled Dalai Lama as the spiritual and political head of the Buddhist culture, the Chinese communist government suppresses allegiance to any outside authority. In the United States, a coalition of religious groups, human rights advocates, and supporters of the Dalai Lama continue to press the US Congress to apply economic sanctions against countries, such as China, that are seen as practising religious persecution.

CONFUCIANISM   An exiled politician and philosopher named Kung-fu-dz (pronounced *Confucius* in English) began teaching his ideas in China nearly 2500 years ago. Today, China is home to most of Confucianism's 225 million followers. Confucian thought is also ingrained in the cultures of Japan, South Korea, and nations with large numbers of ethnic Chinese, such as Singapore.

South Korean business practice reflects Confucian thought in its rigid organizational structure and unswerving reverence for authority. Whereas Korean employees do not question strict chains of command, non-Korean managers and workers often feel differently. Efforts to apply Korean-style management in overseas subsidiaries have caused some high-profile disputes with US executives and even physical confrontations with factory workers in Vietnam.

Buddhism instructs its followers to live a simple life void of materialistic ambitions. Buddhism also teaches that seeking pleasure for the human senses causes suffering. But as globalization pries open Asia's markets, the products of Western multinationals are streaming in. Here a young Buddhist monk passes in front of an advertisement for Heineken beer. Do you think Asian cultures can modernize while retaining their traditional values and beliefs?

Source: Emmanuel Dunand/AFP/Getty Images Inc.

Some observers contend that the Confucian work ethic and educational commitment helped spur East Asia's phenomenal economic growth. But others respond that the link between culture and economic growth is weak. They argue that economic, historical, and international factors are at least as important as culture. They say Chinese leaders distrusted Confucianism for centuries because they believed that it stunted economic growth. Likewise, many Chinese despised merchants and traders because their main objective (earning money) violated Confucian beliefs. As a result, many Chinese businesspeople moved to Indonesia, Malaysia, Singapore, and Thailand, where they launched successful businesses. Today, these countries (along with Taiwan) are financing much of China's economic growth.

JUDAISM   More than 3000 years old, Judaism was the first religion to preach belief in a single God. Nowadays, Judaism has roughly 18 million followers worldwide. In Israel, Orthodox ("fully observant") Jews make up 12 percent of the population and constitute an increasingly important economic segment. In Jerusalem, there is even a modelling agency that specializes in casting Orthodox Jews in ads aimed both inside and outside the Orthodox community. Models include scholars and one rabbi. In keeping with Orthodox principles, women model only modest clothing and never appear in ads alongside men.

Employers and human resource managers must be aware of important days in the Jewish faith. Because the Sabbath lasts from sundown on Friday to sundown on Saturday, work schedules might need adjustment. Devout Jews want to be home before sundown on Fridays. On the Sabbath itself, they do not work, travel, or carry money. Several other important observances are Rosh Hashanah (the two-day Jewish New Year, in September or October), Yom Kippur (the Day of Atonement, 10 days after New Year), Passover (which celebrates the Exodus from Egypt, in March or April each year), and Hanukkah (which celebrates an ancient victory over the Syrians, usually in December).

Marketers must take into account foods that are banned among strict Jews. Pork and shellfish (such as lobster and crab) are prohibited. Meat is stored and served separately from milk. Other meats must be slaughtered according to a practice called *shehitah*. Meals prepared according to Jewish dietary traditions are called *kosher*. For example, most airlines offer *kosher* meals for Jewish passengers on their flights.

SHINTO   Shinto (meaning "way of the gods") arose as the native religion of the Japanese. But today Shinto can claim only about 4 million strict adherents in Japan. Because modern Shinto preaches patriotism, it is sometimes said that Japan's real religion is nationalism. Shinto teaches sincere and ethical behaviour, loyalty and respect toward others, and enjoyment of life.

Shinto beliefs are reflected in the workplace through the traditional practice of lifetime employment (although this is waning today) and through the traditional trust extended between firms and customers. Japanese competitiveness in world markets has benefited from loyal workforces, low employee turnover, and good labour–management cooperation. The phenomenal success of many Japanese companies in recent decades gave rise to the concept of a Shinto work ethic, certain aspects of which have been emulated by Western managers.

Quick Study

1. What are the main beliefs of each of the seven religions presented above?
2. In what ways does religion affect international business activities?
3. Identify the dominant religion in each of the following countries: (a) Brazil, (b) China, (c) India, (d) Ireland, (e) Mexico, (f) Russia, and (g) Thailand.

Personal Communication

communication
System to convey thoughts, feelings, knowledge, and information through speech, writing, and actions.

People in every culture have a **communication** system to convey thoughts, feelings, knowledge, and information through speech, writing, and actions. Understanding a culture's spoken language gives us great insight into why people think and act the way they do. Understanding a culture's body language helps us avoid sending unintended or embarrassing messages. Let's examine each of these forms of communication more closely.

SPOKEN AND WRITTEN LANGUAGE Spoken and written language is the most obvious difference we notice when travelling in another country. We overhear and engage in a number of conversations and read many signs and documents to find our way. Knowledge of a people's language is often essential for achieving success in international business; understanding its language is the key to deeply understanding a culture.

Linguistically different segments of a population are often culturally, socially, and politically distinct. Malaysia's population is composed of Malay (60 percent), Chinese (30 percent), and Indian (10 percent). Although Malay is the official national language, each ethnic group speaks its own language and continues its traditions. The United Kingdom includes England, Northern Ireland, Scotland, and Wales. The native languages of Ireland and Scotland are dialects of *Gaelic*, and the speaking of *Welsh* in Wales predates the use of English in Britain. After decades of decline, Gaelic and Welsh are staging comebacks on radio and television, and in school curricula. Read the Global Challenges feature, titled "Speaking in Fewer Tongues," to learn about endangered languages around the world.

Implications for Managers The importance of understanding local languages is becoming increasingly apparent on the Internet. Roughly two-thirds of all Web pages are in English, but around three-quarters of all Internet users are non-native English speakers. Software solutions providers are assisting companies from English-speaking countries in adapting their Web sites for global e-business. Web surfers from cultures across the globe bring their own specific tastes, preferences, and buying habits online with them. The company that can provide its customer in Mexico City, Paris, or Tokyo with a quality buying experience in his or her native language will have an edge on the competition.

Language proficiency is crucial in production facilities where non-native managers are supervising local employees. One North American manager in Mexico was confused when his seemingly relaxed and untroubled workers went on strike. The problem lay in different cultural perspectives. Mexican workers generally do not take the initiative in problem solving and

---

Global Challenges   Speaking in Fewer Tongues

One day this year, somewhere in the world, an old man or woman will die and with them will go their language. Dozens of languages have just one native speaker still living, and some blame globalization. Here are the facts, the consequences, and the challenge.

- **Some Are Losing.** Of the world's roughly 6000 languages, about 90 percent have fewer than 100 000 speakers. By the end of this century, more than half of the world's languages may be lost; perhaps fewer than 1000 will survive. One endangered language is Aramaic, a 2500-year-old Semitic language that was once the major language in the Middle East.

- **Some Are Gaining.** Even as minority languages die out, three languages continue to grow in popularity: Mandarin, Spanish, and English. English has emerged as the universal language of business, higher education, diplomacy, science, popular music, entertainment, and international travel. More than 70 nations give special status to English, and roughly one-quarter of the world's population is fluent or competent in it.

- **The Consequences.** The loss of a language can mean the loss of a people's culture because it is the vehicle for cultural, spiritual, and intellectual life. What is lost includes prayers, myths, humour, poetry, ceremonies, conversational styles, and terms for emotions, behaviours, and habits. When a language dies, all these must be expressed in a new language with different words, sounds, and grammar. The result is that much of a culture can simply vanish.

- **The Challenge.** Linguists are concerned that such a valuable part of human culture could vanish. The impending loss of more languages has linguists creating videotapes, audiotapes, and written records of endangered tongues before they disappear. Communities themselves are also taking action. In New Zealand, Maori communities set up nursery schools called *kohanga reo*, or "language nests," that are staffed by elders and conducted entirely in Maori.

- **Want to Know More?** Visit the Linguistic Society of America (www.lsadc.org), European Bureau for Lesser Used Languages (www.eblul.org), and Foundation for Endangered Languages (www.ogmios.org).

workplace complaints. Workers concluded the plant manager knew, but did not care, about their concerns because he did not question employees about working conditions.

American-born Thomas Kwan, who now works for a health products company in Shanghai, China, says similar scenarios occur there. "Whereas Americans are encouraged to challenge their boss to explain things, I have to ask Chinese staff what they think and encourage them to speak up. A lot of [expatriate] managers fail in China because they don't understand that Chinese don't tell you what they think," he says.[9]

Marketers prize insights into the interests, values, attitudes, and habits of teenagers. Habbo (www.habbo.com), the world's largest virtual hangout for teens, surveyed more than 50 000 teenagers in 31 countries to learn how they communicate with each other. The study found that although 72 percent of teens have active e-mail accounts, 76 percent communicate with friends primarily through instant messaging. Teens reserve e-mail for nonpersonal needs such as school, work, and corresponding with family members. Knowledge of these habits helps marketers to better target promotions.[10]

Language Blunders   Advertising slogans and company documents must be translated carefully so messages are received precisely as intended. There are many stories of companies making terrible language blunders in their international business dealings. General Motors' Chevrolet division (www.chevrolet.com) made perhaps the most well-known blunder when it first launched its Chevrolet Nova in Spanish-speaking markets. The company failed to notice beforehand that "No va" means "No go" in Spanish. Chevrolet had far greater success when it renamed the car *Caribe* (piranha)—the voraciously carnivorous freshwater fish native to South America that attacks and destroys living animals! In Sweden, Kellogg (www.kellogg.com) had to rename its Bran Buds cereal because the Swedish translation came out roughly as "burned farmer." And then there's the entrepreneur in Miami who tried to make the most of a visit to the United States by the pope of the Roman Catholic Church. He quickly began printing T-shirts for Spanish-speaking Catholics that should have read, "I saw the Pope (el Papa)." But a gender error on the noun resulted in T-shirts proclaiming "I saw the Potato (la Papa)"![11] Other translation blunders include the following:

- An English-language sign in a Moscow hotel read, "You are welcome to visit the cemetery where famous Russian composers, artists, and writers are buried daily except Thursday."
- A sign for English-speaking guests in a Tokyo hotel read, "You are respectfully requested to take advantage of the chambermaids."
- An airline ticket office in Copenhagen read in English, "We take your bags and send them in all directions."
- A Japanese knife manufacturer labelled its exports to the United States with "Caution: Blade extremely sharp! Keep out of children."
- Braniff Airlines' English-language slogan "Fly in Leather" was translated as "Fly Naked" in Spanish.

Such blunders are not the exclusive domain of humans. The use of machine translation—computer software used to translate one language into another—is booming along with the explosion in the number of non-native English speakers using the Internet. One search engine allows its users to search the Internet in English and Asian languages, translate Web pages, and compose an e-mail in one language and send it in another. The computers attempted a translation of the following: "The Chinese Communist Party is debating whether to drop its ban on private-enterprise owners being allowed to join the Party." And it came up with this in Chinese: "The Chinese Communist Party is debating whether to deny its ban in join the Party is allowed soldier enterprise owners on." Various other machine translators turned the French version of "I don't care" ("*Je m'en fou*") into "I myself in crazy," "I of insane," and "Me me in madman."

lingua franca

Third or "link" language understood by two parties who speak different native languages.

Lingua Franca   A **lingua franca** is a third or "link" language understood by two parties who speak different native languages. The original *lingua franca* arose to support ancient trading activities and contained a mixture of Italian and French, along with Arabic, Greek, and Turkish. Although only 5 percent of the world's population speaks English as a first language, it is the most common *lingua franca* in international business, followed closely by French and Spanish.

The Cantonese dialect of Chinese spoken in Hong Kong and the Mandarin dialect spoken in Taiwan and on the Chinese mainland are so different that a *lingua franca* is often preferred.

And, although India's official language is Hindi, its *lingua franca* among the multitude of dialects is English because it was once a British colony. Yet many young people speak what is referred to as "Hinglish"—a combination of Hindi, Tamil, and English words mixed within a single sentence. Multinational corporations sometimes choose a *lingua franca* for official internal communications because they operate in many nations, each with its own language.

Companies that use English for internal correspondence include Philips (www.philips.com) (a Dutch electronics firm), Asea Brown Boveri (www.abb.ca) (a Swiss industrial giant), and Alcatel-Lucent (www.alcatel-lucent.com) (a French telecommunications firm). Executives of Japan's number one Internet shopping site, Rakuten (www.rakuten.co.jp), announced in 2010 that it will officially adopt English because of its pervasiveness on the Internet. All executive meetings are to be held in English and all internal documents will eventually be written in English. The company expects the move to "improve its employees' abilities and broaden their perspectives."[12]

BODY LANGUAGE **Body language** communicates through unspoken cues, including hand gestures, facial expressions, physical greetings, eye contact, and the manipulation of personal space. Similar to spoken language, body language communicates both information and feelings, and differs greatly from one culture to another. Italians, French, Arabs, and Venezuelans, for example, animate conversations with lively hand gestures and other body motions. Japanese and Koreans, although more reserved, communicate just as much information through their own body languages; a look of the eye can carry as much or more meaning as two flailing arms.

> **body language**
> Language communicated through unspoken cues, including hand gestures, facial expressions, physical greetings, eye contact, and the manipulation of personal space.

Most body language is subtle and takes time to recognize and interpret. For example, navigating the all-important handshake in international business can be tricky. In the United States, it is a firm grip and can include several pumps of the arm. But in the Middle East and Latin America, a softer clasp of the hand with little or no arm pump is the custom. And in some countries, such as Japan, people do not shake hands at all but bow to one another. Bows of respect carry different meanings, usually depending on the recipient. Associates of equal standing bow about 15 degrees toward one another. But proper respect for an elder requires a bow of about 30 degrees. Bows of remorse or apology should be about 45 degrees.

Proximity is an extremely important element of body language to consider when meeting someone from another culture. If you stand or sit too close to your counterpart (from their perspective), you may invade their personal space and appear aggressive. If you remain too far away, you risk appearing untrustworthy. For North Americans, a distance of about 19 inches is about right between two speakers. For Western Europeans, 14 to 16 inches seems appropriate, but someone from the United Kingdom might prefer about 24 inches. Koreans and Chinese are likely to be comfortable about 36 inches apart; people from the Middle East will close the distance to about 8 to 12 inches.

Physical gestures often cause the most misunderstanding between people of different cultures because they can convey very different meanings. The thumbs-up sign is vulgar in Italy and Greece but means "all right" or even "great" in the United States.

Physical gestures reflect centuries of cultural differences. Forming the thumb-and-index circle in most of Europe and in the United States means "okay"; in Germany it's a very rude gesture. Tapping one's nose in England and Scotland means "You and I are in on the secret"; in nearby Wales it means "You're very nosy." Tapping one's temple in much of Western Europe means "You're crazy"; in the Netherlands it means "You're very clever."

Sources: (left) foto.fritz/Shutterstock; (centre) Stephen Orsillo/Shutterstock; (right) ostill/shutterstock.

Quick Study

1. Define *communication*. Why is knowledge of a culture's spoken language important for international business?

2. Describe the threat faced by endangered languages. What is being done to help them survive?

3. What is a *lingua franca*? Describe its implications for conducting international business.

4. Why is *body language* important for international business? Give several examples of how it differs across cultures.

Education

Education is crucial for passing on traditions, customs, and values. Each culture educates its young people through schooling, parenting, religious teachings, and group memberships. Families and other groups provide informal instruction about customs and how to socialize with others. In most cultures, intellectual skills such as reading and mathematics are taught in formal educational settings. Two important topics in education are education level and brain drain.

EDUCATION LEVEL   Data that a government provides on its people's education level must be taken with a grain of salt. Comparisons from country to country can be difficult because many nations rely on literacy tests of their own design. Although some countries administer standardized tests, others require only a signature as proof of literacy. Yet searching for untapped markets or new factory locations can force managers to rely on such undependable benchmarks. As you can see from Table 2.1, some countries have further to go than others in increasing national literacy rates.

TABLE 2.1	Literacy Rates of Selected Countries
Country	**Adult Literacy Rate (Percentage of People Age 15 and up)**
Mali	31
Sierra Leone	42
Central African Rep.	56
Bangladesh	57
Timor-Leste	58
Nepal	60
Nigeria	61
Ghana	67
Egypt	72
Guatemala	75
Iraq	78
El Salvador	84
Saudi Arabia	87
Puerto Rico	90
Brazil	90
Mexico	93
Vietnam	93
Colombia	93
China	94

Source: Based on *World Development Indicators 2012,* World Bank Web site (www.worldbank.org).

The table shows that China and Brazil, which are major emerging markets, have a 6 and 10 percent illiteracy rate (respectively). Around 800 million adults remain illiterate worldwide. Although global illiteracy rates are higher for women, the gap with men is closing. Globally, the average literacy rate for youth (ages 15–24) is lowest in Sub-Saharan Africa, at 72 percent; South Asia has the second lowest youth literacy rate, at 79 percent, followed by the Arab world, at 87 percent.[13]

Countries with poorly educated populations attract the lowest-paying manufacturing jobs. Nations with excellent programs for basic education tend to attract relatively good-paying industries. Those that invest in worker training are usually repaid in productivity increases and rising incomes. Meanwhile, countries with skilled, highly educated workforces attract all sorts of high-paying jobs, often called "brainpower" industries.

Emerging economies in Asia owe much of their rapid economic development to solid education systems. Hong Kong, South Korea, Singapore, and Taiwan focus on rigorous mathematical training in primary and secondary schooling. University education concentrates on the hard sciences and aims to train engineers, scientists, and managers. On the other hand, some experts say China's rote-learning education system graduates many bright engineers but few managers. This could pose problems for China as quality managers are what the country needs to take its economy to a higher level.[14]

THE "BRAIN DRAIN" PHENOMENON   The quality of a nation's education system is related to its level of economic development. **Brain drain** is the departure of highly educated people from one profession, geographic region, or nation to another. Over the years, political unrest and economic hardship forced many Indonesians to flee their homeland for other nations, particularly Hong Kong, Singapore, and the United States. Most of Indonesia's brain drain occurred among Western-educated professionals in finance and technology—exactly the people needed for economic development.

brain drain
Departure of highly educated people from one profession, geographic region, or nation to another.

Many countries in Eastern Europe experienced high levels of brain drain early in their transition to market economies. Economists, engineers, scientists, and researchers in all fields fled westward to escape poverty. But as these nations continue to liberalize, some are luring professionals back to their homelands—a process known as *reverse brain drain.*

Physical and Material Environments

The physical environment and material surroundings of a culture heavily influence its development and pace of change. In this section, we first look at how physical environment and culture are related, and then we explore the effect of material culture on business.

PHYSICAL ENVIRONMENT   Although the physical environment affects a people's culture, it does not directly determine it. Two aspects of the physical environment that heavily influence a people's culture are topography and climate.

Topography   All the physical features that characterize the surface of a geographic region constitute its **topography**. Some surface features such as navigable rivers and flat plains facilitate travel and contact with others. By contrast, treacherous mountain ranges and large bodies of water can discourage contact. Cultures isolated by topographical features can find themselves less exposed to the cultural traits of other peoples, which can mean slower cultural change.

topography
All the physical features that characterize the surface of a geographic region.

Topography can affect consumers' product needs. For example, there is little market for Honda scooters (www.honda.com) in most mountainous regions because their engines are too small. These are better markets for the company's more rugged, manoeuvrable motorcycles with larger engines. Thinner air at higher elevations might also entail modifications in carburetor design for gasoline-powered vehicles.

Topography can have a profound impact on personal communication in a culture. For example, mountain ranges and the formidable Gobi Desert consume two-thirds of China's land surface. Groups living in the valleys of these mountain ranges hold on to their own ways of life and speak their own languages. Although the Mandarin dialect was decreed the national language many years ago, the mountains, desert, and vast expanse of China still impair personal communication and, therefore, the proliferation of Mandarin.

Climate   Climate affects where people settle and helps direct systems of distribution. In Australia, for example, intensely hot and dry conditions in two large deserts and jungle conditions in the northeast pushed settlement to coastal areas. These climatic conditions, combined with the higher cost of land transport, means coastal waters are still used to distribute products between distant cities.

Climate plays a large role in lifestyle and work habits. The heat of the summer sun grows intense in the early afternoon hours in the countries of southern Europe, northern Africa, and the Middle East. For this reason, people often take afternoon breaks of one or two hours in July and August. People use this time to perform errands, such as shopping, or even take short naps before returning to work until about 7 or 8 p.m. Companies doing business in these regions must adapt to this local tradition.

Climate also affects customs such as the type of clothing people wear. People in many tropical areas wear little clothing and wear it loosely because of the warm, humid climate. In the desert areas of the Middle East and North Africa, people also wear loose clothing, but they wear long robes to protect themselves from intense sunshine and blowing sand.

material culture

All the technology used in a culture to manufacture goods and provide services.

MATERIAL CULTURE   All the technology used in a culture to manufacture goods and provide services is called its **material culture**. Material culture is often used to measure the technological advancement of a nation's markets or industries. Generally, a firm enters a new market under one of two conditions: demand for its products has developed or the infrastructure is capable of supporting production operations.

Many regions and nations lack the most basic elements of a modern society's material culture. For example, companies are not flocking to the Southeast Asian nation of Myanmar because the nation lacks both sufficient product demand and an adequate infrastructure. Political and social problems under a repressive military government have stalled Myanmar's economic development. Yet technology is helping some nations at the bottom of the global economic pyramid break down barriers that keep their people mired in poverty.

Uneven Material Culture   Material culture often displays uneven development across a nation's geography, markets, and industries. For example, much of China's recent economic progress is occurring in coastal cities. Shanghai has long played an important role in China's international trade because of its strategic location and its superb harbour on the East China Sea. Although it is home to only 1 percent of the total population, Shanghai accounts for about 5 percent of China's total output—including about 12 percent of both its industrial production and its financial-services output.

Members of the "2010 Chinese Root-Seeking Tour" pose for photos under an old tree in the Temple of Heaven in Beijing, China. The summer camp program attracts more than 6000 overseas Chinese youths from 51 countries and regions each year. It is designed to educate young people in the cultural traditions of their Chinese ancestors. Organizers hope that by gaining a better understanding of Chinese history and culture, these youths will grow to become good cross-cultural communicators between China and other nations.

Source: Wang Yongji/Xinhua/ Photoshot/Newscom.

Likewise, Bangkok, the capital city of Thailand, houses only 10 percent of the nation's population but accounts for about 40 percent of its economic output. Meanwhile, the northern parts of the country remain rural, consisting mostly of farms, forests, and mountains.

Quick Study

1. Why is the education level of a country's people important to international companies?
2. What is meant by the terms *brain drain* and *reverse brain drain*?
3. How are a people's culture and physical environment related?
4. What is the significance of *material culture* for international business?

Classifying Cultures

Throughout this chapter, you've seen how cultures can differ greatly from one another. People living in broadly different cultures tend to respond differently in similar business situations. There are two widely accepted ways to classify cultures based on differences in characteristics such as values, attitudes, social structure, and so on. Let's now take a detailed look at each of these tools: the Kluckhohn–Strodtbeck and Hofstede frameworks.

Kluckhohn–Strodtbeck Framework

The **Kluckhohn–Strodtbeck framework** compares cultures along six dimensions. It studies a given culture by asking each of the following questions:[15]

Kluckhohn–Strodtbeck framework
Framework for studying cultural differences along six dimensions, such as focus on past or future events and belief in individual or group responsibility for personal well-being.

- Do people believe that their environment controls them, that they control the environment, or that they are part of nature?
- Do people focus on past events, on the present, or on the future implications of their actions?
- Are people easily controlled and not to be trusted, or can they be trusted to act freely and responsibly?
- Do people desire accomplishments in life, carefree lives, or spiritual and contemplative lives?
- Do people believe that individuals or groups are responsible for each person's welfare?
- Do people prefer to conduct most activities in private or in public?

CASE: DIMENSIONS OF JAPANESE CULTURE By providing answers to each of these six questions, we can briefly apply the Kluckhohn–Strodtbeck framework to Japanese culture:

1. *Japanese believe in a delicate balance between people and environment that must be maintained.* Suppose an undetected flaw in a company's product harms customers using it. In many countries, a high-stakes class-action lawsuit would be filed against the manufacturer on behalf of the victims' families. This scenario is rarely played out in Japan. Japanese culture does not feel that individuals can possibly control every situation but that accidents happen. Japanese victims would receive heartfelt apologies, a promise it won't happen again, and a relatively small damage award.
2. *Japanese culture emphasizes the future.* Because Japanese culture emphasizes strong ties between people and groups, including companies, forming long-term relationships with people is essential when doing business there. Throughout the business relationship, Japanese companies remain in close, continuous contact with buyers to ensure that their needs are being met. This relationship also forms the basis of a communication channel by which suppliers learn about the types of products and services buyers would like to see in the future.
3. *Japanese culture treats people as quite trustworthy.* Business dealings among Japanese companies are based heavily on trust. Once an agreement to conduct business has been made, it is difficult to break unless there are extreme uncontrollable factors at work. This is due to the fear of "losing face" if one cannot keep a business commitment. In addition to business applications, society at large reflects the Japanese concern for

trustworthiness. Crime rates are quite low, and the streets of Japan's largest cities are very safe to walk at night.

4. *Japanese are accomplishment-oriented—not necessarily for themselves, but for their employers and work units.* Japanese children learn the importance of groups early by contributing to the upkeep of their schools. They share duties such as mopping floors, washing windows, cleaning chalkboards, and arranging desks and chairs. They carry such habits learned in school into the adult workplace, where management and labour tend to work together toward company goals. Japanese managers make decisions only after considering input from subordinates. Also, materials buyers, engineers, designers, factory floor supervisors, and marketers cooperate closely throughout each stage of a product's development.

5. *Japanese culture emphasizes individual responsibility to the group and group responsibility to the individual.* This trait has long been a hallmark of Japanese corporations. Traditionally, subordinates promise hard work and loyalty, and top managers provide job security. But to remain competitive internationally, Japanese companies have eliminated jobs and moved production to low-wage nations like China and Vietnam. As the tradition of job security falls by the wayside, more Japanese workers now consider working for non-Japanese companies, whereas others find work as temporary employees. Although this trait of loyalty is diminishing somewhat in business, it remains a very prominent feature in other aspects of Japanese society, especially family.

6. *The culture of Japan tends to be public.* You will often find top Japanese managers located in the centre of a large, open-space office surrounded by the desks of many employees. By comparison, Western executives are often secluded in walled offices located on the perimeter of workspaces. This characteristic reaches deep into Japanese society— consider, for example, Japan's continued fondness for public baths.

Hofstede Framework

Hofstede framework
Framework for studying cultural differences along five dimensions, such as individualism versus collectivism and equality versus inequality.

The **Hofstede framework** compares cultures along five dimensions.[16] Dutch psychologist Geert Hofstede developed the framework from a study of more than 110 000 people working in IBM subsidiaries (www.ibm.com) in 40 countries and a follow-up study of students in 23 countries. Let's examine each of these dimensions in detail.[17]

1. *Individualism versus collectivism.* This dimension identifies the extent to which a culture emphasizes the individual versus the group. Individualist cultures (those scoring high on this dimension) value hard work and promote entrepreneurial risk taking, thereby fostering invention and innovation. Although people are given freedom to focus on personal goals, they are held responsible for their actions. That is why responsibility for poor business decisions is placed squarely on the shoulders of the individual in charge. At the same time, higher individualism may be responsible for higher rates of employee turnover.

   On the contrary, people in collectivist cultures (those scoring low on this dimension) feel a strong association to groups, including family and work units. The goal of maintaining group harmony is probably most evident in the family structure. People in collectivist cultures tend to work toward collective rather than personal goals and are responsible to the group for their actions. In turn, the group shares responsibility for the well-being of each of its members. Thus, in collectivist cultures, success or failure tends to be shared among the work unit, rather than any particular individual receiving all the praise or blame. All social, political, economic, and legal institutions reflect the group's critical role.

2. *Power distance.* This dimension conveys the degree to which a culture accepts social inequality among its people. A culture with large power distance tends to be characterized by much inequality between superiors and subordinates. Organizations tend also to be more hierarchical, with power deriving from prestige, force, and inheritance. This is why executives and upper management in cultures with large power distance often enjoy special recognition and privileges. On the other hand, cultures with small power distance display a greater degree of equality, with prestige and rewards more equally shared between superiors and subordinates. Power in these cultures (relative to cultures with large power distance) is seen to derive more from hard work and entrepreneurial drive and is therefore often considered more legitimate.

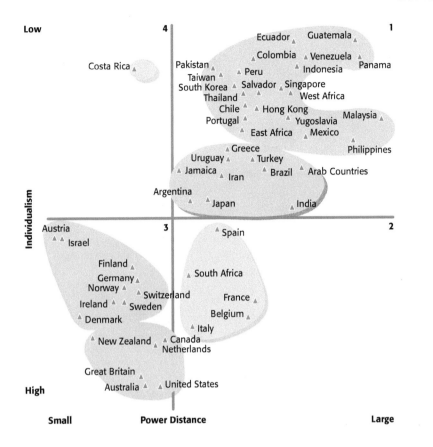

FIGURE 2.2

Power Distance and Individualism versus Collectivism

Source: Based on Geert Hofstede, "The Cultural Relativity of Organizational Practices and Theories," *Journal of International Business Studies,* Fall 1983, p. 82.

Figure 2.2 shows how various countries rank according to these first two dimensions: power distance and individualism versus collectivism. What is striking about this figure is the tight grouping of nations within the five clusters (plus Costa Rica). You can see the concentration of mostly African, Asian, Central and South American, and Middle Eastern nations in Quadrant 1 (cultures with relatively larger power distance and lower individualism). By contrast, Quadrants 3 and 2 comprise mostly the cultures of Australia and the nations of North America and Western Europe. These nations had the highest individualism scores, and many had relatively smaller power distance scores.

3. ***Uncertainty avoidance.*** This dimension identifies the extent to which a culture avoids uncertainty and ambiguity. A culture with large uncertainty avoidance values security and places its faith in strong systems of rules and procedures in society. It is perhaps not surprising then that cultures with large uncertainty avoidance normally have lower employee turnover, more formal rules for regulating employee behaviour, and more difficulty implementing change. Cultures scoring low on uncertainty avoidance tend to be more open to change and new ideas. This helps explain why individuals in this type of culture tend to be entrepreneurial and organizations tend to welcome the best business practices from other cultures. Because people tend to be less fearful of change, however, these cultures can also suffer from higher levels of employee turnover.

Figure 2.3 plots countries according to the second and third dimensions: power distance and uncertainty avoidance. Although the lines of demarcation are somewhat less obvious in this figure, patterns do emerge among the six clusters (plus Jamaica). Quadrant 4 contains nations characterized by small uncertainty avoidance and small power distance, including Australia, Canada, Jamaica, the United States, and many Western European nations. Meanwhile, Quadrant 2 contains many Asian, Central American, South American, and Middle Eastern nations—nations having large power distance and large uncertainty avoidance indexes.

4. ***Achievement versus nurturing.*** This dimension captures the extent to which a culture emphasizes personal achievement and materialism versus relationships and quality of life. Cultures scoring high on this index tend to be characterized more by personal assertiveness and the accumulation of wealth, typically translating into an entrepreneurial drive. Cultures

FIGURE 2.3

Power Distance and Uncertainty Avoidance

Source: Based on Geert Hofstede, "The Cultural Relativity of Organizational Practices and Theories," *Journal of International Business Studies,* Fall 1983, p. 84.

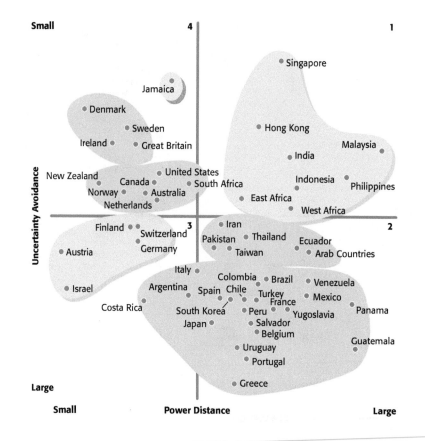

scoring low on this dimension generally have more relaxed lifestyles, wherein people are more concerned about caring for others as opposed to material gain.

5. ***Long-term orientation.*** This dimension indicates a society's time perspective and an attitude of overcoming obstacles with time, if not with will and strength. It attempts to capture the differences between Eastern and Western cultures. A high-scoring culture (strong long-term orientation) values respect for tradition, thrift, perseverance, and a sense of personal shame. These cultures tend to have a strong work ethic because people expect long-term rewards from today's hard work. A low-scoring culture is characterized by individual stability and reputation, fulfilling social obligations, and reciprocation of greetings and gifts. These cultures can change more rapidly because tradition and commitment are not impediments to change.

Locate your country in Figures 2.2 and 2.3. In your personal experience, do you agree with the placement of your nation in these figures? Do you believe managers in your country display the types of behaviours depicted on each dimension just described?

Quick Study

1. What six dimensions comprise the *Kluckhohn–Strodtbeck framework* for classifying cultures?
2. What are the five dimensions of the *Hofstede framework* for classifying cultures?
3. Briefly explain how each framework can be used to analyze a culture.

International Human Resource Management

Perhaps the most important resource of any successful business is the people who comprise it. If a company gives its human resource management practices the importance they deserve, it can have a profound impact on performance. Highly trained and productive employees who are proficient in their duties allow a company to achieve its business goals both domestically and internationally. **Human resource management (HRM)** is the process of staffing a company and ensuring that employees are as productive as possible. It requires managers to be effective in recruiting, selecting, training, developing, evaluating, and compensating employees and in forming good relationships with them.

International HRM differs considerably from HRM in a domestic setting because of differences in national business environments. There are concerns over the employment of **expatriates**— citizens of one country who are living and working in another. Companies must deal with many issues when they have expatriate employees on job assignments that could last several years. Some of these issues are related to the inconvenience and stress of living in an unfamiliar culture.

Training and development programs must often be tailored to local practices. Some countries, such as Germany and Japan, have extensive vocational-training schools that turn out graduates ready to perform their jobs proficiently. Finding well-qualified managerial workers in those markets is relatively easy. By contrast, developing a production facility in many emerging markets requires far more basic training of workers. For example, workers in China work hard and tend to be well educated. But because China lacks an advanced vocational training system like those in Germany and Japan, Chinese workers tend to require more intensive on-the-job training. Recruitment and selection practices must also be adapted to the host nation's hiring laws. Hiring practices regarding non-discrimination among job candidates must be carefully monitored so that the company does not violate such laws. And companies that go abroad to lower labour expenses then adjust pay scales and advancement criteria to suit local customs.

International Staffing Policy

The customary means by which a company staffs its offices is called its **staffing policy**. Staffing policy is greatly influenced by the extent of a firm's international involvement. There are three main approaches to the staffing of international business operations—*ethnocentric*, *polycentric*, and *geocentric*. Although we discuss each of these approaches as being distinct from one another, companies often blend different aspects of each staffing policy in practice. The result is an almost infinite variety of international staffing policies among international companies.

Ethnocentric Staffing

In **ethnocentric staffing**, individuals from the home country manage operations abroad. This policy tends to appeal to companies that want to maintain tight control over decision making in branch offices abroad. Accordingly, those companies work to formulate policies designed to work in every country in which they operate. But note that firms generally pursue this policy in their international operations for top managerial posts—implementing it at lower levels is often impractical.

ADVANTAGES OF ETHNOCENTRIC STAFFING   Firms pursue this policy for several reasons. First, locally qualified people are not always available. In developing and newly industrialized countries, there is often a shortage of qualified personnel that creates a highly competitive local labour market.

Second, companies use ethnocentric staffing to recreate local operations in the image of home-country operations. Especially if they have climbed the corporate ladder in the home office, expatriate managers tend to infuse branch offices with the corporate culture. This policy is important for companies that need a strong set of shared values among the people in each international office—such as firms implementing global strategies. For example, Mihir Doshi was born in Bombay, but his family moved to the United States in 1978. Doshi graduated from New York University and became a naturalized US citizen in 1988. In 1995 he became executive director of Morgan Stanley's (www.ms.com) operations in India. "Mentally," he reports, "I'm very American. Here, I can be Indian. What the firm gets is somebody to indoctrinate Morgan Stanley culture. I provide the link."[18]

By the same token, a system of shared values is important when a company's international units are highly interdependent. For instance, fashioning branch operations in the image of home-office operations can also ease the transfer of special know-how. This advantage is particularly valuable when that know-how is rooted in the expertise and experience of home-country managers.

Finally, some companies feel that managers sent from the home country will look out for the company's interests more earnestly than will host-country natives. Japanese companies are

human resource management (HRM)
Process of staffing a company and ensuring that employees are as productive as possible.

expatriates
Citizens of one country who are living and working in another.

staffing policy
Customary means by which a company staffs its offices.

ethnocentric staffing
Staffing policy in which individuals from the home country manage operations abroad.

notorious for their reluctance to place non-Japanese managers at the helm of international offices. And when they do appoint a foreigner, they often place a Japanese manager in the office to monitor important decisions and report back to the home office. Companies that operate in highly nationalistic markets and those worried about industrial espionage also typically find an ethnocentric approach appealing.

DISADVANTAGES OF ETHNOCENTRIC STAFFING Despite its advantages, ethnocentric staffing has its negative aspects. First, relocating managers from the home country is expensive. The bonuses that managers often receive for relocating plus relocation expenses for entire families can increase the cost of a manager several times over. Likewise, the pressure of cultural differences and long periods away from relatives and friends can contribute to the failure of managers on international assignments.

Second, an ethnocentric policy can create barriers for the host-country office. The presence of home-country managers in the host country might encourage a "foreign" image of the business. Lower-level employees might feel that managers do not really understand their needs because they come from another culture. Occasionally they are right: Expatriate managers sometimes fail to integrate themselves into the local culture. And if they fail to overcome cultural barriers, they typically fail to understand the needs of their local employees and those of their local customers.

Polycentric Staffing

polycentric staffing
Staffing policy in which individuals from the host country manage operations abroad.

In **polycentric staffing**, individuals from the host country manage operations abroad. Companies can implement a polycentric approach for top and mid-level managers, for lower-level staff, or for non-managerial workers. It is well suited to companies who want to give national units a degree of autonomy in decision making. For example, polycentric staffing is commonly used in retail and food franchise operations. This policy does not mean that host-country managers are left to run operations in any way they see fit. Large international companies usually conduct extensive training programs in which host-country managers visit home offices for extended periods. This exposes them to the company's culture and specific business practices. Small and medium-sized companies can find this policy expensive, but being able to depend on local managers who fully understand what is expected of them can far outweigh any costs.

ADVANTAGES AND DISADVANTAGES OF POLYCENTRIC STAFFING Polycentric staffing places managerial responsibility in the hands of people intimately familiar with the local business environment. Managers with deep cultural understanding of the local market can be an enormous advantage. They are familiar with local business practices and can read the subtle cues of both verbal and nonverbal language. They need not overcome any cultural barriers created by an image of being an outsider, and they tend to have a better feel for the needs of employees, customers, and suppliers.

Another important advantage of polycentric staffing is elimination of the high cost of relocating expatriate managers and families. This benefit can be extremely helpful for small and medium-sized businesses that cannot afford the expenses associated with expatriate employees.

The major drawback of polycentric staffing is the potential for losing control of the host-country operation. When a company employs natives of each country to manage local operations, it runs the risk of becoming a collection of discrete national businesses. This situation might not be a problem when a firm's strategy calls for treating each national market differently. It is not a good policy, however, for companies that are following global strategies. If these companies lack integration, knowledge sharing, and a common image, performance will surely suffer.

Geocentric Staffing

geocentric staffing
Staffing policy in which the best-qualified individuals, regardless of nationality, manage operations abroad.

In **geocentric staffing**, the best-qualified individuals, regardless of nationality, manage operations abroad. The local operation may choose managers from the host country, from the home country, or from a third country. The choice depends on the operation's specific needs.

This policy is typically reserved for top-level managers. However, as you learned in this chapter's opening case, Cirque du Soleil has successfully applied geocentric staffing in all levels of the business.

ADVANTAGES AND DISADVANTAGES OF GEOCENTRIC STAFFING   Geocentric staffing helps a company develop global managers who can adjust easily to any business environment—particularly to cultural differences. This advantage is especially useful for global companies trying to break down nationalistic barriers, whether between managers in a single office or between different offices. One hope of companies using this policy is that a global perspective among its managers will help them seize opportunities that may otherwise be overlooked.

The downside of geocentric staffing is the expense. Understandably, top managers who are capable both of fitting into different cultures and being effective at their jobs are highly prized among international companies. The combination of high demand for their skills and their short supply inflates their salaries. Moreover, there is the expense of relocating managers and their families—sometimes every year or two.

Quick Study

1. List several ways in which *human resource management* differs in the international versus domestic environment.
2. What are the three different types of international *staffing policies* that companies can implement?
3. Identify the advantages and disadvantages of each type of international staffing policy.

Recruiting and Selecting Human Resources

Naturally, companies try to recruit and select qualified managers and non-managerial workers who are well suited to their tasks and responsibilities. But how does a company know the number of managers and workers it needs? How does it recruit the best available individuals? How does it select from the pool of available candidates? In this section, we explore some answers to these and other important questions about recruiting and selecting employees.

Human Resource Planning

Recruiting and selecting managers and workers requires **human resource planning**—the process of forecasting a company's human resource needs and its supply. The first phase of HR planning involves taking an inventory of a company's current human resources—that is, collecting data on every employee, including educational background, special job skills, previous jobs, language skills, and experience living abroad.

The second phase of HR planning is estimating the company's future HR needs. For example, consider a firm that plans to sell its products directly to buyers in a new market abroad. Will it create a new operation abroad and staff it with managers from the home office, or will it train local managers? Will it hire its own local sales force, or will it hire a distributor? Likewise, manufacturing or assembling products in an international market requires factory workers. A company must decide whether to hire these people itself or to subcontract production to other producers—thus eliminating the need for it to hire factory workers. This decision frequently raises ethical questions: Are the employees being treated fairly? Will they be exploited? Are the working conditions offered by the subcontractor good? For example, Apple (www.apple.com) sent a team of investigators to China to look into charges of sweatshop-like conditions at a company manufacturing Apple's iPod. The company that Apple investigated was a division of the world's largest contract electronics manufacturer, Hon Hai Precision Industry.[19]

human resource planning
Process of forecasting a company's human resource needs and its supply.

Another example on this topic involves Levi Strauss (www.levistrauss.com). When apparel contractors in Bangladesh admitted that they hired children, Levi Strauss demanded that they comply with local regulations. Unfortunately, it turned out that many of the under-age workers were their families' sole sources of support. So Levi's struck a deal: Contractors agreed to continue paying wages to the youngsters while they went to school and then they would be rehired when they reached age 14. Levi's paid for them to attend school until they came of age.

In the third phase of HR planning, managers develop a plan for recruiting and selecting people to fill vacant and anticipated new positions, both managerial and non-managerial. Sometimes, a firm must also make plans for reducing its workforce—a process called *decruitment*—when current HR levels are greater than anticipated needs. Planning for decruitment normally occurs when a company decides to discontinue manufacturing or selling in a market. Unfortunately, the decision by global companies to shift the location of manufacturing from one country to another can also result in lost jobs. Let's now take a closer look at the recruitment and selection processes.

Recruiting Human Resources

recruitment
Process of identifying and attracting a qualified pool of applicants for vacant positions.

The process of identifying and attracting a qualified pool of applicants for vacant positions is called **recruitment**. Companies can recruit internally from among their current employees or look to external sources.

CURRENT EMPLOYEES Finding an international manager among current employees is easiest for a large company with an abundance of internal managers. Likely candidates within the company are managers who were involved in previous stages of an international project—say, in *identifying* the new production site or potential market. It is likely that these individuals have already made important contacts inside the host country, and they have already been exposed to its culture.

RECENT COLLEGE GRADUATES Companies also recruit from among recent college graduates who have come from other countries to attend college in the firm's home country. This is a particularly common practice among companies in the United States. Over a one-year period, these new hires receive general and specialized training, and then are given positions in their native countries. As a rule, they learn about the organization's culture and the way in which it conducts business. Most important, perhaps, is their familiarity with the culture of the target market, including its customs, traditions, and language.

LOCAL MANAGERIAL TALENT Companies can also recruit local managerial talent. Hiring local managers is common when cultural understanding is a key job requirement. Hiring local managers with government contacts can speed the process of getting approvals for local operations. In some cases, governments force companies to recruit local managers so that they can develop their own internal pools of managerial talent. Governments sometimes also restrict the number of international managers that can work in the host country.

NON-MANAGERIAL WORKERS Companies typically recruit locally for non-managerial positions because there is often little need for highly specialized skills or training. However, a specialist from the home country is typically brought in to train people chosen for more demanding positions.

Firms also turn to the local labour market when governments restrict the number of people allowed into the host country for work purposes. Such efforts are usually designed to reduce unemployment among the local population. On the other hand, countries sometimes permit the importation of non-managerial workers. Kuwait, a wealthy oil-producing country in the Middle East, has brought in large numbers of non-managerial workers for its blue-collar and technical jobs. Many of these workers come from Egypt, India, Lebanon, Pakistan, and the Philippines in search of jobs or higher wages.

selection
Process of screening and hiring the best-qualified applicants with the greatest performance potential.

Selecting Human Resources

The process of screening and hiring the best-qualified applicants with the greatest performance potential is called **selection**. The process for international assignments includes measuring a person's ability to bridge cultural differences. Expatriate managers must be able to adapt to a new way of life in the host country. Conversely, native host-country managers must be able to work effectively with superiors who have different cultural backgrounds.

In the case of expatriate managers, cultural differences between home country and host country are important factors in their potential success. Culturally sensitive managers increase the likelihood that a company will achieve its international business goals. Recruiters can assess cultural sensitivity by asking candidates questions about their receptiveness to new ways of doing things and questions about racial and ethnic issues. They can also use global aptitude tests such as the one mentioned in the Web Site Report exercise at the end of this chapter.

It is also important to examine the cultural sensitivity of each family member who will be going to the host country. The ability of a family member (particularly a spouse) to adapt to a new culture can be a key factor in the success or failure of an expatriate manager.

Culture Shock

Successful international managers typically do not mind, and often enjoy, living and working outside their native lands. In extreme cases, they might even be required to relocate every year or so. These individuals are capable of adapting quickly to local conditions and business practices. Such managers are becoming increasingly valuable with the emergence of markets in Asia, Central and Eastern Europe, and Latin America. They are also helping to create a global pool of managers who are ready and willing to go practically anywhere on short notice. The size of this pool, however, remains limited because of the difficulties that many people experience in relocating to unfamiliar cultures.

Living in another culture can be a stressful experience. Selecting managers comfortable travelling to and living in unfamiliar cultures, therefore, is an extremely important factor when recruiting for international posts. Set down in the midst of new cultures, many expatriates experience **culture shock**—a psychological process affecting people living abroad that is characterized by homesickness, irritability, confusion, aggravation, and depression. In other words, they have trouble adjusting to the new environment in which they find themselves. *Expatriate failure*—the early return by an employee from an international assignment because of inadequate job performance—often results from cultural stress. The higher cost of expatriate failure is convincing many companies to invest in cultural-training programs for employees sent abroad.

culture shock
Psychological process affecting people living abroad that is characterized by homesickness, irritability, confusion, aggravation, and depression.

Reverse Culture Shock

Ironically, expatriates who successfully adapt to new cultures often undergo an experience called **reverse culture shock**—the psychological process of re-adapting to one's home culture. Because values and behaviour that once seemed so natural now seem so strange, reverse culture shock may be even more disturbing than culture shock. Returning managers often find that either no position or merely a "standby" position awaits them in the home office. Companies often do not know how to take full advantage of the cross-cultural abilities developed by managers who have spent several potentially valuable years abroad. It is not uncommon for expatriates to leave their companies within a year of returning home because of difficulties blending back into the company culture.

reverse culture shock
Psychological process of re-adapting to one's home culture.

Moreover, spouses and children often have difficulty leaving the adopted culture and returning home. For many Japanese employees and their families, re-entry into Japanese culture after a work assignment in North America can be particularly difficult. The fast pace of business and social life in North America, plus the relatively high degree of freedom and independence for women, contrasts with life in Japan. Returning Japanese expatriates can find it difficult to adjust back to life in Japan after years of living in North America.

DEALING WITH REVERSE CULTURE SHOCK The effects of reverse culture shock can be reduced. Home-culture reorientation programs and career-counselling sessions for returning managers and their families can be highly effective. For example, the employer might bring the entire family home for a short stay several weeks before the official return. This kind of trip allows returnees to prepare for at least some of the reverse culture shock that may await them.

Good career development programs can help companies retain valuable managers. Ideally, the career development plan was worked out before the employee went abroad and revised before his or her return. Some companies work with employees before they go abroad to plan career paths of up to 20 years within the company. Mentors who have previously gone abroad and had to adjust on returning home can also be assigned to returning managers. The mentor becomes a confidant with whom the expatriate manager can discuss particular problems related to work, family, and readjusting to the home culture.

Cultural Training

Ideally, everyone involved in business should be culturally literate and prepared to go anywhere in the world at a moment's notice. Realistically, many employees and many companies do not need or cannot afford to be entirely literate in another culture. The extent of a company's international involvement demands a corresponding level of cultural knowledge from its employees. Companies whose activities are highly international need employees with language fluency and in-depth experience in other countries. Meanwhile, small companies or those new to international business can begin with some basic cultural training. As a company increases its international involvement and cross-cultural contact, employees' cultural knowledge must keep pace.

As we see in Figure 2.4, companies use many methods to prepare managers for an international assignment. These methods tend to reflect a manager's level of international involvement. The goal is to create informed, open-minded, flexible managers with a level of cultural training appropriate to the duties required of them.

ENVIRONMENTAL BRIEFINGS AND CULTURAL ORIENTATIONS *Environmental (area) briefings* constitute the most basic level of training—often the starting point for studying other cultures. Briefings include information on local housing, health care, transportation, schools, and climate. Such knowledge is normally obtained from books, films, and lectures. *Cultural orientations* offer insight into social, political, legal, and economic institutions. Their purpose is to add depth and substance to environmental briefings.

CULTURAL ASSIMILATION AND SENSITIVITY TRAINING *Cultural assimilation* teaches the culture's values, attitudes, manners, and customs. So-called guerrilla linguistics, which involves learning some phrases in the local language, is often used at this stage. It also typically includes role-play exercises: the trainee responds to a specific situation to be evaluated by a team of judges. This method is often used when someone is given little notice of a short stay abroad and wishes to take a crash course in social and business etiquette and communication. *Sensitivity*

FIGURE 2.4

International Assignment Preparation Methods

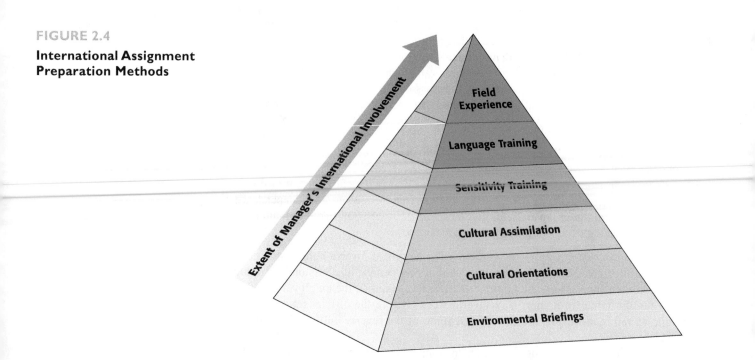

training teaches people to be considerate and understanding of other people's feelings and emotions. It gets the trainee "under the skin" of the local people.

LANGUAGE TRAINING   The need for more thorough cultural preparedness brings us to intensive *language training*. This level of training entails more than memorizing phrases for ordering dinner or asking directions. It gets a trainee "into the mind" of local people. The trainee learns more about why local people behave as they do. This is perhaps the most critical part of cultural training for long-term assignments.

A survey of top executives found that foreign-language skills topped the list of skills needed to maintain a competitive edge. According to the survey, 31 percent of male employees and 27 percent of female employees lacked foreign-language skills. To remedy this situation, many companies either employ outside agencies that specialize in language training or they develop their own programs. Employees at 3M Corporation (www.3m.com) developed a third way. They created an all-volunteer "Language Society" composed of current and retired employees and family members. About 1000 people are members, and the group offers classes in 17 languages taught by 70 volunteer employee teachers. The society meets 45 minutes per week and charges a nominal $5 membership fee. Officials at 3M say that the society nicely complements the company's formal language education program.[20]

FIELD EXPERIENCE   *Field experience* means visiting the culture, walking the streets of its cities and villages, and becoming absorbed by it for a short time. The trainee gets to enjoy some of the unique cultural traits and feel some of the stresses inherent in living in the culture.

Finally, remember that spouses and children also need cultural training. Training for them is a good investment.

Employee Compensation

Essential to good international HRM is a fair and effective compensation (reward) system. Such a system is designed to attract and retain the best and brightest employees and to reward them for their performance. Because a country's compensation practices are rooted in its culture and legal and economic systems, determining compensation can be complicated. For example, base pay accounts for nearly all employee compensation in some countries. In others, bonuses and fringe benefits account for more than half of a person's compensation.

Managerial Employees

Naturally, compensation packages for managers differ from company to company and from country to country. Good packages are fairly complicated to design, for several reasons. Consider the effect of *cost of living*, which includes factors such as the cost of groceries, dining out, clothing, housing, schooling, health care, transportation, and utilities. Quite simply, it costs more to live in some countries than in others. Moreover, within a given country, the cost of living typically varies from large cities to rural towns and villages. Most companies add a certain amount to an expatriate manager's pay to cover greater cost-of-living expenses. On the other hand, managers who are relocating to lower cost-of-living countries are typically paid the same amount that they were receiving at the home office—otherwise, they would be financially penalized for accepting an international job assignment.

Companies must cover other costs incurred by expatriate managers even when the cost of living abroad is lower than at home. One important concern for relocating managers is the quality of local education. In many cases, children cannot immediately enter local classes because they do not speak the local language. In such instances, most companies pay for private-school education.

BONUS AND TAX INCENTIVES   Companies commonly offer managers inducements to accept international postings. The most common is a financial bonus. This bonus can be in the form of a one-time payment or an add-on to regular pay—generally 15 to 20 percent. Bonuses for managers who are asked to go into a particularly unstable country or one with a very low standard of living often receive *hardship pay*.

Managers can also be attracted by another income-related factor. For example, the US government permits citizens working abroad to exclude $82 000 of "foreign-earned income" from their taxable income in the United States—even if it was earned in a country with no income tax. But earnings over that amount are subject to income tax, as are employee benefits such as free housing.[21]

CULTURAL AND SOCIAL CONTRIBUTORS TO COST   Culture also plays an important role in the compensation of expatriate managers. Some nations offer more paid holidays than others. Many offer free medical care to everyone living and working there. Granted, the quality of locally available medical care is not always good. Many companies, therefore, have plans to take seriously ill expatriates and family members home or to nearby countries where medical care is equal to that available in the home country.

Companies that hire managers in the local market might encounter additional costs engendered by social attitudes. For instance, in some countries employers are expected to provide free or subsidized housing. In others the government obliges employers to provide paid maternity leaves of up to one and a half years. Government-mandated maternity leaves vary significantly across European countries. Although not all such costs need to be absorbed by companies, they do tend to raise a country's cost of doing business.

Managers recruited from within the host country generally receive the same pay as managers who work for local companies. Yet they often receive perks not offered by local firms. And some managers are required to visit the home office at least several times per year. If time allows, many managers will make these into short vacations by taking along their families and adding a few extra days onto the length of the trip.

Quick Study

1. Identify the types of training and development used for international managers.
2. Describe each type of cultural training used to prepare managers for international assignments.
3. What variables are involved in decisions regarding employee compensation for managers?

Bottom Line for Business

As globalization continues to draw companies into the international arena, understanding local culture can give a company an advantage over rivals. By avoiding ethnocentric thinking, managers can avoid mistakenly disregarding the beneficial aspects of other cultures. By contrast, culturally literate managers who understand local needs and desires bring their companies closer to customers and, therefore, increase their competitiveness. They can become more effective marketers, negotiators, and production managers. Let's explore several areas in which culture has a direct impact on international business activity.

Marketing and Cultural Literacy

Many international companies operating in local markets abroad take advantage of the public relations value of supporting national culture. Some of India's most precious historical monuments and sites are crumbling due to a lack of government funds for upkeep. Companies are helping the government to maintain key sites and are earning the goodwill of the people.

This chapter introduced the Kluckhohn–Strodtbeck and Hofstede frameworks for classifying cultures. Local culture is important for a company exploring international markets for its products. We see the significance of power distance in the export of luxury items. A nation with a large power distance accepts greater inequality among its people and tends to have a wealthy upper class that can afford luxury goods. Thus, companies marketing products such as expensive jewellery, high-priced cars, and even yachts could find wealthy market segments within relatively poor nations.

Work Attitudes and Cultural Literacy

National differences in work attitudes are complex and involve other factors in addition to culture. Perceived opportunity for financial reward is no doubt a strong element in attitudes toward work in any culture. Research suggests both North American and German employees work longer hours when there is a greater likelihood that good performance will lead to promotion and increased pay. Yet this appears relatively less true in Germany, where wages are less variable and job security and jobless benefits (such as free national health care) are greater. Thus, other aspects of German society are at least as important as culture in determining work attitudes. The culturally literate manager understands the complexity of national workplace attitudes and would incorporate this knowledge into reward systems.

Expatriates and Cultural Literacy

As stated in our discussion of classifying cultures, people living in broadly different cultures tend to respond differently in similar business situations. This is why companies that send personnel abroad to unfamiliar cultures are concerned with cultural differences. A Norwegian manager working in Japan for a European car manufacturer, but whose colleagues were mostly Japanese, soon became frustrated with the time needed to make decisions and take action. The main cause for his frustration was that the uncertainty avoidance index for Japan is much larger than that in his native Norway (see Figure 2.3). In Japan, a greater aversion to uncertainty led to the need for a greater number of consultations than would be needed in the home market. The frustrated manager eventually left Japan to return to Europe.

Gender and Cultural Literacy

In Japan, men traditionally hold nearly all positions of responsibility. Women generally serve as office clerks and administrative assistants until their mid- to late 20s, when they are expected to marry and then focus on tending to family needs. Although this is still largely true today, progress is being made in expanding the role of women in Japan's business community. Women own nearly a quarter of all businesses in Japan, but many of these businesses are very small and have little economic clout. Greater gender equality prevails in Australia, Canada, Germany, and the United States, but women in these countries still tend to earn less money than men in similar positions.

Chapter Summary

1. **Describe culture and explain the significance of both national culture and subcultures.**
   - *Culture* is the set of values, beliefs, rules, and institutions held by a specific group of people.
   - Managers should try to avoid *ethnocentricity* (the tendency to view one's own culture as superior to others) and develop *cultural literacy* (detailed knowledge necessary to function effectively in another culture).
   - We are conditioned to think in terms of national culture—that is, to equate a nation-state and its people with a single culture.
   - Governments promote national culture and intervene in business to protect it from the influence of other cultures.
   - Most nations are also home to numerous *subcultures*—groups of people who share a unique way of life within a larger, dominant culture.
   - Subcultures contribute greatly to national culture and must be considered in marketing and production decisions.

2. **Identify the components of culture and describe their impact on international business.**
   - *Aesthetics* help determine which colours and symbols will be effective in promotions and advertising.
   - *Values* influence a people's *attitudes* toward time, work and achievement, and cultural change.
   - Knowledge of *manners* and *customs* is necessary for negotiating, marketing products, and managing operations in other cultures.
   - *Social structure* affects business decisions including production-site selection, advertising methods, and the costs of doing business in a country.
   - Different *religions* take different views of work, savings, and material goods.
   - Understanding a people's system of *personal communication* provides insight into their values and behaviour.
   - A culture's *education* level affects the quality of the workforce and a people's standard of living.
   - *Physical* and *material environments* influence work habits and preferences for products such as clothing and food.

3. **Describe cultural change and explain how companies and culture affect each other.**
   - *Cultural change* occurs when people integrate into their culture the gestures, material objects, traditions, or concepts of another culture through *cultural diffusion*.
   - Globalization and technology are increasing the pace of cultural change around the world.
   - Companies influence culture when they import new products, policies, and business practices into a host country.
   - Companies should try to avoid *cultural imperialism*—the replacement of one culture's traditions, folk heroes, and artifacts with substitutes from another.
   - Cultures affect management styles, work scheduling, and reward systems.
   - Adapting to local cultures around the world means heeding the maxim "Think globally, act locally."

4. **Explain how the physical environment and technology influence culture.**
   - A people's *physical environment* includes *topography* and climate and how people relate to their surroundings.
   - Cultures isolated by topographical barriers, such as mountains or seas, normally change relatively slowly, and their languages are often distinct.
   - Climate affects a people's work hours, clothing, and food.
   - *Material culture* refers to all the technology a culture uses to manufacture goods and provide services, and it can be uneven within a nation.
   - Businesspeople measure material culture to determine whether a market has developed adequate demand for a company's products and whether it can support production activities.

5. Describe the two main frameworks used to classify cultures and explain their practical use.
   - The *Kluckhohn–Strodtbeck framework* compares cultures along six dimensions by seeking answers to questions on topics including a people's (1) relation to the environment; (2) focus on past, present, or future; (3) trustworthiness; (4) desire for accomplishment; (5) group–individual responsibility; and (6) public versus private nature.
   - The *Hofstede framework* compares cultures along five dimensions including a people's (1) individualism versus collectivism; (2) power distance; (3) uncertainty avoidance; (4) achievement vs. nurturing; and (5) long-term orientation.
   - Taken together, these frameworks help companies understand many aspects of a culture, including risk taking, innovation, job mobility, team cooperation, pay levels, and hiring practices.

6. Explain the three different types of staffing policies used by international companies.
   - *Ethnocentric staffing* means staffing operations outside the home country with home-country nationals; it can give a company tight control over subsidiary decision making.
   - *Polycentric staffing* means staffing operations with host-country natives; it can give subsidiaries some autonomy in decision making.
   - *Geocentric staffing* means staffing operations with the best-qualified individuals, regardless of nationality; it is typically reserved for top-level managers.

7. Describe the recruitment and selection issues facing international companies.
   - Large companies often recruit international managers from within the ranks of existing employees, but smaller companies may need to hire outside managers.
   - International students who have graduated from colleges abroad can be hired, trained locally, and posted in their home countries.
   - Local managerial talent may be recruited in the host country to obtain people with an understanding of the local culture and political system; this is often required when a company engages extensively in manufacturing or marketing abroad.

8. Explain how companies compensate managers and workers in international markets.
   - An effective compensation policy takes into account local cultures, laws, and practices; key issues are base pay, bonuses, and fringe benefits.
   - Managerial compensation packages may need adjustment to reflect the local cost of living and, perhaps, the cost of education.
   - *Bonus payments* or hardship pay may be needed to entice managers to accept international assignments.

Key Terms

aesthetics 49	ethnocentric staffing 73	popular custom 54
attitudes 51	ethnocentricity 46	recruitment 76
body language 65	expatriates 73	reverse culture shock 77
brain drain 67	folk custom 54	selection 76
caste system 56	geocentric staffing 74	social group 55
class system 57	Hofstede framework 70	social mobility 56
communication 62	human resource management	social stratification 56
cultural diffusion 52	(HRM) 73	social structure 55
cultural imperialism 52	human resource planning 75	staffing policy 73
cultural literacy 47	Kluckhohn–Strodtbeck framework 69	subculture 48
cultural trait 52	lingua franca 64	topography 67
culture 46	manners 54	values 50
culture shock 77	material culture 68	
customs 54	polycentric staffing 74	

Talk It Over

1. Two students are discussing the various reasons why they are not studying international business. "International business doesn't affect me," declares the first student. "I'm going to stay here, not work in some foreign country." "Yeah, me neither," agrees the second. "Besides, some cultures are real strange. The sooner other countries start doing business our way, the better." What counterarguments can you present to these students' perceptions?

2. In this exercise, two groups of four students each will debate the benefits and drawbacks of individualist versus collectivist cultures. After the first student from each side speaks, the second student questions the opponent's arguments, looking for holes and inconsistencies. A third student attempts to reply to these counterarguments. Then, a fourth student summarizes each side's arguments. Finally, the class votes on which team presented the more compelling case.

3. Many Japanese companies use ethnocentric staffing policies in international operations. Why do you think Japanese companies prefer to have Japanese in top management positions? Would you recommend a change in this policy?

Take It to the Web

1. **Video Report.** Visit YouTube (www.youtube.com) and type "cross-cultural business" into the search engine. Watch one of the videos from the results of your search and then summarize it in a half-page report. Reflecting on the contents of this chapter, which components of culture can you identify in the video? How might a company engaged in international business use the information contained in the video?

2. **Web Site Report.** Culture affects the product a company sells in a market or region, how it markets the product, its human resource practices, and so on. It is increasingly important that managers have cultural understanding of their markets in this age of globalization.

   Select a well-known multinational company and visit its Web site. Locate the section of the Web site that tells about the company's activities (usually titled "About Us"). Report on the (1) main products or services the company offers; (2) extent to which the company pursues international business operations (often expressed as percentage of sales or assets); (3) ways that the company has adapted to cultures around the world; and (4) general policies it follows in doing business internationally.

   Regarding its Internet presence, does the company offer its Web site in another widely spoken language? Find and click on several of the company's other national Web sites. What kinds of products are advertised on the home page of the different sites? Can you identify how the company adapts its Web site to suit cultural preferences?

Culture Makes or Breaks the Deal

The Middle East has not traditionally been a hotbed for manufacturing. The economic strength of the region over the past 50 years has come from other areas such as resource extraction, agriculture, and trade. Manufacturing has been left to those parts of the world with fewer resources to exploit and more human resources to draw from. Thus OMNI Oil Technologies' plan to design and manufacture tools for the oil and gas industry in the Middle East was a unique and challenging vision.

OMNI Oil Technologies was established in 2004 in Dubai, United Arab Emirates, the gateway to the Middle East. This global city has earned a tremendous reputation by creating a thriving centre of commerce, trade, and entertainment. Many international visitors have experienced the architectural wonders of Dubai, from the sail-shaped Burj al-Arab hotel to the spectacular 163-storey Burj Khalifa, the tallest building in the world.

For OMNI, a company created by Arabian engineers from Schlumberger (a leading supplier to the oil and gas industry), Dubai was a comfortable fit culturally. But the decision to set up an advanced manufacturing centre in Dubai was a considerable business risk. It had never been done in the region before, and there was no supply-chain base to justify a manufacturing company. However, OMNI became the first cutting-edge oil and gas technology and manufacturing centre in the Middle East.

In 2008, OMNI came to Canada with the goal of penetrating the burgeoning oil and gas industry. Why? Besides envisioning a market for their products, OMNI's CEO and CFO both had children attending school in Canada; they had developed relationships with friends in Canada; and they had experienced a culture of openness and innovation. OMNI set up a partnership with a manufacturing company in the Toronto area that had similar Arab cultural roots and a sales office in Calgary, with an Egyptian manager who had moved to Canada to represent OMNI in the market.

After a year of trying to sell their product on the Canadian market, OMNI realized they were out of sync with the culture and style of doing business in Western Canada. For example, OMNI's

Middle Eastern style was to start later in the day, to conduct most of their business over meals rather than in an office setting, and to adopt a relaxed attitude about following the terms of a contract.

To improve their business prospects in Canada and to penetrate the Canadian market, OMNI hired Rainmaker Global Business Development (www.rainmaker-gbd.com), a Canadian firm specializing in global business development. Rainmaker provided an effective evaluation of the marketplace for OMNI and worked with them to clinch their first sales in Western Canada. As a result, OMNI began working with an established tool manufacturer in Airdrie, Alberta.

Rainmaker's understanding of and connection to the local subculture opened up the field for OMNI, and they have since had success in the Canadian market. OMNI has now been acquired by a New York–based private equity group and has merged with four other oilfield service companies to form a global oilfield products company called Tercel. Tercel sells globally diversified oilfield products in 14 countries, servicing all major oil regions in the world.

Thinking Globally

1. What could OMNI have done differently when setting up in Canada to accelerate their market entry?
2. What are some of the cultural challenges OMNI faced when entering the Canadian market?
3. What cross-cultural factors may have influenced OMNI's market entry into Canada?
4. If you were to do a Hofstede analysis, what would you define as the main cultural differences between the United Arab Emirates and Canada?

Sources: This case was developed from information provided by Mr. Clark Grue, president and CEO of Rainmaker Global Business Development, and is based on his personal experience and knowledge of OMNI Oil Technologies, January 2013; Oil & Gas Middle East staff, "Omni Oil Technologies Supplies Drilling Tools," arabianbusiness.com, November 14, 2005.

CHAPTER THREE

Politics and Law

Learning Objectives

After studying this chapter, you should be able to

1. Describe each main type of political system.

2. Identify the origins of political risk and how managers can reduce its effects.

3. Describe each main type of legal system and the important global legal issues.

4. Explain how international relations affect international business activities.

A LOOK BACK

Chapter 2 explored the main elements of culture and showed how they affect business practices. We learned about different methods used to classify cultures and how these methods can be applied to business.

A LOOK AT THIS CHAPTER

This chapter explores the roles of politics and law in international business. We begin by explaining different types of political systems and how managers cope with political risk. We then examine several kinds of legal systems and how international relations affect business.

A LOOK AHEAD

Chapter 4 discusses ethics, ethical behaviour, and ethical dilemmas that may arise when conducting business globally. We also examine corporate social responsibility and sustainable practices in international business.

Source: ShutterStock.

PepsiCo's Global Challenge

PURCHASE, New York—Entrepreneurial despite its enormity, PepsiCo's (www.pepsico.com) sales grew an amazing 13 percent annually for nearly half a century. To keep sales bubbling, PepsiCo is targeting international sales, which comprise 40 percent of total revenue, and investing aggressively in India, which ranks among its top 10 markets and its three fastest-growing countries. PepsiCo needed the approval of India's government to increase its investment there by nearly a third in an effort to triple its revenue in the country by 2015.

Source: NATALIA KOLESNIKOVA/AFP/Getty Images/Newscom.

Like all companies operating internationally, PepsiCo must carefully navigate unfamiliar political and legal systems. If PepsiCo's bottling operations in India were to drain the water table to unacceptable levels, it would face the wrath of India's regulators and its people. And British regulators, for example, would pull PepsiCo's Baked Lays brand of chips off store shelves if it failed to live up to its health claims. PepsiCo knows that today companies are expected to be model citizens wherever they operate.

PepsiCo's CEO Indra Nooyi (pictured here) says the company has no choice but to move its product line in healthier directions. She introduced the motto "Performance with Purpose" to reflect how the company is transforming its global businesses. She wants the company to balance its drive for profits with making healthier snacks, decreasing its impact on the environment, and taking care of its workforce. Born and raised in India, Nooyi believes it is essential that "we use corporations as a productive player in addressing some of the big issues facing the world."

Nooyi also helped spark "green" initiatives at PepsiCo. She proved that investments in water- and heat-related conservation projects can be worthy endeavours. In addition to their environmental benefits, those projects now save the company $55 million annually. Nooyi says, "Companies today are bigger than many economies. We are little republics. We are engines of efficiency. If companies don't do [responsible] things, who is going to?" As you read this chapter, consider how companies adapt to different political and legal systems worldwide.[1]

Chapter 2 explained that an understanding of culture contributes to success in the international marketplace. Another crucial element of success is political and legal savvy. Businesses involved internationally need to overcome some tricky political and legal situations in other countries. This is true for both brick-and-mortar and online companies. Although the Web shrinks the distance between two points, it still matters where those two points are located. The Internet community consists of about 250 country domains and dozens of political and legal environments.

Just as brick-and-mortar companies have always adapted to local politics and laws in the global marketplace, so too do Internet companies. Yahoo! (www.yahoo.com) held back certain news stories from its Web site in China, though the stories appeared on the company's US site. Rupert Murdoch's News Corp. (www.newscorp.com) removed BBC news (www.bbc.co.uk) from its Asian television broadcasts because it occasionally criticized China. Barnes & Noble (www.bn.com) and Amazon (www.amazon.com) stopped selling the English-language version of *Mein Kampf* to Germans when the German government complained—although it's illegal only to sell the German-language version. A statement by Barnes & Noble read, "Our policy with regard to censorship remains unchanged. But as responsible corporate citizens, we respect the laws of the countries where we do business." And a broad spectrum of German politicians and citizens decried Google's (www.google.com) plan to introduce its mapping service called Street View there in 2010. Memories of secret police prying into personal lives under past dictatorial and fascist regimes make Germans fearful of allowing the entire world to see photos of their homes and gardens on the Internet.[2]

Understanding the nature of politics and laws in other countries lessens the risks of conducting international business. In this chapter, we present the basic differences between political and legal systems around the world. We explain how disputes arising from political and legal matters affect business activities and how companies can manage the associated risks. We close this chapter by briefly discussing the interaction between business and international relations.

Political Systems

political system

Structures, processes, and activities by which a nation governs itself.

A **political system** includes the structures, processes, and activities by which a nation governs itself. Japan's political system, for instance, features a *Diet* (Parliament) that chooses a prime minister who will carry out the operations of government with the help of cabinet ministers. The *Diet* consists of two houses of elected representatives who enact the nation's laws. These laws affect the personal lives of people living in and visiting Japan, as well as the activities of companies doing business there.

Politics and Culture

Politics and *culture* are closely related. A country's political system is rooted in the history and culture of its people. Factors such as population, age and race composition, and per capita income influence a country's political system.

Consider the case of Switzerland, where the political system actively encourages all eligible members of society to vote. By means of *public referendums*, Swiss citizens vote directly on many national issues. The Swiss system works because Switzerland consists of a relatively small population living in a small geographic area. Contrast this practice with that of most other democracies, in which representatives of the people, not the people themselves, vote on specific issues.

Political Participation

We can characterize political systems by *who* participates in them and *to what extent* they participate. *Participation* occurs when people voice their opinions, vote, and show general approval or disapproval of the system.

Participation can be wide or narrow. Wide participation occurs when people who are capable of influencing the political system make an effort to do so. For example, most adults living in Canada have the right to participate in the political process by voting in elections. Narrow participation occurs when few people participate. In Kuwait, for example, only citizens who can prove Kuwaiti ancestry participate in the political process.

Tellers count ballot papers at a voting station in Conakry, Guinea, in June of 2010. Guineans voted in the West African nation's first democratic election since independence in 1958, hoping to end half a century of military and civilian dictatorships. Early reports from individual voting stations indicated a massive turnout in the crucial election. How do you think wide participation can benefit a country and its people?

Source: SEYLLOU/AFP/Getty Images/ Newscom.

Political Ideologies

We can arrange the world's three political ideologies on a horizontal scale, with two on either end and one in the middle:

- At one extreme lies *totalitarianism*—the belief that every aspect of people's lives must be controlled for a nation's political system to be effective. Totalitarianism disregards individual liberties and treats people as slaves of the political system. The state reigns supreme over institutions such as family, religion, business, and labour. Totalitarian political systems include authoritarian regimes such as communism and fascism.
- At the other extreme lies *anarchism*—the belief that only individuals and private groups should control a nation's political activities. An anarchist views public government as unnecessary and unwanted because it tramples personal liberties.
- Between totalitarianism and anarchism lies *pluralism*—the belief that both private and public groups play important roles in a nation's political activities. Each group (consisting of people with different ethnic, racial, class, and lifestyle backgrounds) serves to balance the power that can be gained by the other. Pluralistic political systems include democracies, constitutional monarchies, and some aristocracies.

To better understand how elements of politics influence national business practices let's now examine two prevalent political systems—*totalitarianism* and *democracy*.

TOTALITARIANISM In a **totalitarian system**, individuals govern without the support of the people, tightly control people's lives, and do not tolerate opposing viewpoints. Nazi Germany under Adolf Hitler and the former Soviet Union under Joseph Stalin are historical examples of totalitarian governments. Today, North Korea is a prominent example of a totalitarian government. Totalitarian leaders attempt to silence those with opposing political views and, therefore, require the near-total centralization of political power. But a "pure" form of totalitarianism is not possible because no totalitarian government is capable of entirely silencing all its critics.

Totalitarian governments tend to share three features:

- ***Imposed Authority***. An individual or group forms the political system without the explicit or implicit approval of the people. Leaders often acquire and retain power through military force or fraudulent elections. In some cases, they come to power through legitimate means but then remain in office after their terms expire.

totalitarian system
Political system in which individuals govern without the support of the people, tightly control people's lives, and do not tolerate opposing viewpoints.

- *Lack of Constitutional Guarantees*. Totalitarian systems deny citizens the constitutional guarantees woven into the fabric of democratic practice. They limit, abuse, or reject concepts such as freedom of expression, periodically held elections, guaranteed civil and property rights, and minority rights.
- *Restricted Participation*. Political representation is limited to parties sympathetic to the government or to those who pose no credible threat. In most cases, political opposition is completely banned, and political dissidents are severely punished.

Let's now take a detailed look at the two most common types of totalitarian political systems: *theocratic* and *secular*.

theocracy

Political system in which a country's religious leaders are also its political leaders.

theocratic totalitarianism

Political system under the control of totalitarian religious leaders.

Theocratic Totalitarianism A political system in which a country's religious leaders are also its political leaders is called a **theocracy**. The religious leaders enforce a set of laws and regulations based on religious beliefs. A political system under the control of totalitarian religious leaders is called **theocratic totalitarianism**.

Iran is a prominent example of a theocratic totalitarian state. Iran has been an Islamic state since the 1979 revolution in which the reigning monarch was overthrown. Today, many young Iranians appear disenchanted with the strict code imposed on many aspects of their public and private lives, including stringent laws against products and ideas deemed too "Western." They do not question their religious beliefs but yearn for a more open society.

secular totalitarianism

Political system in which leaders rely on military and bureaucratic power.

Secular Totalitarianism A political system in which political leaders rely on military and bureaucratic power is called **secular totalitarianism**. It takes three forms: *communist*, *tribal*, and *right-wing*.

Under *communist totalitarianism* (here referred to simply as *communism*), the government maintains sweeping political and economic powers. The Communist Party controls all aspects of the political system, and opposition parties are given little or no voice. In general, each party member holding office is required to support all government policies, and dissension is rarely permitted. **Communism** is the belief that social and economic equality can only be obtained by establishing an all-powerful Communist Party and by instituting **socialism**—an economic system in which the government owns and controls all types of economic activity. This includes granting the government ownership of the means of production (such as capital, land, and factories) and the power to decide what the economy produces and the prices at which goods are sold.

communism

Belief that social and economic equality can be obtained only by establishing an all-powerful Communist Party and by granting the government ownership and control over all types of economic activity.

socialism

An economic system in which the government owns and controls all types of economic activity.

However, important distinctions separate communism from socialism. Socialism generally refers to an economic system, while communism usually refers to both an economic and a political system. Communists follow the teachings of Marx and Lenin, believe that a violent revolution is needed to seize control over resources, and wish to eliminate political opposition. Socialists believe in none of these. Thus, communists are socialists, but socialists are not necessarily communist.

Under *tribal totalitarianism*, one tribe (or ethnic group) imposes its will on others with whom it shares a national identity. Tribal totalitarianism characterizes the governments of several African nations, including Burundi and Rwanda. When the European colonial powers departed Africa, many national boundaries were created with little regard to ethnic differences among the people. People of different ethnicities found themselves living in the same nation, whereas members of the same ethnicity found themselves living in different nations. In time, certain ethnic groups gained political and military power over other groups. Animosity among them often erupted in bloody conflict.

Although tribalism plays a role in many of Africa's civil conflicts, it is not always the most significant factor. To explore the economic and social costs of civil wars (particularly in Africa) and how developed nations can help put an end to them, see the Global Challenges feature, titled "From Civil War to Civil Society ."

Under *right-wing totalitarianism*, the government endorses private ownership of property and a market-based economy but grants few (if any) political freedoms. Leaders generally strive for economic growth while opposing *left-wing totalitarianism* (communism). Argentina, Brazil, Chile, and Paraguay all had right-wing totalitarian governments in the 1980s.

Despite the inherent contradictions between communism and right-wing totalitarianism, China's political system is currently a mix of the two ideologies. China's leaders are engineering high economic growth by implementing certain characteristics of a capitalist economy while retaining a hard line in the political sphere. The Chinese government is selling off money-losing,

Global Challenges   From Civil War to Civil Society

Today, most wars occur *within* nations that were once controlled and stabilized by colonial powers. If these nations are to prosper from globalization, they must break the vicious cycle whereby conflict causes poverty and poverty causes conflict.

- **War's Root Causes.** Although tribal or ethnic rivalry is typically blamed for starting civil wars, the most common causes are poverty, low economic growth, and dependency on natural resource exports. In fact, the poorest one-sixth of humanity endures four-fifths of the world's civil wars. Still, religious differences increasingly underlie civil conflicts.

- **What's at Stake?** It appears that pitched battles in Bunia, a city in eastern Congo, are rooted in ethnic conflict. Yet the Hema and the Lendu tribes only began annihilating each other when neighbouring Uganda (to control mineral-rich Bunia) started arming rival militias in 1999. In the Darfur region of Sudan, Arab Muslims battle black non-Muslims. Depending on whom you ask, the conflict began as a fight over pastures and livestock or the oil beneath them. Meanwhile, foreign investors remain wary.

- **What Is Lost?** On average, a civil conflict lasts eight years. And apart from the terrible human cost in lives and health, there is also a financial cost. Health costs are $5 billion per conflict because of collapsed health systems and forced migrations (which worsen and spread disease). Gross domestic product (GDP) falls by 2.2 percent, and another 18 percent of income is spent on arms and militias. Full economic recovery takes a decade, which reduces output by about 105 percent of the nation's pre-war GDP.

- **The Challenge.** Recent research offers several solutions to this global challenge. Because the risk of civil war is cut in half when income per person doubles, conflicts may be *prevented* by funnelling more aid to poor nations. Also, war might be *limited* by restricting a nation in conflict from spending the proceeds from its exports on munitions or by lowering the world market price of those exports. Finally, to *halt* nations from slipping back into civil war, health and education aid could be increased after war ends or a foreign power could intervene to keep the peace.

- **Want to Know More?** Visit the Centre for the Study of African Economies at Oxford University (www.csae.ox.ac.uk), the Copenhagen Consensus Center (www.copenhagenconsensus.com), and the World Bank Conflict Prevention and Post-conflict Reconstruction Unit (www.worldbank.org).

Sources: "Unloved for Trying to Keep the Peace," *The Economist*, April 17, 2010, pp. 51–52; "More than Sectarian Strife," *The Economist* (www.economist.com), April 13, 2010; "Putting the World to Rights," *The Economist* (www.economist.com), June 3, 2004; Paul Collier and Anke Hoeffler, *The Challenge of Reducing the Global Incidence of Civil War* (Oxford: Copenhagen Consensus, March 2004); Copenhagen Consensus Center (www.copenhagenconsensus.com).

state-run companies and encouraging investment needed to modernize its factories. But China's government still has little patience for dissidents who demand greater political freedom, and it does not allow a completely free press.

Doing Business in Totalitarian Countries   What are the costs and benefits of doing business in a totalitarian nation? On the plus side, international companies can be relatively less concerned with local political opposition to their activities. On the negative side, they might need to pay bribes and kickbacks to government officials. Refusal to pay could result in loss of market access or even forfeiture of investments in the country.

In any case, doing business in a totalitarian country can be a risky proposition. In a country such as Canada, laws regarding the resolution of contractual disputes are quite specific. In totalitarian nations, the law can be either vague or nonexistent, and people in powerful government positions can interpret laws largely as they please. In China, for instance, it may not matter so much what the law states but rather how individual bureaucrats interpret the law. The arbitrary nature of totalitarian governments makes it hard for companies to know how laws will be interpreted and applied to their particular business dealings. In Venezuela, some North American businesses, particularly in the oil and gas industry, have been victims of the political system in the last few years. To learn more about Venezuela's political system, see the Political Systems in Times of Change section later in this chapter.

Companies that operate in totalitarian nations are sometimes criticized for lacking compassion for people hurt by the oppressive policies of their hosts. Executives must decide whether to refrain from investing in totalitarian countries—and miss potentially profitable opportunities—or invest and bear the brunt of potentially damaging publicity. There are no simple answers to this controversial issue, which amounts to an ethical dilemma.

Quick Study

1. What is a *political system*? Explain the relation between political systems and culture.
2. Identify the three main features of *totalitarianism*.
3. Briefly explain each form of totalitarianism.
4. How might a totalitarian government affect business activities?

---

democracy

Political system in which government leaders are elected directly by the wide participation of the people or by their representatives.

DEMOCRACY   A **democracy** is a political system in which government leaders are elected directly by the wide participation of the people or by their representatives. Democracy differs from totalitarianism in nearly every respect. The foundations of modern democracy go back at least as far as the ancient Greeks.

The Greeks tried to practise a *pure* democracy, one in which all citizens participate freely and actively in the political process. But a pure democracy is more an ideal than a workable system for several reasons. Some people have neither the time nor the desire to get involved in the political process. Also, citizens are less able to participate completely and actively as a population grows and as the barriers of distance and time increase. Finally, leaders in a pure democracy may find it difficult or impossible to form cohesive policies because direct voting can lead to conflicting popular opinion.

representative democracy

Democracy in which citizens elect individuals from their groups to represent their political views.

Representative Democracy   For practical reasons, most nations resort to a **representative democracy**, in which citizens elect individuals from their groups to represent their political views. These representatives then help govern the people and pass laws. The people re-elect representatives they approve of and replace those they no longer want representing them.

Representative democracies strive to provide some or all of the following:

- *Freedom of Expression*. A constitutional right in most democracies, freedom of expression ideally grants the right to voice opinions freely and without fear of punishment.
- *Periodic Elections*. Each elected representative serves for a period of time, after which the people (or electorate) decide whether to retain that representative. Three examples of periodic elections include the Canadian federal election to the House of Commons, the French presidential elections (held every five years), and the Mexican presidential elections (held every six years).
- *Full Civil and Property Rights*. Civil rights include freedom of speech, freedom to organize political parties, and the right to a fair trial. Property rights are the privileges and responsibilities of owners of property (homes, cars, businesses, and so forth).
- *Minority Rights*. In theory, democracies try to preserve peaceful coexistence among groups of people with diverse cultural, ethnic, and racial backgrounds. Ideally, the same rights and privileges extend legally to each group, no matter how few its members.
- *Nonpolitical Bureaucracies*. The bureaucracy is the part of government that implements the rules and laws passed by elected representatives. In *politicized bureaucracies*, bureaucrats tend to implement decisions according to their own political views rather than those of the people's representatives. This clearly contradicts the purpose of the democratic process.

Despite such shared principles, countries vary greatly in the practice of representative democracy. Britain, for example, practises *parliamentary democracy*. The nation divides itself into geographical districts, and people in each district vote for competing *parties* rather than individual candidates. But the party that wins the greatest number of legislative seats in an election does not automatically win the right to run the country. Rather, a party must gain an *absolute majority*—that is, the number of representatives that a party gets elected must exceed the number of representatives elected among all other parties.

Freedom of expression is a fundamental right that most democracies strive to uphold. On the International Day of Press Freedom, a woman in Tegucigalpa, Honduras, wears tape on her mouth to show support for the right of freedom of expression. To limit and tightly control the news that ordinary people receive, some countries block or scramble the reception of foreign broadcasts from all sorts of media. In what ways do you think freedom of expression can benefit a society?

Source: DANIEL MENDOZA/ picture-alliance/dpa/Newscom.

If the party with the largest number of representatives lacks an absolute majority, it can join with one or more other parties to form a *coalition government*. In a coalition government, the strongest political parties share power by dividing government responsibilities among themselves. Coalition governments are often formed in Italy, Israel, and the Netherlands, where a large number of political parties make it difficult for any single party to gain an absolute majority.

Nations also differ in the relative power that each political party commands. In some democratic countries, a single political party has effectively controlled the system for decades. In Japan, for example, the Liberal Democratic Party (which is actually conservative) enjoyed nearly uninterrupted control of the government since the 1950s. In Mexico, the Institutional Revolutionary Party (PRI) ran the country for 70 years until 2000, when Vicente Fox from the conservative National Action Party (PAN) won the presidency. Felipe Calderon, also from PAN, assumed office on December 1, 2006.

Doing Business in Democracies   Democracies maintain stable business environments primarily through laws that protect individual property rights. In theory, commerce prospers when the **private sector** includes independently owned firms that seek to earn profits. Capitalism is the belief that ownership of the means of production belongs in the hands of individuals and private businesses. **Capitalism** is also frequently referred to as the *free market*. (We cover the economics of communism and capitalism in Chapter 5.)

private sector
Segment of the economic environment comprising independently owned firms that seek to earn profits.

capitalism
Belief that ownership of the means of production belongs in the hands of individuals and private businesses.

Bear in mind that although participative democracy, property rights, and free markets tend to encourage economic growth, they do not always do so. For instance, although India is the world's largest democracy, it experienced slow economic growth for decades until recently. Meanwhile, some countries achieved rapid economic growth under political systems that were not truly democratic. The four tigers of Asia—Hong Kong, Singapore, South Korea, and Taiwan—built strong market economies in the absence of truly democratic practices.

Political Systems in Times of Change

People around the world are demanding wider participation in the political process and forcing a move toward more democratic systems. Capitalism also seems to have won the battle over communist totalitarianism and economic socialism. Shortly after the former Soviet Union implemented its twin policies of *glasnost* (political openness) and *perestroika* (economic reform), its totalitarian government crumbled. Communist governments in Central and Eastern Europe fell soon after, and today countries such as the Czech Republic, Hungary, Poland, Romania, and

Ukraine have republican governments. There are far fewer communist nations than there were two decades ago, although North Korea remains hard-line communist today.

Venezuela is a current example of a political system undergoing change that affects both domestic and foreign businesses. Venezuela became a democracy in 1999 with the democratic election of Hugo Chavez and enacted a new constitution on December 20, 1999. Although some people view Venezuela as a communist country, in reality it is neither democratic nor communist. Venezuela holds periodic elections—the last federal election was held in April 2013—one of the characteristics of a democracy. Venezuelans also have the freedom to organize political parties. For example, there were eight candidates from different parties in the 2012 federal elections. Private ownership is permitted in some industries in Venezuela. Yet, according to a report from Human Rights Watch, the government under Hugo Chavez systematically restricted the right to free expression, curtailed workers' freedom of association, and undercut the ability to protect human rights. This trend is seen in the 2010 laws adopted by the Venezuelan legislature that gave the government more power to restrict civil rights. The current Venezuelan judicial system also fails to protect the fundamental rights established in the democratic Venezuelan constitution. However, with the death of Hugo Chavez in March 2013, the Venezuelan political system is once more in a state of flux and may undergo further changes in the near future, depending on the decisions of its newly elected president.[3]

Other than Venezuela, one of the most closely watched nations in terms of its political change is China. After 1949, when the communists defeated the nationalists in China's civil war, China imprisoned or exiled most of its capitalists. But private businesspeople are now allowed to join China's Communist Party, and workers can now elect local representatives to the official trade union. These moves represent the leadership's struggle to maintain order in the face of increasingly rapid economic and social change. Part of the reason for this move was explained in a government report that spoke of problems facing the nation. Difficulties reported include the collapse of state-owned industry, a social safety net unable to cope with millions of unemployed, poor relations with the nation's ethnic minorities, an unjust legal system, and an increasingly restless rural population.

Quick Study

1. What is *democracy*? Explain the differences between *democracy* and *totalitarianism*.
2. What five freedoms does a representative democracy strive to provide its people?
3. How might a democratic government affect business activities in a nation?
4. Does Venezuela have a democratic or totalitarian political system?

Political Risk

political risk
Likelihood that a society will undergo political changes that negatively affect local business activity.

All companies doing business domestically or internationally confront **political risk**—the likelihood that a society will undergo political changes that negatively affect local business activity. Political risk abroad affects different types of companies in different ways. It can threaten the market of an exporter, the production facilities of a manufacturer, or the ability of a company to extract profits from a country in which they were earned. A solid grasp of local values, customs, and traditions can help reduce a company's exposure to political risk.

Map 3.1 shows that political risk levels vary from nation to nation. Some of the factors included in this assessment of political risk levels include government stability, internal and external conflict, military and religion in politics, corruption, law and order, and bureaucracy quality.

Types of Political Risk

The broadest categories of political risk reflect the range of companies affected. *Macro risk* threatens the activities of all domestic and international companies in every industry. Examples include an ongoing threat of violence against corporate assets in a nation and a rising level of government corruption. *Micro risk* threatens companies only within a particular industry (or more narrowly defined group). For example, an international trade war in steel affects the operations of steel producers and companies that require steel as an input to their business activities.

In addition to these two broad categories, we can classify political risk according to the actions or events that cause it to arise, including:

- Conflict and violence
- Terrorism and kidnapping
- Property seizure
- Policy changes
- Local content requirements

CONFLICT AND VIOLENCE Local conflict can strongly discourage international companies from investing in a nation. Violent disturbances impair a company's ability to manufacture and distribute products, obtain materials and equipment, and recruit talented personnel. Open conflict also threatens a company's physical assets (such as offices and factories) and the lives of its employees.

Conflict arises from several sources. First, it may arise from people's resentment toward their own government. When peaceful resolution of disputes between people (or factions) and the government fails, violent attempts to change political leadership can ensue. ExxonMobil (www.exxonmobil.com) suspended production of liquid natural gas at its facility in Indonesia's Aceh province when separatist rebels targeted the complex with their violence.

Second, conflict can arise over territorial disputes between countries. For example, a dispute over the Kashmir territory between India and Pakistan resulted in major armed conflict between their two peoples several times. And a border dispute between Ecuador and Peru caused these South American nations to go to war three times—most recently in 1995.

Third, disputes among ethnic, racial, and religious groups may erupt in violent conflict. Indonesia comprises 13 000 islands, more than 300 ethnic groups, and some 450 languages. Years ago, Indonesia's government relocated people from crowded, central islands to less popu-lated remote ones, but without regard to ethnicity and religion. Violence among them later dis-placed more than 1 million people. Companies doing business in Indonesia today still face the possibility of ethnic and religious violence disrupting business operations.

TERRORISM AND KIDNAPPING Terrorist activities are means of making political statements. Groups dissatisfied with the current political or social situation sometimes resort to terrorist tactics to force change through fear and destruction. On September 11, 2001, the world witnessed terrorism on a scale like never before. Two passenger planes were flown into the twin towers of the World Trade Center in New York City, one plane was crashed into the Pentagon in Washington, DC, and one plane crashed in a Pennsylvania field. The terrorist group Al-Qaida claimed responsibility for those US attacks and more recent attacks around the world. The terror organization's stated goals are to drive Western influence out of Muslim nations and to implement Islamic law.

Kidnapping and the taking of hostages for ransom may be used to fund a terrorist group's activities. Executives of large international companies are often prime targets for kidnappers because their employers have "deep pockets" to pay large ransoms. Latin American countries have some of the world's highest kidnapping rates, and Mexico City is at or near the top of the list of cities with the highest kidnapping rates. Annual security costs for a company with a sales office in Bogotá, Colombia, can be $125 000 and up to $1 million for a company with operations in rebel-controlled areas. Top executives are forced to spend about a third of their time coordinat-ing their company's security in Colombia. A medium-sized firm that has 5 to 10 employees travelling to Latin America for a week at a time could carry $10 million in kidnap and ransom insurance for around $5000 a year.[4]

When high-ranking executives are required to enter countries with high kidnapping rates, they should enter unannounced, meet with only a few key people in secure locations, and leave just as quickly and quietly. Some companies purchase kidnap, ransom, and extortion insurance, but security experts say that training people to avoid trouble in the first place is a far better invest-ment. For additional ways managers can stay safe during overseas assignments, see the Global Manager's Briefcase, titled "Your Global Security Checklist."

Global Manager's Briefcase   Your Global Security Checklist

- **Getting There.** Take nonstop flights when possible as accidents are more likely during takeoffs and landings. Move quickly from an airport's public and check-in areas to more secure areas beyond passport control. Report abandoned packages to airport security.
- **Getting Around.** Kidnappers watch for daily routines. Vary the exit you use to leave your house, office, and hotel, and vary the time that you depart and arrive. Drive with your windows up and doors locked. Swap cars with others occasionally, or take a cab one day and ride the tram/subway the next. Be discreet regarding your itinerary.
- **Keep a Low Profile.** Don't draw attention by pulling out a large wad of currency or paying with large denominations. Avoid public demonstrations. Dress like the locals when possible and leave expensive jewellery at home. Avoid loud conversation and being overheard. If you rent an automobile, avoid the flashy and choose a local, common model.
- **Guard Personal Data.** Be friendly but cautious when answering questions about you, your family, and your employment. Keep answers short and vague when possible. Give out your work number only—all family members should do the same. Don't list your home or mobile phone numbers in directories. Do not carry items in your purse or wallet that contain your home address, family pictures, contact information for friends, and so on.
- **Use Caution.** Be cautious if a local asks directions or the time—it could be a mugging ploy. When possible, travel with others and avoid walking alone after dark. Avoid narrow, dimly lit streets. If you get lost, act as if you know where you are, and ask directions from a place of business, not passersby. Beware of offers by drivers of unmarked or poorly marked cabs.
- **Know Emergency Procedures.** Be familiar with the local emergency procedures before trouble strikes. Keep phone numbers of police, fire, your hotel, your nation's embassy, and a reputable taxi service in your home and with you at all times.

PROPERTY SEIZURE   Governments sometimes seize the assets of companies doing business within their borders. Asset seizures fall into one of three categories: *confiscation*, *expropriation*, or *nationalization*.

The forced transfer of assets from a company to the government *without compensation* is called **confiscation**. Usually the former owners have no legal basis for requesting compensation or the return of assets. The 1996 Helms–Burton Law allows US businesses to sue companies from other nations that use their property that Cuba confiscated in its 1959 communist revolution. The Cuban government faces nearly 6000 company claims valued at $20 billion. But US presidents repeatedly waive the law so as not to harm the nation's relations with other countries.[5]

The forced transfer of assets from a company to the government *with compensation* is called **expropriation**. The expropriating government normally determines the amount of compensation. There is no framework for legal appeal, and compensation is typically far below market value. Today, governments rarely resort to confiscation or expropriation because these acts can force companies to leave the nation and can jeopardize future investment in the country. For example, Argentina's Congress passed a bill in May 2012 ordering the expropriation of YPF, the country's biggest oil company, causing international concern and market uncertainty.[6]

Whereas expropriation involves one or several companies in an industry, **nationalization** means government takeover of an *entire* industry. Nationalization is more common than confiscation and expropriation. Likely candidates for nationalization include industries important to a nation's security and those that generate large revenues. In recent years, Venezuela's President Hugo Chavez nationalized that country's telephone, electricity, and oil industries and threatened to nationalize many more. Businesses from other countries reacted to these moves by not investing in Venezuela. In general, a government may nationalize an industry to:

1. Use subsidies to protect an industry for ideological reasons.
2. Save local jobs in an ailing industry to gain political clout.
3. Control industry profits so they cannot be transferred to low-tax-rate countries.
4. Invest in sectors, such as public utilities, that private companies cannot afford.

confiscation

Forced transfer of assets from a company to the government without compensation.

expropriation

Forced transfer of assets from a company to the government with compensation.

nationalization

Government takeover of an entire industry.

The extent of nationalization varies widely from country to country. Whereas the governments of Cuba, North Korea, and Vietnam control practically every industry, those of the United States and Canada own very few. Many countries, including France, Mexico, Poland, and India, try to strike a balance between government and private ownership.

POLICY CHANGES   Government policy changes are the result of a variety of influences, including the ideals of newly empowered political parties, political pressure from special interests, and civil or social unrest. One common policy tool restricts ownership to domestic companies or limits ownership by nondomestic firms to a minority stake. This type of policy restricted PepsiCo's (www.pepsico.com) ownership of local companies to 49 percent when it first entered India.

The telecommunications industry is highly regulated worldwide, with domestic governments typically restricting foreign ownership. For example, Canada limits foreign ownership to 20 percent of voting shares in facilities-based carriers, with 80 percent of the board membership required to be Canadian citizens. Foreigners are limited to less than 47 percent of voting shares of a telecommunication common carrier, with the exclusion of small firms holding less than 10 percent of the total Canadian market. In Brazil's public telecommunication services, there is a 49 percent limit on foreign ownership. China has a 49 percent limit, and India limits foreign ownership in this industry to 74 percent. For a full list, visit the Information and Communications Technology (ICT) regulation toolkit (www.ictregulationtoolkit.org).[7]

Other policies relate to cross-border investments. Facing a slowdown in the technology sector, Taiwan's businesses and politicians called for a scrapping of the nation's "go slow, be patient" policy with China. That policy capped investments in mainland China at $50 million and banned investments in infrastructure and industries sensitive for national security reasons. Taiwan's government created a new policy called, "active opening, effective management," which reduced restrictions on cross-border investment.

LOCAL CONTENT REQUIREMENTS   Laws stipulating that a specified amount of a good or service be supplied by producers in the domestic market are called **local content requirements**. These requirements can force companies to use locally available raw materials, procure parts from local suppliers, or employ a minimum number of local workers. They ensure that international companies foster local business activity and help ease regional or national unemployment. They also help governments maintain some degree of control over international companies without resorting to extreme measures such as confiscation and expropriation.

local content requirements
Laws stipulating that a specified amount of a good or service be supplied by producers in the domestic market.

But local content requirements can jeopardize an international firm's long-term survival. First, a company required to hire local personnel might be forced to take on an inadequately trained workforce or take on excess workers. Second, a company made to obtain raw materials or parts locally can find its production costs rise or its product quality decline. The NAFTA rules governing tariffs specify a certain percentage of NAFTA content to be considered as "made in NAFTA," with the product then receiving preferential tariffs or duty exemptions. For example, to import a car from the United States to Canada, 62.5 percent of the value of the car must originate within NAFTA. If the car does not meet the local content requirement, import duty must be paid.

Managing Political Risk

International companies benefit from monitoring and attempting to predict political changes that can negatively affect their activities. When an international business opportunity arises in an environment plagued by extremely high risk, simply not investing in the location may be the wisest course of action. Yet when risk levels are moderate and the local market is attractive, international companies find other ways to manage political risks. Let's now examine the three main methods of managing political risk: *adaptation*, *information gathering*, and *political influence*.

ADAPTATION   *Adaptation* means incorporating risk into business strategies, often with the help of local officials. Companies can incorporate risk by means of four strategies:

- *Partnerships* help companies leverage expansion plans. They can be informal arrangements or include joint ventures, strategic alliances, and cross-holdings of company stock.

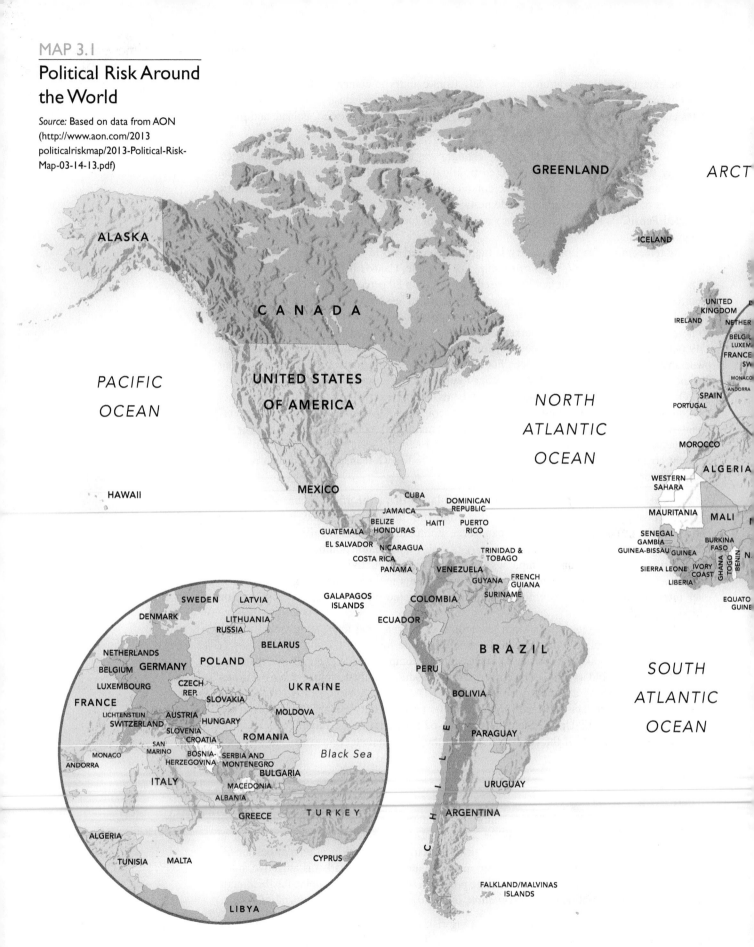

MAP 3.1

Political Risk Around the World

Source: Based on data from AON (http://www.aon.com/2013 politicalriskmap/2013-Political-Risk-Map-03-14-13.pdf)

C OCEAN

NORWAY

SWEDEN

FINLAND

ESTONIA

LATVIA

LITHUANIA

RUSSIA

MARK

BELARUS

IDS

POLAND

RMANY

UKRAINE

RG

CZECH
REP.

SLOVAKIA

AUSTRIA

HUNGARY

MOLDOVA

SLOVENIA

ROMANIA

CROATIA

BOSNIA
HERZEGOVINA

SERBIA AND
MONTENEGRO

BULGARIA

ITALY

MACEDONIA

GEORGIA

ALBANIA

GREECE

TURKEY

AZERBAIJAN

ARMENIA

NISIA

CYPRUS

SYRIA

LEBANON

IRAQ

ISRAEL

JORDAN

KUWAIT

LIBYA

EGYPT

QATAR

SAUDI
ARABIA

UNITED ARAB
EMIRATES

OMAN

GER

CHAD

SUDAN

ERITREA

YEMEN

RIA

DJIBOUTI

SOMALIA

CENTRAL AFRICAN
REPUBLIC

MEROON

ETHIOPIA

CONGO
REPUBLIC

UGANDA

KENYA

BON

CONGO
DEMOCRATIC
REPUBLIC
(ZAIRE)

RWANDA

BURUNDI

TANZANIA

ANGOLA

ZAMBIA

MALAWI

MOZAMBIQUE

NAMIBIA

ZIMBABWE

BOTSWANA

MADAGASCAR

MAURITIUS

RÉUNION

SWAZILAND

SOUTH
AFRICA

LESOTHO

RUSSIA

KAZAKHSTAN

MONGOLIA

UZBEKISTAN

KYRGYZSTAN

TURKMENISTAN

TAJIKISTAN

AFGHANISTAN

IRAN

PAKISTAN

CHINA

NORTH
KOREA

SOUTH
KOREA

JAPAN

NEPAL

BHUTAN

INDIA

BANGLADESH

MYANMAR
(BURMA)

LAOS

HONG KONG

THAILAND

VIETNAM

CAMBODIA

TAIWAN

PHILIPPINES

SRI
LANKA

BRUNEI

MALAYSIA

SINGAPORE

INDONESIA

PAPUA
NEW
GUINEA

SOLOMON
ISLANDS

INDIAN

OCEAN

PACIFIC

OCEAN

AUSTRALIA

VANUATU

FIJI

NEW
CALEDONIA

NEW
ZEALAND

Level of risk

- very high
- high
- moderate
- low
- very low
- no data available

Partnering helps a company to share the risk of loss, which is especially important in emerging markets. If partners own shares (*equity*) in local operations, they get cuts of the profits; if they loan cash (*debt*), they receive interest. Local partners who can help keep political forces from interrupting operations include firms, trade unions, financial institutions, and government agencies.

- *Localization* entails modifying operations, the product mix, or some other business element—even the company name—to suit local tastes and culture. For example, MTV (www.mtv.ca) demonstrates its sensitivity to local cultural and political issues by localizing certain aspects of its programming to suit regional and national tastes. McDonald's (www.mcdonalds.com) offers different menu options in several countries, taking into account local flavour preferences and religious diet restrictions. For example, in India McDonald's restaurants do not sell Big Macs because the Hindu people have a religious taboo against eating beef. Instead, the company offers a hamburger called the "Maharaja Mac," which is basically a Big Mac made with lamb or chicken. A vegetarian option called McAloo Tikki, made from potatoes mixed with Indian spices, is also available. In Germany, McDonald's offers beer. In Japan, the company offer shrimp burgers and a green tea–flavoured milkshake. In Costa Rica, you can order Gallo Pinto (rice and beans), and the list goes on.[8]

- *Development assistance* lets an international business assist the host country or region in improving the quality of life for locals. For example, by helping to develop distribution and communications networks, both a company and a nation benefit. Royal Dutch/Shell (www.shell.com), the oil company, is working in Kenya to increase the incomes of poor villagers and triple the average period of food security.[9] Canon (www.canon.com), the Japanese copier and printer maker, practises *kyosei* ("spirit of cooperation") to press local governments to make social and political reforms.

- *Insurance* against political risk can be essential to companies entering risky business environments. Export Development Canada (EDC) is the largest political risk insurance provider in Canada. EDC can insure a company for up to 90 percent of its losses resulting from breach of contract, expropriation, political violence, currency conversion or transfer, repossession, and non-payment by a government. To learn more about EDC's insurance solutions, visit www.edc.ca/insuranceform.

One way to lessen political risk is to offer development assistance to poor communities. Here, students get advice from an experienced businessman at the Branson School of Entrepreneurship in Johannesburg, South Africa. The school is named for Richard Branson, founder of the Virgin Group (www.virgin.com). Branson's not-for-profit foundation, Virgin Unite, strives to educate and inspire young leaders to unlock the potential of South Africa's youth.

Source: Louise Gubb/Corbis.

INFORMATION GATHERING International firms attempt to gather information that will help them predict and manage political risk. Two sources that companies use to conduct accurate political risk forecasting are:

- *Current Employees with Relevant Information.* Employees who have worked in a country long enough to gain insight into local culture and politics are often good sources of information. Individuals who formerly had decision-making authority while on international assignment probably had contact with local politicians and other officials. Yet it is important that an employee's international experience be recent because political power in a nation can shift rapidly and dramatically.
- *Agencies Specializing in Political-Risk Services.* These include banks, political consultants, news publications, and risk-assessment services. Many of these agencies publish reports detailing national levels and sources of political risk. Small companies that cannot afford to pay for some of these services can consider the many free sources of information available, notably from their federal governments. Government intelligence agencies are excellent and inexpensive sources to consult.

POLITICAL INFLUENCE Managers must work within the established rules and regulations of each national business environment. Business law in most nations undergoes frequent change, with new laws being enacted and existing ones modified. Influencing local politics means dealing with local lawmakers and politicians directly or through lobbyists. **Lobbying** is the policy of hiring people to represent a company's views on political matters. Lobbyists meet with a local public official to influence his or her position on issues relevant to the company. The ultimate goal of the lobbyists is to get favourable legislation enacted and unfavourable legislation rejected. Lobbyists also work to convince local officials that a company benefits the local economy, environment, workforce, and so on.

Bribes often represent attempts to gain political influence. In Canada, **Bill S-21**, enacted in 1999, forbids Canadians (individuals or companies) from bribing foreign governments and public officials, and laundering properties and proceeds. A bribe constitutes "anything of value"— money, gifts, and so forth—and cannot be given to any "foreign government official" empowered to make a "discretionary decision" that may be to the payer's benefit. The law also requires firms to keep accounting records that reflect their international activities and assets. (We discuss corruption further in Chapter 4.)

lobbying
Policy of hiring people to represent a company's views on political matters.

Bill S-21
A 1999 Bill that forbids Canadians (individuals or corporations) from bribing foreign government officials, and laundering properties and proceeds.

In our discussion of political systems and how companies deal with political uncertainty, we touched on several important legal issues. Although there is a good deal of overlap between a nation's political and legal systems, they are distinct. Let's now examine several types of legal systems and how they influence the activities of international companies.

Quick Study

1. What are the five main types of *political risk*? How might each affect international business activities?
2. Identify several steps managers can take to stay safe while on an international assignment.
3. Distinguish among *confiscation*, *expropriation*, and *nationalization*.
4. What three methods can businesses use to manage political risk?

Legal Systems

legal system
Set of laws and regulations, including the processes by which a country's laws are enacted and enforced, and the ways in which its courts hold parties accountable for their actions.

A country's **legal system** is its set of laws and regulations, including the processes by which its laws are enacted and enforced, and the ways in which its courts hold parties accountable for their actions. Many cultural factors—including ideas on social mobility, religion, and individualism—influence a nation's legal system. Likewise, many laws and regulations are enacted to safeguard cultural values and beliefs. For several examples of how legal systems differ from nation to nation, see this chapter's Culture Matters feature titled "Playing by the Rules ."

A country's political system also influences its legal system. Totalitarian governments tend to favour public ownership of economic resources and enact laws limiting entrepreneurial behaviour.

Culture Matters   Playing by the Rules

Understanding legal systems in other countries begins with an awareness of cultural differences. Here are snapshots of several nations' legal environments:

- **Japan.** Japan's harmony-based, consensus-driven culture considers court battles a last resort. But with growing patent disputes and a rise in cross-border mergers, Japan is discovering the value of lawyers. Japan has just 22 000 licenced attorneys compared with more than 100 000 lawyers in Canada and 4000 Quebec notaries. Japan is now minting thousands of new lawyers every year. Japanese businesses now litigate disputes that once might have been settled between parties.

- **Saudi Arabia.** Islam permeates every aspect of Saudi Arabia and affects its laws, politics, economics, and social development. Islamic law is grounded in religious teachings contained in the Koran and governs both criminal and civil cases. The Koran, in fact, is considered to be Saudi Arabia's constitution. The king and the council of ministers exercise all executive and legislative authority within the framework of Islamic law.

- **China.** Factory workers in China must sometimes endure military-style drills, verbal abuse, and mockery. But labour groups are winning higher wages, better working conditions, and better housing from a flock of lawyers and law students who hold free seminars and argue labour cases in China's courts. Inadequate protection of workers' rights is slowly giving way to better conditions for China's 169 million factory workers.

- **Mexico.** The legal system is derived from the Greek, Roman, and French legal systems. It is also influenced by colonial Spanish law, which includes several legal codes. One distinctive feature of the legal system in Mexico is that an individual is deemed guilty until proven otherwise, and the death penalty doesn't exist.

- **Want to Know More?** Visit Davis LLP legal advisors (www.davis.ca/en/practice-area/japan), the Embassy of Saudi Arabia (www.saudiembassy.net), China Development Gateway (http://en.chinagate.cn), and Mexico Online (www.mexonline.com).

Sources: David Barboza, "Scrutiny of China's Grim Factories Intensifies After Suicides," *The New York Times* (www.nytimes.com), June 6, 2010; "Light and Death," *The Economist* (www.economist.com), May 27, 2010; "Our Women Must Be Protected," *The Economist*, April 26, 2008, pp. 64–65; "Japan: Lawyers Wanted. No, Really," *Bloomberg Businessweek* (www.businessweek.com), April 3, 2006; "Japan," Davis LLP (www.davis.ca/en/practice-area/japan), June 21, 2012; "Mexican Legal System Overview," *Mexico Online*, (www.mexonline.com/lawreview.htm), June 25, 2012.

By contrast, democracies tend to encourage entrepreneurial activity and protect business with strong property-rights laws. The rights and responsibilities of parties to business transactions also differ from nation to nation. Political systems and legal systems, therefore, are naturally interlocked. A country's political system inspires and endorses its legal system, and its legal system legitimizes and supports its political system.

Legal systems are frequently influenced by political moods and upsurges of **nationalism**—the devotion of a people to their nation's interests and advancement. Nationalism typically involves intense national loyalty and cultural pride, and is often associated with drives toward national independence. In India, for example, most business laws originated when the country was struggling for "self-sufficiency." As a result, the legal system tended to protect local businesses from international competition. Although years ago India had nationalized many industries and closely scrutinized business applications, today its government is embracing globalization by enacting pro-business laws.

With that brief introduction, let's now examine the key characteristics of each type of legal system in use around the world (*common law*, *civil law*, and *theocratic law*), and discuss the key legal issues facing international companies.

> **nationalism**
> Devotion of a people to their nation's interests and advancement.

Common Law

The practice of common law originated in eleventh-century England and was adopted in that nation's territories worldwide. The Canadian legal system, therefore, is based largely on the common law tradition (although civil law is practised in Quebec). A **common law** legal system reflects three elements:

- *Tradition.* A country's legal history
- *Precedent.* Past cases that have come before the courts
- *Usage.* How laws are applied in specific situations

> **common law**
> Legal system based on a country's legal history (tradition), past cases that have come before its courts (precedent), and how laws are applied in specific situations (usage).

Under common law, the justice system decides cases by interpreting the law on the basis of tradition, precedent, and usage. Yet each law may be interpreted somewhat differently in each case to which it is applied. In turn, each new interpretation sets a precedent that may be followed in later cases. As new precedents arise, laws are altered to clarify vague wording or to accommodate situations not previously considered.

Business contracts tend to be lengthy in common-law nations (especially the United States) because they must consider many possible contingencies and many possible interpretations of the law in case of a dispute. Companies devote considerable time to devising clear contracts and spend large sums of money on legal advice. On the positive side, common-law systems are flexible. Instead of applying uniformly to all situations, laws take into account particular situations and circumstances. The common-law tradition prevails in Australia, Britain, Canada, Ireland, New Zealand, the United States, and some nations of Asia and Africa.

Civil Law

The origins of the civil law tradition can be traced to Rome in the fifth century BCE. It is the world's oldest and most common legal tradition. A **civil law** system is based on a detailed set of written rules and statutes that constitute a legal *code*. Civil law can be less adversarial than common law because there tends to be less need to interpret what a particular law states. Because all laws are codified and concise, parties to contracts tend to be more concerned only with the explicit wording of the code. All obligations, responsibilities, and privileges follow directly from the relevant code. Less time and money are typically spent, therefore, on legal matters. But civil law systems can ignore the unique circumstances of particular cases. Civil law is practiced in Cuba, Puerto Rico, Quebec, all of Central and South America, most of Western Europe, and many nations in Asia and Africa.

> **civil law**
> Legal system based on a detailed set of written rules and statutes that constitute a legal code.

Theocratic Law

A legal tradition based on religious teachings is called **theocratic law**. Three prominent theocratic legal systems are Islamic, Hindu, and Jewish law. Although Hindu law was restricted by India's 1950 constitution, in which the state appropriated most legal functions, it does persist as a cultural and spiritual force. Likewise, although Jewish law remains a strong religious force, it has served few legal functions since the eighteenth century, when most Jewish communities lost their judicial autonomy.

Islamic law is the most widely practised theocratic legal system today. Islamic law was initially a code governing moral and ethical behaviour, and was later extended to commercial

> **theocratic law**
> Legal system based on religious teachings.

transactions. It restricts the types of investments companies can make and sets guidelines for business transactions. According to Islamic law, for example, banks cannot charge interest on loans or pay interest on deposits. Instead, banks receive a portion of the profits earned by investors who borrow funds and pay depositors from these earnings. Likewise, because the products of alcohol- and tobacco-related businesses violate Islamic beliefs, firms abiding by Islamic law cannot invest in such companies.

Quick Study

1. What is meant by the term *legal system*?
2. Explain the role of *nationalism* in politics.
3. Identify the main features of each type of legal system (*common*, *civil*, and *theocratic law*).

Standardization

Companies must adapt to dissimilar legal systems because there is no clearly defined body of international law that all nations accept. There is a movement toward *standardizing* the interpretation and application of laws in more than one country, but this does not involve standardizing entire legal systems. Enduring differences in legal systems, therefore, can force companies to continue the costly practice of hiring legal experts in each country where they operate.

Still, international treaties and agreements exist in intellectual property rights, antitrust or antimonopoly regulation, taxation, contract arbitration, and general matters of trade. International organizations that promote standardization include the United Nations (UN) (www.un.org), the Organisation for Economic Cooperation and Development (OECD) (www.oecd.org), and the International Institute for the Unification of Private Law (www.unidroit.org). The European Union is standardizing parts of its members' legal systems to facilitate commerce in Western Europe.

Intellectual Property

intellectual property
Property that results from people's intellectual talent and abilities.

Property that results from people's intellectual talent and abilities is called **intellectual property**. It includes graphic designs, novels, computer software, machine-tool designs, and secret formulas, such as that for making Coca-Cola or the Kentucky Fried Chicken recipe. Technically, it results in *industrial property* (in the form of either a *patent* or a *trademark*) or *copyright* and confers a limited monopoly on its holder.

property rights
Legal rights to resources and any income they generate.

Most national legal systems protect **property rights**—the legal rights to resources and any income they generate. Similar to other types of property, intellectual property can be traded, sold, and licensed in return for fees and/or royalty payments. Intellectual property laws are designed to compensate people whose property rights are violated.

Intellectual property laws differ greatly from nation to nation. Business Software Alliance (BSA) (www.bsa.org), the trade body for business software makers, participates in an annual study of software piracy rates around the globe. Globally, software piracy averages around 42 percent and costs business software makers about $63 billion annually.[10] According to the BSA 2012 study, 40 percent of Canadian users admit they pirate software. Table 3.1 shows piracy rates for some nations included in the BSA study. As these figures suggest, the laws of some countries are softer than the laws of some other nations. Software companies in the European Union continually lobby their governments to pressure other nations to adopt stronger laws.

China currently has the most blatant piracy problem in the world. In 2011, the Chinese illegal software market was worth almost $9 billion (see Table 3.1), while the legal software market generated only $3 billion, suggesting a piracy rate of 77 percent. Although peddlers of pirated CDs and DVDs usually operate openly from sidewalk kiosks in China, the Chinese government did take measures to tackle piracy when China hosted the Summer Olympics in 2008. Their effort was a test case in fighting piracy in the YouTube era of video sharing. Richard Cotton, a general legal counsel at NBC, says, "[Chinese officials] recognize the future of the Chinese economy depends on innovation and creativity, and they have to protect the [intellectual property] that drives it."[11]

TABLE 3.1	Top 20 Economies in Commercial Value of Pirated Software		
	Pirated Value ($M)	Legal Sales ($M)	Piracy Rate
US	$9773	$41 664	19%
China	$8902	$2 659	77%
Russia	$3227	$1 895	63%
India	$2930	$1 721	63%
Brazil	$2848	$2 526	53%
France	$2754	$4 689	37%
Germany	$2265	$6 447	26%
Italy	$1945	$2 107	48%
UK	$1943	$5 530	26%
Japan	$1875	$7 054	21%
Indonesia	$1467	$ 239	86%
Mexico	$1249	$ 942	57%
Spain	$1216	$1 548	44%
Canada	$1141	$3 085	27%
Thailand	$852	$ 331	72%
South Korea	$815	$1 223	40%
Australia	$763	$2 554	23%
Venezuela	$668	$ 91	88%
Malaysia	$657	$ 538	55%
Argentina	$657	$ 295	69%

Source: Based on the *Ninth Annual BSA and IDC Global Software Piracy Study* (Washington, D.C.; Business Software Alliance, May 2012), Table 1, p. 1 (www.bsa.org/globalstudy).

Even though international piracy continues, the Uruguay Round of multilateral trade negotiations took an important step toward controlling the practice: The *Agreement on Trade-Related Aspects of Intellectual Property Rights* (TRIPS) was created to help standardize intellectual property rules around the world and to protect intellectual property rights. This initiative benefits society because it encourages the development of new technologies and other creations. TRIPS supports the specific articles on intellectual property in both the Paris and the Berne Conventions, and in certain instances takes a stronger stand on intellectual property protection.

Under the umbrella of the United Nations, the World Intellectual Property Organization (WIPO) (www.wipo.int) promotes innovation and creativity through an international intellectual property system. WIPO administers 24 multilateral treaties; aids companies to obtain global protection for new inventions, brands, and designs; and provides access to its intellectual property (IP) database, among other services.

INDUSTRIAL PROPERTY   **Industrial property** includes patents and trademarks, which are often a firm's most valuable assets. Laws protecting industrial property are designed to reward inventive and creative activity. Industrial property is protected internationally under the *Paris Convention for the Protection of Industrial Property* (www.wipo.int), to which nearly 100 countries are signatories.

industrial property
Patents and trademarks.

A **patent** is a right granted to the inventor of a product or process that excludes others from making, using, or selling the invention. Canadian patent law is similar to the systems of most developed nations and offers patent protection for 20 years. A patent is granted to the inventor who first files an application; 18 months after an application is filed, the document is made public in order to promote knowledge sharing (www.cipo.ic.gc.ca). Canadian patent law provisions parallel those of the World Trade Organization (WTO), the international organization that regulates trade between nations. The WTO (www.wto.org) typically grants patents for a period of 20 years. The 20-year term begins when a patent application is filed with a country's patent office, not when it is finally granted. Patents can be sought for any invention that is new, useful,

patent
Property right granted to the inventor of a product or process that excludes others from making, using, or selling the invention.

and not obvious to any individual of ordinary skill in the relevant technical field. Patents motivate companies to pursue inventions and make them available to consumers because they protect investments companies make in research and development.

trademark
Property right in the form of words or symbols that distinguish a product and its manufacturer.

Trademarks are words or symbols that distinguish a product and its manufacturer. The Nike (www.nike.com) "swoosh" is a trademark, as is the name "Lexus" (www.lexus.com). Trademark law creates incentives for manufacturers to invest in developing new products. It also benefits consumers because they know what to expect when they buy a particular brand. In other words, you would not expect a canned soft drink labelled "Coca-Cola" to taste like one labelled "Sprite."

Trademark protection typically lasts indefinitely, provided the word or symbol continues to be *distinctive*. Ironically, this stipulation presents a problem for companies such as Coca-Cola (www.coca-cola.com) and Xerox (www.xerox.com), whose trademarks "Coke" and "Xerox" have evolved into *generic* terms for all products in their respective categories. Trademark laws differ from country to country, though some progress toward standardization is occurring. The European Union, for example, opened a trademark-protection office to police trademark infringement against firms that operate in any EU country.

Designers who own trademarks, such as Chanel (www.chanel.com), Christian Dior (www.dior.com), and Gucci (www.gucci.com), have long been plagued by shoddily made counterfeit handbags, shoes, shirts, and other products. But, recently, pirated products of equal or nearly equal quality are turning up, especially in Italy. Most Italian owners of luxury brands of leather goods and jewellery, for example, outsource production to small manufacturers. It is not hard for these same artisans to counterfeit extra copies of a high-quality product. Bootleg copies of a Prada (www.prada.com) backpack that costs $500 in New York can be bought for less than $100 in Rome. Jewellery shops in Milan can buy fake watches labelled Bulgari (www.bulgari.com) and Rolex (www.rolex.com) for $300 and sell them retail for $2500. For a Canadian example, read the Canada Goose case at the end of this chapter.

copyright
Property right giving creators of original works the freedom to publish or dispose of them as they choose.

COPYRIGHTS **Copyright** gives creators of original works the freedom to publish or dispose of them as they choose. A copyright is typically denoted by the well-known symbol ©, a date, and the copyright holder's name. A copyright holder has the legal rights to:

- Reproduce the copyrighted work
- Derive new works from the copyrighted work
- Sell or distribute copies of the copyrighted work
- Perform the copyrighted work
- Display the copyrighted work publicly

Copyright holders include artists, photographers, painters, literary authors, publishers, musical composers, and software developers. Works created after January 1, 1978, are automatically copyrighted for the creator's lifetime plus 50 years. Publishing houses receive copyrights for either 75 years from the date of publication or 100 years after creation, whichever comes first. Copyrights are protected under the **Berne Convention** (www.wipo.int), an international copyright treaty, and the 1954 Universal Copyright Convention. More than 50 countries abide by one or both of these treaties.

Berne Convention
International treaty that protects copyrights.

A copyright is granted for the *tangible expression* of an idea, not for the idea itself. For example, no one can copyright the idea for a movie about the sinking of the *Titanic*. But once a film is made that expresses its creator's treatment of the subject, that film can be copyrighted.

Perhaps the most well-known song around the world, "Happy Birthday to You," is actually protected by US copyright law. The song was composed in 1859 and copyrighted in 1935. Although the copyright was set to expire in 2010 on the song's 75th copyright birthday, the take over US Congress extended it until 2030. Time Warner owns the copyright and stands to gain as much as $20 million from the extension.

Product Safety and Liability

Product safety laws in most countries set standards that manufactured products must meet. **Product liability** holds manufacturers, sellers, individuals, and others responsible for damage, injury, or death caused by defective products. Injured parties can sue for monetary compensation through *civil* lawsuits and for fines or imprisonment through *criminal* lawsuits.

product liability
Responsibility of manufacturers, sellers, individuals, and others for damage, injury, or death caused by defective products.

Developed nations have the toughest product liability laws, while developing and emerging countries have the weakest laws. Business insurance costs and legal expenses are greater in nations with strong product liability laws, where damage awards can be large. Likewise, enforcement of product liability laws differs from nation to nation. In the most developed nations, for example, tobacco companies are regularly under attack for the negative health effects of tobacco and nicotine. But critics say that the tobacco industry markets aggressively to women and children in developing countries where regulations are weak and many people do not know that smoking is dangerous.[12]

In Canada, product safety and liability are regulated by the *Canada Consumer Product Safety Act* (CCPSA), which is administered by Health Canada. Its purpose is to protect the public by addressing and preventing dangers to human health or safety posed by consumer products in Canada. For example, the following products are banned in Canada: baby walkers, infant self-feeding devices, jequirity beans, lawn darts with elongated tips, and polycarbonate baby bottles containing BPA. For a full list of banned products, consult the Health Canada site (www.hc-sc.gc.ca). Caution is advised for consumers purchasing from foreign online sites, as it is the consumer's responsibility to make sure the product is not banned in Canada. Restricted items will be seized by customs.

Taxation

National governments use income and sales taxes for many purposes. They use tax revenue to pay government salaries, build military capabilities, and shift earnings from people with high incomes to the poor. Nations may also tax imports to make them more expensive and give locally made products an advantage among price-sensitive consumers.

Nations pass indirect taxes, called "consumption taxes," which help pay for the consequences of using particular products. Consumption taxes on products such as alcohol and tobacco help pay the health-care costs of treating illnesses that result from using these products. Similarly, gasoline taxes help pay for road and bridge repairs needed to counteract the effects of traffic and weathering.

Many countries impose a **value added tax (VAT)**—a tax levied on each party that adds value to a product throughout its production and distribution. The VAT in Canada is known as the goods and services tax (GST). In provinces such as Prince Edward Island, New Brunswick, Nova Scotia, Newfoundland and Labrador, and Ontario, a harmonized sales tax (HST) is charged. This reflects a combination of the GST and the provincial sales tax, and is typically 13 percent.[13] Supporters of the VAT system contend that it distributes taxes on retail sales more evenly between producers and consumers. Suppose, for example, that a shrimper sells the day's catch of shrimp for $1 per kilogram and that the country's VAT is 10 percent (see Table 3.2). The shrimper, processor, wholesaler, and retailer pay taxes of $0.10, $0.07, $0.11, and $0.10, respectively, for the value that each adds to the product as it makes its way to consumers. Consumers pay no additional tax at the point of sale because the government has already collected taxes from each party in the value chain. Still, consumers end up paying the tax because producers and distributors must increase prices to compensate for their tax burdens. So that the poor are not overly burdened, many countries exclude the VAT on certain items such as children's clothing. In Canada, GST (VAT) is usually excluded on groceries, prescription drugs, medical devices, outbound and inward transportation, and the export of certain goods and services.

value added tax (VAT)
Tax levied on each party that adds value to a product throughout its production and distribution.

Antitrust (Antimonopoly) Regulations

Laws designed to prevent companies from fixing prices, sharing markets, and gaining unfair monopoly advantages are called **antitrust (antimonopoly) laws**. These laws try to provide consumers with a wide variety of products at fair prices. The United States and the European Union are the world's strictest antitrust regulators. In Japan, the Fair Trade Commission enforces antitrust laws but is often ineffective because *absolute proof* of wrongdoing is needed to bring charges.

antitrust (antimonopoly) laws
Laws designed to prevent companies from fixing prices, sharing markets, and gaining unfair monopoly advantages.

TABLE 3.2	Effect of Value-Added Taxes (VAT)			
Production Stage	**Selling Price**	**Value Added**	**10% VAT**	**Total VAT**
Shrimper	$1.00	$1.00	$0.10	$0.10
Processor	1.70	0.70	0.07	0.17
Wholesaler	2.80	1.10	0.11	0.28
Retailer	3.80	1.00	0.10	0.38

Companies based in strict antitrust (antimonopoly) countries often argue that they are at a disadvantage against competitors whose home countries condone *market sharing*, whereby competitors agree to serve only designated segments of a certain market. That is why firms in strict antitrust or antimonopoly countries often lobby for exemptions in certain international transactions. Small businesses also argue that they could better compete against large international companies if they could join forces without fear of violating antitrust (antimonopoly) laws.

In the absence of a global antimonopoly enforcement agency, international companies must concern themselves with the antitrust (antimonopoly) laws of each nation where they do business. In fact, a nation (or group of nations) can block a merger or acquisition between two nondomestic companies if those companies do a good deal of business there. This happened to the proposed $43 billion merger between General Electric (GE) (www.ge.com) and Honeywell (www.honeywell.com). GE wanted to marry their manufacture of airplane engines to Honeywell's production of advanced electronics for the aviation industry. Although both companies are based in the United States, together they employed 100 000 Europeans. GE alone earned $25 billion in Europe the year before the proposed merger. The European Union blocked the merger because it believed the result would be higher prices for customers, particularly airlines.

To learn about several agencies responsible for the enforcement of business laws in Canada, see this chapter's Entrepreneur's Toolkit, titled "The Long Arm of the Law."

Quick Study

1. What are *intellectual property rights*? What is the significance of such rights?
2. Explain the term *industrial property*. What are its two types?
3. What is a *copyright*? Explain its importance to international business.
4. Identify the ramifications of antitrust (antimonopoly) laws and product liability laws?

Entrepreneur's Toolkit The Long Arm of the Law

Most governments have agencies designed to monitor the nation's business environment and enforce its laws. Several important Canadian agencies that entrepreneurs and small business owners can consult for free legal information are as follows:

- **Canadian Intellectual Property Office (CIPO).** CIPO is a special operating agency (SOA) associated with Industry Canada and is responsible for the administration and processing of intellectual property in Canada. CIPO issues patents and registers trademarks. On CIPO's Web site (www.cipo.ic.gc.ca), you can find information on how to fill out a trademark application, as well as information on trademarks, patents, copyrights, and industrial design databases. CIPO also disseminates intellectual property information.
- **Health Canada.** Health Canada administers the *Canada Consumer Product Safety Act* (CCPSA). CCPSA protects the public from injury and death associated with consumer products. It also provides information

for businesses regarding noncompliant or banned products.
- **Competition Bureau.** The Competition Bureau (www.competitionbureau.gc.ca) is an independent law enforcement agency whose goal is to ensure that Canadian businesses and consumers prosper in a competitive and innovative marketplace.
- **Canadian Trade Commissioner Service (TCS).** TCS provides Canadian businesses with advice on foreign markets, including step-by-step guides on exporting to specific markets. TCS can assist companies with the commercialization of Canadian innovations abroad and the sourcing of innovative technologies and partnerships.
- **Want to Know More?** Visit the Web sites of the following government agencies: CIPO (www.cipo.ic.gc.ca), Health Canada CCPSA (www.hc-sc.gc.ca), the Competition Bureau (www.competitionbureau.gc.ca); and the Canadian Trade Commissioner Service (www.tradecommissioner.gc.ca).

Sources: Canadian Intellectual Property Office Web site (www.cipo.ic.gc.ca); Health Canada Web site (www.hc.sc.gc.ca); Competition Bureau Web site (www.competitionbureau.gc.ca); Canadian Trade Commissioner Service Web site (www.tradecommissioner.gc.ca).

Business and International Relations

The political relations between a company's home country and the nations in which it does business affect its international business activities. Favourable political relationships foster stable business environments and increase international cooperation in many areas, including the development of international communications and distribution infrastructures. In turn, a stable environment requires a strong legal system through which disputes can be resolved quickly and fairly. In general, favourable political relations lead to increased business opportunities and lower risk.

The way a country is perceived has a strong effect on the country's ability to compete for investment and to export its goods and services, and can make a significant difference in the success of its businesses. In partnership with Gfk Roper, a world-renowned consulting company, policy advisor Simon Anholt led the development of an index called "The Anholt-GfK Roper Nation Brands Index." This index measures the power and quality of each country's brand image by combining six dimensions: exports, governance, culture and heritage, people, tourism, and investment and immigration. Six European countries are listed in the top ten. Canada ranked sixth, indicating that the country possesses a strong reputation in the combined dimensions. In particular, Canada ranks highest in the immigration dimension, as it is recognized for its liberal immigration policy and high quality of life. Additionally, Canada is well known around the world for its natural beauty; it is considered rich in its cultural heritage; and it has a strong governance reputation. No Latin American, African, or Middle Eastern countries appeared in the top ten; the only Asian country in the top ten was Japan. To learn more about the Anholt-GfK Roper Nation Brands Index visit (www.gfk.com).[14]

To generate stable business environments, some countries have turned to *multilateral agreements*—treaties concluded among several nations, each of whom agrees to abide by treaty terms even if tensions develop. According to the European Union's founding treaty, goods, services, and citizens of member nations are free to move across members' borders. Every nation must continue to abide by such terms even if it has a conflict with another member. For instance, although Britain and France disagree on many issues, neither can treat goods, services, and citizens coming and going between their two nations any differently than it treats any other member nation's goods, services, and citizens. See Chapter 8 for a detailed presentation of the European Union.

The United Nations

Although individual nations sometimes have the power to influence the course of events in certain parts of the world, they cannot monitor political activities everywhere at once. The **United Nations (UN)** (www.un.org) was formed after the Second World War to provide leadership in fostering peace and stability around the world. The UN and its many agencies provide food and medical supplies, educational supplies and training, and financial resources to poorer member nations. The UN receives its funding from member contributions based primarily on gross national product (GNP). Practically all nations in the world are UN members—except for several small countries and territories that have observer status.

The UN is headed by a secretary general who is elected by all members and serves for a five-year term. The UN system consists of six main bodies:

- All members have an equal vote in the *General Assembly*, which discusses and recommends action on any matter that falls within the UN Charter. It approves the UN budget and the makeup of the other bodies.
- The *Security Council* consists of 15 members. Five (China, France, the United Kingdom, Russia, and the United States) are permanent. Ten others are elected by the General Assembly for two-year terms. The council is responsible for ensuring international peace and security, and all UN members are supposed to be bound by its decisions.
- The *Economic and Social Council,* which is responsible for economics, human rights, and social matters, administers a host of smaller organizations and specialized agencies.
- The *Trusteeship Council* consists of the five permanent members of the Security Council and administers all trustee territories under UN custody.

United Nations (UN)
International organization formed after the Second World War to provide leadership in fostering peace and stability around the world.

- The *International Court of Justice* consists of 15 judges elected by the General Assembly and Security Council. It can hear disputes only between nations, not cases brought against individuals or corporations. It has no compulsory jurisdiction, and its decisions can be, and have been, disregarded by specific nations.
- Headed by the secretary general, the *Secretariat* administers the operations of the UN.

An important body within the UN Economic and Social Council is the United Nations Conference on Trade and Development (UNCTAD) (www.unctad.org). The organization has a broad mandate in the areas of international trade and economic development. It hosts conferences on pressing development issues including entrepreneurship, AIDS, poverty, and national debt. Certain conferences are designed to develop the business management skills of individuals in developing nations.

Another important organization related to international business is the International Trade Centre (ITC) (www.intracen.org). The ITC's goal is "to assist developing and transition countries to achieve sustainable development through exports." This objective is achieved through partnerships that provide sustainable and inclusive development solutions to the private sector, trade support institutions, and policy makers.

Quick Study

1. Why are international relations among countries important to international business?
2. Many people question the existence of the United Nations (UN). Do you think the existence of the UN is useful for business?

Bottom Line   for Business

Differences in political and legal systems present both opportunities and risks for international companies. Gaining complete control over events in even the most stable national business environment is extremely difficult because of the intricate connections among politics, law, and culture. Still, understanding these connections is the first step in managing the risks of doing business in unfamiliar environments.

Implications for Business in Totalitarian Nations

Political opposition to business from nongovernmental organizations is extremely unlikely if a totalitarian nation sanctions that particular commercial activity. Bribery and kickbacks to government officials will likely prevail, and refusal to pay tends not to be an option. As such, business activities in totalitarian nations are inherently risky. Business law in totalitarian nations is either vague or nonexistent, and interpretation of the law is highly subjective. Finally, certain groups criticize companies for doing business in or with totalitarian nations, saying they are helping sustain oppressive political regimes.

Implications for Business in Democracies

Democracies tend to provide stable business environments through laws that protect individual property rights. Commerce should prosper when the private sector comprises independently owned firms that exist to make profits. Although participative democracy, property rights, and free markets tend to encourage economic growth, they do not always do so. India is the world's largest democracy, yet its economy grew very slowly for decades. Meanwhile, some countries achieved rapid economic growth under political systems that were not genuinely democratic.

Which Type of Government Is Best for Business?

Do democratic governments provide more "stable" national business environments than totalitarian ones? Although democracies pass laws to protect individual civil liberties and property rights, totalitarian governments could also grant such rights. The difference is that whereas democracies strive to guarantee such rights, totalitarian governments retain the power to repeal them whenever they choose.

As for a nation's rate of economic growth, we can say only that a democracy does not guarantee high rates of economic growth and that totalitarianism does not doom a nation to slow economic growth. An economy's growth rate is influenced by many variables other than political and civil liberties, including its tax system, openness toward investment, availability of capital, and extent of trade and investment barriers.

Implications of Legal Issues for Companies

A nation's political system is naturally intertwined with its legal system. Its political system inspires and endorses its legal system, which legitimizes and supports the political system. Flexible business strategies help companies operate within the political and legal frameworks of nations. An area in which political and legal environments have important implications is copyright law. People today share digital files worldwide for free and directly with one another through the Internet. The introduction of a new digital technology can devastate a business because it can spread worldwide in days. Managers will benefit if they have a solid grasp of how legal systems affect company operations and strategy.

Chapter Summary

1. Describe each main type of political system.
    *   A *political system* consists of the structures, processes, and activities by which a nation governs itself.
    *   In a *totalitarian system*, individuals govern without the support of the people, tightly control people's lives, and do not tolerate opposing viewpoints.
    *   Totalitarian governments tend to impose authority, lack constitutional guarantees, and restrict participation.
    *   Under *theocratic totalitarianism*, a country's religious leaders enforce laws and regulations based on religious and totalitarian beliefs.
    *   Under *secular totalitarianism*, political leaders rely on military and bureaucratic power.
    *   Secular totalitarianism takes three forms: *communist totalitarianism*, *tribal totalitarianism*, and *right-wing totalitarianism*.
    *   In a *democratic system*, leaders are elected directly by the wide participation of the people or by their representatives.
    *   Most democracies are *representative democracies*, in which citizens elect individuals from their groups to represent their political views.
    *   Representative democracies strive to provide freedom of expression, periodic elections, full civil and property rights, minority rights, and nonpolitical bureaucracies.

2. Identify the origins of political risk and how managers can reduce its effects.
    *   *Political risk* is the likelihood that a society will undergo political changes that negatively affect local business activity.
    *   *Macro risk* threatens the activities of all domestic and international companies in every industry, whereas *micro risk* threatens companies only within a particular industry or more narrowly defined group.
    *   Five actions or events that cause political risk are conflict and violence, terrorism and kidnapping, property seizure, policy changes, and local content requirements.
    *   The seizure of assets by a local government can take one of three forms: *confiscation* (forced transfer of assets without compensation), *expropriation* (forced transfer with compensation), or *nationalization* (forced takeover of an entire industry).
    *   Managers can reduce the effects of political risk through *adaptation* (incorporating risk into business strategies), *information gathering* (monitoring local political events), and *political influence* (such as by *lobbying* local political leaders).
    *   Bill S-21 forbids Canadians (individuals or corporations) from bribing foreign government and officials, and laundering property and proceeds.

3. Describe each main type of legal system and the important global legal issues.
    *   A country's *legal system* is its set of laws and regulations, including the processes by which its laws are enacted and enforced and the ways in which its courts hold parties accountable for their actions.
    *   *Common law* is a legal system based on a country's legal history (tradition), past cases that have come before its courts (precedent), and how laws are applied in specific situations (usage).
    *   *Civil law* is a system based on a detailed set of written rules and statutes that constitute a legal code, from which flows all obligations, responsibilities, and privileges.
    *   *Theocratic law* is a system based on religious teachings.
    *   Businesses prefer a legal system that protects *property rights* (legal rights to resources and any income they generate) and *intellectual property* (property that results from people's intellectual talent and abilities).
    *   Intellectual property takes the form of *industrial property* (a patent or trademark) or copyright.
    *   Many nations have *product liability laws* (responsibility for damage, injury, or death caused by defective products) and *antitrust (antimonopoly) laws* (designed to prevent companies from fixing prices, sharing markets, and gaining unfair monopoly advantages).

4. Explain how international relations affect international business activities.
   - Political relations between a company's home country and those with which it does business strongly affect its international activities.
   - In general, favourable political relations lead to increased opportunity and stable business environments.
   - A nation's branding has a strong effect on the country's ability to compete for investments and to export its goods and services.
   - The mission of the *United Nations (UN)* is to provide leadership in fostering peace and stability around the world.
   - Although its global peacekeeping efforts have had mixed results, the UN helps poor nations by providing food and medical supplies, educational supplies and training, and financial resources.

Key Terms

antitrust (antimonopoly) laws 107	intellectual property 104	representative democracy 92
Berne Convention 106	legal system 102	secular totalitarianism 90
Bill S-21 101	lobbying 101	socialism 90
capitalism 93	local content requirements 97	theocracy 90
civil law 103	nationalism 103	theocratic law 103
common law 103	nationalization 96	theocratic totalitarianism 90
communism 90	patent 105	totalitarian system 89
confiscation 96	political risk 94	trademark 106
copyright 106	political system 88	United Nations (UN) 109
democracy 92	private sector 93	value added tax (VAT) 107
expropriation 96	product liability 106	
industrial property 105	property rights 104	

Talk It Over

1. The Internet and the greater access to information it can provide are forcing politicians to change their methods of governing. How might the Internet change totalitarian political systems, such as North Korea? What might the Web's future expansion mean for nations with theocratic systems, such as Iran? How might technology change the way that democracies function?

2. Under a totalitarian political system, the Indonesian economy grew strongly for 30 years. Meanwhile, the economy of the world's largest functioning democracy, India, performed poorly for decades until recently. Relying on what you learned in this chapter, do you think the Indonesian economy grew despite or because of a totalitarian regime? What might explain India's relatively poor performance under a democratic political system?

3. Consider the following statement: "Democratic political systems, as opposed to totalitarian ones, provide international companies with more stable environments in which to do business." Do you agree? Why or why not? Support your argument with specific country examples.

Take It to the Web

1. **Video Report.** Visit YouTube (www.youtube.com) and type "politics and law" into the search engine. Watch one of videos from the results of your search and then summarize it in a half-page report. Reflecting on the contents of this chapter, which components of politics and law can you identify in the video? How might a company engaged in international business act on the information contained in the video?

2. **Web Site Report.** To attract investment from domestic and foreign companies, nations compete against each other to provide top-notch services.
   Visit the main government portal of Hong Kong, SAR (www.gov.hk). Can you identify several sections of the site that are government-to-business activities and government-to-citizen dealings? List the types of services that would be available to you as (1) a citizen of Hong Kong, (2) a tourist going to visit Hong Kong, (3) a person thinking of starting a business in Hong Kong, and (4) a company currently operating in Hong Kong. What additional services should the government offer on its Web site that it does not currently provide?

3. **Web Site Report.** Visit the International Trade Centre Web site (www.intracen.org) and select a country from the "ITC by Country" list. Open the trade and tariff graphs. Summarize the data and compare it to Canada's data. Present a one-page report on your findings.

Pirates of Globalization

It pays to remember that old Latin phrase, *caveat emptor* ("let the buyer beware") when tackling the production of counterfeit products on a global scale. Sophisticated pirates routinely violate patents, trademarks, and copyrights to churn out high-quality fakes of the best-known brands. Trademark counterfeiting amounts to between 5 and 7 percent of world trade or around $600 billion a year! Phony products appear in many industries, including computer software, films, books, music CDs, and pharmaceutical drugs. Fake computer chips, broadband routers, and computers cost the electronics industry alone up to $100 billion annually. And the amount of counterfeit medicines making their way into Europe is constantly growing.

Traditionally peddled by sidewalk vendors and in back-street markets, counterfeiters now employ the latest technology. Just as honest businesses do, they are using the Internet to slash the cost of distributing their fake goods. All merchandise on some Internet sites is counterfeit, and even legitimate Web site operators, such as eBay (www.ebay.com), have difficulty rooting out pirates.

Counterfeit products, commonly called "knockoffs," have become global—counterfeiting is one of the fastest growing economic crimes of our times. A Canadian outerwear company that has become a victim of knockoff products is Toronto-based Canada Goose. Founded in 1957, the company began exporting to the United States, Japan, Sweden, and Antarctica in 2000. By 2009, Canada Goose products were being sold in 40 countries worldwide.

Canada Goose is now recognized internationally as the world's leading manufacturer of extreme weather outwear. But fame has come at a cost: Canada Goose's product reputation and brand integrity is being compromised by counterfeiters. The counterfeited products are usually non-functional versions made with inferior materials. Counterfeiting these specialized products is not only illegal but also dangerous. For example, some of the fake products are filled with feather mulch that may contain bacteria, fungi, and mildew, posing a health risk. Equally or even more serious, consumers who purchase these knockoff products risk freezing to death in extreme weather conditions if their clothing is inadequate. Canada Goose knockoffs are manufactured in Asia, and sold online and in the flea markets of Shanghai, Beijing, and Bangkok. Hundreds of fake online Web sites with names such as canada-goose-finland.com, canadagoose-france.fr, and canda-goose.org have been created specifically to sell Canada Goose imitations—in one month, the company discovered 20 000 fake versions of their products.

Another industry hard hit by counterfeiters is the automotive parts industry, which loses around $12 billion annually to phony goods. Counterfeiters are making fake batteries, windshields, brakes, fluids, filters, and spark plugs. The problem is causing fears of lawsuits because of malfunctioning counterfeits and concerns of lost revenue for producers of the genuine articles. For example, if someone is in an accident because of a counterfeit product, legitimate manufacturers need to prove the product is not their own. Car manufacturers list potentially harmful fakes such as brake linings made of compressed sawdust and transmission fluid that is nothing more than cheap oil with added dye. Boxes bearing legitimate-looking labels make it difficult for consumers to tell the difference between a fake and the real deal. More fake products are recently coming into North America, but the larger market for consumption remains the Middle East.

China, India, South Korea, Malaysia, Taiwan, and Thailand are all leading sources of counterfeit products. Lax anti-piracy regulations and booming economies in China and India mean potential intellectual-property traps await companies doing business in these emerging markets. For example, Indian law gives international pharmaceutical firms five- to seven-year patents on *processes used to manufacture drugs—but not on the drugs themselves.* This lets Indian companies modify the patented production processes of international pharmaceutical companies to create only slightly different drugs.

In China, political protection for pirates of intellectual property remains fairly common. Government officials, people working for the government, and even the People's Liberation Army (China's national army) operate factories that churn out pirated goods; others operate on government-owned land. Criminals are often connected to political leaders and receive legal protection from prosecution. An international company has difficulty fighting piracy in China because filing a lawsuit can severely damage its business relations there.

Yet international opinion is divided on the root causes of rampant intellectual property violations in China. Some argue that Chinese legislation is vaguely worded and difficult to enforce. Others say that China's intellectual property laws and regulations are fine, but poor enforcement is to blame for high rates of piracy. Amazingly, China's regulatory body sometimes allows a counterfeiter to remove an infringing trademark and still sell the substandard good.

Thinking Globally

1. What actions can companies and governments take to ensure that products cannot be easily pirated? Be specific.
2. Do you think that the international business community is being too lax about the abuse of intellectual property rights? Are international companies simply afraid to speak out for fear of jeopardizing access to attractive markets?

3. Increased digital communication may pose a threat to intellectual property because technology allows people to create perfect clones of original works. How do you think the Internet is affecting intellectual property laws?

4. Research Canada Goose's current counterfeiting situation. What actions has the company taken to reduce this problem? If you were hired as a consultant for Canada Goose, what other recommendations would you give, based on what you learned in this chapter?

Sources: Rachael King, "Fighting a Flood of Counterfeit Tech Products," *Bloomberg Businessweek* (www.businessweek.com), March 1, 2010; Andrew Willis, "Europe Awash in Counterfeit Drugs," *Bloomberg Businessweek* (www.businessweek.com), December 8, 2009; International Chamber of Commerce Commercial Crime Services Web site (www.icc-ccs.org); Canada Goose Web site (www.canada-goose.com); Canadian Press, "Canada Goose Targets Counterfeit Knockoffs," *The Hamilton Spectator*, February 23, 2012.

CHAPTER FOUR

International Ethics

Learning Objectives

After studying this chapter, you should be able to

1. Explain ethics, ethical behaviour, ethical dilemmas, and codes of ethics.

2. Understand the different philosophies of ethics and how international business managers apply them to their decision-making processes.

3. Explain corporate social responsibility, understand the concept of sustainability and sustainable practices, and provide examples of international businesses that apply these concepts.

4. Understand the principles of responsible investment.

A LOOK BACK

Chapter 3 looked at the roles of politics and law in international business. We learned about the different types of political systems and how managers cope with political risk. We also examined several kinds of legal systems and how international relations affect business.

A LOOK AT THIS CHAPTER

This chapter begins with a discussion of ethics and ethical behaviour, and explores why ethical dilemmas arise. It focuses on understanding the different philosophies of ethics and how international business managers apply them to their decision-making processes. Understanding ethics is key to success in international business because what is considered right and wrong varies, depending upon the country's cultural, political, and legal systems. This chapter also examines corporate social responsibility and sustainable practices in international business.

A LOOK AHEAD

Chapter 5 discusses the world's different economic systems. We learn about emerging markets and development, and explore challenges facing countries that are transforming their economies into free markets.

Source: ShutterStock.

Air Canada's Corporate Social Responsibility

MONTREAL, Quebec—Air Canada (www.aircanada.com) is Canada's largest airline, operating in both domestic and international markets. Established by the Canadian government as Trans-Canada Air Lines in 1937, the company was renamed Air Canada in 1964 and became fully privatized in 1989. Today Air Canada is the fifteenth largest commercial airline in the world with revenues of $12.1 billion, employs 27 000 people, and flies to more than 175 destinations on five continents.

The company's business strategy strives to balance economic, environmental, and social considerations by focusing on four areas: safety, the environment, employees, and the community. In 2011, Air Canada published its first report focused on corporate sustainability initiatives.

Safety is Air Canada's first priority. The company is committed to providing a safe travel and work environment, and encourages employees to correct suboptimal conditions and behaviours. Air Canada's pilot selection and training process is one of the most rigorous in the industry. The company's safety focus extends throughout the supply chain to include manufacturers, suppliers, and distributors.

Source: Reproduced with the permission of Air Canada.

To lessen its environmental impact, Air Canada works to reduce energy use, lower carbon dioxide emissions, decrease aircraft noise, and curtail waste. The company's average fuel efficiency has improved by 33 percent since 1990; between 2006 and 2011 it reduced carbon dioxide emissions by over 318 000 tonnes.

Air Canada strives to create safe, fair, and rewarding working conditions for its employees. Some initiatives in this regard include maintaining a defined benefit pension plan for most of its unionized workers, actively recruiting First Nations people, and promoting talent from within.

Air Canada engages in various activities in the community, including charity and broad-based enrichment programs. For example, through the "Every Bit Counts" program, small change can be donated on board and at select airports, and is given to the Children's Miracle Network for pediatric hospitals across Canada. Air Canada also sponsors many sports and cultural organizations, including the National Hockey League, the Toronto International Film Festival, and various regional symphony orchestras and museums.

As you read this chapter, consider how ethics, corporate social responsibility, and sustainable practices affect the activities of international companies.[1]

We learned in previous chapters that when a company goes global, its managers often encounter unfamiliar cultural rules that govern human behaviour. Although legal systems set boundaries for lawful individual and corporate behaviour, they are inadequate for dilemmas of ethics and social responsibility. Frameworks for business law vary in strength from country to country. Unfortunately, the quest for profits may entice a company to exploit differences in legal standards by locating certain business operations in nations where they will be less scrutinized. In this way, national legal differences can become ethical issues for managers.

We begin this chapter by defining ethics and ethical behaviour. Next we examine ethical dilemmas and discuss the importance of developing a code of ethics to guide and encourage employees to behave ethically. We then present the different philosophies regarding ethics and how international business managers apply them in their decision-making processes. We also look at corporate social responsibility (CSR) and the issues related to this topic, as well as discuss the concept of sustainability and sustainable practices in international business. We close the chapter by explaining the principles of responsible investment.

Ethics, Ethical Behaviour, Ethical Dilemmas, and Codes of Ethics

ethics

Moral obligation to separate right from wrong.

Ethics is the moral obligation to separate right from wrong. Ethics can also be defined as the set of moral principles or values that defines right or wrong for a person or group. Ethics seeks to resolve questions dealing with human morality. Acts can be legal or illegal. While illegal acts should not be difficult to resolve through law enforcement, legal acts can sometimes present ethical challenges, meaning that an act can be legal but unethical.

For example, it is clearly unethical for the chief executive officer (CEO) of a company to use the company's corporate jet to travel for personal reasons such as going on vacation. However, some may consider it unethical for a CEO to use the corporate jet for business travel when the distance is short and drivable. In this situation, more information is needed before deciding if the CEO's approach was ethical or unethical. For instance, if using the jet for business purposes frees up time for the CEO to work or improves his or her ability to do business upon arrival, then the cost may be justifiable.

Ethics is a dynamic and individual concept strongly influenced by societal governance, laws, regulations, and codes of conduct, also known as codes of ethics. Ethical conduct is not a guaranteed formula for profits or sustainability; on the other hand, the lack of ethical behaviour, particularly in light of social scrutiny, is a recipe for failure.[2]

ethical behaviour

Personal behaviour in accordance with guidelines for good conduct or morality.

Ethical behaviour is personal behaviour in accordance with guidelines for good conduct or morality. Culture often establishes the limits on what are considered acceptable and unacceptable behaviours; it pressures individuals and groups into accepting and following certain behaviours. These limits are typically established to ensure uniform practice among members of a society. For example, in Spain it is acceptable or considered ethical behaviour for debt collectors to shame or embarrass debtors into paying their bills. In the United Kingdom, by contrast, publicly humiliating debtors is considered unprofessional and an unfair business practice. In Canada and the United States, it is illegal to harass debtors by publicizing their circumstances to friends and acquaintances.[3] As you can see, different cultures have different acceptable ethical behaviours.

Given that ethical behaviours vary, it is not uncommon for ethical dilemmas to occur. Ethical dilemmas are not legal questions. When a law exists to guide a manager toward a legally correct action, that path must be followed. In an ethical dilemma, there is no right or wrong decision. There are alternatives, however, that may be equally valid in ethical terms depending on one's perspective.

Ethical Dilemmas

Competition pressure, survival in the market, sky-scraping business goals, and pressure to meet unrealistic business deadlines influence the moral relationships between companies, clients, potential clients, and the communities where they have business operations. It is in this type of environment where ethical dilemmas emerge in business.

An **ethical dilemma** occurs when moral imperatives are in conflict. A moral or ethical dilemma may be understood as *"the process of moral judgment on appropriateness or inappropriateness of some action, activity, or decision of an institution and/or individual, with appreciation of basic moral standards and information about the facts concerning the actions which are the subject of discussion."*[4]

These conflicts are called ethical dilemmas because they are situations in which the individual may have two choices, neither of which resolves the situation in an ethically acceptable way, or situations in which any possible resolution is morally intolerable.

The process of resolving ethical dilemmas involves understanding the context in which the dilemma occurred. It is important for the individual making the decision to understand the facts, values, principles, and moral obligations with regards to the case. Usually ethical dilemmas involve a conflict between the individual's personal needs and the needs of others. There is no clear formula or model to resolve an ethical dilemma, but the following are some guidelines and questions to ask before making a decision.

- Is the proposed action legal?
- Is the decision a fair and balanced one? Consider this question not only in terms of the individual involved but also for all other stakeholders, both in the short and the long term.
- Does the situation justify the action?
- How will this decision make me feel about myself?
- How would I feel if my decision were to be published in the newspaper? Or if my family found out about it?

Below you will find examples of ethical dilemmas that business people may face when doing business abroad or when assigned to international operations. Try to use the guidelines presented above to decide what you would do in each situation.

- You are a Canadian citizen recently assigned to be the manager of distribution in a European country where bribery is widely practised. Your job description includes responsibility for accepting shipments as they enter the local port authority. On your first trip down to the docks to sign for a shipment, the customs agent in charge asks for a "tip" to clear the goods for pickup. The value of the incoming shipment is around $150 000. Knowing that the government has recently launched an initiative to reduce corruption, how do you react? If additional information would be helpful to you, what would it be?
- You are the CEO of a major Canadian apparel company that contracts work to garment manufacturers abroad. Employees of the contractors report 20-hour workdays, pay below the minimum wage, overcrowded living conditions, physically abusive supervisors, and confiscation of their passports. Contractors and government officials say local labour laws are adhered to and enforced. You send inspectors to the factories abroad, but they uncover no labour violations. A labour-advocacy group claims that supervisors coached workers to lie to your inspectors about conditions and threatened workers with time in makeshift jails without food if they talked. How do you handle this situation? Do you implement some type of monitoring system? Do you help the factories improve conditions, withdraw your business, or do nothing? How might your actions affect your relations with the factory owners and your ability to do business in the country?
- You are the vice president of international operations for a large pharmaceutical firm that manufactures an anti-malarial drug. Your firm is considering opening up a factory in a small Central American nation where malaria is common. The operation will be a cooperative venture between your firm and the local government. The majority of the people in that country cannot afford the medicine because of the high import tariffs. Yet, if your plan goes through, more than 200 jobs will be created and the drug's international price will drop by more than 50 percent. In a final meeting with a senior government official, the gentleman informs you that if you pay him $500 000 cash, the deal will go through. What issues must you consider? What do you do?
- You are the president of a firm that publishes textbooks for medical students in more than 30 languages. On a recent trip to a university in a developing country (with a GDP per capita of under $1000 per year), you discover that students are using bound photocopies of

ethical dilemma
Situation where moral imperatives are in conflict. There is no right or wrong decision.

your best-selling medical textbook. Speaking with several students, you find out that if the students were required to pay for the actual books, they could not afford medical school. Witnessing the clear copyright violation firsthand, how do you react? What possible courses of action might you take?

- You are the proprietor of a fledging computer graphics company in Shanghai, China. The sophisticated business application software you need for your business normally sells for 2900 renminbi (around $350) at computer stores in Shanghai. But with an income of just over $5000 a year, you cannot afford to buy the original graphics software for your business. A friend has told you she can get you all the software you need, and more, at a nearby street market for only $40. Because very few people buy official software, you know the authorities will not punish you if you are caught. Is it unethical for you to purchase the pirated software? Do you believe you are justified in doing so?

- You are the CEO of a major pharmaceutical firm that holds worldwide patents on several highly successful drugs. Your company invests heavily to develop its drugs because patents allow it to recoup its investment. But your firm has come under pressure from competitors selling cheaper alternatives and from politicians and nongovernmental groups to supply drugs to people in poor nations at reduced prices. Several senior executives in your company feel the firm is unfairly being asked to discount its drugs that treat diseases afflicting people of poor nations. Some executives suggest the firm should focus on drugs to treat diseases (such as heart disease and cancer) that occur mostly in wealthy nations, but you are uneasy with such a move. Would such a course of action be ethical? Diseases such as AIDS, cancer, and heart disease all kill their victims. Should drugs for only certain diseases be exempt from patent protection?

The best advice for companies wanting to reduce ethical dilemmas is to start by selecting and hiring ethical employees. To facilitate finding such candidates, the company can perform personality-based integrity tests in the recruitment phase and ask behavioural questions in the interview process. Companies should also establish codes of ethics, train their employees to make ethical decisions, and create an ethical climate. To establish an ethical climate, managers and business leaders must act ethically and persuade those under their supervision to behave in the same manner. The company also needs to actively promote its ethics programs, encourage employees to report ethics violations, and sanction the violators.

Ethical dilemmas can also arise if a company finds itself obliged to deal with organized crime, such as the Mafia. To read about a similar criminal organization operating in Japan, see this chapter's Global Challenges feature, titled "The Global Con."

Codes of Ethics

code of ethics
Set of guidelines established by an organization to help their employees or members behave in accordance with the organization's values and ethical standards.

Companies and professional organizations in Canada and around the world have been adopting codes of ethics for many years. A **code of ethics** is a set of guidelines established by an organization to help its employees or members behave in accordance with the organization's values and ethical standards. Increasingly, multinational corporations are following this practice and publishing codes of ethics. A corporate code of ethics defines the expected ethical behaviour for all members of the corporation.

For the most part, corporate codes of ethics are completely voluntary, meaning that their establishment, implementation, and enforcement depend on the firm's management team. These codes are normally written or developed by the board of directors, the CEO, top management, or, in smaller companies, by the owner(s).

What comprises a code of ethics? Companies usually include statements related to expected conduct and values that are considered acceptable, such as integrity, professionalism, and other such behaviours. They may also include statements prohibiting certain behaviours, such as illegal activities, bribery, theft, and the use of company property for personal reasons.

Codes of ethics can be as detailed as the company or organization wants them to be. Some codes are short one-page statements of principles, such as the code from the Canadian Bookkeepers Association (CBA) shown on page 123. Others may be longer documents or publications, such as *What We Stand For*, the code of business ethics and code of conduct published by Export Development Canada (EDC) (www.edc.ca). EDC's code explains all the policies and procedures that govern its employees' behaviour, defining exactly what

Global Challenges   The Global Con

Canadian exporters to Japan encounter various economic, political, and cultural challenges. But companies looking to enter the Japanese market should also be aware of the *yakuza* (the Japanese mafia) and come up with strategies to avoid stumbling into their sphere of influence.

- **What Is the *Yakuza*?** The Japanese *yakuza* is a large criminal network with a formidable influence due to its connections with businesses in Japan and around the world, as well as with high-ranking politicians. Claiming to be over 300 years old, the organization traces its origins to the *machi-yakko*, who protected their villages against roving bandits. The *yakuza* has a family-like hierarchical structure, based on an *oyabun–kobun* (father–son) relationship that demands absolute loyalty and obedience. Because many *yakuza* members come from poor, unstable backgrounds, membership in the organization is often looked upon as way to secure a better life.

- **What Are Some *Yakuza* Characteristics?** The *yakuza* see themselves as outsiders (*yakuza* literally represents the numbers adding up to a losing hand in a traditional card game) Tattoos are a common practice. They are usually elaborate, often covering the whole body with designs such as dragons, flowers, land- or seascapes, and gang insignia. The *yakuza* are also known for *yubizume*, the punishment dealt to members who disobey or displease their boss: amputation of parts of the fingers, a ritual dating back to the time of the samurai.

- **How Large Is the *Yakuza* and What Does It Do?** Japan has around 110 000 *yakuza* members, organized into about 2500 "families." The *yakuza* has strong, historical political ties to Japan's right-wing nationalists and supported the Japanese war effort during the Second World War. Its criminal activities include corporate extortion, gambling, smuggling, loan sharking, money laundering, drug dealing, stock manipulation, tourist scams, sex tours, prostitution, slavery, pornography, and gun running.

- **What Sectors of the Economy Are Affected by the *Yakuza*?** According to investigators, the *yakuza* operates in almost all sectors of the Japanese economy. The organization is deeply involved in the corporate world and is active in other areas such as construction, real estate, sports and entertainment, and transportation. It has been estimated that nearly 50 percent of companies in Japan have some relations with the *yakuza*, and some companies are fully controlled by the organization.

- **How Does the *Yakuza* Control Companies?** Corporate extortion is one of the *yakuza*'s most lucrative criminal operations. A small number of shares in the target company are bought up—just enough to ensure entry to shareholders' meetings. Then, armed with incriminating information about the company and its officials (such as illegal business practices, subpar standards in factories, damaging personal information, and so on), the *yakuza* pay a visit to management and demand payments on threat of public disclosure. If management refuses to pay, *yakuza* members known as *sokaiya* (meeting men) go to a shareholders' meeting and shout out their damaging secrets. Because embarrassment and shame are intolerable in Japanese culture, Japanese executives often succumb to the *yakuza*'s demands.

- **Does the *Yakuza* Operate Outside of Japan?** The *yakuza* have an international presence, and can be found in countries in Asia, Western Europe, North and South America, and the Mid-Pacific. The organization is especially prominent in areas where large ethnic Japanese populations are present, such as in Brazil, where *yakuza* members can be found in the capital São Paulo.

- **What Is Being Done to Combat the *Yakuza*?** In 2010 and 2011, laws were enacted in Osaka and Tokyo to try to combat *yakuza* influence by making it illegal for any company to do business with the *yakuza*. Some Japanese companies are offering jobs to *yakuza* members if they leave the organization, while communities are beginning to banish *yakuza* social clubs from their neighbourhoods. But the *yakuza* remains a formidable criminal organization not to be underestimated.

Sources: Anthony Bruno, "The Yakuza," *Crime Library*, www.trutv.com/library/crime/gangsters_outlaws/gang/yakuza/1.html; Victoria Chemko, "The Japanese Yakuza Influence on Japan's International Relations and Regional Politics," www.conflicts.rem33.com/images/yett_secu/yakuza_chemko.htm, 2002.

operating ethically means for this government agency. The code discusses legal and ethical business conduct, environmental and social risk management, prohibitions against bribery and corruption, respect for human rights, and anti–money laundering and anti-terrorist measures. It also provides guidance on how to avoid conflicts of interest and how to handle confidential information. Moreover, EDC's code explicitly states that employees who fail to comply with the code will be subject to disciplinary measures, including the possibility of termination of employment.[5]

Most large international corporations have codes of ethics in place. For example, Petro-Canada, now the Canadian retail brand for Suncor, has a code of conduct (sustainability.suncor .com) as detailed as Export Development Canada's code. Petro-Canada's code includes a message from the CEO, a statement of the company's principles and values, criteria for ethical decision making, and policies governing personal and business integrity, ethical conduct in the workplace, and ethical use of company property and information. To ensure that Petro-Canada employees read and understand the code of conduct, the company has an online training course that all employees are required to complete.[6]

A code of ethics is no guarantee that a corporation or its employees and stakeholders will behave ethically. However, it does provide guidelines for acceptable ethical conduct and may discourage unethical behaviour, especially if there is evidence that disciplinary measures will be enforced.

For a checklist on how to ensure ethical behaviour when operating internationally, see this chapter's Entrepreneur's Toolkit, titled "Tips for Combating Corruption in International Business."

Quick Study

1. Define *ethics* and *ethical behaviour*.
2. What are the benefits of having a code of ethics in place for companies operating in foreign markets?
3. Can a company guarantee that its employees or its stakeholders will act ethically by having a code of ethics in place? Why or why not?

Entrepreneur's Toolkit

Tips for Combating Corruption in International Business

- **Put the Right Policies and Practices in Place.** Companies with operations in several countries can prevent corruption by putting the right policies and practices in place. For instance, providing employees with a code of ethics and training on potential ethical issues is a good preventative move. Be clear on the consequences that employees will face if they behave unethically, and enforce the rules for backsliders.

- **Do an Audit.** An audit is necessary to monitor compliance, so make sure you set one up. For example, Export Development Canada (EDC) requires anti-corruption declarations from exporters who apply for accounts receivable insurance.

- **Perform Your Own Reference Checks.** If you are planning on hiring an agent abroad, you still need to perform your own reference checks, even if the

referral initially came from the Canadian Embassy or a business colleague. You also need to understand the agent's compensation—specifically, what he or she is permitted to use the money for.

- **Keep a Professional Distance.** Don't become excessively familiar with business contacts. Learn about their background; indicate that you don't have the authority on certain decisions; avoid private meetings outside business locations; and avoid offers to do you small favours.

- **Want to Know More?** To find out more about corruption, visit the Export Development Canada (EDC) Web site at www.edc.ca/EN/About-Us/Corporate-Social-Responsibility and click on "Business Ethics." You'll learn to recognize red flags that warn you to be vigilant, and you can take a quiz on safeguarding your company from corruption.

Source: "Combating Corruption in International Business," *Export Wise,* Fall 2012, pp. 26–27.

Code of Professional Standards

A member shall practice public relations according to the highest professional standards.
Members shall conduct their professional lives in a manner that does not conflict with the public interest and the dignity of the individual, with respect for the rights of the public as contained in the Constitution of Canada and the Charter of Rights and Freedoms.

A member shall deal fairly and honestly with the communications media and the public.
Members shall neither propose nor act to improperly influence the communications media, government bodies or the legislative process. Improper influence may include conferring gifts, privileges or benefits to influence decisions.

A member shall practice the highest standards of honesty, accuracy, integrity and truth, and shall not knowingly disseminate false or misleading information.
Members shall not make extravagant claims or unfair comparisons, nor assume credit for ideas and words not their own.
Members shall not engage in professional or personal conduct that will bring discredit to themselves, the Society or the practice of public relations.

A member shall deal fairly with past or present employers/clients, fellow practitioners and members of other professions.
Members shall not intentionally damage another practitioner's practice or professional reputation. Members shall understand, respect and abide by the ethical codes of other professions with whose members they may work from time to time.

Members shall be prepared to disclose the names of their employers or clients for whom public communications are made and refrain from associating themselves with anyone who would not respect such policy.
Members shall be prepared to disclose publicly the names of their employers or clients on whose behalf public communications is made. Members shall not associate themselves with anyone claiming to represent one interest, or professing to be independent or unbiased, but who actually serves another or an undisclosed interest.

A member shall protect the confidences of present, former and prospective employers/ clients.
Members shall not use or disclose confidential information obtained from past or present employers/ clients without the expressed permission of the employers/clients or an order of a court of law.

A member shall not represent conflicting or competing interests without the expressed consent of those concerned, given after a full disclosure of the facts.
Members shall not permit personal or other professional interests to conflict with those of an employer/client without fully disclosing such interests to everyone involved.

A member shall not guarantee specified results beyond the member's capacity to achieve.

Members shall personally accept no fees, commissions, gifts or any other considerations for professional services from anyone except employers or clients for whom the services were specifically performed.

Source: Canadian Public Relations Society.

Philosophies of Ethics

There are four commonly cited philosophies of business ethics: the Friedman view, the cultural relativist view, the righteous moralist view, and the utilitarian view.

The *Friedman view*—named for its main supporter, the late economist Milton Friedman— says that a company's sole responsibility is to maximize profits for its owners (or shareholders) while operating within the law.[7] Imagine a company that moves its pollution-generating operations from a country having strict and expensive environmental protection laws to a country having no such laws. Managers subscribing to the Friedman philosophy would applaud this decision. They would argue that the company is doing its duty to increase profits for owners and, moreover, is operating within the law in the foreign country. Many people disagree with this argument and say the discussion is not *whether* a company has corporate social responsibility obligations but *how* it will fulfill them.

A company following Friedman's philosophy might also decide to move its operations to a developing nation to reduce labour costs by paying the minimum wage stipulated in the host-country law and not a loonie more. That company will most likely ask its employees to work the maximum number of hours per week stipulated in the host-country labour law, which in many cases is higher than the maximum allowed in North America or in some northern European nations. For instance, a French company using this approach would justify moving its manufacturing operations to Mexico, where the minimum wages are significantly lower than in France and the number of hours of work per week permitted are much higher than the 35 maximum allowed under French law.

The *cultural relativist view* says that a company should adopt local ethics wherever it operates because all belief systems are determined within a cultural context. Cultural relativism sees truth, itself, as relative and argues that right and wrong are determined within a specific situation. The expression "When in Rome, do as the Romans do" captures the essence of cultural relativism. Consider a company that opens a factory in a developing market and, following local customs, employs child labourers. The cultural relativist manager would argue that the company is acting appropriately and in accordance with local standards of conduct. Many people find this line of ethical reasoning appalling.

Consider another example: A company opens a factory in a developing country known to have high levels of corruption and bribery, and its managers and employees pay large amounts of money in "tips," otherwise called bribes, to gain government contracts. The cultural relativist would approve because "everyone does it." Or think about a company that pays an organization such as the Mafia in order to operate in the country without issues.

The *righteous moralist view* says that a company should maintain its home-country ethics wherever it operates because the home-country's view of ethics and responsibility is superior to others' views. Imagine a company that expands from its developed-country base to an emerging market where local managers commonly bribe officials. Suppose headquarters detests the act of bribery and instructs its subsidiary managers to refrain from bribing any local officials. In this situation, headquarters is imposing its righteous moralist view on local managers.

Now consider the righteous moralist view from another angle. A company opens a manufacturing facility in an emerging market and decides to implement its home-country corporate social responsibility initiatives. It donates to local charities and works to improve the local community by building schools or hospitals, even though these types of initiatives are not common practice among its competitors operating in the same emerging market.

The *utilitarian view* says that a company should behave in a way that maximizes "good" outcomes and minimizes "bad" outcomes wherever it operates. The utilitarian manager asks the question, "What outcome should I aim for?" and answers, "That which produces the best outcome for all affected parties." In other words, utilitarian thinkers say the right behaviour is that which produces the greatest good for the greatest number. Consider, again, the righteous moralist company above that instructs its employees not to bribe local officials in the emerging market. Now suppose a manager learns that by bribing a local official, the company will finally obtain permission to expand its factory and create 100 well-paying jobs for the local community. If the manager pays the bribe based on her calculations that more people will benefit than will be harmed by the outcome, she is practicing utilitarian ethics.

Although businesses develop guidelines and policies regarding ethical behaviour and social responsibility, issues arise on a daily basis that can cause dilemmas for international managers.

Quick Study

1. What are the four commonly cited philosophies of business ethics?
2. You are the manager of an oil and gas company that is considering drilling in a wildlife preserve abroad. You decide to go ahead with the project because the economic benefits of job creation outweigh the costs of environmental degradation. Which philosophy are you using to justify your decision?
3. Your manager or supervisor tells you to "do whatever it takes to meet the goals as long as it's legal." What ethical approach do you think he or she favours?

Corporate Social Responsibility and CSR Issues

In addition to the need for individual managers to behave ethically, businesses are expected to exercise **corporate social responsibility (CSR)**—the practice of companies going beyond legal obligations to actively balance commitments to investors, customers, other companies, and communities. Corporate social responsibility includes a wide variety of activities, including giving to the poor, building schools in developing countries, and protecting the global environment.

We can think of CSR as consisting of three layers of activity. The first layer is *traditional philanthropy*, whereby a corporation donates money and, perhaps, employee time toward a specific social cause. The second layer is related to *risk management*, whereby a company develops a code of conduct that it will follow in its global operations and agrees to operate with greater transparency. The third layer is *strategic CSR*, in which a business builds social responsibility into its core operations to create value and build competitive advantage.[8]

Companies should not produce public relations campaigns that present a business as socially responsible if it does not truly embrace CSR principles. Conscientious business leaders realize that the future of their companies rests on healthy workforces and environments worldwide. For example, soft-drink makers support all sorts of environmental initiatives because they understand their futures depend on an ample supply of clean drinking water. Let's now discuss CSR as it pertains to bribery and corruption, labour conditions and human rights, fair trade practices, and sustainability.

Bribery and Corruption

Similar to other cultural and political elements, the prevalence of corruption varies from nation to nation. In certain countries, bribes are routinely paid to distributors and retailers to push a firm's products through distribution channels. Bribes can mean the difference between obtaining an important contract and being completely shut out of a market. But corruption is detrimental to society and business. Among other things, corruption can send resources toward inefficient uses, hurt economic development, distort public policy, and damage national integrity.

Map 4.1 shows how countries rate on their perceived levels of corruption. The higher a country's score on the Corruption Perceptions Index (CPI), the less corrupt it is perceived to be by international managers. What stands out immediately on this map is that the least developed nations tend to be perceived as being most corrupt (such as Haiti, much of Africa, North Korea, Venezuela, Russia, and areas in the Middle East). This reflects the hesitancy on the part of international companies about investing in corrupt economies. Among the countries perceived as having the least corruption are Denmark, Finland, New Zealand, Sweden, Singapore, Switzerland, Australia, Norway, Canada, and The Netherlands. All these countries are considered developed nations or advanced economies.

Enron Corporation made history when it acknowledged in a US federal filing that it had overstated its earnings. Investors fled in droves as Enron stock became worthless and the company went bankrupt. Although executives had earned millions over the years in salaries and bonuses, Enron's rank-and-file employees saw their retirement savings disappear as the firm disintegrated. European banks lost around $2 billion that they had lent to Enron and its subsidiaries. Chairman of the Board Kenneth Lay (now deceased) and Chief Executive Officer Jeffrey Skilling were convicted on criminal charges. Then a criminal indictment was filed against accounting firm Arthur Andersen, Enron's auditor, for shredding documents related to its work for Enron. With its reputation irreparably damaged, Andersen also collapsed.

The financial losses and diminished confidence in business that resulted from Enron's collapse prompted the US Congress to pass the *Sarbanes-Oxley Act* (Sarbox) on corporate governance. The law established new, stringent accounting standards and reporting practices for US firms. Around the world, governments, accounting standards boards, other regulators, and interest groups also won the fight for higher standards and more transparent financial reporting by companies. Businesses worldwide received the message that fudging the accounting numbers, misrepresenting the firm's financial health, and running a company in that grey area between right and wrong is unethical and, now, increasingly, illegal.

Some people have since complained about the financial burden that companies face in conforming to the requirements of these laws. Regulators, securities experts, and scholars find themselves pitted against chief financial officers—many of whom say that regulatory laws should be

corporate social responsibility (CSR)

Practice of companies going beyond legal obligations to actively balance commitments to investors, customers, other companies, and communities.

MAP 4.1

Corruption
Perceptions Index

Source: Based on data from
Transparency International (http://
www.transparency.org/cpi2012/results)

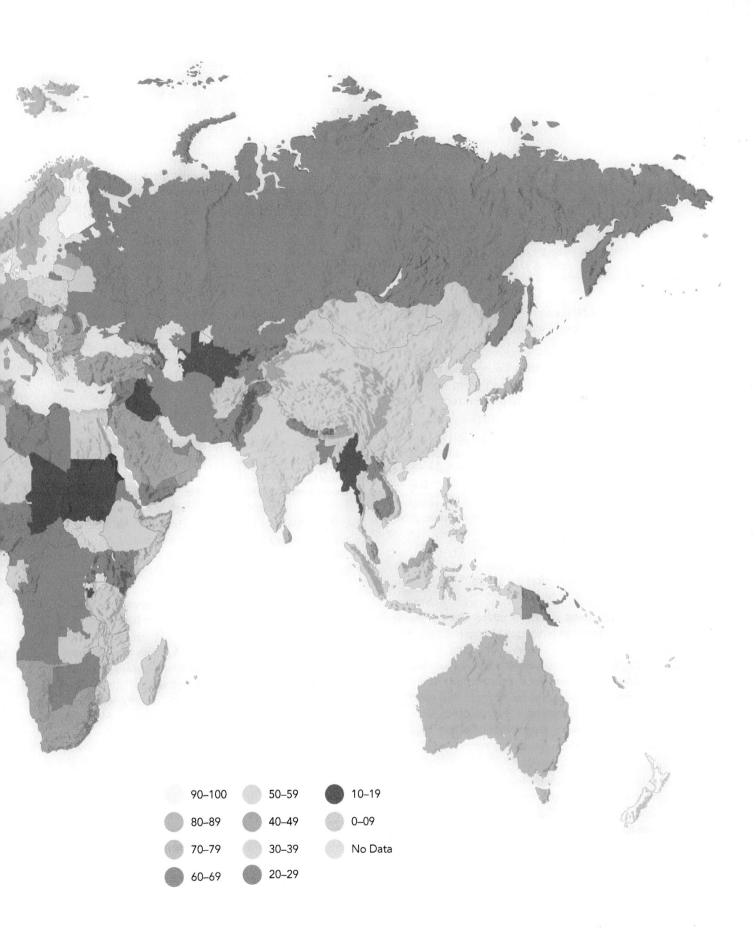

90–100	50–59	10–19	
80–89	40–49	0–09	
70–79	30–39	No Data	
60–69	20–29		

reformed or repealed because the costs outweigh the benefits. But legislators are not backing down. Suddenly, directors on the boards of companies no longer just rubber stamp strategies and policies, but are required to take a far more active part in company operations, to the point where, as one expert on corporate governance quipped, being a director is "a job now."[9]

For further information on bribery and corruption, see this chapter's Global Manager's Briefcase, titled "Who Is Bribing Whom?"

Labour Conditions and Human Rights

To fulfill their responsibilities to society, companies are monitoring the actions of their own employees and the employees of companies with whom they conduct business. Pressure from human rights activists drove conscientious apparel companies to introduce codes of conduct and

---

Global Manager's Briefcase   Who Is Bribing Whom?

It is well known that business in a majority of countries in the world is conducted through "mordida," "payola," or "bribes."

- **Evidence Shows That Bribes Are on the Rise.** According to a 2010 Ernst & Young report, the cost of bribes has increased from 5 percent of a contract's value in the 1980s to about 20 percent today.

- **Well-Known Multinational Corporations Have Been Accused of Bribery.** In April 2012, *The New York Times* reported that Walmart had paid over US$24 million in bribes in an attempt to gain market dominance in Mexico. As a result, Walmart shares fell by almost 5 percent. In February 2013, Giuseppe Orsi, CEO of Italian aerospace and defence group Finmeccanica SpA, was arrested for allegedly paying €51 million in bribes to help his company sell 12 military helicopters to India. Finmeccanica shares fell 7 percent immediately after the arrest.

- **Canadian Businesses Are Not Exempt.** Although Canada is perceived as a highly ethical country, managers of some Canadian businesses have tried to eliminate political risk by using bribery. For example, Quebec engineering and construction firm SNC-Lavalin fired its Tunisian-born head of global construction, Riadh Ben Aïssa, over allegations that he had paid $56 million in bribes to secure contracts in North Africa. Some of these payments were apparently authorized by CEO Pierre Duhaime, who subsequently resigned.

- **Internal Company Investigations Won't Solve the Problem.** Although internal Walmart investigators found evidence of widespread bribery in its Mexican subsidiary, the company's top executives chose to shut down the investigation. They focused on damage control rather than on eliminating corruption—even promoting one of the main managers involved to a high position in the company—until the story was made public in the press. In the SNC-Lavalin case, the company launched an internal investigation and fired several "rogue" employees, but was careful to deflect blame away from the company itself. However, an April 2012 RCMP raid of SNC's offices in Montreal suggested that charges were possible.

- **Countries Need to Enforce and Upgrade Anti-Bribery Laws.** According to a *Globe and Mail* report, "the companies snared by authorities are only a tiny fraction of the global bribery bonanza." Most of the 33 Organisation of Economic Co-operation and Development (OECD) member countries have made no bribery prosecutions. Although the Canadian anti-bribery law, the *Corruption of Foreign Public Officials Act*, came into effect in 1999 and was amended in June 2013, enforcement has been limited. To date, only three convictions have been registered. The first, in 2005, was minor and resulted in a $25 000 fine (less than the bribe involved) for a small Alberta pipeline maintenance company that pleaded guilty to bribing a US border official. The second, in 2011, fined oil and gas exploration company Niko Resources Ltd. $9.5 million for bribing an official in Bangladesh. The third (the first case to go to trial and the first individual prosecuted) convicted Nazir Karigar, agent for Ottawa-based security company Cryptometrics Canada, of offering bribes to Air India officials in an attempt to win a security technology contract with the airline.

- **Bribes Do Major Damage to Countries with Emerging Economies by Acting as a Barrier to Entry.** A UK study of 98 companies operating in Brazil concluded that corruption interfered with a company's entry into a new market more than any other factors. If companies are to succeed overseas, anti-bribery laws must be enforced. Bribery is difficult to eradicate, but all countries and companies should work toward that goal.

Source: Eric Reguly, "Don't be naive, Bribery is everywhere", *The Globe and Mail*, May 24, 2012.

monitoring mechanisms for their international suppliers. Levi-Strauss (www.levistrauss.com) pioneered the use of practical codes to control working conditions at contractors' facilities. The company does business only with partners who meet its "Terms of Engagement," which sets minimal guidelines regarding ethical behaviour, environmental and legal requirements, employment standards, and community involvement.[10]

Consider one case publicized by human rights and labour groups investigating charges of worker abuse at the factory of one of Nike's Vietnamese suppliers. Twelve of 56 female employees reportedly fainted when a supervisor forced them to run around the factory as punishment for not wearing regulation shoes. Nike confirmed the report and, in suspending the supervisor, took steps to implement practices more in keeping with the company's home-country ethics.

International law says that only nations can be held liable for human rights abuses. But activist groups can file a lawsuit against a business for an alleged human rights violation. In the United States, this can be done under the Alien Tort Claims Act by alleging a company's complicity in the abuse. Yahoo! (www.yahoo.com) felt the power of this law when two Chinese dissidents were jailed after the company gave data it had on them to Chinese authorities. Yahoo!

Source: Megapress/Alamy.

reached an out-of-court settlement with the families of the jailed men. And despite denials of any responsibility in the matter, US oil company Unocal, now part of Chevron (www.chevron.com), settled out of court over allegations of complicity in government soldiers' abuse of villagers during construction of an oil pipeline in Myanmar in the 1990s.

In 2013, Canada's Joe Fresh (the clothing brand owned by Loblaw) got caught in the spotlight over a human rights issue when the building housing its Bangladesh manufacturing operation collapsed. The incident is considered the deadliest for Bangladesh's clothing industry. Joe Fresh vowed to help improve working conditions in Bangladesh and promised to work with its vendors to improve the health and safety standards by making sure its products are produced in a socially responsible manner.[11]

Fair Trade Practices

fair trade

A trading partnership, based on dialogue, transparency, and respect, that seeks greater equity in international trade and contributes to sustainable development by offering better trading conditions to, and securing the rights of, marginalized producers and workers.

According to the World Fair Trade Organization (www.wfto.com), "**fair trade** is a trading partnership, based on dialogue, transparency, and respect, that seeks greater equity in international trade. It contributes to sustainable development by offering better trading conditions to, and securing the rights of, marginalized producers and workers."[12]

Second Cup (www.mysecondcup.com), headquartered in Mississauga, Ontario, with over 430 cafés in 18 countries, works hard to operate in a socially responsible manner by incorporating fair trade into its business practices.[13] The specialty coffee and café franchisor is a leader in the ethical sourcing of its supplies. Its coffees are primarily sourced from the Rainforest Alliance (www.rainforest-alliance.org), an international nonprofit organization that works to conserve biodiversity and promote the rights and well-being of workers, their families, and communities. Farm workers on Rainforest Alliance certified farms benefit from safe working conditions, enjoy dignified housing and medical care, and have access to schools for their children.[14]

Sustainability

sustainability (sustainable development)

Development that meets the needs of the present without compromising the economy or the social and natural environments for future generations.

Concern for the environment and ecosystems is no longer left to government agencies and non-governmental organizations. Today companies pursue "green" initiatives to reduce their toll on the environment *and* to reduce operating costs and boost profit margins. A 1987 report published by the World Commission on Environment and Development (WCED), titled *Our Common Future* (also known as the Brundtland report), defined and popularized the term "sustainable development" or sustainability as "development that meets the needs of the present without compromising the ability of future generations to meet their own needs."[15]

Sustainability (sustainable development) is comprised of three main pillars: economic development, social equity, and environmental protection. Economic sustainability refers not only to corporate financial success, but also to the ability of nonprofit organizations to attain funding and cover costs on an ongoing basis. Social sustainability encompasses the humanitarian side of societies, including medical and educational access, and also the broader issues created by poverty. Environment sustainability focuses on the impact of organizations on the quality and quantity of natural resources.[16]

During the past 20 years, corporations have adopted sustainability practices to demonstrate their commitment to the environment. Take Loblaw Companies Limited (Loblaw), for example. Loblaw (www.loblaw.ca), Canada's largest food (and now drugstore) retailer, employs more than 134 000 full-time and part-time employees; it is one of Canada's largest private-sector employers, and a significant importer of international products and food. Loblaw has adopted numerous environmental initiatives, including the commitment to source 100 percent of the seafood sold in its stores from sustainable sources. As Canada's largest purchaser of seafood, Loblaw collaborates with the World Wildlife Fund (WWF), the Marine Stewardship Council (MSC), and government agencies. Sustainable seafood purchasing practices imply that the seafood caught or farmed will be maintained at healthy population levels, without harming international ecosystems.

Loblaw has received recognition from environment groups for its efforts. Gerald Butts, president and CEO of the WWF Canadian division, stated, "Loblaw has developed the most aggressive sustainable seafood commitment in the world. Through its collaboration within the supply chain, investment in education, and stakeholder and government engagement, Loblaw is driving large-scale transformational change."[17]

CARBON FOOTPRINT   **Carbon footprint** is the environmental impact of greenhouse gases (measured in units of carbon dioxide) that results from human activity. It consists of two components:

- *Primary Footprint.* Direct carbon dioxide emissions from the burning of fossil fuels, including domestic energy consumption and transportation (such as electricity and gasoline).
- *Secondary Footprint.* Indirect carbon dioxide emissions from the whole life cycle of products (from their manufacture to eventual breakdown).[18]

Four Seasons Hotels and Resorts (www.fourseasons.com) is a trendsetter in reducing its carbon footprint as well as in other sustainability practices. Founded in 1961 and based in Canada, the luxury chain is actively engaged in sustainable practices that conserve natural resources and reduce environmental impact in its 85 properties located worldwide. Examples of its green strategies include paperless planning, opportunities to donate used decorations and display materials, local printing services to lower transportation impact, local and seasonal menus, reuse of guest room linens, on-site recycling, and composting.

In 2011 Four Seasons launched its 10 Million Trees program, committing the company to plant 10 million trees around the world. Already Four Seasons' 35 000 employees worldwide are hard at work to meet this goal. Trees play a vital role in the overall health of the planet, with deforestation causing an increase in the amount of carbon dioxide released into the

carbon footprint

The environmental impact of greenhouse gases (measured in units of carbon dioxide) that results from human activity.

A man uses an electric cable to plug in a hybrid Toyota Prius at a charging station in Strasbourg, France. Many people believe that globalization and economic development take a toll on the environment. Companies are working to create all sorts of "green" products to reduce the impact of modern economies on our ecosystem. Besides car manufacturers, can you think of other types of companies that are working to become more environmentally responsible?

Source: Rolf Haid/dpa/picture-alliance/ Newscom.

atmosphere. Carbon dioxide emissions are linked to many environmental problems, from global warming to severe changes in rainfall patterns and water levels. Planting trees will help offset these emissions, because trees store large amounts of carbon dioxide. According to Trees Ontario (www.treesontario.ca), an acre of trees can absorb 2.6 tonnes of carbon dioxide in one year—the same amount a car produces driving about 42 000 kilometres. Through 10 Million Trees, Four Seasons "hopes to raise awareness, education, conservation, and preservation efforts for trees."[19]

Companies at the leading edge of the green movement are printing a number on their products that represents the grams of carbon dioxide emitted from producing and shipping them to retailers. The number signifies the environmental impact of all the materials, chemicals, and so on, used in producing and distributing a good. For example, the United Kingdom's number-one selling snack food brand, Walker (www.walkers.co.uk), stamps "75g" on its packets of cheese- and onion-flavoured potato chips, or *crisps*—meaning 75 grams of carbon dioxide were emitted in producing and shipping each packet. Footwear and clothing maker Timberland (www.timberland.com) is implementing a different system. It labels its products with a score ranging from 0 to 10. A score of "0" means producing and shipping a product emitted less than 2.5 kilograms of carbon dioxide; a product with a score of "10" emitted 100 kilograms of carbon dioxide—roughly equivalent to driving a car 380 kilometres.[20]

Another trendsetter in reducing its carbon footprint is Marriott International (www.marriott.com). The hotel company's employee cafeteria replaced paper and plastic containers with real plates and biodegradable potato-based containers called Spudware. Marriott gave employees reusable plastic water bottles and let them exchange burnt-out regular bulbs, from work or home, for energy-saving compact fluorescent bulbs. The company also has green ambassadors who remind employees to print documents double-sided and to turn off lights and electronic devices not in use.[21]

Boisset Family Estates (www.boisset.com), France's third-largest winery, initiated an eco-smart alternative to the glass bottle. Boisset uses aluminum-coated paperboard similar to containers commonly used for juices and milk. Besides protecting the product from oxidation and making it easier to chill, the new packaging helps the environment and improves company profits. It used to take 28 trucks to haul enough empty glass bottles to the winery to package the same volume of wine that today takes just one truck of empty cartons. After the cartons are filled, one truck now hauls away what used to take three trucks. The savings in materials, fuel, and equipment are significant.[22]

Employees of Four Seasons in Nevis planting trees as part of the company's 10 Million Trees program.

Source: Tara MacIntyre/Four Seasons Resort Nevis.

On a national level, the German government has gone greener than most others. Germany's energy law guarantees operators of windmills and solar generators prices that are above the market rate for as long as 20 years. That law, combined with German expertise in aerodynamics, is making the country a global leader in renewable energy. Today 60 companies in Germany specialize in wind systems. Former East Germany is nicknamed Solar Valley because of the large number of companies that manufacture solar cells there. Germany's green-energy sector employs more than 235 000 people and generates $33 billion in sales annually.[23]

Quick Study

1. What is *corporate social responsibility*?
2. What is the *Corruption Perception Index*?
3. What is *sustainability*? Name three companies applying sustainable practices.

The Principles of Responsible Investment

The psychological foundation of ethical responsibility is the feeling of responsibility. Previously in the chapter, we defined corporate social responsibility (CSR) and discussed examples of companies applying this concept in different ways.

Many companies that establish CSR programs do so voluntarily or because they have been pressured to do so by nongovernmental organizations (NGOs), the local community where they operate, or their consumers.

The **Principles of Responsible Investment (PRI)**, a set of socially responsible investment principles created in 2006, is another instrument to encourage companies to behave ethically. The main objectives of the PRI are to protect the world's assets by applying social responsibility to investments and to assist investors to achieve better long-term investments and create sustainable markets.

The PRI were developed between April 2005 and January 2006 through a UN-instigated process in which representatives of large investment firms from more than 12 countries, as well as

Principles of Responsible Investment (PRI)
Principles created to protect the world's assets by applying social responsibility to investments.

experts from the investment industry, NGOs, government agencies, academics, and individuals from civil society participated. The PRI were launched by former UN Secretary-General Kofi Annan at the New York Stock Exchange in April 2006.[24]

The PRI Initiative, a UN-supported international body of investors who are signatories to the principles, "aims to help investors integrate the consideration of environmental, social, and governance (ESG) issues into investment decision making and ownership practices across all asset classes and regions, and in so doing, help contribute to the creation of a sustainable financial system."[25]

There are six principles, each defining specific actions. They were designed to be applied by all investors, with a special focus on fiduciary institutions with long-term perspectives. The six principles are as follows:

> **Principle 1:** We will incorporate ESG issues into investment analysis and decision-making processes.
> **Principle 2:** We will be active owners and incorporate ESG issues into our ownership policies and practices.
> **Principle 3:** We will seek appropriate disclosure on ESG issues by the entities in which we invest.
> **Principle 4:** We will promote acceptance and implementation of the Principles within the investment industry.
> **Principle 5:** We will work together to enhance our effectiveness in implementing the Principles.
> **Principle 6:** We will each report on our activities and progress towards implementing the Principles.[26]

What are the benefits for the signatories? First, implementing the principles should ultimately result in increased returns and lower risk. Why? Because by applying the principles, investors will have a more complete understanding of a range of material issues. A second benefit is "being part of a global network, with opportunities to pool resources and influence to engage with companies on ESG issues, lowering costs for signatories to undertake stewardship activities."[27] Finally, signatories may improve their reputation or public image, as they will be seen as socially responsible companies.

Unveiling of the PRI at the New York Stock Exchange in 2006, attended by founding PRI signatories and former UN secretary-general Kofi Annan.

Source: UNPRI.

Signatories commit to completing the annual reporting framework. The process is mandatory, because it helps signatories and the PRI Initiative to evaluate progress in implementing the six principles. However, there are no legal or regulatory sanctions associated with the principles. Compliance is voluntary and aspirational. But a company that does not comply may be publicly delisted from the PRI Initiative, which could affect the company's reputation. In other words, noncompliance can have reputational risks.

Quick Study

1. What is the main objective of the Principles of Responsible Investment (PRI)?
2. What are the benefits for the signatories?
3. What are the sanctions for not complying with the PRI?

Bottom Line for Business

This completes our chapter coverage of international ethics. We have seen that ethical behaviour varies among cultures, that there are different philosophies of ethics companies can adopt to implement their business objectives, and that ethical issues are becoming increasingly important for any company wanting to operate or invest internationally.

What Ethics Philosophy Should a Company Use?

Canadian companies operating abroad need to be aware of the ethics philosophy normally applied in the country where they want to conduct business. However, a company should not blindly follow the behaviour of other companies in that country without understanding the consequences. Specifically, Canadian companies need to be cautious about applying cultural relativism. For example, a company could decide to pay bribes to secure building permits in a country such as Mexico because their business people see that bribery is a common practice in that country. However, if a business person from a Canadian company is caught bribing a public official abroad, he or she can be prosecuted in Canada. Bribery is a criminal offence in Canada, and Canadians (and Canadian companies) are subject to Canadian law.

Implications of Ethical Issues for Companies

Probably every international company of at least moderate size has a policy for corporate social responsibility (CSR). Traditionally, companies practised CSR through old-fashioned philanthropy. Indeed, donating money and time toward solving social problems helped society and bolstered a company's public image. Companies later developed codes of conduct for their global operations to ensure they were good citizens wherever they operated. Today companies search for ways to use CSR to create value and build competitive advantage. Key CSR issues include labour conditions, human rights, bribery, corruption, fair trade practices, and the environment.

Bribery and corruption are major issues for businesses in the international arena. According to the Corruption Perception Index, Canada is perceived as one of the least corrupt countries in the world. Canadian businesses planning to invest or establish operations abroad will most likely have to deal with higher levels of corruption almost anywhere they decide to go. These companies need to train their managers and employees in ethical decision making to prepare them for the ethical dilemmas they will face in new circumstances. Companies should also reward their personnel for moral courage.

Implications of the Principles of Responsible Investment for Companies

The Principles of Responsible Investment (PRI) have been in operation for seven years. There are currently over 1200 signatories from 50 countries, with total assets under management in excess of $32 trillion. What are the implications for international businesses? If a company is looking for an investor to expand its operations globally, investors will increasing require the company to disclose its commitment to environmental, social, and governance (ESG) issues. The company's level of commitment will most likely affect the decision to provide funding or not. In addition, failure to take environmental and social risks into consideration can lead to a long-term loss for the company, not only to its reputation but also to its value. Some PRI signatories have already disinvested from companies that have practices inconsistent with the PRI. Arms manufacturing companies are one example of the type of companies affected.

In Canada, PRI signatories include the British Columbia Municipal Pension Plan, the Canada Pension Plan Investment Board, the Ontario Teachers' Pension Plan, and the Native Benefits Plan, to name a few.

Chapter Summary

1. Explain ethics, ethical behaviour, ethical dilemmas, and codes of ethics.
   - *Ethics* is the moral obligation to separate right from wrong.
   - *Ethical behaviour* is personal behaviour in accordance with guidelines for good conduct or morality.
   - *Ethical dilemmas* are situations where moral imperatives are in conflict; there is no right or wrong decision.
   - The best advice for companies wanting to reduce ethical dilemmas is to start by selecting and hiring ethical employees. Companies should also establish codes of ethics, train their employees to make ethical decisions, and create an ethical climate.
   - A *code of ethics* is a set of guidelines established by an organization to help their employees or members behave in accordance with the organization's values and ethical standards.
   - Companies include statements related to expected behaviour and values that are considered acceptable in their codes of ethics. Including statements prohibiting certain behaviours is recommended.

2. Understand the different philosophies of ethics and how international business managers apply them to their decision-making processes.
   - The *Friedman view* says that a company's sole responsibility is to maximize profits for its owners while operating within the law.
   - The *cultural relativist view* says that a company should adopt local ethics wherever it operates.
   - The *righteous moralist view* says that a company should maintain its home-country ethics wherever it operates.
   - The *utilitarian view* says that a company should behave in a way that maximizes "good" outcomes and minimizes "bad" outcomes wherever it operates.

3. Explain corporate social responsibility, understand the concept of sustainability and sustainable practices, and provide examples of international businesses that apply these concepts.
   - *Corporate social responsibility* is the practice of companies going beyond legal obligations to actively balance commitments to investors, customers, other companies, and communities.
   - Most companies focus their corporate social responsibilities in the areas of bribery and corruption, labour conditions and human rights, fair trade practices, and sustainability.
   - The Corruption Perceptions Index (CPI) rates countries on their perceived level of corruption.
   - Some of the most corrupt countries and regions of the world are Haiti, much of Africa, North Korea, Venezuela, Russia, and areas in the Middle East.
   - Among the countries perceived as having the least corruption are Denmark, Finland, New Zealand, Sweden, Singapore, Switzerland, Australia, Norway, Canada and The Netherlands.
   - Bribes do major damage to emerging countries by acting as a barrier to entry.
   - International law says that only nations can be held liable for human rights abuses.
   - *Fair trade* is a trading partnership, based on dialogue, transparency and respect, that seeks greater equity in international trade. It contributes to sustainable development by offering better trading conditions to, and securing the rights of, marginalized producers and workers.
   - *Sustainability* initiatives are business practices which meet the needs of the present without compromising the economy, society, or environment for future generations.
   - *Carbon footprint* is the environmental impact of greenhouse gases (measured in units of carbon dioxide) that results from human activity.

4. Understand the principles of responsible investment.
   - The *Principles of Responsible Investment (PRI)* are principles created to protect the world's assets by applying social responsibility to investments.
   - The PRI were launched by former UN Secretary-General Kofi Annan at the New York Stock Exchange in April 2006.

- There are six principles each defining specific actions.
- Implementing the principles should ultimately result in increased returns and lower risk.
- There are no legal or regulatory sanctions associated with the principles. Compliance is voluntary and aspirational.

Key Terms

carbon footprint   131
code of ethics   120
corporate social responsibility
  (CSR)   125

ethics   118
ethical behaviour   118
ethical dilemma   119
fair trade   129

Principles of Responsible Investment
  (PRI)   133
sustainability (sustainable
  development)   129

Talk It Over

1. Two owners of small businesses are discussing the various reasons why they don't apply corporate social responsibility to their business practices. "It's too expensive to implement;" "The costs outweigh the benefits;" "It's not required by law." What counterarguments can you present to these business owners' perceptions?
2. Consider the following statement: "Developed countries provide international business with more secure environments in which to operate." Do you agree? Why or why not? Support your argument with specific country examples. Hint: This topic relates to corruption and the Corruption Perception Index (CPI).
3. "A company's sole responsibility is to maximize profits for its owners while operating within the law." Do you agree with this statement? Why or why not? Hold a debate in class on the benefits and drawbacks of applying this philosophy. Opposing arguments should focus on CSR and sustainability.

Take It to the Web

1. **Video Report.** Visit the Web site for Transparency International (www.transparency.org). Click on "What We Do" on the menu bar and choose "Research"; then click on "Corruption Perceptions Index." Watch the video and summarize it in a half-page report. Think about what you have learned in this chapter. Which concepts in the chapter can you identify in the video? How might a company engaged in international business act on the information contained in the video?
2. **Web Site Report.** In this chapter, we've seen how corporate social responsibility and sustainability are changing business and society. Select a Canadian company that interests you and visit its Web site. Research the company's involvement in corporate social responsibility and sustainability initiatives. Does the company have a code of ethics? Is it a signatory to the Principles of Responsible Investment? Write a summary of your findings and include key Web sites that you found helpful. Do you think the company is doing enough in terms of CSR and sustainability? If you were hired as a consultant, what advice would you give to the company's managers about these issues?

Digging Deep for CSR

Mining is an important sector in Canada's resource-based economy, and Canada is the world's largest exporter of metals and minerals, exporting to over 100 countries globally. The Canadian mining sector also has over $129 billion worth of investments abroad.

Like other sectors, the mining industry is concerned with sustainable development, in particular environmental and health and safety issues. Although the Canadian government participates in various bilateral and regional initiatives and is committed to "promote the sustainable development of minerals and metals," Canadian mining companies have been involved in international controversies.

Still a benchmark for severity, the mining disaster created in 1996 by Canadian company Marcopper Mining Corporation was one of the worst ever seen in the Philippines—where Canada is the second biggest investor in mines (behind Australia). The Canadian-owned mine leaked toxic mine waste into Marinduque province's Boac River, still contaminated today.

Publicly listed Canadian mining company TVI Pacific Inc. is working to change this negative reputation through its Philippine affiliate, TVI Resource Development Philippines Inc. (TVIRD). TVIRD is a Filipino corporation with projects on Mindanao and Panay islands. Its first operation, located in Canatuan, Siocon, Zamboanga del Norte, began mining gold and silver in 2004, and moved on to copper and zinc in 2009. Shortly after work began in Canatuan, TVIRD came face to face with its first big CSR challenge: The 508-hectare mining concession granted to the company by the Philippine government fell within the ancestral domain of the Subanon indigenous people.

In the early years, there was some conflict. Subanon elders felt that Mount Canatuan, considered sacred to their people, had been desecrated. Some local people accused TVIRD of polluting the Siocan River. Others were concerned about excessive force employed against protesters by the company's security.

Throughout, TVIRD worked to put into practice its CSR policy which states: "TVIRD is committed to exploration and mining practices that promote transparency, responsible stewardship of the environment, and the inalienable rights to life, dignity, and sustainable development in its host communities."

TVIRD pointed out that the chemicals in the Siocon River came from an illegal mining operation that had preceded TVIRD's arrival on the scene. Nevertheless, the company took measures to clean up the river. TVIRD also established a sustainability program for Canatuan, encompassing such areas as livelihood, health and sanitation, education, environmental management and protection, and human resource development.

One of TVIRD's sustainable livelihood initiatives in Canatuan is its Farmer-Instructor-Technician (FIT) program. Under the FIT program, the formerly semi-nomadic Subanons are encouraged to change their traditional way of farming to an irrigated multi-cropping method using rice terrace techniques. As part of its health and sanitation program, TVIRD set up a medical clinic with a full-time doctor, nurse, and midwife in Canatuan, bringing medical care to communities that previously had had no access to medical services. TVIRD also participated with the Philippine government in a regional campaign to eradicate lymphatic filariasis (a mosquito-borne disease common in the area) and carried out medical missions to remote communities.

Although mining affects the environment in both the short and the long term, TVIRD's environmental management and protection program aims "to minimize its impact footprint, to implement appropriate and best practice measures to control the impacts, and to promote restoration and rehabilitation that best support the needs of the community and the natural environment." Measures include tailings management, water quality monitoring, protection of land and water habitats to preserve the region's biodiversity, and reforestation. Since 2004, TVIRD has planted almost 380 000 seedlings as part of its rehabilitation program.

TVIRD has received many awards for its CSR initiatives in the Philippines. In 2011 the company received the Titanium Award for Environmental Management and three other safety awards; in 2012 TVIRD was awarded the Safest Mining Operations Award, the Platinum Award for Excellence in Environmental Management, the Safest Surface Mining Operation Award, and the Safest Mineral Processing–Concentrator Category Award. TVIRD also received the Gaward Kalinga Award, given by the Philippines Department of Labour and Employment in recognition of outstanding achievement in the area of response to the health and safety needs of workers, workplaces, and the community.

Based on its CSR record in Canatuan, TVIRD has now received certification from the National Commission on Indigenous Peoples (NCIP) in the Philippines, showing that the company has fulfilled the requirement of free prior informed consent from the Subanon people in support of its operations.

The Canatuan mine is slated for final closure in 2014. One of the TVIRD's goals is "to return the Canatuan mine to its natural and stable state, thereby making it available to the Subanons for other uses."

Thinking Globally

1. Which ethical philosophy is TVIRD using in the Philippines?
2. Name a few of TVIRD's corporate social responsibility initiatives.
3. Do you think TVIRD is applying the concept of sustainability in its operations?

Sources: Natural Resources Canada, "Canadian Mining Assets Abroad," Information Bulletin (www.nrcan.gc.ca/minerals-metals/publications-reports/4425#F1), January 2012; Natural Resources Canada, "The Minerals and Metals Policy of the Government of Canada," (www.nrcan.gc.ca/minerals-metals/policy/bulletin/minerals-metals-policy/3309); Karol Anne M. Ilagan, "12 Years After Mining Disaster: Chronic Illnesses on the Rise in Marcopper Towns," Philippine Centre for Investigative Journalism (PCIJ) (www.pcij.org), November 3, 2008; TVIRD, "Once Again—TVIRD Declared 'Best of the Best,'" (www.tviphilippines.com/articlet.php?id=392), November 22, 2012; Isa Lorenzo and Philip Ney, "The Canadian Quandary," PCIJ (www.pcij.org), December 29, 2008; TVI Resource Development Philippines Inc. Web site (www.tviphilippines.com), various reports.

CHAPTER FIVE

Economics and Emerging Markets

Learning Objectives

After studying this chapter, you should be able to

1. Describe what is meant by a centrally planned economy and explain why its use is declining.

2. Identify the main characteristics of a mixed economy and explain the emphasis on privatization.

3. Explain how a market economy functions and identify its distinguishing features.

4. Describe the different ways to measure a nation's level of development.

5. Discuss the process of economic transition and identify the obstacles for business.

A LOOK BACK

Chapter 4 presented the different approaches to ethics that companies may take. We learned that the definition of ethical behaviour can vary from country to country. Ethical dilemmas often occur in international business, and we studied ways to overcome them. We also explored how international businesses use corporate social responsibility to act ethically.

A LOOK AT THIS CHAPTER

This chapter explains the key differences between centrally planned, mixed, and market economies. We also explore economic development and the challenges facing emerging markets and those transforming their economies into free markets.

A LOOK AHEAD

Chapter 6 introduces us to a major form of international business activity—international trade. We examine the patterns of international trade and outline several theories that attempt to explain why nations conduct trade.

Source: ShutterStock.

Datawind

MONTREAL, Quebec—Datawind (www.datawind.com) was founded in 2000 in Montreal by brothers Suneet and Raja Singh Tuli, both Indian-born Canadian citizens. Prior to 2011, Datawind, registered in the United Kingdom, was a relatively unknown wireless device maker. However, when Suneet learned that the Indian government was calling for bids to build an inexpensive tablet computer for the Indian market, the company's fate changed.

India, a country of approximately 1.2 billion people, is one of the biggest emerging markets in the world. It has the fastest-growing mobile market on the planet. Over 800 million people in India have mobile phones, with over 10 million signing up each month. The opportunity is enormous if companies can provide products for the masses at low prices. This is exactly what Datawind did, winning the contract with its $52 per unit bid.

Why was this deal important? The Indian government's goal is to provide a tablet to the country's 80 to 100 million high school students to incorporate IT into Indian education and increase the use of digital textbooks. Consequently, the government subsidized the tablet, reducing the consumer price to $35.00 to make it available to lower-income families. Since the success of this huge contract, Datawind has become known worldwide as the company manufacturing the cheapest tablet on earth. It has subsequently received potential offers from Thailand for 10 million tablets and Turkey for 15 million. Other countries including Sri Lanka, Trinidad and Tobago, Panama, and Egypt have also expressed interest.

Source: STR/epa/Corbis.

The current version of the tablet is called Aakash2 ("sky"). Designed and developed in Canada, the components are sourced globally, and the device is manufactured and programmed in India. Datawind has entered into a strategic alliance with Reverse Language Technologies Pvt Ltd of Bangalore to ensure that Aakash2 tablets are available in all major languages of India and the world. Datawind's CEO Suneet believes that technology should reach every corner of the globe and that price and language should not be a barrier. As you read this chapter, consider the importance of economic development and how companies can help improve a nation's living standards.[1]

Similar to culture and systems of politics and law, economic systems differ from country to country. In Chapter 2, we saw that one defining element of a culture is its tendency toward *individualism* or *collectivism*. In Chapter 3, we saw how a people's history and culture influence the development of their political and legal systems. In Chapter 4, we studied how ethical behaviour varies among countries. In this chapter, we investigate the linkages between culture and economic systems.

National culture can have a strong impact on a nation's economic development. In turn, the development of a country's economy can dramatically influence many aspects of its culture. Economic systems in individualist cultures such as Canada tend to provide incentives and rewards for individual business initiative. Collectivist cultures tend to offer fewer such incentives and rewards. For example, in individualist cultures, *entrepreneurs*—businesspeople who accept the risks and opportunities involved in creating and operating new business ventures—tend to be rewarded with relatively low tax rates or government grants that encourage their activities.

We begin this chapter by introducing the world's different economic systems and exploring the links between culture and economics. We then examine economic development and ways of classifying nations using several indicators of development. We conclude by looking at how countries in transition are implementing market-based economic reforms and the challenges they face. Throughout the chapter, we will encounter anecdotes of how *emerging markets* are faring in their economic development efforts.

Economic Systems

economic system
Structure and processes that a country uses to allocate its resources and conduct its commercial activities.

A country's **economic system** consists of the structure and processes that it uses to allocate its resources and conduct its commercial activities. No nation is either completely individualist or completely collectivist in its cultural orientation. Likewise, the economies of all nations display a blend of individual and group values. In other words, no economy is entirely focused on individual reward at the expense of social well-being. Nor is any economy so completely focused on social well-being that it places no value on individual incentive and enterprise.

Yet every economy displays a *tendency* toward individualist or collectivist economic values. We can arrange national economies on a horizontal scale that is anchored by two extremes. At one end of the scale is a theoretical pure centrally planned economy; at the other end is a theoretical pure market economy; and in between is a mixed economy (see Figure 5.1). Let's now explore the workings of *centrally planned*, *mixed*, and *market economies*.

Centrally Planned Economy

centrally planned economy
Economic system in which a nation's land, factories, and other economic resources are owned by the government, which plans nearly all economic activity.

A **centrally planned economy**, also known as a command economy, is a system in which a nation's land, factories, and other economic resources are owned by the government. The government makes nearly all economy-related decisions—including who produces what and the prices of products, labour, and capital. Central planning agencies specify production goals for factories and other production units, and they even decide prices. In the former Soviet Union, for example, communist officials set prices for milk, bread, eggs, and other essential goods. The ultimate goal of central planning is to achieve a wide range of political, social, and economic objectives by taking complete control over the production and distribution of a nation's resources. Today, North Korea is an example of a centrally planned economy.

ORIGINS OF THE CENTRALLY PLANNED ECONOMY   Central planning is rooted in the ideology that the group's welfare is more important than individual well-being. Just as collectivist cultures emphasize group over individual goals, a centrally planned economy strives to achieve economic and social equality.

FIGURE 5.1

Range of Economic Systems

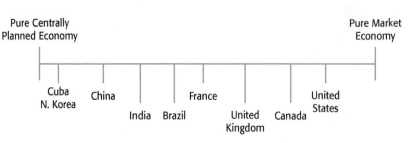

German philosopher Karl Marx popularized the idea of central economic planning in the nineteenth century. Marx formulated his ideas while witnessing the hardship endured by the working class people in Europe during and after the Industrial Revolution. Marx argued that the economy could not be reformed, but that it must be overthrown and replaced with a more equitable "communist" system. (See the discussion of communism in Chapter 3.)

Different versions of Marx's ideas were implemented in the twentieth century by means of violent upheaval. Revolutions installed totalitarian economic and political systems in Russia in 1917, China and North Korea in the late 1940s, and Cuba in 1959. By the 1970s, central planning was the economic law in lands stretching across Central and Eastern Europe (Albania, Bulgaria, Czechoslovakia, East Germany, Hungary, Poland, Romania, and Yugoslavia), Asia (Cambodia, China, North Korea, and Vietnam), Africa (Angola and Mozambique), and Latin America (Cuba and Nicaragua).

DECLINE OF CENTRAL PLANNING   In the late 1980s, nation after nation began to dismantle communist central planning in favour of market-based economies. Economists, historians, and political scientists attribute the decline of centrally planned economies to a combination of several factors.

Failure to Create Economic Value   Central planners paid little attention to the task of producing quality goods and services at the lowest possible cost. In other words, they failed to see that commercial activities succeed when they create economic value for customers. Along the way, scarce resources were wasted in the pursuit of commercial activities that were not self-sustaining.

Failure to Provide Incentives   Government ownership of economic resources drastically reduced incentives for businesses to maximize the output obtained from those resources. Except for aerospace, nuclear power, and other sciences (in which government scientists excelled), there were few incentives to create new technologies, new products, and new production methods. The result was little or no economic growth and consistently low standards of living.

As the world's most closed economy, North Korea has earned its nickname, "The Hermit Kingdom." For the most part, its policy of *juche* (self-reliance) is causing extreme hardship for North Korea's citizens. The combination of recurring floods and droughts, a shortage of fertilizers, and a lack of farm machinery restrain the nation from reaching its peak food production potential. As a result, North Korea often must rely on aid from abroad to feed its people.

Failure to Achieve Rapid Growth   Leaders in communist nations took note of the high rates of economic growth in places such as Hong Kong, Singapore, South Korea, and Taiwan—called Asia's four tigers. That a once-poor region of the world had so rapidly achieved such astounding growth awakened central planners to the possibilities. They realized that an economic system based on private ownership fosters growth much better than one hampered by central planning.

North Korea, once again, provides us with a good example. Each year for a decade until 1999, the North Korean economy contracted. Out of desperation, the country's leaders quietly allowed limited free market reforms and small bazaars soon dotted the countryside. Street-corner currency exchanges sprang up to help facilitate a tiny but growing trade with bordering Chinese merchants. Impoverished North Koreans could buy mobile phones and found hope for a better life in DVDs of South Korean soap operas. But a disastrous attempt to reform its currency dealt a serious setback to North Korea's experiment with the free market.[2] For now, at least, the last green shoots of capitalism in North Korea seem to be coming from its Kaesong Industrial Complex along its border with South Korea. The one-of-a-kind industrial park buses in around 500 South Korean managers daily to manage approximately 51 452 North Korean factory workers. But its future is uncertain amid volatile relations between the North and South and because many South Korean businesses involved in the project are losing money. One example of the uncertain environment is spontaneous tax increases. On October 2012, 8 companies out of the 123 South Korean companies received unannounced tax collection notices, a unilateral decision made by the North Koreans.[3]

Failure to Satisfy Consumer Needs   People in centrally planned economies were tired of a standard of living that had slipped far below that found in market economies. Ironically, although central planning was conceived as a means to create a more equitable system of distributing wealth, too many central planners failed to provide even basic necessities such as adequate food, housing, and medical care. Underground (shadow) economies for all kinds of goods and services flourished and, in some cases, even outgrew "official" economies. Prices of goods on the black market were much higher than the official (and artificial) prices set by governments.

Although farming is a high-tech endeavour in the world's most advanced nations today, it is labour-intensive and inefficient in North Korea. The government's failed communist economic policies hamper development and are at the root of its inability to afford fertilizers and modern machinery that could boost food production. Seemingly endless famines and economic collapse have cut North Korea's life expectancy by more than six years to 60 years for men and 69 years for women.

Source: Lindsay Hebberd/Corbis

Emerging Market Focus: China

China began its experiment with central planning in 1949, when communists defeated the nationalists in a long and bloody civil war. Today, the country's leaders describe its economic philosophy as "socialism with Chinese characteristics," also known as state capitalism. This is a unique economic model combining socialism and capitalism, in which the state fosters commercial economic activity while maintaining the conditions of wage labour. The state dominates the economy by owning controlling shares of publicly listed corporations, acting as a large stakeholder. In addition the communist party maintains ultimate authority over virtually all economic decision making.[4]

There is possibly no country on earth that has done more for its people economically over the past two decades than China. Glistening skyscrapers now dominate the Shanghai and Beijing cityscapes, where most people have good job prospects. The country's immense population, rising incomes, and expanding opportunities are attracting huge sums of investment.

EARLY YEARS From 1949 until reforms were initiated in the late 1970s, China had a unique economic system. Agricultural production was organized into groups of people who formed production "brigades" and production "units." Communes were larger entities responsible for planning agricultural production quotas and industrial production schedules. Rural families owned their homes and parcels of land on which to produce particular crops. Production surpluses could be consumed by the family or sold at a profit on the open market. In 1979 China initiated agricultural reforms that strengthened work incentives in this sector. Family units could then grow whatever crops they chose and sell the produce at market prices.

At about the same time, township and village enterprises (TVEs) began to appear. Each TVE relied on the open market for materials, labour, and capital, and used a nongovernmental distribution system. Each TVE employed managers who were directly responsible for profits and losses. The government initially regarded TVEs as illegal and unrelated to the officially sanctioned communes. But they were legalized in 1984 and helped lay additional groundwork for a market economy.

PATIENCE AND *GUANXI* If there is one trait that is needed by all private companies in China, it is patience. Despite obvious ideological differences between itself and the private sector, China's Communist Party is trying very hard to appear well suited to running the country. Karl Marx once summed up communism as the "abolition of private property," and the name of China's

Communist Party (in Chinese characters) literally means "common property party." But business was officially embraced when the Communist Party allowed businesspeople to become party members. Private property is now an accepted concept (though property rights violations are commonplace), which encouraged Chinese companies to invest in innovation. For example, in 2011 the Chinese telecommunications firm ZTE Corporation filed the most applications for patents under the international Patent Cooperation Treaty, administered by the World Intellectual Property Organization (WIPO). In addition, China had a 33.4 percent increase overall in the number of applications that year. Huawei Technologies, also a Chinese company, ranked as the world's third-largest applicant for patents.[5]

A personal touch is another necessary ingredient for success in China. Initially, and in line with communist ideology, non-Chinese companies were restricted from participating in China's economy. But since the mid-1980s, outsiders have enjoyed ever-greater opportunities to create joint ventures with local partners. One of the most important factors in forming a successful venture in China is *guanxi*—the Chinese term for "personal relationships." To learn more about the secrets of *guanxi*, see this chapter's Global Manager's Briefcase, titled "Guidelines for Good *Guanxi*."

CHALLENGES AHEAD FOR CHINA   Despite the global recession, China's economy continues to reform itself, growing at between 8 and 10 percent annually and becoming a player in foreign direct investment. *Political and social problems*, however, pose threats to China's future economic performance. Skirmishes between secular and Muslim Chinese in western provinces still occur, although less frequently today. Meanwhile, for the most part, political leaders restrict advanced democratic reforms. Protests sporadically arise from time to time whenever ordinary Chinese citizens grow impatient with political progress. In addition, the current political party has many factional divisions, with junior members pushing for a reduction in corruption and greater market influence.

Global Manager's Briefcase   Guidelines for Good *Guanxi*

- **Importance of Contacts, Not Contracts.** In China, face-to-face communication and personal relationships take priority over written contracts. Mu Dan Ping of Ernst & Young (www.ey.com) offers this diagram to show the different priorities:

  United States (applies for Canada):
  Reason → Law → Relationship

  China: Relationship → Reason → Law

  Managers from North America look for rationale or reason first, wondering if there is a market with profit potential. If so, they want a legal contract before spending time on a business relationship. But the Chinese need to establish a trust relationship first and then look for common goals as a reason for doing business. For them, legal contracts are just a formality, serving to ensure mutual understanding.

- **Pleasure Before Business.** Experts advise managers to leave the sales pitch on the back burner and follow the lead of their Chinese hosts. If seeking partnerships in China, one cannot overlook the importance of personal relationships. Companies that send their top performers to wow Chinese businesspeople with savvy sales pitches can return empty-handed—friendship comes before business in China.

- **Business Partners Are Family Members Too.** The importance of family means visiting managers should never turn down invitations to partake in a Chinese executive's family life. Lauren Hsu, market analyst for Kohler Company (www.kohler.com), was responsible for researching and identifying potential joint venture partners in China. She once went bowling with the partner's daughter and then to a piano concert with the entire family. Two years of meetings and visits to get acquainted eventually resulted in a joint venture deal.

- **Cultural Sensitivity.** China is not a single market but many different regional markets with different cultures and even different languages. Bob Wilner, of McDonald's Corporation (www.mcdonalds.com), went to China to learn how Chinese people are managed. "Unlike the way we cook our hamburgers exactly the same in all 101 countries," says Wilner, "the way we manage, motivate, reward, and discipline is more sensitive to the culture." Wilner and other McDonald's managers developed that sensitivity only through repeated visits to China.

Source: "The Panda Has Two Faces," *The Economist*, April 3, 2010, p. 70; Paul Maidment, "China's Legal Catch-22," *Forbes* (www.forbes.com), February 17, 2010; Frederik Balfour, "You Say *Guanxi*, I say Schmoozing," *Bloomberg Businessweek* (www.businessweek.com), November 8, 2007.

Another potential problem is *unemployment*. Intensified competition and the entry of international companies into China are placing greater emphasis on efficiency and the cutting of payrolls in some industries. But the biggest contributor to the unemployed sector seems to be migrant workers. Hundreds of thousands of workers have left their farms and now go from city to city searching for better-paying factory work or construction jobs. Unhappiness with economic progress in the countryside and the misery of migrant workers are serious potential sources of social unrest for the Chinese government. And although factory workers are striking with greater frequency, they are mostly trying to recover ground lost by mandatory pay freezes during the economic crisis of 2008–2009.[6]

China has developed its own approach to innovation. First, *flexible networks* fuelled by *guanxi* help companies to reduce costs and increase flexibility. Chinese companies spread their production contracts over a large number of parts suppliers and can then increase or decrease orders as demand dictates. Second, some companies exploit China's lax enforcement of property rights to quickly copy new, pricey global products and make cheaper versions available to Chinese consumers. These companies employ *bandit* or *guerilla innovation* to continually learn innovative ways to produce goods at lower cost, though they clearly violate the original producer's property rights.[7]

Other major challenges include poverty, a cultural bias in favour of men, and the environment. A recent survey showed that most Chinese households have a low savings rate, indicating that the majority of the population do not have money to spend. This issue needs to be addressed if China wants to move toward a consumer-based economy. But perhaps the biggest challenge ahead is securing food, water, and clean air for the 1.35 billion population. For instance, Beijing and other parts of northeastern China are already water-stressed, and air-quality is "abysmal" in cities such as Chongquing and Chengdu.[8]

Another key issue is *reunification* of "greater China." China regained control of Hong Kong in 1997 after 99 years under British rule. For the most part, China has kept its promise of "one country, two systems." Although the economic (and to a lesser extent political) freedoms of people in Hong Kong would remain largely intact, the rest of China would continue along lines drawn by the communist leadership. China also regained control of its southern coastal territory of Macao in 1999. Only a one-hour ferry ride from Hong Kong, Macao was under Portuguese administration since it was founded in 1557. Although Macao's main function used to be that of trading post, today it serves mainly as a gambling outpost and is referred to as "Asia's Vegas."[9]

Any chance of Taiwan's eventual reunification with the Chinese mainland depends on how China manages Hong Kong and Macao. For now, reunification seems more likely as economic ties between China and Taiwan grow steadily. Taiwan scrapped a 50-year ban that capped the size of investments in China and eased restrictions on direct financial flows between Taiwan businesses and the mainland. China and Taiwan have currently adopted a new policy, "viable diplomacy," designed to replace hostility between the two countries with pragmatic dialogue and support a more proactive diplomacy internationally. The entry of both China and Taiwan into the World Trade Organization (www.wto.org) in recent years has encouraged further integration of their two economies. Also, in August 2012 the two countries signed an investment protection pact.

Quick Study

1. Define *economic system*. What is the relation between culture and economics?
2. What is a *centrally planned economy*? Describe the link between central planning and communism.
3. Identify several factors that contributed to the decline of centrally planned economies.
4. Describe China's experience with central planning and the challenges it faces.

mixed economy

Economic system in which land, factories, and other economic resources are rather equally split between private and government ownership.

Mixed Economy

A **mixed economy** is a system in which land, factories, and other economic resources are rather equally split between private and government ownership. In a mixed economy, the government owns fewer economic resources than does the government in a centrally planned economy.

Yet in a mixed economy, the government tends to control the economic sectors that it considers important to national security and long-term stability. Such sectors usually include iron and steel manufacturing (for building military equipment), oil and gas production (to guarantee continued manufacturing and availability), and automobile manufacturing (to guarantee employment for a large portion of the workforce). Many mixed economies also maintain generous welfare systems to support the unemployed and provide health care for the general population.

Mixed economies are found all around the world: Denmark, France, Germany, Norway, Spain, and Sweden in Western Europe; India, Indonesia, Malaysia, Pakistan, and South Korea in Asia; Argentina, Brazil, and Colombia in South America; Mexico in North America; and South Africa. Although all governments of these nations do not centrally plan their economies, they all influence economic activity by means of special incentives, including hefty subsidies to key industries and significant government involvement in the economy.

ORIGINS OF THE MIXED ECONOMY   Advocates of mixed economies contend that a successful economic system not only must be efficient and innovative but also should protect society from the excesses of unchecked individualism and organizational greed. The goal is to achieve low unemployment, low poverty, steady economic growth, and an equitable distribution of wealth by means of the most effective policies.

Proponents argue that nations with mixed economies should not dismantle their social-welfare institutions but modernize them so they contribute to national competitiveness. Austria, the Netherlands, and Sweden are taking this route. In the Netherlands, labour unions and the government agreed to an epic deal involving wage restraint, shorter working hours, budget discipline, new tolerance for part-time and temporary work, and the trimming of social benefits. As a result, unemployment in the Netherlands is 5.6 percent. By comparison, unemployment in Spain and Greece is around 26 percent, and the average jobless rate for all European Union nations is around 10.7 percent.[10]

DECLINE OF MIXED ECONOMIES   Many mixed economies are remaking themselves to more closely resemble free markets. When assets are owned by the government, there seems to be less incentive to eliminate waste or to practise innovation. Extensive government ownership on a national level tends to result in a lack of accountability, rising costs, defective products, and slow economic growth. Many government-owned businesses in mixed economies need large infusions of taxpayer money to survive as world-class competitors, which raises taxes and prices for goods and services. Underpinning the move toward market-based systems is the sale of government-owned businesses.

Move Toward Privatization   Citizens of many European nations prefer a combination of rich benefits and higher unemployment to the somewhat lower jobless rates and smaller social safety net of Canada. In France, for instance, the French electorate continues to hold fast to a deeply embedded tradition of social welfare and job security in government-owned firms. Many French believe the social security and cohesion benefits of a more collectivist economy outweigh the efficiency advantages of an individualist one. Yet such attitudes are costly in terms of economic efficiency.

The selling of government-owned economic resources to private operators is called **privatization**. Privatization helps eliminate subsidized materials, labour, and capital formerly provided to government-owned companies. It also curtails the practice of appointing managers for political reasons rather than for their professional expertise. To survive, newly privatized companies must produce competitive products at fair prices because they are subject to the forces of the free market. The overall aim of privatization is to increase economic efficiency, boost productivity, and raise living standards.

privatization
Policy of selling government-owned economic resources to private operators.

Emerging Market Focus: India

India began its transition to a mixed economy in 1947, adopting a democratic government after it gained independence from Britain. At first, the country operated a centrally planned type of economy with state-owned companies. However, the various regulations and bureaucratic red tape, called "Licence Raj," made it difficult to set up and run a business. The country basically continued in this manner from 1947 to 1990, even though Prime Minister Rajiv Ghandi introduced small reforms during the 1980s to reduce the red tape and promote the software and tele-communication industries. Regardless, during these four decades India's economy stagnated, and low annual growth rates prevailed.

A park along the Thames River in London, England, buzzes with activity on a sunny afternoon. The UK government sold off many of its state-owned companies to improve efficiency and productivity. Today, the UK economy lies between the more collectivist economies of continental Europe and one of the more individualist—Canada. What is your personal view regarding the balance between individualist and collectivist government policies?

Source: Jose Fuste Raga/Corbis.

In 1991, Prime Minister Narasimha Rao initiated a trade liberalization process by abolishing the Licence Raj system, which ended several monopolies. An ambitious economic reform program was implemented to reduce the fiscal deficit, privatize the public sector, and increase infrastructure investment. At the same time, trade reforms and foreign direct investment regulations changed to open the economy to foreign investors. For example, the new rules gave an automatic approval to foreign investment of up to 51 percent of the ownership in an Indian company; 100 percent foreign ownership was permitted in certain industries. Other reforms implemented since 1991 include establishing a national stock exchange and making the rupee (Indian currency) convertible. Special economic zones were created, and major investments in infrastructure were made. Various laws have also been passed, such as the Right to Information Act, giving timely access to government information and promoting transparency and accountability, and the Right to Education Act, making education a fundamental right of all children aged between 6 and 14. These reforms have had a positive impact on foreign direct investment.

Today India is one of the fastest developing economies in the world and has achieved annual growth rates above 6 percent since 2003. In 2009 and 2010—while most of the world was undergoing a severe economic crisis—India's annual growth rate was 8.4 percent. Still, India's economy is far from a free market economy, as you will learn in the Economic Freedom section later in this chapter.

CHALLENGES AHEAD FOR INDIA India does not yet have a well-functioning legal and regulatory framework, despite progress made in this regard. Judicial procedures are costly and subject to political pressure. Huge efforts have been made to privatize the country, but there are still many state-owned enterprises. Subsidies remain high, creating a large budget deficit. The government continues to control prices on a number of products; the average tariffs to import products are at 8 percent; and complex nontariff barriers are still in place. Intellectual and property rights are not well protected, and high levels of corruption persist. The labour market is underdeveloped, and a substantive informal sector remains. In summary, India has many challenges to overcome, challenges that hinder international trade and investment, and stand in the way of India becoming a developed nation with a full market economy.

Emerging Market Focus: Brazil

Brazil began its transition to a democracy in 1985, after 21 years (1964–1985) under an authoritarian military regime. Although provincial and federal elections were held between 1985 and

A typical street in India.

Source: Don MacMillan

1989, many of the elected politicians in power at that time still belonged to the old military regime. In 1989, Fernando Collor de Mello was elected president of Brazil in Brazil's first democratic presidential election since the military dictatorship. During his term of office, Collor de Mello battled a huge national debt and hyperinflation, which at times reached rates of 25 percent per month. However, he managed to privatize fifteen companies. Accused of corruption, Collor de Mello resigned in 1992 and was later prosecuted and convicted.

From 1995 to 2003 under President Fernando Cardoso, Brazil went through a major economic transformation that saw a reduction of trade barriers and an increase in international cooperation. Cardoso's term was marked by advances in the promotion and protection of human rights and by a deepening of the privatization program in such areas as steel milling, telecommunications, and mining. Cardoso's successor, Lula da Silva, was elected in 2003 and served until 2011. During Lula's presidential term, Brazilian foreign trade increased dramatically, changing deficits to surpluses; as a result, Brazil's external vulnerability was reduced. During this period, Brazil's financial, economic, and risk indicators improved, and its annual growth rates between 2.6 and 3 percent made Brazil the largest economy in Latin America. Nevertheless, the country still faced problems such as high interest rates, high unemployment, poverty, social inequality, poor infrastructure, and rampant corruption. Dilma Rousseff, Brazil's first female president, was elected in 2011. Her government is currently focused on reducing inflation, tightening Brazil's monetary policy, maintaining and extending social programs to raise the standard of living, and improving Brazil's infrastructure.

This Port of Santos, Brazil, is currently considered the busiest container port in Latin America.

Source: Caio Brecco

CHALLENGES AHEAD FOR BRAZIL Brazil has not yet established a full market economy and needs to overcome several issues before it can be considered a free economy. High inflation and unemployment, both at 6 percent, continue to plague the country. It has an overly bureaucratic regulatory system: Starting up a business or even obtaining a permit is a long process. Labour regulations are rigorous, and corruption remains a problem, although protection of intellectual property rights has improved. The average tariffs to import products into Brazil are at 7.6 percent; nontariff barriers and antidumping measures are also a concern for importers. Foreign investment is still restricted in some sectors, and Brazil's tax system is complex. However, major infrastructure investments are underway as Brazil prepares to host the 2014 World Cup and the 2016 Olympic games. Despite its challenges, Brazil's economy is one of the fastest growing in the world and is forecast to become one of the five largest economies in the coming decades.

Market Economy

In a **market economy**, the majority of a nation's land, factories, and other economic resources are privately owned, either by individuals or businesses. This means that who produces what and the prices of products, labour, and capital in a market economy are determined by the interplay of two forces:

- **Supply:** the quantity of a good or service that producers are willing to provide at a specific selling price
- **Demand:** the quantity of a good or service that buyers are willing to purchase at a specific selling price

market economy
Economic system in which the majority of a nation's land, factories, and other economic resources are privately owned, either by individuals or businesses.

supply
Quantity of a good or service that producers are willing to provide at a specific selling price.

demand
Quantity of a good or service that buyers are willing to purchase at a specific selling price.

As supply and demand change for a good or service, so does its selling price. The lower the price, the greater will be the demand for a product; the higher its price, the lower will be the demand for it. Likewise, the lower a product's price, the smaller the quantity that producers will supply; the higher the price, the greater the quantity they will supply. In this respect, what is called the "price mechanism" (or "market mechanism") dictates supply and demand.

Market forces and uncontrollable natural forces can affect prices for many products, particularly commodities. Chocolate lovers, for example, should consider how the interplay of several forces affects the price of cocoa, the principal ingredient in chocolate. Suppose cocoa consumption suddenly rises in large cocoa-consuming nations such as Britain and Japan. Suppose further that disease and pests plague crops in cocoa-producing countries such as Brazil, Ghana, the Ivory Coast, and Indonesia. As worldwide consumption of cocoa begins to outstrip production, market pressure is felt on both the demand side (consumers) and the supply side (producers). Falling worldwide reserves of cocoa then force the price of cocoa higher.

ORIGINS OF THE MARKET ECONOMY   Market economics is rooted in the belief that individual concerns should be placed above group concerns. According to this view, the group benefits when individuals receive incentives and rewards to act in certain ways. It is argued that people take better care of property they own and that individuals have fewer incentives to care for property under a system of public ownership.

Laissez-Faire Economics   For many centuries, the world's dominant economic philosophy supported government control of a significant portion of a society's assets and government involvement in its international trade. But in the mid-1700s a new approach to national economics called for less government interference in commerce and greater individual economic freedom. This approach became known as a *laissez-faire* system, loosely translated from French as "allow them to do [without interference]."

Canada and the United States are examples of contemporary market economies. It is no accident that both these countries have individualist cultures (although to a somewhat lesser extent in Canada). As much as an emphasis on individualism fosters a democratic form of government, it also supports a market economy.

FEATURES OF A MARKET ECONOMY   To function smoothly and properly, a market economy requires three things: *free choice*, *free enterprise*, and *price flexibility*.

- *Free choice* gives individuals access to alternative purchase options. In a market economy, few restrictions are placed on consumers' ability to make their own decisions and exercise free choice. For example, a consumer shopping for a new car is guaranteed a variety from which to choose. The consumer can choose among dealers, models, sizes, styles, colours, and mechanical specifications such as engine size and transmission type.
- *Free enterprise* gives companies the ability to decide which goods and services to produce and the markets in which to compete. Companies are free to enter new and different lines of business, select geographic markets and customer segments to pursue, hire workers, and advertise their products. They are, therefore, guaranteed the right to pursue interests profitable to them.
- *Price flexibility* allows most prices to rise and fall to reflect the forces of supply and demand. By contrast, nonmarket economies often set and maintain prices at stipulated levels. Interfering with the price mechanism violates a fundamental principle of the market economy.

GOVERNMENT'S ROLE IN A MARKET ECONOMY   In a market economy, the government has relatively little direct involvement in business activities. Even so, it usually plays four important roles: *enforcing antitrust (antimonopoly) laws*, *preserving property rights*, *providing a stable fiscal and monetary environment*, and *preserving political stability*. Let's look briefly at each of these activities.

Enforcing Antitrust (Antimonopoly) Laws   When one company is able to control a product's supply—and, therefore, its price—it is considered a monopoly. *Antitrust (antimonopoly) laws* are designed to encourage the development of industries with as many competing businesses as the market will sustain. (These laws are explained fully in Chapter 3.) In competitive industries, prices are kept low by the forces of competition. By enforcing antitrust (antimonopoly) laws, governments prevent trade-restraining monopolies and business combinations that exploit consumers and constrain the growth of commerce.

In Canada, the Competition Act is a federal law aimed at preventing anti-competitive practices, which applies, with few exceptions, to all businesses in the country. It is administered and enforced by the Competition Bureau. Note that in Canada a monopoly is not in itself illegal; what is illegal and will be investigated under the Competition Act is abuse of a dominant position resulting in a substantial restriction on competition. For example, a company or group of companies that dominated 60 percent or more of market share in any particular area would be investigated by the Competition Bureau.[11]

One of the newest antimonopoly laws in the world is China's Antimonopoly Law. Based on EU and German competition law, it came into effect on August 1, 2008, emerging as an important competition law for international businesses with activities in China. The Antimonopoly Law features three broad rules governing conduct, mergers, and administrative power: It prohibits restrictive agreements and the abuse of a dominant market position; articulates merger rules to control large mergers and acquisitions; and prohibits the abuse of administrative power that leads to restrictions on competition. The National Development and Reform Commission (NDRC) is one of the agencies that enforce this law. In one case, the NDRC took action against state-owned salt companies for violating the law against abuse of dominant market position and for using their exclusive operation rights to jeopardize consumers' interests.[12]

Preserving Property Rights   A smoothly functioning market economy rests on a legal system that safeguards individual property rights. By preserving and protecting individual property rights, governments encourage individuals and companies to take risks such as investing in technology, inventing new products, and starting new businesses. Strong protection of property rights ensures entrepreneurs that their claims to assets and future earnings are legally safeguarded. This protection also supports a healthy business climate in which a market economy can flourish.

Providing a Stable Fiscal and Monetary Environment   Unstable economies are often characterized by high inflation and unemployment. These forces create general uncertainty about a nation's suitability as a place to do business. Governments can help control inflation through effective *fiscal policies* (policies regarding taxation and government spending) and *monetary policies* (policies controlling money supply and interest rates). A stable economic environment helps companies make better forecasts of costs, revenues, and the future of the business in general. Such conditions reduce the risks associated with future investments, such as new product development and business expansion.

Preserving Political Stability   A market economy depends on a stable government for its smooth operation and, indeed, for its future existence. Political stability helps businesses engage in activities without worrying about terrorism, kidnappings, and other political threats to their operations. (See Chapter 3 for extensive coverage of political risk and stability.)

ECONOMIC FREEDOM   So far we have discussed the essence of market economies as being grounded in freedom: free choice, free enterprise, free prices, and freedom from direct intervention by government. Map 5.1 classifies countries according to their levels of economic freedom. Factors making up each country's rating include trade policy, government intervention in the economy, property rights, black markets, and wage and price controls. Most developed economies are rated completely "free" or "mostly free." For example, according to the 2013 Index of Economic Freedom, Canada is the sixth-freest economy in the world, with an overall score of 79.4. Canada performs well in freedom from corruption, financial freedom, and regulation transparency. Canada has sound public finance management and a strong, stable democratic political system. The index refers to Canada as "one of the world's leading free market economies." However, Canada still has federal and provincial nontariff barriers, restrictions on agricultural products imports, import licensing in certain industries, and restrictions on foreign direct investment in sectors such as the media, telecommunications, fishing, mining, and aviation.

Overall, as you can see in Map 5.1, the scale tips toward a lack of economic freedom around the world, with most emerging markets and developing nations rated "mostly unfree" or "repressed." Included in the "mostly unfree" category are Brazil, Russia, India, and China (the BRIC countries), all ranked much lower than Canada. Brazil ranks number 100, with an overall economic freedom score of 57.7, due to poor-quality government services and a judicial system that is vulnerable to political influence and corruption. Russia, ranking number 139 with an overall score of 51.1, lacks investment and financial freedom, and has persistent high corruption. India, at number 119 with a score of 55.2, has a restricted regulatory environment, an inefficient judicial system, and high levels of corruption. The legal framework is particularly weak in India, where it can take almost 200 days to obtain a construction permit. China's overall score is just 51.9, because it is only nominally open to foreign investment, lacks transparency, has a complex and arbitrary regulatory framework, and is riddled with bureaucracy and rife with corruption. In addition, the Chinese courts have an inconsistent record in protecting the legal rights of foreigners.

As a final point, recall from Chapter 3 that the connection between political freedom and economic growth is not at all certain. Likewise, we can say only that countries with the greatest economic freedom *tend to have* the highest standards of living, whereas those with the lowest freedom *tend to have* the lowest standards of living. But greater economic freedom does not *guarantee* a high per capita income. A country can rank very low on economic freedom yet have a higher per capita income than a country with far greater freedom.

Quick Study

1. What is a *mixed economy*? Explain the origin of mixed economies.
2. Explain the changes occurring in mixed economies and the role of *privatization*.
3. Define what is meant by *market economy*, and identify its three required features.
4. Explain government's role in a market economy. How are economic freedom and living standards related?
5. Do you consider Canada a mixed economy or a market economy?

Development of Nations

The economic well-being of one nation's people as compared with that of another nation's people is reflected in the country's level of **economic development**. It reflects several economic and human indicators, including its economic output (agricultural and industrial), infrastructure (power and transportation facilities), and its people's physical health and level of education. Cultural, political, legal, and economic differences among nations can cause great differences in economic development.

economic development
Measure for gauging the economic well-being of one nation's people as compared with that of another nation's people.

Economic development is an increasingly important topic for international businesspeople as companies pursue business opportunities in emerging markets. Although much of the population in these countries is poor, there are often a thriving middle class and ambitious development programs.

Productivity is a key factor that drives economic growth and rising living standards. Productivity is simply the ratio of outputs (what is created) to inputs (resources used to create output). We can speak about the productivity of a business, an industry, or an entire economy. For a company to boost its productivity, it must increase the value of its outputs using the same amount of inputs; create the same value of outputs with fewer inputs; or do both at the same time.

Raising living standards in an economy depends in large part on unlocking the gains that productivity offers. Mixed economies in Western Europe continue to privatize state-owned companies to boost productivity and competitiveness. Former centrally planned economies in Eastern Europe implemented free market reforms to raise living standards. Even North Korea (with one of the lowest standards of living outside Africa) is being compelled to consider economic reform.

As the poorest nations invest in the fundamental drivers of productivity growth (such as basic infrastructure), the richest nations exploit the latest technological advancements. Information technology is driving productivity gains in online customer service, online purchasing of materials and parts, outsourcing operations, and other areas of business. To read more about the factors that influence productivity and economic development, see this chapter's Culture Matters feature, titled "Foundations of Development."

Managers can use a variety of measures to estimate a country's level of economic development. But it is wise to consider a combination of measures when analyzing potential markets because each measure has advantages and disadvantages. Let's now take a look at a few of the main gauges of economic development.

UN World Risk Index

Recently the United Nations developed a World Risk Index. The index uses four indicators to define countries at risk for natural disasters: exposure to natural hazards, susceptibility, coping capacities, and adaptive strategies. How does this index relate to a nation's economic development status? More developed nations are usually better able to cope and adapt faster in the event of a natural disaster. The implications for business are enormous. Investing in a country ranking in the top 15 highest risk countries should be considered very carefully. Included in the top 10 countries with the highest risk are Vanuatu, Tonga, Philippines, Guatemala, Bangladesh, Solomon Islands, Costa Rica, Cambodia, Timor-Leste, and El Salvador. According to the UN

MAP 5.1

Countries Ranked by Level of Economic Freedom

Source: Based on data from The Heritage Foundation (http://www.heritage.org/index/heatmap)

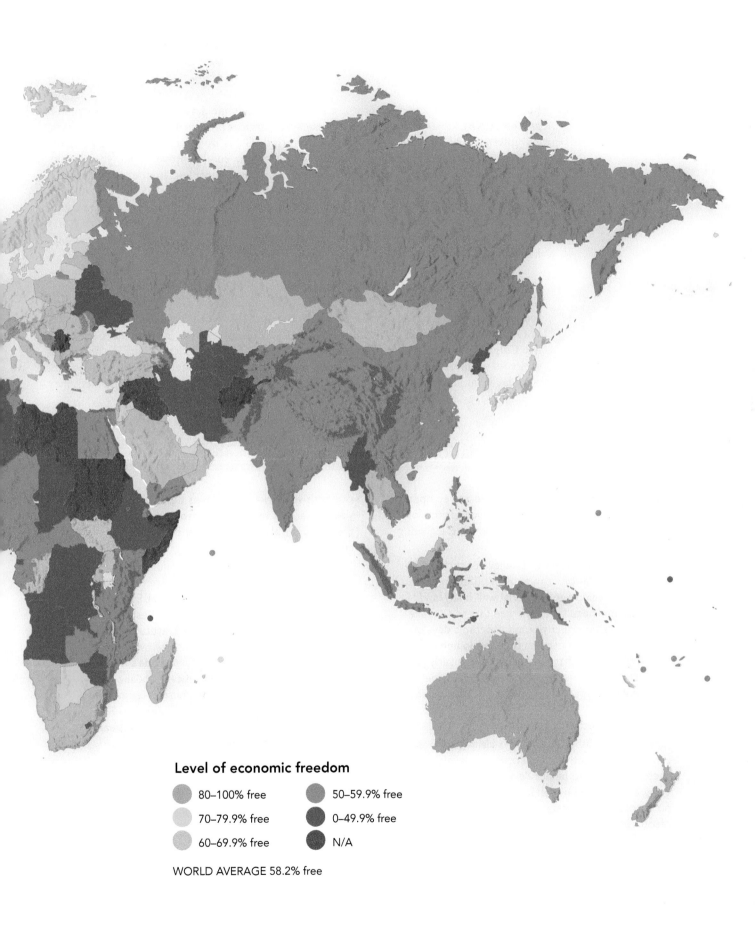

Level of economic freedom

- 80–100% free
- 70–79.9% free
- 60–69.9% free
- 50–59.9% free
- 0–49.9% free
- N/A

WORLD AVERAGE 58.2% free

World Risk Index, Chile is an example of a country with "strong governance in preparing for disasters." Haiti, on the other hand, is labelled as a "fragile state."[13]

National Production

Recall from Chapter 1 that the broadest measure of economic development is *gross national product (GNP)*, which is the value of all goods and services produced by a country's domestic and international activities over a one-year period. *Gross domestic product (GDP)* is the value of all goods and services produced by a domestic economy over a one-year period. GDP is a narrower figure that excludes a nation's income generated from exports, imports, and the international operations of its companies. A country's *GDP per capita* is simply its GDP divided by its population. GNP per capita is calculated similarly. Both GDP per capita and GNP per capita measure a nation's income per person. Map 5.2 shows how the World Bank (www.worldbank.org) classifies countries according to gross national income per capita (a term it uses).

Marketers often use GDP or GNP per capita figures to determine whether a country's population is wealthy enough to begin purchasing its products. For example, the Asian nation of Myanmar (Burma), with a GDP per capita of about $120 per year, is very poor. Here, you won't find computer companies marketing laptops or designer-apparel firms selling expensive clothing. Yet several large makers of personal-care products are staking out territory in Myanmar. Companies like Colgate-Palmolive (www.colgate.com) and Unilever (www.unilever.com) are traditional explorers of uncertain but promising markets in which they can offer relatively inexpensive, everyday items such as soap and shampoo. As multinational companies enter such markets, they

---

Culture Matters   Foundations of Development

Why are certain nations more productive and competitive than others? Researchers debate which aspects of a nation might influence economic development, including the following:

- **Culture.** Some researchers believe cultural differences among nations can explain differences in economic development, material well-being, and socioeconomic equity. They argue that any culture can attain high productivity and economic development if it values the benefits that development brings. Critics say that this perspective unfairly judges other cultures. They argue that each culture defines its own values, practices, goals, and ethics, and that Western nations should not impose their concept of "progress" on other cultures.

- **Geography.** Other researchers claim geography is central to productivity and economic development. Factors thought to hinder development include being a landlocked nation far from the coast, having poor access to markets, possessing few natural resources, and having a tropical climate. But Hong Kong, Singapore, South Korea, and Taiwan built

competitive market economies despite their small size and lack of vast natural resources. Each of these nations also threw off dependence on a colonial power.

- **Innovation.** Nations that want to join the European Union (EU) must satisfy strict and innovative requirements. A by-product is that Eastern Europe's culture is moving closer to Western Europe's along with shifting habits, attitudes, and values. In emerging markets today, innovation is being driven by ambition to improve one's lot in life and fear of being replaced by an even cheaper production location. Home-grown businesses in emerging markets have developed $3000 autos, $300 computers, and $30 mobile phones that appeal to consumers at home and abroad.

- **Want to Know More?** Visit the Culturelink Network (www.culturelink.org); the Observatory of Cultural Policies in Africa (ocpa.irmo.hr); the North-South Institute (www.nsi-ins.ca); or read the books *The Other Side of Innovation* and *Innovation Reverse* by Vijay Govindarajan.

Source: "The World Turned Upside Down," *The Economist*, April 17, 2010, pp. 3–6; Mark Johnson, "Innovation in Emerging Markets," *Bloomberg Businessweek* (www.businessweek.com), May 28, 2010; William Fischer, "Dealing with Innovation from Emerging Markets," IMD Web site (www.imd.ch/research/challenges), November 2008.

often try to satisfy the needs of people who live at the *bottom of the pyramid*—the world's poorest populations with the least purchasing power.

Although GDP and GNP are the most popular indicators of economic development, they have several important drawbacks. We detail each of these in the following sections.

UNCOUNTED TRANSACTIONS   For a variety of reasons, many of a nation's transactions do not get counted in either GDP or GNP. Some activities not included are:

- Volunteer work
- Unpaid household work
- Illegal activities such as gambling and black market (underground) transactions
- Unreported transactions conducted in cash

In some cases, the unreported (shadow) economy is so large and prosperous that official statistics such as GDP per capita are almost meaningless. In the case of Myanmar, economists report that official numbers mask a thriving shadow economy driven by differences between official and black-market currency exchange rates. In many wealthy nations the shadow economy is from one-tenth to one-fifth as large as the official economy. But in more than 50 countries, the shadow economy is at least 40 percent the size of documented GDP. In the Eurasian country of Georgia, for example, unreported transactions are estimated to equal as much as 73 percent of reported transactions. While Georgia's official GDP is around $24.5 billion, its shadow economy is worth another $14.8 billion.[14] According to a report from the Spanish bank Banco Bilbao Vizcaya Argentaria (BBVA), the shadow economy in the seven largest countries in Latin America (Argentina, Bolivia, Brazil, Chile, Colombia, Mexico, and Peru) represents on average 39 percent of the GDP.

One way in which goods and services flow through shadow economies is through *barter*—the exchange of goods and services for other goods and services instead of money. In one classic incident, Pepsi-Cola (www.pepsi.com) traded soft drinks in the former Soviet Union for 17 submarines, a cruiser, a frigate, and a destroyer. Pepsi then converted its payment into cash by selling the military goods as scrap metal.[15] Russians still use barter extensively because of a lack of currency. In another classic, but bizarre, case, the Russian government paid 8000 teachers in the Altai republic (about 2980 km east of Moscow) their monthly salaries with 15 bottles of vodka each. Teachers had previously refused an offer to receive part of their salaries in toilet paper and funeral accessories.[16]

QUESTION OF GROWTH   Gross product figures do not tell us whether a nation's economy is growing or shrinking—they are simply a snapshot of one year's economic output. Managers will want to supplement this data with information on expected future economic performance. A nation with moderate GDP or GNP figures inspires greater investor confidence and attracts more investment if its expected growth rate is high.

PROBLEM OF AVERAGES   Recall that per capita numbers give an average figure for an entire country. These numbers are helpful in estimating national quality of life, but averages do not give us a very detailed picture of development. Urban areas in most countries are more developed and have higher per capita income than rural areas. In less advanced nations, regions near good harbours or other transportation facilities are usually more developed than interior regions. Likewise, an industrial park that boasts companies with advanced technology in production or design can generate a disproportionate share of a country's earnings.

For example, GDP or GNP per capita figures for China are misleading because Shanghai and coastal regions of China are far more developed than the country's interior. Although luxury cars are sold in many of China's coastal cities and regions, bicycles and simple vehicles are still the transportation of choice in China's interior.

PITFALLS OF COMPARISON   Country comparisons using gross product figures can be misleading. When comparing gross product per capita, the currency of each nation being compared must be translated into another currency unit (usually the dollar) at official exchange rates. But official exchange rates only tell us how many units of one currency it takes to buy one unit of another. They do not tell us what that currency can buy in its home country. Therefore,

MAP 5.2

Gross National Income

Source: Gross National Income, from The
World Bank Group, http://data.worldbank.
org/indicator/NY.GNP.PCAP.PP.CD/
countries?display=map

GREENLAND

ARCT

ICELAND

UNITED
KINGDOM

IRELAND   NETHER

BELGIU
LUXEMI

FRANCE
SW

MONACO
ANDORRA

SPAIN

PORTUGAL

MOROCCO

ALGERIA

WESTERN
SAHARA

MAURITANIA   MALI

SENEGAL
GAMBIA
GUINEA-BISSAU GUINEA

BURKINA
FASO

N

SIERRA LEONE IVORY
COAST

GHANA
TOGO
BENIN

LIBERIA

EQUATO
GUINE

ALASKA

C A N A D A

UNITED STATES
OF AMERICA

PACIFIC

OCEAN

NORTH

ATLANTIC

OCEAN

HAWAII

MEXICO

CUBA

DOMINICAN
REPUBLIC

JAMAICA

BELIZE   HAITI   PUERTO
HONDURAS   RICO

GUATEMALA

EL SALVADOR NICARAGUA

COSTA RICA

PANAMA

TRINIDAD &
TOBAGO

VENEZUELA

GUYANA   FRENCH
GUIANA

SURINAME

GALAPAGOS
ISLANDS

COLOMBIA

ECUADOR

B R A Z I L

SOUTH

ATLANTIC

OCEAN

PERU

BOLIVIA

SWEDEN   LATVIA

DENMARK

LITHUANIA
RUSSIA

BELARUS

NETHERLANDS

BELGIUM GERMANY POLAND

LUXEMBOURG CZECH
REP.

UKRAINE

FRANCE

LICHTENSTEIN AUSTRIA   MOLDOVA
SWITZERLAND   HUNGARY
SLOVENIA

SLOVAKIA

C
H
I
L
E

PARAGUAY

MONACO
ANDORRA

SAN
MARINO

CROATIA   ROMANIA

BOSNIA-
HERZEGOVINA SERBIA

Black Sea

URUGUAY

ITALY   MONTENEGRO   BULGARIA
MACEDONIA
ALBANIA

ARGENTINA

ALGERIA

GREECE

T U R K E Y

TUNISIA   MALTA

CYPRUS

FALKLAND/MALVINAS
ISLANDS

LIBYA

ARCTIC OCEAN

NORWAY
SWEDEN
FINLAND
DENMARK
ESTONIA
LATVIA
LITHUANIA
RUSSIA
BELARUS
GERMANY
POLAND
NETHERLANDS
CZECH REP.
SLOVAKIA
UKRAINE
LUXEMBOURG
AUSTRIA
HUNGARY
MOLDOVA
SLOVENIA
ROMANIA
CROATIA
BOSNIA-HERZEGOVINA
SERBIA
MONTENEGRO
BULGARIA
GEORGIA
ITALY
MACEDONIA
ALBANIA
GREECE
TURKEY
ARMENIA
AZERBAIJAN
TUNISIA
CYPRUS
SYRIA
LEBANON
ISRAEL
IRAQ
JORDAN
KUWAIT

RUSSIA

KAZAKHSTAN

MONGOLIA

UZBEKISTAN
KYRGYZSTAN
TURKMENISTAN
TAJIKISTAN

AFGHANISTAN

IRAN

PAKISTAN

NEPAL
BHUTAN

BANGLADESH

CHINA

NORTH
KOREA

SOUTH
KOREA

JAPAN

TAIWAN

PACIFIC
OCEAN

LIBYA
EGYPT
SAUDI
ARABIA
QATAR
UNITED ARAB
EMIRATES
OMAN

INDIA

MYANMAR
(BURMA)
LAOS

THAILAND
VIETNAM
CAMBODIA

PHILIPPINES

NIGER
CHAD
SUDAN
ERITREA
YEMEN
DJIBOUTI
NIGERIA
CENTRAL AFRICAN
REPUBLIC
SOUTH
SUDAN
CAMEROON
ETHIOPIA
SOMALIA

SRI
LANKA

CONGO
REPUBLIC
UGANDA
GABON
CONGO
DEMOCRATIC
REPUBLIC
(ZAIRE)
RWANDA
BURUNDI
KENYA
TANZANIA

BRUNEI
MALAYSIA
SINGAPORE

INDONESIA

INDIAN
OCEAN

PAPUA
NEW
GUINEA

SOLOMON
ISLANDS

ANGOLA
ZAMBIA
MALAWI
MOZAMBIQUE
NAMIBIA
ZIMBABWE
BOTSWANA
MADAGASCAR
MAURITIUS
RÉUNION

VANUATU
FIJI

SWAZILAND
SOUTH
AFRICA
LESOTHO

AUSTRALIA

NEW
CALEDONIA

NEW
ZEALAND

Gross National Income (GNI)
in US dollars

7490 or more

2350–7490

1110–2350

430–1110

less than 430

no data available

to understand the true value of a currency in its home country, we apply the concept of *purchasing power parity*.

Purchasing Power Parity

purchasing power

Value of goods and services that can be purchased with one unit of a country's currency.

Using gross product figures to compare production across countries does not account for the different cost of living in each country. **Purchasing power** is the value of goods and services that can be purchased with one unit of a country's currency. **Purchasing power parity (PPP)** is the relative ability of two countries' currencies to buy the same "basket" of goods in those two countries. This basket of goods is representative of ordinary, daily-use items such as apples, rice, soap, toothpaste, and so forth. Estimates of gross product per capita at PPP allow us to see what a currency can actually buy in real terms.

purchasing power parity (PPP)

Relative ability of two countries' currencies to buy the same "basket" of goods in those two countries.

Let's now see what happens when we compare the wealth of several countries to that of Canada by adjusting GDP per capita to reflect PPP. If we convert Canadian dollars to US dollars at official exchange rates, we estimate Canada's GDP per capita at $50 345. This is higher than the official GDP per capita of the United States ($48 112). But adjusting Canada's GDP per capita for PPP gives us a revised figure of just $39 660, which is lower than the US GDP figure of $48 820. Why the difference? GDP per capita at PPP is lower in Canada because of Canada's higher cost of living. It simply costs more to buy the same basket of goods in Canada than it does in the United States. The opposite phenomenon occurs in Mexico. Because the cost of living there is lower than in Canada, Mexico's GDP per capita rises from $10 047 to $15 390 when PPP is considered (see Table 5.1).[17]

BIG MAC INDEX   An informal way of measuring the PPP is the Big Mac Index (see Table 5.2). It was introduced by *The Economist* in 1986 and is published every year. McDonald's is a global multinational that produces the Big Mac in about 120 countries. *The Economist* Big Mac Index is based on the theory of purchasing power parity (PPP). In this index, the "basket" is a McDonald's Big Mac. By comparing actual exchange rates with PPPs, the index indicates whether a currency is under- or overvalued.

For example, the cheapest burger in the chart is in India, at $1.50, compared with an average Canadian price of $5.26 or a Swedish price of $6.16. This implies that the rupee (India's currency) is undervalued by about 60 percent. On the same basis, the Swedish Kronor (SEK) is overvalued by around 60 percent. We conclude that the Canadian loonie was overvalued against the US dollar.[18]

TABLE 5.1	GDP Per Capita (Current US$) and GNI PPP (Current International $) 2011	
Country	**GDP per capita**	**GNI PPP per capita**
Norway	$98 102	$61 460
Switzerland	$83 383	$52 570
Denmark	$59 852	$41 900
Canada	$50 345	$39 660
United States	$48 112	$48 820
Japan	$45 903	$35 330
United Kingdom	$39 038	$36 010
Russia	$13 089	$20 560
Brazil	$12 594	$11 420
Mexico	$10 047	$15 390
China	$5445	$8390
India	$1489	$3590

Source: Based on data obtained from *World Development Indicators 2011*, The World Bank (www.worldbank.org), Table GDP per capita and PPP per capita.

TABLE 5.2	Big Mac Index 2012
Country	**dollar_price**
India	1.50
South Africa	1.82
Hong Kong	2.19
Malaysia	2.30
Canada	5.26
Sweden	6.16
Switzerland	6.72
Venezuela	7.15
Norway	7.51

Source: "The Big Mac Index," *The Economist,* January 12, 2012.

Quick Study

1. What is meant by the term *economic development*? Explain the relationship between productivity and living standards.
2. Describe two measures of economic development, and list their advantages and disadvantages.
3. Explain the concept of *purchasing power parity*. What are its implications for a nation's *relative* income per capita?
4. Explain the concept of the Big Mac Index. What are the implications for a Canadian business trying to export its products?

Human Development

The purchasing power parity concept does a fairly good job of revealing differences between national levels of economic development. Unfortunately, it is *a poor indicator of a people's total well-being*. Table 5.3 shows how selected countries rank according to the United Nations' **Human Development Index (HDI)**—the measure of the extent to which a government equitably provides its people with a long and healthy life, an education, and a decent standard of living.

Table 5.3 also illustrates the inequality that can be present within a country in terms of the distribution of health and well-being, education, and income. This second measure, called the Inequality-Adjusted Human Development Index (IHDI), was introduced in 2011. For example, in 2011 Canada ranked sixth in the overall HDI, but came in twelfth in the IHDI because Nunavut and Prince Edward Island have lower levels of development than the rest of the country. Table 5.3 shows that in 2013 Canada ranked eleventh in the HDI but thirteenth in the inequality-adjusted HDI. China is another striking example: It ranked 67th in the inequality-adjusted HDI but 101st in the overall HDI. The table illustrates the huge difference in HDI values between the very high-ranking countries such as Norway and Australia, and the emerging economies such as Brazil, Russia, India, and China (the BRIC countries). Perhaps most remarkable is the column showing each nation's life expectancy at birth. We see that people from first-ranked Norway have a life expectancy that is 26 years longer than people from last-ranked Niger.

Unlike other measures we have discussed, the HDI looks beyond financial wealth. By stressing the human aspects of economic development, it demonstrates that high national income alone does not guarantee human progress—although the importance of national income should not be underestimated. Countries need money to build good schools, provide quality health care, support environmentally friendly industries, and underwrite other programs designed to improve the quality of life.

Human Development Index (HDI)

Measure of the extent to which a government equitably provides its people with a long and healthy life, an education, and a decent standard of living.

TABLE 5.3	Human Development Index (HDI)			
HDI Rank	**Country**	**HDI Value**	**Inequality-Adjusted HDI Rank**	**Life Expectancy at Birth (Years)**
Very High Human Development				
1	Norway	0.955	1	81.3
2	Australia	0.938	2	82.0
3	United States	0.937	16	78.7
4	Netherlands	0.921	4	80.8
5	Germany	0.920	5	80.6
10	Japan	0.912	–	83.6
11	Canada	0.911	13	81.1
26	United Kingdom	0.875	19	80.3
45	Argentina	0.811	43	76.1
High Human Development				
55	Russian Federation	0.788	–	69.1
59	Cuba	0.780	–	79.3
61	Mexico	0.775	55	77.1
Medium Human Development				
101	China	0.699	67	73.7
119	Botswana	0.634	–	53.0
136	India	0.554	91	65.8
Low Human Development				
161	Haiti	0.456	120	62.4
186	Niger	0.304	131	55.1

Source: Based on data obtained from the *Human Development Report 2013* (United Nations Development Programme, New York, NY) (www.undp.org), Summary, pp. 16–18.

The spread of communicable diseases in the world's poorest nations is especially worrying. These diseases cause human and economic loss, social disintegration, and political instability. The health-care costs required to combat such diseases can significantly impair national development. To read about the costs of three particularly lethal diseases, see the Global Challenges feature, titled "Public Health Goes Global."

Classifying Countries

Nations are commonly classified as being *developed*, *newly industrialized*, or *developing*. These classifications are based on indicators such as national production, portion of the economy devoted to agriculture, amount of exports in the form of industrial goods, and overall economic structure. There is no single, agreed-upon list of countries in each category, however, and borderline countries are often classified differently in different listings. Let's take a closer look at each of these classifications.

developed country

Country that is highly industrialized and highly efficient, and whose people enjoy a high quality of life.

DEVELOPED COUNTRIES A country that is highly industrialized and highly efficient and whose people enjoy a high quality of life is a **developed country**. People in developed countries usually receive the finest health care and benefit from the best educational systems in the world. Most developed nations also support aid programs for helping poorer nations to improve their economies and standards of living. Countries in this category include Australia, Canada, Japan, New Zealand, the United States, and all Western European nations.

newly industrialized country (NIC)

Country that has recently increased the portion of its national production and exports derived from industrial operations.

NEWLY INDUSTRIALIZED COUNTRIES A country that has recently increased the portion of its national production and exports derived from industrial operations is a **newly industrialized country (NIC)**. The NICs are located primarily in Asia and Latin America. Most listings of NICs include

Global Challenges — Public Health Goes Global

Three communicable diseases present a serious global challenge. Beyond the human suffering, these diseases dim hopes for economic development in poor nations and put a drag on the global economy.

- **HIV/AIDS.** This disease has killed nearly as many people as the plague that struck fourteenth-century Europe. AIDS has already killed at least 22 million worldwide, and at least 40 million are infected with HIV/AIDS. In Africa alone, 20 million have died and 30 million are infected. In Sub-Saharan Africa, 22.9 million are living with the disease, and almost 90 percent of the 16.6 million children orphaned by AIDS live in this region. The disease has cut GDP growth by 2.6 percent in some African countries and could *decrease* South Africa's average household income 8 percent by 2013.

- **Tuberculosis.** Each year, tuberculosis (TB) kills 1.4 million people and sickens another 8.7 million. More than 90 percent of TB cases occur in low- and lower-middle-income countries across Southeast Asia, Eastern Europe, and Sub-Saharan Africa. The largest numbers of cases are found in China and in India, which accounts for almost 40 percent alone. TB is on the rise because of economic hardship, broken health systems, and the emergence of drug-resistant TB. This disease depletes the incomes of the poorest nations by about $12 billion.

- **Malaria.** According to the World Health Organization 2012 report, malaria kills 660 000 people per year and sickens another 219 million. Malaria is prevalent in Africa, where 90 percent of the deaths occur. The countries with the higher number of cases in the world are Nigeria, Congo, Tanzania, Uganda, Mozambique, and the Ivory Coast. In the worst affected African nations, malaria costs about 1.3 percent of GDP. The disease remains inextricably linked with poverty.

- **The Challenge.** To combat *HIV/AIDS*, rich nations could donate money for training doctors and nurses in poor nations and invest more in research. To battle *tuberculosis*, more aid money could purchase drugs that cost just $10 per person for the full six- to eight-month treatment. To fight *malaria*, better distribution of insecticide-treated bed nets could reach the 98 percent of Africa's children who do not sleep under such nets.

- **Want to Know More?** Visit the Global Business Coalition (www.businessfightsaids.org); the Global Fund to Fight AIDS, Tuberculosis, and Malaria (www.theglobalfund.org); the Malaria Foundation International (www.malaria.org); and the World Health Organization TB site (www.who.int/tb).

Sources: Malaria 2012 Report, World Health Organization (www.who.int/malaria); *Global Tuberculosis Report 2012,* World Health Organization (www.who.int/tb); Avert Website (www.avert.org/africa-hiv-aids-statistics.htm); "Altogether Now," *The Economist* (www.economist.com), June 3, 2010; Tom Randall, "J&J, Sanofi, Pfizer Speed Testing for New Tuberculosis Drug," *Bloomberg Businessweek* (www.businessweek.com), March 18, 2010; "Twenty-Five Years of AIDS," *The Economist,* June 3, 2006, pp. 24–25; Malaria Foundation International (www.malaria.org), various reports.

Asia's "four tigers" (Hong Kong, South Korea, Singapore, and Taiwan), Brazil, China, India, Malaysia, Mexico, South Africa, and Thailand. Depending on the pivotal criteria used for classification, a number of other countries could be placed in this category, including Argentina, Brunei, Chile, the Czech Republic, Hungary, Indonesia, the Philippines, Poland, Russia, Slovakia, Turkey, and Vietnam.

When we combine newly industrialized countries with countries that have the potential to become newly industrialized, we arrive at a category often called **emerging markets**. Generally, emerging markets have developed some (but not all) of the operations and export capabilities associated with NICs. Debate continues, however, over the defining characteristics of such classifications as *newly industrialized country* and *emerging market*.

emerging markets
Newly industrialized countries plus those with the potential to become newly industrialized.

DEVELOPING COUNTRIES A nation that has a poor infrastructure and extremely low personal incomes is called a **developing country** (also called a *less-developed country*). Developing countries often rely heavily on one or a few sectors of production, such as agriculture, mineral mining, or oil drilling. They might show potential for becoming newly industrialized countries, but they typically lack the necessary resources and skills to do so. Most lists of developing countries include many nations in Africa, the Middle East, and the poorest formerly communist nations in Eastern Europe and Asia.

developing country
Nation that has a poor infrastructure and extremely low personal incomes. Also called a less-developed country.

Developing countries (and NICs as well) are sometimes characterized by a high degree of **technological dualism**—use of the latest technologies in some sectors of the economy coupled with the use of outdated technologies in others. By contrast, developed countries typically incorporate the latest technological advancements in all manufacturing sectors.

technological dualism
Use of the latest technologies in some sectors of the economy coupled with the use of outdated technologies in other sectors.

Quick Study

1. Explain the value of the *Human Development Index (HDI)* in measuring a nation's level of development.
2. How are communicable diseases devastating human and economic development in some poor nations?
3. Identify the main characteristics of (a) developed countries, (b) newly industrialized countries, (c) emerging markets, and (d) developing countries.

Economic Transition

economic transition
Process by which a nation changes its fundamental economic organization and creates new free-market institutions.

Over the past two decades, countries with centrally planned economies have been remaking themselves in the image of stronger market economies. This process, called **economic transition**, involves changing a nation's fundamental economic organization and creating entirely new free-market institutions. Some nations take transition further than others do, but the process typically involves several key reform measures:

- Stabilize the economy, reduce budget deficits, and expand credit availability.
- Allow prices to reflect supply and demand.
- Legalize private business, sell state-owned companies, and support property rights.
- Reduce barriers to trade and investment, and allow currency convertibility.

Obstacles to Transition

Transition from central planning to free-market economics generates tremendous international business opportunities. Yet difficulties arising from years of socialist economic principles hampered progress from the start, and some countries still endure high unemployment rates. In many nations undergoing transition, worries over employment affect children as well as adults, which troubles social experts. Surveys find that when children in transition countries are asked what kind of country they want to live in, employment and the economy are primary concerns.

Let's examine the key remaining obstacles for countries in transition: lack of managerial expertise, shortage of capital, cultural differences, and environmental degradation.

LACK OF MANAGERIAL EXPERTISE In central planning, there was little need for production, distribution, and marketing strategies or for trained individuals to devise them. Central planners formerly decided all aspects of the nation's commercial activities. There was no need to investigate consumer wants and no need for market research. And little thought was given to product pricing or to the need for experts in operations, inventory, distribution, or logistics. Factory managers at government-owned firms had only to meet production requirements set by central planners. In fact, some products rolled off assembly lines merely to be stacked outside the factory because knowing where they were to go after production—and who took them there—was not the factory manager's job.

Recent years, however, are seeing higher quality management in transition countries. Reasons for this trend include improved education, opportunities to study and work abroad, and changes in work habits caused by companies investing locally. Some managers from former communist nations are even finding managerial opportunities with large multinational companies in Western Europe and North America.

SHORTAGE OF CAPITAL Not surprisingly, economic transition is expensive. To facilitate the process and ease the pain, governments usually spend a great deal of money to:

- Develop a telecommunications and infrastructure system, including highways, bridges, rail networks, and sometimes subways.
- Create financial institutions, including stock markets and a banking system.
- Educate people in the ways of market economics.

The governments of many countries in transition cannot afford all the investments required of them. Outside sources of capital are available, however, including national and international companies, other governments, and international financial institutions, such as the World Bank, the International Monetary Fund (IMF), and the Asian Development Bank. Some transition countries owe substantial amounts of money to international lenders, but this is less of a problem today than it was earlier in the era of transition economies.[19]

CULTURAL DIFFERENCES   Economic transition and reform make deep cultural impressions on a nation's people. As we saw in Chapter 2, some cultures are more open to change than others. Likewise, certain cultures welcome economic change more easily than others do. Transition replaces dependence on the government with greater emphasis on individual responsibility, incentives, and rights. But sudden deep cuts in welfare payments, unemployment benefits, and guaranteed government jobs can present a major shock to a nation's people.

Importing modern management practices into the culture of a transition country can be difficult. South Korea's Daewoo Motors (www.daewoo.com) faced a culture clash when it entered Central Europe. Korea's management system is based on a rigid hierarchical structure and an intense work ethic. Managers at Daewoo's car plants in South Korea arrived early for work to stand and greet workers at the company gates. But problems arose when Daewoo's managers did not fully comprehend the culture at its factories in Central Europe. Daewoo bridged the cultural and workplace gaps by sending Central European workers to staff assembly lines in Korea, and sent Korean managers and technicians to work in Central and Eastern Europe.

ENVIRONMENTAL DEGRADATION   The economic and social policies of former communist governments in Central and Eastern Europe were disastrous for the natural environment. The direct effects of environmental destruction were evident in high levels of sickness and disease, including asthma, blood deficiencies, and cancer—which lowered productivity in the workplace. Countries in transition often suffer periods during which the negative effects of a market economy seem to outweigh its benefits. In other words, it is hard to enjoy a larger pay cheque when smokestacks are polluting the air and the parks and rivers are polluted. Commuters can suffer carbon monoxide poisoning, and children can get lead poisoning from flaking house paint.

Emerging Market Focus: Russia

Russia's experience with communism began in 1917. For the next 75 years, factories, distribution, and all other facets of operations, as well as the prices of labour, capital, and products, were controlled by the government. While China was experimenting with private farm ownership and a limited market-price system, Russia and other nations in the Soviet Union remained staunchly communist under a system of complete government ownership. The total absence of market institutions meant that, unlike China, Russia endured massive political change along with economic reform when it embarked on its transition.

ROUGH TRANSITION   In the 1980s, the former Soviet Union entered a new era of freedom of thought, freedom of expression, and economic restructuring. For the first time since 1917, people could speak freely about their lives under economic socialism, and speak freely they did. People vented their frustrations over a general lack of consumer goods, poor-quality products, and long lines at banks and grocery stores.

But transition away from government ownership and central planning has been challenging. Except for politicians, bureaucrats, and wealthy businesspeople (called "oligarchs" in Russia), ordinary people are having difficulty maintaining their standard of living and affording many basic items. Some Russians are doing well financially because they were factory managers under the old system and retained their jobs in the new system. Others have turned to the black market to amass personal wealth. Still others are working hard to build legitimate companies but find themselves forced into making "protection" payments to organized crime.

An opaque legal system, rampant corruption, and shifting business laws make Russia a place where non-Russian businesspeople must operate cautiously. Yet some ambitious, foreign entrepreneurs are not deterred by such obstacles. For some insights on how brave entrepreneurs can do business in today's Russia, see the Entrepreneur's Toolkit, titled "Russian Rules of the Game."

CHALLENGES AHEAD FOR RUSSIA   As in so many other transitional economies, Russia needs to foster *managerial talent*. Years of central planning delayed the development of managerial skills needed in a market-based economy. Russian managers must improve their skills in every facet of management practice, including financial control, research and development, human resource management, and marketing strategy.

Political instability, especially in the form of intensified nationalist sentiment, is another potential threat to progress. Strong ethnic and nationalist sentiments in the region can cause misunderstandings to quickly spiral out of control. The lack of security for Russia's nuclear weapons stockpile is also a potential cause of instability. These weapons in the hands of terrorists would threaten global security.

An *unstable investment climate* is another concern within the international business community. Tense uneasiness characterizes relations between Russia's government and its business community. The uneasiness stems from the Russian government's attacks on both business owners that disagree with official policy and on businesses it wants to control.

The root of many of Russia's problems appears to be *corrupt law enforcement*. Officials of the government, such as the Russian Interior Ministry, are accused of raiding the offices of companies for documents and computers. Records are then falsified and signatures forged to make it appear that another company—one controlled by government officials—has massively overpaid taxes and is due a government refund. Meanwhile, the owners and managers of the raided businesses often find themselves behind Russian prison bars.[20]

The Russian government confiscated oil giant Yukos and threw its chief, Mikhail Khodorkovsky, in jail on charges of fraud, embezzlement, and tax evasion. Observers of events in Russia say that Khodorkovsky's problems were based in his refusal to bow to Russia's bureaucrats and that he ran Yukos as if it were a private company. He also tried to create a new class of people in Russia who would one day push for political reforms there by financing boarding schools for orphans, computer classes for village schools, and civil-society programs for journalists and politicians. His actions clearly made him a threat to the state.[21] If Russia truly wishes to become a location of choice for international companies, it will need to meddle less in business and begin to safeguard property rights.

Quick Study

1. What are several reform measures involved in *economic transition*?
2. Describe some of the remaining obstacles to businesses in transitional economies.
3. Explain Russia's experience with economic transition.

Entrepreneur's Toolkit   Russian Rules of the Game

Although business in Russia can be brutal at times, some go-getting entrepreneurs and small business owners are venturing into this rugged land. If you are one of them, or just an interested observer, here are a few pointers on doing business in Russia.

- **Getting Started.** A visit to your country's local chamber of commerce in Russia should be high on your list. The best organized and managed of these hold regularly scheduled luncheons at which you can make contacts with Russians and others wanting to do business. They might also offer programs on getting acquainted with the business climate in Russia. Many businesses get started in Moscow, St. Petersburg, or Vladivostok, depending in part on their line of business.
- **Be Adventurous.** The kind of person who will succeed in Russia thrives on adventure and enjoys a challenge. He or she also should not demand predictability in day-to-day activities—Russia is anything but predictable. Initially, knowledge of Russian is helpful though not essential, but eventual proficiency

will be necessary. Prior experience working and living in Eastern Europe would be a big plus.

- **Office Space.** Doing business in Russia demands a personal touch. Locating an office in Russia is crucial if you eventually want to receive income from your operations. Your office does not need to be a suite off Red Square. Almost any local address will do, and a nice flat can double as an office at the start. For business services, upscale hotels commonly have business centres in them. Eventually, renting an average Russian-style office would be more than adequate.
- **Making Deals.** Business in Russia takes time and patience. The Russian negotiating style, like the country itself, is tough and ever changing. During negotiations, emotional outbursts, walkouts, or threats to walk out should not be unexpected from your Russian counterparts. Finally, signed contracts in Russia are not always followed to the letter, as your Russian associate may view new circumstances as a chance to renegotiate terms. All in all, the personalities of individuals involved in business dealings counts for much in Russia.

Bottom Line for Business

This completes our four-chapter coverage of national business environments. This chapter showed us that economic freedom tends to generate higher standards of living. This relation is causing mixed economies to remove unnecessary regulation and government interference. Formerly centrally planned economies continue free market reforms to drive domestic entrepreneurial activity and attract international investors. These trends are changing the face of global capitalism. Two topics are likely to dominate conversations on development—the race between China and India, and the productivity gap between the United States and Europe. For Canadians, a third topic under discussion is Canada's low productivity rate, which impairs its competitiveness in the global economy.

Economic Development in China vs. India

Both China and India have immense potential for growth, and it is only a matter of time before each has a middle class larger than the entire North American population. Whether the organic-led path of India or the investment-led path of China is best for a particular nation depends on that nation's circumstances.

Every nation on earth has so far followed a path to development that relied on its natural resources and/or its relatively cheap labour—the model China is following. The money turning China into the world's factory is coming from foreign companies, which is doing little to help China create its own powerful multinationals. Also, China's top-down approach to development and India's bottom-up approach reflect their political systems: India is a democracy, and China is not. Although China is growing rapidly, it needs home-grown entrepreneurs and Western-style managerial skills to take it to the next level of global competitiveness.

If India can achieve sustained economic growth, it will become the first developing nation to advance economically by relying on the brainpower of its people. India's growth came largely from native competitive firms in cutting-edge, knowledge-based industries. Although India has a long reputation for high taxes and burdensome regulations, it also has had the foundations of a market economy, such as private enterprise, democratic government, and Western accounting practices. India also has a relatively advanced legal system, fairly efficient capital markets, and many talented entrepreneurs.

Productivity in the United States vs. Europe

Productivity growth is a key driver of living standards in any nation. Although productivity growth in Europe kept pace with that in the United States for decades, it has fallen behind in recent years. In fact, while US productivity growth hovers above 3 percent, the rate in Europe's main economies is a little more than half that. But why is there a productivity gap at all?

Several explanations have been proposed. First, despite its benefits, information technology (IT) spending in Europe lags behind that in the United States. Europeans may be discouraged from spending on IT for reasons related to European business law. Second, stronger labour laws in Europe relative to the United States make it more difficult and costly to shed workers. Thus, even if European companies invest in IT to increase labour productivity, overall productivity gains may be hampered by their inability to rid themselves of excess workers. Third, although the US tech sector is a big driver behind higher US productivity growth, the tech sector in Europe is far smaller by comparison. Fourth, although spending on research and development (R&D) is a big boost to productivity growth, Europe spends far less overall on R&D.

Strong productivity growth means higher profits, better living standards, and stable prices. Many European officials are calling for a greater shift toward free market reform to boost productivity growth rates. European officials understand that robust productivity growth is the only way for their citizens to close the gap with their US counterparts.

Productivity Lag in Canada

Unlike the United States, Canada's productivity rate is only about 0.88 percent. According to a Deloitte report called *The Future of Productivity: Clear Choices for a Competitive Canada*, the biggest threat to the standard of living in Canada is its declining productivity. The main factors identified are risk aversion, low export activity, weak R&D, and long-term government strategy.

The Deloitte report points out that Canada's labour costs have increased 23 percent since 2000. Probable causes include companies' reluctance to invest in labour-saving machinery and equipment that would make employees more productive; inflexible labour contracts; and the high value of the Canadian dollar relative to the US dollar.

Canada's financial sector, although it successfully weathered the recent economic crisis, lags in productivity. This may be due to Canadian banks' focus on retail banking rather than investment banking, which is more risky but also more productive in terms of value produced for hours worked.

Compared to other Western nations, Canada has a relatively high number of fast-growing start-ups and new businesses. However, many of these companies fail to live up to their promise. Of Canadian service companies in business for five or more years, for example, only 2.66 percent maintained high growth.

Recommendations for Canadian businesses are to go national and global rather than stay local; to invest in new equipment and technology; to search out and retain talented and skilled employees; to create strategic relationships (clusters) that will augment the capabilities of both partners in such areas as distribution channels, equipment, expertise, and so forth; and to innovate and invest in R&D. For its part, government needs to develop strategies to encourage business growth and investment in Canada.[22]

Chapter Summary

1. **Describe what is meant by a centrally planned economy and explain why its use is declining.**
   - In a *centrally planned economy*, the government owns land, factories, and other economic resources and plans nearly all economic-related activities.
   - The philosophy of central planning stresses the group over individual well-being and strives for economic and social equality.
   - One reason for the decline of central planning is that scarce resources were wasted because central planners paid little attention to product quality and buyers' needs.
   - Second, a lack of incentives to innovate resulted in little or no economic growth and consistently low standards of living.
   - Third, central planners realized that other economic systems were achieving far higher growth rates for other countries.
   - Fourth, consumers became fed up with a lack of basic necessities such as adequate food, housing, and health care.

2. **Identify the main characteristics of a mixed economy and explain the emphasis on privatization.**
   - In a *mixed economy*, land, factories, and other economic resources are split between private and government ownership.
   - In mixed economies, governments tend to control economic sectors crucial to national security and long-term stability.
   - Proponents of mixed economies say that a successful economic system must be not only efficient and innovative, but must also protect society from unchecked individualism and organizational greed.
   - Many mixed economies are engaging in *privatization* (the sale of government-owned economic resources) to become more efficient in how they use resources.

3. **Explain how a market economy functions and identify its distinguishing features.**
   - In a *market economy*, private individuals or businesses own the majority of land, factories, and other economic resources.
   - Economic decisions in a market economy are influenced by the interplay of *supply* and *demand*.
   - Market economics is rooted in the belief that individual concerns are paramount and that the group benefits when individuals receive proper incentives and rewards.
   - To function smoothly, a market economy requires free choice (in buyers' purchasing options), free enterprise (in producers' competitive decisions), and price flexibility (reflecting supply and demand).
   - Government's role in a market economy involves enforcing antitrust (antimonopoly) laws, preserving property rights, providing a stable fiscal and monetary environment, and preserving political stability.

4. **Describe the different ways to measure a nation's level of development.**
   - *Economic development* refers to the economic well-being of one nation's people compared with that of another nation's people.
   - The United Nations developed a World Risk Index. The index uses four indicators to define countries at risk of natural disasters, including exposure, susceptibility, coping capacity, and adaptive capacity.
   - One method for gauging economic development is *national production*, which includes measures such as *gross national product* and *gross domestic product*.
   - A second method is *purchasing power parity (PPP)*, which refers to the relative ability of two countries' currencies to buy the same "basket" of goods in those two countries.
   - Purchasing power parity is used to correct international comparisons made at official exchange rates.
   - The Big Mac Index, based on the theory of *purchasing power parity (PPP)*, uses a McDonald's Big Mac as the "basket" for comparison purposes.
   - A third method is the United Nations' *Human Development Index (HDI)*, which measures the extent to which a people's needs are satisfied and addressed equally across the population.

5. Discuss the process of economic transition and identify the obstacles for business.
   - *Economic transition* is the process whereby a nation changes its fundamental economic organization to create free-market institutions.
   - Economic transition typically involves five reform measures: (1) macroeconomic stabilization; (2) liberalization of economic activity; (3) legalization of private enterprises and privatization of state-owned enterprises; (4) removal of barriers to free trade, investment, and currency flows; and (5) development of a social welfare system.
   - One remaining obstacle to transition is a *lack of managerial expertise* because central planners made virtually all business decisions.
   - A second obstacle is a *shortage of capital* to pay for new communications and infrastructure, new financial institutions, and education.
   - A third obstacle is *cultural differences* between transition economies and the West that can make introducing modern management practices difficult.
   - A fourth obstacle is *environmental degradation* that can lower productivity due to poor health conditions.

Key Terms

centrally planned economy 142	economic transition 164	privatization 147
demand 150	emerging markets 163	purchasing power 160
developed country 162	Human Development Index (HDI) 161	purchasing power parity (PPP) 160
developing country 163	market economy 150	supply 150
economic development 153	mixed economy 146	technological dualism 163
economic system 142	newly industrialized country (NIC) 162	

Talk It Over

1. The Internet has penetrated many aspects of business and culture in developed countries, but it is barely available in many poor countries. Do you think this technology will widen the economic development gap between rich and poor countries? Why or why not? Is there a way for developing countries to use such technologies as tools for economic development?

2. Imagine that you are the director of a major international lending institution supported by funds from member countries. What one area in newly industrialized and developing economies would be your priority for receiving development aid? Do you suspect that any member country will be politically opposed to aid in this area? Why or why not?

3. Two students are discussing the pros and cons of different measures of economic development. "GDP per capita," declares the first, "is the only true measure of how developed a country's economy is." The second student counters: "I disagree. The only true measure of a country's economic development is its people's quality of life, regardless of its GDP." Why is each of these students incorrect?

Take It to the Web

1. **Video Report.** Visit YouTube (www.youtube.com) and search for the video called "William Easterly and Dambiso Moyo: Emerging Economies 2013." Watch the video, and then summarize it in a half-page report. Think about what you have learned in this chapter. Which components of economic systems and economic development can you identify in the video? How might a company engaged in international business act on the information contained in this video?

2. **Web Site Report.** Governments across Western Europe are privatizing state-owned companies, and nations in Eastern Europe are transitioning toward market-based economies.

   Go to the European Union (EU) Web site (europa.eu), and search for information regarding its progress on issues presented in this chapter. Possible topics include privatization, economic and social development, global competition, and national infrastructure. For the topic(s) of your choice, what are the EU's goals? What specific policies will help the EU achieve those goals? Does the EU directly address the challenges (such as increased competition) that globalization presents to its companies?

   Some countries (such as Estonia, Hungary, and Poland) outperformed others (such as Bulgaria and Romania) during their post-communist transitions. For your topic(s), what specific policies does the EU have in place to help nations in transition develop? Identify as many economic, social, and cultural efforts as you can.

Practising International Management Case

Cuba Comes Off Its Sugar High

When the Soviet Union still existed, Cuba would barter sugar with its communist allies in return for oil and other goods. But when the Soviet Union crumbled in 1989, Cuba had to say good-bye to its preferential barter rates and Soviet subsidies. The only option left to Cuba's leader, Fidel Castro, was to sell the nation's sugar on the open market. But whereas sugar exports earned Cuba $5 billion in 1990, they earned a paltry $20 million in 2006. Production fell from a peak of more than 8 million tons in 1989 to around 1 million tons in 2010. With decreasing revenues on world markets, falling production, and inefficient sugar mills that guzzle expensive oil, Castro had no choice but to shut down about half the island-nation's mills. Today, Cuba remains a *net sugar importer*, and power is now in the hands of Fidel's brother, Raul.

With the remaining state-owned industrial dinosaurs wheezing away and the economy under immense strain, Castro opened up key state industries to non-Cuban investment. As a result, joint ventures became a key plank in the effort to prop up Cuba through limited economic reforms. The money came chiefly from Canada, Mexico, and Europe—all of whom benefited from the absence of Cuba's neighbour and nemesis, the United States, which has maintained a trade embargo against Cuba since 1962. Much of the investment occurred in another commodity that Cuba has to offer the world—nickel. Cuba holds 30 percent of the world's reserves of nickel, which is used in stainless steel and other alloys, and it exports 75 percent of its nickel to Europe. One of the biggest mining firms active in Cuba today is Canada's Sherritt International Corporation (www.sherritt.com). Sherritt's flag flutters outside the island's biggest nickel mine, and Sherritt rigs are reviving output from old oil fields. After turning around the ailing nickel mine at Moa, Sherritt received Castro's go-ahead to develop beach resorts and beef up communications and transport networks.

Although international concerns like Sherritt are free to invest in Cuba, they face some harsh realities and restrictions. Although Castro allowed a bit of capitalism into his communist haven, Cuba is burdened with complex and contradictory rules and regulations. And once foreigners begin to figure out the rules, the government changes them. "There are times when the Cubans seem to go out of their way to create obstacles," complained one European businessman. "They need us, we can do business here, so I don't understand what the problem is." But it seemed Cuba's government was going to do little to help.

Ricardo Elizondo came to Cuba from Mexico to help manage his company's stake in ETECSA, Cuba's national telecommunications firm. Elizondo reports that anyone who wants to do business in Cuba must accept the reality of partnership with a socialist state. Cuba lacks a legal system to enforce commercial contracts, it lacks a banking system to offer credit, and there are no private-property rights. One thing the government doesn't lack is plenty of labour laws—and these are onerous. Non-Cuban partners cannot hire, fire, or even pay workers directly. They must pay the government to provide labourers who, in turn, are paid only a fraction of these payments. Human rights group Freedom House (www.freedomhouse.org) says one company paid the Cuban government $9500 per year per worker, but the workers received only $120 to $144 per year. Meanwhile, there are reports that an average of 1.2 buildings collapse in central Havana every day.

Why do companies investing in Cuba put up with such restrictions? For one thing, they are getting a great return on their investment. "Cuba's assets are incredibly cheap, and the potential return is huge," says Frank Mersch, VP at Toronto's Altamira Management (www.altamira.com), which holds 11 percent of Sherritt. Analysts say that Cuba is offering outsiders deals with rates of return up to 80 percent a year. Moreover, international investors acknowledge that the Castro brothers' regime cannot last forever. In a post-Castro era, the United States may end its embargo; in which case, property prices would soar. Companies such as Sherritt and ETECSA, who stepped in first, will have gained a valuable toehold in what could be a vibrant market economy.

Thinking Globally

1. Why do you think the Cuban government requires non-Cuban businesses to hire and pay workers only through the government? Do you think it is ethical for non-Cuban businesses to enter into partnerships with the Cuban government? Why or why not?

2. Do some research on Cuba, and describe a scenario for economic transition in the event that the current regime collapses. How do you think transition to a market economy in Cuba would differ from the experiences of Russia and China?

3. How might a Canadian company and its shareholders be affected by the US anti-Cuba Act?

4. The United States is Canada's largest trading partner. Some Canadian businesses with large investments in the United States may want to support the US embargo on Cuba in order to protect their US investments. Can a Canadian company be sanctioned for honouring the US embargo? Please justify your answer.

Sources: Archibald Ritter, "Cuba in the 2010s: Creative Reform or Geriatric Paralysis?" *Focal Point,* April 2010, pp. 12–13; "U.S. Is $500 Million Supermarket to Cuba," CNBC Web site (www.cnbc.com), May 27, 2010; Steve LeVine and Geri Smith, "New Cuba Policy Is No Business Home Run," *Bloomberg Businessweek* (www.businessweek.com), April 15, 2009; Cuba Coverage on the Foreign Policy Blogs Network (cuba.foreignpolicyblogs.com), various reports and data.

Teaming Up CROSS-CULTURAL BUSINESS

For the countries you are studying, list several of their peoples' manners and customs. What values do people hold dear? Describe their attitude toward time, work, and cultural change. What religions are practised there? What language(s) are spoken? What ethnicities reside in the nation, and do they form distinct subcultures? Describe the nation's social structure and its education system. Turn to Figures 2.2 and 2.3, and either:

a. explain why you think the nation appears where it does, or
b. identify where you think it belongs on the figure and explain why.

Politics and Law

For the countries you are studying, what type of political and legal systems do they have? Do free elections take place? Is the government heavily involved in the economy? Is the legal system effective and impartial? Do political and legal conditions suggest the country could be a potential market? If so, for what kinds of goods or services might the market be appealing? What is the level of corruption in the nation? Is legislation pending that may be relevant to international companies?

International Ethics

For each of the countries your team is researching, answer the following questions: What is the corruption perception index score? What ethical dilemmas or challenges might you encounter in the country? Are there examples of CSR being applied by local companies?

Economics and Emerging Markets

For each of the countries your team is researching, answer the following questions: What type of economic system does it have? Has it always had this type of economic system? Is it a developed, newly industrializing, emerging, or developing country? How does it rank on the various measures of economic development? Has it undergone any form of economic transition within the past 20 years? If so, how has that transition affected the culture and the country's political, legal, and economic systems?

CHAPTER SIX

International Trade

Learning Objectives

After studying this chapter, you should be able to

1. Describe the relationship between international trade volume and world output, and identify overall trade patterns.

2. Describe the political, economic, and cultural motives behind governmental intervention in trade.

3. List and explain the methods governments use to promote and restrict international trade.

4. Describe mercantilism and explain its impact on world powers and their colonies.

5. Explain the theories of absolute advantage and comparative advantage.

6. Explain the factor proportions and international product life cycle theories.

7. Explain the new trade and national competitive advantage theories.

A LOOK BACK

Chapters 2, 3, 4, and 5 examined cultural, political, legal, ethical, and economic differences among countries. We covered these differences early because of their important influence on international business activities.

A LOOK AT THIS CHAPTER

This chapter begins our study of the international trade and investment environment. We explore the oldest form of international business activity—international trade. We discuss the benefits and volume of international trade. We also examine the motives for government intervention in trade and the tools nations use to accomplish their goals. Finally, we survey the major theories that explain why international trade occurs.

A LOOK AHEAD

In Chapter 7 we continue our discussion of the international business environment. We explore recent patterns of foreign direct investment, theories that explain the trends and patterns, and the role of government in influencing investment flows.

Source: ShutterStock.

From Bentonville to Fuzhou

BENTONVILLE, Arkansas—Walmart (www.walmart.com) first became an international company in 1991 when it built a new store near Mexico City, Mexico. Today, Walmart has around 4200 stores in the United States, 380 in Canada, and 6400 stores in 25 other countries. With more than $443.9 billion in sales globally, Walmart is the world's largest company by revenue—yet it is based in a state in which chickens outnumber people. Pictured here is a Walmart store in the city of Fuzhou in the province of Fujian, China.

Source: Newscom.

Aggressive global expansion by Walmart (and similar firms) is helping boost international trade. To win over customers as it extends its reach around the world, Walmart relies on the slogan: "Save Money. Live Better." To fulfill its promise and deliver the lowest priced goods, Walmart sources inexpensive merchandise from low-cost production locations such as China. The discount retailer has played a big part in increasing Chinese imports to the NAFTA countries in recent years. In fact, if Walmart were a country, it would be China's sixth largest trading partner. The actions of Walmart and other global firms have propelled world exports of goods and services to record levels.

Growth in international trade is increasing interdependence between China and the rest of the world. Walmart and others are quickly transforming China into the world's factory. China's international trade is expanding at a rate that is about two to three times faster than trade growth for the rest of the world. Around 18 percent of Japan's imports come from China, and about 11 percent of all goods imported by Canada are Chinese-made. Yet, China's imports are also growing. China imports wood, wood pulp, ores, charcoal, water purification systems, oil and gas technologies, and mineral fuels from Canada. China is also becoming a larger market for Walmart and other Western consumer-goods businesses.

As you read this chapter, consider why nations trade and how the ambitions of firms such as Walmart are driving growth in world trade.[1]

P eople around the world are accustomed to purchasing goods and services produced in other countries. In fact, many consumers get their first taste of another country's culture through merchandise purchased from that country. Chanel No. 5 (www.chanel.com) perfume evokes the romanticism of France. The fine artwork on Imari porcelain conveys the Japanese attention to detail and quality.

In this chapter, we explore international trade in goods and services. We begin by examining the benefits, volume, and patterns of international trade. We then discuss the motives for government intervention in trade and the tools that nations use to accomplish their international trade goals. We explore a number of important theories that explain why nations trade with one another.

Overview of International Trade

international trade
Purchase, sale, or exchange of goods and services across national borders.

The purchase, sale, or exchange of goods and services across national borders is called **international trade**. This is in contrast to domestic trade, which occurs between different states, regions, or cities within a country.

In recent years, nations that embrace globalization are seeing trade grow in importance for their economies. One way to measure the importance of trade to a nation is to examine the volume of an economy's trade relative to its total output. Map 6.1 shows each nation's trade volume as a share of its gross domestic product (GDP). Trade as a share of GDP is defined as the sum of exports and imports (of goods and services) divided by GDP. Recall that GDP is the value of all goods and services produced by a domestic economy over a one-year period. Map 6.1 demonstrates the value of trade passing through some nations' borders actually exceeds the amount of goods and services that they produce (the "over 100 percent" category).

Benefits of International Trade

International trade is opening doors to new entrepreneurial opportunity across the globe. It also provides a country's people with a greater choice of goods and services. Because Japan, for example, has a dense population with limited territory, it cannot grow enough fruits and vegetables to feed its population. Japan sells electronics, cars, and auto parts (which it produces in abundance) to Canada. It then uses the proceeds from the sale of products derived from electronics and other goods to buy Canadian-grown fruits, vegetables, and beef. Thus, people in Japan get food products they would otherwise not have. Likewise, although Canada has an automotive industry, the cars and auto parts products imported from Japan might be of a certain quality or have a differentiated feature that fills a gap in the Canadian marketplace.

International trade is an important engine for job creation in many countries. The Department of Foreign Affairs and International Trade Canada estimates that 20 percent of all jobs in Canada are directly or indirectly derived from exports. According to Statistics Canada, over 150 000 business establishments were engaged in goods importing in 2009. These businesses hired over 33 percent of the Canadian labour force.[2]

Volume of International Trade

The value and volume of international trade continues to increase. Today world merchandise exports are valued at more than $18 trillion, and service exports at $4.1 trillion.[3] Table 6.1 shows the world's largest exporters of merchandise and services. Perhaps not surprisingly, China ranks first in commercial services exports and second in merchandise imports (behind the United States).

Most of world merchandise trade is composed of trade in manufactured goods. The dominance of manufactured goods in the trade of merchandise has persisted over time and will likely continue to do so. The reason is its growth is much faster than trade in the two other classifications of merchandise—mining and agricultural products. Although the importance of trade in services is growing for many nations, it tends to be relatively more important for the world's richest countries. Trade in services accounts for around 20 percent of total world trade.

TRADE AND WORLD OUTPUT   The level of world output in any given year influences the level of international trade in that year. Slower world economic output slows the volume of international trade, and higher output propels greater trade. Trade slows in times of economic recession because when people are less certain about their own financial futures they buy fewer domestic and imported products. Another reason output and trade move together is that a country

TABLE 6.1	World's Top 15 Exporters and Importers								

Rank	Exporters	Value	Share	Annual percentage change	Rank	Importers	Value	Share	Annual percentage change
1	China	1578	10.4	31	1	United States	1968	12.8	23
2	United States	1278	8.4	21	2	China	1395	9.1	39
3	Germany	1269	8.3	13	3	Germany	1067	6.9	15
4	Japan	770	5.1	33	4	Japan	693	4.5	25
5	Netherlands	572	3.8	15	5	France	606	3.9	8
6	France	521	3.4	7	6	United Kingdom	558	3.6	15
7	Korea, Republic of	466	3.1	28	7	Netherlands	517	3.4	17
8	Italy	448	2.9	10	8	Italy	484	3.1	17
9	Belgium	411	2.7	11	9	Hong Kong, China	442	2.9	25
						– retained imports[a]	116	0.8	31
10	United Kingdom	405	2.7	15	10	Korea, Republic of	425	2.8	32
11	Hong Kong, China	401	2.6	22	11	Canada[b]	402	2.6	22
	– domestic exports[a]	18	0.1	7					
	– re-exports[a]	383	2.5	23					
12	Russian Federation	400	2.6	32	12	Belgium	390	2.5	11
13	Canada	387	2.5	22	13	India	323	2.1	25
14	Singapore	352	2.3	30	14	Spain	312	2.0	6
	– domestic exports	183	1.2	32					
	– re-exports	169	1.1	28					
15	Mexico	298	2.0	30	15	Singapore	311	2.0	26
						– retained imports[c]	142	0.9	24

[a] Secretariat estimates.

[b] Imports are valued f.o.b.

[c] Singapore's retained imports are defined as imports less re-exports.

Source: WTO Secretariat, *"The World Trade Report 2011",* Appendix Table 3 http://www.wto.org/english/res_e/booksp_e/anrep_e/world_trade_report11_e.pdf. Reprinted with permission of the World Trade Organization.

in recession also often has a currency that is weak relative to other nations. This makes imports more expensive relative to domestic products. (We discuss the relation between currency values and trade in Chapter 9.) In addition to international trade and world output moving in lockstep fashion, trade has consistently grown faster than output.

International Trade Patterns

Exploring the volume of international trade and world output provides useful insights into the international trade environment, but it does not tell us who trades with whom. It does not reveal whether trade occurs primarily between the world's richest nations or whether there is significant trade activity involving poorer nations.

Customs agencies in most countries record the destination of exports, the source of imports, and the physical quantities and values of goods crossing their borders. Although this type of data is sometimes misleading, customs data does reflect overall trade patterns among nations. For example, governments sometimes deliberately distort the reporting of trade in military equipment or other sensitive goods. In other cases, extensive trade in unofficial (underground) economies can distort the real picture of trade between nations.

Large ocean-going cargo vessels are needed to support these patterns in international trade and deliver merchandise from one shore to another. In fact, more than 90 percent of global trade is carried by sea, typically in containers. As a whole, the developing countries' share of global

MAP 6.1

Importance of Trade

http://data.worldbank.org/indicator/TG.VAL.
TOTL.GD.ZS/countries?display=map

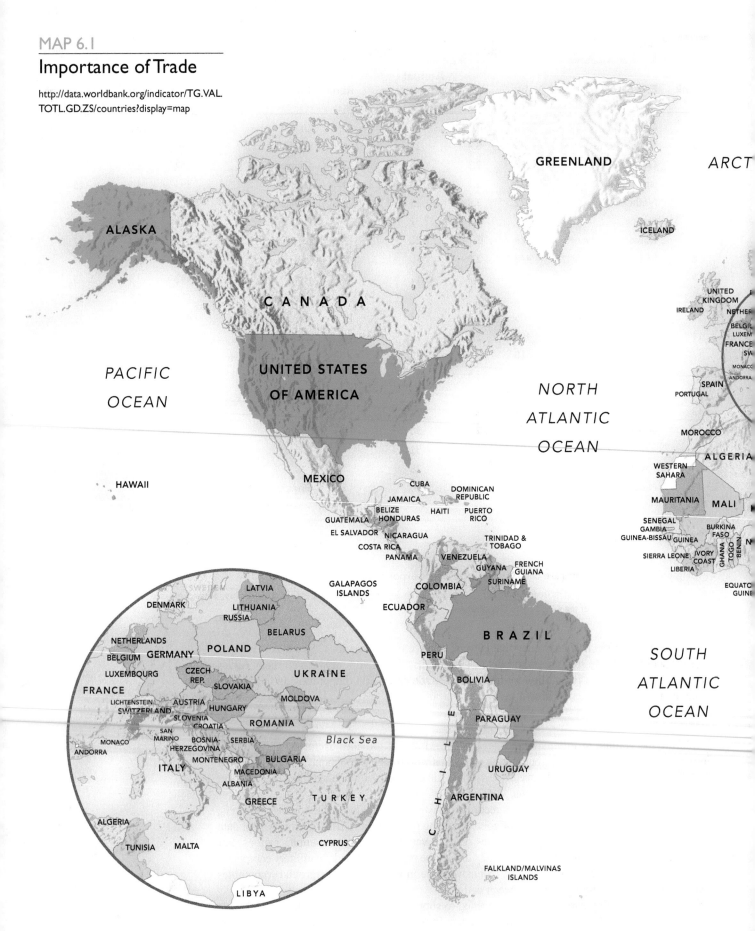

Trade as a percent of GDP

- over 100%
- 75%–100%
- 50%–74%
- 25%–49%
- less than 25%
- no data available

shipping is rising, and today accounts for around 60 percent of all goods. Yet, global merchant shipping companies are feeling the pinch of higher oil prices, resulting in importers absorbing a portion of the higher shipping costs. The increasing cost of transportation is creating a trend where companies are deciding to switch production closer to home, reducing the need for additional merchant shipping capacity.[4]

WHO TRADES WITH WHOM? There has been a persistent pattern of merchandise trade among nations. Trade between the world's high-income economies accounts for roughly 60 percent of total world merchandise trade. Two-way trade between high-income countries and low- and middle-income nations accounts for about 34 percent of world merchandise trade. Meanwhile, merchandise trade between low- and middle-income nations accounts for only about 6 percent of total world trade. These figures reveal the low purchasing power of the world's poorest nations and indicate their general lack of economic development.

Map 6.2 shows intra-regional and extra-regional trade data (in percentages and billion dollars) for the major regions of the world's economy. What immediately stands out is the number representing intra-regional trade for Asia. This number tells us that 52 percent of Asia's exports are destined for other Asian nations. The percentage has not increased much, however, in the last decade. But if we analyze the amount in billions of dollars, Asian intra-regional trade has more than doubled. Asian's extra-regional trade has also increased significantly in billions of dollars. As these nations' economies grow, it will become increasingly important for managers to fully understand how to do business in Asia. For some pointers on doing business in Pacific Rim nations, see this chapter's Global Manager's Briefcase, titled "Doing Business in the Pacific Rim."

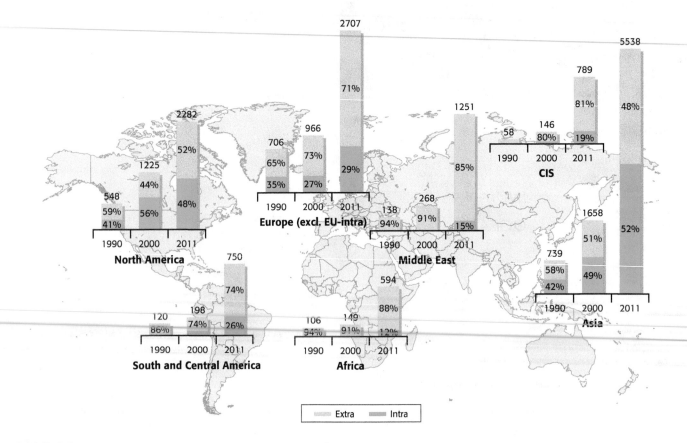

MAP 6.2

Intra-Regional and Extra-Regional Merchandise Exports 1990–2011 (Billion Dollars and Percentage)

Source: WTO Secretariat, *"The World Trade Report 2011"*, Map B.2, p. 69 http://www.wto.org/english/res_e/booksp_e/anrep_e/world_trade_report11_e.pdf. Reprinted with permission of the World Trade Organization.

In contrast, intra-regional exports account for only 12 percent of all exports in Africa and 15 percent of intra-regional exports in Middle East. Another important observation is that North America's total exports in billions of dollars have not increased as much as all the other regions in the past decade. All the developing regions (South and Central America, the Middle East, and Asia) increased their total exports considerably in comparison with the previous decade.

Trade Dependence and Independence

Countries differ in the extent of their trade interdependencies. Some nations depend almost entirely on trade with one other country, whereas some nations depend on no single trade partner. Complete independence was considered desirable from the sixteenth century through much of the eighteenth century. Some remote island nations were completely independent simply because they lacked methods of transportation to engage in trade. But today isolationism is generally considered undesirable.

Trade between most nations today is characterized by a certain degree of interdependency. Companies in advanced nations trade a great deal with companies in other advanced nations. The level of interdependency between pairs of countries often reflects the amount of trade that occurs between a company's subsidiaries in the two nations.

EFFECT ON DEVELOPING AND TRANSITION NATIONS   Developing and transition nations that share borders with developed countries are often dependent on their wealthier neighbours. Trade dependency has been a blessing for many Central and Eastern European nations. A large number of joint ventures now bridge the borders between Germany and its neighbours— Germany recently had more than 6000 joint ventures in Hungary alone. Germany also is the single most important trading partner of the Central and Eastern European nations that recently joined the European Union (www.europa.eu). To gain an advantage over the competition, German firms are combining German technology with relatively low-cost labour in Central and Eastern Europe. For example, Opel (www.opel.com), the German division of General Motors Corporation (www.gm.com), built a $440 million plant in Szentgotthard, Hungary, to make parts for and assemble its Astra hatchbacks destined for export.

| Global Manager's Briefcase | Doing Business in the Pacific Rim |

To do business effectively in Asian countries that rim the Pacific Ocean, remember that Asian customers are as diverse as their cultures, and aggressive sales tactics do not work. Before going to visit these countries, it is helpful to review some general rules:

1. **Make Use of Contacts.** Asians prefer to do business with people they know. Cold calls and other direct-contact methods seldom work. Meeting the right people in an Asian company often depends on having the right introduction. If the person with whom you hope to do business respects your intermediary, chances are that he or she will respect you.

2. **Carry Bilingual Business Cards.** To make a good first impression, have bilingual cards printed even though many Asians speak English. It shows both respect for the language and a commitment to doing business in a country. It also translates your title into the local language. Asians generally are not comfortable until they know your position and whom you represent. They prefer to deal with officials who have higher-level positions. Consider this preference when assigning titles to your representatives abroad.

3. **Respect, Harmony, Consensus.** Asian cultures command respect for their achievements in music, art, science, philosophy, business, and more. Asian businesspeople are tough negotiators, but they dislike argumentative exchanges. Harmony and consensus are the bywords in Asia, so be patient but firm.

4. **Drop the Legal Language.** Legal documents are subordinate to personal relationships. Asians tend not to like detailed contracts and will often insist that agreements be left flexible so that adjustments can be made easily to fit changing circumstances. It's important to foster good relations based on mutual trust and benefit. The importance of a contract in many Asian societies is not what it stipulates but rather who signed it.

5. **Build Personal Rapport.** Social ease and friendship are prerequisites to doing business across most of Asia. As much business is transacted at informal dinners as in corporate settings, so accept invitations, and be sure to reciprocate.

DANGERS OF TRADE DEPENDENCY   The dangers of trade dependency become apparent when a nation experiences economic recession or political turmoil, which then also harms dependent nations. Trade dependency is a concern in Mexico, which for 30 years was a favourite destination for the investments of US companies. Mexican factories assemble all sorts of products headed for the US market, including refrigerators, mobile phones, and many types of garments. But corruption and drug-related violence are forcing some companies to abandon Mexico for locations in Asia and Europe, which is leaving many unemployed people in their wake. Although trade dependency was a blessing for Mexico for years, it is now feeling the pain as some companies shift jobs out of the country. Likely the best way for Mexico to cope with its dependency on the United States is to improve its competitiveness and make it the preferred destination among emerging markets for US companies.[5] Canada has traditionally been dependent upon trade with the United States. Therefore, Canada's economy suffers every time there is an economic recession in the United States, such as the one in 2009. More recently, the Canadian government has actively sought new trade agreements with other nations such as India, Japan, Korea, the European Union, Singapore, Morocco, and so forth. (We identify the current trade agreements between Canada and the Americas in Chapter 8).

Quick Study

1. What portion of world trade occurs in (a) merchandise and (b) services?
2. What is the relation between trade and world output?
3. Describe the broad pattern of *international trade*.
4. Why is a nation's level of trade dependence or independence important?

Why Do Governments Intervene in Trade?

free trade

Pattern of imports and exports that occurs in the absence of trade barriers.

The pattern of imports and exports that occurs in the absence of trade barriers is called **free trade**. Despite the advantages of open and free trade among nations, governments have long intervened in the trade of goods and services. Why do governments impose restrictions on free trade? In general, they do so for reasons that are political, economic, or cultural—or some combination of the three. Countries often intervene in trade by strongly supporting their domestic companies' exporting activities. But the more emotionally charged intervention occurs when a nation's economy is underperforming. In tough economic times, businesses and workers often lobby their governments for protection from imports that are eliminating jobs in the domestic market. Let's take a closer look at the political, economic, and cultural motives for intervention.

Political Motives

Government officials often make trade-related decisions based on political motives because a politician's career can depend on pleasing voters and getting re-elected. Yet a trade policy based purely on political motives is seldom wise in the long run. The main political motives behind government intervention in trade include protecting jobs, preserving national security, responding to other nations' unfair trade practices, and gaining influence over other nations.[6]

PROTECT JOBS   Short of an unpopular war, nothing will oust a government faster than high rates of unemployment. Thus, practically all governments become involved when free trade creates job losses at home. Groups opposed to globalization often say that globalization eliminates jobs in developed nations by sending well-paying jobs abroad to developing countries. (See Chapter 1.) A common example is Western companies' practice of outsourcing business services such as call centre jobs to Asia, particularly India. In Canada, an Industry Canada policy paper discussing responses to offshore outsourcing warns against taking protective measures such as trade restrictions, industrial targeting (allocating government funds to specific firms or industries), and Buy-Canada programs. Instead various policies to make Canada more competitive are recommended, including investment incentives, and subsidies for innovation and retention of knowledge workers.[7]

PRESERVE NATIONAL SECURITY Industries considered essential to national security often receive government-sponsored protection. This is true for both imports and exports.

National Security and Imports Certain imports are often restricted in the name of preserving national security. In the event that a war would restrict their availability, governments must have access to a domestic supply of certain items such as weapons; fuel; and air, land, and sea transportation. Many nations continue to search for oil within their borders in case war disrupts its flow from outside sources. Legitimate national security reasons for intervention can be difficult to argue against, particularly when they have the support of most of a country's people.

Some countries claim national security is the reason for fierce protection of their agricultural sector, for food security is essential at a time of war. France has been criticized by many nations for ardently protecting its agricultural sector. French agricultural subsidies are intended to provide a fair financial return for French farmers, who traditionally operate on a small scale and therefore have high production costs and low profit margins. But many developed nations are exposing agribusiness to market forces and prompting their farmers to discover new ways to manage risk and increase efficiency. Innovative farmers are experimenting with more intensive land management, high-tech precision farming, and greater use of biotechnology.

Yet protection from import competition does have its drawbacks. Perhaps the main one is the added cost of continuing to produce a good or provide a service domestically that could be supplied more efficiently from abroad. Also, a policy of protection may remain in place much longer than necessary once it is adopted. Thus, policy makers should consider whether an issue truly is a matter of national security before intervening in trade.

National Security and Exports Governments also have national security motives for banning certain defence-related goods from export to other nations. Most industrialized nations have agencies that review requests to export technologies or products that are said to have *dual uses*—meaning they have both industrial and military applications. Products designated as dual use are classified as such and require special governmental approval before export can take place.

Products on the dual-use lists of most nations include nuclear materials; technological equipment; certain chemicals and toxins; some sensors and lasers; and specific devices related to weapons, navigation, aerospace, and propulsion. Bans on the export of dual-use products were strictly enforced during the Cold War years between the West and the former Soviet Union. Whereas many countries relaxed enforcement of these controls in recent years, the continued threat of terrorism and fears of weapons of mass destruction are renewing support for such bans.

Nations also place certain companies and organizations in other countries on a list of entities that are restricted from receiving their exports.

RESPOND TO "UNFAIR" TRADE Many observers argue that it makes no sense for one nation to allow free trade if other nations actively protect their own industries. Governments often threaten to close their ports to another nation's ships or to impose extremely high tariffs on its goods if the other nation does not concede on some trade issue that is seen as being unfair. In other words, if one government thinks another nation is not "playing fair," it will often threaten to retaliate unless certain concessions are made.

GAIN INFLUENCE Governments of the world's largest nations may become involved in trade to gain influence over smaller nations. The United States goes to great lengths to gain and maintain control over events in all of Central, North, and South America, and the Caribbean basin.

The United States has banned all trade and investment with Cuba since 1962 in the hope of exerting political influence against its communist leaders. Designed to pressure Cuba's government to change, the policy caused ordinary Cubans to suffer.[8]

Economic Motives

Although governments intervene in trade for highly charged cultural and political reasons, they also have economic motives for their intervention. The most common economic reasons for nations' attempts to influence international trade are the protection of young industries from competition and the promotion of a strategic trade policy.

PROTECT INFANT INDUSTRIES According to the *infant industry argument*, a country's emerging industries need protection from international competition during their development phase until they become sufficiently competitive internationally. This argument is based on the idea that infant industries need protection because of a steep learning curve. In other words, only as an industry grows and matures does it gain the knowledge it needs to become more innovative, efficient, and competitive.

Although this argument is conceptually appealing, it does have several problems. First, the argument requires governments to distinguish between industries that are worth protecting and those that are not. This is difficult, if not impossible, to do. For years, Japan has targeted infant industries for protection, low interest loans, and other benefits. Its performance on assisting these industries was very good through the early 1980s but has been less successful since then. Until the government achieves future success in identifying and targeting industries, supporting this type of policy remains questionable.

Second, protection from international competition can cause domestic companies to become complacent toward innovation. This can limit a company's incentives to obtain the knowledge it needs to become more competitive. The most extreme examples of complacency are industries within formerly communist nations. When their communist protections collapsed, nearly all companies that were run by the state were decades behind their competitors from capitalist nations. To survive, many government-owned businesses required financial assistance in the form of infusions of capital or outright purchase.

Third, protection can do more economic harm than good. Consumers often end up paying more for products because a lack of competition typically creates fewer incentives to cut production costs or improve quality. Meanwhile, companies become less competitive and more reliant on protection. Protection in Japan created a two-tier economy where, in one tier, highly competitive multinationals faced rivals in overseas markets and learned to become strong competitors. In the other tier, domestic industries were made noncompetitive through protected markets, high wages, and barriers to imports.

Fourth, the infant industry argument also says that it is not always possible for small, promising companies to obtain funding in capital markets, and thus they need financial support from their government. However, international capital markets today are far more sophisticated than in the past, and promising business ventures can normally obtain funding from private sources.

PURSUE STRATEGIC TRADE POLICY Government intervention can help companies take advantage of economies of scale and be the first movers in their industries. First-mover advantages result because economies of scale in production limit the number of companies that an industry can sustain.

Benefits of Strategic Trade Policy Advocates claim that strategic trade policies helped South Korea build global conglomerates (called *chaebol*) that dwarf competitors. For years, South Korean shipbuilders received a variety of government subsidies, including low-cost financing. The *chaebol* helped South Korea to emerge strongly from the global economic crisis because of their market power and the wide range of industries in which they compete. Such policies had spin-off effects on related industries, and local suppliers to the *chaebol* are now thriving.[9]

Drawbacks of Strategic Trade Policy Although it sounds as if strategic trade policy has only benefits, there can be drawbacks as well. Lavish government assistance to domestic companies in the past caused inefficiency and high costs for both South Korean and Japanese companies. Large government concessions to local labour unions hiked wages and forced Korea's *chaebol* to accept low profit margins.[10]

In addition, when governments decide to support specific industries, their choice is often subject to political lobbying by the groups seeking government assistance. It is possible that special interest groups could capture all the gains from assistance with no benefit for consumers. If this were to occur, consumers could end up paying more for lower-quality goods than they could otherwise obtain.

Cultural Motives

Nations often restrict trade in goods and services to achieve cultural objectives, the most common being protection of national identity.

French law bans foreign-language words from virtually all business and government communications, radio and TV broadcasts, public announcements, and advertising messages—at least whenever a suitable French alternative is available. You can't advertise a *best-seller*; it has to be a *succès de librairie*. You can't sell *popcorn* at *le cinéma*; French moviegoers must snack on *maïs soufflé*. The Higher Council on French Language works against the inclusion of so-called "Franglais" phrases such as *le marketing*, *le cash flow*, and *le brainstorming* into commerce and other areas of French culture. (Similarly, Quebec passed the Charter of the French Language, otherwise known as Bill 101, into law, making French the official language of Quebec. Quebec's Office québécois de la langue française monitors linguistic issues in the province.) Not to be outdone by neighbouring France, German bureaucrats plan to exchange governmental use of English words with German ones, replacing "brainstorming" with *ideensammlung* and "meeting points" with *treffpukte*.[11]

Canada also tries to mitigate the cultural influence of entertainment products imported from the United States. Canada requires at least 35 percent of music played over Canadian radio to be by Canadian artists. In fact, many countries are considering laws to protect their media programming for cultural reasons.

Quick Study

1. What are some political reasons why governments intervene in trade? Explain the role of national security concerns.
2. Identify the main economic motives for government trade intervention. What are the drawbacks of each method of intervention?
3. What cultural motives do nations have for intervening in *free trade*?

Methods of Promoting Trade

In the previous discussion, we alluded to the types of instruments governments use to promote or restrict trade with other nations. The most common instruments that governments use are shown in Table 6.2. In this section, we examine methods of trade promotion. We cover methods of trade restriction in the next section.

Subsidies

Financial assistance to domestic producers in the form of cash payments, low-interest loans, tax breaks, product price supports, or other forms is called a **subsidy**. Regardless of the form a subsidy takes, it is intended to assist domestic companies in fending off international competitors. This can mean becoming more competitive in the home market or increasing competitiveness in international markets through exports. It is nearly impossible to calculate the amount of subsidies a country offers its producers because of their many forms. This makes the work of the World Trade Organization difficult when it is called upon to settle arguments over subsidies (see Chapter 1 for a discussion on the World Trade Organization).

subsidy
Financial assistance to domestic producers in the form of cash payments, low-interest loans, tax breaks, product price supports, or other forms.

TABLE 6.2	Methods of Promoting and Restricting Trade
Trade Promotion	**Trade Restriction**
Subsidies	Tariffs
Export financing	Quotas
Foreign trade zones	Embargoes
Special government agencies	Local content requirements
	Administrative delays
	Currency controls

DRAWBACKS OF SUBSIDIES Critics say that subsidies encourage inefficiency and complacency by covering costs that truly competitive industries should be able to absorb on their own. Many believe subsidies benefit companies and industries that receive them but harm consumers because they tend to be paid for with income and sales taxes. Thus, although subsidies provide short-term relief to companies and industries, whether they help a nation's citizens in the long term is questionable.

Some observers say that far more devastating is the effect of subsidies on farmers in developing and emerging markets. We've already seen that many wealthy nations award subsidies to their farmers to ensure an adequate food supply for their people. These subsidies worth billions of dollars make it difficult, if not impossible, for farmers from poor countries to sell their unsubsidized (that is, more expensive) food on world markets, it is said. Compounding the plight of these farmers is that international organizations are forcing their nations to eliminate trade barriers. The economic consequences for poor farmers in Africa, Asia, and Latin America are higher unemployment and poverty.[12]

Subsidies can lead to an overuse of resources, negative environmental effects, and higher costs for commodities. As fuel prices soared in China, governments fearing inflation and street protests increased their heavy subsidies of energy. China's fuel subsidies for a single year were estimated at a whopping $40 billion. These subsidies eliminate incentives to conserve fuel and drive fuel prices higher. Whereas countries without fuel subsidies saw steady or falling demand, subsidizing countries saw rising demand that threatened to outstrip growth in global fuel supplies.[13]

Export Financing

Governments often promote exports by helping companies finance their export activities. They can offer loans that a company could otherwise not obtain or charge them an interest rate that is lower than the market rate. Another option is for a government to guarantee that it will repay the loan of a company if the company should default on repayment; this is called a *loan guarantee*.

Many nations have special agencies dedicated to helping their domestic companies obtain export financing. Export Development Canada (EDC) is Canada's export credit agency and is wholly owned by the government of Canada. As a financially self-sustained crown corporation, EDC offers financing both to Canadian companies and the buyers of Canadian companies. EDC offers credit insurance, bonding, and political risk insurance, among other international trade services (www.edc.ca).

Another wholly owned Canadian agency that provides export financing is Business Development Bank of Canada (BDC). It plays a key role in delivering financial and consulting services to small and medium-sized businesses in Canada (www.bdc.ca). BDC offers up to $100 000 in long-term financing to protect the company's cash flow, expansion financing, and re-advances on any repaid portion of the loan.

Foreign Trade Zones

foreign trade zone (FTZ)
Designated geographic region through which merchandise is allowed to pass with lower customs duties (taxes) and/ or fewer customs procedures.

Most countries promote trade with other nations by creating what is called a **foreign trade zone (FTZ)**—a designated geographic region through which merchandise is allowed to pass with lower customs duties (taxes) and/or fewer customs procedures. Increased employment is often the intended purpose of foreign trade zones, with a by-product being increased trade. A good example of a foreign trade zone is Turkey's Aegean Free Zone, in which the Turkish government allows companies to conduct manufacturing operations free from taxes.

Customs duties increase the total amount of a good's production cost and increase the time needed to get it to market. Companies can reduce such costs and time by establishing a facility inside a foreign trade zone. A common purpose of many companies' facilities in such zones is final product assembly.

China has established a number of large foreign trade zones to reap the employment advantages they offer. Goods imported into these zones do not require import licences or other documents, nor are they subject to import duties. International companies can also store goods in these zones before shipping them to other countries without incurring taxes in China. Moreover, five of these zones are located within specially designated economic zones in which local governments can offer additional opportunities and tax breaks to international investors.

Another country that has enjoyed the beneficial effects of foreign trade zones is Mexico. Decades ago, Mexico established such a zone along its northern border with the United States. Creation of the zone caused development of companies called *maquiladoras* along the border inside Mexico. The *maquiladoras* import materials or parts duty free, process them to some extent, and export them duty free back to the country of origin. The program has expanded rapidly over the five decades since its inception, employing hundreds of thousands of people from all across Mexico who move north looking for work.

The closest initiative to a foreign trade zone in Canada is at CentrePort Canada (www.centreport.ca) located in Winnipeg, Manitoba. CentrePort Canada is an inland port offering companies a single-window access to FTZ benefits. The program is a combination of the Export Distribution Centre (EDC) program and the Duty Deferral Program, administered by the Canada Revenue Agency (CRA) and the Canadian Border Services Agency (CBSA). CentrePort's single window has a designated contact in both CBSA and CRA. CentrePort's FTZ program is focused on companies that export the bulk of their production and has constraints on the permitted amount of value added.

Special Government Agencies

The governments of most nations have special agencies responsible for promoting exports. Such agencies can be particularly helpful to small and medium-sized businesses that have limited financial resources. Government trade promotion agencies often organize trips for trade officials and businesspeople to visit other countries to meet potential business partners and generate contacts for new business. They also typically open trade offices in other countries. These offices are designed to promote the home country's exports and introduce businesses to potential partners in the host nation. Government trade promotion agencies typically do a great deal of advertising in other countries to promote the nation's exports. In Canada, companies have access to EDC and BDC (described previously in this chapter under export financing). In addition, the Canadian Trade Commissioner Service (TCS) provides Canadian businesses with on-the-ground intelligence and practical advice on foreign markets to help them achieve their trade goals (www.tradecommissioner.gc.ca).

Governments not only promote trade by encouraging exports but also can encourage imports that the nation does not or cannot produce. For example, the Japan External Trade Organization (JETRO) (www.jetro.go.jp) is a trade promotion agency of the Japanese government. The agency coaches small and medium-sized overseas businesses on the protocols of Japanese deal making, arranges meetings with suitable Japanese distributors and partners, and even assists in finding temporary office spaces.

Quick Study

1. How do governments use *subsidies* to promote trade? Identify the drawbacks of subsidies.
2. How does export financing promote trade? Explain its importance to small and medium-sized firms.
3. Define the term *foreign trade zone*. How can it be used to promote trade?
4. How can special government agencies help promote trade?

Methods of Restricting Trade

Earlier in this chapter, we looked at the political, economic, and cultural reasons for governmental intervention in trade. In this section, we discuss the methods governments can use to restrict unwanted trade. There are two general categories of trade barriers available to governments. A **tariff** is a government tax levied on a product as it enters or leaves a country. A tariff increases the price of an imported product *directly* and, therefore, reduces its appeal to buyers. A nontariff barrier limits the availability of an imported product, which increases its price *indirectly* and,

tariff
Government tax levied on a product as it enters or leaves a country.

therefore, reduces its appeal to buyers. Let's take a closer look at tariffs and the various types of nontariff barriers.

Tariffs

We can classify a tariff into one of three categories. An *export tariff* is levied by the government of a country that is exporting a product. Countries can use export tariffs when they believe an export's price is lower than it should be. Developing nations whose exports consist mostly of low-priced natural resources often levy export tariffs. A *transit tariff* is levied by the government of a country that a product is passing through on its way to its final destination. Transit tariffs have been almost entirely eliminated worldwide through international trade agreements. An *import tariff* is levied by the government of a country that is importing a product. The import tariff is by far the most common tariff used by governments today.

We can further break down the import tariff into three subcategories based on the manner in which it is calculated. An **ad valorem tariff** is levied as a percentage of the stated price of an imported product. A **specific tariff** is levied as a specific fee for each unit (measured by number, weight, and so forth) of an imported product. A **compound tariff** is levied on an imported product and calculated partly as a percentage of its stated price and partly as a specific fee for each unit. Let's now discuss the two main reasons why countries levy tariffs.

PROTECT DOMESTIC PRODUCERS   Nations can use tariffs to protect domestic producers. For example, an import tariff raises the cost of an imported good and increases the appeal of domestically produced goods. In this way, domestic producers gain a protective barrier against imports. Although producers that receive tariff protection can gain a price advantage, in the long run protection can keep them from increasing efficiency. A protected industry can be devastated if protection encourages complacency and inefficiency, and the industry is later thrown into the lion's den of international competition. Mexico began reducing tariff protection in the mid-1980s as a prelude to NAFTA negotiations, and many Mexican producers went bankrupt despite attempts to grow more efficient.

GENERATE REVENUE   Tariffs are also a source of government revenue, but mostly among developing nations. The main reason is that less-developed nations tend to have less formal domestic economies that lack the capability to record domestic transactions accurately. The lack of accurate record keeping makes collection of sales taxes within the country extremely difficult. Nations solve the problem by simply raising their needed revenue through import and export tariffs. As countries develop, however, they tend to generate a greater portion of their revenues from taxes on income, capital gains, and other economic activity.

The discussion so far leads us to question who benefits from tariffs. We've already learned the two principal reasons for tariff barriers—protecting domestic producers and raising government revenue. On the surface it appears that governments and domestic producers benefit. We also saw that tariffs raise the price of a product because importers typically charge a higher price to recover the cost of this additional tax. Thus, it appears on the surface that consumers do not benefit. As we also mentioned earlier, there is the danger that tariffs will create inefficient domestic producers that may go out of business once protective import tariffs are removed. Analysis of the total cost to a country is far more complicated and goes beyond the scope of our discussion. Suffice it to say that tariffs tend to exact a cost on countries as a whole because they lessen the gains that a nation's people obtain from trade.

Quotas

A restriction on the amount (measured in units or weight) of a good that can enter or leave a country during a certain period of time is called a **quota**. After tariffs, quotas are the second most common type of trade barrier. Governments typically administer their quota systems by granting quota licences to the companies or governments of other nations (in the case of import quotas) and domestic producers (in the case of export quotas). Governments normally grant such licences on a year-by-year basis.

REASON FOR IMPORT QUOTAS   A government may impose an *import quota* to protect its domestic producers by placing a limit on the amount of goods allowed to enter the country. This

---

ad valorem tariff
Tariff levied as a percentage of the stated price of an imported product.

specific tariff
Tariff levied as a specific fee for each unit (measured by number, weight, and so forth) of an imported product.

compound tariff
Tariff levied on an imported product and calculated partly as a percentage of its stated price and partly as a specific fee for each unit.

quota
Restriction on the amount (measured in units or weight) of a good that can enter or leave a country during a certain period of time.

helps domestic producers maintain their market shares and prices because competitive forces are restrained. In this case, domestic producers win because their market is protected. Consumers lose because of higher prices and limited selection attributable to lower competition. Other losers include domestic producers whose own production requires the import subjected to a quota. Companies relying on the importation of so-called intermediate goods will find the final cost of their own products increase.

Historically, countries placed import quotas on the textile and apparel products of other countries under the Multi-Fibre Arrangement. This arrangement at one time affected countries accounting for more than 80 percent of world trade in textiles and clothing. When that arrangement expired in 2005, many textile producers in poor nations such as Mexico feared the loss of jobs to China. But some countries with a large textile industry, such as Bangladesh, are benefiting from cheap labour and the reluctance among purchasers to rely exclusively on China for all its inputs.

REASONS FOR EXPORT QUOTAS   There are at least two reasons why a country imposes *export quotas* on its domestic producers. First, it may wish to maintain adequate supplies of a product in the home market. This motive is most common among countries that export natural resources that are essential to domestic business or the long-term survival of a nation.

Second, a country may limit the export of a good to restrict its supply on world markets, thereby increasing the international price of the good. This is the motive behind the formation and activities of the Organization of Petroleum Exporting Countries (OPEC) (www.opec.org). This group of nations from the Middle East and Latin America attempts to restrict the world's supply of crude oil to earn greater profits.

Voluntary Export Restraints   A unique version of the export quota is called a **voluntary export restraint (VER)**—a quota that a nation imposes on its own exports, usually at the request of another nation. Countries normally self-impose a voluntary export restraint in response to the threat of an import quota or total ban on the product by an importing nation. The classic example of the use of a voluntary export restraint is from the 1980s when Japanese carmakers were making significant market share gains in the United States. The closing of US carmakers' production facilities in the United States was creating a volatile anti-Japan sentiment among the population and the US Congress. Fearing punitive legislation if Japan did not limit its automobile exports to the United States, the Japanese government and its carmakers self-imposed a voluntary export restraint on cars headed for the United States.

voluntary export restraint (VER)
Unique version of export quota that a nation imposes on its own exports, usually at the request of an importing nation.

Vietnamese women manufacture woven rugs at a craft centre in Hoi An, Vietnam. Across Vietnam, hundreds of small clothing factories have thrived following removal of worldwide import quotas allowed under the Multi-Fibre Agreement. Under the MFA, wealthy nations guaranteed imports of textiles and garments from poor countries under a quota system. Under what conditions do you think nations should be allowed to impose import quotas?

Source: David R. Frazier/Newscom.

Consumers in the country that imposes an export quota benefit from lower-priced products (due to their greater supply) as long as domestic producers do not curtail production. Producers in an importing country benefit because the goods of producers from the exporting country are restrained, which may allow them to increase prices. Export quotas hurt consumers in the importing nation because of reduced selection and perhaps higher prices. Yet export quotas might allow these same consumers to retain their jobs if imports were threatening to put domestic producers out of business. Again, detailed economic studies are needed to determine the winners and losers in any particular export quota case.

tariff-quota

Lower tariff rate for a certain quantity of imports and a higher rate for quantities that exceed the quota.

TARIFF-QUOTAS A hybrid form of trade restriction is called a **tariff-quota**—a lower tariff rate for a certain quantity of imports and a higher rate for quantities that exceed the quota. Figure 6.1 shows how a tariff-quota actually works. Imports entering a nation under a quota limit of, say, 1000 tonnes are charged a 10 percent tariff. But subsequent imports that do not make it under the quota limit of 1000 tonnes are charged a tariff of 80 percent. Tariff-quotas are used extensively in the trade of agricultural products. Many countries implemented tariff-quotas in 1995 after their use was permitted by the World Trade Organization.

Embargoes

embargo

Complete ban on trade (imports and exports) in one or more products with a particular country.

A complete ban on trade (imports and exports) in one or more products with a particular country is called an **embargo**. An embargo may be placed on one or a few goods, or it may completely ban trade in all goods. It is the most restrictive nontariff trade barrier available, and it is typically applied to accomplish political goals. Embargoes can be decreed by individual nations or by supranational organizations such as the United Nations. Because they can be very difficult to enforce, embargoes are used less today than they have been in the past. One example of a total ban on trade with another country is the US embargo on trade with Cuba. Although some medicines and foods are now allowed to enter Cuba from the United States, US tourists are not legally able to vacation in Cuba.

Local Content Requirements

Recall from Chapter 3 that *local content requirements* are laws stipulating that producers in the domestic market must supply a specified amount of a good or service. These requirements can state that a certain portion of the end product consists of domestically produced goods or that a certain portion of the final cost of a product has domestic sources.

The purpose of local content requirements is to force companies from other nations to use local resources in their production processes—particularly labour. Similar to other restraints on imports, such requirements help protect domestic producers from the price advantage of companies based in other, low-wage countries. Today, many developing countries use local content requirements as a strategy to boost industrialization. Companies often respond to local content requirements by locating production facilities inside the nation that stipulates such restrictions.

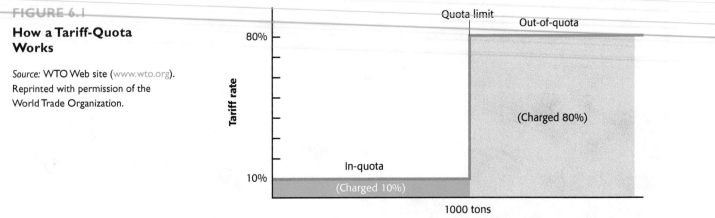

FIGURE 6.1

How a Tariff-Quota Works

Source: WTO Web site (www.wto.org). Reprinted with permission of the World Trade Organization.

Although many people consider music the universal language, not all cultures are equally open to the world's diverse musical influences. To prevent Anglo-Saxon music from invading French culture, French law requires radio programs to include at least 40 percent French content. Such local content requirements are intended to protect both the French cultural identity and the jobs of French artists against other nations' pop culture that may wash up on French shores.

Administrative Delays

Regulatory controls or bureaucratic rules designed to impair the flow of imports into a country are called **administrative delays**. This nontariff barrier includes a wide range of government actions, such as requiring international air carriers to land at inconvenient airports, requiring product inspections that damage the product itself, purposely understaffing customs offices to cause unusual time delays, and requiring special licences that take a long time to obtain. The objective of all such administrative delays for a country is to discriminate against imported products—it is, in a word, protectionism.

administrative delays
Regulatory controls or bureaucratic rules designed to impair the flow of imports into a country.

Currency Controls

Restrictions on the convertibility of a currency into other currencies are called **currency controls**. A company that wishes to import goods generally must pay for those goods in a common, internationally acceptable currency such as the US dollar, European Union euro, or Japanese yen. Generally, it must also obtain the currency from its nation's domestic banking system. Governments can require companies that desire such a currency to apply for a licence to obtain it. Thus, a country's government can discourage imports by restricting who is allowed to convert the nation's currency into the internationally acceptable currency.

Another way governments apply currency controls to reduce imports is by stipulating an exchange rate that is unfavourable to potential importers. Because the unfavourable exchange rate can force the cost of imported goods to an impractical level, many potential importers simply give up on the idea. Meanwhile, the country will often allow exporters to exchange the home currency for an international currency at favourable rates to encourage exports.

currency controls
Restrictions on the convertibility of a currency into other currencies.

Quick Study

1. How do *tariffs* and *quotas* differ from one another? Identify the different forms each can take.
2. Describe how a *voluntary export restraint* works and how it differs from a quota.
3. What is an *embargo*? Explain why it is seldom used today.
4. Explain how local content requirements, administrative delays, and currency controls restrict trade.

Theories of International Trade

Trade between different groups of people has occurred for many thousands of years. But it was not until the fifteenth century that people tried to explain why trade occurs and how trade can benefit both parties to an exchange. Figure 6.2 shows a timeline of when the main theories of international trade were proposed. Efforts to refine existing trade theories and to develop new ones continue today. Let's now discuss the first theory developed to explain why nations should engage in international trade—*mercantilism*.

Mercantilism

The trade theory that nations should accumulate financial wealth, usually in the form of gold, by encouraging exports and discouraging imports is called **mercantilism**. It states that other measures of a nation's well-being, such as living standards or human development, are irrelevant. Nation-states in Europe followed this economic philosophy from about 1500 to the late

mercantilism
Trade theory that nations should accumulate financial wealth, usually in the form of gold, by encouraging exports and discouraging imports.

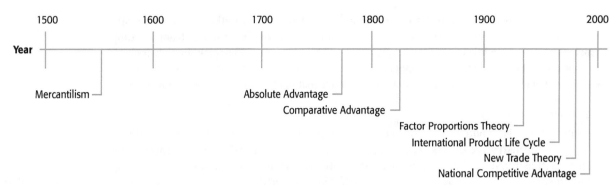

FIGURE 6.2
Trade Theory Timeline

1700s. The most prominent mercantilist nations included Britain, France, the Netherlands, Portugal, and Spain.

HOW MERCANTILISM WORKED   When navigation was a fairly new science, Europeans explored the world by sea and claimed the lands they encountered in the name of the European monarchy that financed their voyage. Early explorers landed in Africa, Asia, and the Americas, where they established colonies. Colonial trade was conducted for the benefit of mother countries, and colonies were generally treated as exploitable resources.

In recent times, former colonies have struggled to diminish their reliance on the former colonial powers. For example, in an effort to decrease their dependence on their former colonial powers, African nations are welcoming trade relationships with partners from Asia and North America. But because of geographic proximity, the European Union is still often preferred as a trading partner.

Just how did countries implement mercantilism? The practice of mercantilism rested upon three essential pillars: trade surpluses, government intervention, and colonialism.

Trade Surpluses   Nations believed they could increase their wealth by maintaining a **trade surplus**—the condition that results when the value of a nation's exports is greater than the value of its imports. In mercantilism, a trade surplus meant that a country was taking in more gold on the sale of its exports than it was paying out for its imports. A **trade deficit** is the opposite condition—one that results when the value of a country's imports is greater than the value of its exports. In mercantilism, trade deficits were to be avoided at all costs.

Government Intervention   Governments actively intervened in international trade to maintain a trade surplus. According to mercantilism, the accumulation of wealth depended on increasing a nation's trade surplus, not necessarily expanding its total value or volume of trade. The governments of mercantilist nations did this by either banning certain imports or imposing various restrictions on them, such as tariffs or quotas. At the same time, they subsidized industries based in the home country to expand exports. Governments also typically outlawed the removal of their gold and silver to other nations.

Colonialism   Mercantilist nations acquired territories (colonies) around the world to serve as sources of inexpensive raw materials and as markets for higher-priced finished goods. These colonies were the source of essential raw materials, including tea, sugar, tobacco, rubber, and cotton. These resources would be shipped to the mercantilist nation, where they were incorporated into finished goods such as clothing, cigars, and other products. These finished goods would then be sold to the colonies. Trade between mercantilist countries and their colonies were a huge source of profits for the mercantilist powers. The colonies received low prices for basic raw materials but paid high prices for finished goods.

The mercantilist and colonial policies greatly expanded the wealth of nations that implemented them. This wealth allowed nations to build armies and navies to control their far-flung colonial empires and to protect their shipping lanes from attack by other nations. It was a source of a nation's economic power that in turn increased its political power relative to other countries. Today, countries seen by others as trying to maintain a trade surplus and expand their national

trade surplus
Condition that results when the value of a nation's exports is greater than the value of its imports.

trade deficit
Condition that results when the value of a country's imports is greater than the value of its exports.

Employees in Mexico churn out all sorts of products destined for the United States. For decades, trade with the United States brought well-paying jobs to ordinary Mexicans, like the man forming athletic shoes shown here. But some of Mexico's garment producers (among others) are moving production to cheaper locations such as China. When this happens, Mexico experiences the negative effects of its dependence on US trade.

Source: © Keith Dannemiller/Corbis.

treasuries at the expense of other nations are accused of practising *neo-mercantilism* or *economic nationalism*.

FLAWS OF MERCANTILISM Despite its seemingly positive benefits for any nation implementing it, mercantilism is inherently flawed. Mercantilist nations believed that the world's wealth was limited and that a nation could increase its share of the pie only at the expense of its neighbours—called a *zero-sum game*. The main problem with mercantilism is that if all nations were to barricade their markets from imports and push their exports onto others, international trade would be severely restricted. In fact, trade in all nonessential goods would likely cease altogether.

In addition, paying colonies little for their exports but charging them high prices for their imports impaired their economic development. Thus, their appeal as markets for goods was less than it would have been if they were allowed to accumulate greater wealth. These negative aspects of mercantilism were made apparent by a trade theory developed in the late 1700s—*absolute advantage*.

Quick Study

1. How did *mercantilism* work? Identify its three essential pillars.
2. What types of policies might a country have in place to be called *neo-mercantilist*?
3. Describe the main flaws of mercantilism. What is meant by the term *zero-sum game*?

Absolute Advantage

Scottish economist Adam Smith first put forth the trade theory of absolute advantage in 1776.[14] The ability of a nation to produce a good more efficiently than any other nation is called an **absolute advantage**. In other words, a nation with an absolute advantage can produce a greater output of a good or service than other nations using the same amount of, or fewer, resources.

absolute advantage
Ability of a nation to produce a good more efficiently than any other nation.

Among other things, Smith reasoned that international trade should not be banned or restricted by tariffs and quotas but allowed to flow as dictated by market forces. If people in different countries were able to trade as they saw fit, no country would need to produce all the goods it consumed. Instead, a country could concentrate on producing the goods in which it holds an absolute advantage. It could then trade with other nations to obtain the goods it needed but did not produce.

Suppose investor Kevin O'Leary wants to install a hot tub in his home. Should he do the job himself or hire a professional installer to do it for him? Suppose O'Leary (who has never installed a hot tub before) would have to take one month off from work and forgo $800 000 in salary to complete the job. On the other hand, the professional installer (who is not a professional investor) can complete the job for $10 000 and do it in two weeks. Whereas O'Leary has an absolute advantage in investing, the installer has an absolute advantage in installing hot tubs. It takes O'Leary one month to do the job the installer can do in two weeks. Thus, O'Leary should hire the professional to install the hot tub to save both time and money resources.

Let's now apply the absolute advantage concept to an example of two trading countries to see how trade can increase production and consumption in both nations.

CASE: RICELAND AND TEALAND   Suppose that we live in a world of just two countries (Riceland and Tealand), with two products (rice and tea), and transporting goods between these two countries costs nothing. Riceland and Tealand currently produce and consume their own rice and tea. The following table shows the number of units of resources (labour) each country expends in creating rice and tea. In Riceland, just one resource unit is needed to produce a tonne of rice, but five units of resources are needed to produce a tonne of tea. In Tealand, six units of resources are needed to produce a tonne of rice, whereas three units are needed to produce a tonne of tea.

	Rice	Tea
Riceland	1	5
Tealand	6	3

Another way of stating each nation's efficiency in the production of rice and tea is:

- In Riceland, 1 unit of resources = 1 tonne of rice or $\frac{1}{5}$ tonne of tea
- In Tealand, 1 unit of resources = $\frac{1}{6}$ tonne of rice or $\frac{1}{3}$ tonne of tea

These numbers also tell us one other thing about rice and tea production in these two countries. Because one unit of resources produces one tonne of rice in Riceland compared with Tealand's output of only $\frac{1}{6}$ tonne of rice, Riceland has an absolute advantage in rice production—it is the more efficient rice producer. However, because one resource unit produces $\frac{1}{3}$ tonne of tea in Tealand compared to Riceland's output of just $\frac{1}{5}$ tonne, Tealand has an absolute advantage in tea production.

Gains from Specialization and Trade   Suppose now that Riceland specializes in rice production to maximize the output of rice in our two-country world. Likewise, Tealand specializes in tea production to maximize the world output of tea. Although each country now specializes and world output increases, both countries face a problem. Riceland can consume only its rice production, and Tealand can consume only its tea production. The problem can be solved if the two countries trade with each other to obtain the good that it needs but does not produce.

Suppose that Riceland and Tealand agree to trade rice and tea on a one-to-one basis—a tonne of rice costs a tonne of tea, and vice versa. Thus, Riceland can produce one extra tonne of rice with an additional resource unit and can trade with Tealand to get one tonne of tea. This is much better than the $\frac{1}{5}$ tonne of tea that Riceland would have gotten by investing that additional resource unit in making tea for itself. Thus, Riceland definitely benefits from the trade. Likewise, Tealand can produce $\frac{1}{3}$ extra tonne of tea with an additional resource unit and trade with Riceland to get $\frac{1}{3}$ tonne of rice. This is twice as much as the $\frac{1}{6}$ tonne of rice it could have produced using that additional resource unit to make its own rice. Thus, Tealand also benefits from the trade. The gains resulting from this simple trade are shown in Figure 6.3.

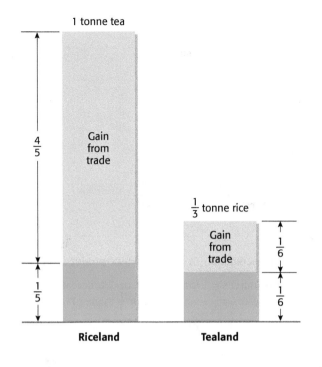

FIGURE 6.3

Gains from Specialization and Trade: Absolute Advantage

Although Tealand does not gain as much as Riceland does from the trade, it does get more rice than it would without trade. The gains from trade for actual countries would depend on the total number of resources each country had at its disposal and the demand for each good in each country.

As this example shows, the theory of absolute advantage destroys the mercantilist idea that international trade is a zero-sum game. Instead, because there are gains to be had by both countries party to an exchange, international trade is a *positive-sum game*. The theory also calls into question the objective of national governments to acquire wealth through restrictive trade policies. It argues that nations should instead open their doors to trade so their people can obtain a greater quantity of goods more cheaply. The theory does not measure a nation's wealth by how much gold and silver it has on reserve but by the living standards of its people.

Despite the power of the theory of absolute advantage in showing the gains from trade, there is one potential problem. What happens if one country does not hold an absolute advantage in the production of any product? Are there still benefits to trade, and will trade even occur? To answer these questions, let's take a look at an extension of absolute advantage: the theory of *comparative advantage*.

Comparative Advantage

An English economist named David Ricardo developed the theory of comparative advantage in 1817.[15] He proposed that, if one country (in our example of a two-country world) held absolute advantage in the production of both products, specialization and trade could still benefit both countries. A country has a **comparative advantage** when it is unable to produce a good more efficiently than other nations but produces the good more efficiently than it does any other good. In other words, *trade is still beneficial even if one country is less efficient in the production of two goods, as long as it is less inefficient in the production of one of the goods.*

Let's return to our hot tub example. Now suppose that O'Leary has previously installed many hot tubs and can do the job in one week—twice as fast as the hot tub installer. Thus, O'Leary now holds absolute advantage in both investing and hot tub installation. Although the professional installer is at an absolute disadvantage in both hot tub installation and investing, he is less inefficient in hot tub installation. Despite his absolute advantage in both areas, however, O'Leary would still have to give up $200 000 (one week's pay) to take time off from investing to complete the work. Is this a wise decision? No. O'Leary should hire the professional installer to do the work for $10 000. The installer earns money he would not earn if O'Leary did the job himself. And Kevin O'Leary earns more money by focusing on his investing than he would save by installing the hot tub himself.

comparative advantage

Inability of a nation to produce a good more efficiently than other nations but an ability to produce that good more efficiently than it does any other good.

Gains from Specialization and Trade   To see how the theory of comparative advantage works with international trade, let's return to our example of Riceland and Tealand. In our earlier discussion, Riceland had an absolute advantage in rice production, and Tealand had an absolute advantage in tea production. Suppose that Riceland now holds absolute advantage in the production of both rice *and* tea. The following table shows the number of units of resources each country now expends in creating rice and tea. Riceland still needs to expend just one resource unit to produce a tonne of rice, but now it needs to invest only two units of resources (instead of five) to produce one tonne of tea. Tealand still needs six units of resources to produce a tonne of rice and three units to produce a tonne of tea.

	Rice	Tea
Riceland	1	2
Tealand	6	3

Another way of stating each nation's efficiency in the production of rice and tea is:

- In Riceland, 1 unit of resources = 1 tonne of rice or $\frac{1}{2}$ tonne of tea
- In Tealand, 1 unit of resources = $\frac{1}{6}$ tonne of rice or $\frac{1}{3}$ tonne of tea

Thus, for every unit of resource used, Riceland can produce more rice and tea than Tealand can—it has absolute advantage in the production of both goods. But if Riceland has absolute advantage in the production of both goods, it can still gain from trading with a less-efficient producer. Although Tealand has absolute disadvantage in both rice and tea production, it has a *comparative* advantage in tea. In other words, although it is unable to produce either rice or tea more efficiently than Riceland, Tealand produces tea more efficiently than it produces rice.

Assume once again that Riceland and Tealand decide to trade rice and tea on a one-to-one basis. Tealand could use one unit of resources to produce $\frac{1}{6}$ tonne of rice. But it would do better to produce $\frac{1}{3}$ tonne of tea with this unit of resources and trade with Riceland to get $\frac{1}{3}$ tonne of rice. By specializing and trading, Tealand gets twice as much rice as it could get if it were to produce the rice itself. There are also gains from trade for Riceland despite its dual absolute advantage. Riceland could invest one unit of resources in the production of $\frac{1}{2}$ tonne of tea. It would do better, however, to produce one tonne of rice with the one unit of resources and trade that rice to Tealand in exchange for one tonne of tea. Thus, Riceland gets twice as much tea through trade than if it were to produce the tea itself. This is in spite of the fact that it is a more efficient producer of tea than Tealand.

The benefits for each country from this simple trade are shown in Figure 6.4. Again, the benefits actual countries obtain from trade depend on the amount of resources at their disposal and each market's desired level of consumption of each product.

Assumptions and Limitations

Throughout the discussion of absolute and comparative advantage, we made several important assumptions that limit real-world application of the theories. First, we assumed that countries are driven only by the maximization of production and consumption. This is often not the case. Governments often get involved in international trade out of a concern for workers or consumers.

Second, the theories assume that there are only two countries engaged in the production and consumption of just two goods. This is obviously not the situation that exists in the real world. There currently are more than 190 countries and a countless number of products being produced, traded, and consumed worldwide.

Third, it is assumed that there are no costs for transporting traded goods from one country to another. In reality, transportation costs are a major expense of international trade for some products. If transportation costs for a good are higher than the savings generated through specialization, trade will not occur.

Fourth, the theories consider labour the only resource used in the production process because labour accounted for a large portion of the total production cost of goods at the time the theories were developed. Moreover, it is assumed that resources are mobile within each nation but cannot be transferred between nations. But labour, and especially natural resources, can be difficult and costly to transfer between nations.

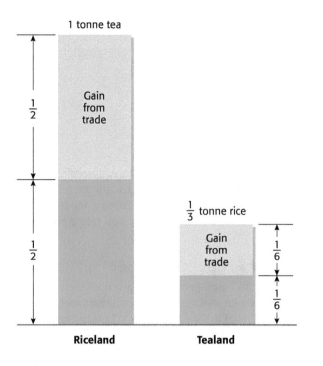

FIGURE 6.4

Gains from Specialization and Trade: Comparative Advantage

Finally, it is assumed that specialization in the production of one particular good does not result in gains in efficiency. But we know that specialization results in increased knowledge of a task and perhaps even future improvements in how that task is performed. Thus, the amount of resources needed to produce a specific amount of a good should decrease over time.

Despite the assumptions made in the theory of comparative advantage, research reveals that it appears to be supported by a substantial body of evidence. Nevertheless, economic researchers continue to develop and test new theories to explain international trade.

Quick Study

1. What is meant by the term *absolute advantage*? Describe how it works using a numerical example.
2. What is meant by the term *comparative advantage*? How does it differ from an absolute advantage?
3. Explain why countries can gain from trade even without having an absolute advantage.

Factor Proportions Theory

In the early 1900s, an international trade theory emerged that focused attention on the proportion (supply) of resources in a nation. The cost of any resource is simply the result of supply and demand: Factors in great supply relative to demand will be less costly than factors in short supply relative to demand. **Factor proportions theory** states that countries produce and export goods that require resources (factors) that are abundant and import goods that require resources in short supply.[16] The theory resulted from the research of two economists, Eli Heckscher and Bertil Ohlin, and is therefore sometimes called the Heckscher–Ohlin theory.

Factor proportions theory differs considerably from the theory of comparative advantage. Recall that the theory of comparative advantage states that a country specializes in producing the good that it can produce more efficiently than any other good. Thus, the focus of the theory (and absolute advantage as well) is on the *productivity* of the production process for a particular good. By contrast, factor proportions theory says that a country specializes in producing and exporting goods using the factors of production that are most *abundant* and thus *cheapest*—not the goods in which it is most productive.

factor proportions theory
Trade theory stating that countries produce and export goods that require resources (factors) that are abundant and import goods that require resources in short supply.

Labour Versus Land and Capital Equipment

Factor proportions theory breaks a nation's resources into two categories: labour on the one hand, land and capital equipment on the other. It predicts that a country will specialize in products that require labour if the cost of labour is low relative to the cost of land and capital. Alternatively, a country will specialize in products that require land and capital equipment if their cost is low relative to the cost of labour.

Factor proportions theory is conceptually appealing. For example, Australia has a great deal of land (nearly 60 percent of which is meadows and pastures) and a small population relative to its size. Australia's exports consist largely of mined minerals, grain, beef, lamb, and dairy products—products that require a great deal of land and natural resources. Australia's imports, on the other hand, consist mostly of manufactured raw materials, capital equipment, and consumer goods—things needed in capital-intensive mining and modern agriculture. But instead of looking only at anecdotal evidence, let's see how well factor proportions theory stands up to scientific testing.

Evidence on Factor Proportions Theory: The Leontief Paradox

Despite its conceptual appeal, factor proportions theory is not supported by studies that examine the trade flows of nations. The first large-scale study to document such evidence was performed by a researcher named Wassily Leontief in the early 1950s.[17] Leontief tested whether the United States, which uses an abundance of capital equipment, exports goods requiring capital-intensive production and imports goods requiring labour-intensive production. Contrary to the predictions of the factor proportions theory, his research found that US exports require more labour-intensive production than its imports. This apparent paradox between the predictions using the theory and the actual trade flows is called the *Leontief paradox*. Leontief's findings are supported by more recent research on the trade data of a large number of countries.

What might account for the paradox? One possible explanation is that factor proportions theory considers a country's production factors to be homogeneous—particularly labour. But we know that labour skills vary greatly within a country—more highly skilled workers emerge from training and development programs. When expenditures on improving the skills of labour are taken into account, the theory seems to be supported by actual trade data. Further studies examining international trade data will help us better understand what reasons actually account for the Leontief paradox.

Because of the drawbacks of each of the international trade theories mentioned so far, researchers continue to propose new ones. Let's now examine a theory that attempts to explain international trade on the basis of the life cycle of products.

International Product Life Cycle

international product life cycle theory

Theory stating that a company will begin by exporting its product and later undertake foreign direct investment as the product moves through its life cycle.

Raymond Vernon put forth an international trade theory for manufactured goods in the mid-1960s. His **international product life cycle theory** says that a company will begin by exporting its product and later undertake foreign direct investment as the product moves through its life cycle. The theory also says that for a number of reasons, a country's export eventually becomes its import.[18]

Although Vernon developed his model around the United States, we can generalize it to apply to any developed and innovative market such as Australia, the European Union, and Japan. Let's examine how this theory attempts to explain international trade flows.

STAGES OF THE PRODUCT LIFE CYCLE   The international product life cycle theory follows the path of a good through its life cycle (from new to maturing to standardized product) to determine where it will be produced (see Figure 6.5). In stage 1, the *new product stage*, the high purchasing power and demand of buyers in an industrialized country drive a company to design and introduce a new product concept. Because the exact level of demand in the domestic market is highly uncertain at this point, the company keeps its production volume low and based in the home country. Keeping production where initial research and development occurred and staying in contact with customers allows the company to monitor buyer preferences and to modify the product as needed. Although initially there is virtually no export market, exports do begin to pick up late in the new product stage.

FIGURE 6.5

International Product Life Cycle

Source: Raymond Vernon and Louis T. Wells, Jr., *The Economic Environment of International Business,* 5e (Upper Saddle River, NJ: Prentice Hall, 1991), p. 85. Reprinted with permission from Pearson Education, Inc.

In stage 2, the *maturing product stage*, the domestic market and markets abroad become fully aware of the existence of the product and its benefits. Demand rises and is sustained over a fairly lengthy period of time. As exports begin to account for an increasingly greater share of total product sales, the innovating company introduces production facilities in the countries with the highest demand. Near the end of the maturity stage, the product begins generating sales in developing nations, and perhaps some manufacturing presence is established there.

In stage 3, the *standardized product stage*, competition from other companies selling similar products pressures companies to lower prices in order to maintain sales levels. As the market becomes more price-sensitive, the company begins searching aggressively for low-cost production bases in developing nations to supply a growing worldwide market. Furthermore, as most production now takes place outside the innovating country, demand in the innovating country is supplied with imports from developing countries and other industrialized nations. Late in this stage, domestic production might even cease altogether.

LIMITATIONS OF THE THEORY Vernon developed his theory at a time when most new products were being developed and sold first in the United States. One reason US companies were strong globally in the 1960s was that their domestic production bases were not destroyed during the Second World War, as was the case in Europe (and to some extent Japan). In addition, during the war, the production of many durable goods in the United States, including automobiles, was shifted to the production of military transportation and weaponry. This laid the foundation for enormous post-war demand for new capital-intensive consumer goods, such as autos and home appliances. Furthermore, advances in technology that were originally developed with military purposes in mind were integrated into consumer goods. A wide range of new and innovative products like televisions, photocopiers, and computers met the seemingly insatiable appetite of consumers.

The theory seemed to explain world trade patterns quite well when the United States dominated world trade. But today the theory's ability to accurately depict the trade flows of nations is weak. New products spring up everywhere as companies continue to globalize their research and development activities.

Furthermore, companies today design new products and make product modifications at a very quick pace. The result is quicker product obsolescence and a situation in which companies replace their existing products with new product introductions. This is forcing companies to introduce products in many markets simultaneously to recoup a product's research and development costs before sales decline and the product is dropped. The theory has a difficult time explaining the resulting trade patterns.

In fact, older theories might better explain today's global trade patterns. Much production in the world today more closely resembles what is predicted by the theory of comparative advantage. Boeing's (www.boeing.com) assembly plant in Everett, Washington, constructs its 747, 767, and 777 wide-body aircraft. The shop floor has wooden crates marked "Belfast, Ireland" containing nose landing-gear doors. On a metal rack, there is a stack of outboard wing flaps from Italy. The entire fuselage of the 777 has travelled in quarter sections from Japan. Its wing tip assembly comes from Korea, its rudders from Australia, and so on.[19] This pattern resembles the theory of comparative advantage in that a product's components are made in the country that can produce them at a high level of productivity. Components are later assembled in a chosen location.

Finally, the theory is challenged by the fact that more companies are operating in international markets from their inception. Many small companies are teaming up with companies in other markets to develop new products or production technologies. This strategy is particularly effective for small companies that would otherwise be unable to participate in international production or sales. French company Ingenico (www.ingenico.com) is a leading global supplier of secure transaction systems, including terminals and their associated software. The company began small and worked with a global network of entrepreneurs who acted as Ingenico's local agents and helped it to conquer local markets. The cultural knowledge embedded in Ingenico's global network helped it to design and sell products appropriate for each market.[20]

The Internet also makes it easier for a small company to reach a global audience from its inception. For a discussion of several pitfalls small companies can avoid in fulfilling their international orders taken on the Internet, see the Entrepreneur's Toolkit, titled "Five Fulfillment Mistakes."

Quick Study

1. What does the *factor proportions theory* have to say about a nation's imports and exports?
2. Identify the two categories of national resources in factor proportions theory. What is the *Leontief paradox*?
3. What are the three stages of the *international product life cycle theory*? Identify its limitations.

New Trade Theory

new trade theory

Trade theory stating that (1) there are gains to be made from specialization and increasing economies of scale, (2) the companies first to market can create barriers to entry, and (3) government may play a role in assisting its home companies.

During the 1970s and 1980s, another theory emerged to explain trade patterns.[21] The **new trade theory** states that (1) there are gains to be made from specialization and increasing economies of scale, (2) the companies first to market can create barriers to entry, and (3) government may play a role in assisting its home companies. Because the theory emphasizes productivity rather than a nation's resources, it is in line with the theory of comparative advantage but at odds with factor proportions theory.

FIRST-MOVER ADVANTAGE   According to the new trade theory, as a company increases the extent to which it specializes in the production of a particular good, output rises because of gains in efficiency. Regardless of the amount of a company's output, it has fixed production costs such as the cost of research and development and the plant and equipment needed to produce the product. The theory states that as specialization and output increase, companies can realize economies of scale, thereby pushing the unit costs of production lower. That is why, as many companies expand, they lower prices to buyers and force potential new competitors to produce at a similar level of output if they want to be competitive in their pricing. Thus, the presence of large economies of scale can create an industry that supports only a few large firms.

first-mover advantage

Economic and strategic advantage gained by being the first company to enter an industry.

A **first-mover advantage** is the economic and strategic advantage gained by being the first company to enter an industry. This first-mover advantage can create a formidable barrier to entry for potential rivals. The new trade theory also states that a country may dominate in the export of a certain product because it has a home-based firm that has acquired a first-mover advantage.[22]

Because of the potential benefits of being the first company to enter an industry, some businesspeople and researchers make a case for government assistance to companies. They say that by working together to target potential new industries, a government and its home companies can take advantage of the benefits of being the first mover in an industry. Government involvement has always been widely accepted in undertakings such as space exploration for national security reasons, but less so in purely commercial ventures. But the fear that governments of other countries might participate with industry to gain first-mover advantages drives many governments into action.

| Entrepreneur's Toolkit | Five Fulfillment Mistakes |

Although there's no way to completely foolproof logistics when selling online, a company should enjoy greater customer satisfaction if it can avoid these five key mistakes.

- **Mistake 1: Misunderstanding the Supply Chain.** How many orders can fulfillment centres fill in an hour, day, and week? How long does it take a package to reach a customer from the fulfillment centre using standard, non-expedited delivery? And how much inventory can the centres receive on any given day? If a company doesn't know the answers, it could be in serious danger of making delivery promises it can't keep.
- **Mistake 2: Overpromising on Delivery.** The entrepreneur owner/manager should not advertise aggressive delivery times without a qualifier for uncontrollable factors, such as the weather. Care must also be taken to ensure that a customer is not promised an unrealistically quick order turnaround time. Flexibility must be built into fulfillment operations.

- **Mistake 3: Not Planning for Returns.** Handling customer returns well can increase repeat business. The internal returns process needs to be organized and not wait until products start coming back to fulfillment centres. Prompt credit to customers can reward the entrepreneurial firm with a reputation as standing behind its products.
- **Mistake 4: Misunderstanding Customer Needs.** Many Internet shoppers are willing to sacrifice shipping speed in exchange for lower shipping costs. Balancing this cost–service differential is an opportunity for online marketers to cut order fulfillment costs.
- **Mistake 5: Poor Internal Communication.** Marketing departments must communicate with logistics people. A public relations nightmare can result if logistics professionals are not told and the big planned marketing push crashes the company Web site.

National Competitive Advantage

Michael Porter put forth a theory in 1990 to explain why certain countries are leaders in the production of certain products.[23] His **national competitive advantage theory** states that a nation's competitiveness in an industry depends on the capacity of the industry to innovate and upgrade. Porter's work incorporates certain elements of previous international trade theories but also makes some important new discoveries.

national competitive advantage theory
Trade theory stating that a nation's competitiveness in an industry depends on the capacity of the industry to innovate and upgrade.

Porter is not preoccupied with explaining the export and import patterns of nations but rather with explaining why some nations are more competitive in certain industries. He identifies four elements present to varying degrees in every nation that form the basis of national competitiveness. The *Porter diamond* consists of (1) factor conditions; (2) demand conditions; (3) related and supporting industries; and (4) firm strategy, structure, and rivalry. Let's take a look at these elements and see how they interact to support national competitiveness.

FACTOR CONDITIONS   Factor proportions theory considers a nation's resources, such as a large labour force, natural resources, climate, or surface features, as paramount factors in what products a country will produce and export. Porter acknowledges the value of such resources, which he terms *basic* factors, but he also discusses the significance of what he calls *advanced* factors.

Advanced Factors   Advanced factors include the skill levels of different segments of the workforce and the quality of the technological infrastructure in a nation. Advanced factors are the result of investments in education and innovation, including worker training and technological research and development. Whereas basic factors can be the initial spark for why an economy begins producing a certain product, advanced factors account for the sustained competitive advantage a country enjoys in that product.

Today, for example, Japan has an advantage in auto production and Canada in the aerospace industry. In the manufacture of computer components, Taiwan reigns supreme, although China is an increasingly important competitor. These countries did not attain their status in their respective areas because of basic factors. For example, Japan did not acquire its advantage in autos because of its natural resources of iron ore—it has virtually none and must import most of the iron it needs. These countries developed their productivity and advantages in producing these products through deliberate efforts.

DEMAND CONDITIONS Sophisticated buyers in the home market are also important to national competitive advantage in a product area. A sophisticated domestic market drives companies to add new design features to products and to develop entirely new products and technologies. Companies in markets with sophisticated buyers should see the competitiveness of the entire group improve. For example, the sophisticated Canadian market for sportswear has given companies based in Canada such as lululemon athletica (www.lululemon.com) an edge in developing new sportswear products.

RELATED AND SUPPORTING INDUSTRIES Companies that belong to a nation's internationally competitive industries do not exist in isolation. Rather, supporting industries spring up to provide the inputs required by the industry. This happens because companies that can benefit from the product or process technologies of an internationally competitive industry begin to form clusters of related economic activities in the same geographic area. Each industry in the cluster serves to reinforce the productivity and, therefore, competitiveness of every other industry within the cluster. For example, Italy is home to a successful cluster in the footwear industry that greatly benefits from the country's closely related leather-tanning and fashion-design industries.

The Canadian province of Ontario is home to the Ontario Food Cluster, the largest food and beverage processing jurisdiction in Canada and the second-largest in North America. The Ontario Food Cluster's mission is to grow its national dominance in the food industry to international dominance.[24] Ontario's expanding agri-food cluster includes internationally focused companies such as General Mills Canada, H.J. Heinz Company of Canada, Labatt Breweries of Canada, Maple Leaf Foods, Kellogg Canada, Saputo, Sleeman Breweries, Dare Foods, Ferrero Canada, Dr. Oetker Canada, McCormick Canada, Cargill Canada, George Weston Ltd., and Unilever. Canada is also home to two wine clusters, one in Ontario's Niagara region and the other in British Columbia's Okanagan region. The BC Okanagan wine cluster has been crucial for growth in the region, prompting the establishment of small wineries that are working together to establish an international reputation for good quality wine by launching a certification system and attracting tourism to the Okanagan.

A relatively small number of clusters usually account for a major share of regional economic activity. They also often account for an overwhelming share of the economic activity that is "exported" to other locations. *Exporting clusters*—those that export products or make investments to compete outside the local area—are the primary source of an area's long-term prosperity. Although demand for a local industry is inherently limited by the size of the local market, an exporting cluster can grow far beyond that limit.[25]

FIRM STRATEGY, STRUCTURE, AND RIVALRY The strategies of firms and the actions of their managers have lasting effects on future competitiveness. Essential to successful companies are managers who are committed to producing quality products valued by buyers while maximizing the firm's market share and/or financial returns. Equally as important is the industry structure and rivalry between a nation's companies. The more intense the struggle to survive among a nation's domestic companies, the greater will be their competitiveness. This heightened competitiveness helps them to compete against imports and against companies that might develop a production presence in the home market.

GOVERNMENT AND CHANCE Apart from the four factors identified as part of the diamond, Porter identifies the roles of government and chance in fostering the national competitiveness of industries.

First, governments, by their actions, can often increase the competitiveness of firms and perhaps even entire industries. Governments of emerging markets could increase economic growth by increasing the pace of privatization of state-owned companies, for example. Privatization forces those companies to grow more competitive in world markets if they are to survive.

Second, although chance events can help the competitiveness of a firm or an industry, it can also threaten it. McDonald's (www.mcdonalds.com) holds a clear competitive advantage worldwide in the fast-food industry. But its overwhelming dominance was threatened by the discovery of mad cow disease several years ago. To keep customers from flocking to the non-beef substitute products of competitors, McDonald's introduced the McPork sandwich and other non-beef products.

There are important implications for companies and governments if Porter's theory accurately identifies the important drivers of national competitiveness. For instance, government policies should not be designed to protect national industries that are not internationally competitive but should develop the components of the diamond that contribute to increased competitiveness.

Quick Study

1. What is the *new trade theory*? Explain what is meant by the term *first-mover advantage*.
2. Describe the *national competitive advantage theory*. What is an "advanced" factor?
3. What are the four elements and two influential factors of the Porter diamond?

Bottom Line for Business

Trade can liberate the entrepreneurial spirit and bring economic development to a nation and its people. As the value and volume of trade continue to expand worldwide, new theories will likely emerge to explain why countries trade and why nations have advantages in producing certain products.

Globalization and Trade

An underlying theme of this book is how companies are adapting to globalization. Globalization and the increased competition it causes are forcing companies to locate particular operations to where they can be performed most efficiently. Firms are doing this either by relocating their own production facilities to other nations or by outsourcing certain activities to companies abroad. Companies undertake such action to boost competitiveness.

The relocation and outsourcing of business activities are altering international trade in both goods and services. In this chapter's opening company profile, we saw that Walmart relies on the sourcing of products from low-cost production locations such as China to deliver low-priced goods. Hewlett-Packard (HP) also makes use of globalization and international trade to minimize costs while maximizing output. The company dispersed the design and production of a new computer server throughout an increasingly specialized electronics-manufacturing system. HP conceptualized and designed the computer in Singapore; engineered and manufactured many parts for it in Taiwan; and assembled it in Australia, China, India, and Singapore. Companies are using such production and distribution techniques to maximize efficiency.

Not only is the production of goods being sent to distant locations, but so too is the delivery of business services, including financial accounting, data processing, and the handling of credit card and insurance inquiries. Even jobs requiring higher-level skills such as engineering, computer programming, and scientific research are migrating to distant locations. The motivation for companies is the same as when they send manufacturing jobs to more cost-effective locations—remaining viable in the face of increasing competitive pressure.

Implications of Trade Protection

Protection of free trade allows firms to move production to locations that maximize efficiency. Yet government interference in the free flow of trade has implications for production efficiency and firm strategy. *Subsidies* often encourage complacency on the part of companies receiving them because they discourage competition. Subsidies can be thought of as a redistribution of wealth in society whereby international firms not receiving subsidies are at a disadvantage. Unsubsidized firms must either cut production and distribution costs, or differentiate in some way to justify a higher selling price.

Import tariffs raise the cost of an imported good and make domestically produced goods more attractive to consumers. But because a tariff can create inefficient domestic producers, deteriorating competitiveness may offset the benefits of import tariffs. Companies trying to enter markets having high import tariffs often produce within that market. *Import quotas* help domestic producers maintain market share and prices by restraining competitive forces. Domestic producers protected by the quota win because the market is protected. Yet other producers that require the import subjected to a quota lose. These companies will need to pay more for their intermediate products or locate production outside the market imposing the quota.

Local content requirements protect domestic producers from producers based in low-cost countries. A firm trying to sell to a market imposing local content requirements may have no alternative but to produce locally. The objective of *administrative delays* is to discriminate against imported products, but it can discourage efficiency. *Currency controls*

(continued)

can require firms to apply for a licence to obtain an internationally accepted currency. The nation thus discourages imports by restricting who is allowed to obtain such a currency to pay for imports. A government may also block imports by stipulating an exchange rate that is unfavourable to potential importers. The unfavourable exchange rate forces the cost of imported goods to an impractical level. The same country then often stipulates an exchange rate that is favourable for exporters.

Government subsidies are typically paid for by levying taxes across the economy. Whether subsidies help a nation's people in the long term is questionable, and they may actually harm a nation. Import tariffs also hurt consumers because they raise the price of imports and protect domestic firms that may raise prices. Import quotas hurt consumers because they lessen competition, boost prices, and decrease selection. Protection tends to lessen the long-term gains a people can obtain from free trade.

Supporting Free Trade

International trade theory is fundamentally no different when it comes to the relocation of services production as compared with the production of goods. As we've seen in this chapter, trade theory tells us that if a refrigerator bound for a Western market can be made more cheaply in China, it should be. The same reasoned logic tells us that if a credit card inquiry from a Western market can be more cheaply (but adequately) processed in India, it should be. In both cases, the importing country benefits from a less-expensive product, and the exporting country benefits from inward-flowing investment and more numerous and better-paying jobs.

Finally, there are policy implications for governments. Although employment in developed countries should not be negatively affected in the aggregate, job dislocation is a concern. Many governments are encouraging lifelong education among workers to guard against the possibility that an individual may become "obsolete" in terms of lacking marketable skills relative to workers in other nations. And no matter how loud the calls for protectionism grow in the service sector, governments will do well to resist such temptations. Experience tells us that erecting barriers to competition results in less competitive firms and industries, greater job losses, and lower standards of living than would be the case under free trade.

Chapter Summary

1. **Describe the relationship between international trade volume and world output, and identify overall trade patterns.**
   - *International trade* is the purchase, sale, or exchange of goods and services across national borders.
   - Trade provides a country's people with a greater choice of goods and services, and is an important engine for job creation in many countries.
   - Merchandise comprises most world trade, although services account for around 20 percent.
   - Slower world economic output slows international trade, and higher output drives greater trade.
   - The pattern of international trade in merchandise is dominated by flows among wealthy nations.

2. **Describe the political, economic, and cultural motives behind governmental intervention in trade.**
   - *Political* motives behind government intervention in trade include (a) protecting jobs, (b) preserving national security, (c) responding to other nations' unfair trade practices, and (d) gaining influence over other nations.
   - *Economic* reasons for government intervention in trade are (a) protection of infant industries and (b) promotion of a strategic trade policy.
   - The *infant industry argument* says that a country's emerging industries need protection from international competition during their development until they become sufficiently competitive, but this may reduce competitiveness and inflate prices.
   - *Strategic trade policy* argues for government intervention to help companies take advantage of economies of scale and be first movers in their industries, but this may cause inefficiency, higher costs, and trade wars.
   - The most common *cultural* motive for trade intervention is protection of national identity.

3. **List and explain the methods governments use to promote and restrict international trade.**
   - A *subsidy* is financial assistance to domestic producers in the form of cash payments, low-interest loans, tax breaks, product price supports, or other forms.
   - Although subsidies are intended to help domestic companies fend off international competitors, critics say that they amount to corporate welfare and are detrimental in the long term.
   - *Export financing* includes loans at below-market interest rates, loans that would otherwise be unavailable, and *loan guarantees* that a government will repay a loan if the company defaults.
   - A *foreign trade zone (FTZ)* is a designated geographic region in which merchandise is allowed to pass through with lower customs duties (taxes) and/or fewer customs procedures.
   - *Special government agencies* organize trips abroad for trade officials and businesspeople and open offices abroad to promote home country exports.
   - A *tariff* is a government tax levied on a product as it enters or leaves a country; its three types are the *export tariff*, *transit tariff*, and *import tariff*.
   - An import tariff can be an *ad valorem tariff*, *specific tariff*, or *compound tariff*.
   - A restriction on the amount of a good that can enter or leave a country during a certain period of time is called a *quota*.
   - *Import quotas* protect domestic producers, whereas *export quotas* maintain adequate supplies domestically or increase the world price of a product.
   - A complete ban on trade with a particular country is an *embargo*.

- *Local content requirements* are laws stipulating that a specified amount of a good or service be supplied by producers in the domestic market.
- Imports can also be discouraged using *administrative delays* (regulatory controls or bureaucratic rules) or *currency controls* (restrictions on currency convertibility).

4. **Describe mercantilism and explain its impact on world powers and their colonies.**
   - *Mercantilism* states that nations should accumulate financial wealth, usually in the form of gold, by encouraging exports and discouraging imports.
   - Mercantilism assumes that a nation increases its wealth only at the expense of other nations—a *zero-sum game*.
   - One key element of mercantilism was to increase wealth by maintaining a *trade surplus*, the condition that results when the value of a nation's exports is greater than the value of its imports.
   - A second key element was to actively intervene in international trade to maintain a surplus.
   - A third key element was the acquisition of colonies to serve as sources of inexpensive raw materials and as markets for higher-priced finished goods.

5. **Explain the theories of absolute advantage and comparative advantage.**
   - The ability of a nation to produce a good more efficiently than any other nation is called an *absolute advantage*, which advocates letting market forces dictate trade flows.
   - Absolute advantage allows a country to produce goods in which it holds an absolute advantage and trade with other nations to obtain goods it needs but does not produce—a *positive-sum game*.
   - A nation holds a *comparative advantage* in production of a good when it is unable to produce the good more efficiently than other nations but can produce it more efficiently than it can any other good.
   - Trade is still beneficial if one country is less efficient in the production of two goods, so long as it is less inefficient in the production of one of the goods.

6. **Explain the factor proportions and international product life cycle theories.**
   - The *factor proportions theory* states that countries produce and export goods that require resources (factors) that are abundant and import goods that require resources that are in short supply.
   - Factor proportions theory predicts a country will specialize in products that require labour if its cost is low relative to the cost of land and capital, and vice versa.
   - The apparent paradox between predictions of the theory and actual trade flows is called the *Leontief paradox*.
   - The *international product life cycle theory* says that a company will begin exporting its product and later undertake foreign direct investment as the product moves through its life cycle.
   - In the *new product stage,* production remains based in the home country; in the *maturing product stage,* production begins in countries with the highest demand; and in the *standardized product stage,* production moves to low-cost locations to supply a global market.

7. **Explain the new trade and national competitive advantage theories.**
   - The *new trade theory* argues that as specialization and output increase, companies realize economies of scale that push the unit costs of production lower.
   - These economies of scale allow a firm to gain a *first-mover advantage*—the economic and strategic advantage gained by being the first company to enter an industry.
   - *National competitive advantage theory* states that a nation's competitiveness in an industry (and, therefore, trade flows) depends on the capacity of the industry to innovate and upgrade.

- The *Porter diamond* identifies four elements that form the basis of national competitiveness: (1) *factor conditions*; (2) *demand conditions*; (3) *related and supporting industries*; and (4) *firm strategy, structure, and rivalry.*
- The actions of *governments* and the occurrence of *chance events* can also affect the competitiveness of a nation's companies.

Key Terms

absolute advantage 191	foreign trade zone (FTZ) 184	quota 186
ad valorem tariff 186	free trade 180	specific tariff 186
administrative delays 189	international product life cycle	subsidy 183
comparative advantage 193	theory 196	tariff 185
compound tariff 186	international trade 174	tariff-quota 188
currency controls 189	mercantilism 189	trade deficit 190
embargo 188	national competitive advantage	trade surplus 190
factor proportions theory 195	theory 199	voluntary export restraint
first-mover advantage 198	new trade theory 198	(VER) 187

Talk It Over

1. If the nations of the world were to suddenly cut off all trade with one another, what products might you no longer be able to obtain in your country? Choose one other country, and identify the products it would need to do without.
2. Many economists believe that China will soon achieve "superpower" status because of its economic reforms, along with the work ethic and high education of its population. How is the rise of China affecting trade among Asia, Europe, and North America?
3. Despite its abundance of natural resources, Brazil was once considered an economic "basket case." Yet in recent years Brazil's economy has performed very well. What forces do you think are propelling Brazil's economic progress?
4. Discuss which industries are Canada's main export industries based on national competitive advantage.

Take It to the Web

1. **Video Report.** Visit YouTube (www.youtube.com). Search for the video called "Global Economics–Global Exchange: Free Trade and Protection." Watch the video, and then summarize it in a half-page report. Reflecting on the contents of this chapter, which components of international trade can you identify in the video? How might a company engaged in international business act on the information contained in the video?
2. **Web Site Report.** Trade theories say that a country gains a competitive advantage in an industry when its companies form a cluster of activities and that governments can help their firms become strong internationally.

The government of France invested heavily in a rather unique public–private venture in Europe called Genopole. Located in a specially designated area within France, the genetic research and development project is designed to thrust France to the forefront of life sciences research. Visit the Web site of Genopole (www.genopole.fr/-Genopole-R-services-.html). Report on (1) the various participants (public and private) involved in the venture, (2) specific types of research (genetics, biotechnology, and so on) the organization carries out, and (3) several specific scientific achievements of the project.

Regarding the aims of Genopole, what does each group offer the cluster to encourage the cross-fertilization of ideas and innovations? Why do you think governments today try to create clusters around groundbreaking research in high-technology products and processes? Do you think governments should undertake such efforts or let markets, on their own, decide who should succeed or fail? Can you identify a cluster in your city? If so, identify its members and the contribution of each to the cluster.

3. **Web Site Report.** Visit the Web site of the World Trade Organization (WTO) (www.wto.org) and the Web sites of business periodicals on the Internet. Identify a case on which the WTO has recently ruled. What countries are involved? List as many cultural, political, or economic reasons you can think of that motivated the country to bring the case. Do you think it was a fair charge, and do you think the ruling was correct? Explain your answer.

Do you think the WTO should have the power to dictate the trade policies of individual nations and punish them if they do not comply? Why or why not? Do you think countries experiencing economic difficulties should be allowed to erect temporary tariff and nontariff barriers? Why or why not? What effect do you think such an allowance would have on the future of the global trading system?

Down with Dumping

"WTO Agrees to Probe EU Duties on Chinese Footwear . . . Canada Launches WTO Challenge to US . . . Mexico Widens Anti-dumping Measure . . . Rough Road Ahead for US-China Trade . . . It Must Be Stopped," are just a sampling of headlines from around the world.

International trade theories argue that nations should open their doors to trade. Conventional free-trade wisdom says that by trading with others, a country can offer its citizens a greater quantity and selection of goods at cheaper prices than it could in the absence of trade. Nevertheless, truly free trade still does not exist because national governments intervene. Despite the efforts of the World Trade Organization (WTO) and smaller groups of nations, governments still cry foul in the trade game. On average, 234 antidumping cases are initiated each year with nearly 70 percent of disputes being settled by negotiation. And whereas the United States and the European Union initiated half of all WTO cases in prior years, they now initiate only about a quarter of all cases.

Canada has also been an active user of the antidumping measures, charging antidumping duties amounting to 91 percent of the export price for certain Chinese seamless carbon, alloy steel, oil, and gas. Moreover, Canada has applied a 193 percent antidumping duty on greenhouse bell peppers from the Netherlands, and a ten-year antidumping duty on imports of flat hot-rolled carbon and alloy steel sheet and strip from South Africa, among many others.

In the past, the world's richest nations would typically charge a developing nation with dumping. But today, developing countries initiate more than half of the cases. China recently launched an inquiry to determine whether synthetic rubber imports (used in auto tires and footwear) from Japan, South Korea, and Russia are being dumped in the country. Mexico expanded coverage of its Automatic Import Advice System. The system requires exporters (from a select list of countries) to notify Mexican officials of the amount and price of a shipment 10 days prior to its expected arrival in Mexico. The 10-day notice gives domestic producers advanced warning of low-priced products so they can report dumping before the products clear customs and enter the market-place. India set up a new government agency to handle antidumping cases. Even Argentina, Indonesia, South Africa, South Korea, and Thailand are using this recently popular tool of protectionism.

Why is dumping so popular? The WTO has made major inroads on the use of tariffs, slashing them across almost every product category in recent years. But it does not have authority to punish companies, only governments. Thus, the WTO cannot make judgments against individual companies that are dumping products in other markets. It can only pass rulings against the government of the country that imposes an antidumping duty. But the WTO allows countries to retaliate against nations whose producers are suspected of dumping when it can be shown that (1) alleged offenders are significantly hurting domestic producers and (2) the export price is lower than the cost of production or lower than the home market price.

Supporters of antidumping tariffs claim that they prevent dumpers from undercutting the prices charged by producers in a target market, driving them out of business. Another claim in support of antidumping is that it is an excellent way of retaining some protection against the potential dangers of totally free trade. Detractors of antidumping tariffs charge that once such tariffs are imposed they are rarely removed. They also claim that it costs companies and governments a great deal of time and money to file and argue their cases. It is also argued that the fear of being charged with dumping causes international competitors to keep their prices higher in a target market than would otherwise be the case. This would allow domestic companies to charge higher prices and not lose market share—forcing consumers to pay more for their goods.

Thinking Globally

1. "You can't tell consumers that the low price they are paying for that fax machine or automobile is somehow unfair. They're not concerned with the profits of some company. To them, it's just a great bargain, and they want it to continue." Do you agree with this statement? Do you think that people from different cultures would respond differently to this statement? Explain your answers.

2. As we have seen, currently the WTO cannot get involved in punishing individual companies—its actions can only be directed toward governments of countries. Do you think this is a wise policy? Why or why not? Why do you think the WTO was not given authority to charge individual companies with dumping? Explain.

3. Identify a recent Canadian antidumping case that was brought before the WTO (different from the ones mentioned in the case). Locate as many articles in the press as you can that discuss the case. Identify the nations, product(s), and potential punitive measures involved. If you were part of the WTO dispute settlement body, would you vote in favour of the measures taken by the retaliating nation? Why or why not?

Sources: Jennifer M. Freedman, "WTO Agrees to Probe EU Duties on Chinese Footwear," *Bloomberg Businessweek* (www.businessweek.com), May 18, 2010; "When Partners Attack," *The Economist* (www.economist.com), February 11, 2010; "Trading Blows," *The Economist* (www.economist.com), December 1, 2009; Frederik Balfour, "Rough Road Ahead for U.S.–China Trade," *Bloomberg Businessweek* (www.businessweek.com), April 4, 2007; Chad P. Bown, "Global Antidumping Database," The World Bank (econ.worldbank.org/ttbd/gad/), 2010.

CHAPTER SEVEN

Foreign Direct Investment

Learning Objectives

After studying this chapter, you should be able to

1. Describe worldwide patterns of foreign direct investment (FDI) and reasons for these patterns.

2. Describe each of the theories that attempt to explain why foreign direct investment occurs.

3. Discuss the important management issues in the foreign direct investment decision.

4. Explain why governments intervene in the free flow of foreign direct investment.

5. Discuss the policy instruments that governments use to promote and restrict foreign direct investment.

A LOOK BACK

Chapter 6 surveyed the major theories that have been developed to explain the patterns of international trade. We examined the important concept of comparative advantage and the conceptual basis for how international trade benefits nations. We discussed the motives and methods of government intervention in trade relations, and looked at the global trading system and how it promotes free trade.

A LOOK AT THIS CHAPTER

This chapter examines another significant form of international business: foreign direct investment (FDI). Again, we are concerned with the patterns of FDI and the theories on which it is based. We also explore why and how governments intervene in FDI activity.

A LOOK AHEAD

Chapter 8 explores the trend toward greater regional integration of national economies. We explore the benefits of closer economic cooperation and examine prominent regional trading blocs that exist around the world.

Source: ShutterStock.

Foreign Takeovers: Nexen

CALGARY, Alberta—Nexen (www.nexeninc.com), founded in 1971 and headquartered in Calgary, is a leading global oil and gas company with three main business streams: traditional oil and gas, oil sands, and shale gas. With onshore production in Western Canada, the United States, Yemen, and Columbia, and offshore operations in the UK North Sea, the Gulf of Mexico, and West Africa, Nexen produces an average of 198 000 barrels of oil equivalent per day. In 2012, almost 70 percent of its production came from its offshore facilities.

Foreign direct investment (FDI) has played a large part in Nexen's exponential growth. Take, for example, its Colombia operations. Colombia's incentives to encourage FDI inflows, such as expedited permitting processes, were a major factor influencing Nexen's decision to invest, as was the free trade agreement between Canada and Colombia. How does Colombia benefit from this deal? Nexen brings specialized technical knowledge to its Colombian shale gas investment and contributes to the community where its facility is located, supporting charitable foundations and local initiatives such as nutrition and education programs.

But FDI can work in both directions. In the summer of 2012, Nexen was an FDI target when the Chinese National Offshore Oil Corporation (CNOOC), the world's largest independent offshore oil and gas producer, offered $15.1 billion as a takeover bid. The deal was approved by the Canadian government at the end of 2012 and by the US government and regulators in February 2013. Nexen's acquisition became the largest influx of FDI into the Canadian economy in modern history.

Source: Todd Korol/Reuters/Corbis.

CNOOC plans to keep Nexen's name, retain the current management team and employees, and build on Nexen's award-wining community projects. How does Canada benefit from this deal? China is the biggest potential market for Canadian products in the world. But the Chinese government waived the possibility of a free trade agreement. However, this deal could improve Canada's relation with China: In September 2012 the two governments concluded negotiations on a Foreign Investment Promotion and Protection Agreement (FIPA)—a first step.

As you read this chapter, consider how government's intervention in foreign direct investment influences international business.[1]

Many early trade theories were created at a time when most production factors (such as labour, financial capital, capital equipment, and land or natural resources) either could not be moved or could not be moved easily across national borders. But, today, all of the above except land are internationally mobile and flow across borders to wherever they are needed. Financial capital is readily available from international financial institutions to finance corporate expansion, and whole factories can be picked up and moved to another country. Even labour is more mobile than in years past, although many barriers restrict the complete mobility of labour.

International flows of capital are at the core of **foreign direct investment (FDI)**—the purchase of physical assets or a significant amount of the ownership (stock) of a company in another country to gain a measure of management control. But there is wide disagreement on what exactly constitutes foreign direct investment. Nations set different thresholds at which they classify an international capital flow as FDI, with most governments setting the threshold between 10 and 25 percent. By contrast, an investment that does not involve obtaining a degree of control in a company is called a **portfolio investment**.

In this chapter, we examine the importance of foreign direct investment to the operations of international companies. We begin by exploring the growth of FDI in recent years and investigating its sources and destinations. We then take a look at several theories that attempt to explain foreign direct investment flows. Next, we turn our attention to several important management issues that arise in most decisions about whether a company should undertake FDI. This chapter closes by discussing the reasons why governments encourage or restrict foreign direct investment and the methods they use to accomplish these goals.

Patterns of Foreign Direct Investment

Just as international trade displays distinct patterns (see Chapter 6), so too does foreign direct investment. In this section, we first take a look at the factors that have propelled growth in FDI over the past decade. We then turn our attention to the destinations and sources of foreign direct investment.

Ups and Downs of Foreign Direct Investment

FDI inflows grew around 20 percent per year in the first half of the 1990s and expanded about 40 percent per year in the second half of the decade. As shown in Figure 7.1, global FDI inflows averaged roughly $580 billion annually between 1995 and 1999. The figure also shows that FDI inflows peaked at around $1.4 trillion in 2000, but then slowed in 2001, 2002, and 2003. Strong economic performance and high corporate profits in many countries lifted FDI inflows in 2004, 2005, 2006, and reached an all-time record of more than $1.9 trillion in 2007.

Global FDI inflows slowed considerably during the global credit crisis of 2008–2009 amid shrinking corporate profits and plummeting stock prices. However, FDI inflows started to recover during 2010 and 2011, and are expected to keep rising as the global economy emerges from recession. The long-term trend points toward greater FDI inflows worldwide, which are expected to reach between $1.7 trillion and $2.1 trillion by the end of 2014. The two main drivers of FDI flows are *globalization* and international *mergers and acquisitions*. Let's now take a closer look at each of these forces.

foreign direct investment (FDI)

Purchase of physical assets or a significant amount of the ownership (stock) of a company in another country to gain a measure of management control.

portfolio investment

Investment that does not involve obtaining a degree of control in a company.

FIGURE 7.1

Yearly FDI Inflows

Source: Based on data from the United Nations Conference on Trade and Development, World Investment Report 2012 (Geneva, Switzerland: UNCTAD). http://www.unctad-docs.org/files/UNCTAD-WIR2012-Full-en.pdf, page 3

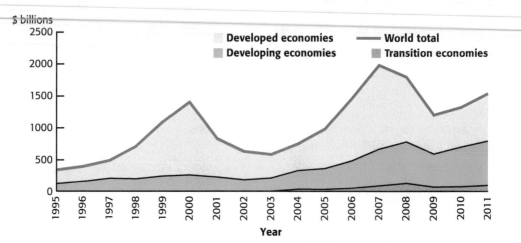

GLOBALIZATION   Recall from Chapters 1 and 6 that years ago, barriers to trade were not being reduced, and new, creative barriers seemed to be popping up in many nations. This presented a problem for companies that were trying to export their products to markets around the world. It resulted in a wave of FDI as many companies entered promising markets to get around growing trade barriers. But then the Uruguay Round of GATT negotiations created renewed determination to further reduce barriers to trade. As countries lowered their trade barriers, companies realized that they could now produce in the most efficient and productive locations and simply export to their markets worldwide. This set off another wave of FDI flows into low-cost, newly industrialized nations and emerging markets. Forces causing globalization to occur are, therefore, part of the reason for long-term growth in foreign direct investment.

Increasing globalization is also causing a growing number of international companies from emerging markets to undertake FDI. For example, companies from Taiwan began investing heavily in other nations two decades ago. Acer (www.acer.com), headquartered in Singapore but founded in Taiwan, manufactures personal computers and computer components. Just 20 years after it opened for business, Acer had spawned 10 subsidiaries worldwide and became the dominant industry player in many emerging markets.

MERGERS AND ACQUISITIONS   The number of *mergers and acquisitions (M&As)* and their exploding values also underlie long-term growth in foreign direct investment. In fact, cross-border M&As are the main vehicle through which companies undertake foreign direct investment. Companies based in developed nations have historically been the main participants behind cross-border M&As, but firms from developing nations are accounting for an ever greater share of global M&A activity. Throughout the past two decades, the value of all M&A activity as a share of GDP rose from 0.3 percent to around 8 percent today. The value of cross-border M&As peaked in 2000 at around $1.2 trillion. This figure accounted for about 3.7 percent of the market capitalization of all stock exchanges worldwide. Reasons previously mentioned for the ups and downs of FDI inflows also cause the pattern we see in cross-border M&A deals (see Figure 7.2). By 2007, the value of cross-border M&As climbed to around $1 trillion, before falling off as the global credit crisis unfolded. Although the current levels have not approached those achieved in 2007, the annual increase in M&As between 2010 and 2011 was very significant, as you can see in Figure 7.2. Megadeals, which have a value over $3 billion, are the main reason for the rising activity. In 2011 the total value of cross-border M&As was $526 billion, an increase from 44 megadeals in 2010 to 62 in 2011. Figure 7.2 also shows the values for greenfield FDI projects, which, in contrast to M&As, remained flat in value terms.[2]

Many cross-border M&A deals are driven by the desire of companies to:

- Get a foothold in a new geographic market.
- Increase a firm's global competitiveness.
- Fill gaps in companies' product lines in a global industry.
- Reduce costs of research and development (R&D), production, distribution, and so forth.

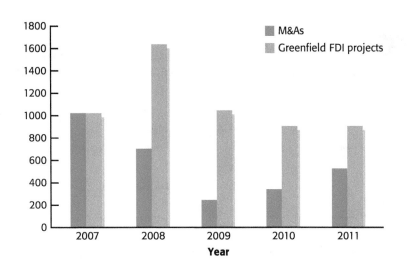

FIGURE 7.2

Value of Cross-Border M&As and Greenfield FDI Projects Worldwide

Source: Based on data from the United Nations Conference on Trade and Development, World Investment Report 2012 (Geneva, Switzerland: UNCTAD). http://www.unctad-docs. org/files/UNCTAD-WIR2012-Full-en. pdf, page 6

Entrepreneurs and small businesses also play a role in the expansion of FDI inflows. There is no data on the portion of FDI contributed by small businesses, but we know from anecdotal evidence that these companies are engaged in FDI. Unhindered by many of the constraints of a large company, entrepreneurs investing in other markets often demonstrate an inspiring can-do spirit mixed with ingenuity and bravado. For an example of an entrepreneur who overcame adverse economic conditions by boldly investing in China, see the Entrepreneur's Toolkit, titled "Canada Metal (Pacific): Surviving in Canada by Investing Abroad."

Worldwide Flows of FDI

Driving FDI growth are more than 82 000 multinational companies with more than 810 000 affiliates abroad, roughly half of which are in developing countries.[3] Developed countries remain the prime destination for FDI because cross-border M&As are concentrated in developed nations. In 2011, developed countries accounted for around 49 percent ($748 billion) of global FDI inflows. By comparison, FDI inflows to developing countries, which comprised 45 percent of global FID inflows, were valued at $684 billion, reaching a record peak. The remaining 6 percent of global FDI inflows went to countries considered as transition economies, the majority of which are located across Southeast Europe and are in various stages of transition from communism to capitalism.

Among developed countries, European Union (EU) nations, the United States, and Japan accounted for the vast majority of world inflows. The EU remains the world's largest FDI recipient, garnering $421 billion in 2011. Behind the large FDI figure for the EU is increased consolidation in Europe among large national competitors and further efforts at EU regional integration.

FDI inflows increased in developing nations in 2011. FDI inflows to developing nations in Asia and in Latin America and the Caribbean increased 10 and 16 percent respectively. Africa, in contrast, declined for the third consecutive year. The less developed countries, which are the poorest, had a decline of 11 percent in FDI inflows.

Canada's Flows of FDI

Canada has generally been losing its attractiveness as a destination for FDI, partially due to the lucrative investment opportunities available in Brazil, Russia, India, and China (the BRIC countries) and the improved manufacturing capability of Mexico. Canada's share of global inward FDI has fallen since the mid-1980s, as firms developed production facilities in the United States or Mexico to serve the North American market. The Organisation for Economic Co-operation and Development (OEDC) considers Canada to be one of the most restrictive countries for FDI. Specifically, Canada is very restrictive in three sectors: finance, transportation, and communications. To learn more about some of these restrictions, see the examples in this chapter's "Management Issues in the FDI Decision" section.

According to Statistics Canada, Canadian FDI abroad and FDI in Canada grew steadily in the 2000s. However, absolute numbers are still modest. It is evident (see Table 7.1) that the United States is still the main source of both inward and outward FDI. Economists generally agree that the FDI flows with emerging markets, particularly countries with which Canada has signed free trade agreements, need to grow in order for Canada to sustain its economic position.

TABLE 7.1	FDI from Canada and into Canada		
FDI from Canada (outward/FDI abroad)*		**FDI into Canada (inward)***	
All countries	$684 496	All countries	$607 497
United States	$276 145	United States	$326 055
Mexico	$ 4 237	Mexico	$ 216
South & Central America	$ 37 849	South & Central America	$ 18 785
Europe	$181 885	Europe	$184 211
Africa	$ 3 054	Africa	$ 3 290
Asia/Oceania	$ 66 065	Asia/Oceania	$ 63 310

*millions of dollars
Source: Statistics Canada, Data from Table CANSIM 376-0051, August 2012.

Entrepreneur's Toolkit

Canada Metal (Pacific): Surviving in Canada by Investing Abroad

Like many Canadian businesses, Canada Metal (Pacific) Ltd. (www.canmet.com), a British Columbia–based manufacturer focused on the recreational boating industry's zinc anode market, was struggling to survive in adverse economic conditions. The company found itself squeezed by the rising Canadian dollar, and its market share was dropping as its biggest customers demanded lower prices. And yet, in 2012 Canada Metal (Pacific) was named the eighteenth most innovative company in British Columbia.

How did John Mitchell, CEO of Canada Metal (Pacific), accomplish this impressive turnaround? An analysis showed the firm needed to build upon an innovative product while addressing cost inefficiencies. The solution? Foreign direct investment. Mitchell decided to focus on opportunities in lower-cost emerging markets to offset uncompetitive labour rates and expand his market reach. After evaluating several possible locations for an offshore manufacturing facility, he decided to invest in China, which offered significant benefits to foreign investors including a seven-year tax exemption.

When investing abroad, companies can decide to acquire another business, rent a facility, create a joint venture, or invest on their own. The latter option is the riskiest move, but also the one that offers a higher level of control and the possibility for greater profits. Mitchell decided to take the bold approach and go solo: He established a wholly owned subsidiary in China. It was an uphill battle, however. "I have a lot more grey hair," says Mitchell. "There were a lot of cultural idiosyncrasies and rules and regulations to learn. But we felt if we could bring down our cost and maintain our quality, we could compete globally."

In the end, Mitchell's bold move was successful. By deciding to invest aboard, Canada Metal (Pacific) doubled its revenue, added new product lines, and increased its number of customers by expanding sales, not only to China but also to Europe and South America.

Canada Metal (Pacific) retains product development in Canada and has over 85 employees in the head office. Mitchell concludes "Had I not expanded, I would have been out of business."

Sources: "Expansion helps B.C. manufacturer navigate economic challenges", *The Globe and Mail* (www.theglobeandmail.com), April 11, 2012; "2012 BC Business Guide to Innovation", Lindsey Peakcock, BC Business (www.bcbusiness.ca).

Quick Study

1. What is the difference between *foreign direct investment* and *portfolio investment?*
2. What factors influence global flows of foreign direct investment?
3. Identify the main destinations of foreign direct investment. Is the pattern shifting?

Explanations for Foreign Direct Investment

So far we have examined the flows of foreign direct investment, but we have not investigated explanations for why FDI occurs. Let's now investigate the four main theories that attempt to explain why companies engage in foreign direct investment.

International Product Life Cycle

Although we introduced the international product life cycle in Chapter 6 in the context of international trade, it is also used to explain foreign direct investment.[4] The **international product life cycle theory** states that a company will begin by exporting its product and later undertake foreign direct investment as a product moves through its life cycle. In the *new product stage*, a good is produced in the home country because of uncertain domestic demand and to keep production close to the research department that developed the product. In the *maturing product stage*, the company directly invests in production facilities in countries where demand is great enough to warrant its own production facilities. In the final *standardized product stage*, increased competition creates pressures to reduce production costs. In response, a company builds production capacity in low-cost developing nations to serve its markets around the world.

international product life cycle theory

Theory stating that a company will begin by exporting its product and later undertake foreign direct investment as the product moves through its life cycle.

Despite its conceptual appeal, the international product life cycle theory is limited in its power to explain why companies choose FDI over other forms of market entry. A local firm in the target market could pay for (license) the right to use the special assets needed to manufacture a particular product. In this way, a company could avoid the additional risks associated with direct investments in the market. The theory also fails to explain why firms choose FDI over exporting activities. It might be less expensive to serve a market abroad by increasing output at the home country factory rather than by building additional capacity within the target market.

The theory explains why the FDI of some firms follows the international product life cycle of their products. But it does not explain why other market entry modes are inferior or less advantageous options.

Market Imperfections (Internalization)

A market that is said to operate at peak efficiency (prices are as low as they can possibly be) and where goods are readily and easily available is said to be a *perfect market*. But perfect markets are rarely, if ever, seen in business because of factors that cause a breakdown in the efficient operation of an industry—called *market imperfections*. **Market imperfections** theory states that when an imperfection in the market makes a transaction less efficient than it could be, a company will undertake foreign direct investment to internalize the transaction and thereby remove the imperfection. There are two market imperfections that are relevant to this discussion—trade barriers and specialized knowledge.

market imperfections
Theory stating that, when an imperfection in the market makes a transaction less efficient than it could be, a company will undertake foreign direct investment to internalize the transaction and thereby remove the imperfection.

TRADE BARRIERS   One common market imperfection in international business is trade barriers, such as tariffs. For example, the North American Free Trade Agreement (NAFTA) stipulates that a sufficient portion of a product's content must originate within Canada, Mexico, or the United States for the product to avoid tariff charges when it is imported to any of these three markets. That is why a large number of Korean manufacturers invested in production facilities in Tijuana, Mexico, just south of Mexico's border with California. By investing in production facilities in Mexico, the Korean companies were able to skirt the North American tariffs that would have been levied if they were to export goods from Korean factories. The presence of a market imperfection (tariffs) caused those companies to undertake foreign direct investment.

SPECIALIZED KNOWLEDGE   The unique competitive advantage of a company sometimes consists of specialized knowledge. This knowledge could be the technical expertise of engineers or the special marketing abilities of managers. When the knowledge is technical expertise, companies can charge a fee to companies in other countries for use of the knowledge in producing the same

Employees from quality control check plasma screens on the production line at a newly opened television assembly plant in Nymburk near Prague, Czech Republic. The plant is a foreign direct investment by a company called Chinese Changhong Europe Electric TV. The plant is Changhong's biggest foreign direct investment in recent times and produces LCD, plasma, and classic televisions. What advantages do you think the Chinese company gained by investing in the Czech Republic?

Source: © Radim Beznoska/epaCorbis.

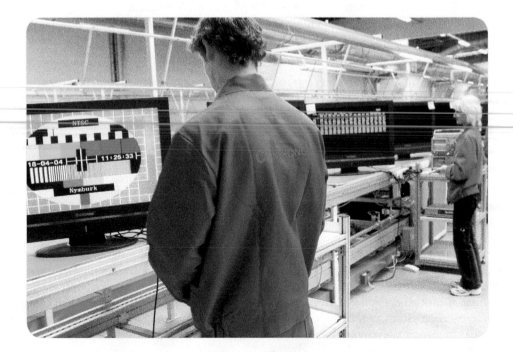

or a similar product. But when a company's specialized knowledge is embodied in its employees, the only way to exploit a market opportunity in another nation may be to undertake FDI.

The possibility that a company will create a future competitor by charging another company for access to its knowledge is another market imperfection that can encourage FDI. Rather than trade a short-term gain (the fee charged another company) for a long-term loss (lost competitiveness), a company will prefer to undertake investment. For example, as Japan rebuilt its industries following the Second World War, many Japanese companies paid Western firms for access to the special technical knowledge embodied in their products. Those Japanese companies became adept at revising and improving many of these technologies and became leaders in their industries, including electronics and automobiles.

Eclectic Theory

The **eclectic theory** states that firms undertake foreign direct investment when the features of a particular location combine with ownership and internalization advantages to make a location appealing for investment.[5] A *location advantage* is the advantage of locating a particular economic activity in a specific location because of the characteristics (natural or acquired) of that location.[6] These advantages have historically been natural resources such as oil in the Middle East, timber in Canada, or copper in Chile. But the advantage can also be an acquired one such as a productive workforce. An *ownership advantage* refers to company ownership of some special asset, such as brand recognition, technical knowledge, or management ability. An *internalization advantage* is one that arises from internalizing a business activity rather than leaving it to a relatively inefficient market. The eclectic theory states that when all of these advantages are present, a company will undertake FDI.

eclectic theory
Theory stating that firms undertake foreign direct investment when the features of a particular location combine with ownership and internalization advantages to make a location appealing for investment.

Market Power

Firms often seek the greatest amount of power possible in their industries relative to rivals. The **market power** theory states that a firm tries to establish a dominant market presence in an industry by undertaking foreign direct investment. The benefit of market power is greater profit because the firm is far better able to dictate the cost of its inputs and/or the price of its output.

One way a company can achieve market power (or dominance) is through **vertical integration**— the extension of company activities into stages of production that provide a firm's inputs (*backward integration*) or absorb its output (*forward integration*). Sometimes a company can effectively control the world supply of an input needed by its industry if it has the resources or ability to integrate backward into supplying that input. Companies may also be able to achieve a great deal of market power if they can integrate forward to increase control over output. For example, they could perhaps make investments in distribution to leapfrog channels of distribution that are tightly controlled by competitors.

market power
Theory stating that a firm tries to establish a dominant market presence in an industry by undertaking foreign direct investment.

vertical integration
Extension of company activities into stages of production that provide a firm's inputs (backward integration) or absorb its output (forward integration).

Quick Study

1. Explain the international *product life cycle theory* of foreign direct investment (FDI).
2. How does the theory of *market imperfections* (internalization) explain FDI?
3. Explain the *eclectic theory*, and identify the three advantages necessary for FDI to occur.
4. How does the theory of *market power* explain the occurrence of FDI?

Management Issues in the FDI Decision

Decisions about whether to engage in foreign direct investment involve several important issues regarding management of the company and its market. Some of these issues are grounded in the inner workings of firms that undertake FDI, such as the control desired over operations abroad or the firm's cost of production. Others are related to the market and industry in which a firm competes, such as the preferences of customers or the actions of rivals. Let's examine each of these important issues.

Control

Many companies investing abroad are greatly concerned with controlling the activities that occur in the local market. Perhaps the company wants to be certain that its product is being marketed in the same way in the local market as it is at home. Or maybe it wants to ensure that the selling price remains the same in both markets. Some companies try to maintain ownership of a large portion of the local operation, say, even up to 100 percent, in the belief that greater ownership gives them greater control.

In some cases, governments are the ones that want to ensure control. For example, the Canadian government considers the broadcasting sector a "sensitive" sector. Its regulatory Broadcasting Act allows foreign broadcasting companies to own a maximum of 20 percent of a broadcaster; foreign ownership of a holding company that owns a broadcaster is limited to 33 percent. The Canadian government wants to ensure that Canada has its own broadcasting system and that the Canadian public has access to Canadian programming created by Canadians. Essentially the Canadian government wants to control the type of programming offered, to provide employment to Canadians in the industry, and to develop and retain programming that promotes Canadian culture.[7]

Yet for a variety of reasons, even complete ownership does not *guarantee* control. For example, the local government might intervene and require a company to hire some local managers rather than bring them all in from the home office. Companies may need to prove a scarcity of skilled local managerial talent before the government will let them bring managers in from the home country. Governments might also require that all goods produced in the local facility be exported so they do not compete with products of the country's domestic firms. For example, in its early years Mexico's "maquiladora" program (the manufacturing program for foreign companies) required that 100 percent of the finished products be exported—even the scrap derivate from the manufacturing process. Benefits for foreign investor(s) were access to low-cost labour, tax incentives, and, in some cases, lower-cost operations, depending on the investor's country of origin.

PARTNERSHIP REQUIREMENTS Many companies have strict policies regarding how much ownership they take in firms abroad because of the importance of maintaining control. In the past, IBM (www.ibm.com) strictly required that the home office own 100 percent of all international subsidiaries. But companies must sometimes abandon such policies if a country demands shared ownership in return for market access.

Some governments saw shared ownership requirements as a way to shield their workers from exploitation and their industries from domination by large international firms. Companies would sometimes sacrifice control to pursue a market opportunity, but frequently they did not. Most countries today do not take such a hard-line stance and have opened their doors to investment by multinational companies. Mexico used to make decisions on investment by multinationals on a case-by-case basis. IBM was negotiating with the Mexican government for 100 percent ownership of a facility in Guadalajara and got the go-ahead only after the company made numerous concessions in other areas. Canada, for example, limits foreign ownership of Canadian air carriers to 25 percent, and no foreigner may control a Canadian air carrier. But companies have found a way to overcome various restrictions by forming partnerships or cooperative alliances such as Star Alliance (www.staralliance.com), a partnership of world-class airlines united to share networks, lounge access, check-in services, ticketing, and so forth. Star Alliance has 28 member companies, including Air Canada, Air China, Air New Zealand, Asiana Airlines, Brussels Airlines, Ethiopian Airlines, Lufthansa, Scandinavian Airlines, South African Airways, Singapore Airlines, TAP Portugal, and United.[8]

BENEFITS OF COOPERATION Many nations have grown more cooperative toward international companies in recent years. Governments of developing and emerging markets realize the benefits of investment by multinationals, including decreased unemployment, increased tax revenues, training to create a more highly skilled workforce, and the transfer of technology. A country known for overly restricting the operations of multinational enterprises can see its inward investment flow dry up. Indeed, restrictive policies of India's government hampered foreign direct investment inflows for many years.

Cooperation also frequently opens important communication channels that help firms to maintain positive relationships in the host country. Both parties tend to walk a fine line—cooperating most of the time, but holding fast on occasions when the stakes are especially high.

Cooperation with a local partner and respect for national pride in Central Europe contributed to the successful acquisition of Hungary's Borsodi brewery (formerly a state-owned enterprise) by Belgium's Anheuser-Busch InBev (www.ab-inbev.com). From the start, Anheuser-Busch InBev wisely insisted it would move ahead with its purchase only if local management would be in charge. Anheuser-Busch InBev then assisted local management with technical, marketing, sales, distribution, and general management training. Borsodi eventually became one of Anheuser-Busch InBev's key subsidiaries and is now run entirely by Hungarian managers.

Purchase-or-Build Decision

Another important matter for managers is whether to purchase an existing business or to build a subsidiary abroad from the ground up—called a *greenfield investment*. An acquisition generally provides the investor with an existing plant, equipment, and personnel. The acquiring firm may also benefit from the goodwill the existing company has built up over the years and, perhaps, brand recognition of the existing firm. The purchase of an existing business may also allow for alternative methods of financing the purchase, such as an exchange of stock ownership between the companies. Factors that can reduce the appeal of purchasing existing facilities include obsolete equipment, poor relations with workers, and an unsuitable location.

Mexico's Cemex, S.A., (www.cemex.com) is a multinational company that made a fortune by buying struggling, inefficient plants around the world and re-engineering them. Chairman Lorenzo Zambrano has long figured the overriding principle was "Buy big globally, or be bought." The success of Cemex in using FDI has confounded, even rankled, its competitors in developed nations. For example, Cemex shocked global markets when it carried out a $1.8 billion purchase of Spain's two largest cement companies, Valenciana and Sanson.

Canada's Scotiabank, also known as the Bank of Nova Scotia (www.scotiabank.com), is recognized as "Canada's International Bank" due to its acquisitions in Latin America, the Caribbean, Europe, and India. By acquiring subsidiaries abroad, Scotiabank has been able to penetrate several foreign markets in a relatively short period of time.

But adequate facilities in the local market are sometimes unavailable and a company must go ahead with a greenfield investment. Because Poland is a source of skilled and inexpensive labour, it is an appealing location for car manufacturers. But the country had little in the way of advanced car-production facilities when General Motors (GM) (www.gm.com) considered investing there. So GM built a $320 million facility in Poland's Silesian region. The factory has the potential to produce 200 000 units annually—some of which are destined for export to

Bombardier started by manufacturing snowmobiles in Quebec in the 1940s. Bombardier's aerospace division started as a result of an acquisition. Today Bombardier is a multinational company with greenfield investments in Mexico, Canada, and the United States. Bombardier Finland is the result of an acquisition of Lynx snowmobiles.

Source: CLEMENT SABOURIN/AFP/ Getty Images/Newscom.

profitable markets in Western Europe. However, greenfield investments can have their share of headaches. Obtaining the necessary permits, financing, and hiring local personnel can be a real problem in some markets.

Production Costs

Many factors contribute to production costs in every national market. Labour regulations can add significantly to the overall cost of production. Companies may be required to provide benefits packages for their employees that are over and above hourly wages. More time than was planned for might be required to train workers adequately to bring productivity up to an acceptable standard. Although the cost of land and the tax rate on profits can be lower in the local market (or purposely lowered to attract multinationals), it cannot be assumed that they will remain constant. Companies from around the world using China as a production base have witnessed rising wages erode their profits as the economy continues to industrialize. Some companies are therefore finding that Vietnam is their low-cost location of choice.

rationalized production
System of production in which each of a product's components is produced where the cost of producing that component is lowest.

RATIONALIZED PRODUCTION   One approach companies use to contain production costs is called **rationalized production**—a system of production in which each of a product's components is produced where the cost of producing that component is lowest. All the components are then brought together at one central location for assembly into the final product. Consider the typical stuffed animal made in China whose components are all imported to China (with the exception of the polycore thread with which it's sewn). The stuffed animal's eyes are moulded in Japan. Its outfit is imported from France. The polyester-fibre stuffing comes from either Germany or the United States, and the pile-fabric fur is produced in Korea. Only final assembly of these components occurs in China.

Although this production model is highly efficient, a potential problem is that a work stoppage in one country can bring the entire production process to a standstill. For example, the production of automobiles is highly rationalized, with parts coming in from a multitude of countries for assembly. When the United Auto Workers (UAW) (www.uaw.org) union held a strike for weeks against General Motors (www.gm.com), many of GM's international assembly plants were threatened. The UAW strategically launched their strike at GM's plant that supplied brake pads to virtually all of its assembly plants throughout North America.

MEXICO'S MAQUILADORA   Stretching 2000 miles from the Pacific Ocean to the Gulf of Mexico, the 210-kilometre–wide strip along the US–Mexican border may well be North America's fastest-growing region. The region's economy encompasses 11 million people and $150 billion in output. The combination of a low-wage economy nestled next to a prosperous giant is now becoming a model for other regions that are split by wage or technology gaps. Some analysts compare the US–Mexican border region to that between Hong Kong and its manufacturing realm, China's Guangdong province. Officials from cities along the border between Germany and Poland studied the US–Mexican experience to see what lessons could be applied to their unique situation.

COST OF RESEARCH AND DEVELOPMENT   As technology becomes an increasingly powerful competitive factor, the soaring cost of developing subsequent stages of technology has led multinationals to engage in cross-border alliances and acquisitions. For instance, huge multinational pharmaceutical companies are intensely interested in the pioneering biotechnology work done by smaller, entrepreneurial start-ups. Convergent Bioscience, a small Toronto company founded in 1995, manufactured some of the highly sophisticated instruments that pharmaceutical companies use to analyze proteins and other large organic molecules called "biologicals." Consequently, the Toronto company, which had invested heavily in R&D, became a target of larger companies interested in its pioneering technology. In 2010, Cell Biosciences (since renamed ProteinSimple), a US company based in Santa Clara, California, acquired Convergent Bioscience for approximately $12 million. In 2011, the same US company also bought Ottawa's Brightwell Technologies, its fourth acquisition in 18 months. Brightwell Technologies was the market leader in micro-flow imaging (MFI), a technique used to detect particles and aggregates in protein-based therapeutics, and its products had been adopted by the world's largest pharmaceutical and biotechnology companies.[9]

One indicator of technology's significance in foreign direct investment is the amount of R&D conducted by companies' affiliates in other countries. The globalization of innovation and the phenomenon of foreign direct investment in R&D are not necessarily motivated by demand factors such as the size of local markets. They instead appear to be encouraged by supply factors, including gaining access to high-quality scientific and technical human capital.

Customer Knowledge

The behaviour of buyers is frequently an important issue in the decision of whether to undertake foreign direct investment. A local presence can help companies gain valuable knowledge about customers that could not be obtained from the home market. For example, when customer preferences for a product differ a great deal from country to country, a local presence might help companies to better understand such preferences and tailor their products accordingly.

Some countries have quality reputations in certain product categories. German automotive engineering, Italian shoes, French perfume, and Swiss watches impress customers as being of superior quality. Because of these perceptions, it can be profitable for a firm to produce its product in the country with the quality reputation, even if the company is based in another country. For example, a cologne or perfume producer might want to bottle its fragrance in France and give it a French name. This type of image appeal can be strong enough to encourage foreign direct investment.

Following Clients

Firms commonly engage in foreign direct investment when the firms they supply have already invested abroad. This practice of "following clients" is common in industries in which producers source component parts from suppliers with whom they have close working relationships. The practice tends to result in companies clustering within close geographic proximity to each other because they supply each other's inputs (see Chapter 6). When Mercedes (www5.mercedes-benz.com) opened its first international car plant in the United States, auto-parts suppliers also moved to the area from Germany—bringing with them additional investment in the millions of dollars. In Canada, Toyota Motor Manufacturing Canada (www.tmmc.ca), a subsidiary of Japan-based Toyota Motor Corporation, recently upgraded and expanded its assembly plants in Cambridge and Woodstock, Ontario. As a result, Arvin Sango, one of Toyota's auto-parts suppliers, also increased its FDI investments by establishing a new production facility in London, Ontario.

Following Rivals

FDI decisions frequently resemble a "follow the leader" scenario in industries having a limited number of large firms. In other words, many of these firms believe that choosing not to make a move parallel to that of the "first mover" might result in being shut out of a potentially lucrative market. When firms based in industrial countries moved back into South Africa after the end of apartheid, their competitors followed. Of course, each market can sustain only a certain number of rivals. Firms that cannot compete choose the "least damaging option." This seems to have been the case for Pepsi (www.pepsi.com), which went back into South Africa in 1994 but withdrew in 1997 after being crushed there by Coke (www.cocacola.com).

In this section, we have presented several key issues managers consider when investing abroad. We will have more to say on this topic in Chapter 11, when we learn about the different entry modes companies use to go international. Meanwhile, you can read more about what managers should consider when going global in the Global Manager's Briefcase, titled "Surprises of Investing Abroad."

Quick Study

1. Why is control important to companies considering the FDI decision?
2. What is the role of production costs in the FDI decision? Define *rationalized production*.
3. Explain the need for customer knowledge, following clients, and following rivals in the FDI decision.

Global Manager's Briefcase   Surprises of Investing Abroad

The decision of whether to build facilities in a market abroad or to purchase existing operations in the local market can be a difficult one. Managers can minimize risk by preparing their companies for a number of surprises they might face.

- **Human Resource Policies.** Companies cannot always import home country policies without violating local laws or offending local customs. Countries have differing requirements for plant operations and their own regulations regarding business operations.

- **Labour Costs.** France has a minimum wage of about $12 an hour, whereas Mexico has a minimum wage of just under $6 a day. But Mexico's real minimum wage is nearly double that due to government-mandated benefits and employment practices. Such differences are not always obvious.

- **Mandated Benefits.** These include company-supplied clothing and meals, required profit sharing, guaranteed employment contracts, and generous dismissal policies.

These costs can exceed an employee's wages and are typically not negotiable.

- **Labour Unions.** In some countries, organized labour is found in nearly every industry and at almost every company. Rather than dealing with a single union, managers may need to negotiate with five or six different unions, each of which represents a distinct skill or profession.

- **Information.** Sometimes there simply is no reliable data on factors such as labour availability, cost of energy, and national inflation rates. These data are generally high quality in developed countries and suspect in emerging and developing ones.

- **Personal and Political Contacts.** These contacts can be extremely important in developing and emerging markets and can be the only way to establish operations. But complying with locally accepted practices can cause ethical dilemmas for managers.

Government Intervention in Foreign Direct Investment

Nations often intervene in the flow of FDI to protect their cultural heritages, domestic companies, and jobs. They can enact laws, create regulations, or construct administrative hurdles that companies from other nations must overcome if they want to invest in the nation. Yet rising competitive pressure is forcing nations to compete against each other to attract multinational companies. The increased national competition for investment is causing governments to enact regulatory changes that encourage investment. As Table 7.2 demonstrates, the vast majority of regulatory changes that governments introduced in recent years are *more favourable to FDI*.

In a general sense, a bias toward protectionism or openness is rooted in a nation's culture, history, and politics. Values, attitudes, and beliefs form the basis for much of a government's position regarding foreign direct investment. For example, South American nations with strong cultural ties to a European heritage (such as Argentina) are generally enthusiastic about investment received from European nations. South American nations with stronger indigenous influences (such as Ecuador) are generally less enthusiastic.

TABLE 7.2 National Regulatory Changes, 2000–2011												
Item	2000	2001	2002	2003	2004	2005	2006	2007	2008	2009	2010	2011
Number of countries that introduced changes	45	51	43	59	80	77	74	49	41	45	57	44
Number of regulatory changes	81	97	94	126	166	145	132	80	69	89	112	67
Liberalization/promotion	75	85	79	114	144	119	107	59	51	61	75	52
Regulation/restriction	5	2	12	12	20	25	25	19	16	24	36	15
Neutral/indeterminate	1	10	3	0	2	1	0	2	2	4	1	0

Source: Based on data from the United Nations Conference on Trade and Development, *World Investment Report 2012* (Geneva, Switzerland: UNCTAD). http://www.unctad-docs.org/files/UNCTAD-WIR2012-Full-en.pdf, page 31.

Opinions vary widely on the appropriate amount of foreign direct investment a country should encourage. At one extreme are those who favour complete economic self-sufficiency and oppose any form of FDI. At the other extreme are those who favour no governmental intervention and booming FDI inflows. Between these two extremes lie most countries, which believe a certain amount of FDI is desirable to raise national output and enhance the standard of living for their people.

Besides philosophical ideals, countries intervene in FDI for a host of very practical reasons. But to fully appreciate those reasons, we must first understand what is meant by a country's *balance of payments*.

Balance of Payments

A country's **balance of payments** is a national accounting system that records all payments to entities in other countries and all receipts coming into the nation. International transactions that result in payments (outflows) to entities in other nations are reductions in the balance of payments accounts and are therefore recorded with a minus sign. International transactions that result in receipts (inflows) from other nations are additions to the balance of payments accounts and thus are recorded with a plus sign.

balance of payments
National accounting system that records all payments to entities in other countries and all receipts coming into the nation.

For example, when a Canadian company buys 40 percent of the publicly traded stock of a Mexican company on Mexico's stock market, Canada's balance of payments records the transaction as an outflow of capital, and it is recorded with a minus sign. Table 7.3 shows the recent balance of payments accounts for Canada. As shown in the table, any nation's balance of payments consists of two major components—the *current account* and *capital account*. Let's describe each of these accounts and discuss how to read Table 7.3.

CURRENT ACCOUNT   The **current account** is a national account that records transactions involving the import and export of goods and services, income receipts on assets abroad, and income payments on foreign assets inside the country. The *goods* account in Table 7.3 includes exports and imports of tangible goods such as computer software, electronic components, and apparel. The *services* account includes exports and imports of services such as tourism, business consulting, and banking services. Suppose a company in Canada receives payment for consulting services provided to a company in another country. The receipt is recorded as an "export of services" and assigned a plus sign in the services account in the balance of payments.

current account
National account that records transactions involving the import and export of goods and services, income receipts on assets abroad, and income payments on foreign assets inside the country.

The *primary income receipts* account includes income earned on Canadian assets held abroad. When a Canadian company's subsidiary in another country remits profits back to the parent in Canada, the receipt is recorded in the income receipts account and given a plus sign. The *primary income payments* account includes income paid to entities in other nations that is earned on assets they hold in Canada. For example, when a French company's Canadian subsidiary sends profits earned in Canada back to the parent company in France, the transaction is recorded in the primary income payments account as an outflow.

A **current account surplus** occurs when a country exports more goods and services and receives more income from abroad than it imports and pays abroad. Conversely, a **current account deficit** occurs when a country imports more goods and services and pays more abroad than it exports and receives from abroad. Table 7.3 shows that Canada had a current account deficit (see the line that reads *Total current account* under the *Balances* section) in the year shown.

current account surplus
When a country exports more goods and services and receives more income from abroad than it imports and pays abroad.

current account deficit
When a country imports more goods and services and pays more abroad than it exports and receives from abroad.

CAPITAL ACCOUNT   The **capital account** is a national account that records transactions involving the purchase or sale of assets. Suppose a Canadian citizen buys shares of stock in a Mexican company on Mexico's stock market. The transaction would show up on the capital accounts of both Canada and Mexico—as an outflow of assets from Canada and an inflow of assets to Mexico. Conversely, suppose a Mexican investor buys real estate in Canada. That transaction also shows up on the capital accounts of both nations—as an inflow of assets to Canada and an outflow of assets from Mexico. Although the balances of the current and capital accounts should be the same, errors are common due to recording methods.

capital account
National account that records transactions involving the purchase or sale of assets.

Reasons for Intervention by the Host Country

A number of reasons underlie a government's decisions regarding foreign direct investment by international companies. Let's now look at the two main reasons countries intervene in FDI flows—to control the *balance of payments* and *to obtain resources and benefits*.

TABLE 7.3	Canada's Balance of Payments Accounts	

Receipts, Payments, and Balances	Current Account and Capital Account	2011
Receipts	Total current account	615 948
	Goods and services	539 289
	Goods	456 518
	Services	82 771
	Primary income	67 837
	Compensation of employees	1 154
	Investment income	66 683
	Secondary income	8 822
	Private transfers	2 180
	Government transfers	6 642
	Capital account	272
Payments	Total current account	668 240
	Goods and services	561 399
	Goods	455 606
	Services	105 793
	Primary income	94 560
	Compensation of employees	3 062
	Investment income	91 498
	Secondary income	12 282
	Private transfers	6 746
	Government transfers	5 536
	Capital account	282
Balances	Total current account	−52 292
	Goods and services	−22 110
	Goods	912
	Services	−23 ,022
	Primary income	−26 723
	Compensation of employees	−1 908
	Investment income	−24 815
	Secondary income	−3 459
	Private transfers	−4 566
	Government transfers	1 106
	Capital account	−10
	Net lending / net borrowing, from current and capital accounts	−52 303

Source: Statistics Canada, Table 376-0101, Balance of International Payments, Current Account and Capital Account, CANSIM Database, 2011.

CONTROL BALANCE OF PAYMENTS   Many governments see intervention as the only way to keep their balance of payments under control. First, because foreign direct investment inflows are recorded as additions to the balance of payments, a nation gets a balance-of-payments boost from an initial FDI inflow. Second, countries can impose local content requirements on investors from other nations coming in for the purpose of local production. This gives local companies the chance to become suppliers to the production operation, which can help reduce the nation's imports and thereby improve its balance of payments. Third, exports (if any) generated by the new production operation can have a favourable impact on the host country's balance of payments.

But when companies repatriate profits back to their home countries, they deplete the foreign exchange reserves of their host countries. These capital outflows decrease the balance of payments of the host country. To shore up its balance of payments, the host nation may prohibit or restrict the nondomestic company from removing profits to its home country.

Alternatively, host countries conserve their foreign exchange reserves when international companies reinvest their earnings. Reinvesting in local manufacturing facilities can also improve the competitiveness of local producers and boost a host nation's exports—thus improving its balance-of-payments position.

OBTAIN RESOURCES AND BENEFITS   Beyond balance-of-payments reasons, governments might intervene in FDI flows to acquire resources and benefits such as technology, management skills, and employment.

Access to Technology   Investment in technology, whether in products or processes, tends to increase the productivity and the competitiveness of a nation. That is why host nations have a strong incentive to encourage the importation of technology. For years, developing countries in Asia were introduced to expertise in industrial processes as multinationals set up factories within their borders. But today some of them are trying to acquire and develop their own technological expertise. When German industrial giant Siemens (www.siemens.com) chose Singapore as the site for an Asia-Pacific micro-electronics design centre, Singapore gained access to valuable technology. To cite another example, Datawind's government-sponsored Aakash tablet is assembled and programmed in India. By having Datawind's tablet manufacturing centre in India, India is gaining access to valuable technology. To read more about Datawind, go back to the opening case in Chapter 5.

A family rides past an advertisement for BlackBerry in India. India's liberal economic policies have caused its inward foreign direct investment to surge. The investments of multinationals bring badly needed jobs. How might such investments affect India's balance of payments?

Source: RAMINDER PAL SINGH/epa/ Corbis.

Management Skills and Employment   As we saw in Chapter 4, many formerly communist nations suffer from a lack of management skills needed to succeed in the global economy. By encouraging FDI, these nations can attract talented managers to come in and train locals, and thereby improve the international competitiveness of their domestic companies. Furthermore, locals who are trained in modern management techniques may eventually start their own local businesses—further expanding employment opportunities. Yet detractors argue that although FDI may create jobs, it may also destroy jobs because less competitive local firms may be forced out of business. Employment was the main reason the Quebec government agreed in 2005 to approve and financially support Japanese-owned Bridgestone-Firestone's Canadian plant expansion. Approximately 1250 jobs were at stake.

Reasons for Intervention by the Home Country

Home nations (those from which international companies launch their investments) may also seek to encourage or discourage *outflows* of FDI for a variety of reasons. But home nations tend to have fewer concerns because they are often prosperous, industrialized nations. For these countries, an outward investment seldom has a national impact—unlike the impact on developing or emerging nations that receive the FDI. Nevertheless, among the most common reasons for discouraging outward FDI are the following:

- *Investing in other nations sends resources out of the home country.* As a result, fewer resources are used for development and economic growth at home. On the other hand, profits on assets abroad that are returned home increase both a home country's balance of payments and its available resources.
- *Outgoing FDI may ultimately damage a nation's balance of payments by taking the place of its exports.* This can occur when a company creates a production facility in a market abroad, the output of which replaces exports that used to be sent there from the home country. For example, if a Toyota manufacturing facility in Canada (www.toyota.ca) fulfills a demand that Canadian buyers would otherwise satisfy with purchases of Japanese-made autos, Japan's balance of payments will correspondingly decrease. However, Japan's balance of payments will increase when its companies repatriate Canadian profits, which helps negate the investment's initial negative balance-of-payments effect. Thus, an international investment might make a positive contribution to the balance-of-payments position of the country in the long term and offset an initial negative impact.
- *Jobs resulting from outgoing investments may replace jobs at home.* This is often the most contentious issue for home countries. The relocation of production to a low-wage nation can have a strong impact on a locale or region. However, the impact is rarely national, and its effects are often muted by other job opportunities in the economy. In addition, there may be an offsetting improvement in home country employment if additional exports are needed to support the activity represented by the outgoing FDI. For example, if Hyundai (www.hyundai.com) of South Korea builds an automobile manufacturing plant in Brazil, Korean employment may increase in order to supply the Brazilian plant with parts.

But foreign direct investment is not always a negative influence on home nations. In fact, under certain circumstances, governments might encourage it. Countries promote outgoing FDI for the following reasons:

- *Outward FDI can increase long-term competitiveness.* Businesses today frequently compete on a global scale. The most competitive firms tend to be those that conduct business in the most favourable location anywhere in the world, continuously improve their performance relative to competitors, and derive technological advantages from alliances formed with other companies. Japanese companies have become masterful at benefiting from FDI and cooperative arrangements with companies from other nations. The key to their success is that Japanese companies see every cooperative venture as a learning opportunity.
- *Nations may encourage FDI in industries identified as "sunset" industries.* Sunset industries are those that use outdated and obsolete technologies or employ low-wage workers with few skills. These jobs are not greatly appealing to countries having industries that pay skilled workers high wages. By allowing some of these jobs to go abroad and retraining workers in higher-paying skilled work, they can upgrade their economies toward "sunrise" industries. This represents a trade-off for governments between a short-term loss of jobs and the long-term benefit of developing workers' skills.

Quick Study

1. What is a country's *balance of payments*? Briefly explain its usefulness.

2. Explain the difference between the *current account* and the *capital account*.

3. For what reasons do *host* countries intervene in FDI?

4. For what reasons do *home* countries intervene in FDI?

Government Policy Instruments and FDI

Over time, both host and home nations have developed a range of methods to either promote or restrict FDI (see Table 7.4). Governments use these tools for many reasons, including improving balance-of-payments positions; acquiring resources; and, in the case of outward investment, keeping jobs at home. Let's take a look at these methods.

Host Countries: Promotion

Host countries offer a variety of incentives to encourage FDI inflows. These take two general forms—financial incentives and infrastructure improvements.

FINANCIAL INCENTIVES Host governments of all nations grant companies financial incentives if they will invest within their borders. One method includes tax incentives, such as lower tax rates or offers to waive taxes on local profits for a period of time—extending as far out as five years or more. A country may also offer *low-interest loans* to investors.

The downside of these types of incentives is they can allow multinationals to create bidding wars between locations that are vying for the investment. In such cases, the company typically invests in the most appealing region after the locations endure rounds of escalating incentives. Companies have even been accused of engaging other governments in negotiations to force concessions from locations already selected for investment. The cost to taxpayers of attracting FDI can be several times what the actual jobs themselves pay—especially when nations try to one-up each other to win investment.

INFRASTRUCTURE IMPROVEMENTS Because of the problems associated with financial incentives, some governments are taking an alternative route to luring investment. Lasting benefits for communities surrounding the investment location can result from making local *infrastructure improvements*—better seaports suitable for containerized shipping, improved roads, and increased telecommunications systems. For instance, Malaysia is carving an enormous Multimedia Super Corridor (MSC) into a region's forested surroundings. The MSC promises a paperless government, an intelligent city called Cyberjaya, two telesuburbs, a technology park, a multimedia university, and an intellectual-property–protection park. The MSC is dedicated to creating the most advanced technologies in telecommunications, medicine, distance learning, and remote manufacturing.

TABLE 7.4	Methods of Promoting and Restricting FDI	
	FDI Promotion	**FDI Restriction**
Host countries	Tax incentives	Ownership restrictions
	Low-interest loans	Performance demands
	Infrastructure improvements	
Home countries	Insurance	Differential tax rates
	Loans	Sanctions
	Tax breaks	
	Political pressure	

Host Countries: Restriction

Host countries also have a variety of methods to restrict incoming FDI. Again, these take two general forms—ownership restrictions and performance demands.

OWNERSHIP RESTRICTIONS   Governments can impose *ownership restrictions* that prohibit nondomestic companies from investing in certain industries or from owning certain types of businesses. Such prohibitions typically apply to businesses in cultural industries and companies vital to national security. For example, as some Islamic countries in the Middle East try to protect traditional values, accepting investment by Western companies is a controversial issue between purists and moderates. Also, most nations do not allow FDI in their domestic weapons or national defence firms. Another ownership restriction is a requirement that nondomestic investors hold less than a 50 percent stake in local firms when they undertake foreign direct investment.

But nations are eliminating such restrictions because companies today often can choose another location that has no such restriction in place. When General Motors was deciding whether to invest in an aging automobile plant in Jakarta, Indonesia, the Indonesian government scrapped its ownership restriction of an eventual forced sale to Indonesians because China and Vietnam were also courting GM for the same financial investment.

PERFORMANCE DEMANDS   More common than ownership requirements are *performance demands* that influence how international companies operate in the host nation. Although typically viewed as intrusive, most international companies allow for them in the same way they allow for home country regulations. Performance demands include ensuring that a portion of the product's content originates locally, stipulating the portion of output that must be exported, or requiring that certain technologies be transferred to local businesses.

Home Countries: Promotion

To encourage outbound FDI, home country governments can do any of the following:

- Offer *insurance* to cover the risks of investments abroad, including, among others, insurance against expropriation of assets and losses from armed conflict, kidnappings, and terrorist attacks.
- Grant *loans* to firms wishing to increase their investments abroad. A home country government may also guarantee the loans that a company takes from financial institutions.
- Offer *tax breaks* on profits earned abroad or negotiate special tax treaties. For example, several multinational agreements reduce or eliminate the practice of double taxation—profits earned abroad being taxed both in the home and host countries.
- Apply *political pressure* on other nations to get them to relax their restrictions on inbound investments. Non-Japanese companies often find it very difficult to invest inside Japan.

Home Countries: Restriction

On the other hand, to limit the effects of outbound FDI on the national economy, home governments may exercise either of the following two options:

- Impose *differential tax rates* that charge income from earnings abroad at a higher rate than domestic earnings.
- Impose outright *sanctions* that prohibit domestic firms from making investments in certain nations.

Quick Study

1. Identify the main methods host countries use to promote and restrict FDI.
2. What methods do home countries use to promote and restrict FDI?

Bottom Line for Business

Companies ranging from massive global corporations to adventurous entrepreneurs all contribute to FDI flows, and the long-term trend in FDI is upward. Here we briefly discuss the influence of national governments on FDI flows and flows of FDI in Asia and Europe.

National Governments and FDI

The actions of national governments have important implications for business. Companies can either be thwarted in their efforts or be encouraged to invest in a nation, depending on the philosophies of home and host governments. The balance-of-payments positions of both home and host countries are also important because FDI flows affect the economic health of nations. To attract investment, a nation must provide a climate conducive to business operations, including pro-growth economic policies, a stable regulatory environment, and a sound infrastructure, to name just a few.

Increased competition for investment by multinationals has caused nations to make regulatory changes more favourable to FDI. Moreover, just as nations around the world are creating free trade agreements (covered in Chapter 8), they are also embracing bilateral investment treaties. These bilateral investment treaties are becoming prominent tools used to attract investment. Investment provisions within free trade agreements are also receiving greater attention than in the past. These efforts to attract investment have direct implications for the strategies of multinational companies, particularly when it comes to deciding where to locate production, logistics, and back-office service activities.

Foreign Direct Investment in Europe

FDI inflows into the developing (transition) nations of Southeast Europe and the Commonwealth of Independent States hit an all-time high in 2008. Countries that recently entered the European Union did particularly well. They saw less investment in areas supporting low-wage, unskilled occupations, and greater investment in higher value-added activities that take advantage of a well-educated workforce.

The main reason for the fast pace at which foreign direct investment is occurring in Western Europe is regional economic integration (see Chapter 8). Some of the foreign investment reported by the European Union certainly went to the relatively less developed markets of the new Central and Eastern European members. But much of the activity occurring among Western European companies is industry consolidation brought on by the opening of markets and the tearing down of barriers to free trade and investment. Change in the economic landscape across Europe is creating a more competitive business climate there.

Foreign Direct Investment in Asia

China attracts the majority of Asia's FDI, luring companies with a low-wage workforce and access to an enormous domestic market. Many companies already active in China are upping their investment further, and companies not yet there are developing strategies for how to include China in their future plans. The "off-shoring" of services will likely propel continued FDI in the coming years, of which India is the primary destination. India's attraction is its well-educated, low-cost, and English-speaking workforce.

An aspect of national business environments that has implications for future business activity is the natural environment. By their actions, businesses lay the foundation for people's attitudes in developing nations toward FDI by multinationals. For example, greater decentralization in China's politics has placed local Communist Party bosses and bureaucrats at the centre of many FDI deals there. These individuals are often more motivated by their personal financial gain than they are worried about pollution. But China's government is increasing spending on the environment, and multinationals are helping in cleaning up the environment.

Chapter Summary

1. **Describe worldwide patterns of foreign direct investment (FDI) and reasons for these patterns.**
   - FDI inflows peaked in 2000 at $1.4 trillion but then slowed through 2003. They then rebounded in 2004, 2005, 2006, and reached a record of more than $1.9 trillion in 2007.
   - Developed countries accounted for around 49 percent ($748 billion) of global FDI inflows.
   - Among developed countries, the European Union (EU), the United States, and Japan account for the majority of FDI inflows. The EU remains the world's largest FDI recipient, garnering $421 billion in 2011.
   - FDI inflows to developing countries were valued at $684 billion in 2011, reaching a record peak.
   - The remaining 6 percent of global FDI inflows went to countries considered as transition economies.
   - *Globalization* and a growing number of *mergers and acquisitions* account for the rising tide of FDI flows.

2. **Describe each of the theories that attempt to explain why foreign direct investment occurs.**
   - The *international product life cycle theory* says that a company begins by exporting its product and later undertakes foreign direct investment as the product moves through its life cycle of three stages: new product, maturing product, and standardized product.
   - *Market imperfections theory* says that when an imperfection in the market makes a transaction less efficient than it could be, a company will undertake foreign direct investment to internalize the transaction and thereby remove the imperfection.
   - The *eclectic theory* says that firms undertake foreign direct investment when the features of a particular location combine with ownership and internalization advantages to make a location appealing for investment.
   - The *market power theory* states that a firm tries to establish a dominant market presence in an industry by undertaking foreign direct investment.

3. **Discuss the important management issues in the foreign direct investment decision.**
   - Although companies investing abroad often wish to *control* activities in the local market, they may be forced to hire local managers or to export all goods produced locally.
   - Acquisition of an existing business is preferred when the existing business entails updated equipment, good relations with workers, and a suitable location.
   - When adequate facilities are unavailable, a company might need to pursue a *greenfield investment*.
   - A local market presence can give a company valuable knowledge of local *buyer behaviour*.
   - Firms commonly engage in FDI when it locates them close to *client* firms and *rival* firms.

4. **Explain why governments intervene in the free flow of foreign direct investment.**
   - *Host nations* receive a *balance-of-payments* boost from initial FDI and from any exports the FDI generates, but they see a decrease in balance of payments when a company sends profits to the home country.
   - FDI in *technology* brings in people with *management skills* who can train locals and increase a nation's productivity and competitiveness.
   - *Home countries* intervene in FDI outflows because they can lower the balance of payments, but profits sent home that are earned on assets abroad increase the balance of payments.
   - FDI outflows may replace jobs at home that were based on exports to the host country and may damage the home nation's balance of payments if they reduce prior exports.

5. Discuss the policy instruments that governments use to promote and restrict foreign direct investment.
   - Host countries can promote FDI inflows by offering companies *tax incentives* (such as lower tax rates or waived taxes), extending *low-interest loans*, and making local *infrastructure improvements*.
   - Host countries can restrict FDI inflows by imposing *ownership restrictions* (prohibitions from certain industries) and by creating *performance demands* that influence how a company can operate.
   - Home countries can promote FDI outflows by offering *insurance* to cover investment risks abroad, granting loans to firms investing abroad, guaranteeing company loans from financial institutions, offering *tax breaks* on profits earned abroad, negotiating special tax treaties, and applying *political pressure* to get other nations to accept FDI.
   - Home countries can restrict FDI outflows by imposing *differential tax rates* that charge income from earnings abroad at a higher rate than domestic earnings and by imposing *sanctions* that prohibit domestic firms from making investments in certain nations.

Key Terms

balance of payments 221	eclectic theory 215	market power 215
capital account 221	foreign direct investment (FDI) 210	portfolio investment 210
current account 221	international product life cycle	rationalized production 218
current account deficit 221	theory 213	vertical integration 215
current account surplus 221	market imperfections 214	

Talk It Over

1. You overhear your superior tell another manager in the company: "I'm fed up with our nation's companies sending manufacturing jobs abroad and offshoring service work to lower-wage nations. Don't any of them have any national pride?" The other manager responds, "I disagree. It is every company's duty to make as much profit as possible for its owners. If that means going abroad to reduce costs, so be it." Do you agree with either of these managers? Why or why not? Now step into the conversation and explain where you stand on this issue.

2. The global carmaker you work for is investing in an automobile assembly facility in Costa Rica with a local partner. Explain the potential reasons for this investment. Will your company want to exercise a great deal of control over this operation? Why or why not? In what areas might your company want to exercise control, and in what areas might it cede control to the partner?

3. This chapter presented several theories that attempt to explain why firms undertake foreign direct investment. Which of these theories seems most appealing to you? Why is it appealing? Can you think of one or more companies that seem to fit the pattern described by the theory? In your opinion, what faults do the alternative theories have?

Take It to the Web

1. **Video Report.** Visit YouTube (www.youtube.com). In the search engine, type "foreign direct investment." Watch one video from the list posted by the Peterson Institute for International Economics, and summarize it in a half-page report. Reflecting on the contents of this chapter, which aspects of foreign direct investment can you identify in the video? How might a company engaged in international business act on the information contained in the video?

2. **Web Site Report.** This chapter presented many reasons why companies directly invest in other nations and factors in the decision of whether and where to invest abroad.

   Research the economy of the Philippines and its neighbours. In what economic sectors is each country strong? Do the strengths of each country really complement one another, or do they compete directly with one another? If you were considering investing in the Philippines, what management issues would concern you? Be specific in your answer. (*Hint*: A good place to begin your research is the CIA's World Factbook at (https://www.cia.gov/library/publications/the-world-factbook).

   In this era of intense national competition to attract jobs, Southeast Asian governments fear losing ground to China in the race for investment. What do you think those governments could do to increase the attractiveness of their homelands for multinationals?

   Find an article on the Internet that describes a company's decision to relocate some or all of its business operations (goods or services). What reasons are stated for the relocation? Was any consideration given to the plight of employees being put out of work?

Is Canada Open for Business?

As you may recall from Chapter 5, Canada is considered one of the freest economies in the world, ranking sixth on the Index of Economic Freedom (published annually by *The Wall Street Journal* and Washington's Heritage Foundation). Although many consider Canada to have a free market economy, no country in the world is a completely "free" market—all governments try to protect or restrict investment in sectors they consider strategic for the country's economy or its national security. In 2010, Canada had to deal with a tough decision that raised the question: Is Canada truly open for business?

The fight was over Potash Corporation of Saskatchewan (Potash Corp), the world's leading producer of potash and key to the economy of Saskatchewan. When Australian-based mining giant BHP Billiton (BHP) suddenly launched a $38.6 billion hostile takeover bid for the Saskatchewan company in August of 2010, both the federal and provincial levels of government got involved.

Why would the acquisition decision not rest solely in the hands of the executives and stakeholders of both companies? The proposed transaction exceeded the CAD $299 million–defined monetary threshold established by the Canadian government for foreign investment, and therefore had to be approved by the Investment Canada Act (ICA).

The Investment Canada Act is designed to ensure that foreign investments benefit Canada economically and contribute to opportunities for employment in Canada. ICA applies to all acquisitions of a Canadian business by non-Canadians, and it conducts a "net benefit test" on any foreign investments that exceed its defined monetary threshold.

Historically, ICA has approved acquisition requests if the investor makes binding commitments that satisfy ICA criteria for net benefit to Canada. To date about 99 percent of applications have been given the green light. As part of its application and review process for the takeover, BHP promised to establish the headquarters of the business in Saskatoon, Saskatchewan, where the president and management group would be located; maintain current levels of employment for at least five years; give up all tax benefits; and sponsor the creation of a Centre of Excellence at the University of Saskatchewan.

To many people's surprise, ICA ruled against BHP's application on the grounds that it did not pass the net benefit test. BHP was given 30 days to make further representations or to submit revised proposals in order to prove a net benefit for Canada. However, BHP refused to make further concessions and dropped the bid.

Many external factors may have influenced ICA's decision. First, potash is considered by many to be a strategic natural resource as countries around the world work to maximize crop yields. The media, therefore, were able to make a case against the acquisition through articles addressing "the loss of a strategic resource to a foreign investor."

Second, it was an election year for both the federal and provincial governments. Brad Wall, then premier of Saskatchewan, voiced his concerns to the federal Minister of Industry and to the public, stating that BHP's bid failed the net benefit test in three areas: jobs and investment, Canadian control of a strategic resource, and provincial revenues—the government stood to lose about $100 million annually in corporate tax.

Certainly the takeover bid had the potential to destabilize Saskatchewan's finances, since Potash Corp is a significant source of tax revenue for the provincial government. The expatriation of revenues was also a concern: If the takeover were to be approved, revenues would go to BHP stakeholders in Australia rather than to Saskatchewan, where profits were being re-invested to fund roads, schools, and hospitals. The revenue to the province also allowed the local government to keep tax levels at a lower rate, which made the local economy more competitive.

Two weeks before the decision date, Premier Wall told the media, "The people of Saskatchewan deserve a potash industry unequivocally managed, operated and marketed for the benefit of Canada and Saskatchewan." Clearly he had done his research: His statement echoed a 2001 statement made by the government of Australia. That year, Shell was denied acquisition of a controlling stake in an Australian natural gas company because it was "in Australia's best interest to have offshore reserves unequivocally managed, operated and marketed for Australia."

Thinking Globally

1. Why do you think BHP was not able to prove a "net benefit" for Canada?
2. Why did ICA approve the acquisition of Nexen but not that of Potash Corp?
3. Was it correct for the Canadian government to restrict FDI in this case? Explain your answer.
4. What are the global implications for Canadian business because of ICA's decision?
5. Do you think the decision might have been different if it had not been an election year?

Sources: Lawson A. W. Hunter, Ashley M. Weber, and Maris Berswick, "A Guide to Navigating Canada's Foreign Ownership Laws for New Investors," *Competition Law International*, January 2012, 8(1), pp. 37–42; Eric J. Dufour and Imran Ahmad, "The Investment Canada Act—Canada's Waking Giant?," International Law Office (www.internationallawoffice.com), November 24, 2010; Don Newman, "The Case Against Selling Saskatchewan's Potash Corp." CBC News (www.cbc.ca), October 1, 2010.

CHAPTER EIGHT

Regional Economic Integration

Learning Objectives

After studying this chapter, you should be able to

1. Define regional economic integration and identify its five levels.

2. Discuss the benefits and drawbacks of regional economic integration and identify the implications for Canadian businesses.

3. Describe regional integration in Europe and its pattern of enlargement.

4. Discuss and analyze regional integration in the Americas, particularly regarding NAFTA and Canada's bilateral trade agreements.

5. Characterize regional integration in Asia and how it differs from integration elsewhere.

6. Describe integration in the Middle East and Africa, and explain the slow progress.

A LOOK BACK

Chapter 7 examined recent patterns of foreign direct investment. We explored the theories that try to explain why it occurs and saw how governments influence investment flows.

A LOOK AT THIS CHAPTER

This chapter explores the trend toward greater integration of national economies. We first examine the reasons why nations are making significant efforts at regional integration. We then study the most prominent regional trading blocs in place around the world today. We identify the types of trade agreements in place between Canada and the Americas, and discuss how they affect Canadian businesses.

A LOOK AHEAD

Chapter 9 begins our inquiry into the international financial system. We describe the structure of the international capital market and explain how the foreign exchange market operates. We also study how exchange rates are used and how they influence the activities of international companies.

Source: ShutterStock.

Bombardier's NAFTA Benefits

MONTREAL, Quebec—Bombardier (www.bombardier.com), founded in 1942 and head-quartered in Montreal, is the third leading company worldwide in the civil aerospace industry, preceded only by Boeing and Airbus. It is the largest provider of equipment and related services in the rail transportation sector and is active in over 60 countries.

Bombardier has numerous plants in Mexico—an ideal business location for reaching both the domestic and the export market. Mexico's geographical proximity to the US market, together with benefits from NAFTA, has furthered Bombardier's international position.

At the Queretaro plant, which has been in operation since 2005, Bombardier produces components for the Learjet 85. The plant employs only Mexican labour to produce fuselage, wings, and electrical harnesses. The Sahagun, Hidalgo, plant produces urban vehicles such as subways, streetcars, suburban trains, one- and two-storey vehicles, mixed-use units, intercity and high-speed trains, coaches, and locomotives. According to Alejandro Gutierrez Marcos, Bombardier's public relations manager, "We are one of the leading companies in the world of transpor-

Source: **Bloomberg via Getty Images.**

tation, and in Mexico we are at the head of the industry. We manage two-thirds of Mexico City's Metro stock, 70 percent of Monterrey's (Nuevo Leon) trains, and 100 percent in Guadalajara (Jalisco)." Bombardier's Latin America division generates between 3 and 5 percent of the company's total earnings, with 95 percent of those earnings coming from Mexico.

The lifting of trade barriers has made it easier to operate throughout the NAFTA region. Bombardier takes advantage of tariff-free access to US and Mexican borders for automotive parts. Other NAFTA benefits for Bombardier in Mexico include access to a qualified, motivated, and trainable workforce at more affordable wages; a viable production cost; and a logistics solution. For instance, products ship from Mexico to Canada in 5 days, compared to 46 days from China. Since Bombardier moved its assembly plants to Mexico from Ireland in 2005, the company has increased its aerospace margins to 8 percent annually. Bombardier further reduced its production costs and logistics by moving the production of rudders from Japan to Queretaro, Mexico, generating a 30 percent savings on parts, even after adding transportation costs.[1]

Regional trade agreements are changing the landscape of the global marketplace. Companies like Bombardier of Canada are finding that these agreements lower trade barriers and open new markets for goods and services. Markets otherwise off-limits because tariffs made imported products too expensive can become quite attractive once tariffs are lifted. But trade agreements can be double-edged swords for many companies. Not only do they allow domestic companies to seek new markets abroad, but they also let competitors from other nations enter the domestic market. Such mobility increases competition in every market that takes part in an agreement.

Trade agreements can allow companies to alter their strategies, sometimes radically. As we will see in this chapter, for example, nations in the Americas want to create a free trade area that runs from the northern tip of Alaska to the southern tip of South America. Companies that do business throughout this region could save millions of dollars annually from the removal of import tariffs under an eventual agreement. Multinationals could also save money by supplying entire regions from just a few regional factories, rather than have a factory in each nation.

We began Part 3 of this book by discussing the gains resulting from specialization and trade. We now show how groups of countries are cooperating to dismantle barriers that threaten these potential gains. In this chapter, we focus on regional efforts to encourage freer trade and investment. We begin by defining *regional economic integration* and describing its five different levels. We then examine the benefits and drawbacks of regional trade agreements in general, and for Canadian businesses in particular. Finally, we explore several long-established trade agreements and several agreements in the early stages of development. We close the chapter with a case study of the softwood lumber dispute between the United States and Canada.

What Is Regional Economic Integration?

regional economic integration (regionalism)
Process whereby countries in a geographic region cooperate to reduce or eliminate barriers to the international flow of products, people, or capital.

The process whereby countries in a geographic region cooperate to reduce or eliminate barriers to the international flow of products, people, or capital is called **regional economic integration (regionalism)**. A group of nations in a geographic region undergoing economic integration is called a *regional trading bloc*.

The goal of nations undergoing economic integration is not only to increase cross-border trade and investment but also to raise living standards for their people. We saw in Chapter 6, for example, how specialization and trade create real gains in terms of greater choice, lower prices, and increased productivity. Regional trade agreements are designed to help nations accomplish these objectives. Regional economic integration sometimes has additional goals, such as protection of intellectual property rights or the environment, or even eventual political union.

Levels of Regional Integration

Since the development of theories demonstrating the potential gains available through international trade, nations have tried to reap these benefits in a variety of ways. Figure 8.1 shows five potential levels (or degrees) of economic and political integration for regional trading blocs. A *free trade area* is the lowest extent of national integration; *political union* is the greatest. Each level of integration incorporates the properties of those levels that precede it.

free trade area
Economic integration whereby countries seek to remove all barriers to trade among themselves, but each country determines its own barriers against non-members.

FREE TRADE AREA   Economic integration whereby countries seek to remove all barriers to trade among themselves, but each country determines its own barriers against non-members, is called a **free trade area**. A free trade area is the lowest level of economic integration that is possible between two or more countries. Countries belonging to the free trade area strive to remove all tariffs and nontariff barriers, such as quotas and subsidies, on international trade in goods and services. However, each country is able to maintain whatever policy it sees fit against non-member countries. These policies can differ widely from country to country. Countries belonging to a free trade area also typically establish a process by which trade disputes can be resolved. The North American Free Trade Agreement (NAFTA)—discussed later in this chapter—is an example of this level of integration.

customs union
Economic integration whereby countries remove all barriers to trade among themselves but erect a common trade policy against non-members.

CUSTOMS UNION   Economic integration whereby countries remove all barriers to trade among themselves, but erect a common trade policy against non-members, is called a **customs union**. Thus, the main difference between a free trade area and a customs union is that the members of a customs union agree to treat trade with all non-member nations in a similar manner. Countries belonging to a customs union might also negotiate as a single entity with other supranational

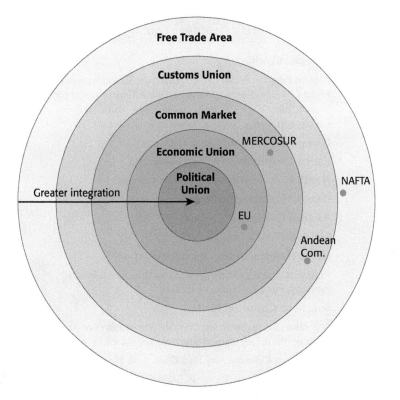

FIGURE 8.1

Levels of Regional Integration

organizations, such as the World Trade Organization. The Andean Community—discussed later in this chapter—became a customs union in 1995.

COMMON MARKET   Economic integration whereby countries remove all barriers to trade and the movement of labour and capital among themselves, but erect a common trade policy against non-members, is called a **common market**. Thus, a common market integrates the elements of free trade areas and customs unions, and adds the free movement of important factors of production: people and cross-border investment. This level of integration is very difficult to attain because it requires members to cooperate to at least some extent on economic and labour policies. Furthermore, the benefits to individual countries can be uneven because skilled labour may move to countries where wages are higher, and investment capital may flow to areas where returns are greater. The Common Market of the South—discussed later in this chapter—is an example of this level of integration.

ECONOMIC UNION   Economic integration whereby countries remove barriers to trade and the movement of labour and capital among members, erect a common trade policy against non-members, and coordinate their economic policies is called an **economic union**. An economic union goes beyond the demands of a common market by requiring member nations to harmonize their tax, monetary, and fiscal policies, and to create a common currency. Economic unions require that member countries concede a certain amount of their national autonomy (or sovereignty) to the supranational union of which they are a part. The only current example of this level of integration in the world is the European Union, which will be discussed later in this chapter.

POLITICAL UNION   Economic and political integration whereby countries coordinate aspects of their economic *and* political systems is called a **political union**. A political union requires member nations to accept a common stance on economic and political matters regarding non-member nations. However, nations are allowed a degree of freedom in setting certain political and economic policies within their territories. Individually, Canada and the United States provide early examples of political unions. In both these nations, smaller states and provinces combined to form larger entities. A group of nations currently taking steps in this direction is the European Union.

Table 8.1 identifies each country involved in the European Union and the members of the main regional trading blocs presented in this chapter. As you work through this chapter, refer back to this table for a quick summary of each bloc's members.

common market

Economic integration whereby countries remove all barriers to trade and the movement of labour and capital among themselves but erect a common trade policy against non-members.

economic union

Economic integration whereby countries remove barriers to trade and the movement of labour and capital among members, erect a common trade policy against non-members, and coordinate their economic policies.

political union

Economic and political integration whereby countries coordinate aspects of their economic *and* political systems.

TABLE 8.1	The World's Main Regional Trading Blocs
EU	**European Union**
	Austria, Belgium, Britain, Bulgaria, Croatia, Czech Republic, Denmark, Estonia, Finland, France, Germany, Greece, Greek Cyprus (southern portion), Hungary, Ireland, Italy, Latvia, Lithuania, Luxembourg, Malta, Netherlands, Poland, Portugal, Romania, Slovakia, Slovenia, Spain, Sweden
EFTA	**European Free Trade Association**
	Iceland, Liechtenstein, Norway, Switzerland
NAFTA	**North American Free Trade Agreement**
	Canada, Mexico, United States
Andean	**Andean Community (CAN)**
	Bolivia, Colombia, Ecuador, Peru
ALADI	**Latin American Integration Association**
	Argentina, Bolivia, Brazil, Chile, Colombia, Cuba, Ecuador, Mexico, Panama, Paraguay, Peru, Uruguay, Venezuela
MERCOSUR	**Southern Common Market**
	Argentina, Brazil, Paraguay, Uruguay, Venezuela (Bolivia, Chile, Colombia, Ecuador, Peru, Guyana and Suirname are associate members)
CARICOM	**Caribbean Community and Common Market**
	Antigua and Barbuda, Bahamas, Barbados, Belize, Dominica, Grenada, Guyana, Haiti, Jamaica, Montserrat, St. Kitts and Nevis, St. Lucia, St. Vincent and the Grenadines, Suriname, Trinidad and Tobago
CACM	**Central American Common Market**
	Costa Rica, El Salvador, Guatemala, Honduras, Nicaragua
FTAA	**Free Trade Area of the Americas**
	Total of 34 nations from Central, North, and South America and the Caribbean
ASEAN	**Association of Southeast Asian Nations**
	Brunei, Cambodia, Indonesia, Laos, Malaysia, Burma (Myanmar), Philippines, Singapore, Thailand, Vietnam
APEC	**Asia Pacific Economic Cooperation**
	Australia, Brunei, Canada, Chile, China, Hong Kong, Indonesia, Japan, South Korea, Malaysia, Mexico, New Zealand, Papua New Guinea, Peru, Philippines, Russia, Singapore, Taiwan, Thailand, United States, Vietnam
CER	**Closer Economic Relations Agreement**
	Australia, New Zealand
GCC	**Gulf Cooperation Council**
	Bahrain, Kuwait, Oman, Qatar, Saudi Arabia, United Arab Emirates
ECOWAS	**Economic Community of West African States**
	Benin, Burkina Faso, Cape Verde, Gambia, Ghana, Guinea, Guinea-Bissau, Ivory Coast, Liberia, Mali, Niger, Nigeria, Senegal, Sierra Leone, Togo
AU	**African Union**
	Total of 54 nations on the continent of Africa

Effects of Regional Economic Integration

Few topics in international business are as hotly contested and involve as many groups as the effects of regional trade agreements on people, jobs, companies, cultures, and living standards. The topic often spurs debate over the merits and demerits of such agreements. On one side of the debate are people who see the bad that regional trade agreements cause; on the other, those who see the good. Each party to the debate cites data on trade and jobs that bolster their positions. They point to companies that have picked up and moved to another country where wages are lower after a new agreement was signed, or to companies that have stayed at home and kept jobs there. The only thing made clear as a result of such debates is that both sides are right some of the time. As we saw in this chapter's opening company profile, Bombardier's business has flourished due to NAFTA. However, Bombardier's relocation of some operations to Mexico did cause job losses in other countries such as Ireland and Japan.

There is also the cultural aspect of such agreements. Some people argue that they will lose their unique cultural identity if their nation cooperates too much with other nations. Let's take a closer look at the main benefits and drawbacks of regional integration.

Benefits of Regional Integration

Recall from Chapter 6 that nations engage in specialization and trade because of the potential for gains in output and consumption. Higher levels of trade between nations should result in greater specialization, increased efficiency, greater consumption, and higher standards of living.

TRADE CREATION Economic integration removes barriers to trade and/or investment for nations belonging to a trading bloc. The increase in the level of trade between nations that results from regional economic integration is called **trade creation**. One result of trade creation is that consumers and industrial buyers in member nations are faced with a wider selection of goods and services not previously available. For example, Canada has many popular brands of beer, including Labatt (www.labatt.com), Molson Canadian (www.molsoncoorscanada.com), and Big Rock (www.bigrockbeer.com). But liquor stores inside Canada also stock a wide variety of lesser-known imported brands of beer, such as Negra Modelo or Dos Equis Lager from Mexico. Certainly, the free trade agreement between Canada, Mexico, and the United States (discussed later in this chapter) created export opportunities for this and other Mexican brands.

trade creation
Increase in the level of trade between nations that results from regional economic integration.

Another result of trade creation is that buyers can acquire goods and services at lower cost after removal of trade barriers such as tariffs. Furthermore, lower-priced products tend to drive higher demand for goods and services because they increase purchasing power.

GREATER CONSENSUS In Chapter 1 we saw how the World Trade Organization (WTO) works to lower barriers on a global scale. Efforts at regional economic integration differ in that they comprise smaller groups of nations—ranging from several countries to as many as 30 or more. The benefit of trying to eliminate trade barriers in smaller groups of countries is that it can be easier to gain consensus from fewer members as opposed to, say, the 159 countries that comprise the WTO.

POLITICAL COOPERATION There can also be *political* benefits from efforts toward regional economic integration. A group of nations can have significantly greater political weight than each nation has individually. Thus, the group, as a whole, can have more say when negotiating with other countries in forums such as the WTO. Integration involving political cooperation can also reduce the potential for military conflict between member nations. In fact, peace was at the centre of early efforts at integration in Europe in the 1950s. The devastation of two world wars in the first half of the twentieth century caused Europe to see integration as one way of preventing further armed conflicts.

EMPLOYMENT OPPORTUNITIES Regional integration can expand employment opportunities by enabling people to move from one country to another to find work or, simply, to earn a higher wage. Regional integration has opened doors for young people in Europe. Forward-looking young people have abandoned extreme nationalism and have taken on what can only be described as a "European" attitude that embraces a shared history. Those with language skills and a willingness to pick up and move to another EU country get to explore a new culture's way of life while earning a living. As companies seek their future leaders in Europe, they will hire people who can think across borders and across cultures.

Drawbacks of Regional Integration

Although regional integration tends to benefit countries, it can also have substantial negative effects. Let's examine each of these potential consequences.

TRADE DIVERSION The flip side of trade creation is **trade diversion**—the diversion of trade away from nations not belonging to a trading bloc and toward member nations. Trade diversion can occur after the formation of a trading bloc because of the lower tariffs charged among member nations. It can actually result in increased trade with a less-efficient producer within the

trade diversion
Diversion of trade away from nations not belonging to a trading bloc and toward member nations.

trading bloc and reduced trade with a more efficient, non-member producer. In this sense, economic integration can unintentionally reward a less efficient producer within the trading bloc. Unless there is other internal competition for the producer's good or service, buyers will likely pay more after trade diversion because of the inefficient production methods of the producer.

A World Bank report caused a stir over the results of the free trade bloc among Latin America's largest countries, MERCOSUR (discussed later in this chapter). The report suggested that the bloc's formation only encouraged free trade in the lowest-value products of local origin, while deterring competition for more sophisticated goods manufactured outside the market. Closer analysis showed that while imports from one member state to another tripled during the period studied, imports from the rest of the world also tripled. Thus, the net effect of the agreement was trade creation, not trade diversion, as critics had charged. Also, the Australian Department of Foreign Affairs and Trade released results of a study that examined the impact of the North American Free Trade Agreement (NAFTA) on Australia's trade with and investment in North America. The study found no evidence of trade diversion following the agreement's formation.[2]

SHIFTS IN EMPLOYMENT Perhaps the most controversial aspect of regional economic integration is its effect on people's jobs. The formation of a trading bloc promotes efficiency by significantly reducing or eliminating barriers to trade among its members. The surviving producer of a particular good or service, then, is likely to be the bloc's most efficient producer. Industries requiring mostly unskilled labour, for example, tend to respond to the formation of a trading bloc by shifting production to a low-wage nation within the bloc.

Yet figures on jobs lost or gained as a result of trading bloc formation vary depending on the source. According to Jeffrey J. Schott from the Peterson Institute for International Economics, net employment rose sharply in all three signatory countries during NAFTA's first 15 years (1993–2008). However, some of the growth that occurred in that period may have been a reflection of the strong economic growth in the United States at the time. By 2008, employment had risen by 25 million people in the United States, 5 million in Canada, and 12 million in Mexico.[3] However, the federation of US unions disputes these figures and claims a loss of jobs due to NAFTA. Trade agreements do cause dislocations in labour markets; some jobs are lost while others are gained.

It is likely that once trade and investment barriers are removed, countries protecting low-wage domestic industries from competition will see these jobs move to the country where wages are lower. This can be an opportunity for workers who lose their jobs to upgrade their skills and gain more advanced job training. This can help nations increase their competitiveness because a more educated and skilled workforce attracts higher-paying jobs than does a less skilled workforce.[4]

LOSS OF NATIONAL SOVEREIGNTY Successive levels of integration require that nations surrender more of their national sovereignty. The least amount of sovereignty that must be surrendered to the trading bloc occurs in a free trade area. By contrast, a political union requires nations to give up a high degree of sovereignty in foreign policy. This is why a political union is so hard to achieve. Long histories of cooperation or animosity between nations do not become irrelevant when a group of countries forms a union. Because one member nation may have very delicate ties with a non-member nation with which another member may have very strong ties, the setting of a common foreign policy can be extremely tricky.

Economic integration is taking place throughout the world because of the benefits and despite the drawbacks of regional trade agreements. Europe, the Americas, Asia, the Middle East, and Africa are all undergoing integration to varying degrees (see Map 8.1). Let's now begin our coverage of specific efforts at economic integration by exploring Europe, which has the longest history and highest level of integration to date.

Quick Study

1. What is the ultimate goal of *regional economic integration*?
2. What are the five levels, or degrees, of regional integration? Briefly describe each one.
3. Identify several potential benefits and several potential drawbacks of regional integration.
4. What is meant by the terms *trade creation* and *trade diversion*? Why are these concepts important?

Integration in Europe

The most sophisticated and advanced example of regional integration that we can point to today is occurring in Europe. European efforts at integration began shortly after the Second World War as a cooperative endeavour among a small group of countries and involved a few select industries. Regional integration now encompasses practically all of Western Europe and all industries.

European Union

In the middle of the twentieth century, many would have scoffed at the idea that European nations, which had spent so many years at war with one another, could present a relatively unified whole more than 50 years later. Let's investigate how Europe came so far in such a relatively short time.

EARLY YEARS   A war-torn Europe emerged from the Second World War in 1945 facing two challenges: (1) it needed to rebuild itself and avoid further armed conflict; and (2) it needed to increase its industrial strength to stay competitive with an increasingly powerful United States. Cooperation seemed to be the only way of facing these challenges. Belgium, France, West Germany, Italy, Luxembourg, and the Netherlands signed the Treaty of Paris in 1951, creating the *European Coal and Steel Community*. These nations were determined to remove barriers to trade in coal, iron, steel, and scrap metal so as to coordinate coal and steel production among themselves, thereby controlling the post-war arms industry.

The members of the European Coal and Steel Community signed the Treaty of Rome in 1957, creating the *European Economic Community*. The Treaty of Rome outlined a future common market for these nations. It also aimed at establishing common transportation and agricultural policies among members. In 1967 the community's scope was broadened to include additional industries, notably atomic energy, and changed its name to the *European Community*. As the goals of integration continued to expand, so too did the bloc's membership. Waves of enlargement occurred in 1973, 1981, 1986, 1995, 2004, and 2007. In 1994 the bloc once again changed its name to the *European Union (EU)*. Today the 27-member European Union (europa.eu) has a population of about 500 million people and a gross domestic product (GDP) of around $16.4 trillion (see Map 8.2).

Over the past two decades, two important milestones contributed to the continued progress of the EU: the *Single European Act* and the *Maastricht Treaty*.

Single European Act   By the mid-1980s, EU member nations were frustrated by remaining trade barriers and a lack of harmony on several important matters, including taxation, law, and regulations. The important objective of harmonizing laws and policies was beginning to appear unachievable. A commission formed to analyze the potential for a common market by the end of 1992 put forth several proposals. The goal was to remove remaining barriers, increase harmonization, and thereby enhance the competitiveness of European companies. The proposals became the *Single European Act* (*SEA*) and went into effect in 1987.

As companies positioned themselves to take advantage of the opportunities that SEA offered, a wave of mergers and acquisitions swept across Europe. Large firms combined their special understanding of European needs, capabilities, and cultures with their advantage of economies of scale. Small and medium-sized companies were encouraged through EU institutions to network with one another to offset any negative consequences resulting from, for example, changing product standards.

Maastricht Treaty   Some members of the EU wanted to take European integration further still. A 1991 summit meeting of EU member nations took place in Maastricht, the Netherlands. The meeting resulted in the *Maastricht Treaty*, which went into effect in 1993.

The Maastricht Treaty had three aims. First, it called for banking in a single, common currency after January 1, 1999, and circulation of coins and paper currency on January 1, 2002. Second, the treaty set up monetary and fiscal targets for countries that wished to take part in monetary union. Third, the treaty called for political union of the member nations—including development of a common foreign and defence policy and common citizenship. Member countries will hold off further political integration until they gauge the success of the final stages of economic and monetary union. Let's take a closer look at monetary union in Europe.

EUROPEAN MONETARY UNION   As stated previously, EU leaders were determined to create a single, common currency. **European monetary union** is the European Union plan that established its own central bank and currency in January 1999. The Maastricht Treaty stated the

European monetary union
European Union plan that established its own central bank and currency.

MAP 8.1

Most Active Economic Blocs

ARCTIC OCEAN

NORWAY
SWEDEN
FINLAND
ESTONIA
LATVIA
DENMARK
LITHUANIA
RUSSIA
BELARUS
NDS
GERMANY
POLAND
JRG
CZECH
REP.
SLOVAKIA
UKRAINE
AUSTRIA
HUNGARY
MOLDOVA
SLOVENIA
ROMANIA
CROATIA
BOSNIA AND
HERZEGOVINA
SERBIA AND
MONTENEGRO
ITALY
MACEDONIA
BULGARIA
ALBANIA
GEORGIA
GREECE
TURKEY
ARMENIA
AZERBAIJAN
UZBEKISTAN
KYRGYZSTAN
TUNISIA
CYPRUS
SYRIA
TURKMENISTAN
TAJIKISTAN
LEBANON
IRAQ
ISRAEL
IRAN
AFGHANISTAN
JORDAN
KUWAIT
LIBYA
EGYPT
QATAR
UNITED ARAB
EMIRATES
PAKISTAN
SAUDI
ARABIA
OMAN
NIGER
CHAD
SUDAN
ERITREA
YEMEN
NIGERIA
DJIBOUTI
CENTRAL AFRICAN
REPUBLIC
ETHIOPIA
SOMALIA
CAMEROON
CONGO
REPUBLIC
UGANDA
GABON
CONGO
DEMOCRATIC
REPUBLIC
(ZAIRE)
RWANDA
BURUNDI
KENYA
TANZANIA
ANGOLA
ZAMBIA
MALAWI
MOZAMBIQUE
NAMIBIA
ZIMBABWE
MADAGASCAR
BOTSWANA
SWAZILAND
SOUTH
AFRICA
LESOTHO

RUSSIA
KAZAKHSTAN
MONGOLIA
CHINA
NORTH
KOREA
SOUTH
KOREA
JAPAN
NEPAL
BHUTAN
INDIA
BANGLADESH
MYANMAR
(BURMA)
LAOS
TAIWAN
THAILAND
VIETNAM
CAMBODIA
PHILIPPINES
SRI
LANKA
BRUNEI
MALAYSIA
SINGAPORE
INDONESIA
PAPUA
NEW
GUINEA
SOLOMON
ISLANDS
VANUATU
FIJI
NEW
CALEDONIA
AUSTRALIA
NEW
ZEALAND

PACIFIC
OCEAN

INDIAN
OCEAN
MAURITIUS
RÉUNION

The most active economic blocs

- EU
- EFTA
- NAFTA
- MERCOSUR
- CARICOM
- CAN
- ASEAN
- APEC
- CER

MAP 8.2

Economic Integration in Europe

economic criteria with which member nations must comply to partake in the single currency, the *euro*. First, consumer price inflation must be below 3.2 percent and must not exceed that of the three best-performing countries by more than 1.5 percent. Second, the debt of government must be 60 percent of GDP or lower. An exception is made if the ratio is diminishing and approaching the 60 percent mark.

Third, the general government deficit must be at or below 3.0 percent of GDP. An exception is made if the deficit is close to 3.0 percent or if the deviation is temporary and unusual. Fourth, interest rates on long-term government securities must not exceed, by more than 2.0 percent, those of the three countries with the lowest inflation rates. Meeting these criteria better aligned countries' economies and paved the way for smoother policy making under a single European Central Bank. The 17 EU member nations that have adopted the single currency are Austria, Belgium, Cyprus, Estonia, Finland, France, Germany, Greece, Ireland, Italy, Luxembourg, Malta, the Netherlands, Portugal, Slovakia, Slovenia, and Spain.

Management Implications of the Euro   The move to a single currency influences the activities of companies within the European Union. First, the euro removes financial obstacles created by the use of multiple currencies. It completely eliminates exchange-rate risk for business deals between member nations using the euro. The euro also reduces transaction costs by eliminating the cost of converting from one currency to another. In fact, the EU leadership estimates the financial gains to Europe could eventually be 0.5 percent of GDP. The efficiency of trade between participating members resembles that of inter-provincial trade in Canada because only a single currency is involved.

Second, the euro makes prices between markets more transparent, making it difficult to charge different prices in adjoining markets. As a result, shoppers feel less of a need to travel to other countries to save money on high-ticket items. For example, shortly before monetary union, a Mercedes-Benz S320 (www5.mercedes-benz.com) cost $72 614 in Germany but only $66 920 in Italy. A Renault Twingo (www.renault.com) that sold for $13 265 in France cost $11 120 in Spain. Car brokers and shopping agencies even sprang up specifically to help European consumers reap such savings. The euro has greatly reduced or eliminated this type of situation.

ENLARGEMENT OF THE EUROPEAN UNION   One of the most historic events across Europe in recent memory was EU enlargement from 15 to 27 members. Croatia, Iceland, Montenegro, Serbia, Turkey, and the former Yugoslav Republic of Macedonia remain candidates for EU membership and are to become members after they meet certain demands laid down by the EU. These so-called *Copenhagen Criteria* require each country to demonstrate that it:

- Has stable institutions, which guarantee democracy, the rule of law, human rights, and respect for and protection of minorities.
- Has a functioning market economy, capable of coping with competitive pressures and market forces within the European Union.
- Is able to assume the obligations of membership, including adherence to the aims of economic, monetary, and political union.
- Has the ability to adopt the rules and regulations of the community, the rulings of the European Court of Justice, and the treaties.

Although it has applied for membership, negotiations for Turkey are expected to be difficult. One reason for Turkey's lack of support in the EU is charges (fair or not) of human rights abuses with regard to its Kurdish minority. Another reason is intense opposition by Greece, Turkey's long-time foe. However, Turkey has a customs union with the EU, and trade between them is growing. Despite disappointment among some EU-hopefuls and intermittent setbacks in the enlargement process, integration will continue, depending upon economic stability in the EU.

STRUCTURE OF THE EUROPEAN UNION   Five EU institutions play particularly important roles in monitoring and enforcing economic and political integration (see Figure 8.2). Two other EU institutions (Ombudsman and Data Protection Supervisor) fulfill secondary and support roles, and are not discussed here.

European Parliament   The European Parliament consists of 766 members elected by popular vote within each member nation every five years. As such, they are expected to voice their particular political views on EU matters. The European Parliament fulfills its role of adopting

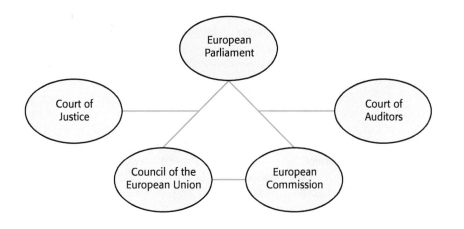

FIGURE 8.2

Institutions of the European Union

EU law by debating and amending legislation proposed by the European Commission. It exercises political supervision over all EU institutions—giving it the power to supervise commissioner appointments and to censure the commission. It also has veto power over some laws (including the annual budget of the EU). There is a call for increased democratization within the EU, and some believe this could be achieved by strengthening the powers of the Parliament. The Parliament conducts its activities in Belgium (in the city Brussels), France (in the city Strasbourg), and Luxembourg.

Council of the European Union The council is the legislative body of the EU. When it meets, it brings together representatives of member states at the ministerial level. The makeup of the council changes depending on the topic under discussion. For example, when the topic is agriculture, the council is composed of the ministers of agriculture from each member nation. No proposed legislation becomes EU law unless the council votes it into law. Although passage into law for sensitive issues such as immigration and taxation still requires a unanimous vote, some legislation today requires only a simple majority to win approval. The council also concludes, on behalf of the EU, international agreements with other nations or international organizations. The council is headquartered in Brussels, Belgium.

European Commission The commission is the executive body of the EU. It comprises commissioners appointed by each member country—larger nations get two commissioners, smaller countries get one. Member nations appoint the president and commissioners after being approved by the European Parliament. It has the right to draft legislation, is responsible for managing and implementing policy, and monitors member nations' implementation of, and compliance with, EU law. Each commissioner is assigned a specific policy area, such as competitive policy or agricultural policy. Although commissioners are appointed by their national governments, they are expected to behave in the best interest of the EU as a whole, not in the interest of their own country. The European Commission is headquartered in Brussels, Belgium.

Court of Justice The Court of Justice is the EU court of appeals and is composed of 28 judges (one from each member nation) and eight advocates general who hold renewable six-year terms. One type of case that the Court of Justice hears is one in which a member nation is accused of not meeting its treaty obligations. Another type is one in which the commission or council is charged with failing to live up to its responsibilities under the terms of a treaty. Like the commissioners, justices are required to act in the interest of the EU as a whole, not in the interest of their own countries. The Court of Justice is located in Luxembourg.

Court of Auditors The Court of Auditors comprises 28 members (one from each member nation) appointed for renewable six-year terms. The court is assigned the duty of auditing the EU accounts and implementing its budget. It also aims to improve financial management in the EU and report to member nations' citizens on the use of public funds. As such, it issues annual reports and statements on implementation of the EU budget. The Court of Auditors is based in Luxembourg, and employs roughly 800 auditors and staff to assist it in carrying out its functions.

Canada–EU Free Trade Agreement Negotiations for a free trade agreement between Canada and the European Union successfully concluded on October 18, 2013, after four years. The main purpose of this agreement is to generate more trade, investment, and jobs on both sides of the Atlantic. Once implemented—by 2015—duties will be eliminated in 98 percent of products. The agreement is expected to increase trade in goods and services by 23 percent or CAD$38 billion. Stephen Harper, Canada's prime minister, believes that the agreement is an historic win for Canada, because it provides Canadian businesses with access to 500 million EU consumers.

European Free Trade Association (EFTA)

Certain nations in Europe were reluctant to join in the ambitious goals of the EU, fearing destructive rivalries and a loss of national sovereignty. Some of these nations did not want to be part of a common market but instead wanted the benefits of a free trade area. So in 1960 several countries banded together and formed the *European Free Trade Association* (*EFTA*) to focus on trade in industrial, not consumer, goods. Because some of the original members joined the EU and some new members joined EFTA (www.efta.int), today the group consists of only Iceland, Liechtenstein, Norway, and Switzerland (see Map 8.2).

Shoppers in Bucharest, Romania, venture into a newly opened mall as they enjoy the fruits of membership in the European Union. Romania and Bulgaria were recently welcomed into the EU, whose membership now totals 27. To balance the divergent national interests of its members, the EU created a unique system of government and designed the role of each EU institution to reflect this balancing act.

Source: AFP PHOTO DANIEL MIHAILESCU/Newscom.

The population of EFTA is around 12.9 million, with a combined GDP of around $869 billion. Despite its relatively small size, members remain committed to free trade principles and raising standards of living for their people. The EFTA and EU created the *European Economic Area (EEA)* to cooperate on matters such as the free movement of goods, persons, services, and capital among member nations. The two groups also cooperate in other areas, including the environment, social policy, and education.

Canada–EFTA Free Trade Agreement The free trade agreement between EFTA and Canada came into force on July 1, 2009. The main purpose of this agreement is to reduce or eliminate duties in a wide range of products, including Canadian agricultural exports. The Canadian government signed this agreement to create new export markets, new customers, and better links to European global supply and value chains, thereby reducing Canada's dependence on exports to the United States. Canadian exports to EFTA countries include nickel, precious stones and metals, and mechanical machinery.

Quick Study

1. Why did Europe initially desire to form a regional trading bloc?
2. Describe the evolution of the European Union. What are its five primary institutions?
3. What is the *European monetary union*? Explain its importance to business in Europe.
4. Briefly describe the European Free Trade Association.

Integration in the Americas

Europe's success at economic integration caused other nations to consider the benefits of forming their own regional trading blocs. Latin American countries began forming regional trading arrangements in the early 1960s, but they made substantial progress only in the 1980s and 1990s. North America was about three decades behind Europe in taking major steps toward economic integration. Let's now explore the major efforts toward economic integration in North, South, and Central America, beginning with North America.

North American Free Trade Agreement (NAFTA)

There has always been a good deal of trade between Canada and the United States. The two countries had in the past established trade agreements in several industrial sectors of their economies, including automotive products. In 1987 Canada and the United States signed a bilateral free trade agreement; the *Canada–United States Free Trade Agreement (CUSFTA)* went into effect in January 1989. The goal was to eliminate all tariffs on bilateral trade between Canada and the United States by 1998.

Accelerating integration in Europe caused new urgency in the task of creating a North American trading bloc that included Mexico. Mexico joined what is now the World Trade Organization in 1987 and began privatizing state-owned enterprises in 1988. Talks among Canada, Mexico, and the United States in 1991 eventually resulted in the formation of the *North American Free Trade Agreement (NAFTA)*. NAFTA (www.nafta-sec-alena.org) became effective on January 1, 1994, and superseded CUSFTA. Today NAFTA comprises a market of 450 million consumers and a GDP of around $18 trillion worth of goods and services (see Map 8.1).[5]

As a free trade agreement, NAFTA seeks to eliminate all tariffs and nontariff trade barriers on goods originating from within North America. The agreement also calls for liberalized rules regarding government procurement practices, the granting of subsidies, and the imposition of countervailing duties. Other provisions deal with issues such as trade in services, intellectual property rights, and standards of health, safety, and the environment.

LOCAL CONTENT REQUIREMENTS AND RULES OF ORIGIN While NAFTA encourages free trade among Canada, Mexico, and the United States, manufacturers and distributors must abide by local content requirements and rules of origin. Although producers and distributors rarely know the precise origin of every part or component in a piece of industrial equipment, they are responsible for determining whether a product has sufficient North American content to qualify for tariff-free status. The producer or distributor must also provide a NAFTA "certificate of origin" to an importer to claim an exemption from tariffs. Four criteria determine whether a good meets NAFTA rules of origin:

- Goods wholly produced or obtained in the NAFTA region (for example, fruits, vegetables, animals born in the NAFTA region, and so forth)
- Goods containing non-originating inputs but meeting Annex 401 origin rules (which cover regional input)
- Goods produced in the NAFTA region wholly from originating materials

- Unassembled goods and goods classified in the same harmonized system category as their parts that do not meet Annex 401 rules but have sufficient North American regional value content

EFFECTS OF NAFTA   Since NAFTA came into effect, trade among the three signatory nations has increased markedly, with the greatest gains occurring between Mexico and the United States. Today the United States exports over three times more to Mexico and Canada than it does to Britain, France, Germany, and Italy combined. Canada is now the second-largest source of US imports (behind China) and the largest market for US exports.

NAFTA helped trade among the three countries to grow from $297 billion in 1993 to around $1 trillion. Since the start of NAFTA, Mexico's exports to the United States jumped to around $211 billion, and US exports to Mexico grew to more than $136 billion.[6] As these numbers suggest, the United States has developed a trade deficit with Mexico. Over the same period, Canada's exports to the United States more than doubled to nearly $300 billion, while US exports to Canada grew to $176 billion. Canada exported very little to Mexico before NAFTA, but afterward exports grew more than threefold, to nearly $2.7 billion.[7]

Overall, NAFTA has increased Canadian trade and investment flows, and productivity has risen. For consumers, NAFTA has provided more choices at competitive prices. Duty-free products or products with reduced tariffs for importers mean cheaper products for consumers, which, together with greater selection, translates into an increase in living standards.[8]

The agreement's effect on employment and wages is not as easy to determine. Although net employment rose sharply in all three countries during the first 15 years of NAFTA, the increase was not only due to NAFTA. The US Trade Representative Office claims that exports to Mexico and Canada support 2.9 million US jobs (900 000 more than in 1993), which pay 13 to 18 percent more than national averages for production workers.[9] But the AFL-CIO group of unions disputes this claim; it argues that, since its formation, NAFTA has cost the United States more than 1 million jobs and job opportunities. According to Foreign Affairs, Trade and Development Canada, one in five jobs in Canada is related in part to trade. More than 4.3 million net new jobs were created in Canada between 1993 and 2008.[10]

NAFTA is a good example of trade diversion. Prior to NAFTA, Canadian and US companies had been establishing manufacturing facilities in Asia; however, after NAFTA came into effect, Mexico became a better option for the location of manufacturing facilities.

Non-NAFTA companies are also investing in Mexico to take advantage of NAFTA's free trade provisions such as reduced or zero duties. In addition, these companies get the benefit of decreased shipping times to the United States and Canada. Transportation costs are also lower from Mexico than from South America or Asia.

NAFTA and the Environment   Opponents claim that NAFTA has damaged the environment, particularly along the United States–Mexico border. Although the agreement included provisions for environmental protection, Mexico is finding it difficult to deal with the environmental impact of greater economic activity. However, Mexico's *Instituto Nacional de Ecologia* (www.ine.gob.mx) has developed an industrial-waste–management program, including an incentive system to encourage waste reduction and recycling. The Mexican government has also created a certification program similar to the International Organization for Standardization (ISO) certification, called *Industria Limpia* (Clean Industry), to assure compliance with environmental norms. The US and Mexican federal governments have invested several billion dollars in environmental protection efforts since the creation of NAFTA.[11] However, the North American Agreement on Environmental Cooperation (NAAEC), an environmental side agreement to NAFTA signed in 1994, was given a limited mandate and a limited budget.

NAFTA's Contentious Clauses   Article 605 of NAFTA, called the "proportional sharing provision," grants NAFTA countries rights in perpetuity to share natural resources. What does this mean for Canada? Under the agreement, two-thirds of Canadian oil needs to be available for export to the United States, even if Canadians experience shortages. Canada must also make the majority of its natural gas supplies available for export to the United States, which accounts for 60 percent of Canada's current natural gas production. Many Canadians think that NAFTA should be renegotiated to eliminate proportionality.

Another controversial section of the NAFTA agreement is Chapter 11, which sets out a framework for investment. Chapter 11 allows corporations or individuals to sue NAFTA member governments for compensation over any government measure that has an effect on their ability to conduct business. For example, US-based Ethyl Corporation sued the Canadian government, claiming that its ban on MMT, a neurotoxin gasoline additive, was an unfair performance requirement. After a NAFTA tribunal ruled against Canada, the Canadian government withdrew the ban and settled out of court for $13 million.[12]

Trade Disputes Within NAFTA   Although theoretically an agreement between three equal parties, NAFTA has huge market size asymmetries. The US market predominance over Mexico and Canada appears to encourage the United States to use tactics such as bans, dumping, and protectionist measures to impose its own trade terms. By its nature, NAFTA runs the risk of becoming an extension of hegemonic US policy. Disputes, such as the softwood lumber case between Canada and the United States (which also involved the World Trade Organization's arbitration system) and the US ban on Mexican trucks operating on US roads, are examples of power-politics prevailing over international trade rules and agreements such as NAFTA.[13]

Besides the claims of job losses and negative environmental impact due to NAFTA and NAFTA's contentious clauses, Canada remains dependent on its trade relationship with the United States. According to Peter Hall, vice-president and chief economist of Export Development Canada, "Canadians know the adage well: The US economy sneezes and we catch pneumonia."[14]

BILATERAL AGREEMENTS BEYOND NAFTA   Although NAFTA has not expanded beyond the original three countries due to opposition groups and political obstacles, each member of NAFTA has entered into bilateral agreements with other countries in the Americas. For example, Canada has signed bilateral free trade agreements with Colombia, Costa Rica, Chile, Peru, and Panama. Canada also concluded negotiations with Honduras in August 2011, although the free trade agreement has yet to come into effect.

The goal of all these agreements is to strengthen economic relations between the two signatory countries by increasing bilateral trade, improving labour and environmental cooperation, and reducing or eliminating duties and non-tariff barriers to trade and investment. The main differences found in the various trade agreements concern the type of goods and services traded.

For instance, major Canadian merchandise exports to Peru are cereals, leguminous vegetables, paper, technical instruments, and machinery. Major imports from Peru consist of gold, zinc and copper ores, oil, animal feed, and vegetables. Canada's key service interests in Peru include oil and gas, mining, engineering, architectural, environmental, distribution, financial, and information technology services.

With Colombia, Canada benefits from exporting cereals, machinery, vegetables, paper and paperboard, and vehicles. Major imports from Colombia consist of mineral fuels and oils, coffee, fruits, and sugar. By signing a free trade agreement with Colombia, Canadian businesses have increased their investments in the Colombian mining, oil, and printing sectors.

The free trade agreement with Panama gives Canadian businesses the opportunity to compete with other exporters such as the United States, Chile, Taiwan, and Singapore, which already have or are seeking preferential agreements with Panama. Canadian businesses export frozen potato products, beans, lentils, pork, malt, beef, electrical and electronic equipment, vehicles, and pharmaceutical equipment to Panama.[15]

For advice from Canadian entrepreneurs with successful businesses in Mexico, see the Entrepreneur's Toolkit titled "Conducting Business in Mexico." Although each culture in Latin America has unique factors, many of the tips found in the Entrepreneur's Toolkit are also true for Colombia, Chile, Peru, Costa Rica, Panama, and Honduras, Canada's other Latin American bilateral partners. These are places where Canadian businesses will most likely aim to expand their operations in the Americas.

The Canadian government has signed bilateral trade agreements beyond the Americas with countries such as Jordan and Israel, as well as with the European Union. It is also actively negotiating other bilateral agreements with several countries including India, Japan, Korea, Morocco, and China. However, these agreements are not "regional trade agreements," which is the focus of this chapter. To learn more about Canada's free trade agreements and ongoing negotiations for new agreements, visit the Foreign Affairs, Trade and Development Canada Web site (www.international.gc.ca), section Negotiations and Agreements.

Entrepreneur's Toolkit — Conducting Business in Mexico

Mexico beckons as a land of untapped opportunity for Canadian business. Even though NAFTA has been in effect for 20 years, Canadian exports to Mexico remain very low, representing less than two percent of Canada's trade worldwide. But, as with conducting business anywhere, opportunity needs to be balanced against the challenges of a particular location. Entrepreneurs who have succeeded in Mexico offer the following advice.

- **Formalities.** Mexican society is quite formal, so it is best to behave in a formal manner unless you know your colleague well. This includes using titles such as Doctor, Mister, *Licenciado* (to address anyone who holds a university degree except an engineer or lawyer), *Ingeniero* (Engineer), and *Abogado* (Lawyer). It's rarely appropriate to use first names unless you are close friends. Remember, Mexico still operates under a class system—respecting the hierarchy is crucial.

- **Business Relationships.** Making money is obviously important and remains the ultimate goal for any business. Still, building personal relationships, establishing good references, and doing favours for others can smooth the way for newcomers. Be careful when asked to do favours, however, as this could be a slippery slope to bribery and corruption. Expect your business set-up to take a long time—you will be dealing with Mexican bureaucracy.

- **Mexican Partners.** The Mexican culture is unique, influenced by its history as a Spanish colony followed by 70 years under one ruling party. Finding a local partner who can understand the inevitable cultural differences that arise, such as expectations about time commitments (although "*mañana*" translates literally as "tomorrow," it really means "later"), language barriers, and observed holidays, is essential. It is also extremely important to demand accountability for results.

- **Local Professionals.** Hiring a Mexican accountant or someone familiar with Mexican laws is a good idea because taxes are different in border and non-border states. A bilingual attorney can also interpret differences between Mexican and Canadian laws. It is also wise to seek help from Export Development Canada (EDC) offices in Mexico City and Monterrey, from the Canadian Chamber of Commerce in Mexico, and from Promexico (the Mexican government institution that promotes trade and investment).

- **Collectivistic Society.** Mexicans are known for being a collectivistic people. In collectivistic societies, family is very important, and people are concerned about the common well-being. Canadian society, on the other hand, is more individualistic, so has different values. (Think back to the discussion in Chapter 2 on the Hofstede framework.)

This toolkit shows that in order to take advantage of regional trade agreements such as NAFTA, companies need to first understand the differences in national business environments and then modify their business practices and strategies accordingly. The toolkit is one more example of how all topics in international business are interrelated.

Quick Study

1. What was the impetus for the formation of the North American Free Trade Agreement (NAFTA)?
2. What effect has NAFTA had on Canadian trade?
3. List the main benefits to Canada from signing free trade agreements with other nations in the Americas.

Andean Community (CAN)

Attempts at integration among Latin American countries had a rocky beginning. The first try, the *Latin American Free Trade Association* (*LAFTA*), was formed in 1961. The agreement first called for the creation of a free trade area by 1971 but then extended that date to 1980. Yet, because of a crippling debt crisis in South America and reluctance on the part of member nations to do away with protectionism, the agreement was doomed to an early demise. Disappointment with LAFTA led to the creation of two other regional trading blocs—the Andean Community and the Latin American Integration Association.

Formed in 1969, the *Andean Community* (in Spanish *Comunidad Andina de Naciones*, or *CAN*) includes four South American countries located in the Andes mountain range—Bolivia, Colombia, Ecuador, and Peru (see Map 8.1). Today the Andean Community (www.comunidadandina.org) comprises a market of around 97 million consumers and a combined GDP of about $220 billion. The main objectives of the group include tariff reduction for trade among member nations, a common external tariff, and common policies in both transportation and certain industries. The Andean Community adopted a common external tariff in 1995, but has not become a common market.

Several factors hamper progress. Political ideology among member nations is somewhat hostile to the concept of free markets and favours a good deal of government involvement in business affairs. Also, inherent distrust among members makes lower tariffs and more open trade hard to achieve. The common market will be difficult to implement within the framework of the Andean Community. One reason is that each country has been given significant exceptions in the tariff structure that they have in place for trade with non-member nations. Another reason is that countries continue to sign agreements with just one or two countries outside the Andean Community framework. Independent actions impair progress internally and hurt the credibility of the Andean Community with the rest of the world.

Latin American Integration Association (ALADI)

The *Latin American Integration Association (ALADI)* was formed in 1980 and today consists of 13 member countries. ALADI is the biggest Latin American trading bloc, representing a market of more than 500 million consumers (www.aladi.org). Because of the failure of the first attempt at integration (LAFTA), the objectives of ALADI were scaled back significantly. The ALADI agreement calls for preferential tariff agreements (*bilateral* agreements) to be made between pairs of member nations that reflect the economic development of each nation. Although the agreement resulted in roughly 24 bilateral agreements and 5 sub-regional pacts, it did not accomplish a great deal of cross-border trade. Dissatisfaction with progress once again caused certain nations to form a trading bloc of their own—the Southern Common Market.

Southern Common Market (MERCOSUR)

The *Southern Common Market* (in Spanish *El Mercado Comun del Sur*, or *MERCOSUR*) was established in 1988 between Argentina and Brazil, but expanded to include Paraguay and Uruguay in 1991 and Venezuela in 2006. Associate members of MERCOSUR (www.mercosur.int) include Bolivia, Chile, Colombia, Ecuador, Peru, Guyana and Suirname (see Map 8.1). Mexico has been granted observer status in the bloc.

Today, with the implementation of a common external tariff (CET), MERCOSUR acts as a customs union and boasts a market of more than 277 million consumers (nearly half of Latin America's total population) and a GDP of around $2.8 trillion. Its first years of existence were very successful, with trade among members growing nearly fourfold. MERCOSUR is progressing on trade and investment liberalization and is emerging as the most powerful trading bloc in all of Latin America. Latin America's large consumer base and its potential as a low-cost production platform for worldwide export appeal to both the European Union and NAFTA. MERCOSUR does not have a common currency or a coordinated monetary policy.

Central America and the Caribbean

Attempts at economic integration in Central American countries and throughout the Caribbean basin have been much more modest than efforts elsewhere in the Americas. Nevertheless, let's look at two efforts at integration in these two regions—CARICOM and CACM.

CARIBBEAN COMMUNITY AND COMMON MARKET (CARICOM) The *Caribbean Community and Common Market (CARICOM)* trading bloc was formed in 1973. There are 15 full members, 5 associate members, and 7 observers active in CARICOM (www.caricom.org). Although the Bahamas is a member of the community, it does not belong to the common market. As a whole, CARICOM has a combined GDP of nearly $30 billion and a market of almost 6 million people.

A key CARICOM agreement calls for establishment of a CARICOM Single Market, which would facilitate the free movement of factors of production including goods, services, capital, and labour. The main difficulty CARICOM will continue to face is that most members trade more with non-members than they do with one another, simply because members do not have the products each other needs to import.

CENTRAL AMERICAN COMMON MARKET (CACM)   The *Central American Common Market* (*CACM*) was formed in 1961 to create a common market among Costa Rica, El Salvador, Guatemala, Honduras, and Nicaragua. Together, the members of CACM (www.sieca.org.gt) comprise a market of 33 million consumers and have a combined GDP of about $120 billion. The common market was never realized, however, because of a long war between El Salvador and Honduras, and guerrilla conflicts in several countries. Yet renewed peace is creating more business confidence and optimism, which is driving double-digit growth in trade between members.

Furthermore, the group has not yet created a customs union. External tariffs among members range between 4 and 12 percent. The tentative nature of cooperation was obvious when Honduras and Nicaragua slapped punitive tariffs on each other's goods during a recent dispute. But officials remain positive, saying that their ultimate goal is European-style integration, closer political ties, and adoption of a single currency—probably the US dollar. In fact, El Salvador has adopted the US dollar as its official currency, and Guatemala already uses the dollar alongside its own currency, the quetzal.

Free Trade Area of the Americas (FTAA)

A truly daunting trading bloc would be the creation of a *Free Trade Area of the Americas* (*FTAA*). The objective of FTAA (www.alca-ftaa.org) is to create the largest free trade area on the planet, stretching from the northern tip of Alaska to the southern tip of Tierra del Fuego, in South America. FTAA would comprise 34 nations and 830 million consumers, with Cuba being the only Western Hemisphere nation excluded from participating. FTAA would work alongside existing trading blocs throughout the region.

The first official meeting, the 1994 Summit of the Americas, created the broad blueprint for the agreement. Nations reaffirmed their commitment to FTAA at the Second Summit of the Americas four years later when negotiations began. The Third Summit of the Americas, hosted in Quebec City in 2001, met with fierce protests. FTAA's ambitious plan means that it will likely be many years before such an agreement can be realized. Currently, FTAA negotiations have ceased, with no dates set for the resumption of talks.

According to Foreign Affairs and International Trade Canada, FTAA would create the world's largest free trade area. With Canadian trade accounting for nearly 40 percent of Canada's economy, Canada would greatly benefit from seeking access to the growing markets of the region.

Quick Study

1. What is the Andean Community? Identify why its progress is behind schedule.
2. Identify the members of the Southern Common Market (MERCOSUR). How has it performed?
3. Characterize economic integration efforts throughout Central America and the Caribbean.
4. What is the objective of the Free Trade Area of the Americas (FTAA)? What are its current prospects for success? How would FTAA benefit Canadian businesses?

Integration in Asia

Efforts at economic and political integration outside Europe and the Americas have tended to be looser arrangements. Let's take a look at important coalitions in Asia and among Pacific Rim nations—the Association of Southeast Asian Nations, the organization for Asia Pacific Economic Cooperation, and the Australian and New Zealand Closer Economic Relations Agreement.

Association of Southeast Asian Nations (ASEAN)

Indonesia, Malaysia, the Philippines, Singapore, and Thailand formed the *Association of Southeast Asian Nations (ASEAN)* in 1967. Brunei joined in 1984, Vietnam in 1995, Laos and Burma in 1997, and Cambodia in 1998 (see Map 8.1). Together, the 10 ASEAN (www.aseansec.org) countries comprise a market of about 560 million consumers and a GDP of nearly $1.1 trillion. The three main objectives of the alliance are to (1) promote economic, cultural, and social development in the region; (2) safeguard the region's economic and political stability; and (3) serve as a forum in which differences can be resolved fairly and peacefully.

The decision to admit Cambodia, Laos, and Burma was criticized by some Western nations. The concern regarding the admittance of Laos and Cambodia stems from their roles in supporting the communists during the Vietnam War. The quarrel with Burma centres on evidence cited by the West of its continued human rights violations. Nevertheless, ASEAN felt that by adding these countries to the coalition, it could counter China's rising strength and its resources of cheap labour and abundant raw materials.

Companies involved in Asia's developing economies are likely to be doing business with an ASEAN member. This is even a more likely prospect as China, Japan, and South Korea accelerate their efforts to join ASEAN. China's admittance would allow the club to bridge the gap between less advanced and more advanced economies. Some key facts about ASEAN that companies should consider are contained in the Global Manager's Briefcase, titled "The Ins and Outs of ASEAN."

Asia Pacific Economic Cooperation (APEC)

The organization for *Asia Pacific Economic Cooperation (APEC)* was formed in 1989. Begun as an informal forum among 12 trading partners, APEC (www.apecsec.org) now has 21 members (see Map 8.1). Together, the APEC nations account for more than 40 percent of world trade and a combined GDP of more than $19 trillion.

The stated aim of APEC is not to build another trading bloc. Instead, it desires to strengthen the multilateral trading system and expand the global economy by simplifying and liberalizing trade and investment procedures among member nations. In the long term, APEC hopes to have completely free trade and investment throughout the region by 2020.

Global Manager's Briefcase   ## The Ins and Outs of ASEAN

Businesses unfamiliar with operating in ASEAN countries should exercise caution in their dealings. Some inescapable facts about ASEAN that warrant consideration are the following.

- **Diverse Cultures and Politics.** The Philippines is a representative democracy, Brunei is an oil-rich sultanate, and Vietnam is a state-controlled communist country. Business policies and protocol must be adapted to each country.

- **Economic Competition.** Many ASEAN nations are feeling the effects of China's power to attract investment from multinationals worldwide. Whereas ASEAN members used to attract around 30 percent of foreign direct investment into Asia's developing economies, it now attracts about half that amount.

- **Corruption and Shadow Markets.** Bribery and shadow (unofficial) markets are common in many ASEAN countries, including Indonesia, Burma, the Philippines, and Vietnam. Corruption studies typically place these countries at or very near the bottom of nations surveyed.

- **Political Change and Turmoil.** Several nations in the region recently elected new leaders. Indonesia in particular has gone through presidents at a fast clip recently. Companies must remain alert to shifting political winds and laws regarding trade and investment.

- **Border Disputes.** Parts of Thailand's borders with Cambodia and Laos are tested frequently. Hostilities break out sporadically between Thailand and Burma over border alignment and ethnic Shan rebels operating along the border.

- **Lack of Common Tariffs and Standards.** Doing business in ASEAN nations can be costly. Harmonized tariffs, quality and safety standards, customs regulations, and investment rules would cut transaction costs significantly.

THE RECORD OF APEC APEC has succeeded in halving members' tariff rates from an average of 15 percent to 7.5 percent. The early years saw the greatest progress, but liberalization received a setback when the Asian financial crisis struck in the late 1990s. APEC is at least as much a political body as it is a movement toward freer trade. After all, APEC certainly does not have the focus or the record of accomplishments of NAFTA or the EU. Nonetheless, open dialogue and attempts at cooperation should continue to encourage progress, however slow.

Further progress may create some positive benefits for people doing business in APEC nations. APEC is changing the granting of business visas so businesspeople can travel throughout the region without obtaining multiple visas. It is recommending mutual recognition agreements on professional qualifications so that engineers, for example, could practise in any APEC country, regardless of nationality. And APEC is ready to simplify and harmonize customs procedures. Eventually, businesses could use the same customs forms and manifests for all APEC economies.

Closer Economic Relations Agreement (CER)

Australia and New Zealand created a free trade agreement in 1966 that slashed tariffs and quotas 80 percent by 1980. The agreement's success encouraged the pair to form the *Closer Economic Relations (CER) Agreement* in 1983 to advance free trade and further integrate their two economies (see Map 8.1).

CER was an enormous success in that it totally eliminated tariffs and quotas between Australia and New Zealand in 1990, five years ahead of schedule. Each nation allows goods (and most services) to be sold within its borders that can be legally sold in the other country. Each nation also recognizes most professionals who are registered to practise their occupation in the other country.

Integration in the Middle East and Africa

Economic integration has not left out the Middle East and Africa, although progress there is more limited than in any other geographic region. Its limited success is due mostly to the small size of the countries involved and their relatively low level of development. The largest of these coalitions are the Gulf Cooperation Council and the Economic Community of West African States.

Gulf Cooperation Council (GCC)

Several Middle Eastern nations formed the *Gulf Cooperation Council (GCC)* in 1980. Members of the GCC are Bahrain, Kuwait, Oman, Qatar, Saudi Arabia, and the United Arab Emirates. The primary purpose of the GCC at its formation was to cooperate with the increasingly powerful trading blocs in Europe at the time—the EU and EFTA. The GCC has evolved, however, to become as much a political entity as an economic one. Its cooperative thrust allows citizens of member countries to travel freely in the GCC without visas. It also permits citizens of one member nation to own land, property, and businesses in any other member nation without the need for local sponsors or partners.

Economic Community of West African States (ECOWAS)

The *Economic Community of West African States (ECOWAS)* was formed in 1975 but restarted efforts at economic integration in 1992 because of a lack of early progress. One of the most important goals of ECOWAS (www.ecowas.int) is the formation of a customs union, an eventual common market, and a monetary union. Together, the ECOWAS nations comprise a large portion of the economic activity in sub-Saharan Africa.

Progress on market integration is almost nonexistent. In fact, the value of trade occurring among ECOWAS nations is just 11 percent of the value that the trade members undertake with third parties. But ECOWAS has made progress in the free movement of people, construction of international roads, and development of international telecommunication links. Some of its main problems are due to political instability, poor governance, weak national economies, poor infrastructure, and poor economic policies.

African Union (AU)

A group of 54 nations on the African continent joined forces in 2002 to create the *African Union (AU)*. Heads of state of nations belonging to the Organization of African Unity paved the way for the AU (www.au.int) when they signed the Sirte Declaration in 1999.

Gwari women carry firewood on their backs in the village of Gwagwalada, which is about 32 kilometres from Abuja in the middle of Nigeria. A growing number of Nigerians from rural areas are beginning to cut down more trees for domestic firewood as an alternative energy following the increase of kerosene prices. Nigeria participates in the regional trading bloc known as ECOWAS to improve the lives of ordinary people, such as the women pictured here.

Source: © Ceorge Esiri/Reuters/Corbis.

The AU is based on the vision of a united and strong Africa, and on the need to build a partnership among governments and all segments of civil society to strengthen cohesion among the peoples of Africa. Its ambitious goals are to promote peace, security, and stability across Africa and to accelerate economic and political integration while addressing problems compounded by globalization. Specifically, the stated aims of the AU are to (1) rid the continent of the remaining vestiges of colonialism and apartheid; (2) promote unity and solidarity among African states; (3) coordinate and intensify cooperation for development; (4) safeguard the sovereignty and territorial integrity of members; and (5) promote international cooperation within the framework of the United Nations.

It is too early to judge the success of the AU, but there is no shortage of opportunities on the continent for it to demonstrate its capabilities. Ethnic violence in the Darfur region of Sudan continues despite heavy involvement by the AU in solving the problem. The people of Africa have much to gain from an effective and successful African Union.

Quick Study

1. Identify the three main objectives of the Association of Southeast Asian Nations.
2. How do the goals of the Asia Pacific Economic Cooperation forum differ from those of other regional blocs?
3. What is the Gulf Cooperation Council? Identify its members.
4. List the aims of both the Economic Community of West African States and the African Union.

Bottom Line for Business

Regional economic integration can expand buyer selection, lower prices, increase productivity, and boost national competitiveness. Yet integration has its drawbacks, and governments and independent organizations work to counter these negative effects. Let's examine the issue of regional integration as it relates to business operations and employment.

Integration and Business Operations

Regional trade agreements are changing the landscape of the global marketplace. They are lowering trade barriers and opening up new markets for goods and services. Markets otherwise off limits because tariffs made imported products too expensive can become attractive after tariffs are lifted. But trade agreements can also be double-edged swords for companies. Not only do they allow domestic companies to seek new markets abroad, but they also let competitors from other nations enter the domestic market. Such mobility increases competition in every market that participates in such an agreement.

Despite increased competition that often accompanies regional integration, there can be economic benefits, such as those provided by a single currency. Companies in the European Union clearly benefit from its common currency, the euro. First, charges for converting from one member nation's currency to that of another can be avoided. Second, business owners need not worry about potential losses due to shifting exchange rates on cross-border deals. Not having to cover such costs and risks frees up capital for greater investment. Third, the euro makes prices between markets more transparent, making it more difficult to charge different prices in different markets. This helps companies compare prices among suppliers of a raw material, intermediate product, or service.

Another benefit for companies is lower or no tariffs. This allows a multinational to reduce its number of factories that supply a region and thereby reap economies of scale benefits. This is possible because a company can produce in one location and then ship products throughout the low-tariff region at little additional cost. This lowers costs and increases productivity.

One potential drawback of regional integration is that lower tariffs between members of a trading bloc can result in trade diversion. This can increase trade with less efficient producers within the trading bloc and reduce trade with more efficient non-member producers. Unless there is other internal competition for the producer's good or service, buyers will likely pay more after trade diversion.

Integration and Employment

Perhaps most controversial is the impact of regional integration on jobs. Companies can affect the job environment by contributing to dislocations in labour markets. The nation that supplies a particular good or service within a trading bloc is likely to be the most efficient producer. When that product is labour intensive, the cost of labour in that market is likely to be quite low. Competitors in other nations may shift production to that relatively lower-wage nation (for example, Mexico) within the trading bloc to remain competitive. This can mean lost jobs in the relatively higher-wage nation (for example, Canada).

Yet job dislocation can be an opportunity for workers to upgrade their skills and gain more advanced training. This can help nations increase their competitiveness because a more educated and skilled workforce attracts higher-paying jobs. An opportunity for a nation to improve its competitiveness, however, is little consolation to people finding themselves suddenly out of work.

Although there are drawbacks to integration, there are potential gains from increased trade such as raising living standards. Regional economic integration efforts are likely to continue rolling back barriers to international trade and investment because of their potential benefits.

Chapter Summary

1. **Define regional economic integration and identify its five levels.**
   - The process whereby countries in a geographic region cooperate with one another to reduce or eliminate barriers to the international flow of products, people, or capital is called *regional economic integration*.
   - *Free trade area:* countries seek to remove all barriers to trade among themselves, but each country determines its own barriers against non-members.
   - *Customs union:* countries remove all barriers to trade among themselves but erect a common trade policy against non-members.
   - *Common market:* countries remove all barriers to trade and the movement of labour and capital among themselves but erect a common trade policy against non-members.
   - *Economic union:* countries remove barriers to trade and the movement of labour and capital among themselves, erect a common trade policy against non-members, and coordinate their economic policies.
   - *Political union:* countries coordinate aspects of their economic *and* political systems.

2. **Discuss the benefits and drawbacks of regional economic integration and identify the implications for Canadian businesses.**
   - *Trade creation* is the increase in trade that results from regional economic integration, which can expand buyer selection, lower prices, increase productivity, and boost national competitiveness.
   - Smaller, regional groups of nations can find it easier to reduce trade barriers than can larger groups.
   - Nations can have more say when negotiating with other countries or organizations, reduce the potential for military conflict, and expand employment opportunities.
   - *Trade diversion* is the diversion of trade away from nations not belonging to a trading bloc and toward member nations; it can result in increased trade with a less-efficient producer within the trading bloc.

3. **Describe regional integration in Europe and its pattern of enlargement.**
   - The *European Coal and Steel Community* was formed in 1951 to remove trade barriers for coal, iron, steel, and scrap metal among the member nations.
   - Following several waves of expansion, broadenings of its scope, and name changes, the community is now known as the *European Union (EU)* and has 28 members.
   - Five main institutions of the EU are the European Parliament, European Commission, Council of the European Union, Court of Justice, and Court of Auditors.
   - The EU single currency has been adopted by 17 member nations, which benefit from elimination of exchange-rate risk and currency conversion costs within the euro zone.
   - The EU signed a free trade agreement with Canada in October 2013 in order to generate more trade, investment, and jobs on both sides of the Atlantic.
   - The *European Free Trade Association (EFTA)* has four members and was created to focus on trade in industrial goods.
   - EFTA has signed a free trade agreement with Canada to create new export markets for Canadian businesses.

4. **Discuss and analyze regional integration in the Americas, particularly regarding NAFTA and Canada's bilateral trade agreements.**
   - The *North American Free Trade Agreement (NAFTA)* began in 1994 among Canada, Mexico, and the United States; it seeks to eliminate all tariffs and nontariff trade barriers on goods originating from within North America.
   - Canada has also signed bilateral agreements with Colombia, Costa Rica, Chile, Peru, and Panama; it has concluded negotiations with Honduras, but that agreement has not yet come into effect.
   - The *Andean Community* was formed in 1969 and calls for tariff reduction for trade among member nations, a common external tariff, and common policies in transportation and certain industries.
   - The *Latin American Integration Association (ALADI)*, formed in 1980 between Mexico and 10 South American nations, has had little impact on cross-border trade.
   - The *Southern Common Market (MERCOSUR)*, established in 1988, acts as a customs union.

- The Caribbean Community and Common Market (CARICOM) trading bloc was formed in 1973, and the Central American Common Market (CACM) was formed in 1961.
5. Characterize regional integration in Asia and how it differs from integration elsewhere.
   - The *Association of Southeast Asian Nations* (*ASEAN*) formed in 1967 and seeks to (1) promote economic, cultural, and social development; (2) safeguard economic and political stability; and (3) serve as a forum to resolve differences peacefully.
   - The organization for *Asia Pacific Economic Cooperation* (*APEC*) was formed in 1989 and strives to strengthen the multilateral trading system and expand the global economy by simplifying and liberalizing trade and investment procedures.
   - The *Closer Economic Relations (CER)* agreement in 1983 between Australia and New Zealand totally eliminated tariffs and quotas between the two economies.
6. Describe regional integration in the Middle East and Africa, and explain the slow progress.
   - Several Middle Eastern nations in 1980 formed the *Gulf Cooperation Council* (*GCC*), which allows citizens of member countries to travel freely without visas and to own properties in other member nations without the need for local sponsors or partners.
   - The *Economic Community of West African States* (*ECOWAS*) formed in 1975, with a major goal being formation of a customs union and an eventual common market.
   - The *African Union (AU)* was started in 2002 among 54 nations to promote peace, security, and stability and to accelerate economic and political integration across Africa.

Key Terms

common market 235	free trade area 234	trade creation 237
customs union 234	political union 235	trade diversion 237
economic union 235	regional economic integration	
European monetary union 239	(regionalism) 234	

Talk It Over

1. Proliferation and growth of regional trading blocs will likely continue into the foreseeable future. At what point do you think the integration process will stop (if ever)? Explain your answer.
2. Some people believe that the rise of regional trading blocs threatens free trade progress made by the World Trade Organization (WTO). Do you agree? Why or why not?
3. Certain groups of countries, particularly in Africa, are far less economically developed than other regions, such as

Europe and North America. What sort of integration arrangement do you think developed countries could create with less developed nations to improve living standards? Be as specific as you can.

4. Should Canada and Mexico seek greater economic integration with the United States, such as a customs or an economic union that would make the US dollar the common currency in the region? Explain and provide pros and cons. What are the economic and political implications?

Take It to the Web

1. **Video Report.** Visit the Foreign Affairs, Trade and Development Canada channel on YouTube (www.youtube.com). Click on "Videos." Watch one video from the list related to regional trade agreements, and summarize it in a half-page report. Reflecting on the contents of this chapter, which aspects of regional integration can you identify in the video? How might a company engaged in international business act on the information contained in the video?
2. **Web Site Report.** Visit the official Web site of Foreign Affairs, Trade and Development Canada (www.international.gc.ca). Click on "Trade" and choose "Opening New Markets" from the drop-down menu. Click on "Free Trade Agreements," and then choose "NAFTA" from the list. Read the NAFTA Background

Information and Institutions of NAFTA. Has NAFTA proved to be a solid foundation for building Canada's future prosperity? How many new jobs have been created in Canada due to NAFTA? Do you think a NAFTA secretariat is needed? Do you think NAFTA is helping lift living standards in Mexico or is it a boon only for Canada and the United States?

Small companies typically have difficulty competing against large multinationals when their governments take part in regional trading blocs. What could governments do to help their small companies compete in such blocs? After all you've read in this chapter about regional trade agreements, what is your assessment of their value? Should their progress continue or be rolled back?

NAFTA Doesn't Guarantee Free Trade After All: United States vs. Canada in the Softwood Lumber Case

NAFTA's main objective was to eliminate all tariffs on trade between member countries, allowing a free flow of goods and services. However, that has not been the case for Canada's softwood lumber exports to the United States.

Only 4 percent of the trade between Canada and the United States is disputed, and 3 percent of those disputes are related to softwood lumber. Why is softwood lumber so important to Canada? Canada is the largest producer of softwood lumber in the world, while the United States is the largest consumer, particularly in the housing market. A trade war related to this single commodity has been going on since 1982. However, Jim Phillips, president and CEO of the Canadian/American Border Trade Alliance, notes that "the first US levy on softwood lumber was actually in 1792." The most recent dispute began in May 2002, when the United States imposed a 27 percent duty on Canadian softwood lumber.

What was the dispute about? The United States claimed that the Canadian lumber industry was subsidized, arguing that the fee Canadian governments charged logging companies to harvest lumber from public lands (called a stumpage fee) was below fair market value. A US coalition of lumber producers wanted the provincial governments to follow the American system and auction off timber rights at market prices. When the provinces refused, the US government imposed its punitive tariff.

Between August 2003 and April 2006, the dispute was presented to a NAFTA panel, the World Trade Organization (WTO), and the US Court of International Trade. On different occasions the NAFTA panel and the WTO made seemingly contradictory rulings on the issue, continuing the dispute. For example, on August 13, 2003, a NAFTA panel ruled that the Canadian lumber industry was subsidized. Two weeks later, the WTO found that the financial benefit to Canadian producers from the stumpage fees was not enough to be considered a subsidy. Both panels concluded that the tariff imposed by the United States was too high. Nonetheless, in February 2006 the US lumber lobby claimed the WTO ruling confirmed that the United States had complied with its international obligations when it applied antidumping duties against Canada. However, in March 2006 a NAFTA panel ruled in Canada's favour.

Finally, at the end of April 2006, Canada and the United States reached an agreement. Bill C-24, legislation to implement the agreement, was introduced in Parliament on September 20, 2006. The purpose of the agreement was to promote a stable bilateral trade environment so that Canadian softwood lumber exporters could prosper. The agreement called for the dismissal of US countervailing and antidumping duty orders and the return of over US$4.5 billion in duties to Canadian exporters. The United States also agreed to third country provisions to cover Canada in case other nations gain US market share at Canada's expense. In return, Canada agreed to impose export duties and volume caps on exports to the United States when the prevailing price of lumber is at or below $355 per thousand board feet. The United States agreed to exempt Atlantic producers and Quebec border mills from this export charge.

The agreement is for a term of seven years, with an option to renew for two more. The agreement also includes a termination clause stating that "either party may at any time after the agreement has been in effect for 18 months, terminate by providing 6 months' notice."

Source: Joe Gough/fotolia.

Thinking Globally

1. Do you think that the softwood lumber case and the subsequent agreement are examples of NAFTA's failure?

2. What are the opportunities and threats that the agreement poses to Canadian producers?

3. Do you think Bill C-24 effectively resolves the softwood lumber dispute? Please explain your reasoning.
4. If you were an international trade manager of a Canadian softwood lumber company, what strategic moves would you make to reduce dependence on the agreement? (Base your response on what you have learned in this chapter.)

Sources: "The Canada-United States Softwood Lumber Agreement: Background," Foreign Affairs, Trade and Development Canada (www.international.gc.ca/controls-controles/softwood-bois_oeuvre/background-generalites); "Prime Minister Announces Canada and U.S. Reach Softwood Deal," Prime Minister's Office Web site (pm.gc.ca/eng/news/2006/04/27/prime-minister-announces-canada-and-us-reach-softwood-deal-0), April 27, 2006; "U.S. Claims Victory in Lumber Case Against Canada," Reuters Canada (ca.reuters.com/article/topNews/idCATRe51P86G20090227), February 26, 2009; Lara L. Sowinski, "Two Opposing Trade Tales," *World Trade*, 2005, 18(11), pp. 55–57; Danny Kucharsky, "Chile's Rising Demand for Canadian Forestry Equipment," *ExportWise*, Winter 2010, pp. 9–13; CBC News, "Softwood Lumber," CBC Web site (www.cbc.ca).

CHAPTER NINE

International Financial Markets and Foreign Exchange

Learning Objectives

After studying this chapter, you should be able to

1. Discuss the purposes, development, and financial centres of the international capital market.

2. Describe the international bond, international equity, and Eurocurrency markets.

3. Discuss the four primary functions of the foreign exchange market.

4. Understand how currencies are quoted and the different rates given.

5. Explain how exchange rates influence the activities of domestic and international companies.

6. Describe the primary methods of forecasting exchange rates.

7. Identify the main instruments of the foreign exchange market.

8. Explain why and how governments restrict currency convertibility.

A LOOK BACK

Chapter 8 introduced the most prominent efforts at regional economic integration occurring around the world. We saw how international companies are responding to the challenges and opportunities that regional integration is creating.

A LOOK AT THIS CHAPTER

This chapter introduces us to the international financial system by describing the structure of international financial markets. We learn first about the international capital market and its main components. We then turn to the foreign exchange market, explaining how it works and outlining its structure. We also study how exchange rates are used and how they influence the activities of international companies.

A LOOK AHEAD

Chapter 10 introduces the topic of the last part of this book—international business management. We will explore the specific strategies and organizational structures that companies use in accomplishing their international business objectives.

Source: ShutterStock.

Wii Is the Champion

KYOTO, Japan—Nintendo (www.nintendo.com) has been feeding the addiction of video gaming fans worldwide since 1989. More than 100 years earlier, in 1889, Fusajiro Yamauchi started Nintendo when he began manufacturing *Hanafuda* playing cards in Kyoto, Japan. Today, Nintendo produces and sells mobile game devices and home game systems, including Wii, Nintendo DS, GameCube, and Game Boy Advance, which feature global icons Mario, Donkey Kong, Pokémon, and others.

Nintendo took the global gaming industry by storm when it introduced the Wii game console. With wireless motion-sensitive remote controllers, built-in Wi-Fi capability, and other features, the Wii outdoes Sony's PlayStation and Microsoft's Xbox game consoles. Nintendo's game called Wii Fit cleverly forces player activity through 40 exercises consisting of yoga, strength training, cardio, and even doing the hula-hoop. Pictured here, Nintendo employees perform a song together as they demonstrate the game "Wii Music."

Yet Nintendo's marketing and game-design talents are not all that affect its performance—so too do exchange rates between the Japanese yen (¥) and other currencies. The earnings of Nintendo's subsidiaries and affiliates outside Japan must be

Source: © Fred Prouser/Reuters/Corbis.

integrated into consolidated financial statements at the end of each year. Translating subsidiaries' earnings from other currencies into a strong yen decreases Nintendo's stated earnings in yen.

Nintendo recently reported annual net income of ¥257.3 billion ($2.6 billion), but it also reported that its income included a foreign exchange loss of ¥92.3 billion ($923.5 million). A rise of the yen against foreign currencies prior to the translation of subsidiaries' earnings into yen caused the loss. As you read this chapter, consider how shifting currency values affect financial performance and how managers can reduce their impact.[1]

Well-functioning financial markets are an essential element of the international business environment. They funnel money from organizations and economies with excess funds to those with shortages. International financial markets also allow companies to exchange one currency for another. The trading of currencies and the rates at which they are exchanged are crucial to international business.

Suppose you purchase an MP3 player imported from a company based in the Philippines. Whether you realize it or not, the price you paid for that MP3 player was affected by the exchange rate between your country's currency and the Philippine peso. Ultimately, the Filipino company that sold you the MP3 player must convert the purchase made in your currency into Philippine pesos. Thus the profit earned by the Filipino company is also influenced by the exchange rate between your currency and the peso. Managers must understand how changes in currency values—and thus in exchange rates—affect the profitability of their international business activities. Among other things, our hypothetical company in the Philippines must know how much to charge you for its MP3 player.

In this chapter, we launch our study of the international financial system by exploring the structure of the international financial markets. The two interrelated systems that comprise the international financial markets are the international capital market and foreign exchange market. We start by examining the purposes of the international capital market and tracing its recent development. We then take a look at the international bond, equity, and Eurocurrency markets, each of which helps companies to borrow and lend money internationally. Next, we explain how currencies are quoted and how exchange rates influence the activities of international businesses. Later, we examine the functioning of the foreign exchange market—an international market for currencies that facilitates international business transactions. We close the chapter by studying how and why governments restrict currency convertibility.

International Capital Market

capital market
System that allocates financial resources in the form of debt and equity according to their most efficient uses.

A **capital market** is a system that allocates financial resources in the form of debt and equity according to their most efficient uses. Its main purpose is to provide a mechanism through which those who wish to borrow or invest money can do so efficiently. Individuals, companies, governments, mutual funds, pension funds, and all types of nonprofit organizations participate in capital markets. For example, an individual might want to buy her first home, a medium-sized company might want to add production capacity, and a government might want to develop a new wireless communications system. Sometimes these individuals and organizations have excess cash to lend, and at other times they need funds.

Here, a customer counts her Philippine pesos after exchanging US dollars at a moneychanger in Manila, the Philippines. The foreign exchange market gives Filipinos working overseas a safe way to wire money to relatives back home. The prices of currencies on the foreign exchange market also help determine the prices of imports and exports. And exchange rates affect the amount of profit a company receives when it translates revenue earned abroad into the home currency.

Source: AFP PHOTO/ROMEO GACAD/Newscom.

Purposes of National Capital Markets

There are two primary means by which companies obtain external financing: *debt* and *equity*. Capital markets function to help them obtain both types of financing. However, to understand the international capital market fully, we need to review the purposes of capital markets in domestic economies. Quite simply, national capital markets help individuals and institutions borrow the money that other individuals and institutions want to lend. Although in theory borrowers could search individually for various parties who are willing to lend or invest, this would be an extremely inefficient process.

ROLE OF DEBT **Debt** consists of loans, for which the borrower promises to repay the borrowed amount (the *principal*) plus a predetermined rate of *interest*. Company debt normally takes the form of **bonds**—instruments that specify the timing of principal and interest payments. The holder of a bond (the *lender*) can force the borrower into bankruptcy if the borrower fails to pay on a timely basis. Bonds issued for the purpose of funding investments are commonly issued by private-sector companies and by municipal, regional, and national governments.

ROLE OF EQUITY **Equity** is part ownership of a company in which the equity holder participates with other part owners in the company's financial gains and losses. Equity normally takes the form of **stock**—shares of ownership in a company's assets that give *shareholders* (*stockholders*) a claim on the company's future cash flows. Shareholders may be rewarded with *dividends*—payments made out of surplus funds—or by increases in the value of their shares. Of course, they may also suffer losses due to poor company performance—and thus decreases in the value of their shares. Dividend payments are not guaranteed but are determined by the company's board of directors and based on financial performance. In capital markets, shareholders can sell one company's stock for that of another or *liquidate* them—exchange them for cash. **Liquidity**, which is a feature of both debt and equity markets, refers to the ease with which bondholders and shareholders may convert their investments into cash.

Purposes of the International Capital Market

The **international capital market** is a network of individuals, companies, financial institutions, and governments that invest and borrow across national boundaries. It consists of both formal exchanges (in which buyers and sellers meet to trade financial instruments) and electronic networks (in which trading occurs anonymously). This market makes use of unique and innovative financial instruments specially designed to fit the needs of investors and borrowers located in different countries that are doing business with one another. Large international banks play a central role in the international capital market. They gather the excess cash of investors and savers around the world and then channel this cash to borrowers across the globe.

EXPANDS THE MONEY SUPPLY FOR BORROWERS The international capital market is a conduit for joining borrowers and lenders in different national capital markets. A company that is unable to obtain funds from investors in its own nation can seek financing from investors elsewhere, making it possible for the company to undertake an otherwise impossible project. The option of going outside the home nation is particularly important to firms in countries with small or developing capital markets of their own. An expanded supply of money also benefits small but promising companies that might not otherwise get financing if there is intense competition for capital.

REDUCES THE COST OF MONEY FOR BORROWERS An expanded money supply reduces the cost of borrowing. Similar to the prices of potatoes, wheat, and other commodities, the "price" of money is determined by supply and demand. If its supply increases, its price—in the form of interest rates—falls. That is why excess supply creates a borrower's market, forcing down interest rates and the cost of borrowing. Projects regarded as infeasible because of low expected returns might be viable at a lower cost of financing.

REDUCES RISK FOR LENDERS The international capital market expands the available set of lending opportunities. In turn, an expanded set of opportunities helps reduce risk for lenders (investors) in two ways:

1. *Investors enjoy a greater set of opportunities from which to choose.* They can thus reduce overall portfolio risk by spreading their money over a greater number of debt and equity instruments. In other words, if one investment loses money, the loss can be offset by gains elsewhere.

debt
Loan in which the borrower promises to repay the borrowed amount (the principal) plus a predetermined rate of interest.

bond
Debt instrument that specifies the timing of principal and interest payments.

equity
Part ownership of a company in which the equity holder participates with other part owners in the company's financial gains and losses.

stock
Shares of ownership in a company's assets that give shareholders a claim on the company's future cash flows.

liquidity
Ease with which bondholders and shareholders may convert their investments into cash.

international capital market
Network of individuals, companies, financial institutions, and governments that invest and borrow across national boundaries.

2. *Investing in international securities benefits investors because some economies are growing while others are in decline.* For example, the prices of bonds in Thailand do not follow bond-price fluctuations in Canada, which are independent of prices in Hungary. In short, investors reduce risk by holding international securities whose prices move independently.

Small would-be borrowers still face some serious problems in trying to secure loans. Interest rates are often high, and many entrepreneurs have nothing to put up as collateral. For some unique methods of getting capital to the owners of small businesses (particularly in developing nations), see this chapter's Entrepreneur's Toolkit, titled "Microfinance Makes a Big Impression."

Forces Expanding the International Capital Market

Around 40 years ago, national capital markets functioned largely as independent markets. But since that time, the amount of debt, equity, and currencies traded internationally has increased dramatically. This rapid growth can be traced to three main factors:

- *Information Technology.* Information is the lifeblood of every nation's capital market because investors need information about investment opportunities and their corresponding risk levels. Large investments in information technology over the past two decades have drastically reduced the costs, in both time and money, of communicating around the globe. Investors and borrowers can now respond in record time to events in the international capital

---

Entrepreneur's Toolkit   Microfinance Makes a Big Impression

Wealthy nations are not the only places where entrepreneurs thrive. Developing nations are teeming with budding entrepreneurs who need just a bit of start-up capital to get off the ground. Here are the key characteristics of microfinance.

- **Overcoming Obstacles.** Obtaining capital challenges the entrepreneurial spirit in many developing countries. If a person is lucky enough to obtain a loan, it is typically from a loan shark, whose sky-high interest rates devour most of the entrepreneur's profits. So microfinance is an increasingly popular way to lend money to low-income entrepreneurs at competitive interest rates (around 10 to 20 percent) without putting up collateral. Now institutions are warming to the idea of "micro savings" so people can manage their small but highly uneven flows of income over time.

- **One for All, and All for One.** Sometimes a loan is made to a group of entrepreneurs who sink or swim together. Members of the borrowing group are joined at the economic hip: if one member fails to pay off a loan, all in the group may lose future credit. Peer pressure and support often defend against defaults, however. Support networks in developing countries often incorporate extended family ties. One bank in Bangladesh boasts 98 percent on-time repayment.

- **No Glass Ceiling Here.** Although outreach to male borrowers is increasing, most microfinance borrowers are female. Women tend to be better at funnelling profits into family nutrition, clothing, and education, as well as into business expansion. The successful use of microfinance in Bangladesh has increased wages, community income, and the status of women. The microfinance industry is estimated at around $8 billion worldwide.

- **Developed Country Agenda.** The microfinance concept was pioneered in Bangladesh as a way for developing countries to create the foundation for a market economy. It now might be a way to spur economic growth in depressed areas of developed nations, such as in decaying city centres. But whereas microfinance loans in developing countries typically average about $350, those in developed nations would need to be significantly larger. A good example of an international nonprofit operating in Canada is the Foundation for International Community Assistance (FINCA), which is a global microfinance organization that provides financial support to low-income entrepreneurs around the world so they can create jobs and improve their standard of living. FINCA's Canadian branch opened in 2009 to provide Canadians with an opportunity to directly help some of the world's poorest people. To learn more about FINCA Canada, visit www.fincacanada.org.

Sources: "FINCA Opens Canadian Outreach Branch," FINCA (www.fincacanada.org), November, 10, 2009; "A Better Mattress," *The Economist,* March 13, 2010, pp. 75–76; Jennifer L. Schenker, "Taking Microfinance to the Next Level," *Bloomberg Businessweek* (www.businessweek.com), February 26, 2008; Steve Hamm, "Setting Standards for Microfinance," *Bloomberg Businessweek* (www.businessweek.com), July 28, 2008; Grameen Bank Web site (www.grameen-info.org), select reports.

market. The introduction of electronic trading after the daily close of formal exchanges also facilitates faster response times.

• *Deregulation.* Deregulation of national capital markets has been instrumental in the expansion of the international capital market. The need for deregulation became apparent in the early 1970s, when heavily regulated markets in the largest countries were facing fierce competition from less regulated markets in smaller nations. Deregulation increased competition, lowered the cost of financial transactions, and opened many national markets to global investing and borrowing. But the pendulum is now swinging the other direction as legislators demand tighter regulation to help avoid another global financial crisis like that of 2008–2009.[2]

• *Financial Instruments.* Greater competition in the financial industry is creating the need to develop innovative financial instruments. One result of the need for new types of financial instruments is **securitization**—the unbundling and repackaging of hard-to-trade financial assets into more liquid, negotiable, and marketable financial instruments (or *securities*). For instance, in Canada, the Canadian Mortgage and Housing Corporation (www.cmhc-schl.gc.ca) provides mortgage insurance and accumulates mortgages into mortgage-backed securities. Most of the major Canadian banks also offer clients mortgage-backed investment opportunities. For example, TD Securities, located in Toronto, has a team with complementary experience in the fields of accounting, corporate law, risk management, credit ratings, fixed income portfolio management, and corporate finance. They focus on traditional asset classes originated by large Canadian and multinational corporations, many of which are important clients of the Toronto-Dominion Bank.[3]

securitization
Unbundling and repackaging of hard-to-trade financial assets into more liquid, negotiable, and marketable financial instruments (or *securities*).

World Financial Centres

The world's three most important financial centres are London, New York, and Tokyo. Toronto usually ranks in the top ten in the world. Traditional exchanges may become obsolete unless they continue to modernize, cut costs, and provide new customer services. In fact, trading over the Internet and other systems might increase the popularity of *offshore financial centres.*

OFFSHORE FINANCIAL CENTRES An **offshore financial centre** is a country or territory whose financial sector features very few regulations and few, if any, taxes. These centres tend to be economically and politically stable, and provide access to the international capital market through an excellent telecommunications infrastructure. Most governments protect their own currencies by restricting the amount of activity that domestic companies can conduct in foreign currencies. So companies can find it hard to borrow funds in foreign currencies and thus turn to offshore centres, which offer large amounts of funding in many currencies. In short, offshore centres are sources of (usually cheaper) funding for companies with multinational operations.

offshore financial centre
Country or territory whose financial sector features very few regulations and few, if any, taxes.

Offshore financial centres fall into two categories:

• *Operational centres* see a great deal of financial activity. Prominent operational centres include London (which does a good deal of currency trading) and Switzerland (which supplies a great deal of investment capital to other nations).

• *Booking centres* are usually located on small island nations or territories with favourable tax and/or secrecy laws. Little financial activity takes place here. Rather, funds simply pass through on their way to large operational centres. Booking centres are typically home to offshore branches of domestic banks that use them merely as bookkeeping facilities to record tax and currency-exchange information. Some important booking centres are the Cayman Islands and the Bahamas in the Caribbean; Gibraltar, Monaco, and the Channel Islands in Europe; Bahrain and Dubai in the Middle East; and Singapore in Southeast Asia.

Quick Study

1. What are the three main purposes of the *international capital market*? Explain each briefly.

2. Identify the factors expanding the international capital market. What is meant by the term *securitization*?

3. What is an *offshore financial centre*? Explain its appeal to businesses.

Global banking giant HSBC recently added Dubai, United Arab Emirates, to its list of key offshore banking centres. The Dubai office will serve customers from the Middle East, North Africa, and Pakistan. HSBC chose Dubai as its offshore centre for Shariah-compliant products and services (those complying with Islamic law). HSBC Bank International is based in Jersey, Channel Islands, and has four other offshore centres located in Jersey, Hong Kong, Miami, and Singapore. Here, employees work in the dealing room of Standard Chartered Bank in Dubai, UAE.

Source: © Ali Haider/epa/Corbis.

Main Components of the International Capital Market

Now that we have covered the basic features of the international capital market, let's take a closer look at its main components: the international bond, international equity, and Eurocurrency markets.

International Bond Market

international bond market
Market consisting of all bonds sold by issuing companies, governments, or other organizations outside their own countries.

The **international bond market** consists of all bonds sold by issuing companies, governments, or other organizations *outside their own countries*. Issuing bonds internationally is an increasingly popular way to obtain needed funding. Typical buyers include medium-sized to large banks, pension funds, mutual funds, and governments with excess financial reserves. Large international banks typically manage the sales of new international bond issues for corporate and government clients.

Eurobond
Bond issued outside the country in whose currency it is denominated.

TYPES OF INTERNATIONAL BONDS   One instrument used by companies to access the international bond market is called a **Eurobond**—a bond issued outside the country in whose currency it is denominated. In other words, a bond issued by a Venezuelan company, denominated in Canadian dollars, and sold in Britain, France, Germany, and the Netherlands (but not available in Canada or to its residents) is a Eurobond. Because this Eurobond is denominated in Canadian dollars, the Venezuelan borrower both receives the loan and makes its interest payments in Canadian dollars.

Eurobonds are popular (accounting for 75 to 80 percent of all international bonds) because the governments of countries in which they are sold do not regulate them. The absence of regulation substantially reduces the cost of issuing a bond. Unfortunately, it increases its risk level—a fact that may discourage some potential investors. The traditional markets for Eurobonds are Europe and North America.

foreign bond
Bond sold outside the borrower's country and denominated in the currency of the country in which it is sold.

Companies also obtain financial resources by issuing so-called **foreign bonds**—bonds sold outside the borrower's country and denominated in the currency of the country in which they are sold. For example, a yen-denominated bond issued by the German carmaker BMW in Japan's domestic bond market is a foreign bond. Foreign bonds account for about 20 to 25 percent of all international bonds.

Foreign bonds are subject to the same rules and regulations as the domestic bonds of the country in which they are issued. Countries typically require issuers to meet certain regulatory requirements and to disclose details about company activities, owners, and upper management. Thus BMW's *samurai bonds* (the name for foreign bonds issued in Japan) would need to meet the same disclosure and other regulatory requirements that Toyota's bonds in Japan must meet. Foreign bonds in Canada are called *maple bonds,* and those in the United Kingdom are called *bulldog bonds*. Foreign bonds issued and traded in Asia outside Japan (and normally denominated in dollars) are called *dragon bonds.*

INTEREST RATES: A DRIVING FORCE   Today, low interest rates (the cost of borrowing) are fuelling growth in the international bond market. Low interest rates in developed nations are resulting from low levels of inflation, but they also mean that investors earn little interest on bonds issued by governments and companies in domestic markets. So banks, pension funds, and mutual funds are seeking higher returns in the newly industrialized and developing nations, where higher interest payments reflect the greater risk of the bonds. At the same time, corporate and government borrowers in developing countries badly need capital to invest in corporate expansion plans and public works projects.

This situation raises an interesting question: How can investors who are seeking higher returns and borrowers who are seeking to pay lower interest rates both come out ahead? The answer, at least in part, lies in the international bond market:

- By issuing bonds in the international bond market, borrowers from newly industrialized and developing countries can borrow money from other nations where interest rates are lower.
- By the same token, investors in developed countries buy bonds in newly industrialized and developing nations in order to obtain higher returns on their investments (although they also accept greater risk).

Despite the attraction of the international bond market, many emerging markets see the need to develop their own national markets because of volatility in the global currency market. A currency whose value is rapidly declining can wreak havoc on companies that earn profits in, say, Indonesian rupiahs but must pay off debts in dollars. Why? A drop in a country's currency forces borrowers to shell out more local currency to pay off the interest owed on bonds denominated in an unaffected currency.

International Equity Market

The **international equity market** consists of all stocks bought and sold outside the issuer's home country. Companies and governments frequently sell shares in the international equity market. Buyers include other companies, banks, mutual funds, pension funds, and individual investors. The stock exchanges that list the greatest number of companies from outside their own borders are Frankfurt, London, and New York. Large international companies frequently list their stocks on several national exchanges simultaneously and sometimes offer new stock issues only outside their country's borders. Four factors are responsible for much of the past growth in the international equity market.

international equity market
Market consisting of all stocks bought and sold outside the issuer's home country.

SPREAD OF PRIVATIZATION   As many countries abandoned central planning and socialist-style economics, the pace of privatization accelerated worldwide. A single privatization often places billions of dollars of new equity on stock markets. When the government of Peru sold its 26 percent share of the national telephone company, Telefonica del Peru (www.telefonica.com.pe), it raised $1.2 billion. Of the total value of the sale, 48 percent was sold in the United States, 26 percent to other international investors, and another 26 percent to domestic retail and institutional investors in Peru.

ECONOMIC GROWTH IN EMERGING MARKETS   Continued economic growth in emerging markets is contributing to growth in the international equity market. Companies based in these economies require greater investment as they succeed and grow. The international equity market becomes a major source of funding because only a limited supply of funds is available in these nations.

ACTIVITY OF INVESTMENT BANKS   Global banks facilitate the sale of a company's stock worldwide by bringing together sellers and large potential buyers. Increasingly, investment banks are searching for investors outside the national market in which a company is headquartered.

In fact, this method of raising funds is becoming more common than listing a company's shares on another country's stock exchange.

ADVENT OF CYBERMARKETS The automation of stock exchanges is encouraging growth in the international equity market. The term *cybermarkets* denotes stock markets that have no central geographic locations. Rather, they consist of global trading activities conducted on the Internet. Cybermarkets (consisting of supercomputers, high-speed data lines, satellite uplinks, and individual personal computers) match buyers and sellers in nanoseconds. They allow companies to list their stocks worldwide through an electronic medium in which trading takes place 24 hours a day.

Eurocurrency Market

Eurocurrency market
Market consisting of all the world's currencies (referred to as "Eurocurrency") that are banked outside their countries of origin.

All the world's currencies that are banked outside their countries of origin are referred to as *Eurocurrency* and trade on the **Eurocurrency market**. Thus Canadian dollars deposited in a bank in Tokyo are called *Euro-Canadian dollars,* and British pounds deposited in New York are called *Europounds*. Japanese yen deposited in Frankfurt are called *Euroyen*, and so forth.

Because the Eurocurrency market is characterized by very large transactions, only the very largest companies, banks, and governments are typically involved. Deposits originate primarily from four sources:

- Governments with excess funds generated by a prolonged trade surplus
- Commercial banks with large deposits of excess currency
- International companies with large amounts of excess cash
- Extremely wealthy individuals

Eurocurrency originated in Europe during the 1950s—hence the "Euro" prefix. Governments across Eastern Europe feared they might forfeit dollar deposits made in US banks if US citizens were to file claims against them. To protect their dollar reserves, they deposited them in banks across Europe. Banks in the United Kingdom began lending these dollars to finance international trade deals, and banks in other countries (including Canada and Japan) followed suit. The Eurocurrency market is valued at around $6 trillion, with London accounting for about 20 percent of all deposits. Other important markets include Canada, the Caribbean, Hong Kong, and Singapore. The exact size of the Eurocurrency market is difficult to determine, because it depends on whether the gross or net size is being discussed. When measuring the market in net size, transfers between banks are eliminated.

APPEAL OF THE EUROCURRENCY MARKET Governments tend to strictly regulate commercial banking activities in their own currencies within their borders. For example, they often force banks to pay deposit insurance to a central bank, where they must keep a certain portion of all deposits "on reserve" in non–interest-bearing accounts. Although such restrictions protect investors, they add costs to banking operations. By contrast, the main appeal of the Eurocurrency market is the complete absence of regulation, which lowers the cost of banking. The large size of transactions in this market further reduces transaction costs. Thus banks can charge borrowers less, pay investors more, and still earn healthy profits.

interbank interest rates
Interest rates that the world's largest banks charge one another for loans.

Interbank interest rates—rates that the world's largest banks charge one another for loans—are determined in the free market. The most commonly quoted rate of this type in the Eurocurrency market is the *London Interbank Offer Rate (LIBOR)*—the interest rate that London banks charge other large banks that borrow Eurocurrency. The *London Interbank Bid Rate (LIBID)* is the interest rate offered by London banks to large investors for Eurocurrency deposits.

An unappealing feature of the Eurocurrency market is greater risk; government regulations that protect depositors in national markets are nonexistent here. Despite the greater risk of default, however, Eurocurrency transactions are fairly safe because the banks involved are large with well-established reputations.

Foreign Exchange Market

foreign exchange market
Market in which currencies are bought and sold and their prices are determined.

Unlike domestic transactions, international transactions involve the currencies of two or more nations. To exchange one currency for another in international transactions, companies rely on a mechanism called the **foreign exchange market**—a market in which currencies are bought and sold and their prices are determined. Financial institutions convert one currency into another at a specific **exchange rate**—the rate at which one currency is exchanged for another. Rates depend on the size of the transaction, the trader conducting it, general economic conditions, and sometimes government mandate.

exchange rate
Rate at which one currency is exchanged for another.

In many ways, the foreign exchange market is like the markets for commodities such as cotton, wheat, and copper. The forces of supply and demand determine currency prices, and transactions are conducted through a process of *bid* and *ask quotes*. If someone asks for the current exchange rate of a certain currency, the bank does not know whether it is dealing with a prospective buyer or seller. Thus it quotes two rates: The *bid quote* is the price at which it will buy, and the *ask quote* is the price at which it will sell. For example, say that the British pound is quoted in Canadian dollars at $1.5375. The bank may then bid $1.5373 to *buy* British pounds and offer to *sell* them at $1.5377. The difference between the two rates is the *bid–ask spread*. Naturally, banks will buy currencies at a lower price than they sell them and earn their profits from the bid–ask spread.

Functions of the Foreign Exchange Market

The foreign exchange market is not really a source of corporate finance. Rather, it facilitates corporate financial activities and international transactions. Investors use the foreign exchange market for four main reasons.

CURRENCY CONVERSION   Companies use the foreign exchange market to convert one currency into another. Suppose a Malaysian company sells a large number of computers to a customer in France. The French customer wants to pay for the computers in euros, the European Union currency, whereas the Malaysian company wants to be paid in its own ringgit. How do the two parties resolve this dilemma? They turn to banks that will exchange the currencies for them.

Companies also must convert to local currencies when they undertake foreign direct investment. Later, when a firm's international subsidiary earns a profit and the company wants to return some of it to the home country, it must convert the local money into the home currency.

CURRENCY HEDGING   The practice of insuring against potential losses that result from adverse changes in exchange rates is called **currency hedging**. International companies commonly use hedging for one of two purposes:

currency hedging
Practice of insuring against potential losses that result from adverse changes in exchange rates.

1. To lessen the risk associated with international transfers of funds
2. To protect themselves in credit transactions in which there is a time lag between billing and receipt of payment

Suppose a South Korean carmaker has a subsidiary in Britain. The parent company in Korea knows that in 30 days—say, on February 1—its British subsidiary will be sending it a payment in British pounds. Because the parent company is concerned about the value of that payment in South Korean *won* a month in the future, it wants to insure against the possibility that the pound's value will fall over that period—meaning, of course, that it will receive less money. Therefore, on January 2, the parent company contracts with a financial institution, such as a bank, to exchange the payment in one month at an agreed-upon exchange rate specified on January 2. In this way, as of January 2, the Korean company knows exactly how many *won* the payment will be worth on February 1.

CURRENCY ARBITRAGE   **Currency arbitrage** is the instantaneous purchase and sale of a currency in different markets for profit. Suppose a currency trader in Toronto notices that the value of the European Union euro is lower in Tokyo than it is in Toronto. The trader can buy euros in Tokyo, sell them in Toronto, and earn a profit on the difference. High-tech communication and trading systems allow the entire transaction to occur within seconds. But note that if the difference between the value of the euro in Tokyo and the value of the euro in Toronto is not greater than the cost of conducting the transaction, the trade is not worth making.

currency arbitrage
Instantaneous purchase and sale of a currency in different markets for profit.

Currency arbitrage is a common activity among experienced traders of foreign exchange, very large investors, and companies in the arbitrage business. Firms whose profits are generated primarily by another economic activity, such as retailing or manufacturing, take part in currency arbitrage only if they have very large sums of cash on hand.

interest arbitrage

Profit-motivated purchase and sale of interest-paying securities denominated in different currencies.

Interest Arbitrage **Interest arbitrage** is the profit-motivated purchase and sale of interest-paying securities denominated in different currencies. Companies use interest arbitrage to find better interest rates abroad than those that are available in their home countries. The securities involved in such transactions include government treasury bills, corporate and government bonds, and even bank deposits. Suppose a trader notices that the interest rates paid on bank deposits in Mexico are higher than those paid in Sydney, Australia (after adjusting for exchange rates). He can convert Australian dollars to Mexican pesos and deposit the money in a Mexican bank account for, say, one year. At the end of the year, he converts the pesos back into Australian dollars and earns more in interest than the same money would have earned had it remained on deposit in an Australian bank.

currency speculation

Purchase or sale of a currency with the expectation that its value will change and generate a profit.

CURRENCY SPECULATION **Currency speculation** is the purchase or sale of a currency with the expectation that its value will change and generate a profit. The shift in value might be expected to occur suddenly or over a longer period. The foreign exchange trader may bet that a currency's price will go either up or down in the future. Suppose a trader in London believes that the value of the Japanese yen will increase over the next three months. She buys yen with pounds at today's current price, intending to sell them in 90 days. If the price of yen rises in that time, she earns a profit; if it falls, she takes a loss. Speculation is much riskier than arbitrage because the value, or price, of currencies is quite volatile and is affected by many factors. Similar to arbitrage, currency speculation is commonly the realm of foreign exchange specialists rather than the managers of firms engaged in other endeavours. To learn more about how speculators can influence the value of a currency, read David Parkinson's article "Speculators Turn Against the Canadian Dollar" published in *The Globe and Mail*.[4]

Quick Study

1. Describe the *international bond market*. What single factor is most responsible for fuelling its growth?
2. What is the *international equity market*? Identify the factors responsible for its expansion.
3. Describe the *Eurocurrency market*. What is its main appeal?
4. For what four reasons do investors use the foreign exchange market?

Foreign exchange brokerage workers in Tokyo, Japan, dress in traditional Japanese kimonos for the first trading day of the year. Around $4 trillion worth of currency is traded on global foreign exchange markets every day.

Source: © Eriko Sugita/Reuters/Corbis.

How the Foreign Exchange Market Works

Because of the importance of foreign exchange to trade and investment, businesspeople must understand how currencies are quoted in the foreign exchange market. Managers must know what financial instruments are available to help them protect the profits earned by their international business activities. They must also be aware of government restrictions that may be imposed on the convertibility of currencies and know how to work around these and other obstacles.

Quoting Currencies

There are two components to every quoted exchange rate: the quoted currency and the base currency. If an exchange rate quotes the number of Japanese yen needed to buy one Canadian dollar (¥/$), the yen is the **quoted currency** and the Canadian dollar is the **base currency**. When you designate any exchange rate, the quoted currency is always the *numerator* and the base currency is the *denominator*. For example, if you were given a yen/cad exchange rate quote of 90/1 (meaning that 90 yen are needed to buy one Canadian dollar), the numerator is 90 and the denominator is 1. We can also designate this rate as ¥90/CAD$.

CALCULATING PERCENT CHANGE Businesspeople and foreign exchange traders track currency values over time as measured by exchange rates because changes in currency values can benefit or harm current and future international transactions. **Exchange-rate risk (foreign exchange risk)** is the risk of adverse changes in exchange rates. Managers develop strategies to minimize this risk by tracking percent changes in exchange rates.

CROSS RATES International transactions between two currencies other than the US dollar often use the dollar as a vehicle currency. For example, a retail buyer of merchandise in the Netherlands might convert its euros (recall that the Netherlands uses the European Union currency) to US dollars and then pay its Japanese supplier in US dollars. The Japanese supplier may then take those US dollars and convert them to Japanese yen. This process was more common years ago, when fewer currencies were freely convertible and when the United States greatly dominated world trade. Today, a Japanese supplier may want payment in euros. In this case, both the Japanese and the Dutch companies need to know the exchange rate between their respective currencies. To find this rate using their respective exchange rates with the US dollar, we calculate what is called a **cross rate**—an exchange rate calculated using two other exchange rates.

Cross rates between two currencies can be calculated using both currencies' indirect or direct exchange rates with a third currency.

SPOT RATES All the exchange rates we've discussed so far are called **spot rates**—exchange rates that require delivery of the traded currency within two business days. Exchange of the two currencies is said to occur "on the spot," and the **spot market** is the market for currency transactions at spot rates. The spot market assists companies in performing any one of three functions:

1. Converting income generated from sales abroad into their home-country currency
2. Converting funds into the currency of an international supplier
3. Converting funds into the currency of a country in which they wish to invest

BUY AND SELL RATES The spot rate is available only for trades worth millions of dollars. That is why it is available only to banks and foreign exchange brokers. If you are travelling to another country and want to exchange currencies at your bank before departing, you will not be quoted the spot rate. Rather, banks and other institutions will give you a *buy rate* (the exchange rate at which the bank will buy a currency) and an *ask rate* (the rate at which it will sell a currency). In other words, you will receive what we described when introducing the foreign exchange market as *bid* and *ask* quotes. These rates reflect the amounts that large currency traders are charging, plus a mark-up.

For example, suppose you are taking a business trip to Spain and need to buy some euros. The bank will quote you exchange rate terms, such as $1.268/78 per €, which means that the bank will buy Canadian dollars at the rate of $1.268/€ and sell them at the rate of $1.278/€.

quoted currency
The numerator in a quoted exchange rate, or the currency with which another currency is to be purchased.

base currency
The denominator in a quoted exchange rate, or the currency that is to be purchased with another currency.

exchange-rate risk (foreign exchange risk)
Risk of adverse changes in exchange rates.

cross rate
Exchange rate calculated using two other exchange rates.

spot rate
Exchange rate requiring delivery of the traded currency within two business days.

spot market
Market for currency transactions at spot rates.

Forward Exchange Rates

forward exchange rate
Exchange rate at which two parties agree to exchange currencies on a specified future date.

forward market
Market for currency transactions at forward exchange rates.

When a company knows that it will need a certain amount of foreign currency on a certain future date, it can exchange currencies using a **forward exchange rate**—an exchange rate at which two parties agree to exchange currencies on a specified future date. Forward exchange rates represent the expectations of currency traders and bankers regarding a currency's future spot rate. Reflected in these expectations are a country's present and future economic conditions (including inflation rate, national debt, taxes, trade balance, and economic growth rate) as well as its social and political situation. The **forward market** is the market for currency transactions at forward exchange rates.

To insure themselves against unfavourable exchange-rate changes, companies commonly turn to the forward market. It can be used for all types of transactions that require future payment in other currencies, including credit sales or purchases, interest receipts or payments on investments or loans, and dividend payments to stockholders in other countries. But not all nations' currencies trade in the forward market, such as countries experiencing high inflation or currencies not in demand on international financial markets.

forward contract
Contract that requires the exchange of an agreed-upon amount of a currency on an agreed-upon date at a specific exchange rate.

derivative
Financial instrument whose value derives from other commodities or financial instruments.

FORWARD CONTRACTS Suppose a Brazilian bicycle maker imports parts from a Japanese supplier. Under the terms of their contract, the Brazilian importer must pay 100 million Japanese yen in 90 days. The Brazilian firm can wait until one or two days before payment is due, buy yen in the spot market, and pay the Japanese supplier. But in the 90 days between the contract date and the due date, the exchange rate will likely change. What if the value of the Brazilian real goes down? In that case, the Brazilian importer will have to pay more reais (plural of real) to get the same 100 million Japanese yen. Therefore, our importer may want to pay off the debt before the 90-day term. But what if it does not have the cash on hand? What if it needs those 90 days to collect accounts receivable from its own customers?

To decrease its exchange-rate risk, our Brazilian importer can enter into a **forward contract**—a contract that requires the exchange of an agreed-upon amount of a currency on an agreed-upon date at a specific exchange rate. Forward contracts are commonly signed for 30, 90, and 180 days into the future, but customized contracts (say, for 76 days) are possible. Note that a forward contract *requires* exchange of an agreed-upon amount of a currency on an agreed-upon date at a specific exchange rate: the bank must deliver the yen, and the Brazilian importer must buy them at the prearranged price. Forward contracts belong to a family of financial instruments called **derivatives**—instruments whose values *derive* from other commodities or financial instruments.

In our example, the Brazilian importer can use a forward contract to pay yen to its Japanese supplier in 90 days. It is always possible, of course, that in 90 days, the value of the real will be lower than its current value. But by locking in at the forward exchange rate, the Brazilian firm protects itself against the less favourable spot rate at which it would have to buy yen in 90 days. In this case, the Brazilian company protects itself from paying more to the supplier at the end of 90 days than if it were to pay at the spot rate in 90 days. Thus it protects its profit from further erosion if the spot rate becomes even more unfavourable over the next three months. Remember, too, that such a contract prevents the Brazilian importer from taking advantage of any increase in the value of the real in 90 days that would reduce what the company owed its Japanese supplier.

Swaps, Options, and Futures

In addition to forward contracts, three other types of currency instruments are used in the forward market: currency swaps, options, and futures.

currency swap
Simultaneous purchase and sale of foreign exchange for two different dates.

CURRENCY SWAPS A **currency swap** is the simultaneous purchase and sale of foreign exchange for two different dates. Currency swaps are an increasingly important component of the foreign exchange market. Suppose a Swedish carmaker imports parts from a subsidiary in Turkey. The Swedish company must pay the Turkish subsidiary in Turkish lira for the parts when they are delivered tomorrow. It also expects to receive Turkish liras for cars sold in Turkey in 90 days. Our Swedish company exchanges kronor for lira in the spot market today to pay its subsidiary. At the same time, it agrees to a forward contract to sell Turkish lira (and buy Swedish kronor) in 90 days at the quoted 90-day forward exchange rate for lira. In this way, the Swedish company uses a swap both to reduce its exchange-rate risk and to lock in the future exchange rate. In this sense, we can think of a currency swap as a more complex forward contract.

CURRENCY OPTIONS Recall that a forward contract *requires* exchange of an agreed-upon amount of a currency on an agreed-upon date at a specific exchange rate. In contrast, a **currency option** is a right, or *option*, to exchange a specific amount of a currency on a specific date at a specific rate. In other words, whereas forward contracts require parties to follow through on currency exchanges, currency options do not.

Suppose a company buys an option to purchase Swiss francs at SF1.02/$ in 30 days. If, at the end of the 30 days, the exchange rate is SF1.05/$, the company would *not* exercise its currency option. Why? It could get SF0.03 more for every dollar by exchanging at the spot rate in the currency market rather than at the stated rate of the option. Companies often use currency options to hedge against exchange-rate risk or to obtain foreign currency.

CURRENCY FUTURES CONTRACTS Similar to a currency forward contract is a **currency futures contract**—a contract requiring the exchange of a specific amount of currency on a specific date at a specific exchange rate, with all conditions fixed and not adjustable.

currency option
Right, or option, to exchange a specific amount of a currency on a specific date at a specific rate.

currency futures contract
Contract requiring the exchange of a specific amount of currency on a specific date at a specific exchange rate, with all conditions fixed and not adjustable.

Quick Study

1. Why is *exchange-rate risk* important to companies?
2. What is meant by the term *cross rate*?
3. Explain how a *spot rate* and *forward exchange rate* are used in the foreign exchange market.
4. What are the main differences between *currency swaps*, *options*, and *futures*?

How Exchange Rates Influence Business Activities

Movement in a currency's exchange rate affects the activities of both domestic and international companies. For example, exchange rates influence demand for a company's products in the global marketplace. A country with a currency that is *weak* (valued low relative to other currencies) will see a decline in the price of its exports and an increase in the price of its imports. Lower prices for the country's exports on world markets can give companies the opportunity to take market share away from companies whose products are priced high in comparison. While their national currency is weak, companies should try to expand their sales abroad to push their exports. However, companies that import products or raw materials need to employ strategies to adjust to a weak currency, such as sourcing domestically for raw materials and components, in order to lower production input costs, avoid exchange rate risk, and shorten the supply chain. These companies should also develop and expand their domestic business; the weak currency gives them a competitive advantage in price over foreign companies whose prices are high because of their relatively strong currencies.

Furthermore, a company improves profits if it sells its products in a country with a *strong* currency (one that is valued high relative to other currencies) while sourcing from a country with a weak currency. For example, if a company pays its workers and suppliers in a falling local currency and sells its products in a rising currency, the company benefits by generating revenue in the strong currency while paying expenses in the weak currency. Yet managers must take care not to view this type of price advantage as permanent because doing so can jeopardize a company's long-term competitiveness.

Exchange rates also affect the amount of profit a company earns from its international subsidiaries. The earnings of international subsidiaries are typically integrated into the parent company's financial statements *in the home currency*. Translating subsidiary earnings from a weak *host* country currency into a strong *home* currency *reduces* the amount of these earnings when stated in the home currency. Likewise, translating earnings into a weak home currency increases stated earnings in the home currency.

devaluation
Intentionally lowering the value of a nation's currency.

revaluation
Intentionally raising the value of a nation's currency.

The intentional lowering of the value of a currency by the nation's government is called **devaluation**. The reverse, the intentional raising of its value by the nation's government, is called **revaluation**. These concepts are not to be confused with the terms *weak currency* and *strong currency*, although their effects are similar.

Devaluation lowers the price of a country's exports on world markets and increases the price of its imports because the value of the country's currency is now lower on world markets. Thus, a government might devalue its currency to give its domestic companies an edge over competition from other countries. But devaluation reduces the buying power of consumers in the nation. It can also allow inefficiencies to persist in domestic companies because there is now less pressure to be concerned with production costs. Revaluation has the opposite effects: it increases the price of exports and reduces the price of imports.

Desire for Stability and Predictability

Unfavourable movements in exchange rates can be costly for domestic and international companies alike. Although methods do exist for insuring against potentially adverse movements in exchange rates, most of these are too expensive for small and medium-sized businesses. Moreover, as the unpredictability of exchange rates increases, so too does the cost of insuring against the accompanying risk. By contrast, *stable* exchange rates improve the accuracy of financial planning and make cash flow forecasts more precise.

Managers also prefer that movements in exchange rates be *predictable*. Predictable exchange rates reduce the likelihood that companies will be caught off-guard by sudden and unexpected rate changes. They also reduce the need for costly insurance (usually by currency hedging) against possible adverse movements in exchange rates. Rather than purchasing insurance, companies would be better off spending their money on more productive activities, such as developing new products or designing more efficient production methods.

Quick Study

1. Why are exchange rates important to managers' decisions?
2. Explain the difference between *devaluation* and *revaluation*.
3. Why is it desirable for exchange rates to be stable and predictable?

Forecasting Exchange Rates

Before undertaking any international business activity, managers should estimate future exchange rates and consider the impact of currency values on earnings. This section explores two distinct views regarding how accurately future exchange rates can be predicted by forward exchange rates—the rate agreed upon for foreign exchange payment at a future date. We also take a brief look at different techniques for forecasting exchange rates.

Efficient Market View

efficient market view
View that prices of financial instruments reflect all publicly available information at any given time.

A great deal of debate revolves around the issue of whether markets themselves are efficient or inefficient in forecasting exchange rates. A market is *efficient* if prices of financial instruments quickly reflect new public information made available to traders. The **efficient market view** thus holds that prices of financial instruments reflect all publicly available information at any given time. As applied to exchange rates, this means that forward exchange rates are accurate forecasts of future exchange rates.

As explained earlier in this chapter, a *forward exchange rate* reflects a market's expectations about the future values of two currencies. In an efficient currency market, forward exchange rates reflect all relevant publicly available information at any given time; they are considered the best possible predictors of exchange rates. Proponents of this view hold that there is no other publicly available information that could improve the forecast of exchange rates over that provided by forward exchange rates. To accept this view is to accept that companies do waste time and money collecting and examining information believed to affect future exchange rates. But there is always a certain amount of deviation between forward and actual exchange rates. The fact that forward exchange rates are less than perfect inspires companies to search for more accurate forecasting techniques.

Inefficient Market View

The **inefficient market view** holds that prices of financial instruments do not reflect all publicly available information. Proponents of this view believe companies can search for new pieces of information to improve forecasting. But the cost of searching for further information must not outweigh the benefits of its discovery.

Naturally, the inefficient market view is more compelling when the existence of private information is considered. Suppose a single currency trader holds privileged information regarding a future change in a nation's economic policy—information that she believes will affect its exchange rate. Because the market is unaware of this information, it is not reflected in forward exchange rates. Our trader will no doubt earn a profit by acting on her store of private information.

Now that we understand the two basic views related to market efficiency, let's look at the specific methods that companies use to forecast exchange rates.

inefficient market view
View that prices of financial instruments do not reflect all publicly available information.

Forecasting Techniques

The issue of whether markets are efficient or inefficient forecasters of exchange rates leads to the question of whether experts can improve on the forecasts of forward exchange rates in *either* an efficient or inefficient market. As we have already seen, some analysts believe that forecasts of exchange rates can be improved by uncovering information not reflected in forward exchange rates. In fact, companies exist to provide exactly this type of service. There are two main forecasting techniques based on this belief in the value of added information—fundamental analysis and technical analysis.

FUNDAMENTAL ANALYSIS **Fundamental analysis** uses statistical models based on fundamental economic indicators to forecast exchange rates. These models are often quite complex, with many variations reflecting different possible economic conditions. These models include economic variables such as inflation, interest rates, money supply, tax rates, and government spending. Such analyses also often consider a country's balance-of-payments situation (see Chapter 7) and its tendency to intervene in markets to influence the value of its currency.

fundamental analysis
Technique that uses statistical models based on fundamental economic indicators to forecast exchange rates.

TECHNICAL ANALYSIS Another method of forecasting exchange rates is **technical analysis**— a technique that uses charts of past trends in currency prices and other factors to forecast exchange rates. Using highly statistical models and charts of past data trends, analysts examine conditions that prevailed during changes in exchange rates, and they try to estimate the timing, magnitude, and direction of future changes. Many forecasters combine the techniques of both fundamental and technical analyses to arrive at potentially more accurate forecasts.

technical analysis
Technique that uses charts of past trends in currency prices and other factors to forecast exchange rates.

Difficulties of Forecasting

The business of forecasting exchange rates is a rapidly growing industry. This trend seems to provide evidence that a growing number of people believe it is possible to improve on the forecasts of exchange rates embodied in forward exchange rates. Difficulties of forecasting remain, however. Despite highly sophisticated statistical techniques in the hands of well-trained analysts, forecasting is not a pure science. Few, if any, forecasts are ever completely accurate because of unexpected events that occur throughout the forecast period.

Beyond the problems associated with the data used by these techniques, failings can be traced to the human element involved in forecasting. For example, people might miscalculate the importance of economic news becoming available to the market, placing too much emphasis on some elements and ignoring others.

Quick Study

1. What are the two market views regarding exchange-rate forecasting? Explain each briefly.
2. Identify the two main methods of forecasting exchange rates. What are the difficulties of forecasting?

Foreign Exchange Market Today

The foreign exchange market is actually an electronic network that connects the world's major financial centres. In turn, each of these centres is a network of foreign exchange traders, currency trading banks, and investment firms. The daily trading volume on the foreign exchange market (comprising currency swaps and spot and forward contracts) had grown by mid-2010 to an unprecedented $4.0 trillion—an amount greater than the yearly gross domestic product of many small nations.[5] Several major trading centres and several currencies dominate the foreign exchange market.

Trading Centres

Most of the world's major cities participate in trading on the foreign exchange market. But in recent years, just three countries have come to account for more than half of all global currency trading: the United Kingdom, the United States, and Japan. Accordingly, most of this trading takes place in the financial capitals of London, New York, and Tokyo.

London dominates the foreign exchange market for historic and geographic reasons. The United Kingdom was once the world's largest trading nation. British merchants needed to exchange currencies of different nations, and London naturally assumed the role of financial trading centre. London quickly came to dominate the market and still does so because of its location halfway between North America and Asia. A key factor is its time zone. Because of differences in time zones, London is opening for business as markets in Asia close trading for the day. When New York opens for trading in the morning, trading is beginning to wind down in London.

Figure 9.1 shows why it is possible to trade foreign exchange 24 hours a day (except weekends and major holidays). Exchanges in at least one of the three major centres (London, New York, and Tokyo) keep the market open for 22 hours a day. Trading does not stop during the two hours these exchanges are closed because other trading centres (including San Francisco and Sydney, Australia) remain open. Also, most large banks active in foreign exchange employ overnight traders to ensure continuous trading. For example, RBC Royal Bank offers a full range of foreign exchange services to corporate and consumer clients.[6]

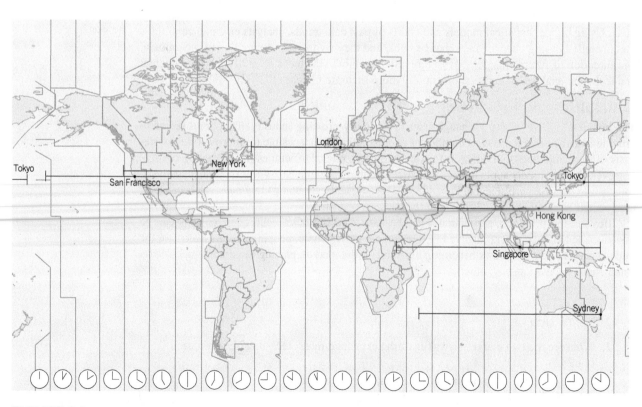

FIGURE 9.1

Financial Trading Centres by Time Zone

| Global Manager's Briefcase | Managing Foreign Exchange |

- **Match Needs to Providers.** Analyze your foreign exchange needs and the range of service providers available. Find a provider that offers the transactions you undertake in the currencies you need, and consolidate repetitive transfers. Many businesspeople naturally look to local bankers when they need to transfer funds abroad, but this may not be the cheapest or best choice. A mix of service providers sometimes offers the best solution.

- **Work with the Majors.** Money-centre banks (those located in financial centres) that participate directly in the foreign exchange market can have cost and service advantages over local banks. Dealing directly with a large trading institution is often more cost effective than dealing with a local bank because it avoids the additional mark-up that the local bank charges for its services.

- **Consolidate to Save.** Save money by timing your international payments to consolidate multiple transfers into one large transaction. Open a local currency account abroad against which you can write drafts if your company makes multiple smaller payments in the same currency. Consider allowing foreign receivables to accumulate in an interest-bearing account locally until you repatriate them in a lump sum to reduce service fees.

- **Get the Best Deal Possible.** If your foreign exchange activity is substantial, develop relationships with two or more money-centre banks to get the best rates. Also, monitor the rates your company gets over time, as some banks raise rates if you're not shopping around. Obtain real-time market rates provided by firms like Reuters and Bloomberg.

- **Embrace Information Technology.** Every time an employee phones, e-mails, or faxes in a transaction, human error could delay getting funds where and when your company needs them. Embrace information technology in your business's international wire transfers and drafts. Automated software programs available from specialized service providers reduce the potential for errors while speeding the execution of transfers.

Important Currencies

Although the United Kingdom is the major location of foreign exchange trading, the US dollar is the currency that dominates the foreign exchange market. Because the US dollar is so widely used in world trade, it is considered a **vehicle currency**—a currency used as an intermediary to convert funds between two other currencies. The currencies most often involved in currency transactions are the US dollar, European Union euro, Japanese yen, and British pound.

vehicle currency
Currency used as an intermediary to convert funds between two other currencies.

OVER-THE-COUNTER MARKET   The **over-the-counter (OTC) market** is a decentralized exchange encompassing a global computer network of foreign exchange traders and other market participants. All foreign exchange transactions can be performed in the OTC market, where the major players are large financial institutions.

The over-the-counter market has grown rapidly because it offers distinct benefits for business. It allows businesspeople to search freely for the institution that provides the best (lowest) price for conducting a transaction. It also offers opportunities for designing customized transactions. For additional ways companies can become more adept in their foreign exchange activities, see this chapter's Global Manager's Briefcase, titled "Managing Foreign Exchange."

over-the-counter (OTC) market
Decentralized exchange encompassing a global computer network of foreign exchange traders and other market participants.

Currency Convertibility

Our discussion of the foreign exchange market so far assumes that all currencies can be readily converted to another in the foreign exchange market. A **convertible (hard) currency** is traded freely in the foreign exchange market, with its price determined by the forces of supply and demand. Countries that allow full convertibility are those that are in strong financial positions and have adequate reserves of foreign currencies. Such countries have no reason to fear that people will sell their own currency for that of another. Still, many newly industrialized and developing countries do not permit the free convertibility of their currencies. Let's now take a look at why governments place restrictions on the convertibility of currencies and how they do it.

convertible (hard) currency
Currency that trades freely in the foreign exchange market, with its price determined by the forces of supply and demand.

Goals of Currency Restriction

Governments impose currency restrictions to achieve several goals. One goal is to preserve a country's reserve of hard currencies with which to repay debts owed to other nations.

Developed nations, emerging markets, and some countries that export natural resources tend to have the greatest amounts of foreign exchange. Without sufficient reserves (liquidity), a country could default on its loans and thereby discourage future investment flows. This is precisely what happened to Argentina several years ago when the country defaulted on its international public debt.

A second goal of currency restriction is to preserve hard currencies to pay for imports and to finance trade deficits. Recall from Chapter 6 that a country runs a trade deficit when the value of its imports exceeds the value of its exports. Currency restrictions help governments maintain inventories of foreign currencies with which to pay for such trade imbalances. They also make importing more difficult because local companies cannot obtain foreign currency to pay for imports. The resulting reduction in imports directly improves the country's trade balance.

A third goal is to protect a currency from speculators. For example, in the wake of the Asian financial crisis years ago, some Southeast Asian nations considered controlling their currencies to limit the damage done by economic downturns. Malaysia stemmed the outflow of foreign money by preventing local investors from converting their Malaysian holdings into other currencies. Although the move also curtailed currency speculation, it effectively cut off Malaysia from investors elsewhere in the world.

A fourth (less common) goal is to keep resident individuals and businesses from investing in other nations. These policies can generate more rapid economic growth in a country by forcing investment to remain at home. Unfortunately, although this might work in the short term, it normally slows long-term economic growth. The reason is that there is no guarantee that domestic funds held in the home country will be invested there. Instead, they might be saved or even spent on consumption. Ironically, increased consumption can mean further increases in imports, making the balance-of-trade deficit even worse.

Policies for Restricting Currencies

Certain government policies are frequently used to restrict currency convertibility. Governments can require that all foreign exchange transactions be performed at or approved by the country's central bank. They can also require import licences for some or all import transactions. These licences help the government control the amount of foreign currency leaving the country.

Some governments implement systems of *multiple exchange rates*, specifying a higher exchange rate on the importation of certain goods or on imports from certain countries. The government can thus reduce importation while ensuring that important goods still enter the country. It also can use such a policy to target the goods of countries with which it is running a trade deficit.

Other governments issue *import deposit requirements* that require businesses to deposit certain percentages of their foreign exchange funds in special accounts before being granted import licences. In addition, *quantity restrictions* limit the amount of foreign currency that residents can take out of the home country when travelling to other countries as tourists, students, or medical patients.

countertrade

Practice of selling goods or services that are paid for, in whole or in part, with other goods or services.

COUNTERTRADE   Finally, one way to get around national restrictions on currency convertibility is **countertrade**—the practice of selling goods or services that are paid for, in whole or in part, with other goods or services. One simple form of countertrade is a *barter* transaction, in which goods are exchanged for others of equal value. Parties exchange goods and then sell them in world markets for hard currency. For example, Cuba once exchanged $60 million worth of sugar for cereals, pasta, and vegetable oils from the Italian firm Italgrani. And Boeing (www.boeing.com) has sold aircraft to Saudi Arabia in return for oil. We detail the many different forms of countertrade in Chapter 11.

Quick Study

1. What are the world's main foreign exchange trading centres? Identify the currencies most used in the foreign exchange market.
2. What are the reasons for restrictions on currency conversion?
3. Identify policies governments use to restrict currency conversion.

Well-functioning financial markets are essential to conducting international business. International financial markets supply companies with the mechanism they require to exchange currencies, and more. Here we focus only on the main implications of these markets for international companies.

International Capital Market and Businesses

The international capital market joins borrowers and lenders in different national capital markets. A company unable to obtain funds in its own nation may use the international capital market to obtain financing elsewhere and allow the firm to undertake an otherwise impossible project. This option can be especially important for firms in countries with small or emerging capital markets.

Similar to the prices of any other commodity, the "price" of money is determined by supply and demand. If its supply increases, its price (in the form of interest rates) falls. The international capital market opens up additional sources of financing for companies, possibly financing projects previously regarded as not feasible. The international capital market also expands lending opportunities, which reduces risk for lenders by allowing them to spread their money over a greater number of debt and equity instruments and to benefit from the fact that securities markets do not move up and down in tandem.

International Financial Market and Businesses

Companies must convert to local currencies when they undertake foreign direct investment. Later, when a firm's international subsidiary earns a profit and the company wishes to return profits to the home country, it must convert the local money into the home currency. The prevailing exchange rate at the time profits are exchanged influences the amount of the ultimate profit or loss.

This raises an important aspect of international financial markets—fluctuation. International companies can use hedging in foreign exchange markets to lessen the risk associated with international transfers of funds and to protect themselves in credit transactions in which there is a time lag between billing and receipt of payment. Some firms also take part in currency arbitrage if there are times during which they have very large sums of cash on hand. Companies can also use interest arbitrage to find better interest rates abroad than those available in their home countries.

Businesspeople are also interested in tracking currency values over time because changes in currency values affect their international transactions. Profits earned by companies that import products for resale are influenced by the exchange rate between their currency and that of the nation from which they import. Managers who understand that changes in these currencies' values affect the profitability of their international business activities can develop strategies to minimize risk.

Chapter Summary

1. Discuss the purposes, development, and financial centres of the international capital market.
   - The international capital market is meant to (1) expand the supply of capital for borrowers, (2) lower interest rates for borrowers, and (3) lower risk for lenders.
   - Growth in the international capital market is due mainly to (1) advances in *information technology*, (2) *deregulation* of capital markets, and (3) innovation in *financial instruments*.
   - London (UK), New York (US), and Tokyo (Japan) are the world's most important financial centres.
   - *Offshore financial centres* handle less business but have few regulations and few, if any, taxes.
2. Describe the international bond, international equity, and Eurocurrency markets.
   - The *international bond market* consists of all bonds sold by issuers outside their own countries.
   - It is growing as investors in developed markets search for higher rates from borrowers in emerging markets and vice versa.
   - The *international equity market* consists of all stocks bought and sold outside the home country of the issuing company.
   - Four factors driving growth in international equity are (1) privatization, (2) greater issuance of stock by companies in emerging and developing nations, (3) greater international reach of investment banks, and (4) global electronic trading.
   - The *Eurocurrency market* consists of all the world's currencies banked outside their countries of origin; its appeal is the lack of government regulation and lower cost of borrowing.

3. Discuss the four primary functions of the foreign exchange market.
   - The *foreign exchange market* is the market in which currencies are bought and sold, and in which currency prices are determined.
   - One function of the foreign exchange market is that individuals, companies, and governments use it, directly or indirectly, to *convert* one currency into another.
   - Second, it is used as a hedging device to *insure against* adverse changes in exchange rates.
   - Third, it is used to *earn a profit* from the instantaneous purchase and sale of a currency (arbitrage) or other interest-paying security in different markets.
   - Fourth, it is used to *speculate* about a change in the value of a currency and thereby earn a profit.

4. Understand how currencies are quoted and the different rates given.
   - When quoting currencies, the base currency is the currency that is to be purchased with another currency.
   - Exchange rates between two currencies can also be found using their respective exchange rates with a common currency; the resulting rate is called a *cross rate*.
   - An exchange rate that requires delivery of the traded currency within two business days is called a *spot rate*.
   - The *forward exchange rate* is the rate at which two parties agree to exchange currencies on a specified future date; it represents the market's expectation of a currency's future value.

5. Explain how exchange rates influence the activities of domestic and international companies.
   - When a country's currency is *weak* (valued low relative to other currencies), the price of its exports on world markets declines (making exports more appealing on world markets) and the price of imports rises. A *strong* currency has the opposite effects.
   - A company can improve profits if it sells in a country with a *strong* currency (one that is valued high relative to other currencies) while paying workers at home in its own weak currency.
   - The intentional lowering of a currency's value by the nation's government is called *devaluation*; this lowers the price of a country's exports on world markets and increases the price of imports.
   - The intentional raising of a currency's value by the nation's government is called *revaluation*; this increases the price of exports and reduces the price of imports.
   - Translating subsidiary earnings from a weak *host* country currency into a strong *home* currency *reduces* the amount of these earnings when stated in the home currency, and vice versa.

6. Describe the primary methods of forecasting exchange rates.
   - A *forward exchange rate* is the rate agreed upon for foreign exchange payment at a future date.
   - The *efficient market view* says that prices of financial instruments reflect all publicly available information at any given time; meaning forward exchange rates accurately forecast future exchange rates.
   - The *inefficient market view* says that prices of financial instruments do not reflect all publicly available information, meaning forecasts can be improved by information not reflected in forward exchange rates.
   - One forecasting technique based on a belief in the value of added information is *fundamental analysis*, which uses statistical models based on fundamental economic indicators to forecast exchange rates.
   - A second forecasting technique is *technical analysis*, which employs charts of past trends in currency prices and other factors to forecast exchange rates.

7. Identify the main instruments of the foreign exchange market.
   - A *forward contract* requires the exchange of an agreed-upon amount of a currency on an agreed-upon date at a specific exchange rate.
   - A *currency swap* is the simultaneous purchase and sale of foreign exchange for two different dates.
   - A *currency option* is the right to exchange a specific amount of a currency on a specific date at a specific rate; it is sometimes used to acquire a needed currency.
   - A *currency futures contract* requires the exchange of a specific amount of currency on a specific date at a specific exchange rate (no terms are negotiable).

8. Explain why and how governments restrict currency convertibility.
- One main goal of currency restriction is that a government may be attempting to preserve the country's hard currency reserves for repaying debts owed to other nations.
- Second, convertibility might be restricted to preserve hard currency to pay for needed imports or to finance a trade deficit.
- Third, restrictions might be used to protect a currency from speculators.
- Fourth, restrictions can be an attempt to keep badly needed currency from being invested abroad.
- Policies used to enforce currency restrictions include (1) government approval for currency exchange, (2) imposed import licences, (3) a system of multiple exchange rates, and (4) imposed quantity restrictions.

Key Terms

base currency 271	efficient market view 274	interest arbitrage 270
bond 263	equity 263	international bond market 266
capital market 262	Eurobond 266	international capital market 263
convertible (hard) currency 277	Eurocurrency market 268	international equity market 267
countertrade 278	exchange rate 269	liquidity 263
cross rate 271	exchange-rate risk (foreign	offshore financial centre 265
currency arbitrage 269	exchange risk) 271	over-the-counter (OTC) market 277
currency futures contract 273	foreign bond 266	quoted currency 271
currency hedging 269	foreign exchange market 268	revaluation 274
currency option 273	forward contract 272	securitization 265
currency speculation 270	forward market 272	spot market 271
currency swap 272	forward exchange rate 272	spot rate 271
debt 263	fundamental analysis 275	stock 263
derivative 272	inefficient market view 275	technical analysis 275
devaluation 274	interbank interest rates 268	vehicle currency 277

Talk It Over

1. What factors do you think are holding back the creation of a truly *global* capital market? How might a global capital market function differently from the present-day international market? (*Hint*: Some factors to consider are interest rates, currencies, regulations, and financial crises for some countries.)

2. The use of different national currencies creates a barrier to further growth in international business activity. What are the pros and cons, among companies *and* governments, of replacing national currencies with regional currencies? Do you think a global currency would be possible someday? Why or why not?

3. Governments dislike the fact that offshore financial centres facilitate money laundering. Do you think that electronic commerce makes it easier or harder to launder money and camouflage other illegal activities? Do you think offshore financial centres should be allowed to operate as freely as they do now, or do you favour regulation? Explain your answers.

Take It to the Web

1. Video Report. Visit YouTube (www.youtube.com) and type "international financial markets" in the search engine. Watch one of videos from the results of your search and then summarize it in a half-page report. Reflecting on the contents of this chapter, which aspects of international financial markets can you identify in the video? How might a company engaged in international business act on the information contained in the video?

2. Web Site Report. Visit the Web site of a financial institution or business periodical that publishes exchange rates among the world's currencies. Compare the performance of the Canadian dollar against the European Union euro since January 2012.

Between that date and now, has the Canadian dollar fallen or risen in value against the euro? What is the exchange rate between the Canadian dollar and the euro?

Conduct Web-based research, to determine what reasons lie behind the exchange rate movement between the Canadian dollar and the euro. Is the shift in the exchange rate due more to movement in the value of the Canadian dollar or the euro? Explain your answer. How has the exchange rate change affected international business activity between Canada and European nations using the euro? Be specific.

Managing an International Business Despite a Strong Loonie

Canada's loonie has strengthened over the past decade, with its value against the US dollar near or above par since 2009. Investors around the world have placed their money in Canada as it currently has a better fiscal environment than the United States, as well as a strong financial sector. As you learned in this chapter, currency values affect financial performance, and managers need to apply certain strategies to reduce the impact of currency fluctuations on profits.

According to Jayson Myers, president and CEO of the Canadian Manufacturers and Exporters, the Canadian dollar has appreciated 62 percent in value since 2002, when it stood at 62 cents (US).

For Canadian citizens who like to travel and shop in the United States, the stronger loonie has made cross-border trips and online shopping more inviting. For exporters, however, the effect has been completely the opposite, as their products have become more expensive, weakening their exports. A 2011 TD Canada Trust Small Business survey performed in Toronto found that 46 percent of exporting business respondents indicated the strong loonie was affecting their profits, and 33 percent said it had caused a fall in customer demand. Since the Canadian dollar's rise, many small businesses have failed, especially those whose only competitive advantage was price. For example, Kirk Forest Products, in operation for 50 years, closed its Nova Scotia Christmas-tree business, blaming the high value of the Canadian dollar. Owner Rick Kirk said the company's costs had gone up 80 percent over five years due to the value of the Canadian dollar alone, and the business could no longer compete.

Small businesses are not the only companies affected by the appreciation of the loonie, however. Large Canadian firms have also been forced to adapt their purchasing and marketing strategies to survive. For example, in October 2010 Maple Leaf Foods announced it was closing some of its plants, along with raising prices, as part of its strategy to cope with a strong loonie. The company is facing growing competition from US food processors that have taken advantage of the strong loonie to export their products into Canada and penetrate the Canadian market.

An Export Development Canada (EDC) survey of Canadian exporters concluded that "the strong Canadian dollar continues to be a primary concern for most Canadian exporters." However, some respondents reported that the strong loonie had served as an incentive to break into new markets and to grow their businesses. More than half the respondents named investing and outsourcing abroad as very effective strategies. Twenty percent of the survey respondents indicated that the high Canadian dollar has caused a fall in their export sales over the past five years, partly due to a decrease in demand for price-sensitive products. However, another 22 percent of those surveyed said that despite the high-value Canadian dollar their export sales have increased. These businesses tended to be ones with high-demand often exclusive products, which were less price sensitive.

When a currency appreciates in value, such as the loonie has appreciated against the US dollar, it forces businesses to rethink the way they operate. TD's senior vice-president of small business banking urges small business owners to approach their banks for advice on how to deal with this situation. One strategy he recommends is to use the opportunity to buy new equipment and supplies from abroad while the loonie is strong.

A business could also employ strategies such as importing more from the United States or from countries with weaker currencies and holding the debt in US funds. Many Canadian businesses are also using the strong loonie to make investments abroad, opening subsidiaries or manufacturing operations in other countries. In this way, they build a natural hedge against currency risks.

The Business Development Bank of Canada (BDC) suggests several ways to structure a business to offset currency fluctuations, including finding foreign suppliers; setting up a foreign bank account to offset currency inflows and outflows; adding foreign operations; and buying and selling currencies using forwards, futures, and options. BDC also proposes using currency options to buy equipment. Let's say you decide to buy a machine for your factory in the United States, and the transaction closes in eight months. An option can protect you against the loonie devaluating during that eight-month period; however, if it appreciates against the US dollar, you can let the option expire and benefit from the higher exchange rate.

In summary, the emergence of the loonie as a strong currency has prompted Canadian businesses to develop new strategies. Canadian exporters and multinationals in Canada are using three main strategies: cutting costs, increasing innovation, and improving operating efficiencies.

Thinking Globally

1. If you were hired by a company that exports only to the United States, what strategies would you recommend the company use to cope with a strong loonie?

2. What strategies do you recommend for companies with price-sensitive products?

3. Do you think a strong loonie is a problem or an opportunity for Canadian exporters? Explain your answer.

Sources: Richard Blackwell, "Thriving in the Era of the Strong Loonie," *The Globe and Mail*, September 26, 2012; Toronto Dominion Bank (TD) "Toronto Small Business Owners Are Cheerful Despite the Strong Dollar Affecting Their Profits," Press Release, TD Web site (td.mediaroom.com), July 5, 2011; Export Development Canada (EDC), "Strong Canadian Dollar: How Canadian Businesses Are Adapting," *ExportWise*, November 30, 2010; CBC News, "Strong Loonie Makes Winners, Losers," CBC News Web site (www.cbc.ca), October 14, 2010; Business Development Bank of Canada (BDC) "Coping with a Strong Canadian Dollar," BDC Web site (www.bdc.ca), February 11, 2010.

Teaming Up INTERNATIONAL TRADE

For the countries you are studying, what trade patterns can you observe? Is there evidence of your product being imported? Exported? List the methods each government uses to promote and restrict trade.

Foreign Direct Investment

For each of the countries your team is researching, answer the following questions: Does it attract large amounts of FDI? Is it a major source of FDI for other nations? What is the nation's balance-of-payments position? What is its current account balance? List some possible causes for its surplus or deficit. How is this surplus or deficit affecting the nation's economic performance? What is its capital account balance? How does the government encourage or restrict trade with other nations?

Regional Economic Integration

For the countries your team is researching, identify any regional integration efforts in which the nation may be participating. What other nations are members? What economic, political, and social objectives drive integration? So far, what have been the positive and negative results of integration? How are international companies (domestic and nondomestic) coping? Explain why companies' coping strategies are, or are not, succeeding.

International Financial Markets and Foreign Exchange

For each of the countries your team is researching, answer the following questions: Does it have a city that is an important financial centre? How has its stock market(s) performed over the past year? What is the exchange rate between its currency and that of your own country? What factors are responsible for the stability or volatility of that exchange rate? Are there any restrictions on the exchange of the nation's currency? How is the forecast for the country's currency likely to influence business activity in its major industries? How have inflation and interest rates affected the nation's exchange rate with other currencies? What impact has the country's exchange rate had on its imports and exports?

CHAPTER TEN

International Strategy and Organization

Learning Objectives

After studying this chapter, you should be able to

1. Explain the stages of identification and analysis that precede strategy selection.

2. Identify the two international strategies and the corporate-level strategies that companies use.

3. Identify the business-level strategies of companies and the role of department-level strategies.

4. Discuss the important issues that influence the choice of organizational structure.

5. Describe each type of international organizational structure and explain the importance of work teams.

A LOOK BACK

Chapter 9 explored how the international capital market and foreign exchange market operate. We examined the factors that affect the determination of exchange rates, studied how exchange rates are used in international business, and discussed international attempts to create a system of stable and predictable exchange rates.

A LOOK AT THIS CHAPTER

This chapter introduces us to the strategies used by international companies. We explore the different types of strategies available to international companies and important factors in their selection. We also examine the organizational structures that companies devise to suit their international operations.

A LOOK AHEAD

Chapter 11 describes the selection and management issues surrounding the different entry modes available to companies going international. We will examine the importance of an export strategy, and the pros and cons of each entry mode.

Source: ShutterStock.

Lululemon's Yoga Apparel—A Global Fashion Statement

VANCOUVER, *British Columbia*—Lululemon Athletica Inc. (www.lululemon.com) is one of the fastest-growing athletic clothing brands in the world. Founded in 1998 in Vancouver, British Columbia, Lululemon now owns over 200 stores in Canada, the United States, Australia, and New Zealand, and has showrooms in London and Hong Kong. Lululemon's global strategy—offering the same line of products worldwide—is paying off: Lululemon's product lines have become "must-have" fashion statements in the worldwide athletic wear market.

Lululemon has had a focus strategy since its inception. At first, the company focused on the needs of yoga practitioners, offering high-quality athletic apparel that allowed its clients to practise their sport comfortably and also look good. Lululemon then expanded its focus to athletic clothing consumers. Part of Lululemon's appeal is its holistic philosophy. Lululemon not only sells clothing, but also promotes self-improvement through exercise and positive thinking, and strives to help its clients find happiness and live their lives to their full potential. The company works hard to provide a warm, homey store experience for its customers—to give them the feeling that the company genuinely cares about their well-being.

Lululemon prides itself on its hyper-local marketing strategy. The company builds its clientele locally by tapping into the interests of individual communities. A key part of Lululemon's marketing strategy is its ambassador program. Local fitness instructors are asked to be ambassadors for the brand; they receive Lululemon merchandise to wear at their classes and, in exchange, provide product feedback and spread the word about the company to their students. Lululemon does not advertise through traditional channels such as TV commercials, radio ads, or newspaper campaigns. However, the company has a strong social media presence on Facebook, Tumblr, Foursquare, Instagram, Pinterest, and Zite, a customized magazine for mobile devices. Lululemon's Facebook page has over 700 000 followers. But relying on word-of-mouth through its ambassadors and its loyal customers remains Lululemon's main marketing strategy. So far, that strategy seems to be working: The company's brand value has nearly tripled since 2010. And Lululemon was named one of the top 10 Best Canadian Brands in 2012.[1]

Source: Mary Altaffer/ASSOCIATED PRESS.

planning
Process of identifying and selecting an organization's objectives and deciding how the organization will achieve those objectives.

strategy
Set of planned actions taken by managers to help a company meet its objectives.

Planning is the process of identifying and selecting an organization's objectives and deciding how the organization will achieve those objectives. In turn, **strategy** is the set of planned actions taken by managers to help a company meet its objectives. The key to developing an effective strategy, then, is to define a company's objectives (or goals) clearly and to plan carefully how it will achieve those goals. This requires a company to undertake an analysis of its own capabilities and strengths to identify what it can do better than the competition. It also means that a company must carefully assess the competitive environment and the national and international business environments in which it operates.

A well-defined strategy helps a company compete effectively in increasingly competitive international markets. It serves to coordinate a company's various divisions and departments so that it reaches its company-wide goals in the most effective and efficient manner possible. A clear, appropriate strategy focuses a company on the activities that it performs best and on the industries for which it is best suited. It keeps an organization away from a future of mediocre performance or total failure. An inappropriate strategy can lead a manager to take actions that pull a company in opposite directions or take it into industries it knows little about.

We begin this chapter by exploring important factors that managers consider when analyzing their companies' strengths and weaknesses. We examine the different international strategies and the corporate-, business-, and department-level strategies that companies implement. Finally, we explore the different types of organizational structures that companies use to coordinate their international activities.

International Strategy

Managers confront similar concerns whether formulating a strategy for a domestic or an international company. Both types of firms must determine what products to produce, where to produce them, and where and how to market them. The biggest difference lies in complexity. Companies considering international production need to select from many potential countries, each likely having more than one possible location. Depending on its product line, a company that wants to market internationally might have an equally large number of markets to consider. Whether it is being considered as a site for operations or as a potential market, each international location has a rich mixture of cultural, political, legal, and economic traditions and processes. All these factors add to the complexity of planning and formulating strategy for international managers.

Strategy Formulation

The strategy-formulation process involves both planning and strategy. Strategy formulation permits managers to step back from day-to-day activities and get a fresh perspective on the current and future direction of the company and its industry. As shown in Figure 10.1, this procedure can be regarded as a three-stage process. Let's now examine several important factors to consider in each stage of this process.

Identify Company Mission and Goals

mission statement
Written statement of why a company exists and what it plans to accomplish.

Most companies have a general purpose for why they exist that they express in a **mission statement**—a written statement of why a company exists and what it plans to accomplish. For example, one company might set out to supply the highest level of service in a *market segment*—a clearly identifiable group of potential buyers. Another might strive to be the lowest-cost supplier in its segment worldwide. The mission statement often guides decisions such as which industries to enter or exit and how to compete in chosen segments.

stakeholders
All parties, ranging from suppliers and employees to shareholders and consumers, who are affected by a company's activities.

TYPES OF MISSION STATEMENTS Mission statements often spell out how a company's operations affect its **stakeholders**—all parties, ranging from suppliers and employees to shareholders and consumers, who are affected by a company's activities. Some companies place corporate brands centre stage and take on the mission of creating well-liked brands above all else. The mission statements of other businesses focus on other issues, including superior shareholder returns, profitability, market share, and corporate social responsibility. Still other companies make their mission to be the interests of consumers. For example, the mission

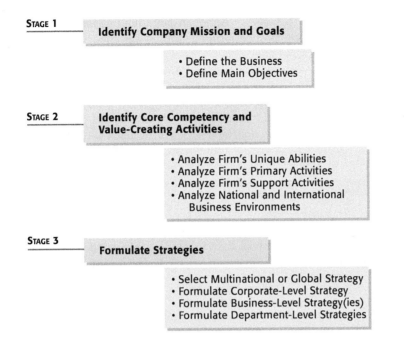

FIGURE 10.1

Strategy Formulation Process

statement of global eye-care company Bausch & Lomb (www.bausch.com) focuses on the customer and reads as follows:

> Bausch & Lomb is solely dedicated to protecting and enhancing the gift of sight for millions of people around the world—from the moment of birth through every phase of life. Our mission is simple yet powerful: Helping you see better to live better.[2]

The mission statement of an international business depends on (among other things) the type of business it is in, the stakeholders it is trying most to satisfy, and that aspect of business most important to achieving its goals. Yet companies must be sensitive to the needs of its different stakeholders in different nations. A company might need to balance the needs of shareholders for financial returns in the home nation, the needs of buyers for good value in a consumer market, and the needs of the public at large where it has a production facility.

Managers must also define the *objectives* they wish to achieve in the global marketplace. Objectives at the highest level in a company tend to be stated in the most general terms. An example of this type of objective is:

> To be the largest global company in each industry in which we compete.

Objectives of individual business units in an organization tend to be more specific. They are normally stated in more concrete terms and sometimes even contain numerical targets. For example, such a mission statement could be stated as follows:

> To mass-produce a zero-pollution emissions automobile by 2015.

Objectives usually become even more precise at the level of individual departments and almost always contain numerical targets of performance. For example, the following could be the objective of a marketing and sales department:

> To increase global market share by five percent in each of the next three years.

Identify Core Competency and Value-Creating Activities

Before managers formulate effective strategies, they must analyze the company, its industry (or industries), and the national business environments in which it is involved. They should also examine industries and countries being targeted for potential future entry. We address the company and its industries in this section and examine the business environment in the next section.

core competency

Special ability of a company that competitors find extremely difficult or impossible to equal.

UNIQUE ABILITIES OF COMPANIES Although large multinational companies are often involved in multiple industries, most perform one activity (or a few activities) better than any competitor does. A **core competency** is a special ability of a company that competitors find extremely difficult or impossible to equal. It is not a skill; individuals possess skills. For example, an architect's ability to design an office building in the Victorian style is a skill. A core competency refers to multiple skills that are coordinated to form a single technological outcome.

Although skills can be learned through on-the-job training and personal experience, core competencies develop over longer periods of time and are difficult to teach. At one point, Canon of Japan (www.canon.com) purchased expertise in optic technology but only later succeeded in developing a variety of products based on optic technology—including cameras, copiers, and semiconductor lithographic equipment. Likewise, Sony (www.sony.com) for decades relied on its core competency in miniaturizing electronic components to fortify its global leadership position in consumer electronics. These companies possessed unique abilities to create superior products and develop their core competencies.

How do managers actually go about analyzing and identifying their firms' unique abilities? Let's explore a tool commonly used by managers to analyze their companies—*value-chain analysis*.

value-chain analysis

Process of dividing a company's activities into primary and support activities and identifying those that create value for customers.

VALUE-CHAIN ANALYSIS Managers must select strategies consistent with their company's particular strengths and the market conditions the firm faces. Managers should also select company strategies based on what the company does that customers find valuable. This is why managers conduct a **value-chain analysis**—the process of dividing a company's activities into primary and support activities, and identifying those that create value for customers.[3]

As we see in Figure 10.2, value-chain analysis divides a company's activities into primary activities and support activities that are central to creating customer value. *Primary activities* include inbound and outbound logistics, production (goods and services), marketing and sales, and customer service. Primary activities involve the creation of the product, its marketing and delivery to buyers, and its after-sales support and service. *Support activities* include business infrastructure, human resource management, technology development, and procurement (sourcing). Each of these activities provides the inputs and infrastructure required by the primary activities.

Each primary and support activity is a source of strength or weakness for a company. Managers determine whether each activity enhances or detracts from customer value, and they incorporate this knowledge into the strategy-formulation process. Analysis of primary and support activities often involves finding activities in which improvements can be made with large benefits. Let's take a look at how managers determine whether an activity enhances customer value.

Primary Activities When analyzing primary activities, managers often look for areas in which the company can increase the value provided to its customers. For example, managers might examine production processes and discover new, more efficient manufacturing methods to reduce production costs and improve quality. Customer satisfaction might be increased by improving logistics management that shortens the time it takes to get a product to the buyer or by providing better customer service.

FIGURE 10.2

Company Value Chain

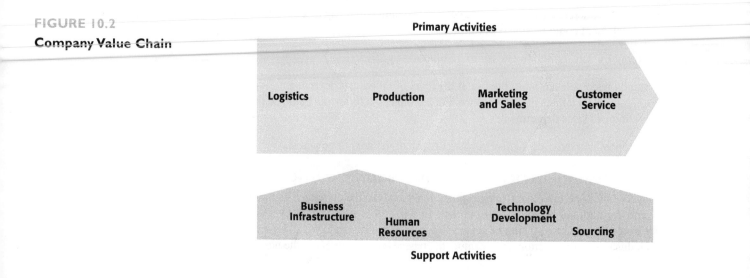

Companies might also lower costs by introducing greater automation into the production process. Computer maker Acer (www.acer.ca) applied a fast-food production model to personal computer manufacturing. Rather than manufacture complete computers in Asia and ship them around the world, Acer first builds components at plants scattered throughout the world. Those components are then shipped to assembly plants, where computers are built according to customer specifications. Acer adopted this approach because there was no longer any value added in simply assembling computers. By altering its production and logistics processes, Acer developed a business model that created value for customers.

Support Activities   Support activities assist companies in performing their primary activities. For example, the actions of any company's employees are crucial to its success. Production, logistics, marketing, sales, and customer service all benefit when employees are qualified and well trained. International companies can often improve the quality of their products by investing in worker training and management development. In turn, ensuring quality can increase the efficiency of a firm's manufacturing, marketing and sales, and customer service activities. Effective procurement (or sourcing) can locate low-cost, high-quality raw materials or intermediate products and ensure on-time delivery to production facilities. Finally, a sophisticated infrastructure not only improves internal communication but also supports organizational culture and each primary activity.

The in-depth analysis of a company that is inherent in the strategy-formulation process helps managers to discover their company's unique core competency and abilities, and to identify the activities that create customer value. For a checklist of issues small companies should consider in a self-analysis of whether it is ready to go global, see this chapter's Entrepreneur's Toolkit, titled "Ask Questions before Going Global."

A company cannot identify its unique abilities in a vacuum, separate from the environment in which it operates. The external business environment consists of all the elements outside a company that can affect its performance, such as cultural, political, legal, and economic forces; workers' unions; consumers; and financial institutions. Let's look at several environmental forces that affect strategy formulation.

NATIONAL AND INTERNATIONAL BUSINESS ENVIRONMENTS   National differences in language, religious beliefs, customs, traditions, and climate complicate strategy formulation. Language differences can increase the cost of operations and administration. Manufacturing processes must sometimes be adapted to the supply of local workers and to local customs, traditions, and practices. Marketing activities sometimes can result in costly mistakes if they do not incorporate cultural differences. For example, a company once decided to sell its laundry detergent in Japan but did not adjust the size of the box in which it was sold. The company spent millions of dollars developing a detailed marketing campaign and was shocked when it experienced disappointing sales. It turned out that the company should have packaged the detergent in smaller containers for the Japanese market. Japanese shoppers prefer smaller quantities because they tend to walk home from the store and have smaller storage areas in tight living quarters. Gerber (www.gerber.com), a major producer of baby food (now part of the food giant Nestlé), made what is today considered a classic mistake in its first attempt to market its products in Africa. The company's traditional advertising strategy in North America had been to place a smiling baby's face on the jar label. However, in Africa many people do not read, so jar labels often have pictures of the jar contents. Consequently, many African consumers thought that Gerber was selling babies in a jar, obviously not the message the company wanted to convey.

Differences in political and legal systems also complicate international strategies. Legal and political processes often differ in target countries to such an extent that firms must hire outside consultants to teach them about the local system. Such knowledge is important to international companies because the approval of the host government is almost always necessary for making direct investments. Companies need to know which ministry or department has the authority to grant approval for a big business deal—a process that can become extremely cumbersome. For example, non-Chinese companies in China must often get approval to conduct business from several separate agencies. The process is further complicated by the tendency of local government officials to interpret laws differently than do bureaucrats in Beijing (the nation's capital).

Different national economic systems further complicate strategy formulation. Negative attitudes of local people toward the impact of direct investment can generate political unrest. Economic philosophy affects the tax rates that governments impose. Whereas socialist economic systems

Entrepreneur's Toolkit	Ask Questions Before Going Global

It seems everywhere a small business turns for advice these days it hears the mantra, "Go global." But any company must have a solid grasp of its capabilities and its product if it's going to be successful in global markets. Here is a brief checklist of issues for small businesses to consider.

- **Are You Ready?** Do you or your key personnel speak other languages? Have you or they lived in other cultures for extended periods? How long has your company been in business? What markets might need what your company sells? Can your business withstand the rough seas of global trade? What specific sales numbers are forecasted? Can you map your global business journey?

- **Is Your Product Ready?** Can your business capitalize on its strengths? Will you need to modify your product or your marketing approach? Will modifying the product or its marketing weaken your offering? Does your product satisfy all local safety standards and other regulations? Can your product

stand up to the competition and to the scrutiny of customers?

- **Is Each Department Ready?** Is your company's infrastructure capable of going global? Does each department (logistics, operations, marketing, sales, service, human resources, collections, and so on) have the resources to handle its international responsibilities? What is your company's financial strategy for international expansion? Can domestic sales support an initial period of money-losing international operations? Is everyone in the company committed to the international effort?

- **Is Your Strategy Ready?** Will your company's international effort conflict with or complement your overall business strategy? Will your company's foreignness be a hindrance, or can it be exploited profitably? Is your business capable of sustaining a lengthy international endeavour? How will your company break into long-established family networks and business relationships?

normally levy high taxes on business profits, free market economies tend to levy lower taxes. The need to work in more than one currency also complicates international strategy. To minimize losses from currency fluctuations, companies must develop strategies to deal with exchange-rate risk.

Finally, apart from complicating strategy, the national business environment can affect the location in which a company chooses to perform an activity. For example, a nation that spends a high portion of its gross domestic product (GDP) on research and development (R&D) attracts high-tech industries and high-wage jobs and, as a result, prospers. By contrast, countries that spend relatively little in the way of R&D tend to have lower levels of prosperity.

Quick Study

1. What are the three stages of the strategy-formulation process? Describe what is involved at each stage.
2. Define what is meant by the term *core competency*. How does it differ from a skill?
3. What is *value-chain analysis*? Explain the difference between primary and secondary activities.
4. How do national and international business environments influence strategy formulation?

Formulate Strategies

As we've already seen, the strengths and special capabilities of an international company, along with the environmental forces it faces, strongly influence its strategy. Let's examine this final stage in the planning and strategy-formulation process.

TWO INTERNATIONAL STRATEGIES Companies engaged in international business activities can approach the market using one of four strategies: *global*, *international*, *multinational*, or *transnational*. These four strategies respond to different levels of cost pressure and need for market responsiveness or adaptation. However, we will focus our discussion on two of these strategies: global, where cost pressure is high but adaptation need is low, and multinational (multidomestic), where adaptation need is high but cost pressure is low. It is important to note that these two strategies do not include companies that export. Exporters do not have foreign direct investments in other national markets and should instead devise an appropriate export strategy (see Chapter 11). Let's now examine what it means for a company to follow a multinational or a global strategy.

Multinational Strategy Some international companies choose to follow a **multinational (multidomestic) strategy**—a strategy of adapting products and their marketing strategies in each national market to suit local preferences. In other words, a multinational strategy is just what its name implies—a separate strategy for each of the multiple nations in which a company markets its products. To implement a multinational strategy, companies often establish largely independent, self-contained units (or subsidiaries) in each national market. Each subsidiary typically undertakes its own product research and development, production, and marketing. In many ways, each unit functions largely as an independent company. Multinational strategies are often appropriate for companies in industries in which buyer preferences do not converge across national borders, such as certain food products and some print media. For example, Canadian company Sun Life Financial (www.sunlife.ca) applies a multinational strategy in all its various markets, both domestic and international. Sun Life Financial specializes in financial services and products such as life insurance, health insurance, pension plans, and disability insurance. Because coverage needs for these types of products vary from country to country due to regulations and cultural patterns, a multinational strategy is the obvious and most successful choice. Sun Life has a specific Web page for each of the different countries it serves, where potential clients can find product information particular to their country. For instance, in the Philippines Sun Life offers a product called Sun Life Shariah to help its clients achieve their financial needs through a product managed according to Shariah principles.

The main benefit of a multinational strategy is that it allows companies to monitor buyer preferences closely in each local market and to respond quickly and effectively to emerging buyer preferences. Companies hope that customers will perceive a tailored product as delivering greater value than do competitors' products. A multinational strategy, then, should allow a company to charge higher prices and/or gain market share.

The main drawback of a multinational strategy is that companies cannot exploit scale economies in product development, manufacturing, or marketing. The multinational strategy typically increases the cost structure for international companies and forces them to charge higher prices to recover such costs. As such, a multinational strategy is usually poorly suited to industries in which price competitiveness is a key success factor. The high degree of independence with which each unit operates also may reduce opportunities to share knowledge among units within a company.

Global Strategy Other companies decide that what suits their operations is a **global strategy**—a strategy of offering the same products using the same marketing strategy in all national markets. Companies that follow a global strategy often take advantage of scale and location economies by producing entire inventories of products or components in a few optimal locations. They also tend to perform product research and development in one or a few locations and typically design promotional campaigns and advertising strategies at headquarters. So-called global products are most common in industries characterized by price competition and, therefore, pressure to contain costs. They include certain electronic components, a wide variety of industrial goods such as steel, and some consumer goods such as paper and writing instruments. Lululelmon, featured in this chapter's opening profile, is an example of a company that successfully uses a global strategy to produce and market its products.

The main benefit of a global strategy is cost savings due to product and marketing standardization. These cost savings can then be passed on to consumers to help the company gain market share in its market segment. A global strategy also allows managers to share lessons learned in one market with managers at other locations.

The main problem with a global strategy is it can cause a company to overlook important differences in buyer preferences from one market to another. A global strategy does not allow a company to modify its products except for the most superficial features, such as the colour of paint applied to a finished product or a small add-on feature. This can present a competitor with an opportunity to step in and satisfy unmet needs of local buyers, thereby creating a niche market.

multinational (multidomestic) strategy
Adapting products and their marketing strategies in each national market to suit local preferences.

global strategy
Offering the same products using the same marketing strategy in all national markets.

FIGURE 10.3

Three Levels of Company Strategy

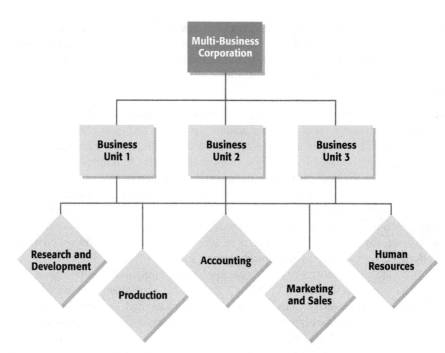

In addition to deciding whether the company will follow a multinational or a global strategy, managers must formulate strategies for the corporation, each business unit, and each department. Let's look closely at the three different levels of company strategy: *corporate-*, *business-*, and *department-level* strategies (see Figure 10.3).

CORPORATE-LEVEL STRATEGIES Companies involved in more than one line of business must first formulate a *corporate-level strategy*. This means, in part, identifying the national markets and industries in which the company will operate. It also involves developing overall objectives for the company's different business units and specifying the role that each unit will play in reaching those objectives. The four key approaches to corporate strategy are *growth*, *retrenchment*, *stability*, and *combination*.

growth strategy

Strategy designed to increase the scale (size of activities) or scope (kinds of activities) of a corporation's operations.

Growth Strategy A **growth strategy** is designed to increase the scale or scope of a corporation's operations. *Scale* refers to the *size* of a corporation's activities, *scope* to the *kinds* of activities it performs. Yardsticks commonly used to measure growth include geographic coverage, number of business units, market share, sales revenue, and number of employees. Lululemon is pursuing a growth strategy in both the scale and scope of its operations by adding stores worldwide and expanding its focus and product lines. (Learn more about the company in this chapter's opening vignette or by visiting Lululemon's Web site at www.lululemon.com).

Organic growth refers to a corporate strategy of relying on internally generated growth. For example, management at 3M (www.3m.com) strongly encourages entrepreneurial activity, often spinning off business units to nurture the best ideas and carry them to completion.

Other methods of growth include mergers and acquisitions, joint ventures, and strategic alliances (see Chapter 11). These tactics are used when companies do not wish to invest in developing certain skills internally or when other companies already do what managers are trying to achieve. Common partners in implementing these strategies include competitors, suppliers, and buyers. Corporations typically join forces with competitors to reduce competition, expand product lines, or expand geographically. A common motivation for joining forces with suppliers is to increase control over the quality, cost, and timing of inputs.

retrenchment strategy

Strategy designed to reduce the scale or scope of a corporation's businesses.

Retrenchment Strategy The exact opposite of a growth strategy is a **retrenchment strategy**—a strategy designed to reduce the scale or scope of a corporation's businesses. Corporations often cut back the *scale* of their operations when economic conditions worsen or competition increases. They may do so by closing factories with unused capacity and laying off workers. Corporations can also reduce the scale of their operations by laying off managers and salespeople in national markets that are not generating adequate sales revenue. Corporations reduce the *scope* of their activities by selling unprofitable business units or those no longer directly related to their overall aims. Weaker competitors often resort to retrenchment when national business environments grow more competitive. For example, Hudson's Bay Company (www3.hbc.com) sold all of its Zellers stores (one of their family brands) to Target (www.target.com), reducing the scope of its activities.

Stability Strategy   A **stability strategy** is designed to guard against change. Corporations often use a stability strategy when trying to avoid either growth or retrenchment. Such corporations have typically met their stated objectives or are satisfied with what they have already accomplished. They believe that their strengths are being fully exploited and their weaknesses fully protected against. They also see the business environment as posing neither profitable opportunities nor threats. They have no interest in expanding sales, increasing profits, increasing market share, or expanding the customer base; at present, they want simply to maintain their present positions.

stability strategy
Strategy designed to guard against change and used by corporations to avoid either growth or retrenchment.

Combination Strategy   The purpose of a **combination strategy** is to mix growth, retrenchment, and stability strategies across a corporation's business units. For example, a corporation can invest in units that show promise, retrench in those for which less exposure is desired, and stabilize others. In fact, corporate combination strategies are quite common because international corporations rarely follow identical strategies in each of their business units.

combination strategy
Strategy designed to mix growth, retrenchment, and stability strategies across a corporation's business units.

BUSINESS-LEVEL STRATEGIES   In addition to stipulating the overall corporate strategy, managers must also formulate separate *business-level strategies* for each business unit. For some companies, this means creating just one strategy. This is the case when the business-level strategy and the corporate-level strategy are one and the same because the corporation is involved in just one line of business. For other companies, this can mean creating dozens of strategies.

The key to developing an effective business-level strategy is deciding on a *general competitive strategy in the marketplace.* Each business unit must decide whether to sell the lowest-priced product in an industry or to integrate special attributes into its products. A business unit can use one of three generic business-level strategies for competing in its industry—*low-cost leadership, differentiation,* or *focus.*[4] These strategies can be applied to practically all firms in all markets worldwide. Let's now explore each of these strategies in detail.

Low-Cost Leadership Strategy   A strategy in which a company exploits economies of scale to have the lowest cost structure of any competitor in its industry is called a **low-cost leadership strategy**. Companies that pursue the low-cost leadership position also try to contain administrative costs and the costs of their various primary activities, including marketing, advertising, and distribution. Walmart (www.walmart.ca) is normally portrayed as an example of a company that successfully employs a low-cost leadership strategy worldwide. Montreal-based wireless device maker Datawind, profiled in the opening vignette of Chapter 5, used a low-cost leadership strategy to win a deal with the Indian government by offering to build the cheapest tablet in the world. Although cutting costs is the mantra for firms that pursue a low-cost leadership position, other important competitive factors such as product quality and customer service cannot be ignored. Factors underlying the low-cost leadership position (efficient production in large quantities) help guard against attack by competitors because of the large upfront cost of getting started. The strategy typically requires a company to have a large market share because achieving low-cost leadership tends to rely on large-scale production to contain costs. One negative aspect of the low-cost leadership strategy is low customer loyalty—all else being equal, buyers will purchase from any low-cost leader.

low-cost leadership strategy
Strategy in which a company exploits economies of scale to have the lowest cost structure of any competitor in its industry.

A low-cost leadership strategy works best with mass-marketed products aimed at price-sensitive buyers. This strategy is often well suited to companies with standardized product and marketing promotions. Two global companies vying for the low-cost leadership position in their respective industries include Casio (www.casio.com) in sports watches and Texas Instruments (www.ti.com) in calculators and other electronic devices.

Differentiation Strategy   A **differentiation strategy** is one in which a company designs its products to be perceived as unique by buyers throughout its industry. The perception of uniqueness can allow a company to charge a higher price and enjoy greater customer loyalty than it could as a low-cost leader. But a perception of exclusivity, or meeting the needs of a small group of buyers, tends to force a company into a lower market-share position. A company using this strategy must develop a loyal customer base to offset its smaller market share and higher costs of producing and marketing a unique product.

differentiation strategy
Strategy in which a company designs its products to be perceived as unique by buyers throughout its industry.

One way products can be differentiated is by improving their reputation for *quality*. Ceramic tableware for everyday use is found at department stores in almost every country. But the ceramic tableware made by Japanese producer Noritake (www.noritake.com) differentiates itself from common tableware by emphasizing its superior quality. The perception of higher quality allows manufacturers to charge higher prices for their products worldwide.

Other products are differentiated by distinctive *brand images*. Armani (www.armani.com) and Donna Karan New York (DKNY) (www.dkny.com), for example, are relatively pricey global clothiers appealing to a young, fashionable clientele. Each is continually introducing new textures and colours that are at once stylish and functional. Lululemon (www.lululemon.com) is rapidly building a worldwide reputation similar to Armani and DKNY, but in the athletic apparel market rather than in high fashion.

Another example is Italian carmaker Alfa Romeo (www.alfaromeo.com), which does not compete in the fiercely competitive mass-consumer segment of the global automobile industry. If it were to do so, it would have to be price-competitive and offer a wider selection of cars. Instead, Alfa Romeo offers a high-quality product with a brand image that rewards the Alfa Romeo owner with status and prestige.

Another differentiating factor is *product design*—the sum of the features by which a product looks and functions according to customer requirements. Special features differentiate both goods and services in the minds of consumers who value those features. Manufacturers can also combine several differentiation factors in formulating their strategies. For example, the designs of Casio (www.casio.com) and other makers of mass-market sports watches stress functionality. The sports watches of TAG Heuer (www.tagheuer.com) of Switzerland, on the other hand, offer class and style in addition to performance. Another example of a company using *product design* as a differentiation strategy is Canada's Palliser Furniture (www.palliser.com). Palliser, a leading producer of furniture, offers its customers a choice of over 250 upholstery fabrics and leathers, and a variety of finishes and options, such as cup holders, wood or metal feet, and different nail head styles, to create their own customized living spaces.

focus strategy

Strategy in which a company focuses on serving the needs of a narrowly defined market segment by being the low-cost leader or by differentiating its product.

Focus Strategy   A **focus strategy** is one in which a company focuses on serving the needs of a narrowly defined market segment by being the low-cost leader or by differentiating its product. Increasing competition often means more products distinguished by price or differentiated by quality, design, and so forth. In turn, a greater product range leads to the continuous refinement of market segments. Today many industries consist of large numbers of market segments and even smaller sub-segments. For example, some firms try to serve the needs of one ethnic or racial group, whereas others, often entrepreneurs and small businesses, focus on a single geographic area.

Johnson & Johnson (J&J) (www.jnj.com) is commonly thought of as being a single, large consumer-products company. In fact, it is a conglomerate of more than 250 operating companies that market an enormous variety of products to a wide array of market segments. Many individual J&J companies try to dominate their segments by producing specialty goods and services. In so doing, they focus on narrow segments using either low-cost leadership or differentiation techniques.[5] We saw how Lululemon applies a focus strategy in this chapter's opening vignette. Blackberry (ca.blackberry.com) is another example of a company that uses a focus strategy. A significant portion of Blackberry's revenue is derived from its focus on serving corporate and government agencies, such as the US Immigration and Customs Enforcement, where its mobile device offers management solutions. A smaller but expanding portion of its revenues comes from sales of the same product line to corporations and consumers in Southeast Asia, particularly in countries such as Indonesia, where it has a dominant market share.[6]

Dollar Tree Canada (www.dollartreecanada.com), formerly called Dollar Giant, uses a low-cost focus strategy. The Vancouver-based company offers general merchandise and everyday consumables all priced at $1.25 (CAD) or less. The company sources inexpensive imported products from low-cost producers in China and other developing countries, and sells them at low prices to the low-income segment of the market.

A focus strategy often means designing products and promotions aimed at consumers who are either dissatisfied with existing choices or who want something distinctive. Consider the highly fragmented gourmet coffee market. One extremely unusual brand of coffee called Kopi Luwak, or civet coffee, sells for up to *$300 per pound*! Civets, or *luwaks* (weasel-like animals found on the Indonesian island of Java), eat coffee berries containing coffee beans. The beans

Employees of China's largest home appliances maker, Haier, work on the refrigerator production line in Qingdao, Shandong province. By analyzing its industry and assets, a company based in an emerging market can determine whether its competitive edge is germane to the local market, or if it is transferable to other markets. Haier is taking the battle for market share to highly industrialized nations and is now the world's fourth largest home-appliances manufacturer—employing more than 50 000 people globally.

Source: Peng Neng/EPN/Newscom.

"naturally ferment" as they pass through the animals' systems and are later recovered. The beans are then washed, roasted, and sold around the world as a specialty coffee.[7]

DEPARTMENT-LEVEL STRATEGIES   Achieving corporate- and business-level objectives depends on effective departmental strategies that focus on the specific activities that transform resources into products. Formulation of *department-level strategies* brings us back to where we began our analysis of a company's capabilities that support its strategy: to the primary and support activities that create value for customers. After managers analyze these activities, they must then develop strategies that exploit their firm's value-creating strengths.

Primary and Support Activities   Each department is instrumental in creating customer value through lower costs or differentiated products. This is especially true of departments that conduct *primary activities.* Manufacturing strategies are obviously important in cutting the production costs of both standardized and differentiated products. They are also crucial to improving product quality. Effective marketing strategies allow companies to promote the differences in their products. A strong sales force and good customer service contribute to favourable images among consumers or industrial buyers and generate loyal customers of both kinds. Efficient logistics in bringing raw materials and components into the factory and getting the finished product out the factory door can result in substantial cost savings.

Support activities also create customer value. For example, research and development identifies market segments with unsatisfied needs and designs products to meet them. Human resource managers can improve efficiency and cut costs by hiring well-trained employees and conducting worker training and management development programs. Procurement tasks provide operations with quality resources at a reasonable cost. Accounting and finance (elements of a firm's infrastructure) must develop efficient information systems to assist managers in making decisions and maintaining financial control, thus having an impact on costs and quality in general.

There are important elements that drive the decisions of world-class companies with regard to strategy formulation. For example, the important *production* issues to consider are the number and dispersion of production facilities and whether to standardize production processes for all markets. The important *marketing* issue is whether to standardize either the physical features of products or their marketing strategies across markets. We present the strategic considerations of production and marketing activities in Chapter 12.

> **Quick Study**
>
> 1. Compare and contrast *multinational strategy* and *global strategy*. When is each appropriate?
> 2. What are the four corporate-level strategies? Identify the main characteristics of each.
> 3. Identify the three business-level strategies. Describe how they differ from one another.
> 4. Explain the importance of department-level strategies. How do primary and support activities help a firm achieve its goals?

International Organizational Structure

organizational structure
Way in which a company divides its activities among separate units and coordinates activities among those units.

Organizational structure is the way in which a company divides its activities among separate units and coordinates activities among those units. If a company's organizational structure is appropriate for its strategic plans, it will be more effective in working toward its goals. In this section, we explore several important issues related to organizational structures and examine several alternative forms of organization.

Centralization Versus Decentralization

A vital issue for top managers is determining the degree to which decision making in the organization will be centralized or decentralized. *Centralized decision making* concentrates decision making at a high organizational level in one location, such as at headquarters. *Decentralized decision making* disperses decisions to lower organizational levels, such as to international subsidiaries.

Should managers at the parent company be actively involved in the decisions made by international subsidiaries? Or should they intervene relatively little, perhaps only in the most crucial decisions? Some decisions, of course, must be decentralized. If top managers involve themselves in the day-to-day decisions of every subsidiary, they are likely to be overwhelmed. For example, managers cannot get directly involved in every hiring decision or assignment of people to specific tasks at each facility. On the other hand, overall corporate strategy cannot be delegated to subsidiary managers because only top management is likely to have the appropriate perspective to formulate corporate strategy.

In our discussion of centralization versus decentralization of decision making, it is important to remember two points:

1. Companies rarely centralize or decentralize all decision making. Rather, they seek an approach that will result in the greatest efficiency and effectiveness.
2. International companies may centralize decision making in certain geographic markets while decentralizing it in others. Numerous factors influence this decision, including the need for product modification and the abilities of managers at each location.

With these points in mind, let's take a look at some specific factors that determine whether centralized or decentralized decision making is most appropriate.

WHEN TO CENTRALIZE Centralized decision making helps coordinate the operations of international subsidiaries. This is important for companies that operate in multiple lines of business or in many international markets. It is also important when one subsidiary's output is another's input. In such situations, coordinating operations from a single, high-level vantage point is more efficient. Purchasing is often centralized if all subsidiaries use the same inputs in production. For example, a company that manufactures steel filing cabinets and desks will need a great deal of sheet steel. A central purchasing department will get a better bulk price on sheet steel than would subsidiaries negotiating their own agreements. Each subsidiary would then benefit by purchasing sheet steel from the company's central purchasing department at lower cost than it would pay in the open market.

Some companies maintain strong central control over financial resources by channelling all subsidiary profits back to the parent for redistribution to subsidiaries based on their needs. This practice reduces the likelihood that certain subsidiaries will undertake investment projects when more promising projects at other locations go without funding. Other companies centrally design policies, procedures, and standards to encourage a single global organizational culture. This policy makes it more likely that all subsidiaries will enforce company rules uniformly. The policy also helps when companies transfer managers from one location to another because uniform policies can smooth transitions for managers and subordinates alike.

WHEN TO DECENTRALIZE   Decentralized decision making is beneficial when fast-changing national business environments put a premium on local responsiveness. Decentralized decisions can result in products that are better suited to the needs and preferences of local buyers because subsidiary managers are in closer contact with the local business environment. Local managers are more likely to perceive environmental changes that managers at headquarters might not notice. By contrast, central managers may not perceive such changes or would likely get a second-hand account of local events. Delayed response and misinterpreted events could then result in lost orders, stalled production, and weakened competitiveness.

Participative Management and Accountability   Decentralization can also help foster participative management practices. The morale of employees is likely to be higher if subsidiary managers and subordinates are involved in decision making. Subsidiary managers and workers can grow more dedicated to the organization when they are involved in decisions related to production, promotion, distribution, and pricing strategies.

Decentralization also can increase personal accountability for business decisions. When local managers are rewarded (or punished) for their decisions, they are likely to invest more effort in making and executing them. Conversely, if local managers must do nothing but implement policies dictated from above, they can attribute poor performance to decisions that were ill-suited to the local environment. When managers are held accountable for decision making and implementation, they typically delve more deeply into research and consider all available options. The results are often better decisions and improved performance.

Coordination and Flexibility

When designing organizational structure, managers seek answers to certain key questions. What is the most efficient method of linking divisions to each other? Who should coordinate the activities of different divisions in order to achieve overall strategies? How should information be processed and delivered to managers when it is required? What sorts of monitoring mechanisms and reward structures should be established? How should the company introduce corrective measures, and whose responsibility should it be to execute them? To answer these types of questions, we must look at the issues of coordination and flexibility.

STRUCTURE AND COORDINATION   As we have seen, some companies have a presence in several or more national business environments—they manufacture and market products practically everywhere. Others operate primarily in one country and export to, or import from, other markets. Each type of company must design an appropriate organizational structure. Each needs a structure that clearly defines areas of responsibility and **chains of command**—the lines of authority that run from top management to individual employees and specify internal reporting relationships. Finally, every firm needs a structure that brings together areas that require close cooperation. For example, to avoid product designs that make manufacturing more difficult and costly than necessary, most firms ensure that R&D and manufacturing remain in close contact.

chains of command
Lines of authority that run from top management to individual employees and specify internal reporting relationships.

STRUCTURE AND FLEXIBILITY   Organizational structure is not permanent but is often modified to suit changes both within a company and in its external environment. Because companies usually base organizational structures on strategies, changes in strategy usually require adjustments in structure. Similarly, because changes in national business environments can force changes in strategy, the same changes will influence company structure. It is especially important to monitor closely the conditions in countries characterized by rapidly shifting cultural, political, and economic environments. Let's now explore four organizational structures that have been developed to improve the responsiveness and effectiveness of companies conducting international business activities.

Types of Organizational Structure

There are many different ways in which a company can organize itself to carry out its international business activities. But four organizational structures tend to be most common for the vast majority of international companies: division structure, area structure, product structure, and matrix structure.

international division structure

Organizational structure that separates domestic from international business activities by creating a separate international division with its own manager.

INTERNATIONAL DIVISION STRUCTURE   An **international division structure** separates domestic from international business activities by creating a separate international division with its own manager (see Figure 10.4). In turn, the international division is typically divided into units corresponding to the countries in which a company is active—say, China, Indonesia, and Thailand. Within each country, a general manager controls the manufacture and marketing of the firm's products. Each country unit typically carries out all of its own activities with its own departments such as marketing and sales, finance, and production.

Because the international division structure concentrates international expertise in one division, divisional managers become specialists in a wide variety of activities such as foreign exchange, export documentation, and host government relations. By consigning international activities to a single division, a firm can reduce costs, increase efficiency, and prevent international activities from disrupting domestic operations. These are important criteria for firms new to international business and whose international operations account for a small percentage of their total business.

An international division structure can, however, create two problems for companies. First, international managers must often rely on home-country managers for the financial resources and technical know-how that give the company its international competitive edge. Poor coordination between managers can hurt the performance not only of the international division but also of the entire company. Second, the general manager of the international division typically is responsible for operations in all countries. Although this policy facilitates coordination across countries, it reduces the authority of each country manager. Rivalries and poor cooperation between the general manager and country managers can be damaging to the company's overall performance.

FIGURE 10.4

International Division Structure

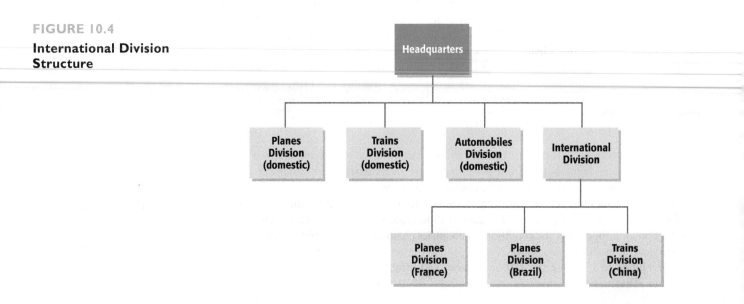

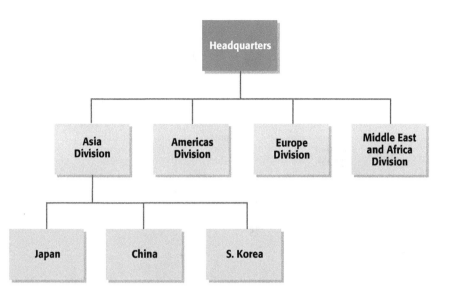

FIGURE 10.5

International Area Structure

INTERNATIONAL AREA STRUCTURE An **international area structure** organizes a company's entire global operations into countries or geographic regions (see Figure 10.5). The greater the number of countries in which a company operates, the greater the likelihood it will organize into regions—say, Asia, Europe, and the Americas—instead of countries. Typically, a general manager is assigned to each country or region. Under this structure, each geographic division operates as a self-contained unit, with most decision making decentralized into the hands of the country or regional managers. Each unit has its own set of departments—purchasing, production, marketing and sales, R&D, and accounting. Each also tends to handle much of its own strategic planning. Management at the parent-company headquarters makes decisions regarding overall corporate strategy and coordinates the activities of various units. For example, BlackBerry (ca.blackberry.com), headquartered in Waterloo, Ontario, operates under an international area structure, with offices in North America, Europe, Asia-Pacific, Latin America, and Africa. BlackBerry United States is located in Irving, Texas; BlackBerry Europe is based in the United Kingdom and serves all the countries in the region; BlackBerry Australia is located in Sydney; and BlackBerry South Africa, located in Johannesburg, provides support for the whole African continent.[8]

international area structure
Organizational structure that organizes a company's entire global operations into countries or geographic regions.

The international area structure is best suited to companies that treat each national or regional market as unique. It is particularly useful when there are vast cultural, political, or economic differences between nations or regions. When they enjoy a great deal of control over activities in their own environments, general managers become experts on the unique needs of their buyers. On the other hand, because units act independently, allocated resources may overlap and cross-fertilization of knowledge from one unit to another may be less than desirable.

GLOBAL PRODUCT STRUCTURE A **global product structure** divides worldwide operations according to a company's product areas (see Figure 10.6). For example, divisions in a computer company might be Internet and Communications, Software Development, and New Technologies. Each product division is then divided into domestic and international units. Each function—R&D, marketing, and so forth—is thus duplicated in both the domestic and international units of each product division. Bombardier (www.bombardier.com) divides its global operations between Aerospace and Transportation. Aerospace is comprised of business, commercial, specialized, and amphibious aircraft divisions as well as an aircraft services and training division, each of which is led by their own president. Transportation is comprised of rail, propulsion and controls, bogies, transportation systems, rail control solutions, and ECO4 technologies, as well as services and maintenance, also led by a president for each product line.

global product structure
Organizational structure that divides worldwide operations according to a company's product areas.

The global product structure is suitable for companies that offer diverse sets of products or services because it overcomes some coordination problems of the international division structure. Bombardier's diversity of products—most of which have a worldwide marketing mandate and a requirement for leadership to ensure rapid product development and focused customer

FIGURE 10.6

Global Product Structure

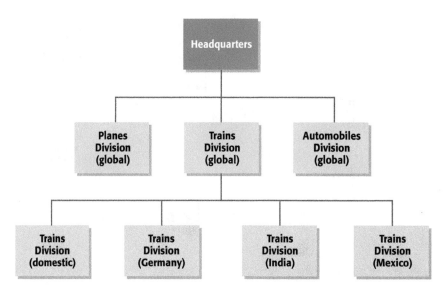

service—make the global product structure its most suitable organizational choice. Because the primary focus is on the product, activities must be coordinated among a product division's domestic and international managers so they do not conflict.

global matrix structure

Organizational structure that splits the chain of command between product and area divisions.

GLOBAL MATRIX STRUCTURE   A **global matrix structure** splits the chain of command between product and area divisions (see Figure 10.7). Each manager reports to two bosses: the president of the product division and the president of the geographic area. A main goal of the matrix structure is to bring together *geographic* area managers and *product* area managers in joint decision making. In fact, bringing together specialists from different parts of the organization creates a sort of team organization. The popularity of the matrix structure has grown among companies trying to increase local responsiveness, reduce costs, and coordinate worldwide operations.

The matrix structure resolves some of the shortcomings of other organizational structures, especially by improving communication among divisions and increasing the efficiency of highly specialized employees. At its best, the matrix structure can increase coordination while simultaneously improving agility and local responsiveness.

However, the global matrix structure suffers from two major shortcomings. First, the matrix form can be quite cumbersome. Numerous meetings are required simply to coordinate the actions

FIGURE 10.7

Global Matrix Structure

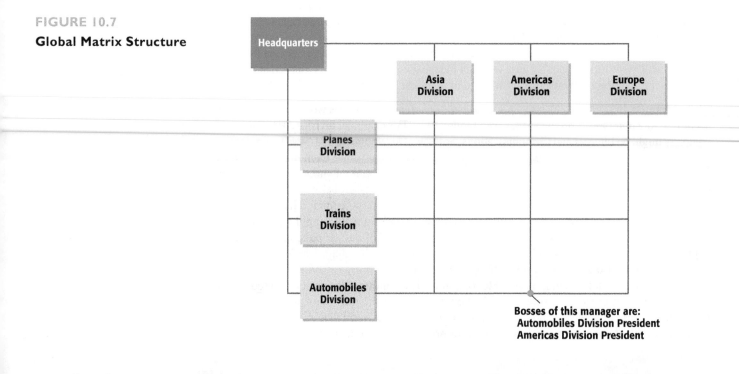

of the various division heads, let alone the activities within divisions. In turn, the need for complex coordination tends to make decision making time consuming and slows the reaction time of the organization. Second, individual responsibility and accountability can become foggy in the matrix organization structure. Because responsibility is shared, managers can attribute poor performance to the actions of the other manager. Moreover, the source of problems in the matrix structure can be hard to detect and corrective action difficult to take.

There are other ways international companies can improve responsiveness and effectiveness. An increasingly popular method among international companies is the implementation of work teams to accomplish goals and solve problems. In the next section, we explore in detail the use of work teams.

Work Teams

Globalization is forcing companies to respond more quickly to changes in the business environment. The formation of teams can be highly useful in improving responsiveness by cutting across functional boundaries, such as that between production and marketing, which slow decision making in an organization. Although a matrix organization accomplishes this by establishing cross-functional cooperation, companies do not always want to change their entire organizational structure to reap the benefits that cross-functional cooperation provides. In such cases, companies can implement several different types of teams without changing the overall company structure.

Work teams are assigned the tasks of coordinating their efforts to arrive at solutions and implementing corrective action. Today, international companies are turning to work teams on an unprecedented scale to increase direct contact between different operating units. Companies are even forming teams to design and implement their competitive strategies. Let's now take a look at several different types of teams—self-managed teams, cross-functional teams, and global teams.

SELF-MANAGED TEAMS A **self-managed team** is one in which the employees from a single department take on the responsibilities of their former supervisors. When used in production, such teams often reorganize the methods and flow of production processes. Because they are "self-managed," they reduce the need for managers to watch over their every activity. The benefits of self-managed teams typically include increased productivity, product quality, customer satisfaction, employee morale, and company loyalty. In fact, the most common self-managed teams in many manufacturing companies are *quality-improvement teams*, which help reduce waste in the production process and, therefore, lower costs.

The global trend toward "downsizing" internal operations to make them more flexible and productive has increased the popularity of teams because they reduce the need for direct supervision. Companies around the world now employ self-managed teams in international operations. Yet research indicates that cultural differences can influence resistance to the concept of self-management and the practice of using teams. Among other things, experts suggest that international managers follow some basic guidelines:[9]

- Use selection tests to identify the employees most likely to perform well in a team environment.
- Adapt the self-managed work-team concept to the national culture of each subsidiary.
- Adapt the process of integrating self-managed work teams to the national culture of each subsidiary.
- Train local managers at the parent company and allow them to introduce teams at a time they feel is most appropriate.

Similarly, the cultural differences discussed in Chapter 2 are important to managers who design teams in international operations. For example, certain cultures are more collectivist in nature. Some cultures harbour greater respect for differences in people's status. In some cultures, people believe the future is largely beyond their personal control. And some cultures display a so-called work-to-live mentality. Researchers say that in these cases conventional management should retain fairly tight authority over teams. But teams are likely to be productive if given greater autonomy in a culture where people are very hardworking.[10]

CROSS-FUNCTIONAL TEAMS A **cross-functional team** is one composed of employees who work at similar levels in different functional departments. These teams work to develop changes in operations and are well suited to projects that require coordination across functions, such as reducing the time needed to get a product from the idea stage to the marketplace. International

self-managed team
Team in which the employees from a single department take on the responsibilities of their former supervisors.

cross-functional team
Team composed of employees who work at similar levels in different functional departments.

companies also use cross-functional teams to improve quality by having employees from purchasing, manufacturing, and distribution (among other functions) work together to address specific quality issues. For the same reason, cross-functional teams can help break down barriers between departments and reorganize operations around processes rather than by functional departments.

global team

Team of top managers from both headquarters and international subsidiaries who meet to develop solutions to company-wide problems.

GLOBAL TEAMS   Finally, large international corporations are creating so-called **global teams**—groups of top managers from both headquarters and international subsidiaries who meet to develop solutions to company-wide problems. For example, Colgate-Palmolive (www.colgatepalmolive.com) created a global team of 150 top executives from around the world to manage its IT strategy and implement IT global projects.

Depending on the issue at hand, team members can be drawn from a single business unit or assembled from several different units. While some teams are disbanded after resolving specific issues, others move on to new problems. The performance of global teams can be impaired by matters such as large distances between team members, lengthy travel times to meetings, and the inconvenience of working across time zones. Companies can sometimes overcome these difficulties, although doing so can be rather costly.

Quick Study

1. What four main types of organizational structure are used in international business?
2. Explain how each type of organizational structure differs from the other three.
3. Identify the three different types of work teams. How does each improve responsiveness and effectiveness?

Bottom Line for Business

Managers have the important and complicated task of formulating international strategies at the levels of the corporation, business unit, and individual department. Managers often analyze their companies' operations by viewing them as a chain of activities that create customer value (value-chain analysis). It is through this process that managers can identify and implement strategies suited to their companies' unique capabilities. The strategies that managers select then determine the firm's organizational structure. National business environments also affect managers' strategy and structure decisions, including whether to alter their products (standardization versus adaptation), where to locate facilities (centralized versus decentralized production), and what

type of decision making to implement (centralized versus decentralized decision making).

The role of managers in formulating strategies and creating the overall organizational structure cannot be overstated. The strategies they choose determine the market segments in which the firm competes and whether it pursues low-cost leadership in its industry or differentiates its product and charges a higher price. These decisions are crucial to all later activities of firms that are going international. They also influence how a company (1) enters international markets; (2) employs its human resources; and (3) manages its day-to-day production, marketing, and other operations.

Chapter Summary

1. Explain the stages of identification and analysis that precede strategy selection.

- *Planning* means identifying and selecting an organization's objectives and deciding how the organization will achieve them.
- *Strategy* is the set of planned actions taken by managers to help a company meet its objectives.
- Prior to formulating strategy, managers must first *identify* the company's mission, goals, core competency, and value-creating activities.
- Managers can identify a company's abilities that create customer value using *value-chain analysis*, which divides a company's activities into *primary* activities and *support* activities that are central to creating value for customers.
- Managers must also analyze the cultural, political, legal, and economic environments.

2. Identify the two international strategies and the corporate-level strategies that companies use.

- A *multinational (multidomestic) strategy* means adapting products and their marketing strategies in each national market to suit local preferences.
- A *global strategy* means offering the same products using the same marketing strategy in all national markets.
- Companies in more than one line of business must formulate a *corporate-level strategy* that encompasses all of the company's different business units.
- A *growth strategy* increases the scale (size of activities) or scope (kinds of activities) of a corporation's operations.
- A *retrenchment strategy* reduces the scale or scope of a corporation's businesses.
- A *stability strategy* guards against change and is used to avoid a corporation's growth or retrenchment.
- A *combination strategy* mixes growth, retrenchment, and stability strategies across a corporation's business units.

3. Identify the business-level strategies of companies and the role of department-level strategies.

- A *low-cost leadership strategy* means exploiting economies of scale to have the lowest cost structure of any competitor in an industry.
- A *differentiation strategy* involves designing products to be perceived as unique by buyers throughout an industry.
- A *focus strategy* means serving the needs of a narrowly defined market segment by being the low-cost leader or by differentiating the product.
- Achieving corporate- and business-level objectives depends on effective *department-level strategies* that focus on the specific activities that create customer value—whether a department conducts *primary* or *support activities*.

4. Discuss the important issues that influence the choice of organizational structure.

- *Organizational structure* is the way in which a company divides its activities among separate units and coordinates activities among those units.
- Important to organizational structure is the degree to which decision making in an organization will be centralized (made at a high level) or decentralized (made at a subsidiary level).
- *Centralized decision making* helps coordinate operations of international subsidiaries, whereas *decentralized decision making* places a premium on local responsiveness.
- When designing organizational structure, managers must consider the issues of *coordination* and *flexibility*.
- Organizational structure must define areas of responsibility and *chains of command*—lines of authority that specify internal reporting relationships.

5. Describe each type of international organizational structure and explain the importance of work teams.

- An *international division structure* separates domestic from international activities by creating a separate division with its own manager.
- An *international area structure* organizes a company's entire global operations into countries or geographic regions, with each division operating as a self-contained unit.
- A *global product structure* divides worldwide operations into product divisions, which are then divided into domestic and international units.

- A *global matrix structure* splits the chain of command and forces each manager and employee to report to two bosses—the general manager of the product division and the general manager of the geographic area.
- *Work teams* are assigned the tasks of coordinating their efforts to arrive at solutions and implementing corrective action; different types are *self-managed teams*, *cross-functional teams*, and *global teams*.

Key Terms

Talk It Over

1. "The elements that affect strategy formulation are the same whether a company is domestic or international." Do you agree or disagree with this statement? Why? Support your argument with examples.

2. "Cultures around the world are becoming increasingly similar, so companies should standardize both their products and global marketing efforts." Do you agree or disagree with this reasoning? Are there certain industries for which it might be more or less true?

3. Continuous advancements in technology are deeply affecting the way international businesses are managed. Do you think technology (the Internet, for example) should radically alter the fundamental strategies and organizational structures of international companies? Or do you think companies can simply graft new strategies and structures onto existing ones? Explain your answers.

Take It to the Web

1. **Video Report.** Visit YouTube (www.youtube.com). Search for the video "The Five Competitive Forces that Shape Strategy" by *Harvard Business Review*. Watch the video, and then summarize it in a half-page report. How might a company engaged in international business act on the information contained in the video?

2. **Web Site Report.** Before the spin-off of Kraft Foods in 2007, Altria Group was the parent company of both Kraft and Philip Morris. Visit the Web site of the Altria Group (www.altria.com). What corporate-level strategies do you think Altria was pursuing in its different businesses prior to the spin-off?

Visit the Web sites of Kraft Foods (www.kraftfoods group.com) and Philip Morris (www.pmi.com)—both their domestic and international operations. What business-level strategies are being pursued by (a) Kraft and (b) Philip Morris?

Why do you think the Altria Group made Kraft its own company? Do you think it had anything to do with the mix of businesses that then-parent Altria Group was involved in? Why or why not? Identify as many stakeholders of Altria, Philip Morris, and Kraft Foods as you can. Aside from past smoking-related lawsuits, are there any trends that encouraged Kraft's independence?

IKEA's Global Strategy

IKEA (www.ikea.com) is a nearly $30 billion global furniture powerhouse based in Sweden. With more than 332 stores in 38 countries, offering 12 000 different products, the company's success reflects founder Ingvar Kamprad's "social ambition" of selling a wide range of stylish, functional home furnishings at prices so low that the majority of people can afford to buy them. The story of Kamprad's success is detailed in a book titled *IKEA: The Entrepreneur, the Business Concept, the Culture.* The store exteriors are painted with Sweden's national colours, bright blue and yellow. Shoppers view furniture in scores of realistic settings arranged throughout the cavernous showrooms.

In a departure from standard industry practice, IKEA's furniture bears names such as "Ivar" and "Sten" as well as model numbers. At IKEA, shopping is very much a self-service activity—after browsing and writing down the names of desired items in the showroom, shoppers pick their furniture off shelves, where they find boxes containing the furniture in kit form. One of the cornerstones of IKEA's strategy is having customers take their purchases home and assemble the furniture themselves, reducing costs and allowing for easier transportation. The typical IKEA store also contains a Swedish-cuisine restaurant, a grocery store called the Swede Shop, a supervised play area for children, and a baby-care room.

IKEA's approach to the furniture business enables it to rack up impressive growth in an industry in which overall sales are flat. Sourcing furniture from more than 2000 suppliers in 50 countries helps the company maintain its low-cost position. IKEA has also opened stores in emerging markets, such as in Central and Eastern Europe. Because many consumers in those regions have relatively low purchasing power, the stores offer a smaller selection of goods, and some of the furniture was designed specifically for the cramped living styles typical in former Soviet bloc countries. Throughout Europe, IKEA benefits from the perception that Sweden is the source of high-quality products. In fact, one of the company's key selling points is its "Swedishness." IKEA also operates in emerging markets like Russia, where its core strategy and anticorruption policies have been effective.

Industry observers predict that the United States will eventually be IKEA's largest market. The company opened its first US store in Philadelphia in 1985, and today has dozens of outlets that generate billions of dollars in sales annually. IKEA's competitors take the company very seriously. Jeff Young, chief operating officer of Lexington Furniture Industries, says, "IKEA is on the way to becoming the Walmart Stores of the home-furnishing industry. If you're in this business, you'd better take a look." Some customers worldwide, however, are annoyed to find popular items sometimes out of stock. Others complain about the long lines resulting from the company's no-frills approach. "The quality of much of what they sell is good," said one shopper, "but the hassles make you question whether it's worth it."

IKEA responds to these complaints through the FAQ section on its Web site, stating that "every effort is made to maintain the availability of items." Since IKEA's products are manufactured all over the world, there may be circumstances that can cause delivery delays.

Also, Goran Carstedt, president of IKEA North America, responds to such criticism by referring to the company's mission. "If we offered more services, our prices would go up," he explains. "Our customers understand our philosophy, which calls for each of us to do a little in order to save a lot. They value our low prices. And almost all of them say they will come back again." To keep them coming back, IKEA is spending millions on advertising to get its message across. Whereas common industry practice is to rely heavily on newspaper and radio advertising, two-thirds of IKEA's North American advertising budget is allocated for TV. IKEA also freely distributes its catalogues, produced in 17 languages for 28 countries. The catalogues are designed not only to feature IKEA's products, but also to give clients or potential clients ideas for room design solutions—a marketing strategy intended to make the catalogues into a resource that customers will keep and reread.

Incredibly, IKEA has also expanded into apartment building. The retail giant has 3500 of its prefab homes throughout Sweden, Norway, Finland, and the United Kingdom. IKEA's BoKlok (meaning "smart living" in Swedish) apartments resemble IKEA's modern furniture. The apartments are designed as open-plan living spaces with high ceilings, windows on three sides, and, of course, pre-fitted IKEA kitchens.

Thinking Globally

1. Has IKEA taken a standardization approach or an adaptation approach in its markets around the world? Do you think the company's approach is the right one for the future? Explain.
2. Which retailers are IKEA's biggest competitors in Canada? Why?
3. When company founder Kamprad decided to expand into China, his decision was not based on market research but, rather, on his own intuition. How well is IKEA doing in China? Did Kamprad's decision pay off?
4. After failing in Japan two decades earlier, IKEA returned in 2006. Conduct some research into how IKEA fared the second time around in Japan. Was IKEA able to avoid the mistakes it made in its first failed attempt?

Sources: Lauren Collins, "House Perfect," *The New Yorker* (www.newyorker.com), October 3, 2011; "The Corruption Eruption," *The Economist*, May 1, 2010, p. 73; Dianna Dilworth, "Ikea Enters UK's Housing Market," *Bloomberg Businessweek* (www.businessweek.com), April 20, 2007; Kerry Capell, "Ikea's New Plan for Japan," *Bloomberg Businessweek* (www.businessweek.com), April 26, 2006; Ikea Web site (www.ikea.com), selected reports and FAQ section.

CHAPTER ELEVEN

Selecting and Managing Entry Modes

Learning Objectives

After studying this chapter, you should be able to

1. Explain how companies use exporting, importing, and countertrade.

2. Explain the various means of financing export and import activities.

3. Describe the different contractual entry modes that are available to companies.

4. Explain the various types of investment entry modes.

5. Discuss the important strategic factors in selecting an entry mode.

A LOOK BACK

Chapter 10 showed us how companies plan and organize themselves for international operations. We explored the different types of strategies and organizational structures that international companies use to accomplish their strategic goals.

A LOOK AT THIS CHAPTER

This chapter introduces the different entry modes companies use to "go international." We discuss the important issues surrounding the selection and management of (1) exporting, importing, and countertrade; (2) contractual entry modes; and (3) investment entry modes.

A LOOK AHEAD

Chapter 12 explains the international marketing efforts of companies. We identify the key elements that influence how companies promote, price, and distribute their products.

Source: ShutterStock.

Spin Master Playing in the Big Leagues

TORONTO, Ontario—Spin Master (www.spinmaster.com), a Toronto-based toy company founded in 1994 by three college friends with only a $10 000 investment, is now the third-largest toy manufacturer in North America, after Mattel and Hasbro. How did the company go from start-up to giant in such a short time? Spin Master grew through successfully selecting and managing different international entry modes.

Spin Master's team of highly creative entrepreneurs made the business-savvy decision to grow through international partnerships, licensing agreements, and acquisitions. For example, the popular action-figure game Bakugan was created through a partnership of Spin Master, Sega Toys Ltd., Nelvana Enterprises Inc., TMS Entertainment, Japan Vistec Inc., and Sega Corporation. The toy was launched in Japan, the United States, and Canada, and became an instant hit, receiving numerous awards including three 2009 Toy of the Year (TOTY) awards.

In 2008, Spin Master launched an entertainment division, teaming up with innovators, inventors, and licensors from all over the world. One of Spin Master's many licensing agreements is with online game developer Mind Candy for the Moshi Monster brand. Under this agreement, Spin Master distributes plush toys and collectable figures—the physical "pet monsters"—in toy stores worldwide. How big is the deal? Mind Candy owns the best-selling children's magazine title in the United Kingdom and markets

Source: Lucas Oleniuk/Toronto Star via Getty Images.

the Moshi Monster brand in 140 countries; its Web site has over 50 million users. Another lucrative licensing deal is between Spin Master and Nickelodeon and Viacom Consumer Products (NVCP), making Spin Master the master global toy licensee for products such as action figures, vehicles, and play sets from the movie *The Last Airbender*, based on Nickelodeon's animated TV series.

Spin Master's acquisitions include several board game titles, making it a dominant player in the game aisles and strengthening its already robust portfolio. The company now has over 900 employees, with offices in Canada, the United States, the United Kingdom, France, Hong Kong, Mexico, and Germany. Spin Master has been named one of Canada's 50 Best Managed Companies and one of Fast Company's 50 Most Innovative Consumer Products Companies.[1]

entry mode

Institutional arrangement by which a firm gets its products, technologies, human skills, or other resources into a market.

The decision of how to enter a new market abroad must take into account many factors, including the local business environment and a company's own core competency. An **entry mode** is the institutional arrangement by which a firm gets its products, technologies, human skills, or other resources into a market. Companies seeking entry to new markets for manufacturing and/or marketing purposes have many potential entry modes at their disposal. The specific mode chosen depends on many factors, including experience in a market, amount of control managers desire, and potential size of the market. In this chapter, we explore the following three categories of entry modes:

1. Exporting, importing, and countertrade
2. Contractual entry
3. Investment entry

Exporting, Importing, and Countertrade

The most common method of buying and selling goods internationally is exporting and importing. Companies often import products in order to obtain less expensive goods or those that are simply unavailable in the domestic market. Companies export products when the international marketplace offers opportunities to increase sales and, in turn, profits. Companies worldwide (from both developed and developing countries) often see North America as a great export opportunity because of the size of the market and the strong buying power of its citizens. According to a recent report from the World Trade Organization, the United States remains the world's biggest trader. Figure 11.1 shows the leading economies of merchandise trade: the United States, China, Germany, Japan, France, and the Netherlands.

Because this chapter focuses on how companies take their goods and services to the global marketplace, this first section concentrates on exporting. We then explain how companies use *countertrade* when cash transactions are not possible and discuss the main export/import financing methods. Importing is a sourcing and inward trade decision for most firms; therefore, importing is not covered in detail in this chapter.

FIGURE 11.1

World Leading Economies of Merchandise Trade

Source: Based on data from International Trade Statistics 2012, World Trade Organization (http://www.wto.org/english/res_e/statis_e/its2012_e/section1_e/i07.xls)

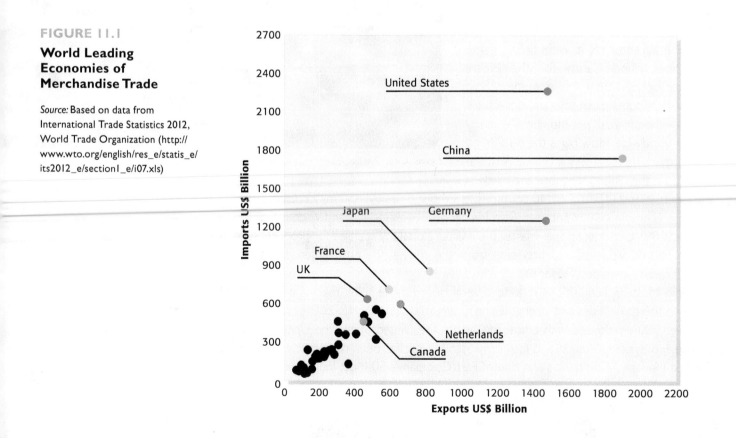

Why Companies Export

In the global economy, companies increasingly sell goods and services to wholesalers, retailers, industrial buyers, and consumers in other nations. Generally speaking, there are three main reasons why companies begin exporting:

1. ***Expand sales.*** Most large companies use exporting as a means of expanding total sales when the domestic market has become saturated. Greater sales volume allows them to spread the fixed costs of production over a greater number of manufactured products, thereby lowering the cost of producing each unit of output. In short, going international is one way to achieve economies of scale.
2. ***Diversify sales.*** Exporting permits companies to diversify their sales. In other words, they can offset slow sales in one national market (perhaps due to a recession) with increased sales in another. Diversified sales can level off a company's cash flow, making it easier to coordinate payments to creditors with receipts from customers.
3. ***Gain experience.*** Companies often use exporting as a low-cost, low-risk way of getting started in international business. Owners and managers of small companies, which typically have little or no knowledge of how to conduct business in other cultures, use exporting to gain valuable international experience.

Developing an Export Strategy: A Four-Step Model

Companies are often drawn into exporting when customers in other countries solicit their goods. In this way, companies become aware of their products' international potential and get their first taste of international business.

Yet a company should not fall into the habit of simply responding to random international requests for its products. A more logical approach is to research and analyze international opportunities and to develop a coherent export strategy. A business with such a strategy actively pursues export markets rather than sitting back and waiting for international orders to come in. Let's take a look at the four steps in developing a successful export strategy.

STEP 1: IDENTIFY A POTENTIAL MARKET To identify whether demand exists in a particular target market, a company should perform market research and interpret the results. Novice exporters should focus on one or only a few markets. For example, a first-time Brazilian exporter might not want to export simultaneously to Argentina, Britain, and Greece. A better strategy would likely be to focus on Argentina because of its cultural similarities with Brazil (despite having a different, though related, language). The company could then expand into more diverse markets after it gains initial international experience in a nearby country. The would-be exporter should also seek expert advice on the regulations and general process of exporting and any special issues related to a selected target market.

STEP 2: MATCH NEEDS TO ABILITIES The next step is to determine whether the company is capable of satisfying the needs of the market. Suppose a market located in a region with a warm, humid climate for much of the year displays the need for home air-conditioning equipment. If a company recognizes this need but makes only industrial-sized air-conditioning equipment, it might not be able to satisfy demand with its current product. But if the company is able to use its smallest industrial air-conditioning unit to satisfy the needs of several homes, it might have a market opportunity. If there are no other options or if consumers want their own individual units, the company will likely need to design a smaller air-conditioning unit or rule out entry into that market.

STEP 3: INITIATE MEETINGS Holding meetings early with potential local distributors, buyers, and others is a must. Initial contact should focus on building trust and developing a cooperative climate among all parties. The cultural differences between the parties will come into play already at this stage. Beyond building trust, successive meetings are designed to estimate the potential success of any agreement if interest is shown on both sides. At the most advanced stage, negotiations take place and details of agreements are finalized.

For example, a group of environmental technology companies in Arizona was searching for markets abroad. A delegation from Taiwan soon arrived in the Arizona desert to survey the group's products. Although days were busy with company visits, formal meetings, and negotiations, evenings were designed to build relationships. There were outdoor barbecues, hayrides, line dancing, and frontier-town visits to give the visitors a feel for local culture and history. To make their counterparts from Taiwan feel comfortable, night-time schedules included visits to karaoke spots and Chinese restaurants where a good deal of singing took place. Follow-up meetings resulted in several successful deals.

STEP 4: COMMIT RESOURCES After all the meetings, negotiations, and contract signings, it is time to put the company's human, financial, and physical resources to work. First, the objectives of the export program must be clearly stated and should extend out at least three to five years. For small firms, it may be sufficient to assign one individual the responsibility for drawing up objectives and estimating resources. Yet as companies expand their activities to include more products and/or markets, many firms discover the need for an export department or division. The head of this department usually has the responsibility (and authority) to formulate, implement, and evaluate the company's export strategy. See Chapter 10 for a detailed discussion of organizational design issues to consider at this stage.

Degree of Export Involvement

Companies of all sizes engage in exporting, but not all companies become involved in exporting to the same extent. Some companies (usually entrepreneurs and small and medium-sized firms) perform few or none of the activities necessary to get their products in a market abroad. Instead, they use intermediaries that specialize in getting products from one market into another. Other companies (usually only the largest companies) perform all of their export activities themselves, with an infrastructure that bridges the gap between the two markets. Let's take a closer look at the two basic forms of export involvement—direct exporting and indirect exporting.

DIRECT EXPORTING Some companies become deeply involved in the export of their products. **Direct exporting** occurs when a company sells its products directly to buyers in a target market. Direct exporters operate in many industries, including aircraft (Bombardier) (www.bombardier.com), industrial equipment (John Deere) (www.deere.com), apparel (Lululemon) (www.lululemon.com), and bottled beverages (Evian) (www.evian.com). Bear in mind that "direct exporters" need not sell directly to *end users*. Rather, they take full responsibility for getting their goods into the target market by selling directly to local buyers and not going through intermediary companies. Typically, they rely on either local *sales representatives* or *distributors*.

direct exporting
Practice by which a company sells its products directly to buyers in a target market.

Sales Representatives A *sales representative* (whether an individual or an organization) represents only its own company's products, not those of other companies. Sales representatives promote those products in many ways, such as by attending trade fairs and making personal visits to local retailers and wholesalers. They do not take title to the merchandise. Rather, they are hired by a company and normally are compensated with a fixed salary plus commissions based on the value of their sales.

Distributors Alternatively, a direct exporter can sell in the target market through *distributors*, who take ownership of the merchandise when it enters their country. As owners of the products, they accept all the risks associated with generating local sales. They sell either to retailers and wholesalers or to end users through their own channels of distribution. Typically, they earn a profit equal to the difference between the price they pay and the price they receive for the exporter's goods. Although using a distributor reduces an exporter's risk, it also weakens an exporter's control over the price buyers are charged. A distributor who charges very high prices can stunt the growth of an exporter's market share. Exporters should choose, if possible, distributors who are willing to invest in the promotion of their products and who do not sell directly competing products.

INDIRECT EXPORTING Some companies have few resources available to commit to exporting activities. Others simply find exporting a daunting task because of a lack of contacts and experience. Fortunately, there is an option for such firms. **Indirect exporting** occurs when a company sells its products to intermediaries who then resell to buyers in a target market. The choice of an intermediary depends on many factors, including the ratio of the exporter's international sales to its total sales, the company's available resources, and the growth rate of the target market. Let's take a closer look at several different types of intermediaries: *agents, export management companies*, and *export trading companies*.

indirect exporting
Practice by which a company sells its products to intermediaries who then resell to buyers in a target market.

Agents Individuals or organizations that represent one or more indirect exporters in a target market are called **agents**. Agents typically receive compensation in the form of commissions on the value of sales. Because establishing a relationship with an agent is relatively easy and inexpensive, it is a fairly common approach to indirect exporting. Agents should be chosen very carefully because it can be costly and difficult to terminate an agency relationship if problems arise. Careful selection is also essential because agents often represent several indirect exporters simultaneously. Agents might focus their promotional efforts on the products of the company paying the highest commission rather than on the company with the better products.

Export Management Companies A company that exports products on behalf of an indirect exporter is called an **export management company (EMC)**. An EMC operates contractually, either as an agent (being paid through commissions based on the value of sales) or as a distributor (taking ownership of the merchandise and earning a profit from its resale).

An EMC will usually provide additional services on a retainer basis, charging set fees against funds deposited on account. Typical EMC services include gathering market information, formulating promotional strategies, performing specific promotional duties (such as attending trade fairs), researching customer credit, making shipping arrangements, and coordinating export documents. It is common for an EMC to exploit contacts predominantly in one industry (say, agricultural goods or consumer products) or in one geographic area (such as Latin America or the Middle East). Indeed, the biggest advantage of an EMC is usually a deep understanding of the cultural, political, legal, and economic conditions of the target market. Company employees work comfortably and effectively in the cultures of both the exporting and the target nation. The average EMC tends to deploy a wide array of commercial and political contacts to facilitate business activities on behalf of its clients.

Perhaps the only disadvantage of hiring an EMC is that the breadth and depth of its service can potentially hinder the development of the exporter's own international expertise. But an exporter and its EMC typically have such a close relationship that an exporter often considers its EMC as a virtual exporting division. When this is the case, exporters learn a great deal about the intricacies of exporting from their EMC. Then, after the EMC contract expires, it is common for a company to go it alone in exporting its products.

Export Trading Companies A company that provides services to indirect exporters in addition to activities directly related to clients' exporting activities is called an **export trading company (ETC)**. Whereas an EMC is restricted to export-related activities, an ETC assists its clients by providing import, export, and countertrade services; developing and expanding distribution channels; providing storage facilities; financing trading and investment projects; and even manufacturing products.

European trading nations first developed the ETC concept centuries ago. More recently, the Japanese have refined the concept, which they call *sogo shosha*. The Japanese ETC can range in size from small, family-run businesses to enormous conglomerates such as Mitsubishi (www.mitsubishi.com), Mitsui (www.mitsui.com), and ITOCHU (www.itochu.co.jp). An ETC in South Korea is called a *chaebol* and includes well-known companies such as Samsung (www.samsung.com) and Hyundai (www.hyundaigroup.com/eng).

Japanese and South Korean ETCs have become formidable competitors because of their enormous success in gaining global market share. These Asian companies quickly came to rival the dominance of the largest US multinationals. ETCs in the United States remain small. The ETC concept has not caught on in the United States as it has in Asia, because Asian governments, financial institutions, and companies have much closer working relationships than their US counterparts. The formation of huge conglomerates that engage in activities ranging from providing financing to manufacturing to distribution is therefore easier to accomplish in Asia.

The Ontario Association of Trading Houses (www.oath.on.ca) is an example of an ETC in Canada. The Association was established in 1996 to promote the trading house sector in Canada; it organizes seminars and workshops to show manufacturers how to increase their exports by using trading houses. Trading houses operate in many industries, including food, textiles, used cars, building equipment, and discount merchandise. Shah Trading Company (www.shahtrading.com) claims to be the largest ethnic food distributor in Canada. Kanus Inc., located in Bedford, Nova Scotia, is a trading house serving a wide range of companies, including those interested in used clothing, cleaning rags, discount merchandise, and used cars.

agents
Individuals or organizations that represent one or more indirect exporters in a target market.

export management company (EMC)
Company that exports products on behalf of indirect exporters.

export trading company (ETC)
Company that provides services to indirect exporters in addition to activities related directly to clients' exporting activities.

Avoiding Export and Import Blunders

There are several errors common to companies new to exporting. First, many businesses fail to conduct adequate market research before exporting. In fact, many companies begin exporting by responding to unsolicited requests for their products. If a company enters a market in this manner, it should quickly devise an export strategy to manage its export activities effectively and not strain its resources.

Second, many companies fail to obtain adequate export advice. National and regional governments are often willing and able to help managers and small-business owners understand and cope with the vast amounts of paperwork required by each country's export and import laws. Naturally, more experienced exporters can be extremely helpful as well. They can help novice exporters avoid embarrassing mistakes by guiding them through unfamiliar cultural, political, and economic environments.

To better ensure that it will not make embarrassing blunders, an inexperienced exporter might also want to engage the services of a **freight forwarder**—a specialist in export-related activities such as customs clearing, tariff schedules, and shipping and insurance fees. Freight forwarders also can pack shipments for export and take responsibility for getting a shipment from the port of export to the port of import. For more information regarding freight forwarders in Canada, visit the Canadian International Freight Forwarders Association Web site (www.ciffa.com). You will be able to find workshops, freight forwarder news, and a directory of all the freight forwarder members.

freight forwarder
Specialist in export-related activities such as customs clearing, tariff schedules, and shipping and insurance fees.

Quick Study

1. Briefly describe each of the four steps involved in building an export strategy.
2. How does direct exporting differ from indirect exporting?
3. Compare and contrast export management companies and export trading companies.

Countertrade

Companies are sometimes unable to import merchandise in exchange for financial payment. The reason is either that the government of the importer's nation lacks the hard currency to pay for imports or that it intentionally restricts the convertibility of its currency. Fortunately, there is a way for firms to trade by using either a small amount of hard currency or even none at all. Selling goods or services that are paid for, in whole or in part, with other goods or services is called **countertrade**. Although countertrade often requires an extensive network of international contacts, even smaller companies can take advantage of its benefits.

Nations that have long used countertrade are found mostly in Africa, Asia, Eastern Europe, and the Middle East. A lack of adequate hard currency often forced those nations to use countertrade to exchange oil for passenger aircraft and military equipment. Today, because of insufficient hard currency, developing and emerging markets frequently rely on countertrade to import goods. The greater involvement of firms from industrialized nations in those markets is expanding the use of countertrade.

countertrade
Practice of selling goods or services that are paid for, in whole or in part, with other goods or services.

TYPES OF COUNTERTRADE There are several different types of countertrade: *barter, counterpurchase, offset, switch trading*, and *buyback*. Let's take a brief look at each of these.

- **Barter** is the exchange of goods or services directly for other goods or services without the use of money. It is the oldest known form of countertrade.
- **Counterpurchase** is the sale of goods or services to a country by a company that promises to make a future purchase of a specific product from that country. This type of agreement is designed to allow the country to earn back some of the currency that it paid for the original imports.

barter
Exchange of goods or services directly for other goods or services without the use of money.

counterpurchase
Sale of goods or services to a country by a company that promises to make a future purchase of a specific product from the country.

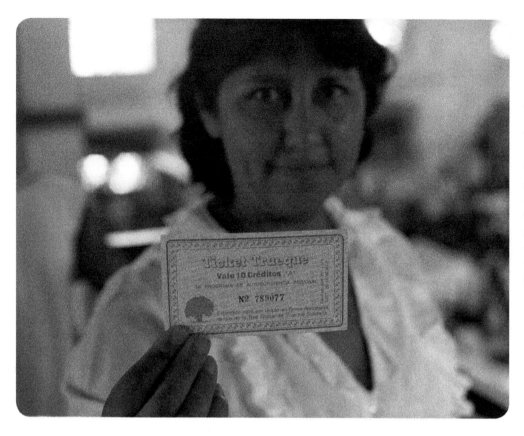

Barter, or *trueque*, became a way of life in Argentina when the nation's economy was mired in a seemingly endless recession. Residents of Buenos Aires, Argentina, bartered goods using "*Ticket Trueque*," or "Barter Vouchers" in English. In the market near Buenos Aires where this woman is working, you can swap music CDs, films on DVD, clothing, fruit, plumbing supplies, vegetables, and much more. Local newspapers run ads for such things as apartments, cars, and washing machines, all offered on a barter basis.

Source: © Neville Elder/Corbis.

- **Offset** is an agreement that a company will offset a hard-currency sale to a nation by making a hard-currency purchase of an unspecified product from that nation in the future. It differs from a counterpurchase in that this type of agreement does not specify the type of product that must be purchased, just the amount that will be spent. Such an arrangement gives a business greater freedom in fulfilling its end of a countertrade deal.
- **Switch trading** is countertrade whereby one company sells to another its obligation to make a purchase in a given country. For example, in return for market access, a firm that wants to enter a target market might promise to buy a product for which it has no use. The company then sells this purchase obligation to a large trading company that makes the purchase itself because it has a use for the merchandise. If the trading company has no use for the merchandise, it can arrange for yet another buyer who needs the product to make the purchase.
- **Buyback** is the export of industrial equipment in return for products produced by that equipment. This practice usually typifies long-term relationships between the companies involved.

Countertrade can provide access to markets that are otherwise off-limits because of a lack of hard currency. It can also cause headaches. Much countertrade involves commodity and agricultural products such as oil, wheat, or corn—products whose prices on world markets tend to fluctuate a good deal. A problem arises when the price of a bartered product falls on world markets between the time that a deal is arranged and the time at which one party tries to sell the product. Fluctuating prices generate the same type of risk that is encountered in currency markets. Managers might be able to hedge some of this risk on commodity futures markets similar to how they hedge against currency fluctuations in currency markets (see Chapter 9).

Export/Import Financing

International trade poses risks for both exporters and importers. Exporters run the risk of not receiving payment after their products are delivered. Importers fear that delivery might not occur once payment is made for a shipment. Export/import financing methods designed to reduce these risks include *advance payment, documentary collection, letter of credit,* and *open account* (see Figure 11.2). Let's now explore each of these methods.

offset
Agreement that a company will offset a hard-currency sale to a nation by making a hard-currency purchase of an unspecified product from that nation in the future.

switch trading
Practice in which one company sells to another its obligation to make a purchase in a given country.

buyback
Export of industrial equipment in return for products produced by that equipment.

FIGURE 11.2

Risk of Alternative Export/Import Financing Methods

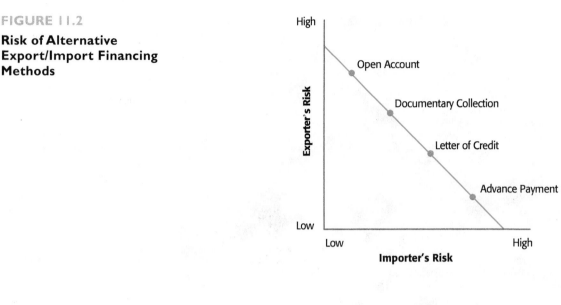

ADVANCE PAYMENT Export/import financing in which an importer pays an exporter for merchandise before it is shipped is called **advance payment**. This method of payment is common when two parties are unfamiliar with each other, the transaction is relatively small, or the buyer is unable to obtain credit because of a poor credit rating at banks. Payment normally takes the form of a wire transfer of money from the bank account of the importer directly to that of the exporter. Although prior payment eliminates the risk of non-payment for exporters, it creates the complementary risk of non-shipment for importers—importers might pay for goods but never receive them. Thus advance payment is the most favourable method for exporters but the least favourable for importers.

DOCUMENTARY COLLECTION Export/import financing in which a bank acts as an intermediary without accepting financial risk is called **documentary collection**. This payment method is commonly used when there is an ongoing business relationship between two parties. The documentary collection process can be broken into three main stages and nine smaller steps (see Figure 11.3).

1. Before shipping merchandise, the exporter (with its banker's assistance) draws up a **draft (bill of exchange)**—a document ordering the importer to pay the exporter a specified sum of money at a specified time. A *sight draft* requires the importer to pay when goods are delivered. A *time draft* extends the period of time (typically 30, 60, or 90 days) following delivery by which time the importer must pay for the goods. (When inscribed "accepted" by an importer, a time draft becomes a negotiable instrument that can be traded among financial institutions.)

2. Following creation of the draft, the exporter delivers the merchandise to a transportation company for shipment to the importer. The exporter then delivers to its banker a set of documents that includes the draft, a *packing list* of items shipped, and a **bill of lading**— a contract between the exporter and shipper that specifies merchandise destination and shipping costs. The bill of lading is proof that the exporter has shipped the merchandise. An international ocean shipment requires an *inland bill of lading* to get the shipment to the exporter's border and an *ocean bill of lading* for water transport to the importer nation. An international air shipment requires an *air waybill* that covers the entire international journey.

3. After receiving appropriate documents from the exporter, the exporter's bank sends the documents to the importer's bank. After the importer fulfills the terms stated on the draft and pays its own bank, the bank issues the bill of lading (which becomes title to the merchandise) to the importer.

Documentary collection reduces the importer's risk of non-shipment because the packing list details the contents of the shipment and the bill of lading is proof that the merchandise was shipped. The exporter's risk of non-payment is increased because, although the exporter retains title to the

advance payment

Export/import financing in which an importer pays an exporter for merchandise before it is shipped.

documentary collection

Export/import financing in which a bank acts as an intermediary without accepting financial risk.

draft (bill of exchange)

Document ordering an importer to pay an exporter a specified sum of money at a specified time.

bill of lading

Contract between an exporter and a shipper that specifies merchandise destination and shipping costs.

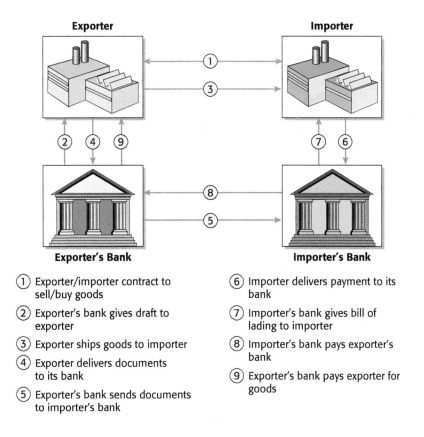

Exporter   **Importer**

Exporter's Bank   **Importer's Bank**

FIGURE 11.3

**Documentary Collection
Process**

① Exporter/importer contract to sell/buy goods

② Exporter's bank gives draft to exporter

③ Exporter ships goods to importer

④ Exporter delivers documents to its bank

⑤ Exporter's bank sends documents to importer's bank

⑥ Importer delivers payment to its bank

⑦ Importer's bank gives bill of lading to importer

⑧ Importer's bank pays exporter's bank

⑨ Exporter's bank pays exporter for goods

goods until the merchandise is accepted, the importer does not pay until all necessary documents have been received. Although importers have the option of refusing the draft (and, therefore, the merchandise), this action is unlikely. Refusing the draft—despite all terms of the agreement being fulfilled—would make the importer's bank unlikely to do business with the importer in the future.

LETTER OF CREDIT   Export/import financing in which the importer's bank issues a document stating that the bank will pay the exporter when the exporter fulfills the terms of the document is called **letter of credit** (**L/C**). A letter of credit is typically used when an importer's credit rating is questionable, when the exporter needs a letter of credit to obtain financing, when the parties involved do not trust each other, and when a market's regulations require it.

Before a bank issues a letter of credit, it checks on the importer's financial condition (see Figure 11.4). Banks normally issue letters of credit only after an importer has deposited on account a sum equal in value to that of the imported merchandise. The bank is still required to pay the exporter, but the deposit protects the bank if the importer fails to pay for the merchandise. Banks will sometimes waive this requirement for their most reputable clients.

There are several types of letters of credit:

- An *irrevocable letter of credit* allows the bank issuing the letter to modify its terms only after obtaining the approval of both exporter and importer.
- A *revocable letter of credit* can be modified by the issuing bank without obtaining approval from either the exporter or the importer.
- A *confirmed letter of credit* is guaranteed by both the exporter's bank in the country of export and the importer's bank in the country of import.

After the issuance of a letter of credit, the importer's bank informs the exporter (through the exporter's bank) that a letter of credit exists and that it may now ship the merchandise. The exporter then delivers a set of documents (according to the terms of the letter) to its own bank. These documents typically include an invoice, customs forms, a packing list, and a bill of lading. The exporter's bank ensures that the documents are in order and pays the exporter.

letter of credit (L/C)

Export/import financing in which the importer's bank issues a document stating that the bank will pay the exporter when the exporter fulfills the terms of the document.

FIGURE 11.4

Letter of Credit Process

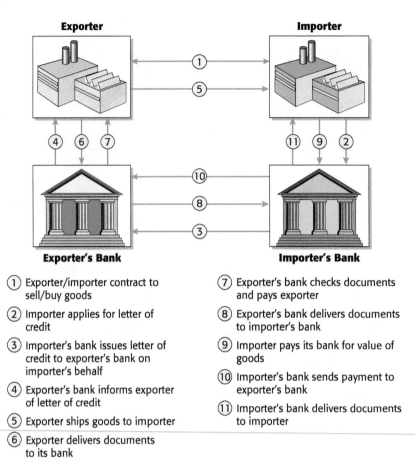

Exporter

Importer

Exporter's Bank

Importer's Bank

1. Exporter/importer contract to sell/buy goods
2. Importer applies for letter of credit
3. Importer's bank issues letter of credit to exporter's bank on importer's behalf
4. Exporter's bank informs exporter of letter of credit
5. Exporter ships goods to importer
6. Exporter delivers documents to its bank

7. Exporter's bank checks documents and pays exporter
8. Exporter's bank delivers documents to importer's bank
9. Importer pays its bank for value of goods
10. Importer's bank sends payment to exporter's bank
11. Importer's bank delivers documents to importer

When the importer's bank is satisfied that the terms of the letter have been met, it pays the exporter's bank. At that point, the importer's bank is responsible for collecting payment from the importer. Letters of credit are popular among traders because banks assume most of the risks. The letter of credit reduces the importer's risk of non-shipment (as compared with advance payment) because the importer receives proof of shipment before making payment. Although the exporter's risk of non-payment is slightly increased, it is a more secure form of payment for exporters because the non-payment risk is accepted by the importer's bank when it issues payment to the exporter's bank.

open account

Export/import financing in which an exporter ships merchandise and later bills the importer for its value.

OPEN ACCOUNT   Export/import financing in which an exporter ships merchandise and later bills the importer for its value is called **open account**. Because some receivables may not be collected, exporters should reserve shipping on open account only for their most trusted customers. This payment method is often used when the parties are very familiar with each other or for sales between two subsidiaries within an international company. The exporter simply invoices the importer (as in many domestic transactions), stating the amount and date due. This method reduces the risk of non-shipment faced by the importer under the advance payment method.

By the same token, the open account method increases the risk of non-payment for the exporter. Thus, open account is the least favourable for exporters but the most favourable for importers. For some insights on how small exporters can increase the probability of getting paid for a shipment, see the Entrepreneur's Toolkit, titled "Collecting International Debts."

Quick Study

1. Why do companies engage in *countertrade*? List each of its five types.
2. What are the four main methods of export/import financing?
3. Describe the various risks that each financing method poses for exporters and importers.

Entrepreneur's Toolkit   Collecting International Debts

What is the point of working hard to make an international sale if the buyer does not pay? There are seldom easy answers when an exporter is stuck without payment. Here are several pointers on what small businesses can do to reduce the likelihood of not receiving payment.

- **Know the Market.** Knowledge of the market you are exporting to is your first and best defence. Understanding its culture, the language spoken, and its legal system is ideal. You should also understand if there is typically a payment lag for business debts and customary debt collection procedures.
- **Keep Up to Date on Problem Countries.** Be aware of countries that commonly cause problems when it comes to debt collection. Regularly consult the many free sources of information available on the Internet to learn which countries are problems. Avoid doing business with them and seek markets elsewhere.
- **Understand the Payment Terms.** Essential to preventing later collection problems is both

parties clearly understanding the payment terms in your export sales agreement. Also be sure the buyer knows precisely when payment is to be issued.
- **Consider Buying Insurance.** If you decide to use an L/C, consider buying a documentary credit insurance policy (DCI) from Export Development Canada (EDC). EDC's DCI policy will cover up to 90 percent of a bank's loss if a foreign buyer's bank defaults on an L/C.[2]
- **Don't Delay Collection.** Do not wait too long to begin collecting a past-due account. Exporters who delay will likely never receive payment. Begin with firmly worded communications via phone, fax, e-mail, and letter.
- **Seek Advice.** Consult an international trade attorney or hire an international debt collection agency if necessary. You may be encouraged to accept arbitration as a way to resolve the issue; it is often your best chance of seeing at least partial payment.

Contractual Entry Modes

The products of some companies simply cannot be traded in open markets because they are *intangible*. Thus a company cannot use importing, exporting, or countertrade to exploit opportunities in a target market. Fortunately, there are other options for this type of company. A company can use a variety of contracts—*licensing, franchising, management contracts*, and *turnkey projects*—to market highly specialized assets and skills in markets beyond its nations' borders.

Licensing

Companies sometimes grant other firms the right to use an asset that is essential to the production of a finished product. **Licensing** is a contractual entry mode in which a company that owns intangible property (the *licensor*) grants another firm (the *licensee*) the right to use that property for a specified period of time. Licensors typically receive royalty payments based on a percentage of the licensee's sales revenue generated by the licensed property. The licensors might also receive a one-time fee to cover the cost of transferring the property to the licensee. Commonly licensed intangible property includes patents, copyrights, special formulas and designs, trademarks, and brand names. Thus licensing often involves granting companies the right to use *process technologies* inherent to the production of a particular good.

> **licensing**
> Practice by which one company owning intangible property (the licensor) grants another firm (the licensee) the right to use that property for a specified period of time.

Here are a few examples of successful licensing agreements:

- Hitachi (Japan) licensed from Duales System Deutschland (Germany) technology to be used in the recycling of plastics in Japan.
- Hewlett-Packard (United States) licensed from Canon (Japan) a printer engine for use in its monochrome laser printers.
- Cirque du Solei (Canada) licensed from Elvis Presley Enterprises subsidiary of CKX, Inc. (United States) Elvis Presley–related intellectual property.

An *exclusive licence* grants a company the exclusive rights to produce and market a property, or products made from that property, in a specific geographic region. The region can be the

cross licensing

Practice by which companies use licensing agreements to exchange intangible property with one another.

licensee's home country or may extend to worldwide markets. A *nonexclusive licence* grants a company the right to use a property but does not grant it sole access to a market. A licensor can grant several or more companies the right to use a property in the same region.

Cross licensing occurs when companies use licensing agreements to exchange intangible property with one another. For example, Fujitsu (www.fujitsu.com) of Japan signed a five-year cross-licensing agreement with Texas Instruments (www.ti.com) of the United States. The agreement allowed each company to use the other's technology in the production of its own goods—thus lowering research and development (R&D) costs. The very extensive arrangement covered all but a few semiconductor patents owned by each company. Because asset values are seldom exactly equal, cross licensing also typically involves royalty payments from one party to the other.

ADVANTAGES OF LICENSING There are several advantages to using licensing as an entry mode into new markets. First, licensors can use licensing to finance their international expansion. Most licensing agreements require licensees to contribute equipment and investment financing, whether by building special production facilities or by using existing excess capacity. Access to such resources can be a great advantage to a licensor who wants to expand but lacks the capital and managerial resources to do so. And because it need not spend time constructing and starting up its own new facilities, the licensor earns revenues sooner than it would otherwise.

Second, licensing can be a less risky method of international expansion for a licensor than other entry modes. Whereas some markets are risky because of social or political unrest, others defy accurate market research for a variety of reasons. Licensing helps shield the licensor from the increased risk of operating its own local production facilities in markets that are unstable or hard to assess accurately.

Third, licensing can help reduce the likelihood that a licensor's product will appear on the black market. The side streets of large cities in many emerging markets are dotted with tabletop vendors eager to sell bootleg versions of computer software, Hollywood films, and recordings of internationally popular musicians. Producers can, to some extent, foil bootleggers by licensing local companies to market their products at locally competitive prices. Royalties will be lower than the profits generated by sales at higher international prices, but lower profits are better than no profits at all—which is what owners get from bootleg versions of their products.

Finally, licensees can benefit by using licensing as a method of upgrading existing production technologies. For example, manufacturers of plastics and other synthetic materials in the Philippines attempted to meet the high standards demanded by the local subsidiaries of Japanese electronics and office equipment producers. To do this, D&L Industries of the Philippines upgraded its manufacturing process by licensing materials technology from Nippon Pigment of Japan.

DISADVANTAGES OF LICENSING There also are important disadvantages to using licensing. First, it can restrict a licensor's future activities. Suppose a licensee is granted the exclusive right to use an asset but fails to produce the sort of results that a licensor expected. Because the licence agreement is exclusive, the licensor cannot simply begin selling directly in that particular market to meet demand itself or contract with another licensee. A good product and lucrative market, therefore, do not guarantee success for a producer entering a market through licensing.

Second, licensing might reduce the global consistency of the quality and marketing of a licensor's product in different national markets. A licensor might find the development of a coherent global brand image an elusive goal if each of its national licensees is allowed to operate in any manner it chooses. Promoting a global image might later require considerable amounts of time and money to change the misconceptions of buyers in the various licensed markets.

Third, licensing might amount to a company "lending" strategically important property to its future competitors. This is an especially dangerous situation when a company licenses assets on which its competitive advantage is based. Licensing agreements are often made for several years and perhaps even a decade or more. During this time, licensees often become highly competent at producing and marketing the licensor's product. When the agreement expires, the licensor might find that its former licensee is capable of producing and marketing a better version of its own product. Licensing contracts can (and should) restrict licensees from competing in the future with products based strictly on licensed property. But enforcement of such provisions works only for identical or nearly identical products, not when substantial improvements are made.

Franchising

Franchising is a contractual entry mode in which one company (the *franchiser*) supplies another (the *franchisee*) with intangible property and other assistance over an extended period. Franchisers typically receive compensation as flat fees, royalty payments, or both. The most popular franchises are those with widely recognized brand names, such as Mercedes (www.mercedes.com), McDonald's (www.mcdonalds.com), and Starbucks (www.starbucks.com). In fact, the brand name or trademark of a company is normally the single most important item desired by the franchisee. This is why smaller companies with lesser known brand names and trademarks have greater difficulty locating interested franchisees.

Franchising differs from licensing in several ways. First, franchising gives a company greater control over the sale of its product in a target market. Franchisees must often meet strict guidelines on product quality, day-to-day management duties, and marketing promotions. Second, although licensing is fairly common in manufacturing industries, franchising is primarily used in service industries such as auto dealerships, entertainment, lodging, restaurants, and business services. Third, although licensing normally involves a one-time transfer of property, franchising requires ongoing assistance from the franchiser. In addition to the initial transfer of property, franchisers typically offer start-up capital, management training, location advice, and advertising assistance to their franchisees.

Some examples of the kinds of companies involved in international franchising include:

- Ozemail (Australia) awarded Magictel (Hong Kong) a franchise to operate its Internet phone and fax service in Hong Kong.
- Jean-Louis David (France) awarded franchises to more than 200 hairdressing salons in Italy.
- Inter Ikea Systems B.V. (The Netherlands) is the owner and franchisor of the Ikea stores. There are franchises in 29 countries.
- New York Fries and South St. Burger Co. (Canada) expanded its poutine-style french fries business to 23 international units in South Korea, United Arab Emirates (UAE), Hong Kong, and Bahrain using franchising. The company also has 195 locations across Canada.

Companies based in the United States dominate the world of international franchising. US companies perfected the practice of franchising in their large, homogeneous domestic market

franchising
Practice by which one company (the franchiser) supplies another (the franchisee) with intangible property and other assistance over an extended period.

Tesco is the largest British-based international grocery and general merchandising retail chain ranked by global sales. Originally specializing in food and drink, it has diversified into areas such as consumer electronics, financial services, movies and music, Internet service, and health insurance. Franchising helps Tesco ensure that individual stores meet company guidelines on matters such as company policies, product offerings, and service. Can you think of other industries that employ franchising?

Source: © Bruce Connolly/Corbis.

having low barriers to interstate trade and investment. Canada is also considered a good candidate for franchising development because a large portion of the population can afford products and services offered by franchises. In addition, there is relatively low income inequality in Canada, and it is considered a service-oriented country, where doing business is relatively safe and easy.[3]

Franchising is growing in the European Union, with the advent of a single currency and a unified set of franchise laws. Many European managers with comfortable early-retirement packages have discovered franchising to be an appealing second career.

Despite projections for robust growth, European franchise managers often misunderstand the franchising concept. One example is when Holiday Inn's franchise expansion in Spain was moving more slowly than expected. According to the company's development director in Spain, Holiday Inn found that it needed to convince local managers that Holiday Inn did not want to "take control" of their hotels.[4] In some eastern European countries, local managers do not understand why they must continue to pay royalties to brand and trademark owners. Franchise expansion in eastern European markets also suffers from a lack of local capital, high interest rates, high taxes, bureaucratic obstacles, restrictive laws, and corruption.[5]

ADVANTAGES OF FRANCHISING   There are several important advantages of franchising. First, franchisers can use franchising as a low-cost, low-risk entry mode into new markets. Companies following global strategies rely on consistent products and common themes in worldwide markets. Franchising allows them to maintain consistency by replicating the processes for standardized products in each target market. Many franchisers, however, will make small modifications in products and promotional messages when marketing specifically to local buyers.

Second, franchising is an entry mode that allows for rapid geographic expansion. Firms often gain a competitive advantage by being first to seize a market opportunity. For example, New York Fries (NYF) (www.newyorkfries.com) of London, Ontario, uses franchising to fuel its international expansion. NYF has successfully entered Hong Kong, the United Arab Emirates, and Bahrain, and is eyeing opportunities in China.[6]

Finally, franchisers can benefit from the cultural knowledge and know-how of local managers. This helps lower the risk of business failure in unfamiliar markets and can create a competitive advantage.

DISADVANTAGES OF FRANCHISING   Franchising can also pose problems for both franchisers and franchisees. First, franchisers may find it cumbersome to manage a large number of franchisees in a variety of national markets. A major concern is that product quality and promotional messages among franchisees will not be consistent from one market to another. One way to ensure greater control is by establishing in each market a so-called *master franchisee*, which is responsible for monitoring the operations of individual franchisees.

Second, franchisees can experience a loss of organizational flexibility in franchising agreements. Franchise contracts can restrict their strategic and tactical options, and they may even be forced to promote products owned by the franchiser's other divisions. For years PepsiCo (www.pepsico.com) owned the well-known restaurant chains Pizza Hut, Taco Bell, and KFC. As part of their franchise agreements with PepsiCo, restaurant owners were required to sell only PepsiCo beverages to their customers. Many franchisees worldwide were displeased with such restrictions on their product offerings and were relieved when PepsiCo spun off the restaurant chains.

Management Contracts

management contract
Practice by which one company supplies another with managerial expertise for a specific period of time.

Under the stipulations of a **management contract**, one company supplies another with managerial expertise for a specific period of time. The supplier of expertise is normally compensated with either a lump-sum payment or a continuing fee based on sales volume. Such contracts are commonly found in the public utilities sectors of developed and emerging markets. Two types of knowledge can be transferred through management contracts—the specialized knowledge of technical managers and the business-management skills of general managers.

Two examples of management contracts include:

- DBS Asia (Thailand) awarded a management contract to Favorlangh Communication (Taiwan) to set up and run a company supplying digital television programming in Taiwan.
- Lyonnaise de Eaux (France) and RWE Aqua (Germany) agreed to manage drinking water quality and client billing, and to maintain the water infrastructure for the city of Budapest, Hungary, for 25 years.

ADVANTAGES OF MANAGEMENT CONTRACTS Management contracts can benefit organizations and countries. First, a firm can award a management contract to another company and thereby exploit an international business opportunity without having to place a great deal of its own physical assets at risk. Financial capital can then be reserved for other promising investment projects that would otherwise not be funded.

Second, governments can award companies management contracts to operate and upgrade public utilities, particularly when a nation is short of investment financing. That is why the government of Kazakhstan contracted with a group of international companies called ABB Power Grid Consortium to manage its national electricity grid system for 25 years. Under the terms of the contract, the consortium paid past wages owed to workers by the government and invested more than $200 million during the first three years of the agreement. The Kazakhstan government had neither the cash flow to pay the workers nor the funds to make badly needed improvements.

Third, governments use management contracts to develop the skills of local workers and managers. ESB International (www.esb.ie) of Ireland signed a three-year contract not only to manage and operate a power plant in Ghana, Africa, but also to train local personnel in the skills needed to manage it at some point in the future.

DISADVANTAGES OF MANAGEMENT CONTRACTS Unfortunately, management contracts also pose two disadvantages for suppliers of expertise. First of all, although management contracts reduce the exposure of physical assets in another country, the same is not true for the supplier's personnel; political or social turmoil can threaten managers' lives.

Second, suppliers of expertise may end up nurturing a formidable new competitor in the local market. After learning how to conduct certain operations, the party that had originally needed assistance may be capable of competing on its own. Firms must weigh the financial returns from a management contract against the potential future problems caused by a newly launched competitor.

Turnkey Projects

When one company designs, constructs, and tests a production facility for a client, the agreement is called a **turnkey (build–operate–transfer) project**. The term *turnkey project* is derived from the understanding that the client, who normally pays a flat fee for the project, is expected to do nothing more than simply "turn a key" to get the facility operating. The company awarded a turnkey project completely prepares the facility for its client.

turnkey (build–operate–transfer) project

Practice by which one company designs, constructs, and tests a production facility for a client firm.

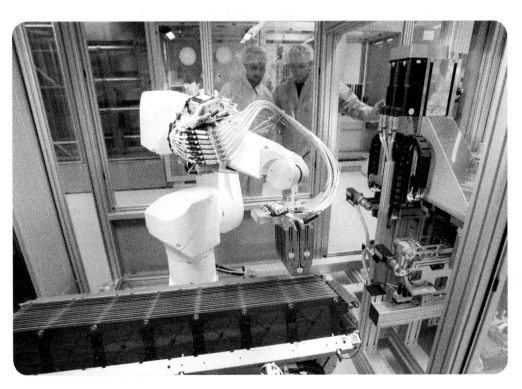

A turnkey project is a venture in which one organization designs, builds, and tests a facility for another, which then merely "turns the key" to get things under way. Here, employees of Solar World monitor the automated refinement process of silicon wafers at the company plant in Freiberg, Germany. The wafers are then integrated into modules at Solar World subsidiaries, which fabricate turnkey-ready solar power plants. What other types of operations are appropriate for a turnkey project?

Source: Matthias Hiekel/Agentur/ Newscom.

Similar to management contracts, turnkey projects tend to be large-scale and often involve government agencies. But unlike management contracts, turnkey projects transfer special process technologies or production-facility designs to the client. They typically involve the construction of power plants, airports, seaports, telecommunication systems, and petrochemical facilities that are then turned over to the client. Under a management contract, the supplier of a service retains the asset—the managerial expertise.

Three examples of international turnkey projects include:

- Telecommunications Consultants India constructed telecom networks in both Madagascar and Ghana—two turnkey projects worth a combined total of $28 million.
- Lubei Group (China) agreed with the government of Belarus to join in the construction of a facility for processing a fertilizer byproduct into cement.
- Greenfield Hydroponic Systems Inc. (Canada), a manufacturer of patented solar and wind-powered portable greenhouses, developed a portable greenhouse in the United States for growing sprouted beans such as lentils, as well as broccoli, radishes, and other organic produce. The project included operations, supplies, marketing, and grower support.[7]

ADVANTAGES OF TURNKEY PROJECTS Turnkey projects provide benefits to providers and recipients. First, turnkey projects permit firms to specialize in their core competencies and to exploit opportunities that they could not undertake alone. ExxonMobil (www.exxonmobil.com) awarded a turnkey project to PT McDermott Indonesia (www.mcdermott.com) and Toyo Engineering (www.toyo-eng.co.jp) of Japan to build a liquid natural gas plant on the Indonesian island of Sumatra. The providers are responsible for constructing an offshore production platform, laying a 100-kilometre underwater pipeline, and building an on-land liquid natural gas refinery. The $316 million project is feasible only because each company contributes unique expertise to the design, construction, and testing of the facilities.

Second, turnkey projects allow governments to obtain designs for infrastructure projects from the world's leading companies. For instance, Turkey's government enlisted two separate consortiums of international firms to build four hydroelectric dams on its Coruh River. The dams combine the design and technological expertise of each company in the two consortiums. The Turkish government also awarded a turnkey project to Ericsson (www.ericsson.com) of Sweden to expand the country's mobile telecommunication system.

DISADVANTAGES OF TURNKEY PROJECTS Among the disadvantages of turnkey projects is the fact that a company may be awarded a project for political reasons rather than for technological know-how. Because turnkey projects are often of high monetary value and awarded by government agencies, the process of awarding them can be highly politicized. When the selection process is not entirely open, companies with the best political connections often win contracts, usually at inflated prices—the costs of which are typically passed on to local taxpayers.

Second, like management contracts, turnkey projects can create future competitors. A newly created local competitor could become a major supplier in its own domestic market and perhaps even in other markets where the supplier operates. Therefore, companies try to avoid projects in which there is danger of transferring their core competencies to others.

Quick Study

1. Identify the advantages and disadvantages of *licensing* for the licensor and the licensee.
2. Describe how *franchising* differs from licensing. What are its main benefits and drawbacks?
3. When is a *management contract* useful? Identify two types of knowledge it is used to transfer.
4. What is a *turnkey project*? Describe its main advantages and disadvantages.

Investment Entry Modes

Investment entry modes entail direct investment in plant and equipment in a country coupled with ongoing involvement in the local operation. Entry modes in this category take a company's commitment in a market to a higher level. Let's now explore three common forms of investment entry: *wholly owned subsidiaries, joint ventures,* and *strategic alliances.*

Wholly Owned Subsidiaries

As the term suggests, a **wholly owned subsidiary** is a facility entirely owned and controlled by a single parent company. Companies can establish a wholly owned subsidiary either by forming a new company and constructing entirely new facilities (such as factories, offices, and equipment) or by purchasing an existing company and internalizing its facilities. Whether an international subsidiary is purchased or newly created depends to a large extent on its proposed operations. When a parent company designs a subsidiary to manufacture the latest high-tech products, it typically must build new facilities. The major drawback of creation from the ground up is the time it takes to construct new facilities, hire and train employees, and launch production.

Conversely, finding an existing local company capable of performing marketing and sales will be easier because special technologies are typically not needed. By purchasing the existing marketing and sales operations of an existing firm in the target market, the parent can have the subsidiary operating relatively quickly. Buying an existing company's operations in the target market is a particularly good strategy when the company to be acquired has a valuable trademark, brand name, or process technology. Another valid reason to purchase an existing company is to take over a competitor, thus increasing market share. For example Target (www.target.ca) entered the Canadian market by acquiring the Zellers stores.

ADVANTAGES OF WHOLLY OWNED SUBSIDIARIES   There are two main advantages to entering a market using a wholly owned subsidiary. First, managers have complete control over day-to-day operations in the target market and access to valuable technologies, processes, and other intangible properties within the subsidiary. Complete control also decreases the chance that competitors will gain access to a company's competitive advantage, which is particularly important if it is technology-based. Managers also retain complete control over the subsidiary's output and prices. Unlike licensors and franchisers, the parent company also receives all profits generated by the subsidiary.

Second, a wholly owned subsidiary is a good mode of entry when a company wants to coordinate the activities of all its national subsidiaries. Companies using global strategies view each of their national markets as one part of an interconnected global market. Thus the ability to exercise complete control over a wholly owned subsidiary makes this entry mode attractive to companies that are pursuing global strategies.

DISADVANTAGES OF WHOLLY OWNED SUBSIDIARIES   Wholly owned subsidiaries also present two primary disadvantages. First, they can be expensive undertakings because companies must typically finance investments internally or raise funds in financial markets. Obtaining the necessary funds can be difficult for small and medium-sized companies but relatively easy for the largest companies.

Second, risk exposure is high because a wholly owned subsidiary requires substantial company resources. One source of risk is political or social uncertainty or outright instability in the target market. Such risks can place both physical assets and personnel in serious jeopardy. The sole owner of a wholly owned subsidiary also accepts the risk that buyers will reject the company's product. Parent companies can reduce this risk by gaining a better understanding of consumers prior to entering the target market.

Joint Ventures

Under certain circumstances, companies prefer to share ownership of an operation rather than take complete ownership. A separate company that is created and jointly owned by two or more independent entities to achieve a common business objective is called a **joint venture**. Joint venture partners can be privately owned companies, government agencies, or government-owned companies. Each party may contribute anything valued by its partners, including managerial talent,

wholly owned subsidiary
Facility entirely owned and controlled by a single parent company.

joint venture
Separate company that is created and jointly owned by two or more independent entities to achieve a common business objective.

marketing expertise, market access, production technologies, financial capital, and superior knowledge or techniques of research and development.

Examples of joint ventures include:

- A joint venture between Suzuki Motor Corporation (Japan) and the government of India to manufacture a small-engine car specifically for the Indian market.
- A joint venture between a group of Indian companies and a Russian partner to produce television sets in Russia for the local market.
- A joint venture between Encana (Canada) and PetroChina (China) to explore and develop Encana's extensive undeveloped Duvernay land holdings in Alberta, Canada.
- A joint venture between Encana (Canada) and Mitsubishi (Japan) to develop a shale gas field in Alberta and British Columbia, Canada.

JOINT VENTURE CONFIGURATIONS As we see in Figure 11.5, there are four main joint venture configurations.[8] Although we illustrate each of these as consisting of just two partners, each configuration can also apply to ventures of several or more partners.

Forward Integration Joint Venture Figure 11.5 (a) outlines a joint venture characterized by *forward integration*. In this type of joint venture, the parties choose to invest together in *downstream* business activities—activities further along in the value system that are normally performed by others. For instance, two household appliance manufacturers opening a retail outlet in a developing country would be a joint venture characterized by forward integration. The two companies now perform activities normally performed by retailers further along in the product's journey to buyers.

Backward Integration Joint Venture Figure 11.5 (b) outlines a joint venture characterized by *backward integration*. In other words, the joint venture signals a move by each company into *upstream* business activities—activities earlier in the value system that are normally performed by others. Such a configuration would result if two steel manufacturers formed a joint venture to mine iron ore. The companies now engage in an activity that is normally performed by mining companies.

FIGURE 11.5

Alternative Joint Venture Configurations

Source: Based on Peter Buckley and Mark Casson, "A Theory of Cooperation in International Business," in Farok J. Contractor and Peter Lorange (eds.), *Cooperative Strategies in International Business* (Lexington, MA: Lexington Books, 1988) pp. 31–53.

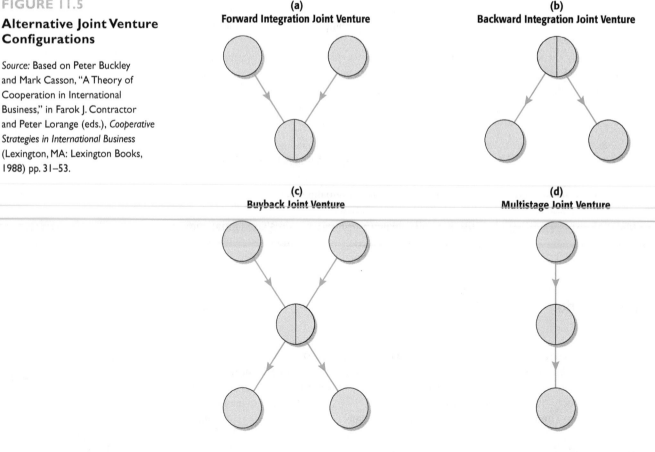

(a)
Forward Integration Joint Venture

(b)
Backward Integration Joint Venture

(c)
Buyback Joint Venture

(d)
Multistage Joint Venture

Buyback Joint Venture   Figure 11.5 (c) outlines a joint venture whose input is provided by, and whose output is absorbed by, each of its partners. A *buyback joint venture* is formed when each partner requires the same component in its production process. It might be formed when a production facility of a certain minimum size is needed to achieve economies of scale but neither partner alone enjoys enough demand to warrant building it. However, by combining resources, the partners can construct a facility that serves their needs while achieving savings from economies of scale production. For instance, this was one reason behind the $500 million joint venture between Chrysler (www.chrysler.com) and BMW (www.bmw.com) to build small-car engines in Latin America. Each party benefited from the economies of scale offered by the plant's annual production capacity of 400 000 engines—a volume that neither company could absorb alone.

Multistage Joint Venture   Figure 11.5 (d) outlines a joint venture that features downstream integration by one partner and upstream integration by another. A *multistage joint venture* often results when one company produces a good or service required by another. For example, a sporting goods manufacturer might join with a sporting goods retailer to establish a distribution company designed to bypass inefficient local distributors in a developing country.

ADVANTAGES OF JOINT VENTURES   Joint ventures offer several important advantages to companies going international. Above all, companies rely on joint ventures to reduce risk. Generally, a joint venture exposes fewer of a partner's assets to risk than would a wholly owned subsidiary—each partner risks only its own contribution. That is why a joint venture entry might be a wise choice when market entry requires a large investment or when there is significant political or social instability in the target market. Similarly, a company can use a joint venture to learn about a local business environment prior to launching a wholly owned subsidiary. In fact, many joint ventures are ultimately bought outright by one of the partners after it gains sufficient expertise in the local market.

Second, companies can use joint ventures to penetrate international markets that are otherwise off-limits. Some governments either require nondomestic companies to share ownership with local companies or provide incentives for them to do so. Such requirements are most common among governments of developing countries. The goal is to improve the competitiveness of local companies by having them team up with and learn from international partner(s).

Third, a company can gain access to another company's international distribution network through the use of a joint venture. The joint venture between Caterpillar (www.caterpillar.com) of the United States and Mitsubishi Heavy Industries (www.mitsubishi.com) of Japan was designed to improve the competitiveness of each against a common rival, Komatsu (www.komatsu.com) of Japan. While Caterpillar gained access to Mitsubishi's distribution system in Japan, Mitsubishi got access to Caterpillar's global distribution network—helping it to compete more effectively internationally.

Finally, companies form international joint ventures for defensive reasons. Entering a joint venture with a local government or government-controlled company gives the government a direct stake in the venture's success. In turn, the local government will be less likely to interfere if it means that the venture's performance will suffer. This same strategy can also be used to create a more "local" image when feelings of nationalism are running strong in a target country.

DISADVANTAGES OF JOINT VENTURES   Among its disadvantages, joint venture ownership can result in conflict between partners. Conflict is perhaps most common when management is shared equally—that is, when each partner supplies top managers in what is commonly known as a "50–50 joint venture." Because neither partner's managers have the final say on decisions, managerial paralysis can result, causing problems such as delays in responding to changing market conditions. Conflict can also arise from disagreements over how future investments and profits are to be shared. Parties can reduce the likelihood of conflict and indecision by establishing unequal ownership, whereby one partner maintains 51 percent ownership of the voting stock and has the final say on decisions. A multiparty joint venture (commonly referred to as a *consortium*) can also feature unequal ownership. For example, ownership of a four-party joint venture could be distributed 20–20–20–40, with the 40 percent owner having the final say on decisions.

Second, loss of control over a joint venture's operations can also result when the local government is a partner in the joint venture. This situation occurs most often in industries considered culturally sensitive or important to national security, such as broadcasting, infrastructure, and defence. Thus a joint venture's profitability could suffer because of local government motives based on cultural preservation or security.

Strategic Alliances

Sometimes companies who are willing to cooperate with one another do not want to go so far as to create a separate jointly owned company. A relationship whereby two or more entities cooperate (but do not form a separate company) to achieve the strategic goals of each is called a **strategic alliance**. Similar to joint ventures, strategic alliances can be formed for relatively short periods or for many years, depending on the goals of the participants. Strategic alliances can be established between a company and its suppliers, its buyers, and even its competitors. In forming such alliances, sometimes each partner purchases a portion of the other's stock. In this way, each company has a direct stake in its partner's future performance. This decreases the likelihood that one partner will try to take advantage of the other.

Examples of strategic alliances include:

- An alliance between Siemens (Germany) and Hewlett-Packard (United States) to create and market devices used to control telecommunications systems
- A strategic alliance between Nippon Life Group (Japan) and Putnam Investments (United States) to permit Putnam to develop investment products and manage assets for Nippon
- A strategic alliance between BASF (Germany) and TenCate (The Netherlands) to develop, produce, and commercialize thermoplastic automotive composites. In this alliance, BASF contributes its know-how in the production of thermoplastic resins, while TenCate provides its manufacturing expertise in composites[9]
- A strategic alliance, called Star Alliance, between several airline carriers including Air Canada to provide easy connections and smooth travel for their passengers in 150 countries

ADVANTAGES OF STRATEGIC ALLIANCES Strategic alliances offer several important advantages to companies. First, companies use strategic alliances to share the cost of an international investment project. For example, many firms are developing new products that not only integrate the latest technologies but also shorten the life spans of existing products. In turn, the shorter life span is reducing the number of years during which a company can recoup its investment. Thus many companies are cooperating to share the costs of developing new products. For example, Toshiba (www.toshiba.com) of Japan, Siemens (www.siemens.com) of Germany, and IBM (www.ibm.com) of the United States shared the $1 billion cost of developing a facility near Nagoya, Japan, to manufacture small, efficient computer memory chips.

Second, companies use strategic alliances to tap into competitors' specific strengths. Some alliances formed between Internet portals and technology companies are designed to do just that. For example, an Internet portal provides access to a large, global audience through its Web site, while the technology company supplies its know-how in delivering, say, music over the Internet. Meeting the goal of the alliance—marketing music over the Web—requires the competencies of both partners.

Finally, companies turn to strategic alliances for many of the same reasons that they turn to joint ventures. Some businesses use strategic alliances to gain access to a partner's channels of distribution in a target market. Other firms use them to reduce exposure to the same kinds of risks from which joint ventures provide protection.

DISADVANTAGES OF STRATEGIC ALLIANCES Perhaps the most important disadvantage of a strategic alliance is that it can create a future local or even global competitor. For example, one partner might be using the alliance to test a market and prepare the launch of a wholly owned subsidiary. By declining to cooperate with others in the area of its core competency, a company can reduce the likelihood of creating a competitor that would threaten its main area of business. Likewise, a company can insist on contractual clauses that constrain partners from competing against it with certain products or in certain geographic regions. Companies are also careful to protect special research programs, production techniques, and marketing practices that are not committed to the alliance. Naturally, managers must weigh the potential for encouraging new competition against the benefits of international cooperation.

As in the case of joint ventures, conflict can arise and eventually undermine cooperation. Alliance contracts are drawn up to cover as many contingencies as possible, but communication and cultural differences can still arise. When serious problems crop up, dissolution of the alliance may be the only option.

Selecting Partners for Cooperation

Every company's goals and strategies are influenced by both its competitive strengths and the challenges it faces in the marketplace. Because the goals and strategies of any two companies are never exactly alike, cooperation can be difficult. Moreover, ventures and alliances often last many years, perhaps even indefinitely. Therefore, partner selection is a crucial ingredient for success. The following discussion focuses on partner selection in joint ventures and strategic alliances. Yet many of the same points also apply to contractual entry modes such as licensing and franchising, for which choosing the right partner is also important.

Every partner must be firmly committed to the goals of the cooperative arrangement. Many companies engage in cooperative forms of business, but the reasons behind each party's participation are never identical. Sometimes, a company stops contributing to a cooperative arrangement once it achieves its own objectives. Detailing the precise duties and contributions of each party to an international cooperative arrangement through prior negotiations can go a long way toward ensuring continued cooperation. For some key considerations in negotiating international agreements, see the Global Manager's Briefcase, titled "Negotiating Market Entry."

Although the importance of locating a trustworthy partner seems obvious, cooperation should be approached with caution. Companies can have hidden reasons for cooperating. Sometimes they try to acquire more from cooperation than their partners realize. If a hidden agenda is discovered during the course of cooperation, trust can break down—in which case the cooperative arrangement is virtually destroyed. Because trust is so important, firms naturally prefer partners with whom they have had a favourable working relationship in the past. However, such arrangements are much easier for large multinationals than for small and medium-sized companies with little international experience and few international contacts.

Global Manager's Briefcase   Negotiating Market Entry

Global business managers must negotiate the terms of many deals. A cooperative atmosphere between potential partners depends on both parties viewing contract negotiations as a success. Managers should be aware of the negotiation process and influential factors. The process normally occurs in four stages.

- **Stage 1: Preparation.** Negotiators must have a clear vision of what the company wants to achieve. Negotiation will vary depending on whether the proposed business arrangement is a one-time deal or just the first phase of a lengthy partnership.
- **Stage 2: Opening Positions.** Discussions begin as each side states its opening position, which is each side's most favourable terms. Positions might emerge gradually to leave negotiators room to manoeuvre.
- **Stage 3: Hard Bargaining.** The relative power of each party is key in the outcome of negotiations. Direct conflict is likely at this stage, and culture plays a role. For example, Chinese negotiators will likely try to avoid conflict and may call off talks if conflict erupts.

- **Stage 4: Agreement and Follow-up.** Negotiations reaching this stage are a success. Whereas Western negotiators view signing contracts as the end of negotiations, most Asian negotiators see contracts as the start of a flexible relationship.

Two key elements influence international business negotiations:

- **Cultural Elements.** Negotiating styles differ from culture to culture. Successful negotiations in Asian cultures mean protecting the other party from losing face (being embarrassed or shamed) and meeting the other party halfway. Yet negotiators in Western cultures typically hope to gain many concessions with little concern for embarrassing the other party.
- **Political and Legal Elements.** Negotiators may have political motives. A rigid public position might be taken to show the company or government officials back home that they are working in the company's or nation's interest. Also, consumer groups and labour unions might lobby government officials to ensure that a proposed agreement benefits them.

Each party's managers must be comfortable working with people of other cultures and travelling to (even perhaps living in) other *national* cultures. As a result, cooperation will go more smoothly and the transition—both in work life and personal life—will be easier for managers who are sent to work for a joint venture. Each partner's managers should also be comfortable working with, and within, one another's *corporate* culture. For example, although some companies encourage the participation of subordinates in decision making, others do not. Such differences often reflect differences in national culture, and when managers possess cultural understanding, adjustment and cooperation are likely to run more smoothly.

Above all, a suitable partner must have something valuable to offer. Firms should avoid cooperation simply because they are approached by another company. Rather, managers must be certain that they are getting a fair return on their cooperative efforts. And they should evaluate the benefits of a potential international cooperative arrangement just as they would any other investment opportunity.

Strategic Factors in Selecting an Entry Mode

The choice of entry mode has many important strategic implications for a company's future operations.[10] Enormous investments in time and money can go into determining an entry mode; therefore, the choice must be made carefully. Several key factors that influence a company's international entry mode selection are the *cultural environment, political and legal environments, market size, production and shipping costs*, and *international experience*. Let's now explore each of these factors.

Cultural Environment

As we saw in Chapter 2, the dimensions of culture—values, beliefs, customs, languages, religions—can differ greatly from one nation to another. In such cases, managers can be less confident in their ability to manage operations in the host country. They can be concerned about the potential not only for communication problems but also for interpersonal difficulties. As a result, managers may avoid investment entry modes in favour of exporting or a contractual mode. On the other hand, cultural similarity encourages confidence and thus the likelihood of investment. Likewise, the importance of cultural differences diminishes when managers are knowledgeable about the culture of the target market.

Political and Legal Environments

As mentioned earlier in this chapter, political instability in a target market increases the risk exposure of investments. Significant political differences and levels of instability cause companies to avoid large investments and to favour entry modes that shelter assets.

A target market's legal system also influences the choice of entry mode. Certain import regulations, such as high tariffs or low quota limits, can encourage investment. A company that produces locally avoids tariffs that increase product cost; it also doesn't have to worry about making it into the market below the quota (if there is one). But low tariffs and high quota limits discourage market entry by means of investment. Also, governments may enact laws that ban certain types of investment outright. For many years, China had banned wholly owned subsidiaries by non-Chinese companies and required that joint ventures be formed with local partners. Finally, if a market is lax in enforcing copyright and patent laws, a company may prefer to use investment entry to maintain control over its assets and marketing.

Market Size

The size of a potential market also influences the choice of entry mode. For example, rising incomes in a market encourage investment entry modes because investment allows a firm to prepare for expanding market demand and to increase its understanding of the target market. High domestic demand in China is attracting investment in joint ventures, strategic alliances, and wholly owned subsidiaries. On the other hand, if investors believe that a market is likely to remain relatively small, better options might include exporting or contractual entry.

Production and Shipping Costs

By helping to control total costs, low-cost production and shipping can give a company an advantage. Accordingly, setting up production in a market is desirable when the total cost of production there is lower than in the home market. Low-cost local production might also encourage contractual entry through licensing or franchising. If production costs are sufficiently low, the international production site might even begin supplying other markets, including the home country. An additional potential benefit of local production might be that managers could observe buyer behaviour and modify products to better suit the needs of the local market. Lower production costs at home make it more appealing to export to international markets.

Companies that produce goods with high shipping costs naturally prefer local production. Contractual and investment entry modes are viable options in this case. Alternatively, exporting is feasible when products have relatively lower shipping costs. Finally, because they are subject to less price competition, products for which there are fewer substitutes or those that are discretionary items can more easily absorb higher shipping and production costs. In this case, exporting is a likely selection.

International Experience

Most companies enter the international marketplace through exporting. As companies gain international experience, they tend to select entry modes that require deeper involvement. But this means businesses must accept greater risk in return for greater control over operations and strategy. Eventually, they may explore the advantages of licensing, franchising, management contracts, and turnkey projects. After businesses become comfortable in a particular market, joint ventures, strategic alliances, and wholly owned subsidiaries become viable options.

This evolutionary path of accepting greater risk and control with experience does not hold for every company. Whereas some firms remain fixed at one point, others skip several entry modes altogether. Advances in technology and transportation are allowing more and more small companies to leapfrog several stages at once. These relationships also vary for each company depending on its product and the characteristics of home and target markets.

Quick Study

1. What is a *wholly owned subsidiary*? Identify its advantages and disadvantages.
2. What is meant by the term *joint venture*? Identify four joint venture configurations.
3. How does a *strategic alliance* differ from a joint venture? Explain the pluses and minuses of such alliances.
4. Discuss the strategic factors to consider when selecting an entry mode.

Bottom Line for Business

This chapter explained important factors in selecting entry modes and key aspects in their management. We studied the circumstances under which each entry mode is most appropriate and the advantages and disadvantages that each provides. The choice of which entry mode(s) to use in entering international markets matches a company's international strategy. Some companies will want entry modes that give them tight control over international activities because they are pursuing a global strategy. Meanwhile, other companies might not require an entry mode with central control because they are pursuing a multinational strategy. The entry mode must also be chosen to align well with an organization's structure.

Chapter Summary

1. **Explain how companies use exporting, importing, and countertrade.**
   - Exporting helps a company to expand sales, diversify sales, or gain experience and represents a low-cost, low-risk way of getting started in international business.
   - A successful export strategy involves (1) identifying a potential market, (2) matching needs to abilities, (3) initiating meetings, and (4) committing resources.
   - *Direct exporting* occurs when a company sells its products directly to buyers in a target market through local *sales representatives* or *distributors*.
   - *Indirect exporting* occurs when a company sells its products to intermediaries (*agents*, *export management companies*, and *export trading companies*) who then resell to buyers in a target market.
   - *Countertrade* is selling goods or services that are paid for with other goods or services; it can take the form of (1) *barter*, (2) *counterpurchase*, (3) *offset*, (4) *switch trading*, and (5) *buyback*.

2. **Explain the various means of financing export and import activities.**
   - With *advance payment* an importer pays an exporter for merchandise before it is shipped.
   - *Documentary collection* calls for a bank to act as an intermediary without accepting financial risk.
   - Under a *letter of credit*, the importer's bank issues a document stating that the bank will pay the exporter when the exporter fulfills the terms of the document.
   - Several types of letters of credit are an *irrevocable letter of credit, a revocable letter of credit*, and a *confirmed letter of credit*.
   - Under *open account,* an exporter ships merchandise and later bills the importer for its value.

3. **Describe the different contractual entry modes that are available to companies.**
   - *Licensing* is a contractual entry mode in which a company that owns intangible property (the *licensor*) grants another firm (the *licensee*) the right to use that property for a specified period of time.
   - *Franchising* is a contractual entry mode in which one company (the *franchiser*) supplies another (the *franchisee*) with intangible property and other assistance over an extended period.
   - A *management contract* enables company to supply another with managerial expertise for a specific period of time and is used to transfer two types of knowledge—the specialized knowledge of technical managers and the business-management skills of general managers.
   - A *turnkey (build–operate–transfer) project* is one in which one company designs, constructs, and tests a production facility for a client.

4. **Explain the various types of investment entry modes.**
   - *Investment entry modes* entail the direct investment in plant and equipment in a country coupled with ongoing involvement in the local operation.
   - A *wholly owned subsidiary* is a facility entirely owned and controlled by a single parent company.
   - A separate company created and jointly owned by two or more independent entities to achieve a common business objective is called a *joint venture*.
   - Joint ventures can involve *forward integration* (investing in downstream activities), *backward integration* (investing in upstream activities), a *buyback joint venture* (input is provided by and output is absorbed by each partner), and *multistage joint venture* (downstream integration by one partner and upstream integration by another).
   - A *strategic alliance* is a relationship in which two or more entities cooperate (but do not form a separate company).

5. Discuss the important strategic factors in selecting an entry mode.
- Managers are typically less confident in their ability to manage operations in unfamiliar cultures and may avoid investment entry modes in favour of exporting or a contractual mode.
- Large political differences and high levels of instability cause companies to avoid large investments and favour entry modes that shelter assets.
- Rising incomes encourage investment entry because investment allows a firm to prepare for expanding market demand and to increase its understanding of the target market.
- Producing locally is desirable when the total cost of production in a market is lower than in the home market and when shipping costs are high.
- Companies tend to make their initial foray into international markets using exporting and select entry modes that require deeper involvement as they gain international experience.

Key Terms

advance payment 314	draft (bill of exchange) 314	licensing 317
agents 311	entry mode 308	management contract 320
barter 312	export management company	offset 313
bill of lading 314	(EMC) 311	open account 316
buyback 313	export trading company (ETC) 311	strategic alliance 326
counterpurchase 312	franchising 319	switch trading 313
countertrade 312	freight forwarder 312	turnkey (build–operate–transfer)
cross licensing 318	indirect exporting 310	project 321
direct exporting 310	joint venture 323	wholly owned subsidiary 323
documentary collection 314	letter of credit (L/C) 315	

Talk It Over

1. Not all companies "go international" by first exporting, then using contracts, and then investing in other markets. How does a company's product influence the process of going international? How (if at all) does technology, such as the Internet, affect the process of going international?

2. "Companies should use investment entry modes whenever possible because they offer the greatest control over business operations." Do you agree or disagree with this statement? Are there times when other types of market entry offer greater control? When is investment entry a poor option?

3. In earlier chapters, we learned how governments get involved in the international flow of trade and foreign direct investment. We also learned how regional economic integration is influencing international business. Identify two market entry modes, and describe how each might be affected by the actions of governments and by increasing regional integration.

Take It to the Web

1. **Video Report.** Visit YouTube (www.youtube.com), and type "entry modes" into the search engine. Watch one video from the list, and then summarize it in a half-page report. Reflecting on the contents of this chapter, which aspects of selecting and managing entry modes can you identify in the video? How might a company engaged in international business act on the information contained in the video?

2. **Web Site Report.** Although forming a joint venture can be advantageous, companies may also encounter challenges and misunderstandings. Marvel Enterprises and Sony formed a 50/50 joint venture that oversees all licensing and merchandising for *Spider-Man*, as well as Sony's animated TV series titled *Spider-Man*. Marvel and Sony became embroiled in a series of lawsuits and counter lawsuits. Perform an Internet search for the name of the joint venture,

"Spider-Man Merchandising L. P.," and locate stories that discuss the lawsuits and their settlement.

What reasons did Marvel give for its initial lawsuit against Sony over its activities? Do you think Marvel was justified in filing suit against Sony? Was it a ruse for Marvel to exact something out of Sony, as some believe? Do you think Sony was right to counter sue as it did? What do you think was the main motivation to form the venture from the perspective of each partner?

Do you think the 50/50 split had anything to do with the joint venture's difficulties? Why or why not? Do you think differences in organizational culture (perhaps rooted in national culture) played any role in the conflict? Do you think anything could have been done during the formation of the joint venture that would have reduced the chances of this dispute arising? Explain.

Practising International Management Case

Telecom Ventures Unite the World

The world of telecommunications is changing. The era of global e-commerce is here, driven by new technologies such as broadband and wireless Internet access that make possible video telephone connections and high-speed data transmission. Annual worldwide revenues for telecommunications services total $600 billion, with international companies accounting for 20 percent of the business.

Market opportunities are opening around the world as post, telephone, and telegraph (PTT) monopolies are undergoing privatization. Since 1998, telecom deregulation has been taking place in earnest in Europe. Meanwhile, governments in developing countries are boosting investments in infrastructure improvements to increase the number of available telephone lines. The demand for telephone service is growing at a sharp pace; international telephone call volume more than doubled over a recent six-year period. The net result of these changes is the globalization of the telecommunications industry. As William Donovan, a vice president at Sea-Land Service, said recently, "I don't want to have to talk to a bunch of different PTTs around the world. I don't want to have to go to one carrier in one country and a second in another just because it doesn't have a presence there."

Several alliances and joint venture partnerships formed between companies hoping to capitalize on the changed market and business environment. France Telecom, Deutsche Telekom, and Sprint created Global One to bring international telecommunications services to multinational companies. As part of the deal, Sprint sold 10 percent of its stock to each of its French and German partners. One hurdle for the company was how to integrate the three partners' communication networks into a unified whole. Start-up costs were high, and the need to communicate in three different languages created some friction among personnel. Early on, lengthy negotiations were required to reach agreement about the value each partner brought to the venture. A former Global One executive noted, "There is no trust among the partners." Other problems included equipment and billing incompatibilities resulting from distribution agreements with telephone monopolies in individual countries. And then there were the financial losses that prompted Sprint chairman William T. Esrey to install Sprint executive Gary Forsee as CEO and president of Global One.

AT&T also depends on various partnership strategies as entry modes. WorldPartners began as an alliance of AT&T, Kokusai Denshin Denwa (KDD) of Japan, and Telecom of Singapore. The goal was to provide improved telecommunications services for companies conducting business globally. Today WorldPartners is composed of 10 companies, including Telecom New Zealand, Telstra (Australia), Hong Kong Telecom, and Unisource.

Unisource is itself a joint venture that originally included Sweden's Telia AB, Swiss Telecom PTT, and PTT Telecom Netherlands. Later, Telefonica de España became an equal equity partner in Unisource. Unisource and AT&T then agreed to form a 60–40 joint venture known as AT&T–Unisource Communications to offer voice, data, and messaging services to businesses with European operations. AT&T would have preferred to form a joint venture with the French or German telephone companies. Yet European regulators, concerned about AT&T's strong brand name and enormous size, refused to approve such a deal.

There was strong logic for the deal. As AT&T–Unisource CEO James Cosgrove explained from headquarters near Amsterdam in Hoofddorp, "You have to be European to play in Europe and yet you have to offer global solutions." Despite the fact that there are five corporate parents, a sense of equality and congeniality has developed. CEO Cosgrove explains, "Working practices of two years have ironed out remarkably well. We have learned that you have to see this thing as a common operation. Otherwise too many bad compromises can be made." The presence of Telefonica de España in the alliance was especially significant for AT&T because of the Spanish company's strong influence in Latin America. Unfortunately, the alliance was weakened when Telefonica decided to ally itself with Concert Communications. To fill the void, AT&T and Italy's Stet announced a new alliance that would expand communication services to Latin America as well as Europe.

The third major telecommunications alliance, Concert Communications, was formed when British Telecommunications PLC bought a 20 percent stake in MCI Communications. Again, the goal of the alliance was to offer global voice and data network services to global corporations.

Thinking Globally

1. What strengths did AT&T bring to its joint venture with Unisource?
2. Can you think of any potential complications that could arise in the AT&T–Unisource joint venture?
3. Assess the formation of Global One, Unisource, and other partnerships discussed in this case in terms of the strategic factors for selecting entry modes identified in the chapter.

Sources: Barbara Martinez, "Sprint Names Its Long-distance Chief to Run Loss-Beset Global One Venture," *The Wall Street Journal*, February 17, 1998, p. B20; Jennifer L. Schenker and James Pressley, "European Telecom Venture with Sprint Hasn't Become the Bully Some Feared," *The Wall Street Journal*, December 23, 1997, p. A11; Alan Cane, "Unisource Partners to Strengthen Ties," *Financial Times*, June 4, 1997, p. 13; Gautam Naik, "Unisource Expected to Merge Operations," *The Wall Street Journal*, June 4, 1997, p. B6.

CHAPTER TWELVE

Developing and Marketing Products

Learning Objectives

After studying this chapter, you should be able to

1. Explain the impact globalization is having on international marketing activities.

2. Describe the types of things managers must consider when developing international product strategies.

3. Discuss the factors that influence international promotional strategies and the blending of product and promotional strategies.

4. Explain the elements that managers must take into account when designing international distribution strategies.

5. Discuss the elements that influence international pricing strategies.

A LOOK BACK

Chapter 11 explained the pros and cons of international entry modes and when each one is most appropriately used. We also described management issues with regard to each entry mode and the important strategic factors in their selection.

A LOOK AT THIS CHAPTER

This chapter explores how globalization and differences in national business environments have an impact on the development and marketing of products internationally. We examine the many variables that must be considered when creating product, promotional, distribution, and pricing strategies.

Source: ShutterStock.

It Gives You Wings

VIENNA, Austria—When Dietrich Mateschitz travelled to Asia on business, he got a taste of some popular energy drinks. Sensing opportunity, he brought a sample of the drinks back to Austria and in 1987 started Red Bull (**www.redbull.com**). Red Bull Energy Drink is now available in more than 160 countries, and sales are in excess of 3.9 billion cans of the raging stuff each year.

Red Bull is identical in every market in which it's sold. The slender red, blue, and silver can packs 8.3 ounces of caffeine, carbohydrates, vitamins, and the amino acid taurine. That's music to the ears of clubgoers, who swear by the drink's ability to keep them going till dawn. Sales are soaring among this crowd, partly due to the word-of-mouth advertising the company gets from loyal customers. Around the world, Red Bull recruits "brand ambassadors" who hand out free samples at events and hires "student managers" who spread the word and drink on campuses.

Red Bull is also racking up double-digit revenue growth with creative TV ads. The ads display the company's "Red Bull Gives You Wings" tag-line as cartoon characters float into the air after downing a can of the sweet drink. Red Bull also sponsors top athletes in racing and sporting events, including snowboarding, hang-gliding, skateboarding, and daredevil stunts. For example, Scott Croxall performs during the "Red Bull Crashed Ice" Ice Cross Downhill Competition in Quebec City.

The company doesn't seem to mind that some people complain about Red Bull's

Source: Robert Wagenhoffer/Corbis.

extreme sweetness. "It's not meant to be a taste drink; you either love us or you hate us," says a spokesperson. Although Denmark, Norway, and Uruguay ban the drink because of its contents, it seems many other people are happily running with the bull. As you read this chapter, think about the many ways in which products are marketed around the world.[1]

n earlier chapters, we emphasized the greater complexity of managing an international business as compared with a purely domestic one. Myriad differences in all aspects of a nation's business environment complicate management. Managing marketing activities that span time zones and cultures can test the most seasoned marketing managers.

We first introduced the concept of globalization and how it affects international business activities in Chapter 1 and returned to this theme in subsequent chapters. We have seen that globalization's impact is not uniform: It affects industries and products in different ways and to varying degrees. Some companies can take advantage of globalization's effects and create a single product that is marketed identically around the world. As we saw in this chapter's opening company profile, Red Bull markets an identical energy drink in the same manner in more than 160 countries around the world. Other companies realize that differences in national business environments are too great to ignore. This group then must create new products, modify promotional campaigns, or adjust their marketing strategies in some other way.

We begin this chapter by taking a brief look at the debate over the extent to which globalization *should* affect marketing strategies. We then describe how marketing internationally differs in terms of how companies create their product strategies, promote and advertise a product, decide on a pricing strategy, and design distribution channels. Throughout the chapter, we examine how globalization on one hand and national differences on the other are having an impact on international marketing activities.

Globalization and Marketing

Globalization is transforming the way in which some products are marketed internationally, but not all. Some companies implement a global strategy that uses similar promotional messages and themes to market the same product around the world. Others find that their products require physical changes to suit the tastes of consumers in markets abroad. Other firms' products need different marketing campaigns to reflect the unique circumstances of local markets. How do managers decide when their marketing strategies need modifying? In this section, we explain the impact of globalization on the standardization-versus-adaptation decision.

Standardization Versus Adaptation

In a well-known article, Harvard economist Theodore Levitt argued that because the world is becoming standardized and homogeneous, companies should market the same products in the same way in all countries.[2] Technology, claimed Levitt, was already causing people's needs and preferences to converge throughout the world. He urged companies to reduce production and marketing costs by standardizing both the physical features of their products and their strategies for marketing them.

Yet, standardization is just one of a number of strategies with which firms successfully enter the international marketplace today. And standardization may not always be the most appropriate strategy. Smaller companies may even be better off adapting to local cultures and exploiting their international image to gain market share locally.

INFLUENCE OF NATIONAL BUSINESS ENVIRONMENTS Consumers in different national markets often demand products that reflect their unique tastes and preferences. Cultural, political, legal, and economic environments have a great deal to do with the preferences of both consumers and industrial buyers worldwide. Recall from Chapter 2 that a culture's aesthetics involves, among other things, preferences for certain colours. Ohio-based Rubbermaid (www.rubbermaid. com) discovered the role of aesthetics as it attempted to increase its international sales. Consumers in the United States prefer household products in neutral blues or almond; in southern Europe, red is the preferred colour. The Dutch want white. In addition, many European cultures perceive plastic products as inferior and want tight lids on metal wastebaskets as opposed to US-style plastic versions with open tops. Just as colour preference varies by culture, so too does colour significance. For example, a Canadian exporter of canned salmon sent an order to China without changing the product label, which showed a white polar bear against a blue background. For Canadians, the image conveys freshness and purity. But in China, blue and white are colours associated with funerals. Chinese consumers, therefore, received the message that the tin contained dead polar bears.[3]

A worker laughs while ironing clothing at the BonWorth clothing factory in Mexico. The company makes clothing for global retailers who intend to sell the same products worldwide without modification. But even globalization in this line of business has its limits. A global retailer must still adapt some aspects of its promotional mix, including its advertising and pricing.

Source: Bob Daemmrich/Corbis.

However, certain products do appeal to practically all cultures. Although it is not a traditional Asian drink, red wine is sweeping Asian markets such as Hong Kong, Singapore, Taiwan, and Thailand. Driving demand are medical studies reporting the health benefits of red wine (the king of Thailand has publicly proclaimed its healthy properties). But other factors—including the fact that red is considered good luck in many Asian cultures—are also at work. Many Asians choose red wine at restaurants because of its image as the beverage of choice for people who are sophisticated and successful. (The same is not true of white wine because from a distance it may resemble water.) Today in Beijing, fashionable young people often give red wine as a housewarming present instead of the traditional favourites of their parents and grandparents.

Product standardization is more likely when nations share the same level of economic development. In years past, consumers in India faced limited options when it came to purchasing automobiles. Most were made in India, were expensive, and were not fuel-efficient. Thanks to steady economic progress over the past two decades, Indian consumers have a better standard of living and more discretionary income. Being able to afford an imported brand-name automobile with a global reputation, such as Suzuki (www.suzuki.co.jp) or Ford (www.ford.com), is more commonplace in Indian cities than it was years ago.

With this brief introduction to some of the issues relevant to international marketing strategy, let's take an in-depth look at the elements that influence a company's *product, promotional, distribution*, and *pricing strategies*.

Developing Product Strategies

Companies can standardize or adapt their products in many alternative ways when they decide to "go international." Let's take a look at some of the factors that influence the standardize-versus-adapt decision as well as several other international product strategy issues.

Laws and Regulations

Companies must often adapt their products to satisfy laws and regulations in a target market. People's tastes also vary across markets, and taste in chocolate is no exception to the rule. A so-called Chocolate War has erupted in the European Union (EU) as it tries to standardize member countries' product content regulations. On one side stand the so-called cocoa purists, including Belgium, France, Germany, Spain, Italy, the Netherlands, Luxembourg, and Greece. Opposite stand Britain, Denmark, Portugal, Austria, Finland, and Sweden—nations who permit manufacturers to add vegetable fats to chocolate products. The purists argue not only that European advertising should restrict the word *chocolate* to 100 percent cocoa products but also that the term *milk chocolate* be outlawed altogether. They want non-pure products labelled something like "chocolate with milk and non-cocoa vegetable fats."

The fact that many developing countries have fewer consumer protection laws creates an ethical issue for some companies. Ironically, lower levels of education and less buying experience mean that consumers in developing countries are more likely to need protection. However, many governments impose fewer regulations in order to hold down production costs and consumer prices. Unfortunately, this can be an invitation for international distributors to withhold full information about products and their potential dangers.

Cultural Differences

Companies also adapt their products to suit local buyers' product preferences that are rooted in culture. Häagen-Dazs (www.haagendazs.com) is an international company that prides itself on its ability to identify the taste preferences of consumers in target markets. It then modifies its base product with just the right flavour to make a product that satisfies consumers' needs. Following years of trial and error developing secret formulas and conducting taste tests, Häagen-Dazs finally launched its green-tea flavour ice cream throughout Japan. The taste is that of *macha* tea—an elite strain of green tea that's been used in elaborate Japanese ceremonies for centuries. Green-tea ice cream was an instant hit and one day may even surpass Häagen-Dazs' perennial flavour champion in Japan—vanilla.

Not all companies need to modify their product to the culture; instead, they may need to identify a different cultural need that it satisfies. Altoids (www.altoids.com), for example, is a British product that has been used for 200 years to soothe upset stomachs. But the company identified a different use for its product in Canada and the United States. Because of its strong flavour, Altoids is sold in the Canadian market as a breath mint and has pushed aside weaker-flavoured candies.

Brand and Product Names

brand name

Name of one or more items in a product line that identifies the source or character of the items.

Several issues related to a company's brand name are important concerns for the day-to-day activities of international managers. A **brand name** is the name of one or more items in a product line that identifies the source or character of the items. When we see a product labelled with a particular brand name, we assign to that product a certain value based on our past experiences with that brand. That is why a brand name is central to a product's personality and the image that it presents to buyers. It informs buyers about a product's source and protects both customer and producer from copycat products. Brand names help consumers to select, recommend, or reject products. They also function as legal property that owners can protect from trespass by competitors.

Indeed, a strong brand can become a company's most valuable asset and primary source of competitive advantage. A consistent worldwide brand image is increasingly important as more consumers and businesspeople travel internationally than ever before. An inconsistent brand name can confuse existing and potential customers. Although companies normally keep their brand names consistent across markets, they can create new product names or modify existing ones to suit local preferences.

Companies also need to review the image of their brand from time to time and update it if it seems old-fashioned. One classic example is that of Lipton (www.lipton.com). The company wanted people to think of Lipton tea as an alternative to colas and other soft drinks. Since the 1890s, Lipton had as its mascot Sir Thomas J. Lipton, the tea maker's founder. But in a major overhaul of the brand, all references to Mr. Lipton were removed because he gave the product a dated image—young people thought of Lipton tea as a drink for their parents' generation. To breathe new life into the brand, Lipton booted the founder in favour of "Tom," a sassy young Briton.

SELECTING INTERNATIONAL BRAND AND PRODUCT NAMES Whether they are standardized or adapted locally, products in international markets need carefully selected names. All company and product brand names (like all nouns) are made up of *morphemes*—semantic elements, or language building blocks, such as the *van* in *advantage*. NameLab (www.namelab.com) is an

A brand name is central to a product's personality and to how buyers perceive it. The brands of all types of global companies blend into the urban surroundings in most nations. Here, Vietnamese people ride motorbikes past a billboard for KFC amid a host of communist flags in Ho Chi Minh City, Vietnam. A strong brand is essential for a global company whether its industry is electronics, delivery services, mobile phones, financial services, or computer software. Why do you think having a global brand image is so important today?

Source: David R. Frazier/ DanitaDelimont.com "Danita Delimont Photography"/Newscom.

identity consultant firm that uses more than 6000 morphemes to develop new product names. NameLab points out that because most Western languages stem from the same linguistic source— Indo-European—companies can create brand names having similar meanings in these nations. *Accu*, for example, connotes *accuracy* in both Western and Japanese cultures. Thus Honda (www.honda.com) created the upscale car division Acura. Other names that are constructed to have similar connotations in many languages or to embody no cultural bias include Compaq (www.compaq.com), Kodak (www.kodak.com), and Sony (www.sony.co.jp).[4] After a name is chosen, companies can survey local native speakers about their reactions to it. These techniques help companies reduce the likelihood of committing potential marketing blunders.

Brand names seldom offend people in international markets, but product names can be highly offensive if they are not carefully researched and selected. Clarks Shoes (www.clarks.com), a British shoe company, once gave a name to a line of shoes that was offensive to the Hindu religious community in Britain. Consequently, the company issued a statement in the British press apologizing for naming some of its products with the names of Hindu Gods Vishnu and Krishna and for offending the British Hindu community. In the future, Clarks Shoes promised to carry out more extensive marketing research before naming its products. Hunt-Wesson, an American food company, experienced brand name troubles when the company decided to enter the Canadian market with its Big John beans line. The company translated "Big John" into French as "Gros Jos," which turned out to be a slang expression for large breasts. Other brand name mishaps for products created in foreign markets and imported into English-speaking countries without changing the name include a Japanese fermented milk drink whose name is pronounced "Kowpis" and a Japanese soft drink named "Mucos."

Other times, product names must be changed, not because they're offensive, but because they mislead consumers. Consider the problem faced by the British beverage and chocolate producer Cadbury (www.cadbury.co.uk), now part of Mondelēz International. When Swiss chocolate manufacturers sued on the grounds that the public was being misled into thinking that Cadbury's Swiss Chalet bar was genuine Swiss chocolate, the company was forced to withdraw the product from the marketplace. A British court confirmed that the name and packaging of the product—the "Swiss" part of the name and the image of a snow-capped Swiss Alp—were likely to mislead consumers. A Quebec company wanting to export the popular Québécois casserole *pâté chinois* would have to change the product's name. "Pâté chinois" means Chinese pie in English, but actually the product is not Chinese nor does it contain Chinese ingredients. In fact, it is commonly known in English as "shepherd's pie."

BEST GLOBAL BRANDS   As we have learned, a brand name is central to a product's personality, and a strong brand name can become a company's most valuable asset. Interbrand (www.interbrand.com), the world's largest brand consultancy firm, developed a ranking for brands called Best Global Brands. To be included in Interbrand's Best Global Brands report, a brand must be global, visible, and financially transparent. This latter criterion excludes such brands as Mars, which does not have publicly available financial data. Brand assessments are based on the financial performance of the branded product or service, the role of the brand in the purchase decision process, and the strength of the brand. Brand strength is determined by both internal factors such as clarity, commitment, protection, and responsiveness; and external factors such as authenticity, differentiation, consistency, presence, and understanding. The top 10 brands in 2013 were Apple, Google, Coca Cola, IBM, Microsoft, General Electric (GE), McDonald's, Samsung, Intel, and Toyota.

Thomson Reuters (www.thomsonreuters.com), ranked 47, is the only Canadian brand included in the 2013 Global Brands report. Specializing in media and intellectual information including financial, tax, and accounting information, Thomson Reuters is valued at $8103 million dollars.[5]

National Image

The value customers obtain from a product is heavily influenced by the image of the country in which it is designed, manufactured, or assembled. We consider the influence of a country's name when thinking of Italian shoes, German luxury cars, and Japanese electronics. This image can be positive for some products but negative for others. For example, the best Russian caviar and vodkas have reputations of quality around the world. The same quality reputation applies for Canada's maple syrup, beef, and ice wine. But how do you feel about Russian automobiles or computers? Attaching "Russia" or "Canada" to certain products is beneficial, whereas attaching it to others could be detrimental.

Because it affects buyers' perceptions of quality and reliability, national image is an important element of product policy. Yet national image can and does change slowly over long periods of time. Decades ago, Japanese products were considered to be of poor quality and rather unreliable. A national effort toward quality improvement and the installation of quality-control procedures by companies then earned Japan a national image for precision and quality products. Once vehicles for budget-conscious consumers, Japanese cars now include some of the finest built luxury autos in the world.

Likewise, years ago Taiwan was known for basic, no-frills items such as toys and industrial products of all sorts. But today many of Taiwan's industries possess a reputation for innovation—designing products that reflect decades of investing in people's research and engineering skills. One company that benefited from an intense devotion to research and development (R&D) is Taiwanese bicycle manufacturer Giant (www.giant-bicycles.com). The company began in Taichung, Taiwan, nearly three decades ago producing bikes under the brand names of other companies. But when the company began to manufacture under its own brand name, it carved itself a solid niche in the mountain bike market. Giant's innovation in using lightweight materials and creating groundbreaking designs even earned it sponsorship of Spain's world-champion racing team. Today, high-tech products, and even those not traditionally thought of as high tech (such as bikes), stamped "Made in Taiwan," command respect in global markets.

Counterfeit Goods and Black Markets

In Chapter 3 we discussed how companies are continually trying to protect their intellectual property and trademarks from counterfeit goods. *Counterfeit goods* are imitation products passed off as legitimate trademarks, patents, or copyrighted works—products that normally enjoy legal protection. Because developing nations often are weakest in enforcing such legal protections, they normally have the most active counterfeiting markets. Countries that top the list for the portion of their markets comprised of counterfeits include China, India, Russia, Thailand, and Turkey.

Counterfeiting is common among highly visible brand-name consumer goods, including watches, perfumes, clothing, movies, music, and computer software. Counterfeit products are typically sold to consumers on what is called the black market—a marketplace of underground

Thousands of fake phones and footwear pile up at a warehouse in China after a massive crackdown on counterfeit goods. Every nation deals with the problem of counterfeit products, though developing countries and emerging markets are most inundated with them. The production of counterfeits affects every product imaginable, including cosmetics, soft drinks, medical devices, auto parts, watches, and household appliances. What could government officials around the world do to better combat counterfeiting?

Source: WENN.com/Newscom.

transactions that typically appears because a product is either illegal (such as counterfeits) or tightly regulated. Tabletop vendors working the back streets of the world's largest cities represent the retail side of the black market. For example, in Sofia, the capital of Bulgaria, you can buy one CD-ROM that contains 50 software applications for $10; buying all the official versions of these products would cost about $5000. In Estonia's Kadaka flea market, you can find the full Microsoft Office (www.microsoft.com) software bundle for around $18—about one-fiftieth of its official selling price. Increasingly, engineered industrial components such as aircraft parts, medicines, and other pharmaceutical products are also becoming targets of counterfeiters.

Counterfeit goods can damage buyers' image of a brand when the counterfeits are of inferior quality—which is nearly always the case. Buyers who purchase an item bearing a company's brand name expect a certain level of craftsmanship and, therefore, satisfaction. But when the product fails to deliver on the expectations, the buyer is dissatisfied, and the company's reputation is tarnished. Japanese motorcycle manufacturers recently saw their sales in China fall sharply, because people were buying near-replicas of their products at discounts of up to 40 percent of the originals. But the counterfeiting problem is more serious today because the Chinese producers are now exporting their motorcycles to other Asian nations. Yamaha (www.yamaha-motor.com), Japan's second-largest motorcycle producer, is considering legal action against one Chinese company. Yamaha officials say that the Chinese company's products resemble its own models right down to the Yamaha name stamped on the side.

Shortened Product Life Cycles

Companies traditionally managed to extend a product's life by introducing it into different markets consecutively. They did this by introducing products in industrialized countries and only later marketing them in developing and emerging markets. Thus, while a product's sales are declining in one market, they might be growing in another.

Advances in telecommunications, however, have alerted consumers around the world to the latest product introductions. Consequently, consumers in developing and emerging markets also demand the latest products and are not happy with receiving what is yesterday's fad in the highly developed nations. Also, the rapid pace with which technological innovation occurs today is shortening the life cycles of products. The actions of international companies themselves actually helped to create this situation. Companies are undertaking new-product development at an increasingly rapid pace and thus shortening the life cycles of their products.

Creating Promotional Strategies

promotion mix
Efforts by a company to reach distribution channels and target customers through communications, such as personal selling, advertising, public relations, and direct marketing.

Promotion mix comprises a company's efforts to reach distribution channels and target customers through communications, such as personal selling, advertising, public relations, and direct marketing. Not surprisingly, promotional activities often receive the greatest attention among marketers because many people, even professionals, tend to equate *marketing* with *promotion*. After we examine two general promotional strategies, we discuss the complications that can arise in international advertising and communications.

Push and Pull Strategies

pull strategy
Promotional strategy designed to create buyer demand that will encourage channel members to stock a company's product.

There are two general promotional strategies that companies can use to get their marketing message across to buyers. They can rely completely on just one of these or use them in combination. A promotional strategy designed to create buyer demand that will encourage channel members to stock a company's product is called a **pull strategy**. In other words, buyer demand is generated in order to "pull" products through distribution channels to end users. Creating consumer demand through direct marketing techniques is a common example of a pull strategy. For example, when Procter & Gamble (www.pg.com) encountered distribution difficulties in trying to introduce Rejoice hair-care products into Asia, the company opted to generate grassroots consumer demand. The company hired a fleet of trucks to drive through village squares and hand out free trial packages to potential end users. In Canada, Dove (www.dove.ca) has created buyer demand by handing out free samples of Dove deodorants at summer festivals.

push strategy
Promotional strategy designed to pressure channel members to carry a product and promote it to final users of the product.

By contrast, a **push strategy** is a promotional strategy designed to pressure channel members to carry a product and promote it to final users. Manufacturers of products commonly sold through department and grocery stores often use a push strategy. For example, manufacturer's sales representatives are constantly calling on Walmart (www.walmart.com) to encourage it to stock the manufacturer's product and give it good visibility. Push strategies are also used for office products, including computers and office furniture. A company's international sales force is the key to successfully implementing a push strategy abroad. For insights into how companies can better manage their salespeople in other cultures, see the Global Manager's Briefcase, titled "Managing an International Sales Force."

Whether the push or pull strategy is most appropriate in a given marketing environment depends on several factors:

- *Distribution System.* Implementing a push strategy can be difficult when channel members (such as distributors) wield a great deal of power relative to that of producers. It can also be ineffective when distribution channels are lengthy: The more levels of intermediaries there are, the more channel members there are who must be convinced to carry a product. In such cases, it might be easier to create buyer demand using a pull strategy than to persuade distributors to stock a particular product.
- *Access to Mass Media.* Developing and emerging markets typically have fewer available forms of mass media for use in implementing a pull strategy. Accordingly, it is difficult to increase consumer awareness of a product and generate product demand. Many consumers in these markets cannot afford cable or satellite television, or perhaps even glossy magazines. In such cases, advertisers might turn to billboards and radio. At other times,

| Global Manager's Briefcase | Managing an International Sales Force |

Today, companies reap a greater portion of their revenues from international sales. How can you become a better global manager of your company's international sales force? Here are some helpful hints on improving the effectiveness of your company's representatives abroad.

- **Know the Sales Scene.** Your company should conduct research before hiring and managing an international sales force. Then formulate a targeted sales strategy and empower your sales force to meet their performance targets. The amount of compensation as well as the way in which it is delivered varies from country to country. For example, in North America a greater portion of salary is based on commission than it is in Europe. Know the salary structure and incentive plans of salespeople with similar jobs at local companies.

- **Research the Customer.** Do not assume that customers abroad have the same needs and preferences as customers at home. Investigate what potential buyers want and how much they are willing to pay. When ECA International (a market information provider) expanded into Asia, it was unsuccessful time and again. The company learned through its sales force that potential customers wanted to buy research piece by piece rather than buy a membership in the company. ECA was able to sell its memberships in Asia after it adapted its methods to suit local buyers.

- **Work with the Culture.** "In order to motivate individuals, you need to set realistic objectives for salespeople, and much of that is culturally bound," says John Wada, sales and marketing director for IOR, a cross-cultural management company. Your company should seek answers to a host of questions. Do people in the local culture feel differently about work teams and competition than your sales force at home? How about schedules and deadlines? Are you moving into a culture where "time is of the essence" or one where time is less important? Your company and its local sales force must understand what is expected of one another.

- **Learn from Your Representatives.** If your salespeople believe they are pushing products that bear no relationship to the local market, their performance will suffer. "I'd do a great job," so the story goes, "but the product just won't sell here." Salespeople may begin focusing on critiquing products rather than selling them. Involve your sales reps in the R&D process so that they have a better sense of what's going on with the product. Perhaps bring your sales force to the home office to learn about your business so they understand their vital link in your company's chain of business activities. Finally, top managers should visit the local office to better comprehend the needs of local customers.

Source: Based on Charlene Marmer Solomon, "Managing an Overseas Sales Force," *World Trade*, Global Sales and Technology Special Section, pp. S4–S6.

gaining wide exposure can be difficult because existing media have only local, as opposed to national, reach. For example, Indonesia did not launch its first nationwide television station until 1994. In yet other situations, advertising certain products on certain media is unlawful. For example, companies that enter Canada or the United States cannot use television or radio to advertise tobacco products.

- *Type of Product.* A pull strategy is most appropriate when buyers display a great deal of brand loyalty toward one particular brand name. In other words, brand-loyal buyers know what brand of a product they want before they go shopping. On the other hand, push strategies tend to be appropriate for inexpensive consumer goods characterized by buyers who are not brand loyal. Low brand loyalty means that a buyer will go shopping for a product, not knowing which brand is best, and simply will buy one of those carried by the retailer or wholesaler. A push strategy is also suited to industrial products because potential buyers usually need to be informed about a product's special features and benefits.

International Advertising

International advertising differs a great deal from advertising in domestic markets. Managers must rely on their knowledge of a market to decide whether an ad is suitable for the company's international promotional efforts. Cultural similarities can mean that ads need only slight modification for different nations, whereas cultural differences may mean that entirely new ads must be created.

Coca-Cola's (www.cocacola.com) classic experience in creating an ad to appeal to Chinese people illustrates the problems that can arise when developing specialized ads. Coca-Cola's desire to create a Coke ad that looked authentically Chinese drew it to Harbin, a city in northeast China. But along the way the bus carrying the crew that was filming the commercial stalled. When the driver lit a fire under the gas tank to thaw the fuel, the horrified crew scrambled off the bus thinking it might explode. The crew stood in biting, subzero temperatures until the bus was once again running—the director's frostbitten nose bears the scars of the adventure. Then when a local older man hired to be in the ad had trouble following the director's instructions, local villagers pointed out why—he was deaf. Finally, the crew had to trudge around in knee-deep snow first to get a field of frozen red pinwheels to spin and then to reorient the whole set so that the wind (which was blowing in an unfavourable direction) could spin the pinwheels. But it appears that Coke's efforts at creating an ad depicting people celebrating Chinese New Year in the traditional manner in a picturesque village paid off. "It made me feel very emotional," said Fang Chuanbao, an office worker in Shanghai who saw the ad. The localized ads exemplify Coke's "think local, act local" mantra, which was pioneered by CEO Douglas Daft as part of an effort to remake Coke into the nimble marketer it once was.[6]

Let's now explore some of the factors involved in the decision of whether to standardize or adapt advertisements.

STANDARDIZING OR ADAPTING ADVERTISEMENTS The vast majority of advertising that occurs in any one nation is produced solely for that domestic audience. But companies that advertise in multiple markets must determine the aspects of the advertising campaign that can be standardized across markets and those that cannot. Companies that do market their products across national boundaries try to contain costs by standardizing as many aspects of their campaigns as possible. However, companies seldom standardize all aspects of their international promotions, for a variety of reasons, including differences in culture and laws.

Firms that standardize advertising often control campaigns from the home office. This policy helps them to project consistent brand images and promotional messages across all markets—the aim of a global strategy (see Chapter 10). Companies can achieve consistency by standardizing their basic promotional message, creative concepts, graphics, and information content. After a company decides to pursue a global marketing strategy, it naturally tries to get the most for its advertising expenditure.

One way companies can reach a global audience is to sponsor global sporting events, such as the Olympics, World Cup Soccer, and Formula One automobile racing. These types of events

The global broadcast of the Olympic Games every four years offers companies a chance to put their messages before an audience of over 3 billion cumulative viewings. The brands of global companies are plastered on signs around the host city and seen worldwide during competitions. Advertising by each individual company can total hundreds of millions of dollars during the Olympic Games.

Source: David Wei/Alamy.

receive heavy media coverage and are often telecast simultaneously in multiple nations. Even posting banners around the venues of such events can boost recognition of a company's brand name by exposing it to perhaps millions of viewers around the world. Viewers in 102 countries see the banners of companies that sponsor Formula One auto racing.

CASE: THE ELUSIVE EURO-CONSUMER   The continuing integration of nations belonging to the European Union is causing many marketers to dream of a day when they can standardize their advertising to appeal to a so-called Euro-consumer. But the Euro-consumer remains a rare, mythical creature that eludes even the world's most clever advertisers.

Some well-known international advertising agencies have tried a pan-European advertising approach, only to fail because of national differences. Consider the experience of the acclaimed Leo Burnett Company (www.leoburnett.com) when it took on the goal of creating a single European campaign for United Distillers' Johnnie Walker (www.johnniewalker.com) whiskey. It took many painful tests and revisions before the ad could be rolled out. In the original ad, the tag line read "The Water of Life" and showed a man attending "the running of the bulls" in Pamplona, Spain. After narrowly escaping being trampled by the bull, the man celebrates with a glass of Johnnie Walker Red Label. But in many countries, the Pamplona setting raised hackles because people said, "The Spanish don't know anything about making good whiskey." Tests of the ad in Germany showed it would not work because to Germans it seemed simply reckless— not a widely admired trait there. Says Jenny Vaughn, worldwide brand director for Johnnie Walker, "Also, because of the German animal rights campaigners, you can't show a goldfish in a goldfish bowl on German television, so a bull run was just not [acceptable]." The tag line "The Water of Life" was baffling in many languages. "People thought it meant watered-down whiskey," said Vaughn, so the line was changed to "Taste Life." Then a voice-over in the ad was incorrectly translated in one language as "when your life flashes in front of you, make sure it's worth watching." In every market the words didn't make sense or the meaning was lost. In Italy the line was totally discarded. In Germany attempts at translation proved so maddening that the line was replaced with "Live every day as if it were your last."

Europe's many languages certainly create thorny translation issues for marketers. Thus, the most successful pan-European ads are those that contain a great deal of visuals, have few written or spoken words, and focus on the product and consumer. One such ad is that for TAG Heuer (www.tagheuer.com) watches, which positions the company's product as competitive and a winner. In the ad, a swimmer is shown racing a shark and a hurdler is shown leaping an oversize razor blade. The highly visual ad gets across the company's message that it is a winner.

Blending Product and Promotional Strategies

When companies extend their marketing efforts internationally, they develop communication strategies that blend product and promotional strategies.[7] A company's communication strategy for a particular market takes into account the nature of the product being marketed and the promotion mix to market it. After we discuss the marketing communication process, we examine five product/promotional methods companies use and the appropriate situation for each.

COMMUNICATING PROMOTIONAL MESSAGES   The process of sending promotional messages about products to target markets is called **marketing communication**. Communicating the benefits of a product can be more difficult in international business than in domestic business for several reasons. Marketing internationally usually means translating promotional messages from one language into another. Marketers must be knowledgeable of the many cultural nuances that can affect how buyers interpret a promotional message. A nation's laws that govern the promotion of products in another country can also force changes in marketing communication.

Marketing communication is typically considered a circular process, as shown in Figure 12.1. The company that has an idea it wishes to communicate is the source of the communication. The idea is *encoded* (translated into images, words, and symbols) into a *promotional message* that the company is trying to get across. The promotional message is then sent to the *audience* (potential buyers) through various *media*. Media commonly used by companies to communicate their promotional messages include radio, television, newspapers, magazines, billboards, and direct mailings. After the audience receives the message, they decode the message and interpret its meaning. Information in the form of *feedback* (purchase or no purchase) then flows back to the source of the message. The decoding process by the audience can be disrupted by the presence of

marketing communication
Process of sending promotional messages about products to target markets.

FIGURE 12.1

Marketing Communications Process

Source: Based on Courtland L. Bovee, John V. Thill, George P. Dovel, and Marian Burk Wood, Advertising Excellence (New York, NY: McGraw-Hill, 1995), p. 14.

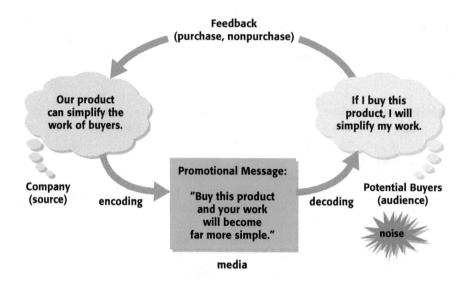

noise—anything that disrupts the audience's ability to receive and interpret the promotional message. By ignoring important cultural nuances, companies can inadvertently increase the potential for noise that can cloud the audience's understanding of their promotional message. For example, language barriers between the company and potential buyers can create noise if a company's promotional message is translated incorrectly into the local language.

PRODUCT/COMMUNICATIONS EXTENSION (DUAL EXTENSION) This method extends the same home-market product and marketing promotion into target markets. Under certain conditions, it can be the simplest and most profitable strategy. For example, because of a common language and other cultural similarities, companies based in English-speaking Canadian provinces can sell the same product with packaging and advertising identical to that in the US market—provided the product is not required by the US government to carry any special statements or warnings. The Canadian companies contain costs by developing a single product and one promotional campaign for both markets. Yet it is important for Canadian companies not to ignore any subtle cultural differences that could cause confusion in interpreting the promotional message.

As the information age continues to knit the world more tightly together, this method will probably grow more popular. Today, consumers in seemingly remote parts of the world are rapidly becoming aware of the latest worldwide fads and fashions. But this strategy appears to be better suited for certain groups of buyers, including brand-conscious teenagers, business executives, and wealthy individuals. The strategy also tends to be better suited for companies that use a global strategy with their products, such as upscale personal items with global brand names—examples include Rolex (www.rolex.com) watches, Hermès (www.hermes.com) scarves and ties, and Coco Chanel (www.chanel.com) perfumes. It can also be appropriate for global brands that have mass appeal and cut across all age groups and social classes—such as Jamieson Vitamins (Canada) (www.jamiesonvitamins.com), Canon (www.canon.com), Mars (www.mars.com), and Nokia (www.nokia.com). The strategy also is useful to companies that are the low-cost leaders in their industries: one product and one promotional message keep costs down.

PRODUCT EXTENSION/COMMUNICATIONS ADAPTATION Under this method, a company extends the same product into target markets but alters its promotion. Communications require adaptation because the product satisfies a different need, serves a different function, or appeals to a different type of buyer. Companies can adjust their marketing communication to inform potential buyers that the product either satisfies their needs or serves a distinct function. This approach helps companies contain costs because the good itself requires no alteration. Altering communications can be expensive, however, especially when cultural differences among target markets are significant. Filming altered ads with local actors and on location can add significantly to promotional costs.

One company that changes its promotional message for international markets is the Japanese retailer Muji (www.muji.ca). Muji offers a wide variety of goods, including writing materials, clothing, and home furnishings inspired by a central theme rooted in centuries of Japanese culture—the simplicity of everyday life. Muji's philosophy is one of selling unbranded quality goods, and company promotions boast the motto "Functional Japanese minimalism for everyone." Its target market in Japan is the average school-aged child and young adult. But Muji's European stores use a different promotional message. Muji's European customers tend to be older and see themselves as sophisticated and stylish buyers of the company's products. In Europe, Muji's promotional message is "shop at a business that has a very respectable brand name"—clearly different from its message in Japan. Also, the company's European customers are not simply buying a product (as do its Japanese customers); they are buying into the traditional Japanese concept of simplicity.[8]

Low economic development also can demand that communications be adapted to suit local conditions. For example, companies in Europe and North America and certain Asian countries can rely on a modern telecommunications system to reach millions of consumers through television, radio, and the World Wide Web. But in developing countries (such as rural parts of India and China), television and radio coverage are limited, and development of the Web is years behind developed nations. Marketers in those countries must use alternative techniques, including door-to-door personal selling and regional product shows or fairs.

PRODUCT ADAPTATION/COMMUNICATIONS EXTENSION Using this method, a company adapts its product to the requirements of the international market while retaining the product's original marketing communication. There are many reasons why companies need to adapt their products. One might be to meet legal requirements in the local market. Moreover, governments can require that firms use a certain amount of local materials, labour, or some other resource in their local production process. If the exact same materials or components are not available locally, the result can be a modified product.

This method can be costly because appropriately modifying a product to suit the needs of local buyers often means the company must invest in production facilities in the local market. If each national market requires its own production facility, cost savings provided by economies of scale in production can be elusive. Still, a company can implement this strategy successfully if it sells a differentiated product for which it can charge a higher price to offset the greater production costs.

PRODUCT/COMMUNICATIONS ADAPTATION (DUAL ADAPTATION) This method adapts both the product and its marketing communication to suit the target market. The product itself is adapted to match the needs or preferences of local buyers. The promotional message is adapted to explain how the product meets those needs and preferences. Because both production and marketing efforts must be altered, this strategy can be expensive; therefore, it is not very common. It can be implemented successfully, however, if a sufficiently large and profitable market segment exists. For example, tire companies selling their products in Canada, such as Toyo Tires (www. toyotires.ca), adapt the product to conform to local weather conditions by offering winter tires instead of just all-season tires. They also adapt their marketing communication by advertising the superior grip of winter tires and their ability to stop the car faster when driving in snow.

PRODUCT INVENTION This method requires that an entirely new product be developed for the target market. Product invention is often necessary when many important differences exist between the home and target markets. One reason for product invention is that local buyers cannot afford a company's current product because of low purchasing power. For example, Honda (www.honda.com) developed a car called "City" for budget-conscious buyers in Southeast Asia and Europe.

Product inventions can also arise because of a lack of adequate infrastructure needed to operate certain products. One day, London inventor Trevor Baylis was watching a television documentary on the difficulty of educating Africans about AIDS because much of the continent did not have the electricity infrastructure or batteries to operate radios. Baylis set to work and developed the Freeplay windup radio—30 seconds of cranking keeps it going for 40 minutes. Baylis and several South African businessmen then formed a company called Bay-Gen Power Corporation in Cape Town, South Africa. The radio was first sold only to relief agencies working in developing nations. But due mostly to word of mouth, it is now popular worldwide among hikers, environmentalists, and even hip shoppers looking for eco-friendly appliances.

> **Quick Study**
>
> 1. Identify several factors that influence the choice between a *push strategy* and a *pull strategy*.
> 2. What issues affect the decision of whether to standardize or adapt international advertising?
> 3. Identify each element in the *marketing communications* process, and describe how they interact.
> 4. What five generic methods are used to blend product and promotional strategies for international markets? Describe each briefly.

Designing Distribution Strategies

distribution
Planning, implementing, and controlling the physical flow of a product from its point of origin to its point of consumption.

Planning, implementing, and controlling the physical flow of a product from its point of origin to its point of consumption is called **distribution**. The physical path that a product follows on its way to customers is called a *distribution channel*. Companies along this channel that work together in delivering products to customers are called *channel members* or *intermediaries*. Bear in mind that manufacturers of goods are not the only producers who need distribution channels. Service providers, such as consulting companies, health-care organizations, and news services, also need distribution (or delivery) systems to reach their customers. In the business of delivering news services over the World Wide Web, channel members involved in getting news from the newsroom to the reader can include, among others, Internet service providers and search engine suppliers.

Companies develop their international distribution strategies based on two related decisions: (1) how to get the goods *into* a country and (2) how to distribute goods *within* a country. Here we focus on distribution strategies within countries.

Designing Distribution Channels

Managers consider two overriding concerns when establishing channels of distribution: (1) the amount of *market exposure* a product needs and (2) the *cost* of distributing a product. Let's now take a look at each of these concerns.

exclusive channel
Distribution channel in which a manufacturer grants the right to sell its product to only one or a limited number of resellers.

DEGREE OF EXPOSURE   In promoting its product to the greatest number of potential customers, a marketer must determine the amount of exposure needed. An **exclusive channel** is one in which a manufacturer grants the right to sell its product to only one or a limited number of resellers. An exclusive channel gives producers a great deal of control over the sale of their product by wholesalers and retailers. It also helps a producer to constrain distributors from selling competing brands. In this way, an exclusive channel creates a barrier that makes it difficult or impossible for outsiders to penetrate the channel. For example, in most countries new car dealerships reflect exclusive distribution—normally, Mitsubishi dealerships cannot sell Toyotas, and General Motors dealers cannot sell Fords.

intensive channel
Distribution channel in which a producer grants the right to sell its product to many resellers.

When a producer wants its product to be made available through as many distribution outlets as possible, it prefers to use an **intensive channel**—one in which a producer grants the right to sell its product to many resellers. An intensive channel provides buyers with location convenience because of the large number of outlets through which a product is sold. It does not create strong barriers to channel entry for other producers nor does it provide much control over reseller decisions, such as what competing brands to sell.

Large companies whose products are sold through grocery stores and department stores typically take an intensive channel approach to distribution. The obstacle for small companies that choose an intensive channel approach is gaining shelf space—especially companies with lesser-known brands. The increasing global trend toward retailers developing their own *private-label brands* (brands created by retailers themselves) exacerbates this problem. In such cases, retailers tend to give their own brands prime shelf space and give lesser-known brands poorer shelf locations that are up high or near the floor. For example, President's

Choice (PC) is a private-label brand of Loblaw Companies Limited, Canada's largest food retailer. PC is available at Loblaws, Loblaw Great Food, Atlantic Superstore, No Frills, Real Canadian Superstore, and so forth. Many of these grocery stores promote themselves and the PC brand through secondary signage as "The Home of President's Choice," clearly giving their own private label an advantage over other brands.

CHANNEL LENGTH AND COST *Channel length* refers to the number of intermediaries between the producer and the buyer. In a *zero-level channel*—which is also called direct marketing—producers sell directly to final buyers. A *one-level channel* places only one intermediary between the producer and the buyer. Two intermediaries make up a *two-level channel*, and so forth. In general, the greater the number of intermediaries in a channel, the more costly it becomes. This happens because each additional member adds a charge for its services onto the product's total cost. This is an important consideration for companies that sell price-sensitive consumer products, such as candy, food, and small household items, which usually compete on the basis of price. Companies that sell highly differentiated products can charge higher prices because of their products' distinctiveness; therefore, they have fewer problems using a channel of several levels.

Influence of Product Characteristics

The value of a product relative to its weight and volume is called its **value density**. Value density is an important variable in formulating distribution strategies. As a rule, *the lower a product's value density, the more localized the distribution system*. Most commodities, including cement, iron ore, and crude oil, have low value-density ratios—they're heavy but not particularly "valuable" if gauged in, say, shipping weight per cubic metre. Relative to their values, the cost of transporting these goods is high. Consequently, such products are processed or integrated into the manufacturing process at points close to their original locations. Products with high value-density ratios include diamonds, emeralds, semiconductors, and premium perfumes. Because the cost of transporting these products is small relative to their value, they can be processed or manufactured in the optimal location and then shipped to market. Because Johnson & Johnson's (www.jnj.com) Vistakon contact lenses have high value density, the company produces and inventories its products in one US location and serves the world market from there. Pilliterri Estates Winery (www.pillitteriicewine.com) is the producer of one of the world's best ice wines, which offer a high value density. The company produces and stores its ice wines in its Niagara-on-the-Lake, Ontario, location because this unique geographic area has the ideal climate for making ice wine.

value density
Value of a product relative to its weight and volume.

When products need to be modified for local markets, companies can design their distribution systems accordingly. Caterpillar (www.cat.com) redesigned its distribution system so that it doubles as the final component in the company's production system. Each national market carries a range of optional product components for Caterpillar's lift trucks. The company ships partially completed lift trucks, along with optional parts, to distribution warehouses in each target market. After a buyer decides what options it desires, final assembly takes place. Caterpillar's distribution warehouses now extend the company's assembly line—allowing the company to maintain or improve service at little cost.

Special Distribution Problems

A nation's distribution system develops over time and reflects its unique cultural, political, legal, and economic traditions. Although each nation's distribution system has its own unique pros and cons, it is the negative aspects of distribution that pose the greatest threat to the business activities of international companies. In some countries, risks arise mostly from the potential for theft and property damage. In others, it is simply the lack of understanding that creates uncertainty and risk. Let's take a look at two special problems that can affect a company's international distribution activities.

LACK OF MARKET UNDERSTANDING Companies can experience a great deal of frustration and financial loss simply by not fully understanding the local market in which they operate. In one now-classic case, Amway Asia Pacific Ltd., the Asian arm of US-based Amway (www.amway.com), learned the hard way the pitfalls of overestimating the knowledge of distributors in emerging markets. The company has a worldwide policy of giving distributors a full refund on its soaps and cosmetics if the distributor's customers are dissatisfied—even if the returned containers are empty. But the policy had some bizarre results shortly after Amway entered China. Word of the guarantee spread quickly. Some distributors repackaged the products in other containers, sold them, and took the original containers back to Amway for a refund. Others scoured garbage bins, gathering bags full of discarded bottles. In Shanghai, returns were beginning to total $100 000 a day. Amway's Shanghai chief Percy Chin admitted, "Perhaps we were too lenient." Amway soon changed its refund policy to allow a refund only for bottles at least half full.[9]

THEFT AND CORRUPTION   A high incidence of theft and corruption can present obstacles to distribution. The distribution system in Russia reflects its roughly 75-year experiment with communism. When Acer Computers (www.acer.com) decided to sell its computers in Russia, it built production facilities in Russia's stable neighbour, Finland, because the company was leery of investing directly in Russia. Acer also considered it too risky to navigate Russia's archaic distribution system on its own. In three years' time, a highway that serves as a main route to get goods overland from Finland to Russia saw 50 Finnish truckers hijacked, two drivers killed, and another two missing. Acer solved its distribution problem by selling its computers to Russian distributors outside its factory in Finland. The Russian distributors, who understood how to negotiate their way through Russia's distribution system, were to deal with distribution problems in Russia.[10]

Quick Study

1. How do *exclusive* and *intensive* channels of distribution differ? Give an example of each.
2. Explain the importance of *value density* to distribution strategy.
3. How might a lack of market understanding, theft, and corruption affect international distribution?

Developing Pricing Strategies

The pricing strategy that a company adopts must match its overall international strategy. The product of a company that is the low-cost leader in its industry usually cannot be sold at a premium price because it likely has few special features and stresses functionality rather than uniqueness. On the other hand, a company that follows a differentiation strategy usually can charge a premium price for its product because buyers value the product's uniqueness. Let's now examine two pricing policies, *worldwide pricing* and *dual pricing*, which companies use in international markets, and then we will explore the important factors that influence managers' pricing decisions.

Worldwide Pricing

worldwide pricing
Policy in which one selling price is established for all international markets.

A pricing policy in which one selling price is established for all international markets is called **worldwide pricing**. In practice, a worldwide pricing policy is very difficult to achieve. First, production costs differ from one nation to another. Keeping production costs the same is not possible for a company that has production bases within each market it serves. As a result, selling prices often reflect these different costs of production.

Second, a company that produces in just one location (to maintain an equivalent cost of production for every product) cannot guarantee that selling prices will be the same in every target market. The cost of exporting to certain markets will likely be higher than the cost of exporting to other markets. In addition, distribution costs differ across markets. Where distribution is efficient, selling prices might well be lower than in locations where distribution systems are archaic and inefficient.

Third, the purchasing power of local buyers must be taken into account. Managers might decide to lower the sales price in a market so that buyers can afford the product and the company can gain market share.

Finally, fluctuating currency values also must be taken into account. When the value of the currency in a country where production takes place rises against a target market's currency, the product will become more expensive in the target market.

Dual Pricing

Because of the problems associated with worldwide pricing, another pricing policy is often used in international markets. A pricing policy in which a product has a different selling price in export markets than it has in the home market is called **dual pricing**. When a product has a higher selling price in the target market than it does in the home market (or the country where production takes place), it is called *price escalation*. It is commonly the result of the reasons just discussed—exporting costs and currency fluctuations.

But sometimes a product's export price is lower than the price in the home market. Under what circumstances does this occur? Some companies determine that domestic market sales are to cover all product costs (such as expenses related to R&D, administration, and overhead). They then require exports to cover only the *additional* costs associated with exporting and selling in a target market (such as tariffs). In this sense, exports are considered a sort of "bonus."

To successfully apply dual pricing in international marketing, a company must be able to keep its domestic buyers and international buyers separate. Buyers in one market might cancel orders if they discover that they are paying a higher price than are buyers in another market. If a company cannot keep its buyers separate when using dual pricing, buyers could potentially undermine the policy through *arbitrage*—buying products where they are sold at lower prices and reselling them where they command higher prices. As is often the case, however, the higher selling price of a product in an export market often reflects the additional costs of transportation to the local market and any trade barriers of the target market, such as tariffs. For arbitrageurs to be successful, the profits they earn must be enough to outweigh these additional costs.

dual pricing
Policy in which a product has a different selling price (typically higher) in export markets than it has in the home market.

Factors That Affect Pricing Decisions

Many factors have an important influence on managers' pricing decisions. We devote the following discussion to four of the most important—transfer prices, arm's-length pricing, price controls, and dumping.

TRANSFER PRICES Prices charged for goods or services transferred among a company and its subsidiaries are called **transfer prices**. It is common for parent companies and their subsidiaries to buy from one another. For example, the parent company often licenses technologies to its subsidiaries in return for royalties or licensing fees. Subsidiaries prefer this route to buying on the open market because they typically receive lower prices. Parent companies then buy finished products from subsidiaries at the stated transfer price.

At one time, companies enjoyed a great deal of freedom in setting their transfer prices. Subsidiaries in countries with high corporate tax rates would reduce their tax burdens by charging a low price for their output to other subsidiaries. The subsidiary lowered the taxes that the parent company must pay by reducing its profits in the high-tax country. Likewise, subsidiaries in countries with low tax rates would charge relatively high prices for their output.

Transfer prices followed a similar pattern based on the tariffs of different nations. Subsidiaries in countries that charged relatively high tariffs were charged lower prices to lower the cost of the goods in the local market. This pattern of transfer prices helped large corporations with many subsidiaries to better manage their global tax burden and become more price-competitive in certain markets.

transfer price
Price charged for a good or service transferred among a company and its subsidiaries.

ARM'S-LENGTH PRICING Increased regulation of transfer pricing practices today is causing reduced freedom in manipulating transfer prices. Many governments now regulate internal company pricing practices by assigning products approximate transfer prices based on their free-market price. Therefore, most international transfers between subsidiaries now occur at a so-called **arm's-length price**—the free-market price that unrelated parties charge one another for a specific product.

Another factor that is increasing the use of arm's-length pricing is pressure on companies to be good corporate citizens in each of their target markets. Developing and emerging

arm's-length price
Free-market price that unrelated parties charge one another for a specific product.

markets are hurt most by lost revenue when international companies manipulate prices to reduce tariffs and corporate taxes. They depend on the revenue for building things such as schools, hospitals, and infrastructure, including telecommunications systems and shipping ports. These items in turn benefit international companies by improving the productivity and efficiency of the local business environment. Indeed, some international companies have even developed codes of conduct specifying that transfer prices will follow the principle of arm's-length pricing.

price controls

Upper or lower limits placed on the prices of products sold within a country.

PRICE CONTROLS   Pricing strategies must also consider the potential for government **price controls**—upper or lower limits placed on the prices of products sold within a country. Upper-limit price controls are designed to provide price stability in an inflationary economy (one in which prices are rising). Companies that want to raise prices in a price-controlled economy must often apply to government authorities to request permission to do so. Companies with good contacts in the government of the target market might be more likely to get a price-control exemption. Those unable to obtain an exemption will typically try to lessen the impact of upper-limit price controls by reducing production costs.

By contrast, lower-limit price controls prohibit the lowering of prices below a certain level. Governments sometimes impose lower-limit prices to help local companies compete against the less expensive imports of international companies. Other times, lower-limit price controls are designed to ward off price wars that could eliminate the competition and thereby give one company a monopoly in the domestic market.

DUMPING   We detailed the practice of dumping in Chapter 1 when discussing the World Trade Organization (WTO), the international body that regulates international trade. Recall that *dumping* occurs when the price of a good is lower in export markets than it is in the domestic market. Accusations of dumping are often made against competitors from other countries when inexpensive imports flood a nation's domestic market. Although charges of dumping normally result from deliberate efforts to undercut the prices of competitors in the domestic market, changes in exchange rates can cause unintentional dumping. When a country's government charges another nation's producers of dumping a good on its market, antidumping tariffs are typically imposed. Such tariffs are designed to punish producers in the offending nation by increasing the price of their products to a fairer level.

Quick Study

1. What is the difference between *worldwide pricing* and *dual pricing*?
2. Explain what is meant by the terms *transfer pricing* and *arm's-length pricing*.
3. How might price controls and dumping affect the pricing decisions of international companies?

Bottom Line   for Business

Despite the academic debate over globalization and the extent to which companies should standardize their international marketing activities, many companies continue to adapt to local conditions. Sometimes this takes the form of only slightly modifying promotional campaigns, and at other times it can require the creation of an entirely new product. The causes of alterations in promotional aspects of marketing strategy can be cultural, such as language differences. They can also be legal, such as requirements to produce locally so as to help ease local unemployment or to spur local industry around the production facility. Other companies are able to reap the rewards of standardization and centralized production that can result from the ability to sell one product worldwide.

Chapter Summary

1. **Explain the impact globalization is having on international marketing activities.**
   - Companies may be able to reduce production and marketing costs by standardizing the physical features of their products and their marketing strategies.
   - Other companies may find that standardization is just one of a number of strategies or that it is not always the best strategy to use.
   - Consumers worldwide appear content with a standardized product in *certain* product categories, but in others they demand products that reflect their unique tastes and preferences.
   - National business environments affect the preferences of both consumers and industrial buyers worldwide, with product standardization more likely when levels of economic development are similar.

2. **Describe the types of things managers must consider when developing international product strategies.**
   - Companies may need to undertake mandatory product adaptation in response to a target market's laws and regulations and to suit cultural differences.
   - Companies try to keep their brand names consistent across markets but will create new product names or modify existing ones to suit local preferences.
   - The image of a nation in which a company designs, manufactures, or assembles a product can influence buyer perception of quality and reliability.
   - Counterfeit goods can damage buyers' image of a brand when the counterfeits are of inferior quality.
   - Shortened product life cycles are affecting decisions of when to market internationally.

3. **Discuss the factors that influence international promotional strategies and the blending of product and promotional strategies.**
   - *Promotion mix* comprises company efforts to reach distribution channels and target customers through communications, such as personal selling, advertising, public relations, and direct marketing.
   - A *pull strategy* creates buyer demand that will encourage channel members to stock a company's product; a *push strategy* pressures channel members to carry a product and promote it to final users of the product.
   - *Product/communications extension* (*dual extension*) extends the same home-market product and marketing promotion into target markets.
   - *Product extension/communications adaptation* extends the same product into new target markets but alters its promotion.
   - *Product adaptation/communications extension* adapts a product to the requirements of the international market while retaining the product's original marketing communication.
   - *Product/communications adaptation* (*dual adaptation*) adapts both the product and its marketing communication to suit the target market.
   - *Product invention* requires that an entirely new product be developed for the target market.

4. **Explain the elements that managers must take into account when designing international distribution strategies.**
   - *Distribution* involves the planning, implementation, and control of the physical flow of a product from its point of origin to its point of consumption; the physical path a product follows to customers is a *distribution channel*.
   - An *exclusive channel* is one in which a manufacturer grants the right to sell its product to only one or a limited number of resellers, which gives wholesalers and retailers significant control over a products' sale.
   - An *intensive channel* is one in which a producer grants the right to sell its product to many resellers, which offers less control over reseller decisions.
   - *Channel length* refers to the number of intermediaries between the producer and the buyer: in a *zero-level channel*, producers sell directly to final buyers; in a *one-level channel*, one intermediary is between producer and buyer, and so forth.

5. Discuss the elements that influence international pricing strategies.
   - *Worldwide pricing* is one selling price for all international markets—a difficult task to achieve in practice.
   - *Dual pricing* means having a different selling price in export markets than in the home market.
   - *Price escalation* occurs when a product has a higher selling price in the target market than it does in the home market (or the country where production takes place).
   - A *transfer price* is the price charged for products sold between a company's divisions or subsidiaries.
   - An *arm's-length price* is the free-market price that unrelated parties charge one another for a specific product.

Key Terms

arm's-length price 351	intensive channel 348	push strategy 342
brand name 338	marketing communication 345	transfer price 351
distribution 348	price controls 352	value density 349
dual pricing 351	promotion mix 342	worldwide pricing 350
exclusive channel 348	pull strategy 342	

Talk It Over

1. Suppose that the product preferences of cultures and people around the world continue to converge. Identify two products that will likely be affected and two products that will likely not be affected by this convergence. For each product, how will the changes influence the marketing manager's job?

2. Price escalation can present serious problems for companies wishing to export their products to other markets under a worldwide pricing policy. How might companies combat the effects of price escalation? List as many possibilities as you can.

Take It to the Web

1. **Video Report.** Visit YouTube (www.youtube.com) and search for "developing and marketing products." Watch one video from the list, and then summarize it in a half-page report. Reflecting on the contents of this chapter, which aspects of developing and marketing products can you identify in the video? How might a company engaged in international business act on the information contained in the video?

2. **Web Site Report.** Companies must carefully consider every facet of marketing, including product, promotional, distribution, and pricing strategies.

   The Web sites of both Adobe (www.adobe.com) and Amazon (www.amazon.com) are reputed to be excellent examples of marketing. Partner with another student, and visit the Web site of one of these companies while your partner visits the other firm's Web site. For the site you chose, what features do you think account for the favourable reputation? Note the different ads on the site, and rate their effectiveness. Compare your findings with those of your partner.

   Now select another international company of your choosing and visit as many of its national Web sites as you can locate. How much freedom do you think the company allows in each nation's Web site design? Why? If you were the CEO of the company, would you follow a similar approach, or would you centralize/ decentralize authority over the Web site's design? How do Adobe and Amazon compare to the apparent freedom (or lack of freedom) that this company allows? Explain your answer.

Psychology of Global Marketing

It's no secret that marketers use a good dose of psychology in both designing and implementing their promotional campaigns—or at least it shouldn't be. But some people, including Gary Rushkin of Washington, DC–based Public Citizen's Commercial Alert (www.commercialalert.org), argue that parents are being duped. "I don't think people understand the extent of psychological tools employed against their kids to whip up their desire to buy products," says Rushkin. "When they find out, they're horrified." Rushkin's organization was behind a letter signed by 60 US psychologists that was sent to the American Psychological Association (www.apa.org) to complain about "the use of psychology to exploit and influence children for commercial purposes."

What was the cause of their fury? Apparently, it was an article by Dr. James McNeal appearing in *Marketing Tools* magazine that described what is called a projective completion test. Suppose a children's TV program is a hit, and boys are buying the company's toy that is tied to the program but girls aren't. To find out why, a company assembles a group of girls. They are given a picture of a boy and girl watching the program in which the boy is asking the girl, "Why do you like watching this program?" The girls' answers help provide clues to how the company can modify its marketing strategy to appeal to girls. Dr. McNeal refers to the method as "good sense and good science." Rushkin counters, "Psychologists are going to have to decide whether psychology is a tool for healing or for exploitation." The American Psychological Association admits that there are currently no guidelines for psychologists working in advertising. In Canada, guidelines have been developed to ensure that advertising to children is treated with sensitivity and respect. Advertisers are self-regulated through Advertising Standards Canada (ASC) and must adhere to the broadcast code for advertising to children.

Still, advertising executives are not just busy creating TV ads. Over a recent one-year period, the number of children's Web sites with no advertising dropped from 10 percent down to 2 percent. In what forms do the promotions appear? One tool is *games*. Roughly 55 percent of all children and teens' Web sites feature games. Ellen Neuborne told her six-year-old that he could choose a candy at the supermarket checkout. With a pack of Sweet Tarts in hand, he broke into a little song-and-dance about the sweets. When asked if that was from the TV commercial, he replied, "No. It's from the Sweet Tarts Internet game." With the use of such games, companies get to spend an extended period of time with kids—far more than they get from a TV ad.

Another tool is *e-mail*. The US Children's Online Privacy Act forbids companies from using e-mail to sell to kids under age 13 without parental permission. But companies get around the problem by having kids e-mail each other. For example, children can go to the Web site (www.sesameworkshop.org) and e-mail a greeting card to a friend that features a Sesame Street character. And then there are the *chat rooms*. Brian Rubash is manager for technical marketing at Tiger electronics (www.tigertoys.com), a division of toy maker Hasbro (www.hasbro.com). He says that he regularly signed on to a newsgroup he found on Yahoo! (www.yahoo.com) to offer product news and answer questions about the i-Cybie robotic dog the company was launching.

European nations have some of the strictest regulations covering marketing to children. However, nations belonging to the European Union (EU) have widely varying rules. For example, Greece bans all TV ads for war toys and bans ads for all other toys between 7 A.M. and 10 P.M. The Dutch-speaking part of Belgium bans TV advertising within five minutes of the start and end of children's programs. But Sweden bans all ads aimed at children under age 12. This means that when kids in Sweden watch the Pokémon cartoon series, they don't hear the closing jingle "Gotta catch' em all" that plays elsewhere.

But the problem for the Swedes (and others with more restrictive bans) is that they can only enforce their laws on programs originating from within the country. They have no power of enforcement over programs broadcast from other nations or from satellite transmissions. That is why the Swedes are pushing for a common restrictive policy toward advertising aimed at children. "They're gradually trying to forge a consensus among the member states," says Stephan Loerke, a lobbyist for the World Federation of Advertisers (www.wfanet.org) in Brussels, Belgium. Although an outright ban like Sweden's is unlikely, partial bans such as that in place in Belgium could be implemented. To forestall stricter EU-wide legislation, advertisers could initiate "voluntary" limits themselves.

Yet some marketers are defending their actions. Advertising executive Geoffrey Roche of Toronto, Ontario, dismissed the influence of psychologists, saying, "They don't have mind-altering powers and kids are a lot smarter than we give them credit for. I don't think there is any way that we, as advertisers, can convince children of anything." According to a privacy rights organization, when children visit commercial Web sites they might fill out surveys or register for memberships, providing the companies with their names and favourite fictional heroes. Then a company could send the child an e-mail pretending to be from the "Hero." This organization believes that younger children are not likely to realize the difference between fiction and reality, so the hero/marketer could have an influential marketing power. However, Roche's statements may apply for older children. Results from a research study called "Young Canadians in a Wired World" showed that the attitudes of children aged 11 to 17 toward online advertising ranged from ambivalent to distrustful.

But Dr. Allen Kanner asks, "If advertising is so ineffective, then why do they spend billions of dollars on it each year?" Dr. Curtis

Haugtvedt, president of the Society for Consumer Psychology, says that although evidence of the negative aspects of advertising does exist, ads can also benefit kids. "Even Barbie has pluses and minuses," says Haugtvedt. "Barbie helps kids imagine and play with one another, but Barbie also portrays the image of a certain body shape." Haugtvedt also stresses the role of guidance in helping kids become responsible consumers, saying, "The child hopefully is not making choices about purchasing things in a vacuum."

Thinking Globally

1. Put yourself in the position of Stephan Loerke of the World Federation of Advertisers. First, make an argument for why the EU should not enact more strict advertising laws. Second, make a case for why advertisers operating in the EU should initiate "voluntary" limits. Third, make a case for why current laws need no modification whatsoever. Which case do you agree with? Which case do you think is the strongest?

2. Certain organizations regularly attack advertisers for their promotional methods. What could the advertising industry do to become a smaller target for such criticisms? Be specific.

3. Some critics charge advertisers with creating wants among consumers rather than helping them satisfy needs. Select a product and describe how, if it were marketed in a developing economy, it could create wants and not satisfy needs. Explain the ethical issues surrounding the decision of whether to market the product in developing nations.

Sources: Steeves, Valerie "Young Canadians in a wired world, Phase III," May 29, 2012, Media Smarts (mediasmarts.ca/research-policy); Ellen Neuborne, "For Kids on the Web, It's an Ad, Ad, Ad, Ad World," *Bloomberg Businessweek* (www.businessweek.com), August 13, 2010; CAB-ARC et al., "Advertising to Children in Canada: A Reference Guide, May 2006, www.cab-acr.ca; Brandon Mitchener, "Banning Ads on Kids' TV," *Wall Street Journal Europe,* May 22, 2001, p. 25; James MacKinnon, "Psychologists Act against Ad Doctors," Adbusters Web site (www.adbusters.org), Piracy Rights Web site (www.piracyrights.org) "Fact Sheet 21: Children's Online privacy: a resource guide for parents".

Teaming Up INTERNATIONAL STRATEGY AND ORGANIZATION

What are the corporate- and business-level strategies that you could apply for your product or service in the two countries selected? In which nations do you currently produce and market your products? Are the production facilities centralized or decentralized? Does your company standardize its products/services or adapt them for different markets? What type of organizational structure does it have? Which of the two types of international strategy does it follow? Does the company make use of work teams?

Selecting and Managing Entry Modes

What method are you going to use to go international? How are you planning to receive payment for the goods or services you offer abroad? Is your company going to use different entry modes in different markets? What factors are influencing your choice of entry mode?

Developing and Marketing Products

For the countries and product or service you selected, determine which of the five types of product and promotion policies is being used: dual extension, product extension/communications adaptation, product adaptation/communication extension, dual adaptation, or product invention. What type is more suitable for your product or service in the two countries you selected?

Endnotes

CHAPTER 1

1. Sara Perez, "YouTube Reaches 4 Billion Views Per Day," *Tech Crunch* Web site (**techcrunch.com**), January 23, 2012; Eliot Van Buskirk, "5-Year-Old YouTube Tops Networks' Primetime with 2 Billion Views," *Wired* Web site (**www.wired.com**), May 17, 2010; "The Five Secrets of YouTube's Success," *Wired*, April 2010, pp. 92–97; Miguel Helft, "YouTube's Quest to Suggest More," *The New York Times* (**www.nytimes.com**), December 30, 2009; Jennifer L. Schenker, "Google Takes YouTube Global," *Bloomberg Businessweek* (**www.businessweek.com**), June 19, 2007; YouTube Web site (**www.youtube.com**), various reports.

2. World Trade Organization (WTO), "Fast-Changing Nature of World Trade Poses New Policy Challenges, Report Says," Press Release, WTO (**www.wto.org**), July 18, 2013.

3. David Kirkpatrick and Adam Lashinsky, "A New Way to Watch TV," *Fortune*, March 17, 2008, pp. 33–40.

4. Anya Kamenetz, "The Power of the Prize," *Fast Company*, May 2008, pp. 43–45; "Facts and Stats," Innocentive Web site (**www.innocentive.com**).

5. Moises Naim, "Post-Terror Surprises," *Foreign Policy* (**www.foreignpolicy.com**), September 1, 2002.

6. Steven Levy, "Tabula Rasa: Why the New Generation of Tablet Computers Changes Everything," *Wired*, April 2010, pp. 74–85.

7. "Google: Search Engine Blocked in Mainland China," CBS News Web site (**www.cbsnews.com**), July 29, 2010.

8. The Simpsons Web site (**www.thesimpsons.com**).

9. The World Trade Organization (WTO) Web site (**www.wto.org**).

10. Ibid.

11. "The Recovery in Trade: Defying Gravity and History," *The Economist* (**www.economist.com**), August 5, 2010.

12. Peter Burrows, "A Videoconference on the Cheap," *Bloomberg Businessweek*, October 6, 2008, p. 56.

13. Rhea Wessel, "Cargo-Tracking System Combines RFID, Sensors, GSM, and Satellite," *RFID Journal* (**www.rfidjournal.com**), January 25, 2008.

14. This discussion is based on "The Globalization Index," *Foreign Policy*, November/December 2007, pp. 68–76; *Foreign Policy* Web site (**www.foreignpolicy.com**), various reports.

15. "KOF Index of Globalization 2012: Economic Crisis Brings Economic Globalization to Fall," Press Release, ETH (**globalization.kof.ethz.ch**), March 16, 2012.

16. This comparison between the first and second ages of globalization is drawn from Thomas L. Friedman, *The Lexus and the Olive Tree* (New York: Anchor Books, 2000), pp. xvi–xix.

17. "Economics A-Z," *The Economist* (**www.economist.com**).

18. For an example of these and other criticisms levelled at Walmart, see Jane Birnbaum, "Corporate Greed vs. Public Good, Where America Shops," AFL-CIO Web site (**www.aflcio.org**).

19. Naomi Klein, "Outsourcing the Friedman," Naomi Klein's Web site (**www.naomiklein.org**).

20. Heather Timmons, "Outsourcing to India Draws Western Lawyers," *The New York Times* (**www.nytimes.com**), August 4, 2010.

21. Data obtained from **www.payscale.com**, June 25, 2012.

22. Marion Jansen, Ralf Peter, and José Manuel Salazar-Xirinachs, "Trade and Employment: From Myths to Facts," International Labour Office, Geneva, Switzerland, 2011 (**www.ilo.org**).

23. The results of these two studies are reported in Daniel W. Drezner, "Bottom Feeders," *Foreign Policy* (**www.foreignpolicy.com**), November 1, 2000.

24. Mattias Lundberg and Lyn Squire, *The Simultaneous Evolution of Growth and Inequality* (Washington, DC: World Bank, 1999) (**www.worldbank.org**).

25. David Dollar and Aart Kraay, *Growth Is Good for the Poor* (Washington, DC: World Bank, 2001) (**www.worldbank.org**).

26. Studies cited in *Poverty in an Age of Globalization* (Washington, DC: World Bank, 2000) (**www.worldbank.org**).

27. As reported in "A Wealth of Data," *The Economist*, July 31, 2010, p. 62.

28. International Monetary Fund, *World Economic Outlook: Growth Resuming, Dangers Remain* (Washington, DC: International Monetary Fund, April 2012); International Monetary Fund Web site (**www.imf.org**).

29. Xavier Sala-i-Martin, "The World Distribution of Income: Falling Poverty and … Convergence, Period," Columbia University (**www.columbia.edu**), working paper, October 9, 2005.

30. Shaohua Chen and Martin Ravallion, "How Well Did the World's Poorest Fare in the 1990s?" *Review of Income and Wealth*, September 2003, 47(3), pp. 283–300.

31. "Debt Relief Under the Heavily Indebted Poor Countries (HIPC) Initiative," International Monetary Fund Web site (**www.imf.org**), March 2008.

32. "Undermining Sovereignty and Democracy," The Ten Year Track Record of the North American Free Trade Agreement series (Washington, DC: Public Citizen's Global Trade Watch, 2004).

33. Stephen Krasner, "Sovereignty," *Foreign Policy*, January/February 2001, pp. 20–29.

34. D. Steven White, "The Top 175 Global Economic Entities, 2010," D. Steven White Web site (**www.dstevenwhite.com**).

35. *Weekend a Firenze* Web site (**www.firenze.waf.it**), select articles.

36. Katherine Scaroow and Carys Mills, "Meet Eight Quintessential Canadian Small Businesses," *The Globe and Mail* (**www.theglobeandmail.com**), June 30, 2011.

CHAPTER 2

1. Cirque du Soleil Web site (**www.cirquedusoleil.com**), various company reports; Deborah Leslie and Norma M. Rantisi, "Creativity and Place in the Evolution of a Cultural industry: The Case of Cirque du Soleil," *Urban Studies*, July 2011, 48(9), pp. 1771–1787; Kelly Nestruck, "How Cirque du Soleil's Hippy Circus Took Over the World," *The Guardian* (**www.guardian.co.uk**), September 4, 2009.

2. Ennio Vita-Finzi provided tips for the Culture Matters section from his personal experience as former trade commissioner for the Ontario government in Milan, San Paulo, Brussels, Paris, and Dallas.

3. Michael R. Solomon, Judith L. Zaichkowsky, and Rosemary Polegato, *Consumer Behaviour*, 4th Canadian Edition

(Toronto, ON: Pearson Education Canada, 2007), Chapter 14; Leon G. Schiffman, Leslie Lazar Kanuk, and Mallika Das, *Consumer Behaviour*, 1st Canadian Edition (Toronto, ON: Pearson Education Canada, 2005), Chapter 10.

4. Leon G. Schiffman, Leslie Lazar Kanuk, and Mallika Das, *Consumer Behaviour*, 1st Canadian Edition (Toronto, ON: Pearson Education Canada, 2005), Chapter 10.

5. Alibaba Web site (**www.alibaba.com**), various company reports.

6. "Tight-Pants Ban Begins in Indonesia District," *AZ Central* Web site (**www.azcentral.com**), May 27, 2010.

7. Lee Berthiaume, "Ottawa Develops Guidelines on Government Gift-giving," *The National Post*, (**www.nationalpost.com**), December 23, 2012.

8. Greg Burke, "Catholics Push Hyundai to Cancel Commercial," Fox News Web site (**www.liveshots.blogs.foxnews.com**), June 14, 2010.

9. Susan Fenton, "Wanted: Manager, Chinese-Speaking Only," *Yahoo News* (**www.yahoo.com**), April 28, 2008.

10. "Habbo's Second Global Youth Survey Reveals the Digital Profiles of Teens Online," Habbo Press Release (**www.habbo.com**), March 4, 2008.

11. "Top Spanish Translation Blunders," SDL Blog (**blog.sdl.com**), January 4, 2010.

12. "Rakuten to Make English Official In-House Language by the End of 2012," *Japan Today* (**www.japantoday.com**), July 1, 2010.

13. Based on *World Development Indicators 2012*, World Bank (**www.worldbank.org**).

14. Susan Fenton, "Wanted: Manager, Chinese-Speaking Only," *Yahoo News* (**www.yahoo.com**), April 28, 2008.

15. Florence Kluckhohn and F. L. Strodtbeck, *Variations in Value Orientations* (Evanston, IL: Harper & Row, 1961).

16. Hofstede's original study has been criticized as having a Western bias, ignoring subcultures, and being outdated as it was conducted in the 1960s and 1970s. See R. Mead, *International Management: Cross-Cultural Dimensions* (Oxford: Basil Blackwell, 1994), pp. 73–75.

17. Geert Hofstede, "The Cultural Relativity of Organizational Practices and Theories," *Journal of International Business Studies*, Fall 1983, pp. 75–89; Geert Hofstede's Web site (**www.geert-hofstede.com**).

18. Barry Newman, "Expat Archipelago: The New Yank Abroad Is the 'Can-Do' Player in the Global Village," *The Wall Street Journal*, December 12, 1995, p. A12.

19. Arik Hesseldahl, "Fixing Apple's 'Sweatshop' Woes," *Bloomberg Businessweek* (**www.businessweek.com**), June 29, 2006.

20. Stephen Dolainski, "Are Expats Getting Lost in the Translation?" *Workforce*, February 1997, pp. 32–39.

21. "Taxing Americans Abroad," *The Economist* (**www.economist. com**), June 24, 2006, p.78.

CHAPTER 3

1. Nanette Byrnes, "Pepsi Brings in the Health Police," *Bloomberg Businessweek*, January 25, 2010, pp. 50–51; Bibhudatta Pradhan and Pooja Thakur, "PepsiCo to Invest $200 Million More in India," *Bloomberg Businessweek* (**www.businessweek.com**), January 9, 2010; Dean Foust, "The Business Week 50," *Bloomberg Businessweek*, Special Report, April 7, 2008, p. 68; Betsy Morris, "The Pepsi Challenge," *Fortune*, March 3, 2008, pp. 54–66; PepsiCo Web site (**www.pepsico.com**), various reports.

2. Annette Weisbach, "Why Germans Want Out of Google's Street View," CNBC Web site (**www.cnbc.com**), August 14, 2010.

3. "World Report 2012: Venezuela," Human Rights Watch (**www. hrw.org/world-report-2012/world-report-2012-venezuela**).

4. E. N. Hester, "Kidnap and Ransom Insurance to the Rescue," Insure.com (**www.insure.com**), January 9, 2010.

5. "Corporate Stakes in Cuba," *Fortune*, May 5, 2008, p. 40.

6. Hugh Bronstein, "Argentina Nationalizes Oil Company YPK," Reuters Web site (**www.reuters.com**), May 4, 2012.

7. Information for Development Program (infoDev) and International Telecommunication Union (ITU), *ICT Regulation Toolkit*, ICT Web site (**www.ictregulationtoolkit.org**).

8. Beatrice Adams, "McDonald's Strange Menu Around the World," Trifter Web site (**trifter.com**), July 19, 2007.

9. Shell Web site (**www.shell.com**).

10. *Ninth Annual BSA and IDC Global Software Piracy Study* (Washington, DC; Business Software Alliance, May 2012), Table 1, p. 1 (**www.bsa.org/globalstudy**).

11. Peter Burrows, "Why China Is Finally Tackling Video Piracy," *Bloomberg Businessweek*, June 9, 2008, p. 73.

12. "Smoking Indonesian Toddler, Ardi, Cuts Back to 15 Cigarettes A Day," *Bintulu News* Web site (**www.bintulu.org**), June 8, 2010.

13. "Value Added Tax (VAT) in Canada," *Economy Watch* (**www. economywatch.com**), June 30, 2010.

14. "America Remains the Most Admired Country Globally in the 2011 Anholt-GfK Roper Nation Brands Index," Press Release, Gfk America (**www.gfkamerica.com/newsroom/press_releases/single_sites/008787/index.en.html**), October, 12, 2011.

CHAPTER 4

1. Air Canada, *Citizens of the World: Air Canada's Corporate Sustainability Report 2011* and *Citizens of the World: Corporate Sustainability Report 2012*, (**www.aircanada.com/en/about/corp_sustainability.html**); Air Canada Web site (**www.aircanada.com**) Corporate Profile, Overview.

2. Terrance P. Power, *International Business: A Canadian Perspective* (Toronto: Thomson Nelson, 2008), Chapter 17, pp. 466–493.

3. Richard M. Steers, Carlos J. Sanchez-Runde, and Luciara Nardon, *Management Across Cultures: Challenges and Strategies* (Cambridge, UK: Cambridge University Press, 2010), pp. 52–53.

4. Radenko Marić and Dragana Bolesnikov, "Moral Dilemmas of Employees in Corporate Business Operations," *Economics and Organizations*, 2008, 5(3), pp. 217–227.

5. Export Development Canada, *What We Stand For: EDC Code of Business Ethics and Code of Conduct*, (**www.edc.ca/EN/Promotions/Documents/code-business-ethics.pdf**).

6. Suncor Energy, *Petro-Canada's Code of Business Conduct* (**sustainability.suncor.com**).

7. Milton Friedman, "The Social Responsibility of Business Is to Increase Its Profits," *The New York Times Magazine*, September 13, 1970.

8. Daniel Franklin, "Just Good Business," *The Economist*, Special Report on Corporate Social Responsibility, January 19, 2008, pp. 3–6.

9. Sarah Johnson, "You Complete My Audit," *CFO Magazine*, May 2010, p. 17; Nanette Byrnes, "Sarbanes-Oxley Lifts Some Directors' Pay Higher Than $1 Million," *Bloomberg Businessweek* (**www.businessweek.com**), February 12, 2010.

10. Levi-Strauss Web site (**www.levistrauss.com**).

11. Daniel Franklin, "A Stitch in Time," *The Economist*, Special Report on Corporate Social Responsibility, January 19, 2008, pp. 12–14; Lindsey Rupp, Arun Devnath, and Sarah Shannon, "Joe Fresh Confirms Clothing Was Produced in Bangladesh Factory that Collapsed, Killing at Least 87," *The Financial Post*, (**www.financialpost.com**), April 24, 2013; "Factory Collapse in Bangladesh," Institute for Global Labour and Human Rights (**www.globallabourrights.org**).

12. World Fair Trade Organization Web site (**www.wfto.org**).

13. Second Cup Web site (**www.mysecondcup.com**).

14. Rainforest Alliance Web site (**www.rainforest-alliance.org**).

15. World Commission on Environment and Development (WCED), *Our Common Future*, (Oxford, UK: Oxford University Press, 1987); John Drexhage and Deborah Murphy for the International Institute for Sustainable Development (IISD), "Sustainable Development: From Brundtland to Rio 2012," Background paper prepared for consideration by the High Level Panel on Global Sustainability at its first meeting, September 19, 2010, United Nations, New York, NY, (**www.un.org/wcm/webdav/site/climatechange/shared/gsp/docs/GSP1-6_BackgroundonSustainableDevt.pdf**).

16. Helen M. Haugh and Alka Talwar, "How Do Corporations Embed Sustainability Across the Organization?", *Academy Of Management Learning and Education,* 9(3), 2010, pp. 384–396.

17. "Loblaw Makes Progress Towards 2013 Sustainable Seafood Commitment," Press Release, Loblaw Web site (**www.loblaw.ca**), June 26, 2012.

18. Carbon Footprint Web site (**www.carbonfootprint.com**).

19. Four Seasons Web site (**www.fourseasons.com**).

20. Heather Green and Kerry Capell, "Carbon Confusion," *Bloomberg Businessweek* (**www.businessweek.com**), March 6, 2008.

21. Michelle Conlin, "Sorry, I Composted Your Memorandum," *Bloomberg Businessweek*, February 18, 2008, p. 60.

22. Alissa Walker, "Spin the Bottle," *Fast Company*, June 2008, pp. 54–55.

23. Jack Ewing, "The Wind at Germany's Back," *Bloomberg Businessweek*, February 11, 2008, p. 68.

24. Ricardo Cuevas and Halia Mayela Valladares Montemayor, "Los Principios de inversion responsable de la ONU bajo la perspectiva de Jonas," *Colombian Accounting Journal, 2008*, 2(2), pp. 113–128.

25. Principles of Responsible Investment Web site (**www.unpri.org**).

26. Ibid.

27. Ibid.

CHAPTER 5

1. Alice Truong, "Take Two: The $35 Tablet Relaunches in India," *Forbes*, September 18, 2012; Datawind Web site (**www.datawind.com**), media reviews; Iain Marlow, "How a Montreal Company Won the Race to Build the World's Cheapest Tablet," *The Globe and Mail* (**www.theglobeandmail.com**), December 29, 2011.

2. "Not Waving. Perhaps Drowning," *The Economist*, May 29, 2010, pp. 23–25.

3. North Korea Economy Watch Web site (**www.nkeconwatch.com**), Archive for Kaesong Industrial Park and diverse articles; Martin Fackler, "A Capitalist Enclave in North Korea Survives," *The New York Times* (**www.nytimes.com**), July 6, 2010.

4. John Garnaut, "National Socialism with Chinese Characteristics," *Foreign Policy* (**www.foreignpolicy.com**), November 15, 2012; "China's State Capitalism: Not Just Tilting at Windmills", *The Economist*, October 6, 2012.

5. "International Patent Filings Set New Record in 2011," Press Release, World Intellectual Property Organization (**www.wipo.int/pressroom**), March 5, 2012.

6. "Socialist Workers," *The Economist* (**www.economist.com**), June 10, 2010.

7. "First Break All the Rules," *The Economist*, April 17, 2010, pp. 6–8.

8. Hilary Whiteman, "Experts Detail 5 Challenges for China," CNN (**www.cnn.com**), November 16, 2012.

9. "Democracy Denied," *The Economist* (**www.economist.com**), January 3, 2008.

10. "November 2012 Euro Area Unemployment Rate at 11.8%, EU27 at 10.7%," Eurostat News Release, European Union (**europa.eu**), January 8, 2013.

11. Information compiled from McCarthy Tetrault Web site (**www.mccarthy.ca**), the *Global Competition Review* (**www.globalcompetitionreview.com**), and the Competition Bureau Web site (**www.competitionbureau.gc.ca**).

12. "Antimonopoly Law in China," Norton Rose Fullbright (**www.nortonrose.com**), March 2012.

13. "2011 UN World Risk Index," United Nations University Institute for Environment and Human Security (**www.ihrrblog.org**), September 26, 2011.

14. "The World Factbook: Georgia," Central Intelligence Agency (**www.cia.gov**), GDP est. 2011; Chris Prentice, "Shadow Economies on the Rise Around the World," *Bloomberg Businessweek* (**www.businessweek.com**), July 29, 2010.

15. Daniel S. Levine, "Got a Spare Destroyer Lying Around? Make a Trade: Embracing Counter Trade as a Viable Option," *World Trade*, June 1997, pp. 34–35.

16. "Central Russian Teachers to Get Paid in Vodka." CNN Web site (**www.cnn.com**), September 1998.

17. Data obtained from the *World Development Indicators 2011*, World Bank (**www.worldbank.org**), Table GDP per capita and PPP per capita.

18. "Big Mac Index," *The Economist* (**www.economist.com**), January 11, 2012.

19. "Another BRIC in the Wall," *The Economist* (**www.economist.com**), April 21, 2008.

20. "Deadly Business in Moscow," *Bloomberg Businessweek*, March 1, 2010, pp. 22–23.

21. "Another Great Leap Forward?" *The Economist*, March 13, 2010, pp. 27–28.

22. "The Future of Productivity: Clear Choices for a Competitive Canada," Deloitte & Touche LLP (**www.productivity.deloitte.ca**), 2012; Kim Hart Macneill, "Declining Productivity Threatens Canadian Competitiveness," *Profit Guide* (**www.profitguide.com**), October 3, 2012.

CHAPTER 6

1. Stephanie Clifford and Stephanie Rosenbloom, "With Backdrop of Glamour, Wal-Mart Stresses Global Growth," *The New York Times* (**www.nytimes.com**), June 4, 2010; Andrew Winston, "Wal-Mart's New Sustainability Mandate in China," *Bloomberg Businessweek* (**www.businessweek.com**), October 28, 2008; Walmart Web site (**www.walmart.com**), select fact sheets; *Canada's State of Trade: Trade and Investment Update 2011*, Department of Foreign Affairs and International Trade Canada, Catalogue No. FR2-8/2011 (**www.international.gc.ca**).

2. Mykyta Vesselovsky et al., *Canada's State of Trade: Trade and Investment Update–2012*, Department of Foreign Affairs and International Trade Canada, Catalogue No. FR2-8/2012 (**www.international.gc.ca**); "A Profile of Canadian Importers,"

Statistics Canada, June 2010 (**www.statcan.gc.ca/pub/65-507-m/ 65-507-m2011011-eng.htm**); Forum for International Trade Training (FITT), *Human Resources: A Vital Driver of Canadian International Trade Capacity and Capability*, FITT (**community.fitt.ca/public/file/Resources/SectorStudy/ Executive_Summary.pdf**), 2011.

3. World Trade Organization (WTO), "Trade Growth to Slow in 2012 After Strong Deceleration in 2011," Press Release 658, WTO (**www.wto.org**), April 12, 2012; WTO, *World Trade Report 2011–The WTO and Preferential Trade Agreements: From Co-existence to Coherence* (Geneva, Switzerland: World Trade Organization, 2011).

4. International Maritime Organization (IMO), "International Shipping Facts and Figures," *Maritime Knowledge Centre*, March 12, 2012.

5. Geri Smith, "NAFTA: Two Mexicos, Two Outcomes," *Bloomberg Businessweek* (**www.businessweek.com**), February 12, 2008; Greg Brosnan, "The U.S. Recession Hits Home—in Mexico," *Bloomberg Businessweek* (**www.businessweek.com**), May 19, 2008.

6. David Leonhardt, "The Politics of Trade in Ohio," *The New York Times* (**www.nytimes.com**), February 27, 2008.

7. Daniel Trefler, *Canadian Policy Response to Offshore Outsourcing* (Ottawa, ON: Industry Canada, 2009) (**publications.gc.ca/ collections/collection_2010/ic/Iu182-1-2009-1-eng.pdf**).

8. "U.S. Is $500 Million Supermarket to Cuba," CNBC Web site (**www.cnbc.com**), May 27, 2010; "Big Brother's Shadow," *The Economist*, August 2, 2008, p. 42.

9. "The Chaebol Conundrum," *The Economist*, April 3, 2010, pp. 14–15.

10. Tariq Hussain, "What's a Chaebol to Do?" *Strategy & Business* (**www.strategy-business.com**), April 3, 2007.

11. "Signs of the Zeitgeist," *The Economist*, May 29, 2010, p. 52.

12. Julio Godoy, "Europe: Subsidies Feed Food Scarcity," *Global Policy Forum* (**www.globalpolicy.org**), April 25, 2008.

13. Keith Bradsher, "Fuel Subsidies Overseas Take a Toll on U.S.," *The New York Times* (**www.nytimes.com**), July 28, 2008.

14. Adam Smith, *The Wealth of Nations*, first published in 1776.

15. David Ricardo, *The Principles of Political Economy and Taxation*, first published in 1817.

16. Bertil Ohlin, *Interregional and International Trade* (Cambridge, MA: Harvard University Press, 1933).

17. Wassily Leontief, "Domestic Production and Foreign Trade: The American Capital Position Re-Examined," *Economia Internazionale*, February 1954, pp. 3–32.

18. Raymond Vernon and Louis T. Wells, Jr., *Economic Environment of International Business*, 7th ed. (Upper Saddle River, NJ: Prentice Hall, 1991).

19. William Greider, *One World, Ready or Not: The Manic Logic of Global Capitalism* (New York: Simon & Schuster, 1997), p. 15.

20. Ingenico Web site (**www.ingenico.com**), select reports and press releases.

21. Elhanan Helpman and Paul Krugman, *Market Structure and Foreign Trade* (Cambridge, MA: MIT Press, 1985).

22. For a detailed discussion of the first-mover advantage and its process, see Alfred D. Chandler, *Scale and Scope* (New York: Free Press, 1990).

23. Michael E. Porter, *The Competitive Advantage of Nations* (New York: Free Press, 1990).

24. "Ontario Food Cluster Declare Increased Hunger for International Business at SIAL Canada 2011," Press Release, Ontario Food Cluster (**www.ontariofoodcluster.com**), May 11, 2011; Ontario Food Cluster Web site (**www.ontariofoodcluster.com**).

25. Michael E. Porter, "Clusters and the New Economics of Competition," *Harvard Business Review* (November–December 1998), pp. 77–90.

CHAPTER 7

1. Nexen Web site (**www.nexeninc.com**), select reports.

2. United Nations Conference on Trade and Development (UNCTAD), *World Investment Report 2012: Towards a New Generation of Investment Policies* (Geneva, Switzerland: UNCTAD, 2012).

3. This section draws on information contained in the *World Investment Report 2009: Transnational Corporations, Agricultural Products and Development* (Geneva, Switzerland: UNCTAD, 2009) and the *World Investment Report 2012: Towards a New Generation of Investment Policies* (Geneva, Switzerland: UNCTAD, 2012).

4. Raymond Vernon and Louis T. Wells, Jr., *Economic Environment of International Business*, 7th ed. (Upper Saddle River, NJ: Prentice Hall, 1991).

5. John H. Dunning, "Toward an Eclectic Theory of International Production," *Journal of International Business Studies*, Spring–Summer 1980, pp. 9–31.

6. For an excellent discussion of the economic benefits provided by particular geographic locations, see Paul Krugman, "Increasing Returns and Economic Geography," *Journal of Political Economy*, June 1991, pp. 483–499.

7. Lawson A. W. Hunter, Ashley M. Weber, and Marisa Berswick, "A Guide to Navigating Canada's Foreign Ownership Laws for New Investors," *Competition Law International*, January 2012, 8(1), pp. 37–42.

8. Ibid.; Star Alliance Web site (**www.staralliance.com**).

9. Dennis and Sandi Jones, "New Frontiers in the Life Sciences: Canadian Companies in China and India," *ExportWise* (**www.exportwise.ca**), Fall 2009, p. 16; "Cell Biosciences Acquires Convergent Bioscience" and "Cell Biosciences Acquires Brightwell Technologies," Press Releases, Cell Biosciences/ProteinSimple (**www.proteinsimple.com**), October 13, 2010 and May 12, 2011; ProteinSimple Web site (**www.proteinsimple.com**), various reports.

CHAPTER 8

1. "Mexico's Partner Bombardier," *Negocios*, January 2010, pp. 15–17; "Bombardier Transport Division: 'On the Right Track…,'" NAFTANow.org (**www.naftanow.org/success/ canada_en.asp**); "Outlook: Aerospace Manufacturing in Mexico," Maquila Reference Web site (**www.maquilareference. com/2013/03/outlook-aerospace-manufacturing-in-mexico**); "Aircraft Production Flying to Mexico," *Industrial Engineer*, June 2008, 40(6), p. 12; Data obtained from Bombardier's Web site (**www.bombardier.com**).

2. Alexander Yeats, "Does Mercosur's Trade Performance Raise Concerns About the Effects of Regional Trade Arrangements?" Policy Research Working Paper 1729, The World Bank, February 1997; Nigel Nagarajan, "MERCOSUR and Trade Diversion: What Do the Import Figures Tell Us?" Economic Papers No. 129, European Commission, July 1998; "NAFTA after Five: The Impact of the North American Free Trade Agreement on Australia's Trade and Investment," Australian Department of Foreign Affairs and Trade (**www.dfat.gov.au**).

3. Data obtained from Jeffrey J. Schott of the Peterson Institute for International Economics, "The North American Free Trade Agreement: Time for a Change," Paper presented at the 7th Annual North American Regional Meeting, Ottawa, November 21–23, 2008 (**www.iie.com/publications/papers/20081218schott.pdf**).

4. "The Dark Side of Globalization," *The Economist*, May 31, 2008, pp. 5–7.

5. "Canada-United States Free Trade Agreement (FTA)" and "North American Free Trade Agreement (NAFTA)," Foreign Affairs, Trade and Development Canada (**www.international. gc.ca/trade-agreements-accords-commerciaux**).

6. Data obtained from the United States–Mexico Chamber of Commerce Web site (**www.usmcoc.org**).

7. Data obtained from Industry Canada (**www.ic.gc.ca**).

8. Data obtained from Foreign Affairs, Trade and Development Canada (**www.international.gc.ca/trade-agreements-accords-commerciaux**).

9. Data obtained from the Office of the United States Trade Representative (**www.ustr.gov**).

10. Data obtained from the AFL-CIO (**www.aflcio.org**) and from "North America Free Trade Agreement (NAFTA): Background Information," Foreign Affairs, Trade and Development Canada (**www.international.gc.ca/trade-agreements-accords-commerciaux/agr-acc/nafta-alena/info**).

11. "NAFTA: Myth vs. Facts," Office of the United States Trade Representative (**www.ustr.gov**), March 2008.

12. "Why It's Time to Renegotiate NAFTA Energy and Trade Agreements," The Council of Canadians (**www.canadians.org**), September 2008; Gordon Laxer and John Dillon, "Over a Barrel: Exiting from NAFTA's Proportionality Clause," Canadian Centre for Policy Alternatives (**www.policyalternatives.ca**) and the Parkland Institute (**www.ualberta.ca/parkland**), May 2008, p. 42.

13. John Patton, "North American Free Trade Agreement (NAFTA) Trade Disputes Attributed to Asymmetric Relationships Leading to the United States' Bad Neighbor Policies with Canada and Mexico," *The Journal of International Management Studies*, August 2010, 5(2), pp. 1–11.

14. Peter Hall, "What's Up Down Mexico Way?" *ExportWise* (**www.exportwise.ca**), Summer 2011, p. 28.

15. Data obtained from Foreign Affairs, Trade and Development Canada (**www.international.gc.ca/trade-agreements-accords-commerciaux/agr-acc/fta-ale**).

CHAPTER 9

1. Martyn Williams, "Nintendo Records a Loss as DS Sales Plummet," *Bloomberg Businessweek* (**www.businessweek.com**), July 29, 2010; Matt Vella, "Wii Fit Puts the Fun in Fitness," *Bloomberg Businessweek* (**www.businessweek.com**), May 21, 2008; Nintendo Web site (**www.nintendo.com**), various articles and annual reports.

2. "Maul Street," *The Economist*, May 15, 2010, pp. 84–85.

3. TD Securities Web site (**www.tdsecurities.com**), Asset Securitization section.

4. David Parkinson, "Speculators Turn Against the Canadian Dollar," *The Globe and Mail* (**www.theglobandmail.com**), March 8, 2013.

5. Bank for International Settlements Web site (**www.bis.org**), Foreign Exchange Statistics section.

6. Royal Bank of Canada (RBC) Web site (**www.rbcroyalbank.com**), Commercial Banking, Foreign Exchange section.

CHAPTER 10

1. Emily Wexler, "Brands of the Year: Lululemon Takes Local to the Next Level," *Strategy* (**strategyonline.ca**), September 28, 2012; Susan Krashinsky, "Lululemon Canada's Fastest-growing Brand," *The Globe and Mail* (**www.theglobeandmail.com**), June 6, 2012; Lululemon Atlethica Web site (**www.lululemon.com**); Advent International Web site (**www.advent-international.com**).

2. Bausch & Lomb Web site (**www.bausch.com**).

3. For an excellent discussion of this approach, see Michael E. Porter, *On Competition* (Boston: Harvard Business School Press, 2008).

4. The discussion of these strategies is based on Michael E. Porter, *Competitive Strategy* (New York: Free Press, 1980), pp. 34–46.

5. Johnson & Johnson Web site (**www.jnj.com**).

6. David Friend, "Blackberry-maker Turns to Complex Market in Southeast Asia to Grow Subscribers," *The Toronto Star* (**www.thestar.com**), January 2, 2013.

7. Norimitsu Onishi, "From Dung to Coffee Brew with No Aftertaste," *The New York Times* (**www.nytimes.com**), April 17, 2010.

8. Blackberry Web site (**ca.blackberry.com**).

9. Bradley L. Kirkman and Debra L. Shapiro, "The Impact of Cultural Values on Employee Resistance to Teams," *Academy of Management Review*, 1997, 22(3), pp. 730–757.

10. Ibid.

CHAPTER 11

1. Spin Master's Web site (**www.spinmaster.com**); Marina Strauss, "How Spin Master Learned to Play with the Giants," *The Globe and Mail* (**www.theglobeandmail.com**), November 1, 2010; Andrew Wahl, "Spin Master, Most Innovative Executive Team," *Canadian Business*, November 23, 2009, 82(20), p. 65; Bernadette Casey, "Fall Toy Show Product Roundup," *License! Global* (**www.licensemag.com**), October, 1, 2009; "Bakugan," *License! Global*, January 2009, p. 27; Douglas Quenqua, "To Create Its Hits, a Company Takes Its Toys on Tour," *The New York Times* (**www.nytimes.com**), June 9, 2008.

2. Export Development Canada (EDC), "Discounting a Letter of Credit Using Documentary Credit Insurance," EDC Web site (**figuide.edc.ca/Content/downloads/cs/cs-dci-en.pdf**).

3. Ilan Alon, *Franchising Globally: Innovation, Learning and Imitation* (Basingstoke, UK: Palgravé Macmillan, 2010), p. 86.

4. David Ing, "Spain Proves Tough to Crack," *Hotel & Motel Management*, September 1997, 212(15), p. 8.

5. Laura Gatland, "Eastern Europe Eagerly Accepts U.S. Franchisors," *Franchise Times*, September 1997, 3(9), p. 17.

6. Sharda Prashad, "New York Fries Heats Up in Hong Kong," *The Globe and Mail* (**www.theglobeandmail.com**), July 1, 2010; New York Fries Web site (**www.newyorkfries.com**), various reports.

7. Data obtained from Greenfield Hydroponic Systems Inc. Web site (**www.greenfield-hydroponics.com**).

8. This classification is made in Peter Buckley and Mark Casson, "A Theory of Cooperation in International Business," in Farok J. Contractor and Peter Lorange (eds.), *Cooperative Strategies in International Business* (Lexington, MA: Lexington Books, 1988), pp. 31–53.

9. "TenCate and BASF Sign Agreement on Strategic Alliance for Thermoplastic Automotive Composites," News Release, Ten Cate Web site (**www.tencate.com**), October 25, 2012.

10. This section is based in part on Franklin R. Root, *Entry Strategies for International Markets* (Lexington, MA: Lexington Books, 1987), pp. 8–21.

CHAPTER 12

1. Alex Duff, "Red Bull's Mark Webber Wins Spanish Formula One Race," *Bloomberg Businessweek* (**www.businessweek.com**), May 9, 2010; Rob Taylor, "Red Bull Drink Lifts Stroke Risk: Australian Study," Thomson Reuters Web site (**www.reuters. com**), August 14, 2008; "Skydiver in Record Channel Flight," *BBC News* (**www.bbc.co.uk**), July 31, 2003; Red Bull Web site (**www.redbull.com**), select reports.

2. To read the original, classic article see Theodore Levitt, "The Globalization of Markets," *Harvard Business Review*, May–June 1983, pp. 92–102.

3. "Top 4 Things to Consider When Designing a Promotional Strategy for the International Market," Trade Ready (**www.tradeready.ca**).

4. NameLab, Inc. Web site (**www.namelab.com**).

5. "Best Global Brands 2013," Interbrand Web site (**www. interbrand.com**).

6. Alessandra Galloni, "Coca-Cola Tests the Waters with Localized Ads in Europe," *The Wall Street Journal* (**www.wsj.com**), July 18, 2001; "Coca-Cola—Windmill," TvSpots.tv (**www.tvspots. tv/video/723**); Jing Wang, *Brand New China: Advertising, Media, and Commercial Culture* (Cambridge, MA: Harvard University Press, 2008), pp. 53–54.

7. This section draws on the classic discussion of these strategies in Warren J. Keegan, *Global Marketing Management*, 5th ed. (Upper Saddle River, NJ: Prentice Hall, 1995), pp. 489–494.

8. Muji Web site (**www.muji.net**), select reports.

9. Craig S. Smith, "In China, Some Distributors Have Really Cleaned Up with Amway," *The Wall Street Journal*, August 4, 1997, p. B1.

10. "Laptops from Lapland," *The Economist*, September 6, 1997, pp. 67–68.

Glossary

Absolute advantage. Ability of a nation to produce a good more efficiently than any other nation.

Ad valorem tariff. Tariff levied as a percentage of the stated price of an imported product.

Administrative delays. Regulatory controls or bureaucratic rules designed to impair the flow of imports into a country.

Advance payment. Export/import financing in which an importer pays an exporter for merchandise before it is shipped.

Aesthetics. What a culture considers "good taste" in the arts, the imagery evoked by certain expressions, and the symbolism of certain colours.

Agents. Individuals or organizations that represent one or more indirect exporters in a target market.

Antidumping duty. Additional tariff placed on an imported product that a nation believes is being dumped on its market.

Antitrust (antimonopoly) laws. Laws designed to prevent companies from fixing prices, sharing markets, and gaining unfair monopoly advantages.

Arm's length price. Free-market price that unrelated parties charge one another for a specific product.

Attitudes. Positive or negative evaluations, feelings, and tendencies that individuals harbour toward objects or concepts.

Balance of payments. National accounting system that records all payments to entities in other countries and all receipts coming into the nation.

Barter. Exchange of goods or services directly for other goods or services without the use of money.

Base currency. The denominator in a quoted exchange rate, or the currency that is to be purchased with another currency.

Berne Convention. International treaty that protects copyrights.

Bill of lading. Contract between an exporter and a shipper that specifies merchandise destination and shipping costs.

Bill S-21. A 1999 Bill that forbids Canadians (individuals or corporations) from bribing foreign government officials and laundering properties and proceeds.

Body language. Language communicated through unspoken cues, including hand gestures, facial expressions, physical greetings, eye contact, and the manipulation of personal space.

Bond. Debt instrument that specifies the timing of principal and interest payments.

Born global firm. Company that adopts a global perspective and engages in international business from or near its inception.

Brain drain. Departure of highly educated people from one profession, geographic region, or nation to another.

Brand name. Name of one or more items in a product line that identifies the source or character of the items.

Buyback. Export of industrial equipment in return for products produced by that equipment.

Capital account. National account that records transactions involving the purchase or sale of assets.

Capital market. System that allocates financial resources in the form of debt and equity according to their most efficient uses.

Capitalism. Belief that ownership of the means of production belongs in the hands of individuals and private businesses.

Carbon footprint. Environmental impact of greenhouse gases (measured in units of carbon dioxide) that results from human activity.

Caste system. System of social stratification in which people are born into a social ranking, or caste, with no opportunity for social mobility.

Centrally planned economy. Economic system in which a nation's land, factories, and other economic resources are owned by the government, which plans nearly all economic activity.

Chains of command. Lines of authority that run from top management to individual employees and specify internal reporting relationships.

Civil law. Legal system based on a detailed set of written rules and statutes that constitute a legal code.

Class system. System of social stratification in which personal ability and actions determine social status and mobility.

Code of ethics. Set of guidelines established by an organization to help their employees or members behave in accordance with the organization's values and ethical standards.

Combination strategy. Strategy designed to mix growth, retrenchment, and stability strategies across a corporation's business units.

Common law. Legal system based on a country's legal history (tradition), past cases that have come before its courts (precedent), and how laws are applied in specific situations (usage).

Common market. Economic integration whereby countries remove all barriers to trade and the movement of labour and capital among themselves but erect a common trade policy against non-members.

Communication. System of conveying thoughts, feelings, knowledge, and information through speech, writing, and actions.

Communism. Belief that social and economic equality can be obtained only by establishing an all-powerful Communist Party and by granting the government ownership and control over all types of economic activity.

Comparative advantage. Inability of a nation to produce a good more efficiently than other nations but an ability to produce that good more efficiently than it does any other good.

Compound tariff. Tariff levied on an imported product and calculated partly as a percentage of its stated price and partly as a specific fee for each unit.

Confiscation. Forced transfer of assets from a company to the government without compensation.

Convertible (hard) currency. Currency that trades freely in the foreign exchange market, with its price determined by the forces of supply and demand.

Copyright. Property right giving creators of original works the freedom to publish or dispose of them as they choose.

Core competency. Special ability of a company that competitors find extremely difficult or impossible to equal.

Corporate social responsibility (CSR). Practice of companies going beyond legal obligations to actively balance commitments to investors, customers, other companies, and communities.

Counterpurchase. Sale of goods or services to a country by a company that promises to make a future purchase of a specific product from the country.

Countertrade. Practice of selling goods or services that are paid for, in whole or in part, with other goods or services.

Countervailing duty. Additional tariff placed on an imported product that a nation believes is receiving an unfair subsidy.

Cross licensing. Practice by which companies use licensing agreements to exchange intangible property with one another.

Cross rate. Exchange rate calculated using two other exchange rates.

Cross-functional team. Team composed of employees who work at similar levels in different functional departments.

Cultural diffusion. Process whereby cultural traits spread from one culture to another.

Cultural imperialism. Replacement of one culture's traditions, folk heroes, and artifacts with substitutes from another.

Cultural literacy. Detailed knowledge about a culture that enables a person to function effectively within it.

Cultural trait. Anything that represents a culture's way of life, including gestures, material objects, traditions, and concepts.

Culture. Set of values, beliefs, rules, and institutions held by a specific group of people.

Culture shock. Psychological process affecting people living abroad that is characterized by homesickness, irritability, confusion, aggravation, and depression.

Currency arbitrage. Instantaneous purchase and sale of a currency in different markets for profit.

Currency controls. Restrictions on the convertibility of a currency into other currencies.

Currency futures contract. Contract requiring the exchange of a specific amount of currency on a specific date at a specific exchange rate, with all conditions fixed and not adjustable.

Currency hedging. Practice of insuring against potential losses that result from adverse changes in exchange rates.

Currency option. Right, or option, to exchange a specific amount of a currency on a specific date at a specific rate.

Currency speculation. Purchase or sale of a currency with the expectation that its value will change and generate a profit.

Currency swap. Simultaneous purchase and sale of foreign exchange for two different dates.

Current account. National account that records transactions involving the import and export of goods and services, income receipts on assets abroad, and income payments on foreign assets inside the country.

Current account deficit. When a country imports more goods and services and pays more abroad than it exports and receives from abroad.

Current account surplus. When a country exports more goods and services and receives more income from abroad than it imports and pays abroad.

Customs. Habits or ways of behaving in specific circumstances that are passed down through generations in a culture.

Customs union. Economic integration whereby countries remove all barriers to trade among themselves but erect a common trade policy against non-members.

Debt. Loan in which the borrower promises to repay the borrowed amount (the principal) plus a predetermined rate of interest.

Demand. Quantity of a good or service that buyers are willing to purchase at a specific selling price.

Democracy. Political system in which government leaders are elected directly by the wide participation of the people or by their representatives.

Derivative. Financial instrument whose value derives from other commodities or financial instruments.

Devaluation. Intentionally lowering the value of a nation's currency.

Developed country. Country that is highly industrialized and highly efficient, and whose people enjoy a high quality of life.

Developing country. Nation that has a poor infrastructure and extremely low personal incomes. Also called less-developed countries.

Differentiation strategy. Strategy in which a company designs its products to be perceived as unique by buyers throughout its industry.

Direct exporting. Practice by which a company sells its products directly to buyers in a target market.

Distribution. Planning, implementing, and controlling the physical flow of a product from its point of origin to its point of consumption.

Documentary collection. Export/import financing in which a bank acts as an intermediary without accepting financial risk.

Draft (bill of exchange). Document ordering an importer to pay an exporter a specified sum of money at a specified time.

Dual pricing. Policy in which a product has a different selling price (typically higher) in export markets than it has in the home market.

Dumping. Exporting a product at a price that is either lower than the price normally charged in the domestic market or lower than the cost of production.

E-business (e-commerce). Use of computer networks to purchase, sell, or exchange products; service customers; and collaborate with partners.

Eclectic theory. Theory stating that firms undertake foreign direct investment when the features of a particular location combine with ownership and internalization advantages to make a location appealing for investment.

Economic development. Measure for gauging the economic well-being of one nation's people as compared with that of another nation's people.

Economic system. Structure and processes that a country uses to allocate its resources and conduct its commercial activities.

Economic transition. Process by which a nation changes its fundamental economic organization and creates new free market institutions.

Economic union. Economic integration whereby countries remove barriers to trade and the movement of labour and capital among members, erect a common trade policy against non-members, and coordinate their economic policies.

Efficient market view. View that prices of financial instruments reflect all publicly available information at any given time.

Embargo. Complete ban on trade (imports and exports) in one or more products with a particular country.

Emerging markets. Newly industrialized countries plus those with the potential to become newly industrialized.

Entry mode. Institutional arrangement by which a firm gets its products, technologies, human skills, or other resources into a market.

Equity. Part ownership of a company in which the equity holder participates with other part owners in the company's financial gains and losses.

Ethical behaviour. Personal behaviour in accordance with guidelines for good conduct or morality.

Ethical dilemmas. Situation where moral imperatives are in conflict. There is no right or wrong decision.

Ethics. Moral obligation to separate right from wrong.

Ethnocentric staffing. Staffing policy in which individuals from the home country manage operations abroad.

Ethnocentricity. Belief that one's own ethnic group or culture is superior to that of others.

Eurobond. Bond issued outside the country in whose currency it is denominated.

Eurocurrency market. Market consisting of all the world's currencies (referred to as "Eurocurrency") that are banked outside their countries of origin.

European monetary union. European Union plan that established its own central bank and currency.

Exchange rate. Rate at which one currency is exchanged for another.

Exchange-rate risk (foreign exchange risk). Risk of adverse changes in exchange rates.

Exclusive channel. Distribution channel in which a manufacturer grants the right to sell its product to only one or a limited number of resellers.

Expatriates. Citizens of one country who are living and working in another.

Export management company (EMC). Company that exports products on behalf of indirect exporters.

Export trading company (ETC). Company that provides services to indirect exporters in addition to activities related directly to clients' exporting activities.

Exports. Goods and services sold abroad and sent out of a country.

Expropriation. Forced transfer of assets from a company to the government with compensation.

Factor proportions theory. Trade theory stating that countries produce and export goods that require resources (factors) that are abundant and import goods that require resources in short supply.

Fair trade. A trading partnership, based on dialogue, transparency, and respect, that seeks greater equity in international trade and contributes to sustainable development by offering better trading conditions to, and securing the rights of, marginalized producers and workers.

First-mover advantage. Economic and strategic advantage gained by being the first company to enter an industry.

Focus strategy. Strategy in which a company focuses on serving the needs of a narrowly defined market segment by being the low-cost leader or by differentiating its product.

Folk custom. Behaviour, often dating back several generations, that is practised by a homogeneous group of people.

Foreign bond. Bond sold outside the borrower's country and denominated in the currency of the country in which it is sold.

Foreign direct investment (FDI). Purchase of physical assets or a significant amount of the ownership (stock) of a company in another country to gain a measure of management control.

Foreign exchange market. Market in which currencies are bought and sold and their prices are determined.

Foreign trade zone (FTZ). Designated geographic region through which merchandise is allowed to pass with lower customs duties (taxes) and/or fewer customs procedures.

Forward contract. Contract that requires the exchange of an agreed-upon amount of a currency on an agreed-upon date at a specific exchange rate.

Forward exchange rate. Exchange rate at which two parties agree to exchange currencies on a specified future date.

Forward market. Market for currency transactions at forward rates.

Franchising. Practice by which one company (the franchiser) supplies another (the franchisee) with intangible property and other assistance over an extended period.

Free trade. Pattern of imports and exports that occurs in the absence of trade barriers.

Free trade area. Economic integration whereby countries seek to remove all barriers to trade among themselves, but each country determines its own barriers against non-members.

Freight forwarder. Specialist in export-related activities such as customs clearing, tariff schedules, and shipping and insurance fees.

Fundamental analysis. Technique that uses statistical models based on fundamental economic indicators to forecast exchange rates.

GDP or GNP per capita. Nation's GDP or GNP divided by its population.

General Agreement on Tariffs and Trade (GATT). Treaty designed to promote free trade by reducing both tariffs and nontariff barriers to international trade.

Geocentric staffing. Staffing policy in which the best-qualified individuals, regardless of nationality, manage operations abroad.

Global matrix structure. Organizational structure that splits the chain of command between product and area divisions.

Global product structure. Organizational structure that divides worldwide operations according to a company's product areas.

Global strategy. Offering the same products using the same marketing strategy in all national markets.

Global team. Team of top managers from both headquarters and international subsidiaries who meet to develop solutions to company-wide problems.

Globalization. Trend toward greater economic, cultural, political, and technological interdependence among national institutions and economies.

Gross domestic product (GDP). Value of all goods and services produced by a domestic economy over a one-year period.

Gross national product (GNP). Value of all goods and services produced by a country's domestic and international activities over a one-year period.

Growth strategy. Strategy designed to increase the scale (size of activities) or scope (kinds of activities) of a corporation's operations.

Hofstede framework. Framework for studying cultural differences along five dimensions, such as individualism versus collectivism and equality versus inequality.

Human development index (HDI). Measure of the extent to which a government equitably provides its people with a long and healthy life, an education, and a decent standard of living.

Human resource management (HRM). Process of staffing a company and ensuring that employees are as productive as possible.

Human resource planning. Process of forecasting a company's human resource needs and its supply.

Imports. Goods and services purchased abroad and brought into a country.

Indirect exporting. Practice by which a company sells its products to intermediaries who then resell to buyers in a target market.

Industrial property. Patents and trademarks.

Inefficient market view. View that prices of financial instruments do not reflect all publicly available information.

Intellectual property. Property that results from people's intellectual talent and abilities.

Intensive channel. Distribution channel in which a producer grants the right to sell its product to many resellers.

Interbank interest rates. Interest rates that the world's largest banks charge one another for loans.

Interest arbitrage. Profit-motivated purchase and sale of interest-paying securities denominated in different currencies.

International area structure. Organizational structure that organizes a company's entire global operations into countries or geographic regions.

International bond market. Market consisting of all bonds sold by issuing companies, governments, or other organizations outside their own countries.

International business. Commercial transaction that crosses the borders of two or more nations.

International capital market. Network of individuals, companies, financial institutions, and governments that invest and borrow across national boundaries.

International division structure. Organizational structure that separates domestic from international business activities by creating a separate international division with its own manager.

International equity market. Market consisting of all stocks bought and sold outside the issuer's home country.

International Monetary Fund (IMF). Agency created to regulate fixed exchange rates and enforce the rules of the international monetary system.

International product life cycle theory. Theory stating that a company will begin by exporting its product and later undertake foreign direct investment as the product moves through its life cycle.

International trade. Purchase, sale, or exchange of goods and services across national borders.

Joint venture. Separate company that is created and jointly owned by two or more independent entities to achieve a common business objective.

Kluckhohn–Strodtbeck framework. Framework for studying cultural differences along six dimensions, such as focus on past or future events and belief in individual or group responsibility for personal well-being.

Legal system. Set of laws and regulations, including the processes by which a country's laws are enacted and enforced, and the ways in which its courts hold parties accountable for their actions.

Letter of credit (L/C). Export/import financing in which the importer's bank issues a document stating that the bank will pay the exporter when the exporter fulfills the terms of the document.

Licensing. Practice by which one company owning intangible property (the licensor) grants another firm (the licensee) the right to use that property for a specified period of time.

Lingua franca. Third or "link" language understood by two parties who speak different native languages.

Liquidity. Ease with which bondholders and shareholders may convert their investments into cash.

Lobbying. Policy of hiring people to represent a company's views on political matters.

Local content requirements. Laws stipulating that a specified amount of a good or service be supplied by producers in the domestic market.

Low-cost leadership strategy. Strategy in which a company exploits economies of scale to have the lowest cost structure of any competitor in its industry.

Management contract. Practice by which one company supplies another with managerial expertise for a specific period of time.

Manners. Appropriate ways of behaving, speaking, and dressing in a culture.

Market economy. Economic system in which the majority of a nation's land, factories, and other economic resources are privately owned, either by individuals or businesses.

Market imperfections. Theory stating that when an imperfection in the market makes a transaction less efficient than it could be, a company will undertake foreign direct investment to internalize the transaction and thereby remove the imperfection.

Market power. Theory stating that a firm tries to establish a dominant market presence in an industry by undertaking foreign direct investment.

Marketing communication. Process of sending promotional messages about products to target markets.

Material culture. All the technology used in a culture to manufacture goods and provide services.

Mercantilism. Trade theory that nations should accumulate financial wealth, usually in the form of gold, by encouraging exports and discouraging imports.

Mission statement. Written statement of why a company exists and what it plans to accomplish.

Mixed economy. Economic system in which land, factories, and other economic resources are rather equally split between private and government ownership.

Multinational (multidomestic) strategy. Adapting products and their marketing strategies in each national market to suit local preferences.

Multinational corporation (MNC). Business that has direct investments abroad in multiple countries.

National competitive advantage theory. Trade theory stating that a nation's competitiveness in an industry depends on the capacity of the industry to innovate and upgrade.

Nationalism. Devotion of a people to their nation's interests and advancement.

Nationalization. Government takeover of an entire industry.

New trade theory. Trade theory stating that (1) there are gains to be made from specialization and increasing economies of scale, (2) the companies first to market can create barriers to entry, and (3) government may play a role in assisting its home companies.

Newly industrialized country (NIC). Country that has recently increased the portion of its national production and exports derived from industrial operations.

Normal trade relations (formerly "most favoured nation status"). Requirement that WTO members extend the same favourable terms of trade to all members as they extend to any single member.

Offset. Agreement that a company will offset a hard-currency sale to a nation by making a hard-currency purchase of an unspecified product from that nation in the future.

Offshore financial centre. Country or territory whose financial sector features very few regulations and few, if any, taxes.

Open account. Export/import financing in which an exporter ships merchandise and later bills the importer for its value.

Organizational structure. Way in which a company divides its activities among separate units and coordinates activities among those units.

Over-the-counter (OTC) market. Decentralized exchange encompassing a global computer network of foreign exchange traders and other market participants.

Patent. Property right granted to the inventor of a product or process that excludes others from making, using, or selling the invention.

Planning. Process of identifying and selecting an organization's objectives and deciding how the organization will achieve those objectives.

Political risk. Likelihood that a society will undergo political changes that negatively affect local business activity.

Political system. Structures, processes, and activities by which a nation governs itself.

Political union. Economic and political integration whereby countries coordinate aspects of their economic and political systems.

Polycentric staffing. Staffing policy in which individuals from the host country manage operations abroad.

Popular custom. Behaviour shared by a heterogeneous group or by several groups.

Portfolio investment. Investment that does not involve obtaining a degree of control in a company.

Price controls. Upper or lower limits placed on the prices of products sold within a country.

Principles of Responsible Investment (PRI). Principles created to protect the world's assets by applying social responsibility to investments.

Private sector. Segment of the economic environment comprising independently owned firms that seek to earn profits.

Privatization. Policy of selling government-owned economic resources to private operators.

Product liability. Responsibility of manufacturers, sellers, individuals, and others for damage, injury, or death caused by defective products.

Promotion mix. Efforts by a company to reach distribution channels and target customers through communications, such as personal selling, advertising, public relations, and direct marketing.

Property rights. Legal rights to resources and any income they generate.

Pull strategy. Promotional strategy designed to create buyer demand that will encourage channel members to stock a company's product.

Purchasing power. Value of goods and services that can be purchased with one unit of a country's currency.

Purchasing power parity (PPP). Relative ability of two countries' currencies to buy the same "basket" of goods in those two countries.

Push strategy. Promotional strategy designed to pressure channel members to carry a product and promote it to final users of the product.

Quota. Restriction on the amount (measured in units or weight) of a good that can enter or leave a country during a certain period of time.

Quoted currency. The numerator in a quoted exchange rate, or the currency with which another currency is to be purchased.

Rationalized production. System of production in which each of a product's components is produced where the cost of producing that component is lowest.

Recruitment. Process of identifying and attracting a qualified pool of applicants for vacant positions.

Regional economic integration (regionalism). Process whereby countries in a geographic region cooperate to reduce or eliminate barriers to the international flow of products, people, or capital.

Representative democracy. Democracy in which citizens elect individuals from their groups to represent their political views.

Retrenchment strategy. Strategy designed to reduce the scale or scope of a corporation's businesses.

Revaluation. Intentionally raising the value of a nation's currency.

Reverse culture shock. Psychological process of re-adapting to one's home culture.

Secular totalitarianism. Political system in which leaders rely on military and bureaucratic power.

Securitization. Unbundling and repackaging of hard-to-trade financial assets into more liquid, negotiable, and marketable financial instruments (or securities).

Selection. Process of screening and hiring the best-qualified applicants with the greatest performance potential.

Self-managed team. Team in which the employees from a single department take on the responsibilities of their former supervisors.

Social group. Collection of two or more people who identify and interact with each other.

Social mobility. Ease with which individuals can move up or down a culture's "social ladder."

Social stratification. Process of ranking people into social layers or classes.

Social structure. A culture's fundamental organization, including its groups and institutions, its system of social positions and their relationships, and the process by which its resources are distributed.

Socialism. An economic system in which the government owns and controls all types of economic activity.

Specific tariff. Tariff levied as a specific fee for each unit (measured by number, weight, and so forth) of an imported product.

Spot market. Market for currency transactions at spot rates.

Spot rate. Exchange rate requiring delivery of the traded currency within two business days.

Stability strategy. Strategy designed to guard against change and used by corporations to avoid either growth or retrenchment.

Staffing policy. Customary means by which a company staffs its offices.

Stakeholders. All parties, ranging from suppliers and employees to stockholders and consumers, who are affected by a company's activities.

Stock. Shares of ownership in a company's assets that give shareholders a claim on the company's future cash flows.

Strategic alliance. Relationship whereby two or more entities cooperate (but do not form a separate company) to achieve the strategic goals of each.

Strategy. Set of planned actions taken by managers to help a company meet its objectives.

Subculture. A group of people who share a unique way of life within a larger, dominant culture.

Subsidy. Financial assistance to domestic producers in the form of cash payments, low-interest loans, tax breaks, product price supports, or other forms.

Supply. Quantity of a good or service that producers are willing to provide at a specific selling price.

Sustainability (sustainable development). Development that meets the needs of the present without compromising the economy or the social and natural environments for future generations.

Switch trading. Practice in which one company sells to another its obligation to make a purchase in a given country.

Tariff. Government tax levied on a product as it enters or leaves a country.

Tariff-quota. Lower tariff rate for a certain quantity of imports and a higher rate for quantities that exceed the quota.

Technical analysis. Technique that uses charts of past trends in currency prices and other factors to forecast exchange rates.

Technological dualism. Use of the latest technologies in some sectors of the economy coupled with the use of outdated technologies in other sectors.

Theocracy. Political system in which a country's religious leaders are also its political leaders.

Theocratic law. Legal system based on religious teachings.

Theocratic totalitarianism. Political system under the control of totalitarian religious leaders.

Topography. All the physical features that characterize the surface of a geographic region.

Totalitarian system. Political system in which individuals govern without the support of the people, tightly control people's lives, and do not tolerate opposing viewpoints.

Trade creation. Increase in the level of trade between nations that results from regional economic integration.

Trade deficit. Condition that results when the value of a country's imports is greater than the value of its exports.

Trade diversion. Diversion of trade away from nations not belonging to a trading bloc and toward member nations.

Trade surplus. Condition that results when the value of a nation's exports is greater than the value of its imports.

Trademark. Property right in the form of words or symbols that distinguish a product and its manufacturer.

Transfer price. Price charged for a good or service transferred among a company and its subsidiaries.

Turnkey (build–operate–transfer) project. Practice by which one company designs, constructs, and tests a production facility for a client firm.

United Nations (UN). International organization formed after World War II to provide leadership in fostering peace and stability around the world.

Value added tax (VAT). Tax levied on each party that adds value to a product throughout its production and distribution.

Value density. Value of a product relative to its weight and volume.

Value-chain analysis. Process of dividing a company's activities into primary and support activities and identifying those that create value for customers.

Values. Ideas, beliefs, and customs to which people are emotionally attached.

Vehicle currency. Currency used as an intermediary to convert funds between two other currencies.

Vertical integration. Extension of company activities into stages of production that provide a firm's inputs (backward integration) or absorb its output (forward integration).

Voluntary export restraint (VER). Unique version of export quota that a nation imposes on its exports, usually at the request of an importing nation.

Wholly owned subsidiary. Facility entirely owned and controlled by a single parent company.

World Bank. Agency created to provide financing for national economic development efforts.

World Trade Organization (WTO). International organization that enforces the rules of international trade.

Worldwide pricing. Policy in which one selling price is established for all international markets.

Name/Company Index